MW00991287

China's Security State
Philosophy, Evolution, and Politics

China's Security State describes the creation, evolution, and development of
Chinese security and intelligence agencies as well as their role in influencing Chinese Communist Party politics throughout the party's history. Xuezhi
Guo investigates patterns of leadership politics from the vantage point of security and intelligence organization and operation by providing new evidence
and offering alternative interpretations of major events throughout Chinese
Communist Party history. This analysis promotes a better understanding of
the CCP's mechanisms for control over both party members and the general
population. This study specifies some of the broader implications for theory
and research that can help clarify the nature of Chinese politics and potential
future developments in the country's security and intelligence services.

Xuezhi Guo is Professor of Political Science and East Asian Studies at Guilford
College.

China's Security State

Philosophy, Evolution, and Politics

XUEZHI GUO

Guilford College, Greensboro, North Carolina

CAMBRIDGE
UNIVERSITY PRESS

CAMBRIDGE
UNIVERSITY PRESS

32 Avenue of the Americas, New York NY 10013-2473, USA

Cambridge University Press is part of the University of Cambridge.

It furthers the University's mission by disseminating knowledge in the pursuit of education, learning and research at the highest international levels of excellence.

www.cambridge.org
Information on this title: www.cambridge.org/9781107688841

© Xuezhi Guo 2012

First published 2012
First paperback edition 2014

A catalogue record for this publication is available from the British Library

Library of Congress Cataloguing in Publication data
Guo, Xuezhi, 1956–
China's security state : philosophy, evolution, and politics / Xuezhi Guo.
p. cm.
Includes bibliographical references and index.
ISBN 978-1-107-02323-9 (hardback)
1. National security – China – History.   2. Intelligence service – China – History.
3. Police – China – History.   4. Zhongguo gong chan dang – History.   I. Title.
JQ1509.5.I6G86   2012
355'.033051–dc23   2012002710

ISBN 978-1-107-02323-9 Hardback
ISBN 978-1-107-68884-1 Paperback

To my father

Contents

Acknowledgments

The research and writing of this book took many years to complete. A book of this breadth of subject matter that deals with the evolution and developments of Chinese Communist Party (CCP) organizations of tremendous size and significance, over a period of some ninety years, owes a great deal to the insights, observations, and analyses of many people – too numerous for all to be mentioned here. I am deeply grateful to the many individuals and organizations that helped me carry out field research and provided financial support and access to information, particularly the many people I met during my field research in China who shared with me their own experiences and insights, and from whom I have learned so much. Although all acknowledged here were helpful, I alone am responsible for any errors and omissions that remain.

Special thanks go to my academic mentor and friend Brantly Womack, who was unstintingly generous for so many years with his time and scholarly advice, always taking an active interest in my work and contributing significantly to it in various ways. I am deeply indebted to Lauren Reed, who made numerous and substantive editorial suggestions; her diligence, knowledge, and judgment gave the process needed direction and energy in the final stages of publication. I am grateful to all those who assisted me during my long years of research at Guilford College. I am profoundly indebted to Adrienne L. Israel, vice president for academic affairs and academic dean of Guilford College, who encouraged me and provided tremendous support for this project from inception to completion. Special appreciation goes to many of my colleagues in both political science and East Asian studies – Kent Chabotar, Ken Gilmore, Kyle Dell, Maria Rosales, Robert Duncan, Victor Archibong, Dottie Borei, and Eric Mortensen. I owe thanks also to many of my colleagues at Guilford College who gave me much encouragement and support – particularly Robert Williams, Dave MacInnes, Kathy Adams, Claire Morse, Teresa Sanford, James Lyons, Jan Prillaman, and Susan McClanahan.

I am deeply indebted to my students at Guilford College, who not only ignited my potential as a teacher but also served as an invaluable source of inspiration, contributed suggestions for my research, asked acute questions, and tracked down sources. I was blessed particularly with excellent student research assistants – Luke Treloar, Daniel Miller, Amanda Speer, Matthew Draelos, Medha Gargeya, and Tahira Siddiqui. Throughout writing the manuscript and preparing it for publication, they were indispensable and creative in collecting materials, checking sources, providing editorial support, preparing bibliographies, and providing technical assistance. Special thanks to my students Jacob R. Rosenberg and Lily C. Wotkyns who have played an essential role in creating an excellent index, which I believe has enhanced the general quality of this book. For the generous financial support that made it possible for me to work on this project, I thank Guilford College for providing the Campbell Fund, Kenan Grant, Faculty Research Funds, and Campbell Travel Grant. Over the course of carrying out the research for this book, the following institutions assisted me by providing research facilities: University of Virginia Library, Duke University Library, and University of North Carolina Library at Chapel Hill. To all of these institutions and their staff I owe a debt of gratitude.

It has been a pleasure to work with the editors at Cambridge University Press; their patience, interest, and expertise are greatly appreciated. They deserve great credit for their indispensable assistance in improving this manuscript and bringing it to publication. I am especially grateful to Robert Dreesen for his commitment to this project and to Abigail Zorbaugh, who has been a wonderful collaborator in the editing and design of the book. I am also extremely grateful for the many useful comments and suggestions made by the expert peer reviewers invited by the Press to evaluate the scholarship that appears in this book. Special thanks also to those who helped bring this book into print. Katherine Faydash edited the manuscript with speedy and patient efficiency and made a painstaking effort to ready the manuscript for publication; working with her has been not only a pleasant experience but also a learning process. I am most grateful to Peggy M. Rote, Senior Project Manager at Aptara Inc., for her dedication in managing the production of the book.

My gratitude also belongs to my family and friends for their tremendous support throughout the years, especially my sister, Yiling, for all the gentle pushes and encouragement. Most of all, I thank my father, Guo Chaozhou, who kindled my interest in history and politics at an early age, and to whom this book is dedicated.

Abbreviations

AB Corps	Anti-Bolshevik Corps
BGC	Beijing Garrison Command
BPS	Bureau of Public Security
BSPS	Brigade of State Political Security
CCP	Chinese Communist Party
CDIC	Central Discipline Inspection Commission
CEC	Committee for Eliminating Counterrevolutionaries
CGB	Central Guard Bureau
CGO	Central General Office
CGR	Central Guard Regiment (Unit 8341)
CID	Central Investigation Department
CMC	Central Military Commission
CPLC	Central Political and Legal Commission
CPPCC	Chinese People's Political Consultative Conference
CPPSF	Chinese People's Public Security Forces
CRG	Cultural Revolution Group
CSC	Central Security Commission
CSWC	Central Special Work Commission
DETST	Department of Eliminating Traitors, Spies, and Trotskyites
ERA	Eighth Route Army
GLF	Great Leap Forward
GMD	Chinese Nationalist Party/Guomindang
GPD	PLA General Political Department
GSD	PLA General Staff Department
ID	Central Committee's Intelligence Department
IRC	Investigation and Research Commission
MPS	Ministry of Public Security
MR	Military Region

MSS	Ministry of State Security
NFA	New Fourth Army
NPC	National People's Congress
PAFC	People's Armed Forces Commission
PAFD	People's Armed Forces Department
PAP	People's Armed Police
PLA	People's Liberation Army
PRC	People's Republic of China
PSD	Political Security Department
SAD	Central Committee's Social Affairs Department
SPSB	State Political Security Bureau
SSD	Special Services Division (Teke)
Sufan	Eliminating counterrevolutionaries

Introduction

This book is not a political history of Chinese security and intelligence apparatuses. Rather, it is an analysis of several interrelated issues at the intersection of security and intelligence apparatuses and elite politics. First, the book analyzes the evolution and development of the Chinese Communist Party's (CCP) security and intelligence organizations during the CCP revolution before 1949, as well as the practices and policies that have controlled those organizations in the People's Republic of China (PRC). Second, it examines the organizations' pursuit of social control over the Chinese populace and their influence over elite politics, a result of the privilege of virtually inscrutable authority. Third, it explores the function of the security and intelligence apparatuses as the paramount shields for protecting the regime and as potent forces guaranteeing compliance to party leadership. Last, it reveals the manner in which the CCP organizes and motivates the security and intelligence organizations to ensure effective social control and the compliance of party and state officials with party discipline. The study of these agencies serves to promote understanding of the CCP's mechanisms for control over party members, military personnel, government officials, and the general population. In addition, this book investigates how security and intelligence apparatuses have been organized, how they have evolved, and how they have operated, with attention to the role they have played in ensuring the CCP's political dominance. Although the role of security and intelligence agencies has largely been hidden from public view,[1] few scholars dispute their importance in CCP politics.[2] In the process of

---

[1] Kenneth Lieberthal, "The Great Leap Forward and the Split in the Yan'an Leadership, 1958–65," in Roderick MacFarquhar (ed.), *The Politics of China: The Eras of Mao and Deng*, p. 146.

[2] Many China studies scholars have provided insight into the crucial role of security apparatuses in CCP politics. See Maurice Meisner, *Mao's China and After: A History of the People's Republic*,

exploring these dimensions, this book highlights important historical activities of and developments in China's security and intelligence agencies, provides a compelling guide to these enigmatic organizations, and suggests a framework for future inquiry.

In the scholarship of communist politics, few institutions have received as much weight but as little weighty analysis as China's security and intelligence agencies and their role in elite politics. Besides substantive monitoring over security and intelligence agencies by party leadership (e.g., Politburo members),[3] there have been specific organizations within both party and army leadership that lead or guide these agencies. These organizations include the Central General Office (*zhongyang bangongting*), the General Staff Department (*zong canmou bu*) of the People's Liberation Army (PLA), the PLA Political Department (*zong zhengzhi bu*), and the General Office of the Central Military Commission (CMC). In addition, Chinese security and intelligence apparatuses are party and government entities that often are categorized as civilian, paramilitary, or military organizations; they therefore are tasked with domestic security and external defense missions. These organizations include the Ministry of Public Security (MPS); the Ministry of State Security (MSS); and the Chinese Armed Forces, which consists of the PLA and the People's Armed Police (PAP). Because the missions and chains of command of each organization are different, some of the functions of the individual entities overlap.[4] Given that Chinese military involvement in politics has a long tradition,[5] the first and foremost military objective of the PLA, according to David M. Finkelstein, "is to be the guardian of the CCP."[6] Moreover, certain central party and governmental organizations have been involved in activities regarding China's security and intelligence services, such as intelligence and counterintelligence, political surveillance, anticorruption, information gathering and analysis, as well as secret operations (mainly designed to exert political influence). These organizations include the Central Discipline Inspection Commission and the Ministry of Supervision;

---

pp. 67–8; Andrew Scobell, *China's Use of Military Force: Beyond the Great Wall and the Long March*, pp. 70–4; Kenneth Lieberthal, "The Great Leap Forward and the Split in the Yan'an Leadership," p. 146; Frederic Wakeman Jr., "Models of Historical Change: The Chinese State and Society, 1839–1989," in Kenneth Lieberthal (ed.), *Perspectives on Modern China: Four Anniversaries*, p. 91; Richard Baum, *Burying Mao: Chinese Politics in the Age of Deng Xiaoping*, p. 410; Robert Weatherley, *Politics in China since 1949: Legitimizing Authoritarian Rule*, p. 67.

[3] This includes Zhou Enlai in the late 1920s, Kang Sheng in the 1940s, and leading party organizations such as the Central Political and Law Commission from the 1980s to the present day.

[4] Dennis J. Blasko, *The Chinese Army Today: Tradition and Transformation for the 21st Century*, p. 16.

[5] George P. Jan, "The Military and Democracy in China," in Stuart S. Nagel (ed.), *Handbook of Global Political Policy*, p. 211.

[6] David M. Finkelstein, "China's National Military Strategy," in James C. Mulvenon, Roy Kamphausen, David Lai, and Andrew Scobell (eds.), *The People's Liberation Army in the Information Age*, p. 109.

the Central Political and Legal Commission; and several subdivisions of the CCP Central Committee, such as the Central Investigation Department (the predecessor of the MSS) and the Central United Front Department. Given that Chinese security and intelligence apparatuses are responsible for protecting party leadership, countering domestic dissent, blocking coups or mass insurrections, preventing external threats to the regime, and conducting foreign operations, they are the CCP's ultimate instruments of state control, and they have been instrumental to the survival of the regime. Thus, it can be argued that security and intelligence apparatuses are an integral and multifaceted part of China's political system: they suppress political opposition, unify party factions, collect information on the political opinions of the Chinese population in country and in the diaspora, and assist the party and government with member supervision and discipline.

The internal security apparatuses such as the paramilitary, civilian police, intelligence services, and civil affairs and emergency rescue forces have increasingly taken the lead in maintaining domestic social order and have facilitated the PLA's transformation into a modern military with a predominately externally oriented mission. These apparatuses, which comprise public security bureaus, state security agencies, judicial and procuratorial organs, and PAP forces, form the first and second lines of internal security; the PLA is the third line.[7] As Murray Scot Tanner indicates, "The Party-state's capacity to successfully carry out its internal security mission by relying overwhelmingly upon its civilian and paramilitary security organs with only limited support from the PLA is critical to freeing the PLA to reform its overwhelming historical orientation toward ground forces, and allow it to modernize and concentrate its resources and capacity on mastering its Taiwan mission as well as its other largely externally-oriented missions."[8]

Specifically, the CCP has established powerful and pervasive internal security apparatuses to ensure political and social dominance, relying greatly on police forces, security apparatuses, intelligence, and justice agencies to deal with internal threats from criminals, mass protests, ethnic separatists, underground religious groups, and political dissidents. The CCP regime is convinced that strengthening internal security is critical to China's long-term prospects for governance and stability. China's internal security institutions encompass six broad areas. The first area includes the myriad police forces, namely, the nationwide public security agencies. Paramilitary forces, including the People's Armed Police, the militia, and the reserve force, constitute the second area. The third area of internal security institutions is the garrison commands of the PLA and other security organizations, and the fourth area is the justice system,

---

[7] Murray Scot Tanner, "How China Manages Internal Security Challenges and Its Impact on PLA Missions," in Roy Kamphausen, David Lai, and Andrew Scobell (eds.), *Beyond the Strait: PLA Missions Other Than Taiwan*, p. 45.

[8] Ibid., p. 40.

which includes public security agencies, the procuratorates, the courts, and the Ministry of Justice.[9] The fifth area includes the internal intelligence organizations, such as the Ministry of State Security, the Ministry of Public Security, and the military intelligence departments (organized as the Second, Third, and Fourth Departments of the PLA's General Staff Department). The sixth area includes the Central Discipline Inspection Commission, the Central Political and Legal Commission, and the Central General Office, which constitute the primary coercive organizations that lead domestic security and intelligence and are responsible for the detention, corruption, and criminal investigation, party supervision, and punishment of party members. In addition, these central organizations ensure civilian oversight of army and police personnel and impose disciplinary sanctions and legal penalties on state officials and party cadres who commit disciplinary violations or crimes.

This book examines the roots of security and intelligence in contemporary China, that is, the legacy of those institutions and the practices inherited from the early communist movement of the 1920s. However, its greater purpose is to analyze how security and intelligence apparatus were created, how they evolved, how they have been shaped by party politics, and how they have influenced the politics of the party elite who wield political power in the most important party organizations Although this study seeks to provide comprehensive research from a historical perspective on China's security and intelligence agencies, its central focus is to investigate the patterns of leadership politics from the vantage point of security and intelligence organizations and operations; it does so by providing detailed information about the structure and operation of these organizations and offering alternative interpretations of major events throughout CCP history. This theoretical and practical investigation supplies the reader with an understanding of the salient dynamics underlying elite politics. From the security and intelligence perspectives, the book specifies some of the broader implications for theory and research that help our understanding of how the security and intelligence services will develop in the future, as well as the nature of Chinese politics. This book therefore seeks to add to the existing body of knowledge regarding the role of security and intelligence organizations in the Chinese communist movement and in party elite politics.

This book makes six major contributions. First, this work is the first full-length scholarly study of Chinese security and intelligence organizations and their role in elite politics. Second, the book presents a broad comparative perspective on key mechanisms used to consolidate power and maintain political control through security and intelligence apparatuses in different communist regimes, particularly the profoundly different roles that Chinese and Soviet security and intelligence organizations have played in politics. Third, it develops an analytical framework that outlines how CCP security and intelligence

---

[9] Although China's criminal justice system has built-in checks and balances, the public security agencies, procuratorate, and courts collaborate with one other to meet party objectives.

agencies function and how their operations affect party politics. Fourth, it offers case studies of the involvement of security and intelligence apparatuses in intraparty conflicts throughout CCP history; these case studies employ new empirical material that is both descriptive and analytic in terms of the various organizations' methods, actions, influences, and relationship to elite politics. Fifth, the book highlights major implications for the future of China's security and intelligence agencies and services. Finally, it provides a guiding framework for future research on this subject and on Chinese politics in general.

Evolution and Features

The emergence of the CCP's security and intelligence apparatuses resulted from the abandonment of the united front between the Chinese Communist Party (CCP) and the Chinese Nationalist Party (Guomindang) in 1927. Although a few security and intelligence organizations had been created in the CCP-led labor unions and in the peasant associations during the early communist movement (mostly to protect regional CCP leaders in places such as Shanghai and Hunan),[10] the CCP leadership did not establish central security and intelligence agencies until the spring of 1927, when Nationalists massacred Communist Party members, thus destroying the previous cooperation between the CCP and the GMD.[11] These new security and intelligence organizations served to provide internal security, maintain discipline within the ranks, protect party leaders and organizations from external threats, sabotage the enemy, and punish traitors.[12] The violence of the GMD against the CCP in the spring of 1927 catalyzed a number of underground groups, which had been formed by survivors of the persecutions and killings in GMD-controlled areas. In response to the violence, CCP leadership established a security and intelligence organization – the Central Committee's Special Services Division (SSD, Teke) – to arrange clandestine meetings and protect party leaders and organizations. The

[10] For example, the Shanghai General Labor Union was established in June 1925 following the May Thirtieth Movement, an incident triggered by anti-imperialist sentiment and fueled by the heroism and radicalism of the Chinese working class. The Department of Policing Duties was one of four departments within the Shanghai General Labor Union (which also included the departments of General Affairs, Communications, and Accounting). See Zhang Guotao, *Wode huiyi* [My reminiscence], vol. 2, p. 429; the departments in charge of the *jiucha* were also created in Guangzhou and Hong Kong after the May Thirtieth Movement. See Tian Min and Xu Jianchuan (eds.), *Gonghui da cidian* [The big dictionary of labor unions], p. 172.

[11] Under the leadership of Chen Duxiu, the CCP followed a policy of collaboration with the Nationalists, as dictated by the Comintern. The failure of the united front resulted directly in Chen's fall from leadership. See William Theodore De Bary, *Sources of East Asian Tradition: The Modern Period*, vol. 2, p. 730.

[12] "Zhongguo renmin jingcha jianshi" bianxiezhu, *Zhongguo renmin jingcha jianshi* [A brief history of Chinese policing], p. 4; Zhongguo renmin gong'an shigao bianxie xiaozu, *Zhongguo renmin gong'an shigao* [Draft of Chinese people's public security history; hereafter, *Gong'an shigao*], pp. 4–20.

SSD's antiespionage network enabled the CCP to access classified information of GMD intelligence organizations and the Shanghai Municipal Police, which controlled the Shanghai International Settlement (where most of the CCP leadership was located at the time).[13] These efforts were intended not only to contend with Nationalist agents and to punish communist turncoats but also as a preventive measure to intimidate those who were disloyal to the party and divulged party secrets.

In the Jiangxi base areas, where the party was to soon establish its government and consolidate control,[14] the Political Security Department (later renamed the State Political Security Bureau) was created in March 1931 through a reorganization of the Commission for Suppressing Counterrevolutionaries (the leading security and intelligence organization that had been established in the base areas in 1929).[15] Anti-counterrevolutionary campaigns in the base areas were launched by the CCP against opposition both outside and inside the revolutionary movement, as the CCP had suffered setbacks as a result of repeated betrayals and the exposure of underground organizations, as well as the political intrigue of noncommunist politicians against the CCP and its leaders.[16] These setbacks that the CCP suffered directly contributed to the large-scale purges and killings launched by political leaders such as Mao Zedong in the Jiangxi base areas. The Futian Incident, in which thousands of Red Army soldiers who mutinied against Mao's leadership were massacred, took place in the context of a hunt to weed out counterrevolutionaries. The CCP believed the soldiers to have been organized by the Anti-Bolshevik Corps, a secret GMD faction that sought to infiltrate the Red Army and communist base areas.[17] Over time, the CCP leadership, controlled by Returned Students, a group of Chinese students who studied in the Soviet Union from the late 1920s until early 1935, sent a large number of followers to the Jiangxi base areas. The Political Security Department (PSD) and State Political Security Bureau (SPSB) of those base areas essentially copied the structure of the Soviet security services, such as the GPU (*Gosudarstvennoe Politicheskoe Upravlenie* – State Political Administration) and the NKVD (*Narodny Komissariat Vnutrennikh Del* – People's Commissariat of Internal Affairs). In this manner the PSD/SPSB amassed an enormous network of agents who penetrated all levels of the Soviet

---

[13] Mu Xin, *Chen Geng tongzhi zai Shanghai: Zai zhongyang teke de douzheng jingli* [Comrade Chen Geng in Shanghai: Battle experience in the Central Special Service Division], p. 22.

[14] In the base areas, the CCP established its guerrilla army and governments by organizing the poor peasants against landlords and rich peasants, often violently.

[15] *Gong'an shigao*, pp. 26–7; Zhonggong zhongyang zuzhi bu [CCP Organization Department] et al., *Zhongguo gongchandang zuzhi shi ziliao* [Reference materials of the history of the CCP organizations; hereafter, *Zuzhi shi ziliao*], vol. 2, p. 354.

[16] Tony Saich and Hans J. Van de Ven, "Regional Variations," in Tony Saich and Hans J. Van de Ven (eds.), *New Perspectives on the Chinese Communist Revolution*, p. 103.

[17] Stephen C. Averill, "The Origins of the Futian Incident," in Tony Saich and Hans Van de Ven (eds.), *New Perspectives on the Chinese Communist Revolution*, pp. 109–10.

Republic in the base areas,[18] the Red Army, and the party itself.[19] The top leadership of the CCP organized the PSD/SPSB in base areas nationwide to train agents to uncover enemy intelligence; to investigate counterrevolutionary activities, espionage, and counterintelligence matters; and to solve cases related to espionage, imprisonment, and execution of anyone considered an enemy or to be training an enemy of the Soviet Republic and the Red Army.

The PSD/SPSB directly commanded local branches at the provincial and county levels and sent special representatives to handle security issues, including by spying on local party and government agencies at the district and township levels.[20] In the Red Army, the PSD and its successor SPSB (the PSD was renamed the SPSB in winter 1931) controlled local branches of the front armies (*fangmian jun*), army groups (*juntuan*), and army corps (*jun*) levels; sent commissioners to supervise the officials and soldiers at the division, regiment, and company levels; and recruited a large number of the secret informers (*wang yuan*) to penetrate every level of the Red Army.[21] The State Political Security Bureau often operated in secrecy for the purpose of protecting the CCP from internal and external threats. Subordinated security departments and commissioners penetrated the entire party and army organizations, holding executive powers to conduct surveillance, investigations, and arrests, as well as to detain suspected party members, army officers, and soldiers. The SPSB aimed to achieve control over every level of the CCP and the Red Army by any means possible, including military operations, torture, and execution of suspected traitors. The SPSB's powers were unlimited and unchecked because the security apparatus received vertical commands from SPSB leadership, and local governments had no authority to intercept decisions or orders.

The use of the party's administrative body, such as the administrative office in charge of the day-to-day operation in the top leadership to control the security and intelligence agencies, began in the winter of 1930, when Mao appointed Gu Bo, general secretary of the General Front Committee and a trusted follower of Mao, to take charge of the leadership security forces. After Mao regained his party leadership position in the winter of 1935, Wang Shoudao, another of Mao's trusted followers and the general secretary of the CCP Central Secretariat, became head of the security forces. In reality, though, the power was in Mao's hands.[22] Following the Sixth Central Committee Plenum in 1938, in

---

[18] The Chinese communists split with the nationalists due to the failure of the First United Front in 1927, the CCP fled from the cities to the countryside, where it founded the semi-autonomous "Chinese Soviet Republic" as well as its local governments.

[19] Ouyang Yi, *Ouyang Yi huiyilu* [Memoirs of Youyang Yi], pp. 125–6.

[20] *Gong'an shigao*, p. 27.

[21] *Ouyang Yi huiyilu*, pp. 125–6.

[22] In October 1935, Mao appointed Wang Shoudao, Mao's longtime trusted follower and the director of the Central Secretary Office, to take charge not only of the confidential materials and communications of the top leadership but also of the SPSB. See *Zuzhi shi ziliao*, vol. 2, pt. 1, p. 87; Fei Yundong and Yu Kuihua, *Zhonggong mishu gongzuo jianshi, 1921–1949*

October 1939, the State Political Security Bureau was abolished and the Social Affairs Department (SAD) was established as the party's leading body for handling security and intelligence for the CCP.[23] The SAD was the Politburo's chief security organization, and it exercised control over both internal and external functions of the party's security, such as protecting party leaders and agencies; conducting surveillance of party members, government, and military organizations; and undertaking espionage operations. As part of the SAD's emphasis on intelligence and espionage, it was also responsible for training security and intelligence personnel.[24] For this purpose, it operated the Northwest Public School, a secret school in Yan'an.[25] The power of the SAD increased in 1941 with an all-out intelligence campaign directed against the Japanese in addition to operations directed against the GMD. The power of the SAD was also enhanced by the Yan'an rectification campaign in which Mao consolidated his ideological domination of the Chinese communist movement and his position of preeminence in the CCP, especially when the campaign escalated into a violent hunt for enemy spies. The violent rectification campaign contributed to overwhelming paranoia in the base areas, where the situation was already tense because of military pressure from the Nationalists. The campaign was a positive-sum game for Mao and Kang Sheng, Mao's "pistol" who had been trained by the Soviet secret police in Moscow before returning to China.[26] Unlike the SPSB, which retained a segmented structure and reported along a vertical chain of command, the activities of the SAD were governed through a complex two-tiered system that horizontally linked area, or "host," party committees with SAD organizations at each level of administration. Even with this additional accountability to party committees, SAD organizations were still under the professional guidance of the next-highest SAD agency.[27] Local party committees were granted control over internal security forces as a result of the party's effort to promote checks and balances for the highly centralized, independent, and secretive Soviet-style internal security system. This was also one of Mao's strategies to undermine the influence of Zhou Enlai and Zhou's followers such as Li Kenong who dominated the central security apparatuses. As such, the origins of local party committee control over internal security, according to Tanner and Green, "lie in classic 'crisis learning' – a major,

[Brief History of the CCP' Secretaries, 1921–1949], pp. 186–7; Wang Jianying, *Zhongguo gongchandang zuzhishi ziliao huibian: Lingdao jigou yange he chengyuan minglu* [A collection of reference materials on party organizational history: The evolution of the leadership structure and the list of its members; hereafter, *Lingdao jigou yangge*], p. 426.

[23] Liu Xingyi, *Yang Qiqing zhuan* [A biography of Yang Qiqing], p. 94

[24] *Gong'an shigao*, p. 80.

[25] Mu Fengyun, *Zoujin yinbi zhanxian* [Getting close to the underground front], pp. 387–8.

[26] David Priestland, *The Red Flag: A History of Communism*, p. 260.

[27] *Yang Qiqing zhuan*, p. 150.

self-inflicted security crisis the Party faced in the late 1930s that caused it to reject USSR-style security work."[28]

The Central General Office (CGO) was founded in Yan'an in 1940 and 1941, when the party was establishing rules and regulations in an effort to "straighten out" the relationships among the various departments of the CCP organs.[29] The goal was to improve the management of logistics and supplies; to systemize and standardize administrative work for all CCP organizations in Yan'an; and to strengthen preexisting regulations regarding the supply and allocation of archives, finances, accounting, and critical party documents.[30] More important, the CGO was responsible for leadership communication, management of the flow of classified and unclassified documents among top leaders, security for top leaders, leadership offices and activities, arrangement of party meetings, and the security of top leaders' residences and travels. These responsibilities and activities demonstrate the CGO's key role in serving top leadership and managing the sensitive administrative and logistical affairs of the entire CCP leadership. Throughout its existence the CGO has been a top administrative body of the party bureaucracy: it is the communication center for top party leaders and the central party apparatus, it coordinates policy implementation and leaders' important affairs, and it serves as a center for providing luxurious benefits and security for high-ranking leaders.[31]

The evolution of the CGO reflects the development of Chinese elite politics: from Mao's reliance on statecraft, coercion, ideology, and charisma to Hu Jintao's emphasis on power sharing, consultation, and consensus building. Between the 1950s and the early 1960s, the CGO was the top administrative agency that served the Politburo and CCP leadership, including the paramount leader, Mao Zedong. Although the CGO was the nerve center that helped Mao communicate with and control high-ranking leaders, it was for the most part directly commanded by top party organs, such as the Politburo and the Central Secretariat. As consensus had been a primary principle of party leadership, the indiscriminate use of the CCP's top organs and security apparatuses in elite conflicts went against party dogma. The Great Leap Forward was disastrous for the Chinese economy, and thus created a near-irreconcilable conflict

---

[28] Murray Scot Tanner and Eric Green, "Principals and Secret Agents: Central versus Local Control over Policing and Obstacles to 'Rule of Law' in China," in Donald C. Clarke (ed.), *China's Legal System: New Developments, New Challenges*, p. 96.
[29] See Shi Zhe, *Zai lishi juren shenbian: Shi Zhe huiyilu* [At the side of a colossus: Memoirs of Shi Zhe; hereafter, *Shi Zhe huiyilu*], pp. 161–5.
[30] See *Shi Zhe huiyilu*, pp. 162–5.
[31] Frederic Wakeman Jr., "Models of Historical Change: The Chinese State and Society, 1839–1989," in Kenneth Lieberthal (ed.), *Perspectives on Modern China: Four Anniversaries*, p. 91.

between Mao and party bureaucrats in the early 1960s.[32] If Mao's withdrawal
from some leading posts (e.g., PRC chairman) and willingness to share responsibilities with his associates in the late 1950s derived from his initiative to
release some of his tedious and time-consuming duties while maintaining the
monopoly of his undisputable power, his withdrawal from party leadership
after the Seven Thousand Cadres Conference in 1962 was because many party
leaders at different levels questioned his ability to lead the national economy.
Although Mao was still venerated as the father of the revolution and there
was no split in the top party leadership,[33] his influence on economic policy had
been greatly eclipsed, and many high-ranking leaders viewed him as unqualified
to lead the nation's economy.[34] A strong sentiment within the leadership was
that China's economic policy needed to be revised and authority over party
bureaucrats restored. These sentiments were most strongly voiced by the frontline leaders, headed by Liu Shaoqi and Deng Xiaoping, in an attempt to lead
a multidimensional "rectification" and economic adjustment. Their attempts
inevitably offended the frustrated Mao, who, because of his responsibility for
the disastrous radical economic policy, was cut out of the state's planning
process.[35] In addition to Mao's emphasis on the importance of ideology (e.g.,
that the CCP should never forget the class struggle), which helped him return to
the political arena, Mao attempted to maintain control over high-ranking party
leaders by dominating the CGO, the CCP organ that had been the key administrative and service body for frontline leaders since the 1940s. The dismissal
of Yang Shangkun, director of the CGO at the time, was undoubtedly part of
Mao's plan to secure control over the high-ranking leaders. With control of the
CGO, Mao could indiscriminately use his personal security forces, retain control over the frontline leaders and party bureaucracy, and monopolize access
to intraparty communication.

The CGO served as Mao's personal tool during the Cultural Revolution;
he called on the CGO when he needed assistance commanding the radical
mass movement, protecting his personal security, ensuring his dominance over
party leadership, punishing or rewarding high-ranking leaders, and controlling
those deemed radicals. The CGO's role changed significantly after the arrest of
the Gang of Four – a group of Maoist radicals, including Jiang Qing, Zhang
Chunqiao, Wang Hongwen, and Yao Wenyuan – and the leadership conflict
between the senior veterans, led by Deng Xiaoping and Hua Guofeng's neo-
Maoist faction. In the post-Deng era, all paramount leaders have taken an

---

[32] For a detailed analysis of the elite conflict in the early 1960s, see Roderick MacFarquhar, *The
Origins of the Cultural Revolution: Vol. 3, The Coming of the Cataclysm 1961–1966*.

[33] Ibid., p. 186.

[34] Liu Yuan and He Jiadong, "'Siqing' yituan" [Doubt about the "Four Cleanup" campaign], in
Wang Guangmei and Liu Yuan (eds.), *Nisuo bu zhidao de Liu Shaoqi* [Liu Shaoqi, whom you
don't know], pp. 95–6.

[35] Ibid.

aggressive stance to control the CGO, in order to influence the elite security forces. As the executive office serving the party chief and as the administrative body of the Politburo, the CGO is responsible for carrying out decisions of the party leadership and for providing services for the coordination, communication, transportation, security, arrangement of meetings, and other party affairs for top leaders.

The CCP security and intelligence organizations discussed here – the Central Committee's Special Services Division, the State Political Security Bureau, the Social Affairs Department, and the Central General Office – all played crucial roles in the evolution of the security and intelligence apparatuses before the People's Republic of China was founded in 1949. These organizations moved beyond security and intelligence functions into any realm in which they could fulfill the party's goals. They led the infiltration of agents into the party's organizations and intelligence agencies, and they played a vital role in assisting the party leadership in completely dominating the party. Not surprisingly, the legacies of the aforementioned pre-PRC security agencies have influenced the CCP security and intelligence organizations that were established after the PRC was founded, including the Ministry of Public Security, the People's Armed Police, the Central Guard Bureau, the Central Guard Regiment (Unit 8341), the Garrison Commands, and the Ministry of State Security.

Mechanisms of the CCP Security and Intelligence Apparatuses

The totalitarian model of employing terror in political rule has been used to describe the Soviet Union, but in contrast, China has never developed a Cheka-like secret police, nor has terror ever been systematically used on the entire population, as was the case in the Soviet Union. Even when terror was used as a form of control in the 1950s, "it was directed not against a hypothetically recalcitrant population in general, but only selected sectors in the specific conjectural campaigns to suppress counter-revolutionaries, remold intellectuals, etc."[36] Similarities do exist with the Soviet Union, though, such as the organization of the population into communal living groups, known as the *danwei* or the commune, in which both coercion and persuasion were used. However, unlike their counterparts in the Soviet Union, the CCP security and intelligence apparatuses never became as powerful and multifaceted as the Soviet security and intelligence agencies Cheka and NKVA. Because of the serious organizational weakness of the Bolsheviks,[37] Soviet communists had to turn to the

---

[36] Raymond W. K. Lau, "Socio-political Control in Urban China: Changes and Crisis," *British Journal of Sociology* 52, no. 4 (December 2001): 606.

[37] The Bolsheviks' weakness lay in their lack of government experience, lack of military experience (before the civil war), or lack of a broad popular base in the countryside.

secret police to fulfill military and government tasks.[38] This was not the case with the CCP.

Throughout most of CCP history, China's security and intelligence organizations have not had the same structure as the Soviet NKVD. At most times, there was not a vertical hierarchical command structure that possessed an enormous network of paid and unpaid agents, penetrating all levels of society and institutions, including the party itself.[39] One explanation for this difference in institutional development may be that in China there exists a long tradition of military personnel and police officers cultivating close relationships with the residents of the area to which they are assigned. Police officers are expected to know all residents in their area personally; they not only are the representatives of the regime in controlling the population but also are the most important link for the regime to connect with society. Their duties prevent and punish crime, yet also promote desirable behavior by counseling people and acting as role models. Other equally, if not more compelling, explanations are that China's top security and intelligence agencies were controlled directly by top leaders and that Mao preferred mass movements to the secret police for his dominance in the leadership. Mao's version of "mass movement," according to Tang Tsou, "referred to collective sociopolitical actions in which either a single class or, more likely, several classes and strata participated."[40] For whatever reason, the leaders of China's security and intelligence agencies did not experience the same fate as those of the Soviet NKVD – Genrikh Iagoda, Nikolai Ezhov, and Lavrentii Beria were all ultimately killed, although Beria survived Stalin by a few months.[41]

Throughout history, the structure of the CCP security and intelligence apparatuses changed as their tasks changed. In the late 1920s and early 1930s, the Central Special Division was an elite force dedicated to eradicating enemy agents and communist turncoats threatening top leaders' security. In the Jiangxi base areas during the 1930s, the State Political Security Bureau (SPSB) was created to suppress counterrevolutionaries and to perform security duties, intelligence services, and law enforcement (e.g., case investigation, policing, prison administration, public safety). In copying the Soviet Cheka and NKVD as Soviet communism had been a guide and an inspiration for the CCP to pursue for China's revolution, the SPSB became an independent organization with a vertical hierarchy over which neither local party committees nor army political departments had any authority. Thus, in the early Chinese communist movement, the Soviet terrorist experience greatly influenced the CCP's security

---

[38] Jonathan R. Adelman, "Soviet Secret Police," in Jonathan Adelman (ed.), *Terror and Communist Politics: The Role of the Secret Police in Communist States*, p. 80.

[39] Peter Kenez, *A History of the Soviet Union from the Beginning to the End*, p. 111.

[40] Tang Tsou, *The Cultural Revolution and Post-Mao Reforms: A Historical Perspective* (Chicago: The University of Chicago, 1986), p. 276.

[41] Ibid., pp. 109–10.

apparatus, and the SPSB carried out mass terror operations and purges, killing tens of thousands of people accused of being members of the Reorganization Clique (*Gaizu pai*) or Third Party, and the AB Corps. The logic behind the mass purges was to eliminate the threat of encirclement by Nationalist armies: hidden enemies in the communist ranks could collaborate with external enemies such as the Nationalists by revealing the CCP's secrets and instigating rebellion against the CCP and therefore pose a threat to the base areas. The SPSB in the base areas hence became a machine of repression of powerful leaders, and it subsequently conducted the most notorious terror operations in the CCP's history: the 1931 campaign against the AB Corps in the Jiangxi base areas; the great suppression of counterrevolutionaries in the Hubei, Henan, and Anhui base areas from 1932 to 1934; and the purges against the Reorganization Clique in the Hunan and Western Hubei base areas from 1932 to 1934. The "crime" of those executed often was not that they were alleged counterrevolutionaries or that they opposed the leadership, but that they disagreed with the opinions of the powerful leaders.

Although the Social Affairs Department (SAD) was originally created in 1939 as an institutional guarantee to ensure Mao's control over the security and intelligence apparatuses, it gradually developed into a powerful and efficient party agency. The SAD was able to ensure the party's control over base areas and facilitate the CCP's infiltration of both GMD- and Japanese-controlled areas. Unlike the SPSB, the activities of the SAD were governed through a complex two-tiered system that horizontally linked each office to local, or "host," party committees. Mao was concerned that a vertical system of organization in the security forces would not allow for effective surveillance by the party committee. He feared that ambitious security leaders might become powerful and independent, thus endangering the legitimacy of the party committee. Mao, of course, continued to use coercive approaches to ensure the compliance of party members and other colleagues, yet he much preferred winning voluntary compliance through persuasive measures and garnering loyalty from associates and party members. Although Mao's dominance of security and intelligence agencies was evident after the PRC was founded, the establishment of the Ministry of Public Security and the Central Investigation Department was an important symbolic step toward the institutionalization of the CCP security apparatuses.

Today, China's intelligence services have retained their conventional functions, such as collecting political and military intelligence, but they have also increased their monitoring of global political and military activities in order to reduce conflicts and to increase cooperation. They have even collected intelligence on "friendly" states and actors. The PLA intelligence organizations engage in defense intelligence, including targeting major actors, early warning, strategic maneuvers, force structure and deployment, weapons development and acquisition, and proliferation of nuclear weapons and missile technology. Despite the overlapping jurisdictions of domestic agencies, the Ministry of State Security actively engages in public security concerns, such as organized crime, international terrorism, drug trafficking, and transnational computer terrorism. However, state security does not deal with common criminals, murderers, child molesters, bandits, and white-collar criminals; these are left to the police and prosecutors. Still, CCP state security is responsible mainly for the security of the regime, and it increasingly arrests and convicts "enemies of the state," which suggests that the state defines political crimes very broadly. As political stability is the top priority of the government, security and intelligence organizations are required to censor information aggressively to monitor political dissidents and antigovernment sentiment. Like the Ministry of Public Security, the MSS has broad authority in domestic intelligence activities, authority so great that it overlaps with the law enforcement responsibilities of the MPS.

The relationship between the Ministry of State Security (MSS) and the police forces was rather complicated and at times quite strained since the MSS was established in June 1983. Western security and intelligence services have experienced similar interinstitutional tensions, but in China such problems were more than merely structural. As an institutionalized apparatus of repression, the MSS encompasses a range of functions, including regular police, political police, and operating intelligence and counterintelligence missions. The MSS is closely tied with the police and is authorized to instruct police to carry out actions of duty such as taking a person into custody and searching cars and houses. However, in reality MSS officials often use police and other agents of the security sector for their own purposes. Although both the MSS and the MPS are militarily organized state security agencies and are responsible for safeguarding the security, rights, and interests of citizens, they primarily protect the party-state's power and the dominance of the CCP. Because their tasks are to repress political opposition against the party and maintain political control over society, their function was essentially political. This explains the high status of the political police in the party-state hierarchy. Still, the economic reforms and increasing openness of the past three decades have brought about certain transparency, efficiency, and effectiveness to the police. Examples of this include the depoliticized efforts to combat terrorism and human trafficking inside and outside the country, as well as having regular professional relationships with counterparts in other countries.

Security and Intelligence Apparatuses and CCP Elite Politics

Throughout the CCP's history, the amount of control over the security and intelligence organizations that a leader has demonstrates how powerfully and effectively he commands the party bureaucracy. Although control of the security and intelligence agencies is the central method for consolidating political power, the ability to employ strategies to create, reorganize, or abolish security and intelligence organizations in accordance with political reality has been a fundamental criterion of being a successful paramount leader in China. In the era of the communist revolution, the dominant leaders relied greatly on their prestige, charisma, personal ties, and status within the revolution to legitimize their command over security and intelligence organizations. After the PRC was founded, this pattern continued, albeit in a slightly different way, as the increasing institutionalization of the CCP promoted power sharing in the leadership in regards to control over security and intelligence organizations. In contrast, the effective control over security and intelligence apparatuses further enhances their prestige, charisma, and influence and thus consolidates their power and dominance among the party leadership.

The CCP security apparatuses engage in protection of the leadership and the regime from enemies who seek its overthrow or weakening. Frequent contact and interaction with the paramount leader was required to ensure that he was well informed. In particular, there were two policy areas Mao thought required his intervention and in which he put the most efforts for his personal involvement: foreign policy and the security apparatus.[42] Mao specifically ordered MPS minister Luo Ruiqing to report all of Luo's work directly to Mao, whereas the MPS was led institutionally by the State Council.[43] One of the important features of Mao's leadership was his guidance of the broad directions in which policy should move and his simultaneous reluctance to assume a specific administrative duty himself. Although he paid great attention to his colleagues' handling of important issues, he was often absent from Beijing and allowed many issues to go forward without intervening. Thus, both the institutional arrangement and Mao's frequent absence gave the party bureaucracy influence and control over the security and intelligence organizations.

China's security and intelligence organizations in the 1950s developed in two directions – one was the party bureaucracy's control over key security and intelligence agencies (e.g., the MPS, the Central Investigation Department) and the other was Mao's surveillance of key security agencies and monopoly over the Central Guard Bureau (also known as the Ninth Bureau of the MPS) and Unit 8341. An important change regarding the security forces occurred in 1953, when the power that controlled these forces became divided. Although Luo Ruiqing was still the most powerful figure in the security forces,[44] the Central General Office (CGO), headed by Yang Shangkun, began to share the security force's managerial responsibilities with Luo. Another portion of the power went to Wang Dongxing, Mao's chief bodyguard, who was appointed to lead the Central Guard Bureau, which was reorganized in 1953 with the removal of responsibility of top leaders from the Eighth Bureau, headed by Liu Wei. In

---

[42] *Gong'an shigao*, p. 338.
[43] According to Luo Ruiqing, the MPS was institutionally a ministry under the authority of the State Council. However, it was a party agency similar to the Social Affairs Department and directly under Mao's command. See Huang Yao and Zhang Mingzhe, *Luo Ruiqing zhuan* [A biography of Luo Ruiqing], pp. 263–5.
[44] He was the most powerful figure in the security forces because of his responsibility in the Ministry of Public Security under the Government Administrative Council and the PLA Public Security Forces.

addition, Yang Shangkun's power was greatly weakened with the merger of the Administrative Department of the Central General Office and the newly established Central Guard Bureau, led by Wang Dongxing. Mao's political strategy was clear when he installed loyalist Wang Dongxing in institutions dominated by those with whom Mao had no strong personal connection. The duties of the Central Guard Bureau or Ninth Bureau of the Ministry of Public Security were intentionally limited mainly to guarding only the top five leaders (and Politburo members who lived in Zhongnanhai), which at the time included Mao, Liu Shaoqi, Zhou Enlai, Zhu De, and Chen Yun. The divided Eighth Bureau retained some of its previous duties, such as guarding ranking leaders other than those previously mentioned. In 1955, Wang Dongxing was appointed vice minister of public security and served as Mao's representative to the Ministry of Public Security; he also continued to serve as Mao's chief bodyguard in Zhongnanhai. Mao's tendency to manipulate the organizational structure of the security apparatuses to personally control the security forces and even establish additional personal security forces demonstrates Mao's desire to have direct control and influence over the security apparatuses. Although having an institutionalized system made it more difficult for him to do this, he deftly adapted to the circumstances and worked within the organizational structure by appointing his closest and most trusted followers – such as Wang Dongxing and Zhang Yaoci, the commander of Unit 8341 – to positions of power.

The increasing influence of the party bureaucracy on the security and intelligence agencies was one of Mao's primary concerns, when he decided to launch the Cultural Revolution. On the eve of the Cultural Revolution, Mao purged the leading figures from the security and intelligence agencies, such as Peng Zhen, mayor of Beijing and a key figure in the Central Secretariat who was assigned to lead the public security, legal, and intelligence agencies; Yang Shangkun, director of the CCP's General Office; and Luo Ruiqing, PLA general chief of staff and former public security minister. Many of Luo's former trusted subordinates who held key positions in the MPS were purged as well. Although Peng's imprisonment was necessary for Mao to sever the link between frontline leaders and the security and intelligence apparatuses, Yang's control of the Central Guard Regiment and Unit 8341, as well as the domestic intelligence agencies, left Mao with only one recourse: to purge Yang and exile him to Guangdong so that he would not become a threat. It is important to note, however, that Mao's increasing dependence on the Central General Office to gain support for the Cultural Revolution pushed him to be extremely concerned about the CGO's loyalty. Therefore, the organizational evolution of the CGO during the early stages of the Cultural Revolution was a process of gradual exclusion of those who were not trusted, as well as a gradual consolidation of Wang Dongxing's power. In addition, Mao's deep distrust of the intelligence agencies resulted in the abolishment of the Central Investigation Department and its merger with the Second Department of the PLA General Staff Department in June 1969.

The organizational merger of the Central Guard Bureau and Unit 8341 in October 1969 was a significant step in Mao's strengthening his control over the security forces. Wang Dongxing was appointed commander of the newly merged Guard Department of the Central General Office. This merger took place in the background of a few key political developments: the Sino-Soviet border dispute was intensifying, Lin Biao was gaining favor in the PLA and among party leadership, and a conflict was developing between Lin's group and the radical Cultural Revolution Group (CRG). After the merger, Wang Dongxing's authority was further strengthened. When it was necessary for the Guard Department to collaborate with other units, such as the Beijing Garrison Command, the Beijing Bureau of Public Security, local public security bureaus, or PLA units, all orders directing these joint efforts originated with the Guard Department headed by Wang. By centralizing power over the security forces in Wang Dongxing's hands, Mao was able to ensure his personal security, control the party bureaucracy, and effectively keep watch over other ranking leaders.

In the post-Mao power struggle between the senior veteran faction led by Deng Xiaoping and the so-called Two Whatevers faction headed by Hua Guofeng, control of security and intelligence organizations became crucial for gaining advantage over political enemies. Before Deng launched the Theoretical Discussions on the "Criteria of Truth" to officially challenge the authority of Hua Guofeng, he attempted to control the security organizations, as he knew this would ensure his dominance among party leadership. Although the security forces still remained organizationally subordinate to the Central General Office, under the dual leadership of the PLA and the Central General Office, Deng moved to establish dominance over the forces by reorganizing the leadership of the security apparatus. The PLA General Staff Department, led by Deng, took full control over both the Central Guard Bureau, and Unit 8341, in an effort to undermine the influence of the CGO as well as Wang's dominance in the security apparatus. This separation was further carried out by appointing Yang Dezhong to lead both the Central Guard Bureau and Unit 8341; Yao Yilin, vice secretary-general of the CCP and former minister of commerce (who had no military background) was appointed to lead the Central General Office. After the PLA's acquisition of the Central Guard Bureau and Unit 8341, the CGO no longer had *de facto* authority over these instrumental elite security forces.

Wang Dongxing lost his power during the Third Plenum, held in December 1978, when Deng Xiaoping emerged victorious from the power struggle and unveiled his vision of economic reform. The Third Plenum also set the tone for further victories by veteran leaders following the reorganization of the security services and the removal of Wang Dongxing. Key followers and subordinates of Wang Dongxing were purged, dismissed, or transferred. Those who served Wang Dongxing but were not charged with wrongdoing were transferred to local military units outside of Beijing, where they were appointed to symbolic positions such as deputy commander of a military district.

Although the Central General Office had become much less powerful and influential than it was under Mao's era, it was still the primary working body for providing services to top party organizations. As the CGO was assigned to serve the Politburo, the Central Secretariat, and the CCP General Secretary, it did not have a clear relationship with Deng Xiaoping, despite the fact that Deng had been recognized as the "core of the collective leadership" at the Third Plenum in 1978.[45] As the CGO no longer held any real power, this left room for the Office of Deng Xiaoping to be established. The office was created to function similarly to the former CGO but specifically to serve Deng. Wang Ruilin, Deng's senior secretary who had served Deng since the early 1950s, was appointed director of the office. At the same time, Wang Ruilin assisted Deng in surveillance of the PLA General Office and the CGO through his role as deputy director of the PLA General Office (1983–1990) and later as deputy director of the CGO (1990–1995). With Wang positioned for intelligence operations, Deng was able to control the CGO and ensure smooth communications with other top leaders.

As the Central General Office was no longer actively involved in elite politics to the extent that it was under Mao's leadership in the Cultural Revolution, it dealt less with elite politics and party infighting because of its limited involvement in communication and interaction among leadership and its limited access to confidential information. Important communications, interactions, and negotiations among top leaders shifted to Deng's confidants and trusted followers – in this case, Yang Shangkun and Wang Ruilin almost exclusively. Because the CGO had become less powerful, it was sheltered from leadership conflicts and changes. Remember, the CGO was created to assist the Politburo and the Central Secretariat in implementing the decisions of top leadership. However, in Deng's era, the CGO served partially as an extension of the Office of Deng Xiaoping, as it was directly supervised by Deng's senior secretary, Wang Ruilin, who was also deputy director of the CGO.

Considering all the changes in organizational structure and the power dynamics involved, it is evident the real authority behind the CGO was not the Politburo, the Central Secretariat, or the general secretary of the party but rather the leading elders, particularly Deng Xiaoping himself. Thus, the functions of the Central General Office in Deng Xiaoping's era gradually diminished, and the CGO evolved into a party organization that mainly provided administrative services to the Central Secretariat and high-ranking leaders. These services included drafting speeches, policy advising, residence allocation, hospital arrangements, lodging in Beijing for business trips of provincial and local party leaders, and arrangement of funerals for deceased veterans. Often, other organizations encroached on their functions, such as the Office of

---

[45] See Li Yan, *Zaisheng zhongguo – zhonggong shiyi jie sanzhong quanhui de qianqian houhou* [Rebirth of China – before and after the Third Plenum of the CCP Eleventh Party Congress], vol. 1 (Beijing: Zhonggong dangshi chubanshe, 1998), pp. 370–71.

Deng Xiaoping and the Political Research Office, headed by Pao Tong under Zhao Ziyang's tenure as the party general secretary.

When senior veterans appointed Jiang Zemin general secretary of the party immediately after the 1989 Tiananmen incident, the CGO gradually became significant in helping Jiang consolidate his power. A very significant turning point in the CGO's history was when Jiang transferred Zeng Qinghong, former vice general secretary of the Shanghai Party Committee, to the Central General Office as its deputy director. Although Wen Jiabao was the director of the CGO at the time, Zeng was in charge of the CGO's most important affairs and he represented the CGO in its service to Jiang Zemin. Because Zeng was assigned by Jiang to assist him in making important decisions and to be involved in supervising party agencies, many functions were added to the responsibilities of the Central General Office, including enacting party rules and regulations and spearheading work related to state legislation.

As the longtime right-hand man of Jiang Zemin and a skillful political operator with strong personal ties to party veterans, military leaders, and the elite group of China's "princelings," a term referring to the descendants of prominent and influential senior CCP officials. Zeng helped Jiang set aside rivals and cultivate ties with many party veterans. He did so by enhancing his influence over the security and intelligence apparatuses and by taking advantage of the decline of veteran leaders' influence, a result of their age and health problems. Perhaps Zeng's most important role as Jiang's aide was his instigation of the removal of the Yang brothers and their followers in 1992 who posed challenges to Jiang's authority in the PLA. In doing so, he was able to eliminate opponents and consolidate Jiang's grip on the military. Later, in 1995, Zeng arrested the mayor of Beijing, Chen Xitong, and subsequently took over the capital and ultimately undermined the influence of Li Peng, thus facilitating Jiang's power grab. Both maneuvers were achieved when Zeng was working in the Central General Office, first as the deputy director and then as director. Zeng's control over the CGO significantly consolidated Jiang's power and strengthened his leadership.

Carrying on Jiang's legacy, Hu Jintao continues to strengthen the power of the CGO. After he was promoted to chairman of the CCP, he made Ling Jihua, a longtime follower, head of the CGO. Although Hu pursues strong personal control over the security and intelligence agencies through the CGO, it is harder for him to do so because of the trend toward institutionalizing the security and intelligence apparatuses. Another possible reason for Hu's lack of influence over the security and intelligence apparatuses is that, historically, Hu has had weak ties with the agencies. Moreover, Hu has remained in the shadow of Jiang Zemin (Hu's predecessor), who held powerful influence over the security and intelligence organizations even after his retirement. Because the intraparty "democracy" based on institutionalizing rules and norms in the party has been considered largely favorable by the party leadership and the general population, it is possible that institutionalizing these organizations will guide the future of security and intelligence in the CCP and engender a profound and lasting change in their structure and operations.

Methodology and Organization of the Study

For most of their existence, the secret world of CCP security and intelligence apparatuses has remained in the shadows because of the lack of transparency in China; as a result, the CCP's operations and activities are unknown to outsiders. Although the release of intelligence and security information has been welcomed, it is just the tip of the iceberg of available material, and only a small portion of the archive has been opened; moreover, our knowledge of CCP's intelligence and security services remains incomplete. This book draws on a wide range of sources from different time periods. The first and most extensively used sources are Chinese-language books, periodicals, and newspapers. During two trips to China, I was able to acquire more than four hundred books, including a number of restricted-circulation materials and books not available to foreigners (*neibu faxing*) and numerous periodicals dealing with the CCP security and intelligence apparatuses and services, as well as with those organizations' relationships to elite politics.

The majority of security and intelligence material released to date concerns the events of the CCP revolution against the Nationalist government and the Japanese during World War II. However, in examining the released records, a number of common themes emerge. Party records from the 1920s and public publications comprise the essential sources, yet the materials released during the Cultural Revolution and in the reform era contain much useful information concerning behind-the-scenes activities. These materials are the bedrock of information for understanding and interpreting leadership conflict of the eras, and thus have been used significantly in this research. However, each category of sources has its strengths and weaknesses, and each is used to different degrees by different authors, but at the very least, quality sources can be used to check the claims of other sources, such as memoirs, news reports, biographies, and other after-the-fact accounts. Sources also complement one another when they provide different perspectives. It is important to use multiple sources on one topic to provide a clearer picture of elite politics.

This research is largely benefited from the rich documentary collections, detailed chronologies, revealing memoirs, and academic histories published in the post-Mao period. These bring a great depth to the current understanding of CCP elite politics – mostly because, even with their flaws, they are more extensive and objective than those released in any previous period. Many outstanding post-Mao materials have been used in this study, including the nine volumes (with four ancillary volumes) of *Reference Materials of the History of the CCP Organizations*, authored by the CCP Organizational Department and others (published by Central Party School Press in 2000); the fourteen volumes of *The Soviet Communist Party, Comintern and Chinese Soviet Movement*, compiled by the CCP Central Party History Research Office (published by Central Documentary Press in 2002), and the eighteen volumes of *A Selection of the CCP Central Committee Documents*, compiled by the Central Archives (published by the Central Party School Press in 1989. I also used comprehensive reference materials, such as *A Collection of Reference Materials about the CCP Organization History: The Evolution of the Leadership Structure and the List of Its Members*, edited by Wang Jianying (published by the Central Party School Press in 1995) and *The PLA Organizational Evolution and the List of Leadership Members at Different Levels*, compiled by the Military Library of the CCP Military Academy (published by Military Science Press in 1990). Moreover, I drew on chronologies such as *Chronicle of Mao Zedong, Chronicle of Liu Shaoqi, Chronicle of Zhou Enlai, Chronicle of Deng Xiaoping*, and the chronicles of many high-ranking leaders, such as Zhu De, Chen Yun, Yang Shangkun, Ren Bishi, Peng Zhen, Peng Dehuai, Ye Jianying, Nie Rongzhen, Dong Biwu, and Luo Ronghuan. I also used the revealing memoirs of top party officials, such as Zhang Guotao, Zhao Ziyang, Yang Shangkun, Bo Yibo, Chen Pixian, Tong Xiaopeng, Deng Liqun, and Song Renqiong; of top military figures, such as Xu Xiangqian, Liu Huaqing, Zhang Zhen; of many PLA generals, such as Huang Kecheng, Xiao Ke, Yang Chengwu, Wu Faxian, Fu Chongbi, Chen Xilian, Liao Hansheng, and Li Zhimin; and of former security and intelligence officers, such as Nie Rongzhen, Wang Fang, Xiong Xianghui, Li Yimin, Li Yimeng, Ouyang Yi, and Wu Lie. I also studied the biographies of high-ranking party and army leaders, such as Mao Zedong, Deng Xiaoping, Ren Bishi, Ye Jianying, Dong Biwu, Zhang Aiping, Yang Yong, as well as of security and intelligence leaders, such as Zhou Enlai, Chen Yun, Kang Sheng, Chen Geng, Luo Ruiqing, Xu Zirong, Yang Qiqing, Li Kenong, Pan Hannian, Zhao Cangbi, Wu Zhong, Pan Yan, and Zhou Chunlin. The personal historical records and personal accounts of important events regarding intraparty conflict and the security and intelligence services provided by the high-ranking leaders and their family members, such as Li Rui, Wu De, and Li Xuefeng, as well as the four volumes of *An Instant in History*, edited by Zhu Chunlin (Volume 1) and Sun Mingshan (published by Qunzhong chubanshe from 1999 to 2004) were useful. Finally, I drew on the memoirs and biographies of the personal secretaries and security guards of the CCP's top leaders, such as Chen Boda, Shi Zhe, Wang Dongxing, Ye Zilong, Zhang Yaoci, Chen Changjiang, Wu Jicheng, and Zhang Yunsheng, as well as the memoirs and personal accounts from a few former party officials and intelligence personnel in exile abroad, such as Xu Jiatun, Li Zhisui, and several intelligence officials who have defected.[46]

---

[46] Among all memoirs written by the high-ranking leaders, Deng Liqun's memoir by far provides the most detailed exposure of the interactions as well as the cooperation and conflicts among the top leaders in the 1980s. In addition, the four volumes of *An Instant in History* covering the memoirs of the public security officers and their family members are undoubtedly the best comprehensive compilation of the CCP's public security history. Moreover, Wu Jicheng's

Nevertheless, the analytical part of this work still has the mark of a young subject. Reliable information is still shrouded in official secrecy. This study references a number of Chinese sources, including biographies and memoirs from security and intelligence personnel, that present fragmented information regarding activities of the former security and intelligence officers. These sources unquestionably are a rich vein of information concerning actors not normally in the public eye. However, many of the released sources also have limitations, given the political constraints concerning sensitive issues, as well as fragmentation, inconsistencies, inaccuracies resulting from biases, and unreliability; therefore, any specific claim from these sources must be treated with caution and must be verified by different sources, especially the richer vein of party documents and materials published in the reform era. In addition, the literature is heavily weighted toward a pro-CCP stance, and very little draws on other perspectives. Thus, these references must be treated carefully and cannot be relied on heavily because they are of variable quality and often unreliable.

Methodologically, a diverse approach to data analysis has been used in this research. The narrative analysis is introduced to find the voice of the involved political figures and participants and to understand the cases in context, including the particularities of time, place, and setting. Statistical analyses based on data collection, analysis, summarization, and interpretation help discover the underlying causes, patterns, relationships, and trends of political events. Network analysis is based on an assumption of the importance of relationships among high-ranking leaders and focuses on the structure of relationships, ranging from casual acquaintances to close bonds. The content analysis that focuses on conceptual analysis and relational analysis establishes the existence and frequency of concepts and examines the relationships among concepts in a text. The multiple-method approaches serve to build as complete a picture of the elite politics as possible by collecting and explaining data from different sources and perspectives.

Moreover, one of the primary intentions of this book is to highlight the rich and diverse collection of security and intelligence records that can be found in the publicly available literature. This research is guided by the principle to use only published work derived from mainly four sources: (1) scholarly books and academic journals; (2) monographs, government documents and reports, military dictionaries, and yearbooks;[47] (3) news reports and published interviews and speeches; and (4) the interviews conducted with CCP historians and the incumbent and retired party and security officers during my research

---

memoir, which records Wu's experience in the Guard Bureau and Unit 8341 during his tenure between the late 1940s and the late 1970s, is the most detailed and objective description of the history of both organizations.

[47] Despite the fact that these works are not academically oriented and are often written in a narrative style, they offer some insight into the CCP's security and intelligence organizations.

in China.[48] To achieve comprehensive coverage of the CCP's security and intelligence organizations as well as of their role in elite politics and Chinese society in general, each chapter deals with a separate theme, with sources indicated in the footnotes, focusing primarily on material available in the public domain. The book seeks to shed light on some of the shadowy aspects of Chinese security and intelligence history, and to provide a framework for all those interested in the history and evolution of Chinese security and intelligence apparatuses and their roles in CCP elite politics.

Chapters 1 and 2 explore the role of the MPS in China's security and intelligence services from a historical perspective. Chapter 3 traces the evolution of the Central Guard Bureau (CGB) since its inception in the late 1940s and examines its organizational makeup and general operations. It focuses on the CGB's role in the central security agencies to highlight key features and characteristics of its importance in politics, including its crucial role in internal surveillance and control involved in its coercive role of the central security apparatus in Zhongnanhai politics. Chapter 4 charts the development of the Central Guard Regiment (CGR), the elite security force that guards top leaders. The CGR has historically played an important role in elite politics, particularly during the leadership conflict and the intraparty power struggle during and after the Cultural Revolution. The role of the armed police is the theme of Chapters 5 and 6, which detail its evolution from its founding and complicated tenure to its significant role quelling social disorder and cracking down on the increasing "mass incidents" during the reform era. Both chapters examine in particular the role of the armed police force, which acts as auxiliaries to the PLA and is one of three paramilitary forces in China – armed police force, the militia, and the reserve force – in performing a wide variety of security duties.

Chapter 7 turns to the analysis of the garrison commands stationed in most major cities, key coastal defense locations, and important strategic military sites. Although garrison commands are responsible for guarding military facilities and for militia and reserve forces, conscription, and the mobilization of military services, they are military police, and so work to maintain social order and discipline among the troops and military personnel stationed in their domains and among military officers and soldiers who are outside of their military barracks on pass, leave, or official duties. Special attention is paid to the Beijing Garrison Command, which has played an important role in guarding high-ranking leaders and the capital city. Chapter 8 is devoted to CCP's intelligence agencies and services during the revolutionary era. Where Chapter 8 provides a historical review of the CCP intelligence organizations that have been used against the GMD, the Japanese, and its own real or assumed

---

[48] In almost all cases, I have refrained from identifying the interviewees by name so as not to compromise the source or to endanger the individual. However, interviews and an in-depth review of relevant document and literature have helped me identify quality information in the process of data collection.

enemies, Chapter 9 focuses on China's intelligence agencies and services in the PRC era, particular on the role of Ministry of State Security (MSS), established in 1983 as part of a large-scale reorganization of China's state apparatus following Deng Xiaoping's introduction of economic reforms. A detailed evaluation of Chinese intelligence organizations and services is also conducted through an examination of the Social Affairs Department; the Central Investigation Department (the predecessors of the MSS); and the Second, Third, and Fourth Departments of the PLA General Staff Department. Chapter 10 assesses the role of the PLA in leading China's security and intelligence services, including the Guard Bureau (under the dual leadership of the PLA General Staff Department and the Central General Office), the General Office of the CMC, and the Security Department of the PLA Political Department. Special attention is paid to the military units guarding the capital, such as the PLA's 38th Army Corps or Group Army.

Finally, in conclusion, the book summarizes the developments of the CCP's security and intelligence organizations to date and considers key features of the CCP's security and intelligence apparatuses in Chinese politics. The chapter discusses significant implications of the increasing challenges that China's security and intelligence organizations have been facing throughout the reform era, as well as the changing role of security and intelligence in the era of Hu Jintao and beyond.

Historical Evolution of Public Security Organizations

The Chinese Communist Party (CCP) has long obsessed over security, intelligence, and law enforcement. When the CCP was established in July 1921, its primary mission was to mobilize and organize the labor movement, mainly focusing on worker strikes in China's major cities. Prime examples are the cases of the great strikes of the Beijing-Hankou railway workers in 1923, the Anyuan railway and coal industrial workers in 1922, and the Kailuan coal mines in 1922. When the labor movement and worker strikes confronted strong resistance from authorities, business owners, and administrations – in the form of political persecution, arrests, and terror against the communist agitators – the CCP established security services within the labor unions in an effort to protect its members and ensure the safety of its organizations. These security services were separated into four spheres of responsibility: policing duty teams (*jiucha dui*), inspection teams (*jiancha dui*), scouting teams (*zhencha dui*), and investigation teams (*diaocha dui*). Principle responsibilities of these teams were to enforce strike laws, maintain strike order, protect the workers' organizations and leaders, punish and execute defectors, and detect and suppress conspiracies. In 1925, when China's warlord authorities had to legitimize the CCP-led General Labor Union as well as its local branches, the department in charge of policing duties (*jiucha*) became a key organization controlled by the party to provide the services for protecting its organizations and reinforcing its programs.[1] These services became the prototypes for the central

---

[1] For example, the Shanghai General Labor Union was established in June 1925 following the May Thirtieth Movement, an incident triggered by the anti-imperialist sentiment and fueled by the heroism and radicalism of the Chinese working class. The Department of Policing Duties was one of four departments within the union (along with General Affairs, Communications, and Accounting). See Zhang Guotao, *Wode huiyi*, vol. 2, p. 429; the departments in charge of the *jiucha* were also created in Guangzhou and Hong Kong after the May Thirtieth Movement. See Tian Min and Xu Jianchuan, *Gonghui da cidian*, p. 172.

committee's Special Services Division (*zhongyang teke*), a well-equipped and organized security apparatus that was founded immediately after the CCP suffered a great loss and a large number of the CCP members were killed following the failure of the CCP-Guomingdang (GMD) united front. The central committee's Special Services Division (SSD, or Teke) played an important role in shaping the philosophy, mechanism, and organizational structure of the later CCP's public security system.

This chapter describes the historical context in which public security organizations emerged and evolved, dating back to the CCP-led labor movement and peasant uprisings of the 1920s. Drawing on historical and critical insights, it examines the domestic and international context and the causes of the CCP's adoption of radical policies in the late 1920s and early 1930s, including the CCP's united front and ensuing conflict with the Nationalists and the enduring intraparty power struggle. It investigates the political, social, and intellectual roots of the communist movement in early CCP history, the early efforts of the CCP to gain national legitimacy through peaceful means and elections, and the dramatic shift toward violent means of power. Through analysis of the historical context and emergence of public security organizations, the chapter demonstrates how the radical nature of the early communist movement partnered with the strong influence of the Soviet model to lay the foundation for CCP security organizations to operate through violent means to ensure the survival and dominance of the CCP.

In particular, this chapter pays attention to the evolution of the CCP's security and intelligence organizations following the assault launched by the Nationalist government against the CCP as a result of the abandoned GMD-CCP united front in 1927, and it outlines the policies of the public security organizations that spurred and shaped the CCP response. The GMD's assault occurred in both urban and rural China, with several rural large-scale GMD encirclements of the Red Army in the late 1920s and early 1930s; they catalyzed an overwhelming CCP response that consisted of violent political campaigns for eliminating counterrevolutionaries (*sufan*) and intraparty conflicts encompassing all CCP base areas, which resulted in large-scale purges and killings of so-called counterrevolutionaries. The responsibilities and authority of public security organizations were greatly enhanced as a result of their leading role in *sufan* campaigns: they managed labor camps and deportation in the 1940s and 1950s, implemented campaigns to suppress counterrevolutionaries such as the "Three-Antis" (anti-corruption, anti-waste, and anti-bureaucratism) and the "Five Antis" (anti-bribery, anti-tax evasion, anti-fraud, anti-embezzlement, and anti-leakage of state secrets) in the early 1950s, and played a vital role in facilitating land reform and collectivization in the late 1940s. In addition to analysis of the principles and philosophy that shaped the radical communist movement, this chapter details the organizational, systemic, large-scale suppression of counterrevolutionaries encouraged by the overwhelming paranoia and zealotry involved in rooting out and punishing "class enemies" in

CCP-controlled areas. Key campaigns of the movement are described in depth, such as the campaign against the so-called Anti-Bolshevik Corps (AB Corps) in the Jiangxi base area, the political purges in the Hubei-Henan-Anhui base area and the Fourth Front Army, the large-scale campaigns against the Reorganization Clique in the Hunan-Hubei border base areas, and the so-called Social Democratic Party in Western Fujian. These violent purges and killings were triggered by the Nationalist military campaigns against the Red Army, the intraparty power struggle, the lack of judicial independence and other checks and balances on executive power, and encouragement and support from Moscow. Although violent political campaigns were launched by dominant base-area party leaders in part to establish authority and consolidate power, *sufan* campaigns did not always benefit the leaders who initiated them; on the contrary, *sufan* campaigns often became a political liability because of overwhelming resentment within the party and armed forces toward the instigators. The violent experience of the early communist movement had a profound impact on party leadership and the evolution of the CCP's security apparatus.

The current public security system originated with the Yan'an (the capital city of the CCP in the late 1930s and most of the 1940s) public security organizations established in the 1940s; its evolution reflects two significant tendencies – gradual departure from the Soviet model and increasing local control over public security organizations in lieu of a centralized authority. Despite the fact that the organizational structure of the Central Committee's Social Affairs Department (SAD), created in 1939, followed that of the Soviet NKVD, the SAD differed significantly from the NKVD in that it rejected the vertical system of command championed by the NKVD. This change occurred when public security organizations were put under the jurisdiction of the SAD, as SAD branches received authority only from two chains of commands: upper-level SAD organizations and the party committees in their units. Another significant evolution of the institutional structure of CCP public security organizations is the transition from oversight by the SAD vertical command system to oversight by local government agencies; this transition began after the civil war in the 1940s. Despite the philosophical and organizational changes that form the history of China's public security organizations, they have consistently been the backbone for maintaining local political and social order.

Committee for Eliminating Counterrevolutionaries

Although the CCP's public security agencies and police organizations were founded during the periods of the Nanchang Uprising and the Guangzhou Uprising in August and December 1927, respectively, their implementation as the party's security apparatuses took place in 1928. The turning point occurred when the CCP bases established organizations to suppress counterrevolutionaries (*sufan*) – that is, Guomindang (GMD) spies, GMD agents, and CCP defectors – in its base areas.[2] Since 1929, the Committee for Eliminating Counterrevolutionaries (CEC) had been established at the CCP provincial level under the Jiangxi Soviet.[3] Although the CEC units were housed under the CCP armed forces, they were not engaged in combat activities like other Red Army units; rather, they focused exclusively on the protection of CCP organs and leaders. The CEC personnel and its informers penetrated almost every level of the Soviet Republic's governments in the Jiangxi base areas and the CCP armed forces. The CEC conducted intelligence, counterintelligence, and investigations, and it carried out arrests, searches, trials, punishments, and executions. As a result of their unchecked power, these powerful security and intelligence agencies, by virtue of the *sufan* campaigns, unleashed their violence on a wide scale. These activities continued until the mid-1930s and resulted in the deaths of tens of thousands of people. Because these organizations were responsible for not only investigation and interrogation but also conviction and execution,[4] they inevitably initiated many questionable persecutions and became the personal tools of dominant leaders against their political foes. The lack of judicial independence caused an increasing tendency toward the expansion of purge campaigns within the CCP organizations and the Red Army.[5]

The Committee for Eliminating Counterrevolutionaries was very much an ad hoc organization, and its power gradually grew in response to various emergencies and threats to the CCP base areas. No formal legislation establishing the CEC was ever enacted, thus giving it a completely extralegal nature. It was meant to serve as an organ of preliminary investigation, but the crimes it was supposed to uncover were not defined and the procedures for handling cases were not set forth, thereby allowing it to function as a temporary organ for waging war against so-called class enemies. Given its militant role and extralegal status, it is not surprising that the CEC acquired powers of summary justice as the threat of counterrevolution and the GMD's political aspirations grew.

In the terror of purges, the natural inclination of a terrorist *sufan* organization, which suspected all citizens indiscriminately, became evident in the political campaigns against the so-called counterrevolutionaries. The CEC had an excuse to arrest people who had committed no crime but who were under suspicion as potential enemies of the CCP. As a result of this summary justice, purges expanded exponentially, but there were also other factors that contributed to their expansion. First, officials of the *sufan* organizations, eager to demonstrate their loyalty and efficiency, felt little restraint in the exercise of their arbitrary powers bestowed by summary justice. Second, the methods employed by the *sufan* organizations fueled expansion of the purges. For example, a confession was usually not considered satisfactory if it failed to name

[2] *Gong'an shigao*, pp. 17–22.
[3] Ibid., p. 21.
[4] Ibid., pp. 22–3.
[5] Ibid., p. 23.

other conspirators, and the list of suspects therefore continuously expanded. Another method was that the arrest of a victim often meant that his or her relatives, friends, and coworkers would also fall under suspicion. Therefore, men and women who feared they themselves were under suspicion preemptively accused others in the hope of gaining their own safety. Zhang Guotao, head of the Hubei-Henan-Anhui base areas, observed how, through the tactics described here, the *sufan* organizations' methods of interrogation bred a "revolutionary red terrorist atmosphere."[6] Under this atmosphere of terror:

> No one dared to voice different opinions. If one did, he or she would suffer punishment. A light punishment was characterized by the accusation of being a "right deviationist"; a severe punishment was characterized by arrest as a member of the counterrevolutionary groups such as the so-called AB Corps and the Reorganization Clique, which could lead to the death penalty.[7]

In the Hubei-Henan-Anhui base areas led by Zhao Guotao, *sufan* campaigns were employed as the means for the top leaders to reorganize the party agencies and the Red Army in an effort to consolidate their power. All army units at the level of battalion and above were reorganized so that officers and soldiers were not familiar with one another. The party's leading agents were organized into inspection groups and then sent to each military unit for supervision. This further promoted the atmosphere of terror, such that even friends and acquaintances did not dare to talk with one another, to prevent being suspected as members of "secret cliques" or those who were engaged in "counterrevolutionary activities."[8] In addition, some CCP leaders were convinced that the terror of violent purges promoted strong combat effectiveness. According to General Li Zhimin, a member of the Commission of Suppression of Counterrevolutionaries in the Fifth Army Group of the Red Army, the officers and soldiers feared being targeted and thus were willing to make sacrifices on the battleground. Sacrifices and bravery were considered ways to prove their innocence and show their superiors and comrades that they were not enemy agents. This led to a perception in the Red Army that "[you would] certainly win a combat in the battleground as long as [you] launched a campaign of purges."[9] This perception also fueled enthusiasm for expanded purges in which more "class enemies" were arrested and executed and better combat effectiveness would be promoted.

The CEC was granted wide powers to eliminate counterrevolutionary outbreaks, perform combat espionage, police the borders of base areas, guard transportation facilities, and execute the government's directives to protect the

---

[6] Liu Xiaonong, "E-yu-wan suqu – Baiqueyuan sufan" [The Hubei-Henan-Anhui base area: Suppression against counterrevolutionaries in Baiqueyuan], in *Wenshi jinghua* [Gems of literature and history], no. 1 (2006), p. 25.

[7] Li Zhimin, *Li Zhimin huiyilu* [Memoirs of Li Zhimin], p. 141.

[8] Xu Xiangqian, *Lishi de huigu* [Historical recollection], vol. 1, pp. 158–9.

[9] *Li Zhimin huiyilu*, p. 141.

revolutionary order. Special military detachments were placed at its disposal. In March 1931, the CEC was abolished and a new agency was created in its place in the Jiangxi base areas. This agency was called the Political Security Department, and it was to function as a branch of the communist government in base areas. In the background of the campaigns to eliminate counterrevolutionaries in CCP base areas was Stalin's power consolidation and radical campaign against the so-called right deviationists within the leadership of the Soviet Union. Although the Nikolai Bukharin-Joseph Stalin alliance in the summer of 1926 helped Stalin successfully defeat the United Opposition, which included such preeminent and influential figures as Grigory Zinoviev, Lev Kamenev, and Leon Trotsky, Stalin turned his gun against Bukharin, a potential political rival, in 1928 and 1929. Stalin was finally able to remove Bukharin from the Politburo in November 1929. Bukharin, a proponent of moderate domestic policies and less extreme views on Western capitalism, was targeted by Stalin as a right deviationist. Distancing himself from Bukharin, Stalin advocated for a radical industrialization and collectivization of the Soviet Union and urged global revolutionary upheaval against the capitalist regime. Stalin's triumph over Bukharin determined the position of the Comintern, which was responsible for guiding the Chinese communist movement. In the tenth plenum of the Comintern's Executive Commission during July 1929, the Comintern emphasized the "danger of right deviationism," further cementing the Chinese communist movement's tendency toward radicalization.[10]

Beginning in July 1929, under the instruction of Stalin, the Comintern began to issue directives to the CCP, demanding that the CCP implement a relentless struggle against the right deviationists and the rich peasants in rural China. In a letter titled "Comintern Executive Commission's Directive to the CCP" sent by the Comintern to the CCP leadership on June 7, 1929, the Comintern pointed out that the CCP leaders, including Mao Zedong, "have committed serious mistakes" regarding the CCP's policy toward rich peasants.[11] When the CCP followed the Comintern's directive to carry out China's rural communist movement, the campaign against rich peasants was tied to the suppression of the AB Corps. In the southwestern Jiangxi base areas, Mao claimed that the

---

[10] "Gongchan guoji he zhongguo gongchandang zhengce zhong 'zuode' qingxiang de jiaqiang" [Strengthening of the "left-wing" tendency in the policy of the Comintern and the CCP], in *Liangong (bu), gongchan guoji yu zhongguo suwei'ai yundong* [The Soviet Communist Party (Bolshevik), Comintern, and Chinese Soviet Movement; hereafter, *Liangong (bu), gongchan guoji*], Zhonggong zhongyang dangshi yanjiushi diyi yanjiubu [First Research Unit of the Research Office of the CCP Party History], ed., *Liangong (bu), gongchan guoji yu zhongguo suwei'ai yundong* [The Soviet Communist Party [Bolshevik], Comintern and Chinese Soviet Movement], vol. 8, pp. 11–12.
[11] "Gongchan guoji zhixing weiyuanhui yu zhongguo gongchandang shu, 1929.6.7" [Comintern executive commission's directive to the CCP, June 7, 1929], in *Liangong (bu), gongchan guoji*, vol. 11, pp. 518–15.

leading organs of the CCP were dominated by the AB Corps at all levels.[12] The Futian Incident was a Red Army rebellion, resulting in an expansion of purges, in the name of eradicating AB Corps members.

Although the causes of the Futian Incident were complicated, at least two key factors triggered it. First, the Futian Incident was a response to the leadership conflict in the Jiangxi base areas. By the summer of 1930, Mao had established a strong leadership position in the communist armed forces in the Jiangxi base areas through his personal influence with powerful military leaders such as Zhu De and Peng Dehui, as well as through the Comintern's endorsement of his authority. Nonetheless, Mao was struggling to ensure the loyalty of his lieutenants and to achieve the compliance of some key army units and leaders, particularly local armed forces and leaders. Mao's primary conflict was with the CCP Jiangxi Acting Commission, headed by Li Wenlin, Duan Liangbi, and other leaders of the local armed forces, the Twentieth Red Army in particular.[13]

The Fourth Red Army, led by Mao and Zhu De, had joined forces with the CCP's local party leadership in southwest Jiangxi as well as with its armed forces – the Second and Fourth Independent Divisions – in Donggu, Jiangxi, in February 1929. However, after joining forces, the leadership of the local party organization in Jiangxi base areas disobeyed the General Front Commission of the Fourth Red Army, led by Mao. This intraparty strife between Mao and party leadership in southwestern Jiangxi intensified in 1929 and 1930. It escalated when party leadership confiscated lands only from rich landlords and the gentry, although Mao had ordered them to confiscate all lands, including those of rich peasants. Another conflict occurred over whether the Red Army should follow Li Lisan's order to attack large cities such as Nanchang or follow Mao's suggestion to take over small cities such as Ji'an. In addition, Mao's effort to reorganize the party organizations in southwestern Jiangxi further exacerbated the tension between Mao and the Jiangxi party leaders. Mao wanted to appoint his trusted followers Liu Shiqi and Zeng Shan to lead the newly established Western Jiangxi Special Commission, which had unified the party organizations in western Jiangxi and at the Hunan-Jiangxi border. The Jiangxi party leaders viewed Mao's initiatives as a conspiracy to establish his dominance in the Jiangxi base areas. For Mao, the most serious challenge to leadership occurred at the Luofang Conference, held in October 1930, when the party and army leadership in southwestern Jiangxi rejected his strategy

---

[12] Yao Jinguo, "Futian shibian shi ruhe dingxing wei fangeming shijian de" [How was Futian Incident determined as counterrevolutionary event?], in *Bai nian chao* [Hundred-year tide], no. 3 (2008), pp. 58–60.
[13] According to Marshal Peng Dehuai, the CCP Jiangxi General Acting Commission was another name for the CCP Jiangxi Provincial Party Commission. See Peng Dehuai, *Peng Dehuai zishu* [Autobiographical notes of Peng Dehuai], p. 163.

of "luring the enemy in deep" when the Red Army was forced to prepare a military campaign against the Nationalist Army.[14]

In early October 1930, Mao had prepared to purge the leading figures in the CCP's southwestern Jiangxi branch. In Mao's letter to the CCP leadership in Shanghai, he expressed the belief that "there has been a severe crisis within the party leadership of the southwest Jiangxi – the rich peasants dominate the leading positions of the party organizations at all levels and a large number of the AB Corps were found in the organizations of the party, the Youth League, the Soviet Government and the Red Army Schools."[15] To "redeem the crisis," Mao decided to launch a large-scale campaign of purges and to pursue "a fundamental change" in the organizations of the party and the Youth League in southwest Jiangxi.[16] Mao targeted Li Wenlin first by using a "receipt," presumably signed by Li Wenlian's father, that was found in a GMD local document as evidence that Li Wenlin was a member of the AB Corps and had established secret communication with the enemy.[17]

The second factor that triggered the Futian Incident was the party's overwhelming fear of the truculent encirclement launched by the Nationalist Army in southwestern Jiangxi. This fear spawned collective paranoia concerning the potential of GMD spies and communist traitors in the Red Army. In General Li Zhimin's words, the Red Army in the base areas "overestimated the severity of the enemy's military campaign."[18] Thus, the Jiangxi base area leaders made a collective effort to reinforce discipline and increase control over the armed

---

[14] "Zhonggong gan xinan tewei baogao – Jiangxi zhengzhi xingshi ji yisan juntuan lai Jiangxi zuozhan yijian" (Report of the CCP Special Committee in southwestern Jiangxi: The political situation in Jiangxi and recommendation for dispatching the First Army Group and Third Army Group for military campaign in Jiangxi, October 25, 1930], in Zhongyang dang'an guan he Jiangxi sheng dang'an guan [The CCP Central Archives and CCP Jiangxi Archive], *Jiangxi geming lishi wenjian huiji, 1930.2* [Compilation of Jiangxi revolutionary historical documents issued in 1930, part 2], internal publication, pp. 123–6; Chen Zhengren, "Huiyi Luofang huiyi, 1967.12" [Recollection of Luofang conference, December 1967], in *Jiangxi dangshi ziliao* [Materials of Jiangxi party history], ed. Zhonggong Jiangxi sheng dangshi yanjiushi, vol. 6, p. 261.

[15] Zhonggong zhongyang wenxian yanjiushi [CCP Central Document Research Office], *Mao Zedong nianpu (1893–1949)* [Chronicle of Mao Zedong, 1893–1949], vol. 1, p. 319; Dai Xiangqing and Luo Huilan, *AB tuan yu Futian shibian* [AB Corps and Futian Incident], p. 90.

[16] *Mao Zedong nianpu*, vol. 1, p. 319; Dai Xiangqing and Luo Huilan, *AB tuan yu Futian shibian*, p. 90; Huang Kecheng, *Huang Kecheng zishu* [Autobiographical notes of Huang Kecheng], p. 84.

[17] An investigation was conducted in 1986 on the "evidence" that had been used against Li Wenlin. The receipt had nothing to do with Li Wenlin's father but rather with a landlord with the same name as Li's father. Li's father did not participate in any organizations like the AB Corps and was not a landlord. See Yu Boliu, "Mao Zedong yu donggu geming genju di de bujie zhiyuan" [Mao Zedong had an indissoluble bond with the Donggu revolutionary base areas], in *Dangshi wenyuan* [Literature circle of party history], no. 3 (2008), pp. 11–14; Gong Chu, *Gong Chu jiangjun huiyilu* [Memoirs of General Gong Chu], vol. 2, p. 353.

[18] *Li Zhimin huiyilu*, pp. 138–9.

units to create a strong combat force to fight against the GMD armies. In addition, the leadership dominated by the nonlocal urban elite (e.g., Mao) in the base areas urgently wanted to establish their authority over local party organs and army units, as well as some rebellious local leaders. In fact, there had been constant and enduring resistance of the urban-oriented, elite-centered political movement to adapt itself to the harsh imperatives of a rural environment and then to transform both that environment and itself in fundamental ways.[19] The Luofang Conference, which triggered the conflict between urban intellectuals and the local rural elite, revealed that urban intellectuals had such difficulty establishing a peasant army because of their inability to adapt to the rural setting and the fact that urban intellectuals played a critical role in shaping communist politics. As a result, leaders at the conference decided to impose more discipline and control over the slack and perfunctory peasant army. They viewed this as a way to deal with sagging morale, to gain loyalty, and to launch the campaign of purges against the rural elite and peasant army officials. At the time when the Red Army in the Jiangxi base areas had to accept battle in haste, the CCP's central leadership was unsatisfied, as pushing military activities in urban China had brought about heavy losses for the Red Army. Some officers and soldiers questioned Mao's strategy of luring the enemy troops in deep, because they did not believe that the strategy could avoid the large-scale military encirclement of the well-equipped GMD.[20] The complaints were perceived as a sign of infiltration and spying by the enemy; thus, the ruthless purges, or "decisive battle of classes" (in Mao's own words), became inevitable.[21]

With security already at risk because of the impending threat from the GMD's encirclement of the base areas, the Futian Incident put the survival of the Red Army in further jeopardy. This explains why CCP leaders felt that the violent suppression of so-called traitors was so imperative. In his comment on the expansion of the purges, Huang Kecheng, political commissar of the Fourth Division of the Third Army Group, pointed out:

Under the military confrontation [between the Red Army and the Nationalist Army], the Red Army on the outside dealt with the encirclement of the mighty Nationalist Army and on the inside had to cope with the Futian Incident – a large-scale and open challenge that split and impaired the Red Army. As chief of the General Front Commission that led the party and the Red Army in the Jiangxi base areas, Mao was thoroughly stunned and therefore believed that there were a large number of counterrevolutionaries who had infiltrated party organizations and the Red Army. He believed the revolutionary career of the party would be ruined if they were not purged. As a result, he mistakenly applied tactics usually reserved for enemies to the intraparty conflict. In addition, Mao authorized Li Shaojiu, a morally questionable and despicable person, to

---

[19] Stephen Averill, "The Origin of the Futian Incident," in *New Perspectives on the Chinese Communist Revolution*, ed. Hans Van De Ven, p. 110.
[20] *Li Zhimin huiyilu*, p. 129.
[21] *Huang Kecheng zishu*, pp. 83–4.

execute the campaign of suppressing counterrevolutionaries. Li Shaojiu did this through acting absurdly and obtaining confessions from victims by compulsion and giving these trumped-up confessions credence. Therefore it is not surprising that the Futian Incident caused the expansion of purges.[22]

According to Huang Kecheng, in addition to Mao's role in expanding the purges, Li Shaojiu, secretary of the General Front Commission, who was in charge of the campaign to suppress counterrevolutionaries, played an important role in the mass killings within the party organizations and the Red Army. In fact, the lack of checks on both the leadership and the security organizations contributed greatly to the Futian Incident and consequently to the expansion of the purges. Only a month after Mao's campaign was launched against the so-called AB Corps, more than 4,400 officers and soldiers – around 11 percent of the total First Front Army – were arrested.[23] According to an official publication, more than two thousand officers and soldiers were killed.[24]

State Political Security Bureau

In March 1931, the CCP Central Bureau in the Jiangxi base areas renamed the Committee for Eliminating Counterrevolutionaries as the Political Security Department (PSD, *zhengzhi baowei chu*). The new department was mainly based on the existing CEC, an indication that the CCP was attempting to legalize the temporary organizations for suppressing counterrevolutionaries as permanent agencies and to strengthen the party's control over security forces.[25] According to the Order to the Organizations of the Red Army and Local Party issued by the Politburo in June 1931, the "work for suppressing counterrevolutionaries must become a continual and systematic effort"; thus, the base areas "must establish the PSD as the specialized organizations" in charge of the effort.[26] When the Chinese Soviet Republic was established in the Jiangxi base areas in the winter of 1931, the PSD was renamed the State Political Security Bureau (SPSB) and the Committee for Eliminating Counterrevolutionaries at the local level was organized as branches thereof.[27] In the 1930s, the PSD and SPSB possessed an enormous network of agents, which penetrated all levels of the CCP and the Red Army. Yet another network in the army functioned to

---

[22] Ibid., p. 85.

[23] Mao Zedong, "Zong qianwei dabian de yi fengxin (12/20/1930)" [A letter: General Front Committee replies for the argument, December 20, 1930], in Zhongguo renmin jiefangjun zhengzhi xueyuan, ed., *Zhonggong dangshi jiaoxue cankao ziliao* [Reference materials of the CCP party-history education], vol. 14, p. 634.

[24] Wen Hong, "Guanyu Futian shibian ji Jaingxi suqu sufan wenti" [Concerning the Futian Incident and the issue of suppressing counterrevolutionaries in Jiangxi], in *Jiangxi wenshi ziliao xuanji* [Selected materials of Jiangxi literature and history], no. 2 (1982), p. 110.

[25] *Gong'an shigao*, pp. 26–7; *Zuzhi shi ziliao*, vol. 2, p. 354.

[26] *Gong'an shigao*, pp. 26–7.

[27] Ibid., 27; *Yang Qiqing zhuan*, p. 42.

ensure the loyalty of the party and the troops – the network of security officers. The PSD and SPSB recruited a large number of informers (*wang yuan*) from the party organizations and the Red Army units. Although these informers looked similar to others and wore military uniforms, they were entirely independent of the high command and reported directly to the PSD or SPSB. The PSD and SPSB officers – special dispatched commissioners (*tepai yuan*) – functioned within military units down to the regiment level, whereas the secret informers (*wang yuan*) were spread throughout every unit from the company level to and below.[28]

Although the PSD and SPSB played a crucial role in continuing the terrorist *sufan* campaigns that it inherited from the Committee for Eliminating Counterrevolutionaries (CEC), Mao's suppression of the AB Corps in Jiangxi base areas was firmly supported by the Comintern that justified Mao's campaign and encouraged a uncompromised position against the rebelled Party members and the Red Army officers and soldiers. According to a memo of the Far East Shanghai Bureau of the Comintern issued on March 28, 1931, the rebellion launched by the Twentieth Army against Mao "was undoubtedly a counter-revolutionary activity plotted by the class enemies as well as their vanguard – the Anti-Bolshevik Corps." The Comintern memo also states that the rebellion aimed to "eliminate the Party's organizations, the Red Army and the leaders of both."[29] The CCP leadership in Shanghai and its three-member delegation in Jiangxi base areas became the instrument of the Comintern to instigate far more radical campaigns for the suppression of the counterrevolutionaries, and further escalated the persecution against the AB Corps. In the summer of 1931, more than two hundred officers of the Twentieth Army at the platoon level and above were executed, and more than 90 percent of the CCP cadres in southwestern Jiangxi were killed, imprisoned, or dismissed.[30]

The campaigns to suppress counterrevolutionaries had developed to uncontrollable levels, such that they became the central task of the party organizations and the Red Army in the Jiangxi base areas. For example, both Qiu Dasan, political commissar of the Twenty-Second Army, and Chen Yi, commander of the Twenty-Second Army, were suspected members of the AB Corps. Chen was able to escape from persecution only after Mao personally intervened.[31] In 1931, about the time the campaigns to suppress counterrevolutionaries became frantic, another large-scale campaign against the Social Democratic Party was

[28] *Ouyang Yi huiyilu*, pp. 125–6.
[29] "Gongchan guoji zhixing weiyuanhui yuandongju guanyu Futian shibian de jueding" [Far East Bureau under Executive Committee of the Comintern regarding decision on Futian Incident], *Liangong (bu), gongchan guoji*, vol. 10, p. 175.
[30] Yao Jinguo, "Futian shibian shi ruhe dingxing wei fangeming shijian de," in *Bainian chao* [Hundred-year tide], no. 3 (2008), pp. 58–60.
[31] "Dangdai zhongguo renwu zhuanji" congshu bianjibu, *Chen Yi zhuan* [A biography of Chen Yi; hereafter *Chen Yi zhuan*], pp. 122, 125–6.

launched in western Fujian. This campaign originated from a slogan that a soldier mistakenly called out in the public gathering commemorating the leaders of the Comintern in western Fujian base areas in early 1931. Not knowing the difference, the soldier called out, "Supporting the Second International!" and "Long live Social Democratic Party!" The CCP leadership tied this to the AB Corps in the Jiangxi base areas to support their assertion that enemies had infiltrated the party organization. Thus, the Red Army and the CCP leadership asked the party organizations and the Red Army in the base areas to "eradicate all counterrevolutionaries in the Red Army, the Soviet governments, and the Party." They insisted on "using the most severe means to deny them from class standing."[32] In this campaign, half the officers at the level of company in the Twelfth Army were executed, and more than six thousand people in the western Fujian base areas were killed after being accused of membership in the Social Democratic Party.[33]

Encouraged by the *sufan* campaigns in Jiangxi and western Fujian, Zhang Guotao initiated a large-scale campaign in the Hubei, Henan, and Anhui base areas and the Fourth Front Army. The *sufan* campaign was triggered by a false confession from the Nationalist captives who were under severe torture. After a series of arrests and extortion, combined with a letter written by chief of the GMD intelligence services to summon Xu Jishen, commander of the Tenth Division of the Fourth Army, a group of officers were forced to "confess" to being members of a secret "military commission" of the Reorganization Clique.[34] In his report to the central party leadership in November 1931, Zhang Guotao, party chief in the Hubei, Henan, and Anhui base areas, was proud of his achievement in the *sufan* campaign in the Hubei, Henan, and Anhui base areas; he said, "The campaign to suppress counterrevolutionaries [in the base areas] has the richer experience than the Futian Incident, which could be used as the experience and lessons for the entire Party, specially for each Soviet base area."[35] In the Hubei, Henan, and Anhui base areas, the great suppression of counterrevolutionaries (*da sufan*), led by Zhang Guotao, purged more than 2,500 officers and soldiers; furthermore, between 60 percent and 70 percent of the officers at the regimental level and above were killed.[36] In this campaign, even Xu Xiangqian, commander of the Fourth Front Army, was

---

[32] Wang Yong, "Minxi genju di 'shehui minzhu dang' yuan'an" [The false case "Social Democratic Party" in the western Fujian base areas], in *Yanhuang chunqiu* [Spring and autumn in China], no. 2 (2004), pp. 27–9.

[33] Ibid., pp. 27–31.

[34] Liu Xiaonong, "E-yu-wan suqu – Baiqueyuan sufan," in *Wenshi jinghua* [Gems of literature and history], no. 1 (2006), pp. 19–28.

[35] Sheng Renxue, *Zhang Guotao wenti yanjiu ziliao* [Research materials of Zhang Guotao case], p. 321.

[36] Xu Xiangqian, *Lishi de huigu*, vol. 1, p. 152; Xiao Ke, "Zhongyang suqu chuqi de sufan yundong" [Suppressing campaign in early period of the central Soviet base areas], in *Dangshi yanjiu ziliao* [Research materials of party history], no. 5 (1982), p. 9.

unable to protect his wife, whom the SPSB had accused of being a member of the Reorganization Clique. She was tortured and executed.[37]

During May 1932, in the Hunan and Hubei border base areas, the campaigns against the Reorganization Clique (*gaizu pai*) were launched by Xia Xi, secretary of the CCP's Central Bureau in the Hunan and western Hubei base areas. According to a false confession from a captured officer of the Nationalist Army, Xia Xi arrested several local party officers who were forced to confess as members of the Reorganization Clique after undergoing severe torture. Within two months, Xia Xi claimed that 90 percent of the party, government, and army leaders in the Hunan and western Hubei base areas were members of the Reorganization Clique. There were four large-scale campaigns to suppress revolutionaries from May 1932 to July 1934, and the first campaign resulted in the death of more than ten thousand party members, army officers, and soldiers.[38] The damage caused by the purges was felt deeply. After July 1934, there were only three thousand to four thousand personnel in the Third Army, a decrease of 25 percent, as a result of the four campaigns.[39]

The CCP allowed the SPSB almost unrestricted powers to persecute those who were perceived as class enemies. Almost all the large-scale purges were supported by the CCP leadership, which further encouraged a much more radical development of the *sufan* campaigns. For example, On March 6, 1932 – a few months after Zhang Guotao launched the campaign to suppress counterrevolutionaries, the party leadership praised the Central Bureau of the Hubei, Henan, and Anhui base areas, led by Zhang Guotao, for the great achievement of "reforming the Party and Soviet government, eradicating the alien class elements, improving the mass work, and promoting and training the new cadres, and making the success and progress of the Hubei-Henan-Anhui base areas."[40] The SPSB in each base area was drawn into the struggles between the party leaders and their opponents, and it was enlisted in the drive toward radical violence against rich peasants. This set the stage for the development of brutal and violent security organizations controlled by dominant leaders in the base areas – millions of innocent people would perish at the hands of those security forces.

---

[37] Xu Xiangqian, *Lishi de huigu*, vol. 1, pp. 162–3.

[38] He Libo, "Xia Xi yu Xiang-e-xi suqu 'sufan'" [Xia Xi and the suppression against counterrevolutionaries in Hunan–western Hubei Soviet base areas], in *Wenshi jinghua* [Gems of literature and history], no. 2 (2006), pp. 23–7.

[39] Ibid., p. 27; Xiao Ke, "Hong er, liu juntuan huishi qianhou – xiangei Ren Bishi, He Long, he Guan Xiangyiny tongzhi" [Before and after the joint force of the Second Army Group and Sixth Army Group – dedicated to comrades Ren Bishi, He Long, and Guan Xiangying], in *Jindai shi yanjiu* [Research of contemporary Chinese history], no. 1 (1980), p. 16. However, this number is questionable, as the loss of the armed personnel was also caused by other factors, such as the successful military campaigns launched by the GMD against the Third Army.

[40] Zhongyang dang'an guan, *Zhonggong zhongyang wenjian xuanji* [Selected CCP central documents; hereafter, *Wenjian xuanji*], vol. 8, p. 146.

The common features of these purges mentioned above were paranoia, zealotry, and excesses involved in the search for counterrevolutionaries. The most frequent methods of the campaign were the use of severe torture to extort a confession, which would then be used to make further arrests, and even to carry out executions, without any concrete evidence. It has mostly been concluded that during this period the AB Corps, the Social Democratic Party, the Reorganization Clique, and other counterrevolutionary organizations never actually existed in any communist base area. Most prosecutions occurred in places where morale was low and party organizations were not strong. Thus, the witch hunts, executions, and torture used to extract confessions from the victims of *sufan* campaigns were introduced to ensure control by party organizations and promote combat forces because the suspected and tortured party members and army soldiers and officials were willing to die in the battlefield to show the party their loyalty and prove their innocence. This was particularly evident in the campaigns against the AB Corps in the Jiangxi Soviet, the Social Democratic Party in western Fujian, and the Reorganization Cliques in the base areas of Hubei, Henan, and Anhui and at the Hunan-Hubei border. The zealotry and excesses further turned into a race among party leadership in each base area, as they competed to achieve "great accomplishments." The idea was that the competition would be justified when the military produced victories against the Nationalist Army.

The purges went to such extremes because there was no mechanism to check potential abuses of power. In the three top regions of the base areas, the top leaders – Mao Zedong, Zhang Guotao, and Xia Xi – had the unchallengeable power to determine the course of the *sufan* campaigns and the fate of anyone under their authority. For example, Xia Xi, as secretary of the CCP Central Bureau, had the final say in all decision making of the CCP's Central Bureau, such that he could implement any policy of his choosing.[41] The special nature of the SPSB allowed it to override decisions of party committees and to function as a personal tool for Mao Zedong, Zhang Guotao, and Xia Xi. Essentially, the SPSB served as a deadly yet fairly successful tool for these leaders to eliminate political rivals, consolidate power, and ensure absolute control over the party and armed forces under their jurisdiction.[42]

Although the terrorist purges in the base areas helped party leaders establish their dominance and consolidate their power, leaders realized that the reliance on violence for the pursuit of power had significant costs. In the spring of 1931, Xiang Ying, acting secretary of the then newly established Central Bureau, was authorized to investigate the Futian Incident. As a result, Mao almost became the target for initiating the arrests of his political opponents that led to the revolt and expanding the purges to consolidate his dominance in the Jiangxi

---

[41] 'Dangdai zhongguo renwu zhuanji' congshu bianjibu, *He Long zhuan* [A biography of He Long], p. 159.
[42] He Libo, "Xia Xi yu Xiang-e-xi suqu 'sufan,'" pp. 22–9.

base areas.[43] At the same time, the institutional changes in the SPSB resulted in checks and balances and aimed to prevent its abuse of power. Despite the powerful role of the SPSB in both the party organizations and Red Army, the SPSB reorganized the original functions of the CEC, creating one department in charge of investigation and interrogation and another department in charge of conviction and execution. This reorganization was a significant step toward a system of checks and balances aimed to prevent the abuse of power by SPSB officials. Although the establishment of the SPSB limited the large-scale arrests and killings engaged in by local party organizations and Red Army units, the PSD and the SPSB grew into a more powerful agency than its predecessors, becoming a key instrument in enforcing party control over party organizations and the Red Army. The expanded campaigns to suppress counterrevolutionaries in Jiangxi were further criticized by Zhou Enlai, secretary of the CCP's Central Bureau in Jiangxi, after he was transferred from Shanghai. In 1932, Zhou Enlai reorganized the SPSB in Jiangxi base areas to bring some form of justice to the unfounded prosecutions and to comfort the families of the victims.[44]

It should be noted that the *sufan* campaigns did not always benefit those leaders who initiated the campaigns. First, although the *sufan* campaigns enabled leaders to eliminate their political opponents and consolidate their power, the campaigns caused overwhelming resentment with the terror they induced and widespread purges. This resentment gave Xiang Ying, acting secretary of the CCP's Central Bureau in the Jiangxi base areas, reason to directly target Mao by criticizing him for committing "mistakes" in the campaign against the AB Corps. According to Xiang Ying, the first mistake was that the campaigns "did not follow the mass line"; they "were undertaken completely by the Red Army or upper-level organizations." The second mistake was that the campaign "acted blindly," and "there were no rules to guide the campaign."[45]

Another criticism of Mao's campaign came from Zhou Enlai, secretary of the Central Bureau in Jiangxi base areas. On August 30, 1931, Zhou wrote to the Central Bureau of the base areas on behalf of the CCP leadership and criticized the *sufan* campaigns against the AB Corps, specifically for "developing toward simplification and expansion."[46] In the Resolution on Work to

---

[43] Dai Xiangqing, "Lun AB tuan he Futian shibian" [Comment on the AB Corps and Futian Incident], in *Zhonggong dangshi yanjiu* [Research of CCP history], no. 2 (1989), p. 26; Wang Fuyi, *Xiang Ying zhuan* [A biography of Xiang Ying], pp. 98–101.

[44] *Chen Yi zhuan*, p. 126.

[45] "Suqu zhongyangju tonggao di erhao – dui Futian shibian de jueyi (January 16 of 1931)" [Number 2 announcement of Central Bureau of the Soviet Base Areas – Decision on Futian Incident, January 16, 1931], in *Zhonggong dangshi jiaoxue cankao ziliao* [Reference materials of the CCP history education], vol. 14, pp. 639–42.

[46] Zhonggong zhongyang wenxian yanjiushi [CCP Central Document Research Office], *Zhou Enlai nianpu, 1898–1949* [Chronicle of Zhou Enlai, 1898–1949] (Beijing: Zhongyang wenxian chubanshe, 1990), p. 212.

Suppress Counterrevolutionaries in the Soviet Base Areas, passed at the Conference of the Central Bureau on January 7, 1932, the campaigns for suppressing counterrevolutionaries were severely criticized. The conference notes read: "because of the incorrect understanding of the AB Corps as well as the counterrevolutionaries, the campaign against the AB Corps was expanded.... It brought about extreme severe mistakes in the methods used in the campaigns and oversimplified the struggle against the AB Corps."[47] According to General Huang Kecheng, Mao's *sufan* campaigns were the reason he quickly lost support among the leadership. Consequently, Mao suffered a setback when the Temporary Center, controlled by returned students, moved to the Jiangxi base areas to squeeze out Mao from leadership.[48] Moreover, the *sufan* campaigns triggered resistance from the army, local party organizations, and the general populace. This is demonstrated by a case in the district of Xianju in Huang'an County of the Hubei, Henan, and Anhui base areas in February 1932: local party leaders, the armed forces, and the general population hid suspected officers, disarmed the local State Political Security Bureau, and shouted the slogan "Down headsman Zhang Guotao!"[49] Another case, during the fall of 1931, in Dongcun of Xingguo, in the Jiangxi base area, occurred when several thousands of villagers voluntarily organized to protect the chairman of the Soviet government from being prosecuted and killed as a suspected member of the AB Corps.[50]

Second, the heavy reliance on the terrorist *sufan* organizations, such as the CEC and the SPSB, in the campaigns to suppress counterrevolutionaries often was a mixed blessing for top leaders. In reality, a *sufan* organization was a double-edged sword that could either greatly benefit a leader or ruin his career. Although the CEC and the SPSB were manipulated by leaders as their own personal tools, the lack of checks and balances created chaotic and unwieldy organizations. Ultimately, the *sufan* organizations came back to haunt the leaders they once supported in the past. Particularly problematic for these leaders was when intimate friends and supporters were accused of being counterrevolutionaries and were sentenced to jail or death. This was a direct result of the forced confessions and naming of coconspirators. Except for top leaders, anyone could become a suspect as long as someone else knew his or her name. For example, Chen Yi, commander of the Twenty-Second Army whom Mao nominated as a member of the CCP Central Bureau in the Jiangxi base area, came under suspicion by a *sufan* organization. To Mao's dismay, Chen had been one of his more loyal supporters. Xu Xianqian, commander of the Fourth Army and a key general on whom Zhang Guotao relied to command the armed forces in the Hubei, Henan, and Anhui base areas, also came under suspicion

[47] *Wenjian xuanji*, vol. 8, pp. 18–9.
[48] *Huang Kecheng zishu*, pp. 99–101.
[49] Yao Jinguo and Su Hang, *Zhang Guotao zhuan* [A biography of Zhang Guotao], pp. 211–12.
[50] Chen Xingeng, *Chise beiju* [Red tragedy], p. 144.

without Zhang Guotao intending it so. The only reason Chen Yi and Xu Xian-qian were not submitted to purges or execution was the personal intervention of Mao and Zhang, respectively.[51] These are prime examples of the *sufan* organizations' wide reach; they knew no limits and were accountable to virtually no one.

In July and August of 1931, Mao began to bring the terrorist *sufan* campaigns to an end. Most likely, this was a result of pressure from other leaders, such as Zhou Enlai and Xiang Ying, as well as overwhelming resentment within the party and the Red Army in the base areas. When Chen Yi wrote to Mao asking for his protection because Li Shaojiu, head of the SPSB, had ordered him to turn himself in, Mao not only protected Chen but also urged him to release suspects from his army unit whom the SPSB had ordered imprisoned.[52] On November 7, 1931, Mao officially ordered the end of the *sufan* campaigns and made an effort to redress the questionable and unjust prosecutions that the SPSB had imposed. In addition, Mao provided five thousand *yuan* as compensation to the family of each victims. He did this only after he was informed by Guo Diren and Zhang Dingchen, two leaders of party organizations in the western Fujian base areas, of the severe damage and loss caused by the *sufan* campaigns.[53] Mao was not the only one with a change of heart. Starting in early 1932, Zhang Guotao also dramatically changed the policy of *sufan* campaigns. He changed course from a focus on the sheer quantity of arrests and killings to quality of confession and prosecution based only on voluntary surrender. In July 1932, Zhang finally phased out completely the *sufan* campaigns in the Hubei, Henan, and Anhui base areas.[54]

It is reasonable to speculate that the end of the *sufan* campaigns came from pressure and overwhelming resentment in the party and the Red Army. Except for the *sufan* campaigns in the Jiangxi base areas, almost all campaigns in other base areas had been officially ended before the mid-1940s. The western Fujian *sufan* campaign was repudiated by the party in January 1932; that of Hunan and western Hubei in May 1934; and that of the Hubei, Henan, and Anhui base areas in June 1945.[55] Despite Mao's increasing weight among the party leadership, which might have prevented anyone from reevaluating

---

[51] Chen Yi was suspected by Li Shaojiu as a leader of the AB Corps. Li Shaojiu, director of the CEC in Jiangxi base areas, personally asked Chen Yi to give himself up to the CEC. After Chen wrote to Mao, Mao protected him. Xu Xiangqian was in the list of the suspected members of the Reorganization Clique, and his wife was arrested and killed by the SPSB, which tried to obtain evidence linking him to Xu. When Zhang Guotao knew that Xu was in danger, Zhang stopped the SPSB from targeting Xu and said, "Xu Xiangqian cannot be touched because he is a person who is very good at combat in battlefield." See *Chen Yi zhuan*, pp. 124–6; Liu Xiaonong, "E-yu-wan suqu – Baiqueyuan sufan," pp. 19–28.

[52] *Chen Yi zhuan*, 126; Wang Hao, *Yige laobing xinzhong de Chen Yi yuanshuai* [Marshal Chen Yi in the heart of an old soldier], pp. 16–18.

[53] Wang Yong, "Minxi genju di 'shehui minzhu dang' yuan'an," pp. 27–31.

[54] *Zhang Guotao zhuan*, p. 212.

[55] He Libo, "Xia Xi yu Xiang-e-xi suqu 'sufan,'" pp. 22–9.

the campaigns in the Jiangxi base areas, he took the initiative and indirectly made a self-criticism in the Yan'an rectification. According to Mao, "the campaigns for suppressing counterrevolutionaries have experienced an extremely painful road," and "the Party suffered setbacks and made mistakes when it was immature."[56] On September 10, 1956, Mao openly admitted that he had "made the mistake in the campaigns of suppressing counterrevolutionaries" and had "mistakenly purged people" when he launched his first campaigns in the Jiangxi base areas.[57]

In fact, the expanded *sufan* campaigns propagated by Mao had become an overwhelming political liability, impinging on his ability to maintain a decent position in the Jiangxi base area leadership, particularly after Zhou Enlai arrived at the base areas and took charge of the CCP Central Bureau there. A huge blow was when Zhou Enlai was appointed to lead the CCP Central Bureau and took over the SPSB and redirected its course. Mao lost leading positions in the party and in the Red Army, and became only a figurehead as the chairman of the Jiangxi Soviet.[58] Zhou made key changes in the leadership of the security apparatus and services after beginning his new post in the Jiangxi base areas. He assigned Li Kenong, one of his trusted assistants, to lead a group to investigate and evaluate the cases in an effort to bring justice to the accused members of the AB Corps in Shicheng, Guangchang, Yudu, and Xingguo.[59] In January 1932, Zhou appointed Wu Defeng as director of the SPSB in the Jiangxi Soviet, a position formerly occupied by Mao's secretary Li Shaojiu. Wu Defeng was also close to Zhou, as he was the director of the Communication Cell of the Central Military Commission, which Zhou had led personally from July 1928 to December 1929.[60] More important, the *sufan* campaigns and their expansion severely undermined the influence over and cohesion within the populace in the base areas. This contributed greatly to the failure of the Red Army in the fifth encirclement campaign launched by the Nationalist Army in October 1933 and early 1934.[61] Unlike other four early encirclement campaigns launched by the GMD in which the CCP was able to avoid significant damage, the fifth campaign was successful due to its new

---

[56] Zhonggong zhongyang dangshi yanjiushi yishi [First Unit of Research Office of CCP Party History], "Zhongguo gongchandang lish (shangjuan)" rogan wenti shuoming [Explanation of several issues regarding the book "Chinese Communist Party History, vol. 1"] (Beijing: Zhonggong dangshi chubanshe, 1991), p. 121.

[57] Mao Zedong, "Guanyu dibajie zhongyang weiyuanhui de xuanju wenti (September 10, 1956)" [Concerning the issue of electing the CCP Central Committee in the Eighth Party Congress], in *Mao Zedong wenji* [Collected works of Mao Zedong], vol. 7, p. 106.

[58] Li Weihan, *Huiyi yu yanjiu* [Recollection and research], vol. 1, p. 338.

[59] Dai Anlin, "Futian shibian yu suqu sufan, [Futian Incident and suppression against counterrevolutionaries in the Soviet base areas], in *Xiang chao* [Hunan tide], no. 6 (2007), p. 30.

[60] *Lingdao jigou yange*, p. 204; Yang Yuying, "Wohe Zhou Xing" [I and Zhou Xing], in Sun Mingshan (ed.), *Lishi shunjian* [An instant in history], vol. 2, p. 483.

[61] Chen Xingeng, *Chise beiju*, pp. 143–4.

strategy and its effective "blockhouse tactics" to force the CCP to flee its base areas for a devastating retreat called the Long March. Neither Mao himself nor official CCP documents hinted that *sufan* campaigns in the Jiangxi base areas caused the CCP's famous retreat, the Long March, but evidence supports this theory. The local populace's support proved important in deciding the outcome when it came to the Nationalists' attack on the Jiangxi base areas in 1934. For example, in some regions, locals fled to GMD-held areas when they learned that the Red Army would be stationed in their villages. Many residents in the base areas refused to support the CCP and the Red Army when the Nationalist Army's Seventy-Seventh Division attacked the base areas.[62]

General Huang Kecheng was convinced that Mao had learned his lesson from the *sufan* campaigns. The experience of the Jiangxi Soviet during 1930 and 1931 pushed Mao to change the course of Jiangxi's *sufan* campaigns and to reject the Soviet model of "red terror" against "class enemies" within the CCP and the Red Army after 1931, when the returned students gradually took control of the Jiangxi base areas. Brantly Womack points out that the foundations of Mao's political thought that contributed to his success in the Chinese revolution took shape in the years before 1935, when "most of his important political concepts germinated,"[63] including the lessons he learned from the *sufan* campaigns. In the Yan'an rectification, Mao enacted the principle of "killing none and arresting few," and he stated that "emphasis should be on the amount of evidence; confessions should not be trusted blindly."[64] Although Mao continually used terror as an instrument of rule in later campaigns,[65] he did try to control the scale and to avoid the campaigns developing into uncontrollable mass killings, as had occurred in the Jiangxi base areas. He seemed to pay much greater attention to the "mass line," the political organizational and leadership method promoted by Mao to arouse the enthusiasm and creativity of the masses, and the cultivation of his personality cult in achieving the rule of the CCP and his dominance over the leadership.[66] As indicated by Huang Kecheng, who was the general chief of staff in 1958 and 1959 and later dismissed at the 1959 Lushan plenum, the rationale was that Mao's reliance on "mass line" and the leadership consensus "guarantees that there will be no death penalty imposed on high-ranking leaders in the leadership conflict and

[62] Ibid., p. 143.
[63] Brantly Womack, *The Foundations of Mao Zedong's Political Thought, 1917–1935*, p. xii.
[64] *Huang Kecheng zishu*, p. 85.
[65] Andrew J. Nathan, *China's Transition*, p. 45.
[66] For example, Mao relied greatly on mass movement politics such as public criticism and self-criticism to achieve the compliance of the party rank and files and the population. As Elizabeth J. Perry and Merle Goldman point out, techniques of mass criticism and self-criticism, which Mao had employed during the Yan'an rectification, "became of central feature of political life in the new People's Republic of China." See Elizabeth J. Perry and Merle Goldman, *Grassroots Political Reform in Contemporary China*, p. 10.

political campaigns, which will leave room for redressing unfounded prosecutions and rehabilitating all parties involved."[67]

The State Political Security Bureau basically copied the structure of the Soviet security services, such as the GPU (State Political Administration) and the NKVD (People's Commissariat of Internal Affairs). When the GPU was renamed NKVD in July 1934, the Soviet secret police became detached from the party and the Politburo, thus transforming into an enormous army. Its branches were all-powerful at the local level, and its "special departments" functioned in all large enterprises and educational establishments.[68] According to the organizational outline of the SPSB, it "was based on top-down command and the subordinates were required to obey their superiors absolutely," and, similar to the party, it was to operate at all levels in the government and the military (including the Central Military Commission). In addition, leaders in the local party, government, and army units had no authority to change or reject the orders issued by the SPSB.[69] The SPSB was the principal instrument of force for maintaining internal control through terror – pervasive clandestine surveillance and secret, arbitrary arrest and condemnation. The SPSB spied on members of the party and the Red Army at all levels. There was a network of informers who fed the SPSB information about suspicious individuals throughout the party and the Red Army. The SPSB-trained security guards were sent not only to protect party and army officials but also to watch them. The functions of the SPSB have been pointed out by General Gong Chu, party chief of the CCP Hunan, Guangdong, and Guangxi base areas:

The principal tasks of the SPSB were to prevent the CCP's enemies from committing counterrevolutionary crimes against the Jiangxi Soviet Government and to crack down on their counterrevolutionary activities. At the same time it was responsible for supervising the Party members, the population, and the CCP leaders. [It] was authorized to arrest, interrogate, and execute anyone who was suspected as a counterrevolutionary. Except the high-ranking officials whose fate would be determined by the Party leadership, the SPSB was allowed to kill anyone without approval.[70]

Li Mingrui, commander of the Seventh Red Army, was killed by his SPSB-trained guard when Li decided to defect to the Nationalist Army in November 1931.[71] Unlike the Committee for Eliminating Counterrevolutionaries (CEC), the SPSB was subject to definite procedural requirements for arrests and executions. Under the CEC, "the agents of the Party, Government, and the Youth League and all mass organizations could freely suppress the counterrevolutionaries and make arrests."[72] The SPSB "was based on a vertical system of

[67] *Huang Kecheng zishu*, p. 85.
[68] Edvard Radzinsky, *Stalin: The First in-Depth Biography Based on Explosive New Documents from Russia's Secret Archives*, trans. H. T. Willetts, pp. 316, 347.
[69] *Gong'an shigao*, pp. 31–2.
[70] Gong Chu, *Gong Chu jiangjun huiyilu*, vol. 2, p. 570.
[71] Ibid., p. 350.
[72] *Wenjian xuanji*, vol. 8, pp. 18–9.

command and its activities often overrode even local party commissions and governments so that it lacked the leadership and supervision" from outside of the SPSB.[73]

Before the SPSB was established, the CCP security and intelligence services were divided into two sections: the base areas led by the CEC and the GMD-held areas led by the central committee's Special Services Division (*zhongyang teke*). The newly established SPSB combined the security and intelligence services of the Jiangxi base areas and GMD held areas, and it took primary authority over the suppression of counterrevolutionaries. Before the establishment of the SPSB, the CEC and the PSD in the Jiangxi base areas were the leading organs that commanded the *sufan* campaigns, with the local party, government, and armed forces assisting in the investigations, arrests, imprisonments, and executions. The creation of the SPSB enabled the party leadership to effectively control the scale and direction of the *sufan* campaigns. Although the party leadership in the Jiangxi base areas continually attempted to suppress counterrevolutionaries, purging and executing accused members of the AB Corps up until the Long March,[74] it limited the *sufan* campaigns to a degree. As Li Yimeng points out, "there was no expansion of the campaigns for suppressing counterrevolutionaries and [the SPSB's] work was relatively smooth."[75] Zhou Enlai was the main architect who organized and recruited leading figures of the SPSB, with Qian Zhuangfei, Li Kenong, Hu Di, and Li Yimeng, the top underground agents in the central committee's Special Services Division, being assigned to head the professional departments of the SPSB.

In the campaigns to suppress counterrevolutionaries during the late 1920s and early 1930s, although the CEC and the SPSB were the main implementers of the campaigns, ironically, most campaign leaders became scapegoats and were consequently punished (Table 1.1). The year 1945 and the early 1950s marked two periods of rehabilitation of the accused, when many officers killed in the *sufan* campaigns were named martyrs, such as Duan Dechang (commander of the Sixth Army) and Xu Jishen (commander of the Twelfth Division of the Fourth Army).[76] These rehabilitations demonstrate the CCP's indirect repudiation of the *sufan* campaigns.

---

[73] *Gong'an shigao*, p. 62.

[74] For example, in May 1932, the State Political Security Bureau was ordered to execute some leading figures in the Jiangxi base areas who were accused of being "prime criminals" of the AB Corps, such as Li Wenlin, Zeng Bingchun, Wang Huai, and Duan Qifeng. See Chen Xingeng, *Chise beiju*, pp. 139–45; Zhonggong Jishui xian dangshiban, "Guanyu Li Wenlin bei cuosha qingkuang de diaocha" [Investigation concerning the situation under which Li Wenlin was mistakenly executed], in *Jiangxi dangshi ziliao* [Materials of Jiangxi party history], Zhonggong Jiangxisheng dangshi yanjiushi (ed.), vol. 1 (1987), p. 326.

[75] Li Yimeng, *Li Yimeng huiyilu* [Memoirs of Li Yimeng], p. 156.

[76] He Libo, "Xia Xi yu Xiang-e-xi suqu 'sufan,'" pp. 22–9; *Anhui ribao* [Anhui daily], September 13, 2009.

TABLE 1.1. *List of the Punished Leaders of the* Sufan *Organizations in CCP Base Areas, 1931–1932*

Name	Position	Base Areas	Punishment	Date Punished
Li Shaojiu	Chairman, CEC	Jiangxi	Dismissal	January 1932
Lin Yizhu	Chairman, CEC	Western Fujian	Execution	September 1931
Jiang Qi	Director, SPSB	Hunan-Western Hubei	Execution	Summer 1933

Source: Gong'an shigao, p. 192; Wang Yong, "Minxi genju di 'shehui minzhu dang' yuan'an," p. 30; He Libo, "Xia Xi yu Xiang-e-xi suqu 'sufan,'" pp. 26–7; Yang Yuying, "Wohe Zhou Xing," in *Lishi shunjian*, vol. 2, Sun Mingshan (ed.), pp. 481–3.

Department of Eliminating Traitors, Spies, and Trotskyites

The Long March from 1934 to 1935 had disastrous consequences for the CCP, including a huge loss of CCP officers and soldiers. Only eight thousand personnel, 25 percent of the total Central Red Army, were able to make it to northern Shaanxi. With this turn of events, the party leadership turned their gaze inward, questioning the *sufan* method of resolving intraparty conflict through violence. The effort to end the ongoing purges launched by local party leaders in northern Shaanxi against several leaders such as Liu Zhidan and Gao Gang was a significant sign that the CCP leadership preferred persuasion with moderate coercion in dealing with the internal conflict. In northern Shaanxi, terror had dissipated, and security forces were brought under the control of party leadership. The establishment of the second united front with the Nationalist Party against the Japanese provided the CCP a relatively peaceful environment for development in northern Shaanxi and thus brought about a changed atmosphere that seemed incompatible with the *sufan* organizations. The second United Front, which was dedicated to ousting the Japanese from China and which lasted from 1937 to 1945, gave the CCP the opportunity to expand its military forces, increase its membership, and successfully project itself to substantial numbers of intellectuals as an enlightened and patriotic party.[77] Mao himself spoke of the need for a change in security services and internal political police. In 1936, after three front armies (First, Second, and Fourth) joined forces in northern Shaanxi, the SPSB branches in these armies were abolished and a new centralized agency was born. In the winter of 1937, the Central Special Work Commission (CSWC) was assigned to take authority over the entire CCP security and intelligence.[78]

In August 1937, after the united front between the CCP and the GMD was established, the Red Army was reorganized as the Eight Route Army of

---

[77] Tony Saich and Hans J. Van de Ven, "Introduction," in *New Perspectives on the Chinese Communist Revolution*, ed. Tony Saich and Hans J. Van de Ven, pp. xiv–xv.

[78] Wang Jun, "Kang Sheng zai zhongyang shehui bu" [Kang Sheng in the Social Affairs Department], in *Bainian chao* [Hundred-year tide], no. 5 (2003), p. 21.

the Nationalist Army. As a result, the Department of Eliminating Traitors, Spies, and Trotskyites (DETST) were created within the units of the Eight Route Army to provide security services for the reorganized communist armed forces and base areas where they were stationed. While the DETST established its main body in the headquarters of the Eight Route Army, branches were also established in the army's three divisions – the 115th Division, the 120th Division, and the 129th Division. The DETST branches were also established in the New Fourth Army (NFA) when the NFA was created, and then dispatched to eastern China in the spring of 1938.[79] At the same time, the different levels of the SPSB also became DETST branches. The DETST had mainly two functions. One was "suppressing sabotage activities by traitors and spies, maintaining order and protecting leaders in the party, army and government." The other was responsibility for "training personnel engaged in security services, including eliminating spies and developing DETST branches."[80] The DETST at each level was in charge of internal security, investigation, interrogation, and execution of spies and agents in the party and the armed forces. In addition, the DETST was responsible for maintaining political and social order, providing security for the local party and government organizations, and establishing public security agencies for the CCP's local authorities.[81]

Japanese operations increasingly threatened the survival of the Eighth Route Army and the CCP guerrilla base areas. Between 1938 and 1940, there were at least 109 campaigns launched by the Japanese Army that severely threatened the survival of the communist armed troops. Obvious physical barriers existed, such as the large number of blockade houses, walls, and ditches that the Japanese Army had built to prevent communist guerrillas from receiving food and supplies from the plains. More significant, however, were the subtler political barriers of power and manipulation. For example, the Japanese established puppet troops and governments in the countryside to encroach upon the communists' domain and undermine their influence. Although the communist troops had a local advantage against the unprepared Japanese in the early stages of the Hundred Regiments' Battle, they suffered heavy losses because of their inferior arms and lack of supplies.[82] For most communist armed forces, according to Nie Rongzhen, commander of the Shanxi-Chahaer-Hebei base areas, the general policy throughout the Sino-Japanese War was to avoid direct confrontation, use guerrilla warfare to surprise and ambush the Japanese troops, and rely on small-scale military attacks against the well-equipped and well-trained Japanese Army.[83] Thus, the intelligence and counterespionage became

---

[79] *Gong'an shigao*, p. 75.

[80] Ibid., pp. 75–6.

[81] *Yang Qiqing zhuan*, p. 83.

[82] Tien-wei Wu, "The Chinese Communist Movement," in James Chieh Hsiung and Steven I. Levine (ed.), *China's Bitter Victory: the War with Japan, 1937–1945*, p. 87.

[83] Nie Rongzhen, *Nie Rongzhen huiyilu* [Memoirs of Nie Rongzhen; hereafter, *Nie Rongzhen huiyilu*], vol. 2, pp. 369–70, 530.

significantly important not only for the survival of the CCP but also for the CCP's pursuit of political and military advantage during the so-called people's war against the Japanese.

Intelligence and counterespionage became even more crucial for the survival of the CCP in the early 1940s when the Japanese took the initiative to secure their supply lines to base areas. In Shaodang in May 1942, Japanese troops launched a campaign to clear communist threats from the supply line, which caused the Shanxi, Chahaer, and Hebei base areas to lose two-thirds of their size and population.[84] Communist troops had to retreat on all fronts, including Japanese-held areas and the communist base areas. In the Japanese-held areas, Japanese troops used the approach of "cleaning villages" (*qing xiang*) and established and developed puppet governments and secret police to ensure their control. They also imposed what they called the *baojia* system, an administrative system organized on the basis of households. The system was effective in controlling the population because an entire group of people could be implicated under just one prosecution. In the partially Japanese-held areas, the primary Japanese initiatives included the policy of "nibbling away" the domain of the communist guerrilla troops by launching military campaigns, establishing fortified points, digging blockaded trenches, and establishing puppet organizations called Associations of Maintenance (*weichi hui*). In the communist base areas, the primary Japanese initiatives were military attacks and terrorist suppression.[85] Therefore, due to the "nibble away" campaign, there existed a huge need for CCP intelligence to find out the Japanese military initiatives and pursue for new domains to compete for political and military advantage with the Nationalist armies.[86]

The campaign against the so-called Trotsky Clique in the CCP originated in Stalin's targeting of his political opponents in the Soviet Union, Leon Trotsky in particular.[87] Stalin's campaign aimed at denigrating the reputation of Trotsky, because Trotsky pursued a genuine Marxist program and embodied the genuine traditions of the October insurrection, continually influencing the Soviet working class and intelligentsia. Trotsky was Lenin's comrade in arms, as well as the leader of the Soviet Red Army, which defeated foreign armies after

---

[84] Ibid., p. 530.

[85] *Gong'an shigao*, pp. 98–9.

[86] In his memoir, Marshal Nie Rongzhen describes in detail how the CCP armed forces survived in the Japanese-controlled areas and how the CCP competed with the Nationalist armies and the variety of local armed groups. See *Nie Rongzhen huiyilu* [Memoirs of Nie Rongzhen], vol. 2, pp. 420–32.

[87] The Chinese Trotskyites refer to two sources of a Trotskyist current in the ranks of the CCP. One was the group of Chinese students who studied at the University of the Toilers of the East and Sun Yat-sen University in Moscow and the other was opposition within the CCP leadership in China to the policy that Sneevliet-Maring had originally advocated and that became official Comintern policy early in 1923. See Robert Jackson, *International Trotskyism, 1929–1985: A Documented Analysis of the Movement*, p. 203.

1918. Stalin established his authority through his dominance of the ideological interpretation of Leninist thought. Representing a variety of bureaucratic centrism, a term that Trotsky used to characterize the political practice of the Stalinist bureaucracy, to destroy the left wing and right wing, and relying on a terror machine to exile, imprison, and murder political opponents, Stalinist bureaucratic centralism undermined the already weak norms of intraparty democracy and it inevitably leads to personal dictatorship. Stalin succeeded in imposing a ruthless dictatorial rule over the Soviet working class. In this way he managed to take over control of the economy and the state apparatus. At the conference of the Comintern on April 21, 1937, leadership of the Comintern agreed on a resolution to condemn Trotsky and Trotskyites, and they ordered all branches of the Comintern "to discuss and research the resolution and launch the struggle against the Trotskyism."[88] Wang Ming and Kang Sheng represented the CCP at the conference. This campaign against the Trotskyites became a weapon Wang Ming used to undermine Mao's influence by attacking Chen Duxiu, chief of the CCP during the 1920s, after Wang returned to Yan'an from Moscow in November 1937.

Chen Duxiu, the principal founder and the main leader of the CCP, was expelled from the party and arrested by the GMD in 1932. Chen wrote to the CCP and asked for the possibility to return to the party after he was released from prison in 1937 with the outbreak of the Sino-Japanese War. To fight the Japanese, the CCP appealed for an anti-Japanese national united front, not only with the GMD government but also with other groups, including the Chinese Trotskyites.[89] Mao allowed Chen Duxiu return to the party as long as Chen "publically [gave] up and firmly oppose[d] the entire theories and actions of Trotskyism, publically announce[d] that [he] [broke] up with Trotskyites, admit[ted] the mistake for joining in the Trotskyist organizations in the past, publically support[ted] the united front policy against the Japanese, and show[ed] his sincerity in supporting the united front in his actions."[90] Mao enthusiastically welcomed Chen's return to the party and ordered the party to establish "a cooperative relationship" with Chen. He proclaimed that if "Chen Duxiu and the Trotskyites are willing to repent and mend their ways," the CCP should cooperate with Chen against their common enemy – the Japanese.[91] The leading weekly theoretical journal of the CCP, *Jiefang* [Liberation], even published a commentary that urged Chen Duxiu "to revive the spirit of a senior soldier for participation in the revolutionary ranks."[92]

[88] See *Jiefang* [Liberation], no. 32, March 5, 1938.
[89] Zhongyang tongzhan bu [Central Department of United Front], *Zhonggong zhongyang kangri minzu tongyi zhanxian wenjian huibian* [Compiled documents of CCP central anti-Japanese national united front], vol. 2, p. 137.
[90] *Wenjian xuanji*, vol. 11, p. 335.
[91] See Zhang Guotao, *Wode huiyi*, vol. 3, p. 422.
[92] "Chen Duxiu xiansheng dao hechu qu" [Where does Mr. Chen Duxiu go?], in *Jiefang* [Liberation], November 20, p. 1937.

Because Mao and Wang Ming competed with each other in the CCP leadership, Wang had a vendetta for Mao. When Wang heard Mao's stand toward Chen, he used it to attack Mao when Wang returned to Yan'an from Moscow in November 1937.[93] On December 4, 1937, Wang published an article in *Jiefang*, condemning Chen Duxiu by tying him to the "Trotskyist bandit." He did this before he released the order from the Comintern regarding the Comintern's position toward the Trotskyites.[94] Wang implied that Mao made a serious "mistake" due to his incapability to lead the party against the Trotskyites and his personal inclination toward Trotskyism. In the Politburo conference of December 9–December 14, Wang was particularly furious at the effort made by the CCP leadership and Mao to engage in dialogue with Chen Duxiu regarding cooperation with Trotskyites. Wang insisted, "We can cooperate with Chiang Kai-shek as well as anti-communist agents of his intelligence services, but not with Chen Duxiu," an implication that the CCP can establish the anti-Japanese united front with anyone but the Trotskyites. Wang further threatened the CCP leadership by saying, "We make the initiative to contact Trotskyites while Stalin was vigorously and speedily suppressing them," and "the consequences are beyond what we could image if Stalin knew [what we have done]."[95] Given Wang Ming's trophy in the Luochuan conference during August 1937 that had been flawed by Trotskyite ideas, there was a ramified Trotskyite conspiracy to infiltrate the CCP and to murder its leaders, and Wang was using Chen Duxiu as a pretext for opposing Mao.[96]

Because of Wang's roles in the Comintern leadership as an executive member and an alternate secretary as well as chief of the CCP's delegation to the Comintern,[97] he understood the policy of the Comintern better than anybody else in the CCP leadership. He used this against Mao, further criticizing Mao of "overemphasizing the CCP's independence and initiative" while participating in the united front. Wang was aware of the significant change of the Comintern's policy after the Comintern's Seventh Congress (July–August 1935) that called for a united front of all elements, classes, and nations in the fight against fascism. When Germany and Japan were increasingly threatening the Soviet Union, Stalin was preoccupied with protecting Soviet national interests, which

[93] John W. Garver, *Chinese-Soviet Relations, 1937–1945: The Diplomacy of Chinese Nationalism*, p. 68.

[94] Wang Ming, "Rikou qinglue de xinjieduan yu zhongguo renmin douzheng de xinshiqi" [New stage of the Japanese envision and the new era of Chinese people's struggle], in *Jiefang* [Liberation], no. 26, December 4, p. 1937.

[95] See Xu Guangshou, "Chen Duxiu 'hanjian' shijian shimo" [Beginning and end of Chen Duxiu "traitor" case], in *Dangshi zonglan* [Over the party history], no. 2 (2007), pp. 41–6.

[96] John W. Garver, *Chinese-Soviet Relations, 1937–1945: The Diplomacy of Chinese Nationalism*, p. 69.

[97] Zhang Jiakang, "Wang Ming yu zhongyang fenting kangli de shi ge yue" [Ten months in which Wang Ming Stood up to the center as an equal], in *Dangshi zongheng* [Over the party history], no. 9 (2007), p. 19.

took his focus away from the internationalist nature of socialism. Wang Ming believed that he should be the instrument of the Comintern for the new policy line to China. Other CCP leaders perceived that Wang's ideas represented Stalin's views well. In his keynote speech to the conference, "How to Continue Resistance and Strive for Victory against the Japanese," Wang proposed a new CCP policy of "everything through the united front." While the conference added Wang Ming, Chen Yun, and Kang Sheng as members to the Central Secretariat, Wang suggested convening the Seventh Party Congress as soon as possible and proposed a list of the "preparation commission," in which he listed himself immediately after Mao. To defeat Mao politically, Wang strove to present an approach to theory that would not only appropriate the united front as his own but also undermine Mao's credibility.

Under Wang Ming's pressure of encouraging the party to take initiative against the Trotskyites at the December conference, the campaign against the Trotskyites became imperative for the CCP.[98] Cooperating with Wang Ming, Kang Sheng wrote an article that tied the Chinese Trotskyites to the Japanese invaders and claimed that Chen Duxiu received a monthly stipend from the Japanese intelligence services. Kang posited that "the order given by the head of Trotskyist bandits to his Chinese followers was to help the Japanese invade China."[99] As deputy chief for the CCP delegation to the Comintern who attempted to implement a purge of the Trotskyites, Kang Sheng supported Wang Ming and was a key vanguardist in the campaign. In early 1938, Kang replaced Zhang Hao as head of the Enemy-Controlled Work Commission and later was appointed as director of the Central Security Commission (*zhongyang baowei weiyuanhui*) – both of which were CCP leading organs in charge of security and intelligence services.[100] In early 1938, one of the emergent tasks for which the Central Security Commission was responsible was screening a large number of newly recruited party members who joined from enemy-controlled areas. Part of the screening process included registering with party organizations and filing forms and reporting personal information such as education, employment history, family background, and social relations. Newcomers were required to provide witnesses to confirm their personal information and receive

---

[98] According to Zhang Guotao, Wang Ming even intimidated the CCP leadership by saying, "There have been so many Trotskyites and counterrevolutionaries in the communist international; are we sure that there is no single Trotskyist in the CCP?" See Zhang Guotao, *Wode huiyi*, vol. 3, pp. 422–3.

[99] Kang Sheng, "Chanchu rikou zhentan minzu gongdi de Trotskyist feitu" [Sweep away the Trotskyist bandits – The Japanese agents and the national public enemies], in *Jiefang* [Liberation], no. 29 (January 28, 1938) and no. 30 (February 8, 1938).

[100] When the Central Security Commission was created in early 1938, Zhou Enlai was its director. After Zhou left Yan'an for Wuhan where he assisted Wang Ming in leading the CCP Yangtzi Bureau, Zhang Hao became its director. Kang Sheng replaced Zhang Hao to take charge of the Central Security Commission after the Sixth Plenum. See *Lingdao jigou yange*, p. 427; *Gong'an shigao*, p. 79.

the party examination. The Central Security Commission would then conduct an investigation based on the reported personal information. The Central Security Commission, controlled by Kang Sheng, expanded its power in October 1939 when the party leadership ordered all local party organizations to establish branches of the Central Security Commission, consisting in each local branch of the local party chief, the director of the Party Organization Department, and the director of the Social Affairs Department.[101]

The Central Security Commission commanded the Department of Eliminating Traitors, Spies, and Trotskyites (DETST), which had three main functions. First, it organized the party, army, and mass organizations against the infiltration of enemy spies and maintained social order in base areas. Under the leadership of DETST, a large number of the commissions in charge of security and eliminating traitors, spies, and Trotskyites (*chujian baowei weiyuanhui*) were created, so that by 1939, more than nine hundred sentry posts had been established in the base areas.[102] Second, the DETST took charge of intelligence, espionage, and counterespionage through dispatching teams of scouts to spy on the enemies' intelligence. This involved secretly sending or recruiting network informers (*wang yuan*) to hide in the party, civil organizations, and army units.[103] This pervasive spy network introduced by Kang Sheng was the embodiment of Soviet-style communism, in which participation from all parts of society was integral to the surveillance system. The agents sent CCP-trained and recruited network informers to observe party members in their daily actions and social relations. Jiang Qing, later Mao's wife and a member of the Gang of Four in the Cultural Revolution, started out as a secret network informer of the Central Security Commission in the Yan'an Luxun Arts Institute.[104] Last, the DETST established agencies to conduct preliminary investigations, make arrests, and manage both detention houses and prisons. In some base areas, such as Shanxi, Chahaer, and Hebei, the DETST established centers to rehabilitate criminals through education, persuasion, labor, and other skills training.[105]

In February 1938, the CCP leadership launched the campaign to eliminate Trotskyites and traitors with the issue of "On the Decision to Expand the Campaign against the Trotskyites and Traitors." Although the nationwide campaign was pushed by the CCP leadership, none of the base areas had carried out a campaign like those launched in the early 1930s in terms of scale and devastating consequences. In the beginning, small-scale purges of Trotskyites with middle or low-level standing in the party typified the campaign. These so-called

---

[101] *Wenjian xuanji*, vol. 12, p. 183.
[102] *Gong'an shigao*, p. 86.
[103] Ibid., pp. 86–7.
[104] Du Chao, "Diaocha Jiang Qing de ren – Xu Jianguo de beiju" [A person who investigated Jiang Qing – The tragedy of Xu Jianguo], in *Wenshi jinghua* [Gems of literature and history], no. 8 (2007), p. 33.
[105] *Gong'an shigao*, pp. 88–9.

Trotskyites were suspected of espionage only because they were historically or currently tied to Trotskyist organizations.[106] Although the campaigns in some regions did attempt to discriminate between Trotskyites and traitors, most of them were used by local leaders to purge their political opponents, people who "held Trotskyist views," and people who "did not get along well with others." The Trotskyites who were convicted, as in central Hebei base areas, had nothing to do with Trotskyites or Trotskyism but were those

who liked to hold different opinions with their superiors, always complained, and who had bad habits. They also exemplified traits characteristic of warlords and guerrilla army members, in that they had shortcomings in aspects of social propriety. In essence, their demeanor bred tensions with others to the point where they became targets for revenge and personal grudge.[107]

In many places, local party organizations used the same methods employed in the early 1930s. These methods relied on severe torture to extort confessions, executing further arrests with those leads and either sentencing jail time or death, all without any concrete evidence. The most severe example of prosecutions without due process was in the hometown of Kang Sheng in the province of Shandong. In this town alone, more than one hundred party members and young intellectuals were charged as Trotskyites and executed.[108]

Consequently, the campaign against the Trotskyites and Traitors was unable to gain popular support within party leadership partially because the purges of the early 1930s were still fresh in their memories. Few of the high-ranking leaders were willing to join the vanguard for these campaigns. This explains why so few high-ranking leaders had been targeted or purged. For example, Zuo Quan, deputy general chief of staff for the Eighth Route Army, was convicted by Wang Ming as a Trotskyist because of his role as "the important member" of the so-called Jiangsu and Zhejiang Association in 1928. Despite the fact that Zuo had always gotten the cold shoulder from the CCP leadership as a suspected Trotskyist since he had returned to China from Moscow, he did not become a target of the campaign. Similarly, Wang Ruofei, secretary of the CCP Center China Work Committee and currently secretary of the North China Work Committee, remained unconvicted, even though he had been charged as a suspected Trotskyist while studying in Moscow in 1930.[109] In addition,

---

[106] Gao Hua, *Hong taiyang shi zenyang shengqi de – Yan'an zhengfeng de lailong qumai* [How did the sun rise over Yan'an? A history of the rectification movement], pp. 440–6.

[107] Li Jinming, *He Long fennu zhizhi jizhong "sutuo"* [He Long indignantly stopped the campaign "suppressing Trotskyites" in the central Hebei], in *Laonian shibao* [Senior times], April 11, 2008, p. 9.

[108] San Mu, "Zuo Quan de liesi yu zixu wuyou de 'tuopai' xianyi" [Zuo Quan's heroic death and unwarranted suspect as a member of the Trotskyist faction], in *Wenshi jinghua* [Gems of literature and history], no. 2 (2003), p. 29.

[109] See Yang Shangkun, "Guanyu 'ershiba ge ban buer shiweike' wenti" [Concerning the issue of 28 and a half Bolsheviks], in *Bainian chao* [Hundred-year tide], no. 8 (2001), p. 17; San Mu, "Zuo Quan de liesi yu zixu wuyou de 'tuopai' xianyi," pp. 26–31.

the campaign confronted strong resistance from some leaders, particularly He Long, commander of the 120th Division of the Eighth Route Army, and Luo Ronghuan, political commissar of the 115th Division of the Eighth Route Army. He Long ordered an end to the campaign in the central Hebei base areas after he took charge in the spring of 1939.[110] Luo Ronghuan terminated the campaign in the Huxi base areas in December 1939.[111] In terms of Zuo Quan's case, he was protected by Peng Dehuai, deputy commander of the Eighth Route Army. Peng not only conveyed to the CCP leadership Zuo Quan's personal appeal for restoring his innocence but also made his own appeal to the Central Secretariat to terminate Zou's case as a suspected Trotskyist.[112] Though still horrific, the campaign was not as widespread or penetrating as political purges that had been launched in the past.

The unpopularity of the campaign also contributed to the decline of Wang Ming's influence and the increase of Mao's power in the CCP leadership. Without a doubt, the Comintern's decision played a significant role in the power struggle between Mao and Wang Ming. Before Wang left Moscow for China, the Comintern had informed him that "the leader of the CCP is Mao Zedong not you" and advised Wang to "humbly" respect Mao.[113] This message, along with the Comintern's reiterations through Wang Jiaxiang and Ren Bishi, was made clear to other top leadership in the party, and so on receiving this news, many high-ranking leaders hastily switched their alliance from Wang Ming to Mao, as in the case of Kang Sheng.[114] The Comintern's position in backing Mao, according to Dieter Heinzig, was greatly derived from the mutual compromises between Stalin and Mao in which "Mao bowed – at least pro forma – to pressure from Moscow to allow the CCP to cooperate with the KMT (GMD) against the Japanese and recognized the KMT as the 'party in power' and Chiang Kaishek as 'leader' of the 'Chinese people'" while Moscow in turn "accepted Mao's demand for the independence of the CCP in the alliance with the KMT – also at least pro forma – and approved Mao's tactic of 'continuous guerrilla warfare' in the countryside with the goal of extending the Communist base even if this would lead to tensions with the KMT, and came to terms with Mao's position as de facto Party leader."[115]

Regardless of the turn of events, Wang Ming continued his politicking. Realizing his disadvantages in competing with Mao directly, Wang attempted to rely

[110] Li Jinming, *He Long fennu zhizhi jizhong "sutuo,"* p. 9.
[111] "Dangdai zhongguo renwu zhuanji" congshu bianjibu, *Luo Ronghuan zhuan* [A biography of Luo Ronghuan], pp. 189–201.
[112] San Mu, "Zuo Quan de liesi yu zixu wuyou de 'tuopai' xianyi," p. 29.
[113] Zhang Jiakang, "Wang Ming yu zhongyang fenting kangli de shi ge yue," p. 19.
[114] Zhonggong zhongyang wenxian yanjiushi, *Ren Bishi zhuan* [A biography of Ren Bishi], rev. ed., p. 525; *Hong taiyang*, pp. 227–8.
[115] Dieter Heinzig, *The Soviet Union and Communist China, 1945–1950: The Arduous Road to the Alliance*, p. 9.

on indirect means to increase his influence in the CCP leadership, such as the effort to push the campaign. To his credit, Wang Ming was successful in dominating the agenda of the CCP leadership during the spring of 1938 with purges of Trotskyites. After the spring of 1938, Wang took a more aggressive stance toward challenging Mao's leadership. In October 1938, the Sixth Plenum was held after the Comintern further emphasized its support of Mao's leadership. The Comintern's stance was reinforced by Dimitrov, the member at the time responsible for Chinese affairs. It was he who asked Wang Jiaxiang to convey the Comintern's message to the CCP leadership: Wang Ming must stop infighting, and Mao should be the party's senior leader. Despite the Comintern's endorsement of Mao's authority, Wang still won overwhelming support from party leadership with the passage of a political resolution that prioritized the campaign to rigorously eliminate spies as one of the "current emergent tasks" of the party. The conference passed the Resolution Regarding Struggle against Traitors, Spies and Trotskyites, which launched the campaign.[116]

Like the CCP armed forces, the CCP local organizations for eliminating traitors, spies, and Trotskyites were established in late 1937. These security agencies served to protect the CCP local governmental branches, and most operated under the name of the United Front. In the areas where the CCP and the GMD worked as a united front, they were called the Commission of War Mobilization, as in central and western Hebei and northeastern Shanxi. In some CCP areas, such as Shandong, they remained the SPSB. In other areas, such as Taihang and Taiyue of Shanxi, southern Hebei, and the border areas of Hebei, Shandong, and Henan, they were known as the Bureau of Public Security, Division of Public Security and the Section of Eliminating Traitors, Spies, and Trotskyites.[117]

Bureau of Public Security

On February 18, 1939, the Central Secretariat decided to establish the Social Affairs Department (SAD) in the CCP's higher-level agencies and the Bureau of Public Security in the CCP-controlled governments in the base areas.[118] The SAD was the organ primarily in charge of the CCP security and intelligence apparatus. The Central Committee's SAD, the newly established security and intelligence agency, was assigned to focus mainly on security functions, including managing the security guards of high-ranking leaders, collecting intelligence, and training security and intelligence personnel. Operating under the direction and jurisdiction of the party leadership, SAD was assigned both internal and external functions: to conduct espionage operations and to conduct

---

[116] San Mu, "Zuo Quan de liesi yu zixu wuyou de 'tuopai' xianyi," pp. 28–9.
[117] *Gong'an shigao*, pp. 76–8.
[118] *Yang Qiqing zhuan*, p. 94

surveillance of all communist party, government, and military organizations.[119] Local security forces were tasked with combating ordinary crime, maintaining social order, and guarding important leaders and government buildings. From the beginning, the SAD had been structured more as an intelligence or counterespionage agency rather than a security services agency for the leadership. As described in the "Decision on the Establishment of the Central Social Affairs Department," issued by the Central Secretariat on February 18, 1939, its five central missions included: (1) initiatives against the enemies' espionages and infiltration into the party; (2) efforts to send its agents to infiltrate the enemies' organizations or recruit communist sympathizes as its agents; (3) the responsibility to inform, alert, and educate party members about the espionage activities of the enemies; and (4) duties in administrating confidential organizations and party top secrets, as well as responsibility for recruiting and training agents.[120]

As the leading agencies of the party at Yan'an and other major base areas, the SAD and its branches had the difficult task of exercising authority over the united front governments, which included communists, Nationalists, and people from other groups. Major base areas, such as the Shaanxi, Gansu, and Ningxia border region and the Shanxi, Chahaer, and Hebei border region were special administrative zones of the Nationalist government. Although the CCP dominated some regions and established governments there, it was required to create law enforcement agencies that publicly were not communist. The Bureau of Public Security was created to achieve this purpose. As indicated by Peng Zhen, party secretary of the CCP's Northern Bureau, the establishment of the Bureau of Public Security was necessary:

The government in the base areas is the united front government without the CCP-led public security organizations. [If someone breaks the law] it is inappropriate to let the Party committee or the army arrest the offenders. Even when there exists a special criminal case, neither the army nor the Party committee is allowed to lead the prosecution. After deliberation, [we decided] to establish the General Bureau of Public Security in the Shanxi-Chahaer-Hebei base areas.[121]

The General Bureaus of Public Security were established in the major CCP base areas and were led by the party committees and the governments of the base areas. Similarly, the organizations of public security were established in all levels of local governments from the district level to the provincial level (Figure 1.1). Organizationally, agencies of public security were subordinate to local governments, but they received professional guidance from the upper-level agencies of public security. There was a clear division of labor and autonomy

[119] Jeffrey Richelson, *Foreign Intelligence Organizations*, p. 274.
[120] *Gong'an shigao*, p. 80.
[121] Ibid., 82.

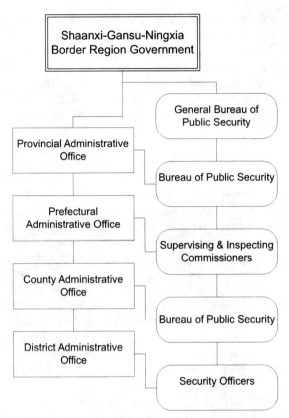

FIGURE I.I. Organizational Structure of the CCP Public Security in Yan'an, 1940s.
Source: *Gong'an shigao*, pp. 84–5.

between the Bureaus of Public Security and the Departments of Eliminating Traitors, Spies, and Trotskyites in the communist armies, such that the General Bureaus of Public Security dealt with security issues only in the government and not in the army. The mutual understanding was that both types of security agencies "should respect the principle of their respective independent work and organizations."[122]

Although the SAD was authorized to lead the CCP intelligence and security services, security services were basically taken over by the local party organizations. Even in the base areas where the central leadership was located, the Department of Security under the government of the Shaanxi, Gansu, and Ningxia border area (its predecessor was the Bureau of Political Security of the CCP Northwestern Bureau) took charge of the security of the CCP Central

[122] Ibid., p. 85.

leadership and the communist government through its local branches throughout the base areas. In Yan'an, the capital city of the CCP, the CCP established the Bureau of Public Security that included the Public Security Office (*zhi'an ke*), Social Affairs Office (*shehui ke*), the Judicial Administration Office (*sifa ke*), Police, the Scout of Cavalry Police, and a local police station (*paichu suo*). The system of public security in Yan'an became the original model of the Bureau of Public Security, local police station, and the uniformed police for the People's Republic of China after 1949.[123]

In the Yan'an rectification, the local public security organ in Yan'an – the Department of Security under the government of the Shaanxi, Gansu, and Ningxia border areas – was the key instrument for arrests, imprisonment, and execution of suspects. Although the SAD was responsible for intelligence and counterespionage across the entire country, the Department of Security in the Shaanxi, Gansu, and Ningxia border areas headed security, intelligence, and counterespionage in those base areas. This included Yan'an, the capital city of the CCP.[124] The Department of Security carried out detentions, arrests, imprisonments, and executions following the orders of Kang Sheng, as on April 1, 1943, when Kang ordered the department to arrest more than two hundred suspects.[125] When the Rescuing Campaign during the Yan'an rectification had grown so extreme that it undermined Mao's effort to unify the party, Kang Sheng became infamous for his excesses and was eventually transferred. Although Mao did write to the Comintern to defend Kang Sheng,[126] he publicly announced the Rescue Campaign as excessive,[127] which implied Kang's excesses and role in promoting many false cases. This shows that Mao used Kang Sheng as a public relations campaign, intending to convince the masses that he was protecting them against power abuses like those of Kang Sheng. Mao's refusal to protect Kang was the source for a popular public opinion that Kang was guilty of leftist deviations and extremism. Although Kang retained his membership in the Politburo, he lost a large amount of votes and failed to keep his post as director of the SAD and the Central Intelligence Department. Kang was exiled to eastern Gansu, western Shanxi, and Bohai, in Shangdong, during 1946–1948, when he was ordered to attend to the local land reform before he was given the post of secretary of the Shangdong Bureau of CCP Central Committee in March 1949.[128]

By 1944, the CCP had begun to take offensive initiatives against the Japanese armies and was striving to gain control over large regions that had been previously controlled by the Japanese. Whenever the CCP armed forces planned

[123] Ibid., p. 74.
[124] Yang Yuying, "Wohe Zhou Xing," p. 492.
[125] *Gong'an shigao*, p. 117.
[126] *Hong taiyang*, pp. 590–1, 603.
[127] Wang Jun, "Kang Sheng zai zhongyang shehui bu," p. 27.
[128] Ibid., p. 28; *Gong'an shigao*, p. 191.

to take over enemy-occupied areas, the security forces or the Bureaus of Public Security were assigned to assist and support the military initiatives of the communist troops. They were responsible for three main tasks:

1. Infiltrating the enemy-controlled areas, executing enemy officers, and instigating a military uprising
2. Providing intelligence regarding enemies' military strength, numbers of troops, weapons, military maneuvers, and particularly detailed information regarding transportation and enemy-controlled cities
3. Cooperating directly with the military actions of the CCP troops[129]

After the CCP armed forces took over a city, the security forces or the Bureaus of Public Security took charge of the security of the newly established communist governments, the consolidation of the new CCP local governments, and the mobilization of the masses to support the CCP army initiatives to take over other cities.[130] In the newly held areas, the security forces were responsible for the following tasks:

1. Quickly establishing or restoring the organizations for the campaign to eliminate traitors, spies, and Trotskyites
2. Mobilizing the masses to capture spies and traitors and imposing the death penalty if the culprit was infamous for his or her guilt of many infamies
3. Registering, investigating, and classifying former officers of the previous governments
4. Suppressing bandits and banning secret-society activities
5. Exposing enemy undercover spies and agents and thwarting their espionage activities
6. Ensuring social security, maintaining social order, and guaranteeing normalcy in daily life[131]

Because the communist-led guerrilla forces had resisted Japanese forces in northern China and Manchuria for nearly a decade, Japan's collapse in August 1945 gave the CCP the opportunity to control vast areas of the countryside. While the communists and Nationalists were executing hastily made plans to expand their territorial control, defense of newly held areas was a priority for the CCP. The party was particularly wary of infiltration and disruptive activities of the GMD intelligence services and of underground agents who could potentially wreak havoc on their territorial expansion.

---

[129] *Gong'an shigao*, p. 124.
[130] Ibid., p. 124.
[131] Ibid., p. 124.

The CCP Police Forces in the 1940s Civil War

In the early 1940s civil war, the CCP was well established in the north and in Manchuria; thus, it was able to organize the communist governments and expand its authority quickly. A large number of the public security organizations were established to take charge of the newly established communist governments. However, Nationalist forces in the nationwide battlefields were on the offensive and communist troops the defensive, because the Nationalists enjoyed a tremendous advantage not only in personnel and equipment but also in considerable international support. For example, they outnumbered communists by three to one, had considerably more artillery, and were backed by the U.S. military. The Nationalists advanced rapidly, occupying many cities and areas controlled by the communists. They had a decisive victory when they captured all the previously communist-held major cities in Manchuria (except Harbin), in addition to Yan'an, the CCP's capital. When the communist armies strategically withdrew to the countryside, the organizations of public security were divided into two – one group accompanied local governments to establish new base areas in the countryside, and the other was to hide in the cities to pursue intelligence and underground activities for the offensive strategy. The Bureaus of Public Security in the newly established base areas mainly focused on safeguarding the base areas by providing intelligence and security services. This allowed the communists to concentrate on the rural areas, where they had a solid base among the peasants, and from where they could regroup and plan counterattacks. Under Nationalist occupation in the cities, CCP organizations of public security continued insurgency tactics. They "punished the spies, split up the enemies, enlisted defectors, protected the masses, abolished the *baojia* system, shielded underground revolutionary activities, performed reconnaissance of the enemy's movements and positions, and cooperated with the major communist forces in military operations."[132]

The GMD lost popular support when its reforms failed and government corruption became rampant. In general, it was an extremely volatile period politically and economically. Joseph W. Esherick has determined that corruption, inflation, and social unrest caused by riots, strikes, demonstrations, protests, and petitions had become a great cancer that undermined the legitimacy of the regime.[133] With the circumstances in their favor, the communists executed counteroffensive attacks, forcing the Nationalists to abandon their plan for a general offensive. Beginning in 1947, the CCP gradually took over the battlefield against demoralized and undisciplined Nationalist troops. By the end of 1947, CCP base areas had expanded to encompass 2.23 million square

---

[132] Ibid., p. 144.
[133] Joseph W. Esherick, "Collapse of the Old Order, Germination of the New: Chinese Society during the Civil War, 1945-1949," in Werner Draguhn and David S. G. Goodman (eds.), *China's Communist Revolutions: Fifty Years of the People's Republic of China*, pp. 30-33.

kilometers. The CCP also controlled 586 cities,[134] and it went on to control Manchuria in early 1948 and central China in late 1948.

A significant evolution in the institutional structure of the CCP's public security organizations was the gradual transition from oversight by party organizations to oversight by CCP local government agencies. By the summer of 1946, the CCP almost completed the system of public security by establishing the General Bureau of the Public Security in each regional bureau of the CCP Central Committee and the Bureaus of Public Security in its local branches at different levels. Although some local branches of the Social Affairs Department were party organizations, and similarly some Bureaus of Public Security were agencies of the local government, many branches of the Social Affairs Department were merged with the Bureaus of Public Security. Three good examples are the SAD: the General Bureau of Public Security of the CCP Shanxi-Hebei-Shandong-Henan Bureau; the SAD: the General Department of Public Security of the CCP Northeast Bureau; and the SAD: the General Bureau of Public Security of the CCP Shanxi-Chahaer-Hebei Bureau. In all three cases, the SAD and the BPS were "the same organization with different names."[135]

A significant organ of each Bureau of Public Security was the main agency responsible for labor camps and deportation. Labor camps were referred to as "Reform through Labor" (*laogai*), and interned millions of defeated GMD officers during the civil war. The camps continued to hold political prisoners when the Ministry of Public Security (MPS) was established in 1949 after the CCP's seizure of power. The CCP had excised the "reform through labor" in the Jiangxi Soviet and the Yan'an base areas during the 1930s and 1940s, and forced labor was the most common type sentence meted out to the counterrevolutionaries.[136] Although there were culturally endemic characteristics such as the heavy emphasis on remolding prisoners' inner thoughts, the CCP's system resembled the Soviet model in several ways, including "the large plurality of convicts sentenced to forced labor as well as the terminology used to describe the forced labor and its supposedly corrective influence on prisoners."[137] After the PRC was founded, reform through labor was directly subordinated to the MPS. The financial and administrative tasks involved in running the labor camps were of critical importance to the MPS. According to an official publication, the reform-through-labor system consisted of a network of several thousand labor camps, factories, and mines that employed a million

---

[134] *Gong'an shigao*, p. 146.
[135] Ibid., pp. 132–8.
[136] See Patricia E. Griffin, *The Chinese Communist Treatment of Counterrevolutionaries: 1924–1949*, pp. 38–39; Qi Li, ed., *Shaan-Gan-Ning bianqu shilu* [True accounts from the Shaanxi-Gansu-Ningxia Border region] (Yan'an: Jiefang she, 1939), p. 35.
[137] Philip F. Williams and Yenne Wu, *The Great Wall of Confinement: The Chinese Prison Camp through Contemporary*, pp. 46, 49.

prisoners.[138] In addition, the MPS played a key role in carrying out the campaign to suppress counterrevolutionaries (*zhenfan*) in the early 1950s. During this period more than 2.6 million people were arrested. Among them 712,000 counterrevolutionaries were executed, 1.29 million were imprisoned, and 1.2 million were subject to control at various times.[139] In addition, the MPS were the vanguard of the 1951 Three-Antis Campaign and Five-Antis Campaign.

Land reform and collectivization launched by the CCP in the late 1940s created an extremely tense struggle in which the CCP public security agencies killed many resisting landlords and rich peasants. In 1947, the CCP's campaign took a distinct leftist turn as the party sought to equalize land rights by confiscating the excess land of landlords and rich peasants and distributing it to the poor. Although some of these excesses were corrected in 1948, "the result was the total eclipse of the power and authority of the rural elite."[140] As the instrument of these campaigns, the local public security agencies played the role of vanguard in reinforcing those policies. They also sent more than 1 million peasants to labor camps. Parallel to land reform and collectivization were a series of campaigns that "eradicated the enemy agents" (*sute*), "exterminated bandits" (*jiaofei*), and "suppressed local tyrants" (*fanba*).[141] After the People's Republic of China was founded, two large-scale campaigns for suppression of counterrevolutionaries were launched. The first one began in October 1950 and lasted for three years. The second one began in the spring of 1955 and ended in late 1956.[142] These campaigns were launched against former officials of the Nationalist Party and the army, rural landlords and gentry, bourgeoisie, businesspeople, former employees of foreign companies, and intellectuals whose loyalty was suspect. The MPS played a vital role in hunting down class enemies and organizing the masses against them. In these political campaigns, the struggle session was a unique method of punishment. Through humiliation, persecution, and/or execution of class enemies, struggle sessions promoted mass participation and enthusiasm, shaped public opinion, and promoted political loyalty from the populace. Although Mao restricted the number of counterrevolutionaries to be killed to less than 0.1 percent of the urban population, he urged the MPS to execute enough counterrevolutionaries so that the executions would reach but not exceed 0.1 percent of the rural

---

[138] Li Yu, *Fendou de zongzhi – xing zhongguo jianyu de wushi si nian* [Pursued objective – Fifty-four years in new China's prisons], in *Fazhi ribao* [Legal system daily], December 28, 2003.

[139] See "Xu Zirong's report on several important statistics since zhenfan, January 14 of 1954," original in the Central Archives quoted from Yang Kuisong, "Reconsidering the Campaign to Suppress Counterrevolutionaries," *China Quarterly*, no. 193 (March 2008), p. 120.

[140] Joseph W. Esherick, "Collapse of the Old Order, Germination of the New: Chinese Society during the Civil War, 1945–1949," in Werner Draguhn and David S. G. Goodman (eds.), *China's Communist Revolutions: Fifty Years of the People's Republic of China*, p. 28.

[141] *Gong'an shigao*, pp. 249–51.

[142] Ibid., pp. 259–78.

population.[143] Mao believed that large-scale killings would intimidate enemies of the CCP so that they would be dissuaded from resisting the newly established People's Republic. Because of the already-pervasive role of the MPS in suppressing counterrevolutionaries, it was natural for the MPS to become the primary instrument for these political campaigns and mass killings.

[143] In rural areas, according to Mao, only execution of more than 0.1 percent of the rural population needed the approval of the CCP Central Bureau. See Mao Zedong, "Zhuanfa xinanju guanyu zhenfan wenti gei chuanbeiqu dangwei de zhishi de piyu" [Remarks on transmitting the directive issued by the CCP Southwest Bureau to the Party Committee of the Northern Sichuan District regarding the issue of suppressing counterrevolutionaries], in Zhonggong zhongyang wenxian yanjiushi, *Jianguo yilai Mao Zedong wengao* [Mao Zedong's manuscripts since the founding of the state; hereafter, *Mao Zedong wengao*], vol. 2, p. 267.

2

From the Social Affairs Department to Ministry of Public Security

The Social Affairs Department (SAD) played an important role in shaping the structure, philosophy, and operating principles of the newly established Ministry of Public Security (MPS) after the CCP took over the government from the Nationalists. One of the first actions of the CCP after coming to power in 1949 was to establish the Ministry of Public Security to address the multifarious security, policing, and intelligence issues. The Ministry of Public Security is China's principal police authority that deals with conventional law enforcement as well as with prosecutions of political crime.[1] Historically, it has had functional departments for areas such as intelligence, police operations, prison administration, political security, economic security, and communications security. Its local branches at various levels are responsible not only for maintaining public order but also for investigating the criminal cases, arresting the suspects and criminals, and undertaking preliminary examinations in criminal cases. The MPS legally is part of the government; in practice, however, it has always fallen under the power of the CCP and thus is one of the tools of coercion that lies in the hands of the party.[2] The direct organizational predecessor of the MPS was the Social Affairs Department, the primary intelligence organization of the CCP and an authority on security and law enforcement. Like the Ministry of State Security, the MPS has authority over Internet security, such as preventing hacking, computer viruses, and other illegal acts, as well as conducting surveillance of dissidents.

---

[1] Richard D. Fisher, *China's Military Modernization: Building for Regional and Global Reach*, p. 32.

[2] Lynn T. White, *Local Causes of China's Intellectual, Legal, and Governmental Reform*, 322; David M. Bachman, *Bureaucracy, Economy, and Leadership in China: The Institutional Origins of the Great Leap Forward*, p. 155.

Although the MPS is directly responsible for maintaining public order and internal security, security detail for elite leaders is also a large part of its duties. Maintaining public order entails apprehending drug traffickers, corrupt officials, and criminals; guarding government and commercial office buildings; directing traffic; and patrolling the streets. Maintaining internal security issues has always been a top priority for the Ministry of Public Security, and the MPS and its local branches oversee internal security issues, which includes maintaining active surveillance over political dissidents, religious groups, radical minority groups, terrorist groups, separatist groups, extremist groups, and "cult" groups, including not only Falun Gong but various traditional Chinese meditation and exercise groups. The MPS also oversees external security, which includes Chinese citizens' travel abroad and foreigners' entry to and exit from the country. Security details involve guarding high-ranking leaders in Beijing and during their international and domestic travels, as well as guarding their residences in Beijing.

In the reform era, the MPS has experienced numerous changes resulting from China's open-door policy, including increasing institutionalization. Moreover, the MPS's approach to social control of the populace has changed significantly from previous eras in that it now heavily emphasizes preventive measures. For example, MPS officers increasingly police the Internet for "undesirable materials" that are considered sources of social instability. They also undertake measures to reeducate [undesirable elements] through labor, the main targets of which are political dissidents, and to disband "cults" and underground churches. The MPS also mediates issues between the populace and the government through the appeals office (*xinfang*), where citizens can file grievances against governmental officials. The MPS derives from a tradition of elite security organizations in the CCP, and control over the populace has always been a principle focus of party leaders. Although the approach to security and intelligence has shifted since the MPS's inception, because of this tradition the MPS places such importance on its duties of public order, internal security, and security of top leaders.

This chapter discusses the evolution and key features of the Ministry of Public Security after it took over most functions of the Social Affairs Department (SAD), which was abolished in 1949. The tendency toward professionalism and institutionalization of public security forces took place after the late 1940s, when the CCP transitioned public security organizations from party to civilian rule following the abolishment of the SAD. The establishment of the Ministry of Public Security was an important step toward institutionalization of the CCP security apparatus, as historically, control over security organizations was reserved solely for dominant party leaders. This development had a profound impact on leadership politics because institutionalization created a persistent but subtle tension between the paramount leader and the party bureaucracy, particularly among security leaders. The collective leadership, which was driven by consensus, albeit suffering from intraparty and governmental tensions, ultimately led to the making of compromises, such as the agreement that the paramount leader would control elite security forces such as the Central Guard Bureau and the Central Guard Regiment while the party, state bureaucracy, and PLA would command other security institutions such as the MPS, the armed police, and the intelligence organizations. While presenting an overview of the important role of the MPS in maintaining political and social order during Mao's era, this chapter analyzes the impact of structural tensions within the MPS on leadership politics. Although the MPS was organizationally under the authority of the State Council and received commands from the Politburo, Mao Zedong personally controlled its Ninth Bureau, and his personal confidant, Wang Dongxing, was directly involved in MPS decision making. Both Deng Xiaoping and Jiang Zemin continued the legacy of personal control over the Ninth Bureau by the paramount leader.

This chapter identifies the characteristics of party norms during the 1950s that shaped MPS operations, advancement, and challenges, and it outlines the MPS's role in elite politics. As consensus was the guiding principle of party leadership early on in the CCP's tenure, the use of the security apparatuses to resolve elite conflicts was done with care and caution. In addition, this chapter analyzes the dominant party norms adapted after the Yan'an rectification to manage intraparty conflict and illustrates the ways in which CCP leadership preferred persuasion together with moderate coercion; moreover, it highlights comparisons with the Soviet experience. In the 1950s and early 1960s, control of the CCP security apparatus shifted toward high-level organizations within the party, where decisions to use the security forces often were based on a consensus among the Politburo, the CCP Central Secretariat, the State Council, and the Central General Office.

Legacy of the Social Affairs Department

The Social Affairs Department was established when Mao was consolidating his position and establishing his dominance in the party by outmaneuvering his opponents during the reorganization of the party and the Red Army following the desperate Long March. In early 1938, following Mao's arrival in northern Shaanxi, the CCP's Central Security Commission (*zhonggong zhongyang baowei weiyuanhui*) was established.[3] The period leading up to the Central Security Commission saw Mao's power grow and an increasingly intense leadership struggle between Mao and Wang Ming, a leader of the Moscow-trained Returned Students faction that had left China in 1931. Wang not only successfully challenged Mao's united front policy (which aimed to maintain the CCP's independence while compromising some party goals) but also gained significant support in his overall policy orientation from several key party leaders, including Zhu De, Peng Dehuai, Ren Bishi, Bo Gu, Xiang Ying, and

---

[3] *Lingdao jigou yange*, p. 427.

Zhou Enlai. Zhou's support was by far the most salient, because his influence among the party's leadership ran deep, and he remained the most influential leader in charge of the CCP security and intelligence services.[4] Wang Ming also used his control of the CCP's Yangtze Bureau to challenge Mao's policy and leadership by attempting to exclude Mao from policy making. Wang's antagonism created considerable political setbacks and embarrassment for Mao,[5] and Wang's actions increasingly frustrated Mao, who complained that "[his] orders could hardly be heard beyond the cave where [he] dwelled."[6] With such a challenge at hand, Mao made several efforts to solidify his leadership by displaying his cooperation with Wang in front of the Comintern so that he could steer Stalin away from having misgivings about Mao's leadership. In addition, Mao attempted to split up the group of returned students by drawing Zhang Wentian, Ren Bishi, and Wang Jiaxiang to his side.[7] Mao's strategy also included an effort to recruit Kang Sheng, a prominent figure in the CCP's security and intelligence apparatus and one of Wang Ming's associates who returned to China with him from Moscow, to manage the newly established CCP Central Security Commission.[8] Mao's initiative to appoint Kang Sheng showed his determination to make a fresh start, without Zhou Enlai in control of the CCP security apparatus.

In February 1939, all levels of the CCP security apparatus were reorganized as the new Social Affairs Department.[9] In October 1939, the CCP Central Security Commission and the Enemy Area Working Commission were combined to form the Social Affairs Department (SAD), with Kang Sheng appointed as the department's head. Kang Sheng's power was further enhanced after he was appointed head of the CCP's Central Committee's Intelligence Department in July 1941.[10] There were several key factors in Mao's use of Kang Sheng: Kang had made a clean break with Wang Ming during the exacerbated conflict among Mao, Wang, and the "two Politburos," in the words of Otto Braun – the first Politburo was led by Mao in Yan'an and the second Politburo by Wang in Wuhan.[11] Kang had been an influential senior party leader in Shanghai; moreover, he had leadership experience in security and intelligence services. Although Mao was not sure how to punish those who posed a threat

---

[4] Gao Wenqian, *Wannian Zhou Enlai* [Zhou Enlai's later years], pp. 64–8.

[5] The Yangtze Bureau forced Mao to accept its decisions; issued several important documents without consulting Mao; and refused to publish Mao's article in *Xinhua Daily*, the CCP's mouthpiece in the GMD areas, in an attempt to undermine Mao's influence. See *Hong taiyang*, pp. 136–62.

[6] Li Weihan, *Huiyi yu yanjiu* [Reminiscence and research], vol. 1, pp. 442–3.

[7] For example, Mao allowed Wang to take charge of drafting the resolution of the December Politburo Conference.

[8] *Lingdao jigou yange*, p. 427.

[9] *Yang Qiqing zhuan*, p. 94.

[10] Ibid., pp. 482, 550.

[11] Otto Braun (Li De), *Zhongguo jishi* [A Comintern agent in China], Li Kuiliu et al. (trans.), p. 282.

to his leadership, he clearly tried to use Kang's experience in Stalin's Great Purge of the 1930s to undermine the influence of his political competitors. When Mao created the General Study Committee to spearhead the Yan'an rectification campaign, he appointed Kang, passing up both the Central Secretariat and the Politburo to lead the effort.[12] During the late 1930s, Mao was managing a variety of factions with a convoluted *guanxi* (relationship) network, yet still his followers never actually took a majority of seats in the leadership. With the Seventh Party Congress scheduled for May 1941, Mao wanted to urgently weaken the influence of his political competitors, especially the group of returned students, led by Wang Ming. In addition, the rectification campaign was accepted by the CCP leadership because of the necessity to "purify" party organizations – in other words, to execute counterintelligence and antiespionage projects. This justification became even more urgent as large numbers of young intellectuals flooded into Yan'an, motivated by patriotism and anti-Japanese sentiment, but also bringing with them an uncertain number of spies sent by either the nationalist government or the Japanese army.

Despite the fact that the SAD's structure was based on that of the Soviet NKVD, it differed significantly from the NKVD, which was based on a vertical system of command. The SAD branches received authority from two chains of command: the upper-level SAD organizations and the same-level party committees. For example, the SAD branches sought advice and suggestions from the upper-level SAD agencies and consulted with local party committees on their campaigns; they also reported the results of their investigations of suspected party members to local party committees. Thus, local party committees, not the upper-level SAD agencies, led the campaigns to eliminate traitors, spies, and Trotskyites. When the CCP issued the document "Resolution on Campaign for Eliminating Traitors, Spies, and Trotskyites" on October 10, 1939, and launched the campaign in all the base areas, it stressed that the party secretaries and the commanders and political commissars in the armed forces must take the lead in the campaign. This demonstrates a clear departure from the Soviet model, in which the security organizations "were divorced from Party leadership and became an independent system."[13]

Thus, the Yan'an rectification campaign was launched in spring 1942, the early stages of which were involved in the assignment of studying 22 documents that included Mao's five articles, Liu Shaoqi's "On the Cultivation of a Communist Member," and Chen Yun's "How to Become a Communist Party Member." The second stage focused on an examination of party cadres *(shengan)*, in which Kang Sheng played a leading role. According to Mao, the rectification campaign served to purify the party from members' thoughts that went against party's spirit and ideology, but the examination of party cadres actually served to screen party members in order to "purify" the party

---

[12] Yang Shangkun, *Yang Shangkun huiyilu* [Memoirs of Yang Shangkun], p. 219.
[13] *Gong'an shigao*, pp. 80–1.

organizations.[14] In the first stage of the Yan'an rectification campaign, Mao attempted to use his writings and speeches to unify the thinking of the whole party, which he hoped would help establish him as the indisputable leader. The second stage was implemented after the so-called standards of true and false were defined to fit Mao's interpretation of assigned readings given to party cadres. In July 1943, the screening of party cadres transformed into purges (*sufan*) known as the rescue campaign (*qiangjiu yundong*).[15] Because Keng Sheng used Stalin-like terror in implementing both the examination of party cadres and the rescue campaign, he confronted strong resistance from party grassroots units and leadership concerning his style of security enforcement.[16] At the Seventh Party Congress, held in April 1945, Kang was severely criticized by many party leaders for his leading role in the investigation of cadres and the rescue campaign, and he fell out of favor with Mao for failing to make substantive change. Kang had falsified cases in the party's grassroots units without making any progress in targeting Mao's high-ranking enemies, such as party leaders from the returned student factions, which was the largest reason for Mao's displeasure with him.[17]

Hence, Kang's loss of power was a direct result of Mao's disappointment and lack of confidence in him. According to Yang Shangkun, Mao was informed by several high-ranking leaders who returned to Yan'an from Moscow about Kang Sheng and Wang Ming's close relationship after Mao had relied on Kang Sheng instead of the Politburo and Central Secretariat to lead the Yan'an rectification. For instance, Kong Yuan, whom Wang and Kang expelled from the party during his studies in the Soviet Union, advised Mao that Kang should not be trusted because he had been a strong supporter of Wang's in Moscow.[18] Thus, Kang gradually lost his influence in the leadership and Li Kenong, acting director of the SAD and one of Zhou Enlai's key assistants, gradually took charge of the SAD and the Central Committee's Intelligence Department (ID). Li Kenong was authorized to clean up the mess that Kang Sheng had left and to redress the falsified cases that his predecessor had litigated.[19] After a short period of exile in the countryside, Kang was transferred to the CCP's East

---

[14] *Yang Shangkun huiyilu*, p. 215.

[15] Shi Zhe, *Zai juren shengbian: Shi Zhe huiyilu* [At the side of a colossus: Memoirs of Shi Zhe; hereafter, *Shi Zhe huiyilu*], pp. 249–50.

[16] Kang's approach to carry out investigation of both the cadres and the rescue campaign was based on the Soviet experience, in which terrorist party organizations were created to target suspected party cadres at the bottom and then trace them to the party leadership. Kang frequently consulted Peter Volajimiluv, the Comintern liaison official in Yan'an, for advice. See *Yang Shangkun huiyilu*, pp. 215–6.

[17] Kang attempted to target several high-ranking leaders, such as Ke Qingshi and Ye Jianying, but none was part of the returned student faction. Kang was forced to stop his investigation of Ke and Ye after Mao intervened. See *Shi Zhe huiyilu*, 259–60; *Yang Shangkun huiyilu*, p. 216.

[18] *Yang Shangkun huiyilu*, p. 219.

[19] Xu Linxiang and Zhu Yu, *Chuanqi jiangjun Li Kenong* [Legendary General Li Kenong], pp. 138–43.

China Bureau, where he was assigned to work as an assistant to Rao Shushi, a former subordinate of his.[20] In May 1948, Li formally replaced Kang as the director of both the SAD and the ID.[21]

The ID was established in September 1941 and was soon incorporated into the SAD. Consequently, the SAD became the sole organization the CCP leadership relied on to direct CCP security and intelligence services.[22] During the Yan'an rectification campaign, the SAD played a leading role by organizing the study groups that investigated party members, detained and arrested suspects, conducted interrogations of those accused, and even executed prisoners. The SAD also dictated security education, by establishing special schools such as the Northwest Public School for training intelligence personnel. For example, Wang Dongxing served in the Northwest Public School as a class adviser and then was transferred to the SAD, where he was appointed deputy director of the Third Office and then director of the Second Office.[23] In addition, the SAD sent personnel to guard key CCP leaders. Chen Long, director of the Third Office of the SAD, was assigned to accompany Mao to Chongqing for the CCP-Guomindang negotiations in 1945. Another example of the burgeoning role of the SAD in the security apparatus was the assignment of Wang Dongxing, director of the Second Office, to guard Zhou Enlai as he returned to Yan'an from northwestern Shanxi Province in April 1947.[24] From leading antiespionage programs and conducting trials to providing education in security studies and security details for key party leaders, the SAD directed all security and intelligence operations.

As the civil war raged during the 1940s, the SAD nurtured the growth of an information network that covered the entire nation, sending personnel to infiltrate key organizations of the Nationalist government and armed forces with the aim of fomenting rebellion within enemy camps. Consequently, the

---

[20] After the party congress was held in April 1945, Kang was sent to eastern Gansu and then northwestern Shanxi to supervise the land reform program launched by the CCP. It is helpful to know the relative positions of Kang and Rao to understand the incredible loss of face Kang experienced after his falling out with Mao. When Kang was associate director of the CCP's accredited delegation to the Comintern, Rao was one of Kang's subordinates, and although Kang had been a Politburo member since November 1937 (when he returned from the Soviet Union), Rao was a member only of the Central Committee. See Wang Jun, "Kang Sheng zai zhongyang shehui bu" [Kang Sheng in the Social Affairs Department], in *Bai nian chao* [Hundred-year tide], no. 5 (2003), pp. 23, 28.

[21] *Lingdao jigou yange*, p. 766.

[22] The Social Affairs Department (SAD) and the Central Intelligence Department were the same organization but had two names. It issued its documents as the SAD when the documents involved security issues and as the Intelligence Department when the documents involved intelligence. See *Li Kenong chuanqi*, p. 236.

[23] Li Yimin, *Li Yimin huiyilu* [Memoirs of Li Yimin], p. 108; Xinghuo liaoyuan bianjibu, *Zhongguo renmin jiefangjun jiangshuai minglu* [Name list of the PLA generals and commanders in chief], vol. 2, p. 635.

[24] Ye Zilong, *Ye Zilong huiyilu* [Memoirs of Ye Zilong], p. 97.

CCP leadership began to rely greatly on the information that the SAD provided for strategic wartime decision making. During the 1940s, the SAD initiated many Nationalist army revolts against the Nationalist Party, including the Nationalist Sixtieth Army in Manchuria, led by Zeng Zesheng; the Nationalist forces in Xikang, headed by Liu Wenhui; the Nationalist forces in Yunnan, led by Lu Han; and the Nationalist forces in northern China, headed by Fu Zuoyi.[25] The increasing importance of the SAD is illustrated by its role after October 1947, when the CCP took over Shijiazhuang in Hebei. This takeover started the CCP's nationwide counteroffensive campaign against the Nationalist forces, which were led by Chiang Kai-shek.

The SAD was authorized to prepare personnel to secure large and medium-size cities once the communist armies took them over. In the spring of 1948 the SAD selected a large number of communist cadres from the CCP's Northwestern Bureau, Northern China Bureau, East China Bureau, and Shanxi-Suiyuan Bureau to take over cities.[26] The SAD also played a key role in securing Beijing's social order by organizing and leading the Beijing Bureau of Public Security and making residential arrangements for high-ranking leaders. In addition, the SAD protected the Central Committee and the PLA headquarters during their move into Beijing.[27]

Ministry of Public Security and the CCP's Elite Politics

The Social Affairs Department of the Central Committee was abolished and its divisions and personnel were absorbed into the Ministry of Public Security (MPS) and the Intelligence Department of the People's Liberation Army in late 1949. The foundation for the Ministry of Public Security was the SAD branch under the CCP's Northern China Bureau and some agencies of the former SAD.[28] This change, according to leaders of the CCP, served to transfer public security operations from the party to the state.[29] The MPS's leadership

[25] Yao Yizhe and Chen Yuhong, *Li Kenong chuanqi*, pp. 260–5; *Chuanqi jiangjun Li Kenong*, pp. 178–88.

[26] Li Haiwen and Wang Yanling, *Shiji duihua – yi xinzhongguo fazhi dianjiren Peng Zhen* [Centurial dialogue – Reminiscing on the founder of the PRC law and legal systems Peng Zhen], p. 35.

[27] *Chuanqi jiangjun Li Kenong*, pp. 191–6; Liu Guangren, Zhao Yimin, and Yu Xingqiang, *Feng Jiping zhuan: Jingdu gong'an juzhang* [A biography of Feng Jiping: Director of public security in the capital], pp. 153–4.

[28] According to the telegram sent by the CCP Central Committee and the CMC on August 9, 1949, the function of the CCP Social Affairs Department would be replaced by two new departments – the Ministry of Public Security and the Ministry of Intelligence. See Wang Zhongfang, "Gong'anbu shi zenyang chengli de" [How was the MPS established?], in *Lishi Shunjian* [An instant in history], Zhu Chunlin (ed.) (Beijing: Qunzhong chubanshe, 1999), p. 5.

[29] Tao Siju, *Xinzhongguo diyiren gong'an buzhang: Luo Ruiqing* [First PRC public security minister: Luo Ruiqing], p. 9.

was chosen from army police-level generals among the five field armies and the Central Military Commission (CMC), indicating a full presentation of the People's Liberation Army. Although party leadership theoretically emphasized diversity in the membership of party organizations (a principle known as *wuhu sihai*, which means "coming from all corners of the country"), in practice it cared more about harmonious relations among members of party organizations. Whenever involved in the transfer of party members, CCP leaders tended to consult with both the transferred cadres and their future colleagues. When a new party agency was established, leaders oftentimes gave top leaders of the new organization the authority to choose their associates. Of the seven associates whom Public Security Minister Luo Ruiqing chose to include in the MPS leadership, four had been Luo's immediate subordinates before the People's Republic of China (PRC) was founded (Table 2.1).[30] Another leader, Wang Zhao, was chosen by Luo in 1953, when Wang returned from Korea after the Korean War. Wang had been one of Luo's close subordinates since 1947, and he quickly became one of his key assistants in the MPS.[31]

The establishment of the Ministry of Public Security was an important step toward the institutionalization of the CCP security apparatus, a sphere historically reserved for the dominant leaders of the party. Although Mao had never hesitated to control the MPS – his leadership of the MPS was one of the two most important aspects to his role as paramount leader (the other being diplomacy), it was predominately the top party organs, such as the Politburo and the Central Secretariat, which led and guided the major security apparatus before the Cultural Revolution. As consensus had been a primary principle of the party leadership, early on in the CCP's tenure, the use of the security apparatus to resolve elite conflicts was careful and cautious.

The dismissal of Gao Gang, director of the State Planning Commission and former chief of the CCP's Northeast Bureau, and Rao Shushi, director of the CCP's Organizational Department and former chief of the CCP's East China Bureau, was the first such conflict in CCP elite politics. When Mao decided to remove Gao and Rao from office, scheduling the Second Plenum of the Seventh Party Congress to attack the two, the Politburo did not order the security

---

[30] Junshi kexueyuan junshi tushuguan [Military Library of the CCP Military Academy], *Zhongguo renmin jiefangjun zuzhi yange he geji lingdao chengyuan minglu* [The PLA organizational evolution and the list of leaders at different levels; hereafter, *Jiefangjun zuzhi yange*], pp. 224–5, 271–2, 829, 842, 849–53; Wang Zhongfang, "Gong'anbu shi zenyang chengli de," pp. 3–7.

[31] Wang Zhao was political commissar of the Fourth Column under the Second Army Group of the North China Military Region, led by Luo Ruiqing, in 1948. When Luo was political commissar of the Nineteenth Army Group of the North China Military Region, Wang was the Political Commissar of the Sixty-Fourth Army Corps, which was subordinate to the Nineteenth Army Group. See *Jiefangjun zuzhi yange*, pp. 842, 852–3, 860. Wang Zhongfang, "Wang Zhao tongzhi yongyuan huozai qinghai renmin xinzhong" [Comrade Wang Zhao lives in the heart of the people in Qinghai forever], in *Lishi shunjian* [An instant in history], Xu Weiwei and Chang Yulan (eds.) (Beijing: Qunzhong chubanshe, 1999), pp. 253–4.

TABLE 2.1. *Career Ties of MPS Leadership Members with Luo Ruiqing, October 1949*

Name	Year Served under Luo	Position under Luo's Direct Supervision	Luo Ruiqing's Position
	1935	Director, Executive Division of the State Political Security Bureau, Third Army Group	Director, Political Department of the Third Group Army
Yang Qiqing	1935–1936	Director, State Political Security Bureau of the Fifteenth Group Army, First Front Army	Director, State Political Security Bureau of the First Front Army
	1943–1944	Director, Division of Eliminating Spies, General Frontline Headquarters, Eighth Route Army	Director, Political Department of General Frontline Headquarters, Eighth Route Army
	1943–1944	Political Commissar, Fifth Military Subdistrict, General Frontline Headquarters, Eighth Route Army	Director, Political Department of General Frontline Headquarters, Eighth Route Army
Xu Zirong	1948	Political Commissar of the Thirteenth Column, the Shanxi-Chahaer-Hebei Field Army	Political commissar, Shanxi-Chahaer-Hebei Field Army; director of political commissar of the Northern China Field Army
	1949	The 61st Army Corps of the Second Army Group, Northern China Military Region	Political commissar, Northern China Military Region
Cai Shunli	1946–1947	Director, Division of Eliminating Spies	Director, Political Department of Shanxi-Chahaer-Hebei Military Region
	1947–1948	Political Commissar of the Ninth Column, the Shanxi-Chahaer-Hebei Field Army	Director of Political Department, Shanxi-Chahaer-Hebei Field Army
	1948[a]	Political Commissar, the Brigade Seventh of the Third Column, Second Army Group of Northern China Military Region	Political Commissar, Second Army Group of Northern China Military Region

(continued)

TABLE 2.1 *(continued)*

Name	Year Served under Luo	Position under Luo's Direct Supervision	Luo Ruiqing's Position
	1949[b]	Deputy Political Commissar, 65th Army Corps of PLA Nineteenth Army Group, North China Military Region	Political commissar, PLA Nineteenth Army Group of North China Military Region
Xu Jianguo	1935	Director, State Political Security Bureau, Third Army Group	Director, Political Department of the Third Army Group
	1937	Director, First Division of Administrative Affairs, Anti-Japanese Military and Political College	Academic Dean, Anti-Japanese Military and Political College

[a] The Second Army Group of Northern China Military Region was established in May 1948.
[b] The Second Army Group of the Northern China Military Region, led by Nie Rongzhen, was renamed the Nineteenth Army Group and transferred to the First Field Army, headed by Peng Dehuai, in April 1949.
Source: Jiefangjun zuzhi yange, pp. 93, 101–3, 224–5, 404, 412–3, 837–43, 847–8, 855–60; Wang Zhongfang, "Gong'anbu shi zenyang chengli de," pp. 3–7.

apparatus to watch or to arrest them. Instead, the MPS was ordered to conduct an investigation to find evidence showing their innocence or guilt in violating party disciplinary standards. Although targeted in the Second Plenum, both Gao and Rao were still protected by their own guards and served by their own secretaries, chefs, and nurses. The MPS was involved in Gao Gang and Rao Shushi's cases only after Gao Gang attempted suicide and Zhou Enlai ordered the MPS to "protect" Gao. To not exacerbate Gao's anxiety and depression, the MPS only sent an officer to guard him.[32]

Likewise, the MPS was not sent to arrest Rao Shushi, who continued to enjoy the protection and services from the Guard Bureau (Eighth Bureau of the MPS) as usual when Mao took the initiative to remove him. Rao was arrested by the MPS in April 1955 only after being accused of involvement with the "criminal" cases concerning Yang Fan, deputy director of Shanghai Public Security, and Pan Hannian, deputy mayor of Shanghai, two former assistants of Rao who had been implicated as traitors of the party. Yang Fan was charged with harboring many Nationalist intelligence agents shortly after the People's Republic of China (PRC) was established; Pan was alleged to have betrayed the party after confessing to having a secret meeting with Wang Jingwei, head of

---

[32] Xin Junsheng, "Wogei Xu Zirong dang mishu" [I was Xu Zirong's secretary], in *Lishi shunjian* [An instant in history], vol. 3, Sun Mingshan (ed.) (Beijing: Qunzhong chubanshe, 2004), p. 388.

the Japanese puppet regime in Nanjing, without reporting it to the party during the Anti-Japanese War. Facing such "crimes," Rao and Pan were probably the highest-level party officials to be imprisoned after the PRC was established. Though prisoners of the CCP, they were well treated while in custody. For example, the party provided Rao Shushi 100 yuan renminbi per month for living expenses, three times the average Chinese worker's monthly income. The party also sent personnel to take care of Rao's personal needs (chefs and secretaries), and even subscribed to newspapers and magazines to entertain their former compatriot.[33] The rejection of terror in the intraparty conflict dominated the elite interaction in the initial years of the PRC, a period viewed by Frederick Teiwes as "a golden age" – a time when leadership relations were marked by a high degree of unity and democracy that contributed to "the overall leniency" in the leadership conflict.[34]

This pattern continued even with the dismissal of Defense Minister Peng Dehuai in September 1959, as the Politburo was cautious of using the security apparatus in leadership conflicts. Peng was dismissed after criticizing Mao's radical Great Leap Forward at the 1959 Lushan plenum. Although Peng was accused as a leader of so-called Anti-Party Clique and the Politburo conducted an investigation of Peng's activities at the Lushan plenum that linked him to the Soviet Union, the Politburo kept his position and salary as a member intact. In addition, he not only was spared surveillance by a security force but also was allowed to stay in his residence in Zhongnanhai. Peng moved out of Zhongnahai only after he repeatedly insisted that he needed to study, and it was no longer appropriate for him to stay once he was no longer defense minister of the PRC. Peng even rejected a luxurious place close to Zhongnanhai chosen by the Central General Office after his request to move was approved. Eventually, he chose the Wujia Garden in a Beijing suburb to escape the city noise and the political turmoil so prevalent in the city.[35]

In the 1950s and early 1960s, the control of the CCP security apparatus shifted toward high-level organizations within the party. Decisions to use the security apparatus often resulted from a consensus among the Politburo, the CCP Central Secretariat, the State Council, and the Central General Office. When Mao accused Gao Gang and Rao Shushi of organizing the Anti-Party Clique and further accused Gao of conspiracy in "fraternizing with foreign countries,"[36] the party leadership ordered the MPS to conduct an investigation to clarify these charges.[37] When the investigation conducted by the MPS revealed Gao's interactions with and lobbying of many high-ranking leaders,

[33] Ibid., p. 387.
[34] Frederick C. Teiwes, *Politics at Mao's Court: Gao Gang and Party Factionalism in the Early 1950s*, pp. 3, 131.
[35] Mao Taiquan et al., *Guofang buzhang chenfu ji* [The ups and downs of a defense minister], pp. 148–9.
[36] Zhang Yuwen, *Siwang Lianmeng: Gao Rao Shijiang Shimo* [Alliance of death: the beginning and end of Gao Gong and Rao Shushi Affairs] (Beijing: Beijing chubanshe, 2000), p. 506.
[37] Xin Junsheng, "Wogei Xu Zirong dang mishu," pp. 386–7.

the party leadership sent an official from the CCP Organizational Department to the MPS to head this part of the investigation. This intervention indicates the party's prudent attitude regarding conflicts among the leadership. In fact, many high-ranking leaders who had been involved in the Gao and Rao affairs, such as Lin Biao, Peng Dehuai, Tao Zhu, and Chen Zhengren, remained in their posts or were not even mentioned. As observed by Chen Junsheng, the secretary of MPS Vice Minister Xu Zirong, who was in charge of the investigation, "I heard that several high-ranking cadres were involved in the Gao and Rao cases and I was of course concerned about their fate; but later developments indicated that they all were unharmed."[38] In 1954, Kang Sheng accused Ling Yun, head of the Bureau of Political Guards under the MPS, of having "political problems" and suggested that the party leadership investigate him. The party leadership decided to ignore Kang's accusation after several high-ranking leaders from different party organs reached a consensus as to Ling's innocence.[39]

Given that the MPS in the 1950s and the early 1960s was not subordinate to any individual party leader (including Mao), professional ethics played an important role in guiding its activities. When Rao Shushi was accused of "surrendering to the enemy" in the 1941 Southern Anhui Incident, Mao labeled Rao a "hidden traitor."[40] After a circumspect investigation, the Ministry of Public Security did not find any evidence that supported this charge and thus indirectly ignored this accusation.[41] Another factor that significantly imperiled Rao Shushi was an incident concerning Pan Hannian. Mao personally ordered the arrest of Pan Hannian and linked Pan with Rao's Counterrevolutionary Clique. Although Mao did not see the need for due process in determining Pan's guilt, there were conflicting voices among the leaders about Pan's case. It could even be argued that these different opinions led to the formation of a special group for investigating the charges against Pan Hannian. Li Kenong, at the time a PLA deputy general staff member and a longtime superior of Pan Hannian, was appointed by Zhou Enlai to lead the investigation in April 1955. The investigation was completed on April 29, 1955; Pan was found not guilty on the basis of the lack of incriminating evidence. Mao was reluctant to accept the verdict, but he allowed the case to be shelved and did not call for further legal proceedings until 1963.[42] While Pan remained imprisoned as a result of Mao's refusal to announce Pan's innocence, and "nobody [in the Politburo]

[38] Ibid., pp. 386–7.
[39] Ling Yun, "Kang Sheng weihe zhizao 'mousha Su Mei an'" [Why did Kang Sheng create the case of "Murdering Su Mei"], in Sun Mingshan (ed.), *Lishi shunjian* [An instant in history], p. 103.
[40] Xiao Nong, "Yijiu wuwu nian Rao Shushi de wenti weihe shengji e'hua?" [Why did the 1955 Rao Shushi case escalate and deteriorate?], in *Dangshi wenyuan* [Literary circles of CCP history], no. 11 (2005), p. 38.
[41] Ibid., p. 38.
[42] Yang Shangkun, *Zhuiyi lingxiu zhanyou tongzhi* [Recollecting leaders, comrades-in-arms, and comrades], pp. 306–11.

could do anything without the authorization of the highest decision maker of the Party [namely, Mao]," Mao approved special and "benevolent" treatment of Pan during his imprisonment.[43]

Ministry of Public Security in the Cultural Revolution

For both Mao and the high-ranking party leaders, controlling the Ministry of Public Security on the eve of the Cultural Revolution was critical for their political survival. Despite the long-standing efforts of Mao to control the MPS, the party bureaucracy had the greater advantage in controlling and influencing the MPS. If institutionalization is the increasing tendency to employ processes on the basis of institutional rule to which officeholders are effectively bound by their office,[44] then the MPS was relatively more institutionalized than most other CCP organizations. As discipline was highly emphasized in the MPS, the party bureaucracy was able to institutionalize the party's values and norms, which in turn strengthened the MPS's loyalty to the party.

Mao's approval to dismiss Luo Ruiqing in December 1965, the PLA general chief of staff and former public security minister, was intended both to remove the danger of a possible split between the PLA leadership due to the growing conflict between Lin Biao and Luo Ruiqing and to abolish the armed public security forces and purge Luo's trusted followers who dominated the leadership of the MPS. The goal of Mao's attempt to reorganize the Ministry of Public Security was to advance and support the Cultural Revolution, but it would not be an easy task. Luo had commanded the MPS for ten years, and he held considerable influence over its leaders at various levels. His removal and the removal of his followers had a massive effect on the organization. Although Xie Fuzhi took over as head of the MPS in September 1959, after Luo was appointed general chief of staff of the PLA, most of Xie's associates were appointed during the period when Luo was the public security minister, and they were Luo's trusted followers who had established close personal ties with Luo. The December 1965 conference in Shanghai was a blow for Luo and all of his close associates, the dismissals of whom played out in various ways.

Xu Zirong, for example, a vice minister of the MPS who had been a close associate of Luo's since the early 1940s, was ordered to go to Shanghai, where he was immediately put under house arrest. In the summer of 1959, when Luo Ruiqing was transferred to the position as PLA general chief of staff following the dismissals of Defense Minister Peng Dehuai and General Chief of Staff

[43] Xin Junsheng, "Wogei Xu Zirong dang mishu," p. 387; Yi Qi, "'Pan Yang anjian' shimo" [Beginning and end of "Pan Yang case"], in *Pan Hannian zai Shanghai* [Pan Hannian in Shanghai; hereafter, *Pan Hannian zai Shanghai*], Zhonggong shanghai shiwei dangsh yanjiushi (ed.) (Shanghai: Shanghai renmin chubanshe, 1996), p. 384.

[44] Robert H. Jackson and Carl G. Rosberg, *Personal Rule in Black Africa: Prince, Autocrat, Prophet, Tyrant*, p. 10.

Huang Kecheng, Xu was the initial candidate for minister of public security.[45] After Xie Fuzhi was appointed minister of public security, Xu frequently consulted Luo for advice regarding many internal affairs of the MPS even though Luo was no longer in charge of the Ministry of Public Security. Luo's trusted followers made Xie Fuzhi a mere figurehead. According to Tao Siju, the conflict between Xie Fuzhi and Xu Zirong began when Xie was transferred to the MPS.[46] Although Luo Ruiqing had left the MPS, he maintained a strong influence and control over the Ministry of Public Security through communications with his trusted followers.

After Luo Ruiqing's dismissal, a large-scale campaign was launched in the Ministry of Public Security against Luo's followers. Immediately after Xu Zirong returned to Beijing, he was no longer allowed to attend MPS leadership meetings or to access party documents. In late May and early June 1966, Xu was officially charged as "a key member of Peng Zhen and Luo Ruiqing's Anti-Party Clique."[47] Following the arrest of Xu Zirong, a large-scale purge was launched in the Ministry of Public Security. Mao was also convinced that Luo Ruiqing had established a powerful influence on the Beijing Bureau of Public Security, a security organization with dual leadership of the MPS and the Beijing municipal government. Thus, the purge extended into the Beijing Bureau of Public Security, to dismiss the followers of Luo Ruiqing and Beijing Mayor Peng Zhen. By May 1966, Feng Jiping and Xin Xiangsheng, two consecutive directors of the Beijing Bureau of Public Security, and thirty-two department heads of the Beijing Bureau of Public Security had been dismissed.[48]

The MPS was reorganized following the purge. In September 1966, several army representatives heading up the Cultural Revolutionary Committee, with the assistance of some leaders from the "rebel" groups, took charge of the MPS's leadership, using military force to impose control. However, the newly established leadership still complained about the enduring influence of the former MPS on the PLA-controlled organization, even though most of the former central, provincial, and local MPS leaders were first sent to cadre schools and then to labor camps in Heilongjiang.[49] However, the reorganized MPS and its branches (bureaus of public security) were still deeply influenced by the established organizational culture, in which they remained instruments of the party; as a result, individual political leaders, including Mao and other radical leaders, had difficulty getting them to join their personal security forces. Although

---

[45] Xin Junsheng, "Wogei Xu Zirong dang mishu," p. 382.
[46] Tao Siju, *Gong'an baowei gongzuo de zhuoyue lingdaoren: Xu Zirong* [An outstanding leader of public security and security guard work: Xu Zirong], pp. 196–7, 265–6.
[47] Ibid., pp. 204–6.
[48] See Cai Mingzhong, "Liu Chuanxin, wei 'siren bang' xunzang de gong'an juzhang" [Director of public security who sacrificed his life for the Gang of Four], in *Yanhuang chunqiu* [Spring and autumn in China], no. 1 (1994), p. 82.
[49] See Mu Fengyun, "Wode wenge shengya" [My life in the Cultural Revolution], in Sun Mingshan (ed.), *Lishi shunjian* [An instant in history], vol. 2 (Beijing: Qunzong chubanshe), pp. 543, 550.

the bureaus of public security did help the Maoist radicals arrest leaders of the conservative organizations defending the United Front Department of the Central Committee, for example, they helped in the conservative counterattack during the February Adverse Current in 1967. Both national and local security forces came under severe attack from the Red Guard for protecting the party's powerful "capitalist roaders" who were betraying the communist revolution, and they were still deeply distrusted by Mao.[50]

On August 7, 1967, one year after Mao launched the Cultural Revolution, Public Security Minister Xie Fuzhi still complained that "Mao Zedong's thought has not become universal" and "he is unable to establish absolute authority in the public security and law enforcement systems."[51] To ensure that the MPS was an effective law enforcement organization, the PLA-led leadership set up several strict rules to limit the impact of the Cultural Revolution on the MPS: MPS personnel had their own mass movement and "revolutionary activities" within the MPS without any connection to the rebels outside of the MPS. Officials in Beijing were not allowed to make political connections with local MPS officials or to critique them, because such critiques and activities related to the Cultural Revolution were limited to officials at the departmental level and above. Officials below the departmental level were required to help officials at the departmental level and above by contributing their comments and criticisms.[52]

Given the significant role that the MPS played as a tool of the proletarian dictatorship, Mao and the radical Maoists did not destroy the MPS, as they did most of the party and governmental organizations. This can be attributed to Mao's concerns about his ability to control the chaos of the Cultural Revolution and his desire to employ the MPS in maintaining social stability. According to Mao, the MPS was "a knife in the hands of the proletariats – it will crack down on enemies and defend the masses if it is employed correctly, and it will hurt [the party] if it is used incorrectly."[53] One of Mao's strategies to control the MPS was to cultivate his relationship with Public Security Minister Xie Fuzhi. Xie was appointed public security minister in September 1959 after Luo Ruiqing replaced PLA General Chief of Staff Huang Kecheng. Xie was also appointed commander and political commissar of the People's Armed Police (renamed the Chinese People's Public Security Forces in January 1963). In 1965, Xue was promoted to vice premier and member of the National Defense Committee.

At the Eleventh Plenum in August 1966, Mao decided to launch the Cultural Revolution, with reorganization of the party's leadership a primary goal. Xue

[50] Frederic Wakeman Jr., "Models of Historical Change: The Chinese State and Society, 1839–1989," in Kenneth Lieberthal, *Perspectives on Modern China: Four Anniversaries*, p. 89.
[51] Zhonggong yanjiu zazhishe, *Zhonggong wenhua dageming zhongyao wenjian huibian* [Compilation of the CCP central documents and materials in the Cultural Revolution], p. 330.
[52] *Yang Qiqing zhuan*, p. 411.
[53] *Zhonggong wenhua dageming zhongyao wenjian huibian*, p. 209.

Fuzhi had become one of the few high-ranking leaders whom Mao trusted. Like Lin Biao, who was promoted as Mao's successor and became the only vice chairman of the CCP, Xie was one of a few beneficiaries of the Eleventh Plenum. Afterward, he was promoted to an alternate member of the Politburo and a member of the Central Secretariat. In the Eleventh Plenum held in August 1966, Xie unreservedly and aggressively aligned with the radicals to gain Mao's favor. At the plenum, Xie was one of Mao's elite followers who cooperated with his attack on senior party leaders.[54] Under this climate of complaint, dissension, confusion, and anxiety regarding the increasing assaults against senior high-ranking leaders, Xie's support of the radicals and attacks on senior leaders did end up increasing Mao's favor for him, as Xie had planned. Essentially, Xie backed Mao in the biggest political comeback of his career (at a time when few others would have considered it), and he won large dividends in networking and status in the years to come.

In particular, Xie led the attack on Deng Xiaoping in order to pander to Mao. Deng had been Xie's superior since the late 1930s, and the bravado of his reversal significantly impressed Mao. It also proved Xie to be a loyal radical, and it became the foundation of the radical clique's treatment of Xie as a political ally.[55] According to Xie, "Deng has given the impression of an image of 'always being correct' in the last thirty years, which has had a significant influence in the Party. That is why there has been such a strong resistance to the movement by the bourgeoisie reactionary line."[56] It didn't stop there. Xie also played a leading role in attacking Liu Shaoqi in a central working meeting immediately after the Eleventh Plenum, slandering Tao Zhu in a Politburo meeting after Tao butted heads with the radicals. Xie not only pandered to favor Mao but also took great strides to please Jiang Qing, too. Once Xie handed over some materials that disclosed Jiang's past in the 1930s and then burned them for good measure.[57] Mao's influence over Xie was so immense that Xie seemingly would do anything to be in Mao's good graces. Having Xie in his camp helped secure the MPS's loyalty to Mao during the Cultural Revolution.

It was not all for naught, however. Mao's strategy to control the MPS during the Cultural Revolution was to strengthen Xie's power and ensure his dominance in the leadership of the apparatus. By December 1966, Xie Fuzhi had been authorized to dismiss those in the MPS leadership who were not his followers, which resulted in the dismissal of the MPS vice ministers Xu Zirong and Ling Yun.[58] By February 1967, five vice ministers and thirty-six

---

[54] Tao Siju, *Xu Zirong zhuan* [A biography of Xu Zirong], 203.

[55] Fu Chongbi, *Fu Chongbi huiyilu* [Memoirs of Fu Chongbi], pp. 184–5; Tao Siju, *Xu Zirong zhuan* [A biography of Xu Zirong], 203.

[56] [Deng] Maomao, *Wode fuqin Deng Xiaoping "Wenge" suiyue* [My father Deng Xiaoping's "Cultural Revolution" years; hereafter, *Deng Xiaoping "Wenge" suiyue*], p. 32.

[57] *Fu Chongbi huiyilu*, pp. 184–5; Tao Siju, *Xu Zirong zhuan*, pp. 203–4.

[58] Mu Fengyun, "Wode wenge shengya," p. 543.

officials at the departmental level of the MPS were dismissed or suspended.[59] Vice Minister Yang Qiqing kept his position only because he had been an assistant to Xie between September 1945 and January 1947. When Xie was the political commissar of the Fourth Column of the Shanxi-Hebei-Shandong-Henan Military Region, headed by Liu Bocheng and Deng Xiaoping, Yang was the associate political commissar and director of the Political Department of the Fourth Column.[60] On August 18, 1966, Mao mustered the Red Guard in Tiananmen Square, and Yang was invited to attend. Mao personally asked Yang Qiqing to support Xie's work with the MPS, leaving him little room to object.[61] To support Xie, Mao also accepted Xie's suggestion to transfer Li Zhen (one of Xie's longtime subordinates) from the Shenyang Military Region to the MPS as Xie's associate. Both Xie and Li came from the 129th Division of the Eighth Route Army and the Second Field Army of the PLA led by Liu Bocheng and Deng Xiaoping. Li was a political commissar of a regiment under the 385th Brigade, headed by Political Commissar Xue Fuzhi during the Sino-Japanese War and had been Xie's close assistant since 1945, when Li served as head of the Political Department of the Sixth Military Subdistrict, led by Xie himself.[62] By the spring of 1950, when Xie was promoted to political commissar of the Third Army Group under the Second Field Army, Li was associate political commissar of the 12th Army Corps, one of three army corps under the Third Army Group.[63] Li Zhen was appointed an MPS vice minister in September 1966, and he became Xie's partner in leading the MPS.[64] Li would not have been transferred if it were not for Xie.[65]

Although Mao tried to rely on Xie Fuzhi to control the MPS, he was still concerned with how the MPS (a conservative and influential governmental institution by nature) could ally with radicals. In fact, party cadres in both the central and the local branches of the MPS were not favored by the radicals and often instigated confrontations with the branches. By the spring of 1967, almost all the remaining MPS vice ministers were dismissed or arrested on charges of "shielding capitalist roaders" – the powerful party leaders who had formed a bourgeois headquarters inside the Central Committee and pursued a revisionist political and organizational line, "committing atrocious counter-revolutionary crimes," and "supporting and colluding with the enemy" (see Table 2.2).[66] Local MPS branches aligned almost overwhelmingly with local

---

[59] *Yang Qiqing zhuan*, p. 423.
[60] *Jiefangjun zuzhi yange*, p. 628; *Yang Qiqing zhuan*, pp. 157–9.
[61] *Yang Qiqing zhuan*, p. 412.
[62] Leng Meng, *Baizhan jiangxing: Zai Liu Bocheng, Deng Xiaoping, Xu Xiangqian huixia*, p. 337; *Jiefangjun zuzhi yange*, p. 420.
[63] *Jiefangjun zuzhi yange*, pp. 673–4.
[64] *Yang Qiqing zhuan*, pp. 423, 432–3.
[65] Leng Meng, *Baizhan jiangxing: Zai Liu Bocheng, Deng Xiaoping, Xu Xiangqian huixia*, p. 337.
[66] *Yang Qiqing zhuan*, pp. 417–21; Yan Youmin, *Gong'an zhanxian wushi nian*, pp. 121–2.

TABLE 2.2. *The MPS Leadership in the Early Cultural Revolution*

Vice Minister (May 1966)[a]	Career Fate
Xu Zirong	Dismissed in September 1966; arrested in January 1967
Yang Qiqing	Arrested in March 1968
Wang Jinxiang	Arrested in September 1967
Liu Fuzhi	Suspended in September 1966
Ling Yun	Suspended in September 1966; arrested in 1967
Yan Youmin	Arrested in March 1968
Yu Sang	Suspended in September 1966
Yin Zhaozhi	Suspended in September 1966

[a] Wang Dongxing was promoted to head of the Central General Office in May 1966 and left the position of vice minister.

Source: "Gong'an dashi ji" [Chronicle of events in public security], in *Renmin gong'an bao* [People's public security daily], http://www.cpd.com.cn/gb/jwcs/2010-09/11/node_256.htm (accessed September 11, 2010); *Yang Qiqing zhuan*, pp. 423, 469; Yan Youmin, *Gong'an zhanxian wushi nian*, p. 119; Wang Tao, "Shenqie huainian jingai de fuqin" [Deeply yearn for the respected and beloved father], p. 713; Tao Siju, *Xu Zirong zhuan*, p. 233.

party leaders against the radical mass rebels who were supported by the Cultural Revolution Group (the radical faction headed by Mao's wife Jiang Qing). In Xie Fuzhi's own words, "From the beginning of the Cultural Revolution to January 1967, the majority of Public Security branches, procuratorial bodies, and courts nationwide were protecting capitalistic roaders and suppressing revolutionary masses."[67]

Another action taken by Mao with respect to the MPS was to impose direct military control over the organization. The transfer of PLA officials to the MPS had been under way since September 1966, when Li Zhen, a deputy political commissar of the Shenyan Military Region, was appointed MPS vice minister and more than 2,700 PLA officers were transferred from local military regions to take charge of the MPS.[68] Following Li Zhen's appointment, Shi Yizhi, political commissar of the 21st Army Corps, became the director of the MPS Political Department in December 1966. As most of the MPS leading figures became targets of the Red Guard and the radical mass organizations, thirty-two PLA officials, including Zeng Wei (political commissar of the Engineering Army under the Beijing Military Region) and Zhao Dengcheng (deputy commander of the 8th Army Corps of the Air Force), were transferred to, and took control of, the MPS.[69] At the same time, forty-one PLA officials of lower rank were transferred to the Ministry of Public Security.[70] Compared to the situation in Beijing, most local branches of the MPS tied themselves to the local party

[67] *Zhonggong wenhua dageming zhongyao wenjian huibian*, p. 329.
[68] *Fu Chongbi huiyilu*, p. 181.
[69] *Gong'an shigao*, pp. 332–3.
[70] Ibid.

organizations against the radical mass rebels and played a leading role in protecting local party leaders. According to Xie Fuzhi, all the MPS branches in the cities and 80 percent of the MPS branches at the county levels did not support the "revolutionary rebels," instead supporting the "conservatives" who associated themselves with local party organizations.[71] This indicates why Mao repeatedly ordered Xie Fuzhi to "smash Public Security branches, procuratorial bodies, and courts."[72] Like the MPS in Beijing, the PLA had been interfering with most MPS local branches since the spring of 1967.[73]

The spring of 1968 saw the reorganization of the MPS's military control. Eleven departments merged into five offices: Political, Administrative, Investigation, Public Security, and Reception that mainly handled complaint letters and visits. The number of MPS personnel was dramatically reduced (through dismissal, exile, or transfer) from around 1,200 to 126 personnel. Two personnel dismissed in this reorganization were Yu Sang and Liu Fuzhi, two of the MPS vice ministers who were sent to labor camps in Heilongjiang and Hubei in March 1969 for reeducation.[74] At the Ninth Party Congress in April 1969, Xie Fuzhi was appointed to the Politburo, and he thereafter promoted his longtime follower Li Zhen to direct the MPS.

In June 1971, the MPS's personnel increased from 126 to 450, a result of its increased role in maintaining social order. Increasing the number of personnel in this way may have contributed to a semblance of party control over the chaotic "civil war" between the rebels and the PLA units. By 1968 the revolutionary committees had gained control over the party bureaucracy from frontline party senior leaders, such that those leaders no longer posed a threat to Mao's utopian socialism. Although some were imprisoned, most were sent to the May Seventh cadre schools (*wuqi ganxiao*), which in actuality were labor camps. More important, the violence and power struggles incited by the rebels at the beginning of the Cultural Revolution was finally put under control. Already by 1971 large numbers of urban youths, mostly consisting of Red Guard, had been sent to the mountains or villages (*shangshan xiaxiang*) for reeducation (*zai jiaoyu*).

Although PLA control of the MPS helped achieve social stability and ensure political order, army officials faced difficulties managing administrative duties that required specialized knowledge and skills. They soon realized that engaging in the administrative work of governmental agencies demanded complicated professional skills; agencies they were expected to operate included various

---

[71] *Zhonggong wenhua dageming zhongyao wenjian huibian*, p. 332.

[72] Mao talked with Xie Fuzhi in person at least eight times about his decision to abolish the Ministry of Public Security and China's legal system. See *Zhonggong wenhua dageming zhongyao wenjian huibian*, p. 332.

[73] Ibid., 329.

[74] Dong Yufeng, "Yichang fan faxisi shencha fangshi de douzheng" [A struggle against fascist-style forms of investigation], in Sun Mingshan (ed.), *Lishi shunjian* [An instant in history], vol. 2 (Beijing: Qunzhong chubanshe, 2001), p. 454.

ministries within the State Council, the Foreign Ministry, and the Ministry of Public Security. For example, in September 1967 an espionage case went unsolved for a long time because the army officials in charge of the MPS and the Beijing Bureau of Public Security lacked the necessary expertise. Eventually, the case was sent outside of the MPS to Yang Qiqing, a dismissed former MPS vice minister.[75] Thus, resuming the functions of these specialized government positions and reinstating previously dismissed party members seemed important to leaders because of the glaring administrative holes, particularly in the security apparatus. In March 1971, the Politburo approved Zhou Enlai's proposal to recover the MPS and reemploy dismissed personnel.[76] In July 1972, the party leadership went further, deciding that the MPS was no longer under military control; the leadership approved the "Suggestions and Report Regarding the Situation of Implementing Cadres Policy in the Public Security System," a document directed by Zhou Enlai that pushed a fast pace for training officials and restoring them to their posts.[77]

Another aspect of removing PLA control and resuming the original functions of the MPS was to return Qincheng Prison to the MPS in January 1973. Qincheng, the only prison under the MPS's jurisdiction, was well known for its reputation as an ultrasecret facility that housed disgraced senior leaders and top political prisoners. It was located north of Beijing in Changping and was designed by Soviet experts, including a number of Soviet gulag engineers. Its design and construction occurred under the auspices as one of the 157 Socialist Construction Projects, supported by the Soviet Union. The prison had a total of four independent compounds, with more than four hundred rooms; the rooms were mainly used to imprison enemy spies and war criminals during the Sino-Japanese War and the CCP-GMD civil war. In 1960, shortly after the prison was complete, war criminals were transferred from Beijing's Gongdelin Prison to Qincheng Prison. Starting in late 1966, with the purges of the Cultural Revolution, many high-ranking leaders became victims of the Cultural Revolution Group and the mass revolutionaries; as a result, the number of political prisoners at Qincheng increased dramatically. To accommodate these prisoners, in 1967 an expansion was planned and a PLA regiment of engineers was sent to the prison to construct additional buildings. The six new buildings were aptly named the Red Buildings because they were used to imprison the leading cadres of the party and government.[78]

Qincheng Prison fell under military control after PLA officials took over leadership of the MPS in the spring of 1967; the Beijing Garrison Command

[75] *Yang Qiqing zhuan*, pp. 434–5.

[76] See "Gong'an dashi ji" [Chronicle of events in public security], in *Renmin gong'an bao* [People's public security daily], http://www.cpd.com.cn/gb/jwcs/2010-09/11/node_256.htm (accessed September 11, 2010).

[77] Ibid.; *Gong'an shigao*, p. 340.

[78] *Yang Qiqing zhuan*, p. 439.

took over the prison on November 7, 1967, controlling it until June 1969.[79] The prison was transferred from the Beijing Garrison Command to the Military Control Committee of the Beijing Bureau of Pubic Security in June 1969.[80] When the MPS personnel were replaced by PLA units, much harsher regulations were imposed on the prisoners.[81] The new regulations allowed jail personnel to abuse and beat the prisoners for the smallest of infractions. In addition, methods such as restricting prisoners' food and water supply became popular ways to treat the prisoners.[82] For example, each prisoner was allowed only one cup of water and ten minutes of exercise per day.[83] Prisoners who fell ill, such as Xu Zirong, a former MPS vice minister, were refused treatment and could be handcuffed day and night, as Xu was. Jail personnel refused to uncuff prisoners even during meals and while sleeping.[84]

Prisoner abuse scandals in Qincheng Prison were exposed by Liu Shuqing, wife of Liu Jianzhang (former vice minister of the Railway Ministry and a prisoner at Qincheng), when she visited her husband in Qincheng Prison. In December 1972 she sent a letter to the Chairman deploring the abhorrent and brutal conditions she witnessed there. Mao's response showed the importance of the issue to him. At one point he indignantly declared: "Who stipulated this fascist-style interrogation? All of [these forms of interrogation] must be abolished!"[85] This letter, along with other information, forced Mao to take action in 1973, when he ended the military's management of the facility. Removing the military from control of Qincheng Prison and resuming the MPS's authority in January 1973 was a crucial step in bringing civil order back to the country. Although PLA officials such as Li Zhen and Shi Zhiyi were still in charge of the MPS, many former MPS employees were "rehabilitated" and returned to their previous posts.[86]

Military control over the MPS was greatly weakened after General Li Zhen, who had taken charge of the MPS in June 1970, committed suicide on October 22, 1973. After Li's death, he was accused of supporting the initiatives of Lin Biao's faction at the 1970 Lushan plenum by secretly colluding with Liu Feng, political commissar of Wuhan Air Force. Liu had been familiar with Li since the late 1930s, when both men served in the 129th Division of the Eighth Route Army. Consequently, the allegations rang true for party members. Li was also involved in a joint effort with Chen Boda and Wu Faxian to frame many party seniors by creating the Special Committee of the Chinese Communist Party.[87]

---

[79] See "Gong'an dashi ji," in *Renmin gong'an bao.*
[80] Ibid.
[81] Dong Yufeng, "Yichang fan faxisi shencha fangshi de douzheng," pp. 453–5.
[82] Li Haiwen and Wang Yanling, *Shiji duihua – yi xinzhongguo fazhi dianjiren Peng Zhen,* p. 91.
[83] Dong Yufeng, "Yichang fan faxisi shencha fangshi de douzheng," p. 455.
[84] Tao Siju, *Xu Zirong zhuan,* p. 210.
[85] Dong Yufeng, "Yichang fan faxisi shencha fangshi de douzheng," p. 457.
[86] Ibid., pp. 457–8.
[87] *Gong'an shigao,* pp. 343–4.

It was not just Li Zhen who was suspected as a supporter of Lin Biao's faction: Zhao Dengcheng, another MPS leader and former deputy army commander of the 8th Army Corps of the Air Force, had been arrested in October 1972 for his involvement in the Lin Biao affair.[88]

It was not until 1975, when Deng Xiaoping took charge of the State Council, that Vice Premier Hua Guofeng was appointed minister of public security and senior MPS leaders, such as Yang Qiqing, Ling Yun, and Yan Youmin, were asked to return to their offices.[89] Although PLA officials, led by Shi Yizhi (former political commissar of the 21st Army Corps), were still in charge of the MPS, the military's influence had been significantly weakened as a result of the gradual return of the former MPS officials. The complete withdrawal of PLA control over the MPS took place after the Cultural Revolution, and Zhao Cangbi was transferred from Sichuan to Beijing to head the MPS in March 1977. Zhao became the key figure for Deng Xiaoping's "reorganizing" program that focused on purging radicals and restoring the normal functions of the party, the government, and the PLA. In May 1977, Shi Yizhi was suspended and investigated by the party.[90]

In September 1977, the leadership of the MPS was completely reorganized, and two veteran leaders – Yu Sang and Yang Qiqing – were appointed vice ministers. The MPS, led by Zhao Cangbi, sent a proposal to Deng Xiaoping recommending the return of all army officials to their previous roles, which Deng approved. At the same time, the army leaders in charge of the MPS during the Cultural Revolution, namely, Li Zhen, Zeng Wei, Shi Yizhi, and Zhao Dengcheng, were accused of "colluding with Jiang Qing and Xie Fuzhi to frame and persecute Party veterans."[91]

When Mao realized that the PLA had grown too strong, another approach he took to weaken powerful local army leaders who had been dominant since the beginning of the Cultural Revolution was to return control of the security forces back to local civilian governments, mainly by resuming operations of the Ministry of Public Security and returning local security forces back to the MPS's jurisdiction. This was accomplished in 1975 when Deng Xiaoping gave the speech "Tasks of the Army's Organization" at a Central Military Commission (CMC) conference. Deng ordered that all local military regions be handed over to the security forces that had been merged with the PLA at the

---

[88] "Lishi de shenpan" bianjizu, *Lishi de shenpan, xuji* [Historical trial, sequel] (Beijing: Qunzhong chubanshe, 1986), pp. 94–115.

[89] *Yang Qiqing zhuan*, p. 458.

[90] Hu Wei, "Siren yiqu, fengfan changcun – shenqie huainian Shi Yizhi tongzhi" [His legacy lives on though he is gone – Deeply yearning for comrade Shi Yizhi], in Chen Feng (ed.), *Xue yu huo de lilian – Shi Yizhi jinian wenji* [Tempered by blood and fire – Collected works commemorating Shi Yizhi], pp. 85–7.

[91] Yu Sang, "Zhao Cangbi tongzhi zhuanlue" [A brief biography of Zhao Cangbi], in Yu Sang (ed.), *Zhao Cangbi zhuanlue ji jinian wenji* [A brief biography of Zhao Cangbi and collected works commemorating Zhao Cangbi], pp. 86–7.

beginning of the Cultural Revolution and be reintegrated with the Ministry of Public Security under the new name the People's Police. Restoring the function of the Ministry of Public Security became a significant part of Deng's holistic party, government, and PLA reorganization program, which entailed restoring political, social, and economic order to the country. This program returned many senior cadres to their posts, including the previously mentioned senior vice ministers of the MPS, such as Yang Qiqing, Yan Youmin, and Ling Yun, who returned to the MPS in October 1975.[92]

After Deng Xiaoping returned the MPS senior leaders to their posts, the party veterans were almost completely poised to take back control of the MPS. The key factor in reclaiming control was appointing Zhao Cangbi as public security minister in March 1977. Zhao later was instrumental in executing Deng Xiaoping's plan to organize the newly established People's Armed Police in the early 1980s. Zhao Cangbi's career had been closely tied to Deng's since 1948, when Zhao was transferred from the Social Affairs Department to serve Deng. After the CCP took over Beijing in 1948, Zhao was dispatched to Beijing, where he managed the Office of Public Security (the Number Three Office) of the Beijing Bureau of Public Security. When the PLA Second Field Army led by Liu Bocheng and Deng Xiaoping took over Nanjing, at the time the capital city of the Nationalist government, Zhao was transferred to Nanjing in April 1949, where he became a leading figure in managing the security forces.[93] Thus, Zhao established his career and personal ties with Deng Xiaoping in Nanjing.

In September 1949, Mao ordered the Second Field Army to head toward Southwest China to conquer the last Nationalist stronghold in China. Zhao was appointed acting director of public security under the Southwest Military and Political Committee headed by Deng Xiaoping. Zhao had been one of the key figures in charge of public security until 1952, when Deng Xiaoping was transferred to Beijing, assisting Deng in suppressing landlords and Nationalist Party remnants to maintain social order in southwestern China. During the Cultural Revolution, Zhao was dismissed after he was accused of being "a diehard follower of Li Jingquan," first party secretary of the CCP Southwest Bureau.[94] After Deng Xiaoping returned to office in 1974 and took charge of the State Council, Zhao Cangbi was appointed member of the Sichuan Provincial Party Secretariat in December 1974 and was promoted again one year later to acting party secretary.[95] After Deng Xiaoping launched the campaign to restore the economy and social order, both Zhao Ziyang, first party secretary of Sichuan, and Zhao Cangbi, acting party secretary of Sichuan, became the leaders of Deng's program. Sichuan became one of the major provinces in which

---

[92] *Yang Qiqing zhuan*, p. 458.
[93] Yu Sang, "Zhao Cangbi tongzhi zhuanlue," pp. 32–47.
[94] Yu Sang, "Zhao Cangbi tongzhi zhuanlue," pp. 73–4.
[95] Ibid., pp. 73–7.

Deng tested his program of "adjustment,"[96] which explains why both Zhao Ziyang and Zhao Cangbi immediately became targets of the radical Maoists after Deng Xiaoping was dismissed in Spring 1976.[97]

In March 1977, Zhao Cangbi was transferred from Sichuan to Beijing, where he was appointed minister of public security. Although there is no evidence to identify Deng's role in Zhao's transfer and promotion, the first important and influential decision made by Zhao after he took over the Ministry of Public Security was to order local public security agencies to rehabilitate all the employees who were dismissed in the wake of Deng's purge. On September 6, 1977, the Ministry of Public Security issued an order that required public security agencies nationwide to study and execute the document "Report regarding Resumption of Publishing Films and Books Containing Comrade Deng Xiaoping's Images and Speeches." Zhao also helped reframe the so-called Tiananmen Incident of the spring of 1976, which directly led to the fall of Deng Xiaoping.[98] Zhao became a primary advocate for Deng Xiaoping by executing Deng's strategy of undermining the PLA's influence in the MPS.[99] On September 12, Deng approved the proposal sent by the MPS to remove PLA personnel from the MPS who had been sent by Mao to take over the MPS at the beginning of the Cultural Revolution. Moreover, all four PLA members who took over leadership of the MPS – Li Zhen, Zeng Wei, Shi Yizhi, and Zhao Dengcheng – were accused of colluding with the Gang of Four against the senior party veterans. According to the MPS's "Report Regarding Li Zhen, Zeng Wei, Shi Yizhi, and Zhao Dengcheng, Who Reorganized the MPS Archives in Order to Frame Central Leadership Members," all four PLA officials in charge of the MPS during the Cultural Revolution were accused of providing the Gang of Four with multitudes of intelligence – it was revealed that they contributed 1,853 pieces of "dark materials" concerning 163 party veterans.[100] As a result of all his work in the MPS reform movement under Deng, Zhao was promoted to member of the CCP Central Committee at the party's congress on September 12, 1982.

The paralysis of many of the MPS's functions and the abolishment of the armed police forces during the Cultural Revolution created chaos in the public

[96] Feng Siping and Zhang Huasu, "Shenqie daonian Zhao Cangbi tongzhi" [Deeply mourning for comrade Zhao Cangbi], in Yu Sang (ed.), *Zhao Cangbi zhuanlue ji jinian wenji*, pp. 263–4.

[97] Both Zhao Ziyang and Zhao Cangbi were charged as "agents of Deng Xiaoping in Sichuan." See Yu Sang, "Zhao Cangbi tongzhi zhuanlue," p. 80; Zhang Zige, "Zhao Cangbi decao xiaoji" [Some of Recorded Zhao Cangbi's Moral Conduct and Personal Integrity], in Yu Sang (ed.), *Zhao Cangbi zhuanlue ji jinian wenji*, p. 260.

[98] Zhao personally led the Bureau of Beijing Public Security in reviewing the Tiananmen Incident and played a vital role in providing evidence proving Deng Xiaoping's innocence. See Yu Sang et al., "Shenqie huainian Zhao Cangbi tongzhi" [Deeply yearning for comrade Zhao Cangbi], Yu Sang (ed.), *Zhao Cangbi zhuanlue ji jinian wenji*, pp. 130–1.

[99] Yu Sang, "Zhao Cangbi tongzhi zhuanlue," pp. 85–7.

[100] Ibid., p. 87.

security system. As the Ministry of Public Security was no longer in charge of the security forces during the Cultural Revolution, the border-guard forces that were under the jurisdiction of the MPS before the Cultural Revolution were severely weakened and did not function well. In 1973, when Marshal Ye Jianying took over the CMC after Lin Biao died, border issues had become a huge problem – "nobody knew when enemies were entering China and nobody knew when bad elements were exiting China," which Ye Jianying described as "having borders without control."[101] To strengthen border control, central party leadership ordered the PLA to return the responsibilities of border control to the MPS, and the former administrative personnel of the MPS were ordered to return to their old positions. At the same time, the PLA also handed back security forces responsible for prison security at the county and city level to the MPS. All this reorganization necessitated that the MPS establish the Bureau of Border Control and the Bureau of the People's Armed Police to be responsible for border control and local prison security.[102] In October 1979, when Zhao Cangbi was in charge of the MPS, Zhao proposed to Deng that reform of the border control system, particularly the establishment of a unique armed force for border control, was needed. In December 1979, the People's Border Control Armed Police was established under the jurisdiction of the MPS, and it later became the base of the People's Armed Police, founded in 1982.[103]

Ministry of Public Security in the Reform Era

The MPS was one of few government organizations that was severely weakened during the Cultural Revolution. In September 1977 when the four key PLA leaders were transferred out of the MPS, the MPS's leadership was reorganized and civilian rule was restored. When the MPS resumed its original functions, it urgently needed to fulfill four tasks to maintain its role in the party. First, it needed to strengthen its leadership and restore the functions of its departments in order to assist in the campaign that party leadership had launched against Maoist radicals and their followers. Second, it needed to redress the large number of fabricated treason cases by rehabilitating the reputation of those who had been accused and disgraced during the Cultural Revolution. Third, it needed to combat rising crime and to ensure social stability. Fourth, it needed to improve its professional skills and to learn advanced technologies so that it could perform its duties of investigation, security, guarding, and border control in the new international and domestic environment.

In spite of high expectations for the MPS's vanguard role in redressing the fabricated treason cases and rehabilitating senior party leaders, the MPS

[101] Ibid., p. 108.
[102] Ibid.
[103] Yu Sang et al., "Shengjie huainian zhao cangbi tongshi," p. 109.

leadership became active only after the Third Plenum in December 1978. This might have contributed to confusion in the MPS leadership with respect to what kinds of cases it should target and what the verdicts should be, considering the power struggle between the veteran leaders, headed by Deng Xiaoping and Chen Yun, and the so-called Two Whatevers campaigners, led by Hua Guofeng and Wang Dongxing. Hua Guofeng was public security minister between 1972 and 1977; therefore, his influence in the MPS was still strong. This is seen in the self-criticism made by Public Security Minister Zhao Cangbi during the Seventeenth National Public Security Conference held in January 1979. According to Zhao, the existing problems in the MPS before the Third Plenum were their "slow response to the battle between 'seeking truth from facts' and 'the Two Whatevers' so that they were unable to 'resist interference from various leaders.'" Consequently, they failed to "do what the Party leadership [mainly the veteran leaders] asked." The veteran leaders, especially Deng Xiaoping, optimistically expected that the MPS would serve as a vanguard against the Maoist radicals and the beneficiaries of the Cultural Revolution. This helps explain why Deng Xiaoping removed all officers from the MPS who joined the Special Case Groups (*zhuan'an zu*), which were formed to investigate or interrogate party veterans during the Cultural Revolution. After December 1979, the MPS played an important role in supporting the veteran leaders against the Two Whatevers, especially their roles in providing evidence that redressed a large number of cases involving senior leaders, including Liu Shaoqi, as well as conducting investigations and preliminary hearings for the trials of the Lin Biao faction and the Gang of Four.

Since Deng Xiaoping launched economic reform in 1979, the MPS has experienced numerous changes that coincided with China's open-door policy. A major change was implemented following the promulgation of the People's Police Law, which restricted the police's power to arrest, investigate crimes, and search suspects. The People's Police Law has detailed provisions on the functions, rights and obligations, and rewards and sanctions of police officers and procurators.[104] In addition, the law requires a court or procuratorate warrant for any planned arrest, and it makes illegal torture of those arrested. A significant organizational change in the post-Mao era regarding the public security system has been the increasing power of local party organizations in controlling local branches of public security. Because social stability has always been a top priority for successful economic reform and the open-door policy, and because local party leaders are responsible for maintaining social order, the local public security branches play a crucial role in local politics. Many public security leaders at the provincial or municipal level not only are members of the party's standing committees but also lead the party's Political and Legal Commission. Although local public security branches are dually led by upper-level public security organizations and local party committees, the local party committees

---

[104] The PRC People's Police Law, *Xinhua*, March 1, 1995.

play a more important role in recruitment, promotion, salary and benefits, and resource allocation than upper-level public security organizations. Murray Scot Tanner and Eric Green point out the powerful historical and institutional factors that reinforce the power that local party officials exercise over police:

Local police in China are "agents" formally subordinate to a variety of central, police and local party-state "principals." An examination of the balance of "power resources" indicates that the center certainly does have important sources of influence. Its major levers are over general policy directives and laws, the appointment of provincial Party secretaries, the organizational structure of provincial bureaus of public security, and overall personnel quotas. But the widespread local disobedience to central directives cited here demonstrates that these resources do not translate into detailed, effective control over local police behavior. The powers in the hands of local party-state leaders – leadership authority, hiring of regular officers, leading cadre management, finance and budgeting, and setting salaries – still loom much larger. They create powerful incentives for local public security officials to obey their local Party "principals" more than either their superior public security "principals" or the Party center. Finally, the variety of legal, administrative, discipline inspection and auditing oversight systems that are supposed to help strengthen central monitoring and access to information for the most part actually end up reinforcing control by local Party committees and PSBs.[105]

The difficulties of state power and control over local public security agencies contribute to the relatively weak and shallow levers of central control over provinces and localities.[106]

The CCP leadership has become increasingly concerned about the strong influence of local party organizations over local public security branches, particularly the role of some local public security organizations in becoming part of the system of protective umbrellas of so-called underworld societies. The protective-umbrellas system is officially defined as "a crime where government employees harbor, provide convenience or illegal protection to underworld societies."[107] In addition to aiding and abetting criminal societies, officials also participate in them. This is a crime in which government officials "organize, lead, and participate in the underworld societies, collude with them and commit the crimes together." It is common for government officials to "use their positions of power to provide underworld organizations with information and lobby for them; they will also hide, destroy or forge evidence for the criminal societies, sometimes going so far as to create obstacles to other government

---

[105] Murray Scot Tanner and Eric Green, "Principals and Secret Agents: Central versus Local Control over Policing and Obstacles to 'Rule of Law' in China," in Donald C. Clarke (ed.), *China's Legal System: New Developments, New Challenges*, pp. 114–5.

[106] Ibid., p. 115.

[107] Liang Qi, "Dangqian chaban shehei 'baohu san' zhiwu fanzui anjian de nandian ji duice" [Difficulties and strategies for current initiatives in investigating job-related crimes that involve the "protective umbrella" for underground societies], in *Renmin jiancha* [People's procuratorial semimonthly], no. 7 (2003), p. 34.

officials who are genuinely investigating these criminal cases. Obstacles are created through obstruction of justice, interference, delay, or refusal to fulfill duties."[108]

The regime has taken action against many of its corrupt officials, especially with the campaign to strike severely (*yanda*) launched in the early 2000s, the effort to dispose of the protective umbrellas has become a fundamental aspect of drumming out rampant corruption. According to an official publication, the government prosecuted about three hundred cases in 2001 relating to criminal societies, of which about two hundred were tied to local party and government authorities that acted as protective umbrellas for criminal societies.[109] Another action taken by the government to stamp out collusion and corruption is the strengthening of the higher-level public security organizations in the oversight of their subordinate branches. Because of the political, organizational, and economic dependence of local public security branches on local party organizations, even if the public security branch personnel are not participating in criminal activity, they often are manipulated into aiding and abetting local party officials. Part of this strengthening includes hiring policies. Since January 2007, all appointments for local public security chiefs must have the approval of their upper-level public security organizations, an effort to prevent the dominance of the local party organizations in the appointment and promotion of local public security leaders.[110]

Another initiative taken by the CCP to reduce the dependence of the local public security branches on the local party organizations while also promoting morale of local public security officials is emphasis on economic benefits for employees. Since almost the beginning of the reform period, the public has been cognizant and critical of the central and local MPS bureaus' inability to deal with rising crime, in addition to their involvement in local corruption scandals since the reforms. The MPS and its local branches have realized that the myriad corruption issues in public security arise from insufficient pay, poor training, and low officer morale, and therefore can be easily addressed. The CCP leadership has attempted to increase pay and improve benefits for public security officers while introducing a mechanism of competition that serves to guarantee the quality of personnel and their training. A landmark initiative on this front occurred in 2007, when daily subsidies for public security officers at the provincial, prefectural, and country levels increased ten times over their previous subsidies.[111] In the early 1990s, a rank system was introduced, and by 2002, 1.7 million police officers under the MPS had been granted police ranks, including 4,000 police commissioners (*jing jian*), 420,000 police supervisors

---

[108] Ibid., p. 34.
[109] Ibid., p. 34.
[110] *Fazhi ribao* [Legal system daily], January 24, 2007.
[111] *Fazhi ribao* [Legal system daily], March 5, 2007.

(*jing du*), 1 million (*jing si*) police superintendents, and 220,000 rank-and-file police officers.[112]

Although the size and scale of the MPS have increased dramatically since 1978, the MPS has undertaken many new responsibilities, including crime prevention, crime suppression, investigation of criminal activities, fighting terrorist activities, counter drug-trafficking activities, maintenance of social order, traffic control, fire control and prevention, security inspection of public information networks, and supervision and instruction of security work in state organizations and nongovernmental organizations. The sheer growth in size of the MPS shows the steps it has taken to improve professionalism since Deng's reorganization. It went from thirteen bureaus in January 1966 to twenty-three bureaus in June 1984.[113] The most significant reform-era reorganizations took place in 1989, 1994, and 1998, when functional departments were redesigned to match the overall development of the MPS during the reform period.[114] Despite that the majority of the MPS's growth taking place in the beginning of the reform period, the need for more advanced public security expertise in the twenty-first century has resulted in considerable growth as well. Since 2000 several departments have been added to the MPS, such as the Bureau of Counterterrorism, the Bureau of Bond Crime Investigation, and the Bureau of Auditing. When the Bureau of Auditing was created in November 2008,[115] the MPS consisted of twenty-seven functional departments, seven administrative departments, and three colleges and universities administratively directly under the control of the MPS (Figure 2.1).

Under the auspices of party veterans, the MPS led several significant initiatives to reform the existing system of security and intelligence services in the post-Mao era. Early initiatives dealt mainly with helping veteran leaders fight the neo-Maoist Two Whatevers faction. Perhaps one of the most important initiatives was to restore the MPS Bureau of Guards (the Eighth Bureau), which Mao had merged with the Ninth Bureau in 1964 to consolidate the power of Wang Dongxing, then leader of the Ninth Bureau. During the Cultural Revolution, Wang was the most powerful figure in the CCP's security and intelligence apparatuses. Wang's dominance over security and intelligence services enabled him to ensure that Mao received unconditional compliance from the party, government, and army leaders (both veteran leaders and radicals) during the Cultural Revolution, yet it also enabled Wang to arrest the Maoist radicals in October 1976.

The veteran leaders took a significant move in 1979 to take control of the leadership of the security and intelligence services. The document "Conference Summary on the Adjustment of the Security Organizations and the

[112] See *Guangzhou ribao* [Guangzhou daily], June 29, 2002.
[113] See "Gong'an dashi ji" [Chronicle of events in public security], in *Renmin gong'an bao*.
[114] Ibid.
[115] Ibid.

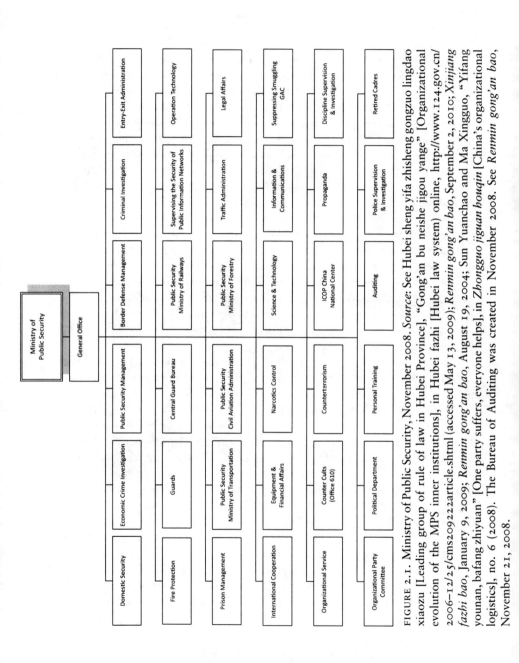

FIGURE 2.1. Ministry of Public Security, November 2008. *Source:* See Hubei sheng yifa zhisheng gongzuo lingdao xiaozu [Leading group of rule of law in Hubei Province], "Gong'an bu neishe jigou yange" [Organizational evolution of the MPS inner institutions], in Hubei fazhi [Hubei law system) online, http://www.124.gov.cn/2006–12/25/cms20922article.shtml (accessed May 13, 2009); *Renmin gong'an bao*, September 2, 2010; *Xinjiang fazhi bao*, January 9, 2009; *Renmin gong'an bao*, August 19, 2004; Sun Yuanchao and Ma Xingguo, "Yifang younan, bafang zhiyuan" [One party suffers, everyone helps], in *Zhongguo jiguan houqin* [China's organizational logistics], no. 6 (2008). The Bureau of Auditing was created in November 2008. See *Renmin gong'an bao*, November 21, 2008.

Improvement of the Security Work," issued by the central party leadership, reestablished the MPS's Eighth Bureau (MPS Guard Bureau) and placed the Central Guard Bureau (traditionally the domain of Wang Dongxing) under the jurisdiction of the MPS.[116] Under the leadership of Deng Xiaoping, the CCP's General Staff Department also resumed its authority over the Central Guard Bureau while keeping the MPS as its superior organizationally. Compared with the MPS Guard Bureau, which took charge of the relevant lower-level high-ranking cadres the Central Guard Bureau was responsible for the security of the top leading figures, mainly Politburo members (Table 2.3).

Still another move reinforced the MPS's authority and power over the security services nationwide in the early stages of reform. In 1977, the CCP leadership issued a document that authorized local MPS branches to manage the security organizations of provincial, autonomous regions, and municipal governments directly under the central government. According to the document issued by party leaders, all responsibilities previously controlled by other security organizations, such as guarding local party and governmental organizations, which PLA units had handled during the Cultural Revolution, must be handed over to local bureaus of public security.[117] This move greatly clarified the organization of security details among the various organizations. Having many security units involved in guarding the same local party organizations and governments had been a prominent feature of the security apparatus during the Cultural Revolution, and it contributed to the chaos of the time. This was the case in Shanghai, where the Shanghai Garrison Command and the 4th Army Corps of the Air Force were both responsible for guarding local party and government organizations and figures.[118]

Given that the MPS was the country's central police authority, some scholars call the MPS as the "Ministry of Police."[119] In the Mao era, the police under the MPS, with ubiquitous, absolute, and unchallengeable power, were

[116] Zhang Qihou, "Zhonggong jianzheng wushi nian gong'an bu fazhan yange" [Development and evolution of MPS in the CCP fifty-year nation building], in Zhongguo dalu wenti yanjiu suo (ed.), *Zhonggong jianzheng wushi nian* [CCP fifty-year nation building], p. 62.

[117] This document was titled "On the Regulations regarding Handing over All Security Units of the Governments at Provinces, Autonomous Regions, and Municipalities Directly under the Central Government to the Bureau of Public Security of the Governments at Provinces, Autonomous Regions, and Municipalities Directly under the Central Government"; it established the authority of the MPS over the security services in local party and government organizations. See Zhang Jing, "Beijing shehui liushi nian" [Sixty years of Beijing's social development], in Lu Xueyi (ed.), *Beijing shehui jianshe liushi nian* [Sixty years of Beijing social construction] (Beijing: Kexue chubanshe, 2008), p. 853. Deng intended to separate local party organs from local PLA units to clarify, streamline, and professionalize the responsibilities of local party, government, and army organs.

[118] Zhou Chunling, *Zhou Chunlin huiyilu* [Memoirs of Zhou Chunling], p. 536.

[119] For example, see Jianfu Chen, "Legal Institutions in the People's Republic of China," in Jianfu Chen, Yuwen Li, and Jan Michiel Otto (eds.), *Implementation of Law in the People's Republic of China*, p. 316.

TABLE 2.3. *Comparison of the Central Guard Bureau and MPS Guard Bureau*

	Central Guard Bureau (Ninth Bureau)	MPS Guard Bureau (Eighth Bureau)
Organizational rank	Deputy military region	Army corps
Feature of organization	Administrative body and security service provider	Administrative body and security service provider
Affiliation	Under dual jurisdiction of both the CMC and the Central General Office; technical guidance from the MPS	Under the MPS
Responsibilities	Provide security services to top party leaders; commands the Central Guard Regiment	Provides macroadministration related to security issues and technical guidance to public security apparatuses nationwide; coordinates security forces from different affiliations; provides security services to central, provincial, municipal, and city leaders; provides security services for important foreign guests
Personages and places for which security detail is provided	Level I Guard: • Party general secretary, president of PRC, Chairman of Central Military Commission (CMC) • Premier • Chairman of NPC • Chairman of the CPPCC • Members of Politburo Standing Committee • Chairman of Central Consultant Committee Level II Guard: • Members of Politburo • Members of Central Secretariat • Secretary of the CDIC Important Buildings/Locations • Zhongnanhai • People's Hall, Mao's Memorial Hall	Level II Guard: • Vice president of PRC • Vice premiers • Vice chairmen of National People's Congress (NPC) • Vice chairmen of Chinese People's Political Consultative Conference (CPPCC) • Vice chairmen of Central Consultant Committee Level III Guard: • Chief judge of Supreme Court • Chief procurator of Supreme Procuratorate Important Buildings/Locations • NPC locations • CPPCC locations/

Source: Wu Jicheng and Wang Fan, *Hongse Jingwei: Zhongyang jingweiju yuan fujuzhang Wu Jicheng huiyilu*, pp. 93–5.

highly centralized, based on the Soviet model, and loyal only to the Party.[120] Deng's reforms focused on decentralizing the police apparatus and promoting professionalism. The PRC's public security forces had experienced decentralization during the Great Leap Forward, during which public security leadership, personnel, and funding underwent wholesale decentralization and local party committees took over security work in their areas.[121] In 1995, the new People's Police Law was established to transform the police force into a professional law enforcement institution; the law is applicable to all police forces, including public security, state security, prisons and labor camps, and courts.[122] The law also defines "the police organization, duties, recruitment, training, powers, disciplinary procedures, and citizen complaint mechanism[s]."[123] The decentralization of the police forces also involved relations between the MPS and the People's Armed Police. Before 1996, the Ministry of Public Security controlled and administrated the PAP. In 1996, the PAP was separated from the MPS and incorporated into the regional military, a condition that qualified the PAP to be located under the direct leadership of the CMC, although it nominally receives continual guidance from the MPS. Because MPS police forces are usually unarmed, whereas PAP police forces are, the MPS does not undertake paramilitary functions. However, with the increasing number and scale of "mass incidents" in the reform era, the MPS must rely greatly on the PAP to control large-scale mass violence.

The MPS created its Bureau for Supervising the Security of Public Information Networks (BSSPIN, *gonggong xinxi wangluo anquan jiancha ju*) in 2000.[124] The tasks of this bureau focus primarily on conducting Internet patrol, monitoring and controlling Internet-based activities engaged in by "hostile" organizations and individuals in and outside China, and watching and reporting on trend-based Internet information that would affect social stability. China's Internet censorship occurs as part of the Golden Shield Project, managed by the MPS, whose "great firewall" functions as a huge national intranet, linked to the World Wide Web through carefully filtered portals.[125] Susan L. Shirk has observed that "the Chinese censors have shown themselves highly capable of controlling Internet content and people's access to information on the Internet" because "China operates the most extensive and technologically sophisticated system of Internet filtering in the world" and employs a large

---

[120] Jack R. Greene, *The Encyclopedia of Police Science*, vol. 1, p. 62.
[121] Murray Scot Tanner and Eric Green, "Principals and Secret Agents: Central versus Local Control over Policing and Obstacles to 'Rule of Law' in China," in Donald C. Clarke (ed.), *China's Legal System: New Developments, New Challenges*, p. 98.
[122] Jianfu Chen, "Legal Institutions in the People's Republic of China," in Jianfu Chen, Yuwen Li, and Jan Michiel Otto (eds.), *Implementation of Law in the People's Republic of China*, p. 316.
[123] Jack R. Greene, *The Encyclopedia of Police Science*, vol. 1, p. 62.
[124] Minxin Pei, *China's Trapped Transition: The Limits of Developmental Autocracy*, p. 86.
[125] Peter Van Ham, *Social Power in International Politics*, p. 101.

network of Internet "nannies," such as managers of Web sites, bulletin boards, and blog platforms, who are assisted by government Internet monitors and citizen vigilantes.[126] Minxin Pei has also pointed out that the PRC has been successful in "minimizing the political impact of the Internet while using the Internet to improve certain aspects of routine administrative functions, such as e-government" through "mobilizing its security resources, imposing stringent regulations, jailing dissidents, and harnessing new technologies."[127]

Authority over and organization of the PAP continues to be a contentious issue for all stakeholders. The MPS seeks continual control over the PAP, yet the PAP struggles for freedom from the MPS's "guidance." The PAP leadership and local units are reluctant to be subordinate to the MPS, yet consensus among the party's leadership supports the MPS's rule over the PAP, as civilian control over the PAP is considered positive and necessary. This principle is reflected in the structure of the PAP, in which the minister of public security is concurrently the first political commissar and the first party secretary of the PAP. Although in 1984 all provincial and municipal party secretaries stepped down from their respective concurrent positions as first political commissars of local military units, effectively ending their supervisory jurisdiction over the local military administration, the ministers of public security continue to keep both positions in the PAP, thus ensuring their supervisory authority. This arrangement did not change even after 1996, when the PAP was integrated into the PLA.[128] Though no longer organizationally controlled by the MPS, the party leadership still wanted the MPS to offer support to the civilian control of the PAP.

The only reason party leaders accepted the position of first party secretary of local army units in the first place was because of Deng's intention to emphasize the party's unilateral authority over the PLA, illustrated by the principle that the party commands the guns. In other words, local party leaders only symbolically led local army units and represented central party leadership in supervising local army units. However, unlike local party leaders, who are not involved in specific responsibilities related to commanding local PLA units, the minister of public security does have specific responsibilities in the PAP, carried out under the authority of two positions in the PAP leadership – first party secretary and first political commissar. This implies that, although the minister of public security may play a symbolic role as first party secretary of the PAP, his or her role as first political commissar renders specific decision-making and administration responsibilities of the PAP to him or her. This organizational system, in which the head of a local MPS branch assumes duties as a key member of local party leadership and as first political commissar of the local PAP unit, occurs nationwide. The regime's reliance on the MPS to reinforce the civilian control over police forces sends a strong message to the PLA and the PAP about the

[126] Susan L. Shirk, *China: Fragile Superpower*, p. 91.
[127] Minxin Pei, *China's Trapped Transition: The Limits of Developmental Autocracy*, p. 85.
[128] *Zuzhi shi*, Ancillary vol. 2, pp. 425–31.

party's ultimate authority over the PAP, although organizationally it makes more sense for the PAP to be under the jurisdiction of the military, for the reasons stated earlier. Thus far, the CCP leadership's insistence on the MPS's control over the PAP has worked in favor of the CCP leadership in achieving its overriding goal of using the security apparatus to maintain its rule and legitimacy.

The Judicial System in Transition

China's justice system in the reform era includes four national agencies: the Ministry of Public Security, the Supreme People's Court, the Supreme People's Procuratorate, and the Ministry of Justice. The highest judicial decision-making body that leads the four national agencies is the Central Political and Legal Commission (CPLC). Compared with the other three agencies, the Ministry of Public Security (MPS) has more judicial power, despite the fact that the MPS is under the control of the State Council. The MPS has traditionally played a much more important role in the CCP justice system than both the Supreme People's Court and the Supreme People's Procuratorate – independent legal institutions that are accountable only to the National People's Congress. Although bureaus of public security had been a central part of all the communist governments in the base areas before the PRC was founded, few CCP-controlled governments had established courts and procuratorates. It was later that these legal organs were intentionally created to promote multilateral authority to be shared with the bureaus of public security. Before the PRC was established, the public security apparatus of the CCP-controlled governments most often took the responsibilities later granted to the courts and the procuratorates.[129] Even for a few years following the founding of the PRC, the public security organs remained the dominant organization in the legal system. By July 1951, all counties nationwide had created bureaus of public security, but only around 300 of 2,200 counties had established procuratorates;[130] courts were faring better, but they still were lagging behind the bureaus of public security – 25 percent of counties still lacked them.[131] In late 1951, following the party's initiative to streamline the organizational structure of the justice system, the newly established procuratorates in some places were abolished and the bureaus of public security director was assigned chief procurator, concurrent to the position of director of bureaus of public security.[132]

---

[129] 'Dong Biwu zhuan' zhuanxie zu, *Dong Biwu zhuan* [A biography of Dong Biwu; hereafter, *Dong Biwu zhuan*], vol. 2, p. 816; Li Haiwen and Wang Yanling, *Shiji duihua – yu xinzhongguo fazhi dianjiren Peng Zhen*, pp. 15–6.

[130] 'Dong Biwu zhuan' zhuanxie zu, *Dong Biwu zhuan*, vol. 2, p. 748.

[131] Ibid., p. 755.

[132] Ibid., p. 818.

After the founding of the PRC, the legal institutions were viewed as an apparatus of the proletarian dictatorship used against the antagonist classes. The courts in the PRC were organized in a four-tier system: grassroots people's courts at the county level, intermediate people's courts at the prefecture level, higher people's courts at the province or large municipality level, and the Supreme People's Court at the national level. Similarly, the CCP established the procuratorates at four levels – county, prefectural, provincial, and central. They were instructed to focus on cases involving counterrevolutionaries – they lodged appeals against unlawful convictions and mistaken sentences. The procuratorates received dual leadership from their corresponding local party committees and the upper-level legal agencies.[133] According to Dong Biwu, president of the People's Supreme Court from 1954 to 1959, the courts were not independent from CCP leadership but rather assisted the party committees. Theoretically, a court was encouraged to report to the next-higher-level party committee if it disagreed with the decision made by its corresponding party committee on an important case, such as one in which the defendant was sentenced with the death penalty.[134] In reality, this seldom occurred, because few court officials were willing to risk their careers for the trouble they could get into with their immediate superiors, the directors of the local party committees. In addition, as the strike-hard mass campaign became the leading CCP initiative for maintaining social order, the courts and the procuratorates became less visible and did not have the same significant impact on the legal process that public security agencies had previously had.

Although the party's role in leading the legal system was undisputable, there was constant debate over whether the legal organs should collaborate or be kept separate to create a system of checks and balances. The debates touched on whether public security agencies, procuratorates, and the courts should supervise one another or jointly handle cases (*lianhe ban'an*), in which case the public security agencies would take the lead. Some cadres in the legal organizations questioned the party's reliance on mass campaigns for administering justice, given the propensity to deal out a large number of unjust sentences. More important, the Great Leap Forward had a significant impact on the evolution of the judiciary system, because with decentralization, local party committees were authorized to take full control of the legal organizations.[135] Personnel of the legal organizations were often forced to cooperate with party leaders, who sometimes resorted to boasting, exaggeration, and lies to bolster their alleged achievements. In 1958, several key figures in the top legal organizations were accused of committing "rightist" mistakes because of their failure to cooperate with the radical campaign, and leaders of the Ministry of Justice were convicted of membership in the Anti-Party Clique; they were subsequently purged.

[133] Ibid., pp. 817–8.
[134] Ibid., pp. 889–90.
[135] Ibid., p. 948.

The lack of supervision from the legal organizations led to a large number of unfounded and unjust arrests, trials, and sentences; from 1957 to 1958 arrests and convictions were three times higher than the second *sufan* campaign in 1955.[136]

China's judicial system modeled the Soviet justice system at the time of the PRC's founding, even though formal law played a much smaller role in the Chinese system than in the Soviet one. Because of the CCP's deep disagreement with the material base of a socialist mode of production that the Soviets exercised,[137] and the growing Sino-Soviet conflict in the late 1950s, Mao favored popular justice over the socialist positivistic notion of law inherited from the Soviet model. Mao's ideology, however, lacked a sense of legality; thus, law and the legal organizations were deemed instruments of the socialist transition. They were charged with inciting social transformation through education, inculcating the masses with communist ethics, and promoting class struggle and mass mobilization.[138]

In 1978, Deng's economic reforms retired both the Soviet model and Maoist radical theory from Chinese politics, to be replaced by a pragmatic approach toward law and the legal system. The Criminal Procedure Law (1979) and the PRC Constitution (1982) formally stipulated mutual checks and supervisions.[139] Another significant change referred to the role of the party committees in leading the legal organizations and the legal process. In the past, all cases a legal organization processed and completed needed to gain approval from the corresponding party committee. Reform made it so this approval was no longer needed. Nonetheless, the party's leadership in deciding on the principles and policies of the justice system was unchallengeable.[140] The goal of Deng's pragmatic policy toward legal reform was to establish a justice system that could effectively help the regime maintain social order and thus ensure the party's dominance in Chinese society. Both Deng and Mao believed that the criminal justice system should be the party's tool for safeguarding the collective public interest, rather than for protecting the rights of the individual, although their methods of protecting public interest were vastly different. Although the constitution that passed in 1978 granted the court jurisdiction over criminals and the procuratorate the power of supervision, it continued to emphasize the

---

[136] Ibid., pp. 959–78.
[137] As John Gittings observes, Mao turned away from the "material base" of production and producers to the intellectual and bureaucratic "superstructure" of politics and culture, which he regarded as lukewarm if not hostile to continuing the revolution. See John Gittings, *The Changing Face of China: From Mao to Market* (New York: Oxford University Press, 2006), p. 39.
[138] Carlos Wing-hung Lo, *China's Legal Awakening: Legal Theory and Criminal Justice in Deng's Era*, p. 10.
[139] *Dong Biwu zhuan*, vol. 2, p. 880.
[140] Ibid., p. 975.

role of the masses in determining the fate of convicted offenders in significant "counterrevolutionary" and criminal cases.[141]

The legal system in China has traditionally been weak and lacking authority.[142] As China has been influenced by a political culture that values community welfare over individual rights,[143] the party's interference with the independence of the judicial system has posed a great obstacle in realizing the rule of law in China. Under a unified political-legal system, the police, procuratorates, and courts are integrated – they serve to achieve the same goal, and therefore are partners instead of adversaries. Thus, there is no separation of powers, only separation of functions, in the Chinese legal system.

The CCP refuses to rely on an external supervision mechanism, such as a public watchdog group, to discipline party officials and the bureaucracy. In Western democracies, the media play an important role in supervising the judicial agencies because public confidence contributes greatly to their legitimacy. Although the media are known to be effective in exposing abuses of power or as a source for expressing public grievances, the CCP has never considered freedom of the press a viable option. In China, the party's propaganda departments supervise media outlets. Because the party censors the media, it poses little threat to the judicial agencies as long as they follow the party unconditionally. Even though they have become fairer and more efficient arbitrators in ordinary cases, the agencies are required to base their handling of cases on the effect that the cases may have on politically or socially sensitive issues, which ends up muddling their judgments.[144]

The procuratorates have no jurisdiction over ordinary violations of discipline by party members or cases that involve administrative rules that are not defined as violations of criminal law. As the party's control over the justice system is unchallengeable, justice agencies are subordinated to the leadership of party committees at all levels, and the officials serving in justice system are ordered to follow the party's command, often in ignorance of the law. Of late, the procuratorates have played an increasingly important role in supporting the Central Discipline Inspection Commission (CDIC) to enhance efforts against abuses of power and corruption among party and government officials. The Supreme People's Procuratorate even has one of its leadership members concurrently appointed as a deputy director of the CDIC. The integration of the procuratorates into the CDIC facilitates the transfer of cases from a disciplinary investigation to a criminal case once the CDIC has grounds to believe that an

---

[141] Zhao Ming, "Cong lishi de shenchu zoulai: Mantan zhuanxing shiqi de dangdai Zhongguo zhengzhi yu sifa gaige" [Coming out from the depths of history: On the reform of contemporary China's political and judicial systems], in *Journal of Political Science and Law*, no. 3 (2008), p. 4.

[142] Susan L. Shirk, *Changing Media, Changing China*, p. 170.

[143] Harry R. Dammer and Jay S. Albanese, *Comparative Criminal Justice Systems*, 4th ed., p. 9.

[144] Benjamin L. Liebman, "China's Courts: Restricted Reform," in Donald C. Clarke (ed.), *China's Legal System: New Developments, New Challenges*, p. 87.

offending official has broken the law. According to a CDIC officer, the CDIC would usually transfer a case of a party or government official to a legal organization when the official received the most severe disciplinary sanction – expulsion from the party. Still, legal agencies may be asked to take over the case if any of the five disciplinary sanctions are given. They are, ranked from least severe to most severe: warning, severe warning, dismissal from leadership position in the party (including demotion to lower positions or having no position), probation of party membership, and expulsion from the party.[145]

Although the post-Mao reforms have made China's justice system more accountable, professional, and transparent, the lack of independence has limited its role in effectively overseeing the government and gaining public trust. Although the party's constitution no longer grants party committees the authority of oversight of legal cases processed by the legal organizations, in reality, party committees often order the legal organizations to report cases. When this occurs, legal organizations are put in a bind in which they have to decide "whether to obey the law or the Party committees."[146] Since the late 1970s, the CCP has relied on the legal organizations to serve its overarching mission – economic reform. Before China launched economic reforms, the court had only two professional departments: the criminal department (*xingshi ting*) and the civil department (*minshi ting*). Since the mid-1980s, the economic department (*jingji ting*) has been created specifically to handle the increasing number of cases related to economic crimes. A large number of regulations and rules have been established to guide international and domestic arbitration in disputes arising from trade, investment, and other economic activities. In many places, the courts are no longer a neutral legal agency but a service center for protecting the interests of business and enterprises, especially state-owned enterprises.

Another challenge that the CCP leadership has been facing is the increasing power of local party and government agencies and the gradual decline of the central leadership's influence over the local legal organizations. Since the 1990s, the localization of legal organizations had become a prominent phenomenon in China; a policy that promotes this is the CCP's separation of local and central government taxes. The separation of taxes encourages local governments to tighten their control over the legal organizations to protect local interests. In addition, the localization of legal organizations challenges the existing system in which the Central Political and Legal Commission (CPLC) controls the justice system through local political and legal commissions. Local party committees use local legal organizations as a bargaining chip to vie for power with the CPLC, because the legal organizations rely on party committees for resources, welfare, and social benefits. An example of a typical

---

[145] *Fazhi wanbao* [Legal evening news], September 29, 2004.
[146] Li Jianming, "Lun dang lingdao xiade sifa duli" [On legal independence under the leadership of the party], in *Zhengzhi yu falu* [Political science and law], no. 2 (2003), pp. 33–41.

case is that of the governor of Xifeng in Liaoning. He ordered the bureau of public security under his jurisdiction to go to Beijing to arrest Zhu Wenna, a journalist for *Faren* [The legal person], a journal sponsored by *Fazhi ribao* [Legal daily], which happens to be the mouthpiece of the Central Political and Legal Commission. Xifeng's governor wanted to arrest Zhu simply because she wrote a report that revealed the county government's abuse of power in dealing with the cost of moving a gas station.[147] It is not an overstatement to say that party leaders at all levels have absolute authority in the political region and level of their domain, to which the legal organizations are not exempt.

China's legal system is attempting to shift from the role of protector of economic development to the vanguard of the "harmonious society" initiated by the "fourth generation" leadership headed by Hu Jintao. This transformation was triggered by three factors. First, China has put tremendous emphasis on economic development since Deng Xiaoping launched economic reforms in 1978. The overwhelming trend in China's reforms has been prioritizing economic development at the cost of ignoring political reform and social fairness. Corresponding to this overarching mission, China's legal system and the rule of law have emphasized economic efficiency as well. As a result, corruption among government and party officials is rampant, the wealth disparity has widened tremendously, and western and inland China fail to experience the same development as the coastal cities, thus undermining the cohesion of the country. The CCP has lost some popular support as a result of the lack of social programs to improve national education, health care, and social welfare. All of these factors have contributed to the growing number of "mass incidents" and mass protests. Compared with Jiang Zemin, who stressed China's rapid economic development, the fourth generation of the CCP leadership, led by Hu Jintao, emphasizes fairness and equity (if not equality), problems that heretofore have been unaddressed as the country barreled forward in pursuit of higher gross domestic product.

Although it is hard to say how effective the legal system can be in supporting the mission to create a harmonious society, public security agencies and other legal organs have supported the party leadership's initiative in at least three ways. First, corruption is being tackled slowly but surely, as the CCP recognizes the impact of corruption on maintaining its legitimacy. Second, laws and regulations have been created or amended to emphasize social protection and welfare. This includes the improvement of China's social security system and extending protection to disadvantaged groups. Third, the legal system has increasingly relied on the new criminal policy of tempering justice with mercy (*kuanyan xiangji*) instead of aggressive crime-fighting measures, such as the former strike-hard campaign. This approach has been applied to various situations, including the resolution of civil disputes through mediation rather than

---

[147] See *Nanfang dushi bao* [Southern metropolitan daily], January 8, 2008.

mere reliance on a court's verdict. The CCP's leadership has placed great importance on ensuring social stability and cultivating a balance between economic growth and social equality and fairness. As such, the legal organizations of the CCP are expected to play an increasingly important role in China's political reform and social transition in the future.

3

Leading Central Security Agency

Central Guard Bureau

The Central Guard Bureau (*zhongyang jingwei ju*) has the main function of providing protection and security to top retired and incumbent leaders of the Politburo Standing Committee, their families, and important foreign leaders.[1] The Central Guard Bureau (CGB) also commands other security units, such as the Central Guard Regiment (CGR), or Unit 8341, and the Beijing Garrison Command, by assigning their elite security corps, which are staffed by active service members, to coordinate and cooperate with military and security agencies to protect top leaders. The CGR's primary responsibility includes providing geographical security support through guarding and protecting a leader's residential area, office areas, facilities, conference halls, and other sites of important events.[2] While the CGR provides geographical security, the CGB provides personalized protection services for central officials by selecting and managing their bodyguards, arranging and supervising security measures to protect them at home and during travels, and coordinating security arrangements with other relevant units.[3] The CGB also maintains high-level contacts

---

[1] Before the Cultural Revolution, the Central Guard Bureau was often called the Guard Bureau of the Central General Office or the Guard Bureau of the PLA General Staff Department because it was assigned the dual leadership of the CGO and the PLA General Staff Department. Although the dual leadership remains, the name of the Central Guard Bureau has been widely used since the Cultural Revolution. In addition, the CGB has been the Ninth Bureau of the MPS since the Ninth Bureau was created in 1953.

[2] Occasionally, the special forces of the Central Guard Regiment engage in special operations. For example, immediately after Lin Biao died in September 1971, the CGR established the Antiaircraft Machine Gun and Antiaircraft Artillery Mobile Detachment against possible attack from Lin Biao's followers in Beijing. See Wu Jicheng and Wang Fan, *Hongse jingwei: Zhongyang jingweiju yuan fujuzhang Wu Jicheng huiyilu* [Red guards: Memoirs of former deputy director of the Central Guard Bureau Wu Jicheng; hereafter, *Wu Jicheng huiyilu*), pp. 195–6.

[3] Wei Li, "The Security Service for Chinese Central Leaders," in *China Quarterly*, no. 143 (September 1995), pp. 815–16.

among senior members of both civilian and military systems regarding security issues.

To assess the importance of the CGB in the central security services and its leading role among central service apparatuses, this chapter investigates the origin and evolution of the CGB and examines its organizational makeup along with its general functions and operations. The CGB, under the distinct leadership of the Central General Office and the PLA General Staff Department, focuses on protecting top leaders by coordinating civilian and military security units and local CCP units, which then focus on protecting top officials by partaking in operations and security measures that involve the presence of agents in close proximity of top leaders, by conducting security surveys of locations to be visited by leaders, and by administering intelligence analysis of present and future threats. Apart from implementing, planning, and coordinating security measures, secret services undertake foreign missions as well. These missions extend to protecting foreign visiting dignitaries, missions in Beijing, and cooperating with the Guard Bureau (Eighth Bureau) of the MPS to carry out those missions.[4] In some cases, a three-tier system of security is necessary, as when the National People's Congress and the Chinese People's Political Consultative Conference take place, in which CGB and CGR personnel, People's Armed Police guards, and MPS Special Forces cooperate and work together to ensure the safety of high-ranking officials. Often in this three-tier system of protection, the CGB and CGR personnel are of the highest caliber and the most important, in that they are the bodyguards of the top leaders. Hence, CGB and CGR personnel must acquire a great level of professional knowledge and skill, and they must have the utmost political loyalty. Their personnel are generally trained by PLA units, which discipline them to acquire the attributes of sacrifice and dedication, through the practical application of martial arts and the core values of honor, courage, and commitment. And although the CGB and CGR personnel are at the top and innermost level of the three-tier security system, the personnel of the People's Armed Police and the MPS occupy the outer second and third tiers of the three-tier security system.[5]

The central security apparatuses, like the traditional palace guards of China – with a tight organizational structure, capacity for coercive action, and access to the emperors – not only have provided protection against external dangers but also have played an important role in internal politics by being instruments or allies in seizing, consolidating, and helping maintain power.[6] This chapter evaluates the role of the central security agencies and its importance by highlighting

---

[4] For example, when President Barack Obama visited China in November 2009, anyone who entered the Beijing International Club where Obama lodged needed permission from the CGB or the Foreign Ministry's Bureau of Foreign Services. See *Xinhua*, November 19, 2009.

[5] See "Lianghui an'bao shexia sancheng jingjie xian, neiyou wujing waiyou gong'an" [Three circles of security lines are set up with the PAP inside and the MPS outside in the two conferences], *Phoenix Satellite Television*, March 4, 2011.

[6] Wei Li, "The Security Service for Chinese Central Leaders," p. 815.

its key features in regard to its role in internal surveillance and control over the coercive actions of the central security apparatuses in Zhongnanhai politics. In addition, this chapter evaluates the dual leadership system designed to ensure high-level recruitment standards, training, discipline, and morale of military units, as well as overall operational and combat effectiveness to maintain control over the security apparatuses. The dual leadership also depends on dual rule and military surveillance that promotes the physical and psychological deterrence of any internal dissidents. Even though the PLA and the ranking military personnel of other organizations involved hold dual or single leadership and preside over the security forces, the personnel of the security forces are generally outside of military control.[7] For this reason, the security forces can possibly be viewed as the political alternative to the regular army, which is the actual fighting force. In other words, the protection forces are more of a political counterweight to the regular army than an alternative fighting force. This chapter also considers the relationship between the CGB and other security forces, particularly the Beijing-based security units that protect the central leadership, such as the Guard Bureau of the MPS, the Central Guard Regiment, the People's Armed Police, and the Beijing Garrison Command. Finally, this chapter analyzes the Central Guard Bureau and its leadership of and dependence on various security institutions and units to protect top CCP leaders and their residences, a system that follows the Soviet model of depending on numerous and varied executive protection forces for guarding top leaders and their residence. In fact, the CBG was once a security agency that organizationally followed the Soviet model of the Ninth Chief Directorate of the KGB; it was also named the Ninth Bureau of the Ministry of Public Security after the Soviet model.

Features, Operations, and Mechanism

The importance of the Central Guard Bureau (CGB) resides in the various responsibilities it holds. First, because the CGB is responsible for the security of top leaders, it manages other security apparatuses to guarantee the safety of those top leaders. Second, CGB personnel play an important role in protecting the lives of top leaders by taking the positions of bodyguards (*tieshen weishi*) and by always assigning a leadership member or top CGB officials to the chief bodyguard post of every top leader. For instance, Li Yinqiao, Li Taihe, and Cheng Yuangong, three senior officials of the CGB, were chief bodyguards of Mao, Liu Shaoqui, and Zhou Enlai. The CGB also guards and protects visiting foreign leaders. For example, in the 1950s when Nikita Khrushchev,

---

[7] For example, although the Central Guard Bureau is under the dual leadership of the PLA and the Central General Office, it operates and recruits its personnel independently as its personnel might come from the PLA, MPS, government agencies, schools, and businesses. The CGB is not a military unit with active-duty service personnel.

Sukarno, and Ho Chi Minh visited China, the CGB officials – Li Shuhuai, Yang Dezhong, and Zhang Wenjian – were the chief bodyguards of these foreign leaders.[8] In the 1950s, the CGB gained increasing assignments and responsibilities as China focused on establishing an international united front against Western industrialized nations. During this time, the United States–led Western industrial nations of the world had issued an embargo on China, which China tried to dismantle by allying with and leading the developing countries against the West. For example, China attempted to ally itself with Indonesia to create a united front by strongly supporting Sukarno's policy of driving the United States and the United Kingdom out of Southeast Asia.[9]

The CGB bodyguards not only command the CGR personnel to guard the residencies of top leaders but also accompany and guard their leaders at all time. These accompanying bodyguards (*suishen jingwei* or *suiwei*) guard leaders inside and outside of their residents, while the leaders travel to places outside of Beijing,[10] during meetings, during outings with friends or family, and while they go to entertainment events. In regard to the accompaniment provided by the CGB, oftentimes individual leaders have no say in whether they would like to be left alone by themselves. For example, Chen Boda acquired CGB bodyguards to accompany him wherever he went because Chen became a member of the Politburo and head of the Central Cultural Revolution Group during the Cultural Revolution. Chen Boda had disliked being accompanied wherever he went and would try to escape from his personal CGB bodyguards. However, although Chen was viewed as an important leftist intellect in CCP history who "played a major role in shaping Mao Zedong thought,"[11] the CGB did not listen to Chen's complaints about the bodyguards accompanying him.[12] Instead, the CGB would order its personnel to lay all irons in the fire to follow him – oftentimes secretly.[13]

Although no institutional relationship has existed between the CGB and the CGR, the CGB is actually the de facto superior of the CGR. The CGB is superior to the CGR in that the leading figures of the CGR are automatically deputy directors of the CGB. The CGB also executes internal surveillance over high-ranking leaders through the appointment of temporary bodyguards to local leaders who visit Beijing or attend other party conferences and events.[14]

[8] *Wu Jicheng huiyilu*, pp. 60, 75–7.
[9] Rizal Sukma, *Indonesia and China: The Politics of a Troubled Relationship*, p. 31.
[10] Chen Changjiang, *Mao Zedong zuihou shinian: Jingwei duizhang de huiyi* [Mao Zedong's last ten years: Recollection of the head of security guards], pp. 1–2.
[11] Bill Brugger and Stephen Reglar, *Politics, Economy and Society in Contemporary China*, p. 228.
[12] *Wu Jicheng huiyilu*, pp. 60, 121–2.
[13] Ibid., pp. 60, 121–2.
[14] Qiao Jinwang, "Lao Qiao a, wenhua da geming ba wo lei kua le" [Old Qiao ah, the Cultural Revolution has tired me out], in Cheng Hua (ed.), *Zhou Enlai he tade mishumen* [Zhou Enlai and his secretaries], (Beijing: Zhongguo guangbo tianshi chubanshe, 1992), p. 429.

Visiting local leaders were never allowed to be accompanied by their personal bodyguards, only by an assigned temporary bodyguard. Moreover, during party conferences and events, the CGB never allowed leaders to bring their personal bodyguards; instead, only secretaries of local party and PLA leaders, such as leaders of military regions, provincial party committees, PLA Air Force, Navy, and the People's Armed Police were allowed in.[15] Thus, by appointing temporary bodyguards to delegates and leaders, the CGB took complete charge over the security of meetings and conferences. In doing so, the Central Guard Bureau coordinated PLA units to guard the areas surrounding the events. For example, before Mao's death, the CCP leadership often arranged leadership conferences in Lushan of Jiangxi, so that the CGB could coordinate the PLA's 20th Army Corps to guard the entrances to Lushan and ensure the security of the surrounding areas.[16] During these conferences, protective operations would be graded on a three-tier scale of A, B, and C. The party chairman and vice chairman would usually be placed under the A tier of high-security protection.[17] Also, although high-ranking leaders were at times allowed to bring their personal bodyguards to informal meetings and events, the CGB would remove arms from the bodyguards and not allow them to enter official meetings and conferences.[18]

The Central Guard Bureau also keeps an eye on and maintains effective control over those high-ranking officials for the paramount leader. In this regard, the CGB is a highly feared security apparatus, falling under the Central General Office's communications and operations sector; it provides personal protection to top leaders and their families by placing "a protective envelope around the central leadership," and the CGB's director "must block any threatening or unwanted contacts or messages."[19] During Mao's era, all top leaders, except Mao, were exposed to and put under the direct surveillance of the CGB and Unit 8341, headed by Wang Dongxing. The bodyguards of the CGB and Unit 8341 were then required to report every suspicious movement to Wang Dongxing. For example, Lin Baio, named by the party as Mao's successor after the party's congress in 1969, was subjected to the same internal surveillance carried out by the CGB and Unit 8341 bodyguards.[20] The paramount leader relies greatly on the CGB and CGR as forces against political opponents, as in the cases of Liu

[15] *Wu Jicheng huiyilu*, p. 164.
[16] Ibid., p. 166.
[17] Ibid., p. 164.
[18] Even Marshal Ye Jianying's bodyguards were not allowed to enter the meetings in which the Hua Guofeng, Ye Jianying, and Wang Dongxing alliance took the initiative to arrest the Gang of Four. See Fan Shuo, *Ye Jianying zai yijiu qiliu nian* [Ye Jianying in 1976], pp. 374–5.
[19] John Wilson Lewis and Litai Xue, *Imagined Enemies: China Prepares for Uncertain War*, p. 103.
[20] After Lin Biao became the only vice chairman of the CCP in the Eleventh Plenum in August 1966, Wang Dongxing sent Han Qingyu, an officer of Unit 8341, to guard Lin Biao. Realizing Mao's move in watching Lin, Lin's wife Ye Qun deeply distrusted Han and tried not to let Han be involved in Lin's security issues and find out secrets in Maojiawan, Lin's residence. See

Shaoqi and Deng Xiaoping, who were put under house arrest during the early stages of the Cultural Revolution.[21] During the Cultural Revolution, the CGB had given orders to Liu Shaoqi's guards to send the radical mass organizations into Liu's residence to physically abuse him.[22] In addition, the CGB assigned temporary bodyguards to high-ranking leaders no matter whether they wanted to be accompanied or "protected" by CGB personnel or whether the high-ranking leaders reported to the Central General Office for their business and personal activities; all CGB personnel were required to follow and report on the activities of top leaders to the CGB. As mentioned before, regardless of Chen Boda's complaints on being accompanied and protected by CGB personnel during personal affairs, the CGB ignored his complaints and continued to have him secretly followed – and the CGB personnel guarded him at all costs.[23] These elite security apparatuses are also crucial forces in the intraparty power struggle, as in the case of the alliance among Hua Guofeng, Ye Jianying, and Wang Dongxing, who used the CGB and the CGR to arrest Maoist radicals in a palace coup that "ended the reign of terror of the Gang of Four in 1976."[24] As did officials of Unit 8341 whom Mao sent to conduct investigations into the general public's reaction to Mao's policies, the CGB personnel became instrumental to Mao as an important source of information and internal intelligence gathering, especially when Mao distrusted his Politburo colleagues and local officials, as when he sent two of his bodyguards, Li Yinqiao and Feng Yaosong, to Shandong to conduct investigations on his behalf.[25]

In the early 1960s, the CGB strengthened its control over high-ranking officials by assigning accompanying bodyguards to high-ranking leaders, even if the leaders already had a personal bodyguard allocated to them by the CGB. These accompanying bodyguards served as Mao's spies to monitor ranking member's activities and to observe the level of personal loyalty between the leaders and their guards. Zhou Enlai's personal guard was Cheng Yuangong; however, the CGB or the MPS Ninth Bureau (both are the same units with different names) appointed Li Shuhuai, deputy director of the Ninth Bureau, as Zhou's accompanying bodyguard. Chen Yi and Luo Ruiqing were also assigned accompanying bodyguards, Wu Jicheng and Qu Qiyu, who were departmental heads of the Ninth Bureau.[26] Marshal Ye Jianying was also assigned the accompanying bodyguards Mu Naichuan and Ma Xijin, who were

Zhang Yunsheng, *Maojiawan jishi: Lin Biao mishu huiyilu* [True account of Maojiawan: The memoirs of Lin Biao's secretary], pp. 243–6.

[21] *Deng Xiaoping "Wenge" suiyue*, pp. 58–61.

[22] Liu Zhende, "Jiyao mishu de huiyi" [Recollections of a confidential secretary], in Huang Zheng (ed.), *Liu Shaoqi de zuihou suiyue* [The last years of Liu Shaoqi] (Beijing: Zhongyang wenxian chubanshe, 2006), p. 99.

[23] *Wu Jicheng huiyilu*, pp. 121–2.

[24] Bruce Gilley, *China's Democratic Future: How It Will Happen and Where It Will Lead*, p. 128.

[25] Quan Yanchi, *Lingxiu lei* [Tears of leaders], pp. 131–2.

[26] *Wu Jicheng huiyilu*, p. 83.

former subordinates of Wang Dongxing when they served at the Central Guard Bureau.

In addition to bodyguards, doctors, nurses, housekeepers, chefs, and drivers were also sent from the Central Guard Regiment, the Bureau of Secretaries, the Bureau of Health, and the Bureau of Living Services, under the Central General Office, to serve and monitor important clients. On orders of the Central General Office, these service members attended meetings and study groups and reported observations to their supervisors regularly. Moreover, all security guards who protected and monitored high-ranking party members were rotated at regular intervals to prevent them from establishing personal relationships with the leaders. Li Wenpu was assigned by the CGB and Unit 8341 to guard Lin Biao after Lin Biao officially became Mao's successor in the Eleventh Plenum held in August 1966. Lin was previously guarded by the CMC General Office but now the CGB and Unit 8341 were also involved in Lin's security. Because of Li's background as a guard from Unit 8341, Ye Qun, Lin's wife and Director of Lin Biao Office, treated Li extremely carefully.[27]

At the dawn of the Cultural Revolution, personal security guards arrested their leaders in their homes on the orders of Wang Dongxing; the arrested leaders included Liu Shaoqi, Deng Xiaoping, and Peng Zhen. Among the personal security guards, anyone who showed sympathy toward those who they guarded were immediately relieved of their posts. In this system, everyone was monitored to such an extent that high-ranking officials were even fearful of crying in their own homes after the Red Guard had begun its campaign, out of concern that their guards, secretaries, nannies, or even their own children might report their weeping to the party organizations or the mass rebels.[28] To the CCP security apparatuses, anything that indicated less than 100 percent support and fervor for the Cultural Revolution was considered a sign of hostility toward the "revolutionary mass movement." Ye Jianying turned on the radio in his home to prevent others from listening in when he had important conversations with others.[29] After Wang Dongxing replaced Yang Shangkun as head of the Central General Office in December 1965 and the Chinese People's Public Security Forces were abolished in June 1966, following the purge of Luo Ruiqing, complete control of the security forces fell to Wang Dongxing. At that time, Wang became the most powerful figure in the CCP security apparatus.

In Mao's era, every top CCP leader in the central security system was served by four types of personnel: bodyguards (*weishi*), security guards (*jingwei renyuan*), doctors and nurses (*yihu renyuan*), and a variety of secretaries

---

[27] See Zhang Ning, *Ziji xie ziji* [One writes oneself], pp. 189–90.
[28] For example, Tan Zhenlin complained that he didn't have a place to cry because his secretaries and children were around him. See *Maojiawan jishi*, p. 94.
[29] Fan Shuo, *Ye Jianying zai yijiu qiliu nian*, pp. 285–6, 306, 320.

(*mishu*).[30] Between four and seven bodyguards were assigned to each top leader; the bodyguards not only provided protection services but also fulfilled basic needs of leaders, from delivering meals to other menial responsibilities of providing clothing, transport, and even clysters (in Mao's case).[31] Also, bodyguards, except the chief bodyguard, were not allowed to carry guns while serving top leaders.[32] The armed security guards in charge of providing security in areas such as the residential compounds of top leaders, offices, facilities, conference halls, and important events were sent by Unit 8341. As for the seven top leaders (Mao, Liu Shaoqi, Zhou Enlai, Zhu De, Chen Yun, Lin Biao, and Deng Xiaoping), each was guarded by a company (later called a detachment) in which the internal-security squad, which comprised about ten soldiers, had direct access to the top leaders.[33] Two types of secretaries, personal and confidential, served top leaders and were in charge of preparing documents for leaders' attendance of the Politburo meetings and of communicating information to other top leaders. In addition, the leaders could temporarily call on the personnel of the party's think tank as their secretaries. For instance, Mao did this when he appointed Chen Boda and Hu Qiaomu as his political secretaries to help him draft party documents and important speeches.[34]

The Central Guard Bureau commands the Central Guard Regiment on behalf of the Central General Office, and doing so is one of its most important responsibilities. The Central General Office (CGO) experienced some difficulties as a civilian organization in attempting to manage a military unit with active-duty service personnel. This led the CGO to let the PLA manage political education, demobilization, recruitment, promotions and demotions, and logistics of the Central Guard Regiment while the Central Guard Bureau, subordinate to the CGO, commanded the Central Guard Regiment and detailed operations and decision making.[35]

Politics of the MPS Ninth Bureau

The creation of the Central Guard Bureau derived from a long-standing CCP tradition in which the party, instead of the military, controls the central security forces. Although in Jiangxi base areas Mao created the Special Service Teams to ensure the leadership's security, his trusted secretaries usually commanded and coordinated the protective operations, as in the case of Gu Bo, who was general secretary of the General Front Committee headed by Mao and a close assistant

[30] Quan Yanchi, *Lingxiu lei*, p. 69.
[31] Ibid., p. 54; Qi Li, *Mao Zedong wannian shenghuo jishi* [Record of events of Mao Zedong's later life], p. 39.
[32] Quan Yanchi, *Lingxiu lei*, p. 54.
[33] Ibid., pp. 54, 82–3.
[34] Ibid., p. 106.
[35] Wang Fan and Dong Ping, *Hongqiang tonghua: Wojia zhuzai zhongnanhai* [Fairy tales within the red wall: My family lived in Zhongnanhai], pp. 176–7.

of Mao's in later 1920s.[36] From 1931 to 1935, the CCP leadership in Shanghai gradually sent the returned students to the Jiangxi base areas and replaced Mao in controlling the Jiangxi base areas. With the returned students, the Soviet-style State Political Security Bureau was introduced into the Jiangxi base areas, and it took charge of central security services. The earliest organization in charge of security services for top leaders in the Jiangxi base areas was the Political Security Department (PSD, *zhengzhi baowei chu*), established in June 1931.[37] Later, the PSD was reorganized as the State Political Security Bureau (SPSB), and its functions were significantly expanded on the basis of the Soviet vertical chain of command; it had unchecked power to suppress any imagined, suspected, or real counterrevolutionary inside or outside the party. In early 1930, when the returned students infiltrated the base areas, the organizational structure of CCP security forces was modeled on that of the Soviet NKVD, which was characterized by a highly centralized and vertical leadership. These forces gradually became powerful paramilitary units controlled by the SPSB. By the time the CCP was forced to retreat from the Jiangxi bases areas and embarked on the Long March, the SPSB had developed into a powerful security apparatus that protected and supervised high-ranking leaders. The SPSB often operated in secrecy to protect against internal and external threats. It was a powerful organization with executive powers to conduct surveillance, investigation, and arrest, and to detain suspected party members, army officers, and soldiers, and its subordinate security departments and commissioners penetrated all party organs and the Red Army. The SPSB aimed to achieve control over every level of the CCP and the Red Army, and it planned to do so by any means possible, including military operations, torture, and execution of suspected traitors.

After the Zunyi Conference, which marked Mao's rise in the CCP leadership and the CCP's increasing independence from the Comintern, Mao again assigned his secretaries to take charge of leading, administrating, and coordinating security services for leaders, as for Wang Shoudao in the late 1930s and early 1940s, and Shi Zhe in early 1940s.[38] The formal party organization that took charge of the top leaders and that led protective operations – the Guard Department (*jingwei chu*) of the Central General Office – was established in the village of Xibaipo in Hebei, where Mao had set up a temporary revolutionary base during the summer of 1948.[39] Wang Dongxing, Mao's chief bodyguard, was appointed to take charge of the Guard Department. As head of the Guard Department, Wang Dongxing commanded the elite security forces and coordinated other civilian and military organizations, such as the armed police; the

[36] Hans J. Van de Ven, "New States of War: Communist and Nationalist Warfare, and State Building, 1928–1934," in Hans J. Van de Ven (ed.), *Warfare in Chinese History*, p. 381; Wu Lie, *Zhengrong suiyue* [The eventful times], p. 44.

[37] *Zhengrong suiyue*, pp. 67–8.

[38] Shi Zhe was Mao's secretary and director of the Office of the Central Bureaucrat. See *Shi Zhe huiyilu*, pp. 169, 240.

[39] *Wu Jicheng huiyilu*, p. 25.

Central Guard Regiment; the Social Affairs Department; the PLA's Northern China Field Army; the Beijing Bureau of Public Security; and the PLA's 207th Division, which provided security for the capital.[40]

The expansion in 1953 of the Central Guard Regiment, a special palace guard unit, enabled Mao to control not only his own security but also that of his top associates who resided in Zhongnanhai. Because Mao was unable to exert control over high-ranking leaders who lived outside Zhongnanhai, this aspect of security and control was instead carried out by the Eighth Bureau of the Ministry of Public Security (also called the Guard Bureau of the MPS), headed by Luo Ruiqing. When the MPS was established in November 1949, it comprised only the MPS General Office (*bangong ting*) and six professional bureaus, including Political Security (*zhengzhi baowei*), Economic Security (*jingji baowei*), Public Security and Administration (*zhi'an xingzheng*), Border Control (*bianfang baowei*), Armed Guard and Protection (*wuzhuang baowei*), and Personnel Administration (*renshi*).[41] The Guard Bureau, or the Eighth Bureau (*jingwei ju*), was added to the MPS in the winter of 1950.[42] Luo's career had been closely tied to Mao's faction: he served in the Fourth Army in the late 1920s, the First Army Group and the First Front Army in the early 1930s, and the North China Field Army in the late 1940s.[43] Mao's choice of Luo Ruiqing, instead of Li Kenong, is often attributed to the strong factional ties between Luo and Mao. Considering that Luo's career always linked him to Mao's factions, Mao was more comfortable trusting Luo than someone who had been tied to other powerful leaders, such as Zhou Enlai or Zhang Guotao. When Mao planned to visit the Soviet Union in the spring of 1948, Luo Ruiqing was chosen to manage his security; the Politburo sent a brigade led by Luo Ruiqing to head Mao's security detail from Shanxi to the border of China and the Soviet Union.[44] Factional politics often played a large role in elite CCP organizations,[45] which motivated party leaders to hire their political followers by both recruiting former subordinates and identifying factional ties between themselves and those who had served in their factions, but not necessarily their immediate subordinates. Oftentimes, factional ties alone became a significant basis for leaders to cultivate and develop personal *guanxi* with other party members.

However, according to Luo's daughter, Luo Diandian, Luo never personally served Mao before Luo became public security minister, despite the fact that Luo's career was closely tied to Mao's faction.[46] Lacking a strong or intimate

---

[40] Ibid., pp. 31–2.
[41] Tao Siju, *Xinzhongguo diyiren gongan buzhang: Luo Ruiqing* [First PRC public security minister: Luo Ruiqing], p. 11.
[42] Tao Siju, *Xu Zirong zhuan* [A biography of Xu Zirong], p. 111.
[43] See (Luo) Diandian, *Feifan de niandai* [Those extraordinary years], pp. 280–2.
[44] *Yang Shangkun huiyilu*, p. 261.
[45] Jing Huang, *Factionalism in Chinese Communist Politics*, pp. 26–106.
[46] *Feifan de niandai*, p. 151.

bond, Luo's loyalty to Mao always remained more institutional than personal. In the early 1950s, the Chinese People's Public Security Forces (CPPSF) and the Ministry of Public Security operated strictly under the command of the CMC and the State Council, although the CPPSF and the Ministry of Public Security were under the authority of Luo Ruiqing in their commitment to keep Mao informed of their work. Although Luo stayed loyal to Mao, he also cared about institutional loyalty to the party, which created conflicts between the two men. For example, Luo supported the CMC in putting the Central Guard Regiment under the administration of the CPPSF, which displeased Mao and was later viewed as Luo's initiative to "enlarge his personal control and influence over security forces nationwide."[47] Furthermore, in 1956, Mao became upset when Luo tried to stop him from swimming in the Yangzi River by using the authority of the party's Central Committee to support his concerns regarding Mao's safety.[48] The Red Guard publication revealed that Luo was involved in the Gao Gang affairs in the early 1950s.[49] Luo's involvement in the affairs might be why Mao summoned Luo to his residence and severely criticized him.[50] The Chairman felt increasingly inconvenienced by Luo and frequently showed his dissatisfaction with him. In the mid-1950s, Luo believed that he had lost Mao's trust and would soon be dismissed.[51] For Mao, Luo Ruiqing was not the ideal follower with whom he could cultivate absolute personal loyalty or entrust with control of his personal security forces. The rise of Wang Dongxing was in response to this need of Mao's to ensure absolute loyalty and to gain absolute control over personal security forces, in order to stay immune from the influence of party bureaucracy.

Wang Dongxing was appointed deputy director of the MPS Eighth Bureau and director of the First Department of the Eighth Bureau, a unit that was responsible for guarding Zhongnanhai when the Eighth Bureau was created in the winter of 1950. An important change regarding the security forces occurred in 1953, when the power that controlled these forces was divided. Although Luo Ruiqing was still the most powerful controlling figure in the central security forces because of his position at the MPS and the PLA Public Security Forces (its predecessor was the Chinese People's Public Security Forces), the Central General Office, headed by Yang Shangkun, shared the security force's

[47] Zhonggong wenhua dageming zhongyao wenjian huibian, p. 28.
[48] See Wang Fan et al., Zhiqing zheshuo [Said by insiders], vol. 1, p. 392.
[49] See Ding Wang, Zhonggong wenhua dageming ziliao huibian [Compilation of materials published in the Cultural Revolution], vol. 1, p. 583.
[50] See Huang Yao and Zhang Mingzhe, Luo Ruiqing zhuan [A biography of Luo Ruiqing], pp. 294–5.
[51] For a long time, according to Ye Zilong, Mao was angry with Luo and refused to talk with him. Luo complained several times that Mao distrusted him and might give him trouble. See Wang Fan et al., Zhiqing zheshuo, p. 392; Zhonggong wenhua dageming zhongyao wenjian huibian, p. 26.

managerial responsibilities with Luo. Interestingly, Wang Dongxing was not only appointed to take control of the Central Guard Bureau[52] but also became a vice minister of the MPS in 1955. In addition, Yang Shangkun's power was greatly divided with the merger of the Administrative Department of the CGO with the newly established Central Guard Bureau, led by Wang Dongxing.[53] Only Wang Dongxing's power was consolidated by these changes. Mao's political patronage was clear with his efforts to install loyalist Wang Dongxing in institutions otherwise dominated by those with whom Mao had not established strong loyalties. This strategy, which Mao referred to as "mixing in sand," was also used to suppress Lin Biao's groups during the Cultural Revolution.[54] Wang's penetration of the Ministry of Public Security was achieved by removing responsibilities from guarding top leaders from the Eighth Bureau, headed by Liu Wei, and creating the Ninth Bureau, led by Wang, in 1953. The duties of the Ninth Bureau of the MPS, also known as the Central Guard Bureau[55] (the same agency but with two names), were specifically limited to guarding the top five leaders: Mao, Liu Shaoqi, Zhou Enlai, Zhu De, Chen Yun, and Politburo members whose residences were in Zhongnanhai. The divided Eighth Bureau retained some of its previous duties, such as guarding ranking leaders other than the top five leaders and the Politburo members in Zhongnanhai.

After the creation of the Ninth Bureau, the Eighth Bureau was assigned to guard the relatively lower-ranking leadership members, such as vice premiers, vice presidents of the central government, vice chairs of the Chinese People's Political Consultative Conference, the president of the Supreme People's Court, and the procurator general of Supreme People's Procuratorate. The Eighth Bureau was also responsible for guarding military leaders of the CMC, important foreign guests, and key military and governmental units.[56] When Wang Dongxing was appointed to the directorship of the Ninth Bureau, he essentially became the only figure in charge of security for the top leaders in Zhongnanhai. Previously, Wang had been under the leadership of the Eighth Bureau. In December 1958, the Ninth Bureau was completely moved to the jurisdiction of the Central General Office.[57] For Mao, moving the power of decision making on Zhongnanhai security from the MPS to the Guard Bureau of the CGO was of great importance. Mao's direct control over top

[52] Ibid. note 1.
[53] *Hongqiang tonghua*, p. 176.
[54] When Mao decided to purge Lin Biao, Mao appointed Li Desheng to the CMC Administrative Office and Ji Dengkui to Beijing Military Region to undermine Lin's influence.
[55] Ibid. note 1.
[56] See *Wu Jicheng huiyilu*, pp. 93–5.
[57] See Hubei sheng yifa zhisheng gongzuo lingdao xiaozu [Leading group of rule of law in Hubei Province], "Gong'an bu neishe jigou yange" [Organizational evolution of the MPS inner institutions], in *Hubei fazhi* [Hubei law system] online, http://www.124.gov.cn/2006–12/25/cms209222article.shtml (accessed May 13, 2009).

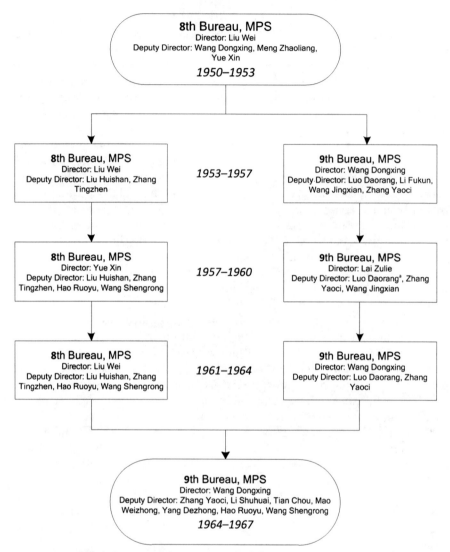

FIGURE 3.1. Ninth Bureau of the MPS (Central Guard Bureau), 1950–67. *Source: Wu Jicheng huiyilu*, pp. 93–5; *Hongqiang tonghua*, pp. 176, 178–9.
[a] After Wang Dongxing was sent to Jiangxi, Luo Daorang was appointed to take charge of the Ninth Bureau for a short period of time.

leaders and certain other lower-ranking leaders was achieved in April 1964, when the Eighth Bureau was abolished and merged into the Ninth Bureau (Figure 3.1).[58]

[58] See *Wu Jicheng huiyilu*, pp. 93–5.

In addition, as the head of Mao's personal security force, Wang Dongxing was specifically responsible for protecting Mao. Wang personally looked after Mao's security, directly ordering both the Central Guard Bureau and Unit 8341 to implement his plans. No one in either the Central Guard Bureau or Unit 8341 was allowed to ask about reasons for their assignment.[59]

Nonetheless, Mao did not hesitate to use punishment to ensure Wang's unconditional obedience. Wang received two severe punishments, first in the 1950s and again in the early 1970s. The first occurred in the mid-1950s, when Mao considered Wang too subservient to the party bureaucracy. Like Luo Ruiqing, Wang reported to Liu Shaoqi on Mao's security issues and relied on the party bureaucracy to restrain any of Mao's activities that could have resulted in security problems. Neither Luo nor Wang were shifting their loyalty to Liu Shaoqi or the party bureaucracy over the Chairman; they simply wanted to rely on the party bureaucracy to ensure the safety and security of the Chairman and to encourage other top leaders to share such responsibilities.[60] When Mao suspected that Wang had shifted his loyalty to the party bureaucracy, he stripped Wang of authority as head of Mao's security guards and sent him to the Central Party Cadre School for "reeducation."[61] Immediately after Wang completed his studies in 1957, Mao approved of Wang's transfer from Beijing to Jiangxi, where he was exiled as one of several vice governors. Mao did not offer Wang the opportunity to return to Beijing until September 1960, when Mao decided to strengthen his personal security against possible challenges from the party bureaucracy. From that point, Wang was extremely careful to serve Mao and show loyalty to the Chairman alone.

Wang's second punishment resulted from his involvement in Lin Biao's conflict with Mao at the 1970 Lushan plenum. Mao became angry when Wang cooperated with Lin and Lin's followers, who were against the Maoist radicals headed by Jiang Qing, Mao's wife. He was also frustrated when Wang supported Lin's suggestion that the chairmanship should remain within the PRC constitution.[62] In the debate over the PRC constitution and whether Lin Biao should be named state chairman if Mao were to refuse to hold the position himself, Wang supported Lin's followers, who were lobbying to secure Lin's

[59] Ibid., p. 162.

[60] See Li Zhisui, *Mao Zedong siren yisheng huiyilu* [The private life of Chairman Mao] (Taipei: Shibao wenhua chuban qiye gufen youxian gongsi, 1994), pp. 175–6.

[61] Ibid., pp. 175–6

[62] After Liu Shaoqi, chairman of the PRC and one of the CCP vice chairmen, was purged in August 1966, Lin Biao replaced Liu as Mao's successor due to Lin's role as sole vice chairman of the CCP (but not chairman of the PRC). By the time when the Lushan plenum took place in August–September 1970, Mao had been warned of Lin's dominance in the PLA and the PLA's powerful role in local politics because the PLA officers led local Revolutionary Committees. Although Mao did not show his position in terms of whether he was unwilling to keep Lin as his successor, he had made the effort to undermine Lin's influence. The debate on the abolishment of a state chairmanship was one of his efforts against Lin Biao.

position as state chair. Mao was particularly concerned about the increasingly close relationship between Wang Dongxing and Lin Biao's group after the 1969 Ninth Party Congress, when Lin's position as Mao's successor was written into the party's constitution.

According to Wu Faxian, Wang Dongxing had been allied politically with Lin Biao's group since the Ninth Party Congress and "was very excited" when Mao said that "only Comrade Lin Biao was qualified if the position of the State Chairman remained."[63] Although Wang knew of Mao's reluctance to resume the post of the state chairmanship, after former PRC chairman Liu Shaoqi was dismissed and died due to persecution, he was obviously unclear how seriously Mao held this position and, therefore, he chose to support Lin Biao to put pressure on Mao to accept Lin's suggestion for resuming the state chairmanship.[64] Although it was not clear what role Mao played in the decision to punish Wang, the Politburo expelled Wang Dongxing from the Central Guard Bureau immediately after the 1970 Lushan plenum. Ji Dengkui was then appointed Mao's chief security guard. When Wang reported to Mao that Ji Dengkui had, on behalf of the Politburo, asked him to hand over his work to Ji, Mao pretended that he knew nothing of it and asked Wang to remain at his position as head of the Central General Office as well as his chief bodyguard.[65] Although Mao accepted Wang's self-criticism and Wang promised that he would not commit such a "mistake" again,[66] Mao's maneuvering of Wang's responsibilities served as a warning to Wang about the consequences of even the semblance of disloyalty and the potential repercussions of such behavior being repeated in the future.

Wang's personal loyalty to Mao was based on the moral dimension of *guanxi*; the obligatory loyalty (*zhong*) that entails a political follower's unconditional support and obedience to his leader. Obligatory loyalty in the Chinese context derives from filial piety, "a belief that an individual has a moral obligation to safeguard the interests and welfare of his leader at any cost, even to the point of sacrificing his own life."[67] Thus, whenever Mao clarified his position, Wang unconditionally followed. When Mao decided to dismiss Liu Shaoqi in 1966 and attack Lin Biao in 1970, Wang followed Mao without hesitation, even though Wang had no personal conflicts with either man. When Wang learned

[63] Wu Faxian, *Suiyue jiannan – Wu Faxian huiyilu* [Difficult years – The memoirs of Wu Faxian; hereafter, *Wu Faxian huiyilu*], vol. 2, pp. 775–6.

[64] See *Wu Jicheng huiyilu*, pp. 171–2.

[65] See *Wu Jicheng huiyilu*, p. 178.

[66] According to party historian Shu Yun, Wang made his self-criticism five times regarding his "mistakes" at the Lushan plenum. In Wang's own words, he "made the inappropriate comments that brought negative effects on the unity [of the party] and the smooth process of the conference" and, more important, "acted as the gunner of counterrevolutionary element Chen Boda." See Shu Yun, *Lin Biao shijian wanzheng diaocha* [The complete investigation on Lin Biao's incident], vol. 1, pp. 269–72; *Wu Jicheng huiyilu*, p. 172.

[67] Xuezhi Guo, "Dimensions of Guanxi in Chinese Elite Politics," *China Journal*, vol. 42 (2001), p. 77.

that Mao was disgusted with the Gang of Four because he believed that they frequently created conflict with members of the Politburo, Wang immediately followed Mao's lead in ordering all personnel of the Central General Office to study Mao's criticism of the Gang of Four. Wang's actions infuriated Jiang Qing, the leader of the Gang of Four, and became the source of the conflict between Wang and the Maoist radicals.

Wang Dongxing built a strong *guanxi* network based on personal loyalty in the security services. He firmly controlled both the Central Guard Bureau and Unit 8341. According to Zhang Yaoci, commander of Unit 8341 and a trusted follower of Wang Dongxing, Unit 8341, the crack army unit charged with guarding CCP's top leaders, had been under the direct leadership of Wang Dongxing (and by extension Mao) since the early 1950s.[68] The quintessential example of this was the successful cooperation between Wang and his trusted followers against the Gang of Four after Mao's death in October 1976. Wang agreed to cooperate with Hua Guofeng and Ye Jianying against the Gang of Four by secretly contacting some of his key assistants and ordering them to monitor the Gang of Four.[69] Wang Dongxing asked Sun Fengshan, Wang Hongwen's bodyguard, to keep close watch over Wang Hongwen, paying particular attention to how frequently Wang Hongwen carried a gun.[70] Among the high-ranking leaders who participated in the political maneuvers against the Gang of Four that eventually defeated the Maoist radicals, Wang was undoubtedly the most important figure leading to the arrest of the Gang of Four because of his role in commanding the central security forces against the Maoist radicals.

Central Guard Bureau under Dual Leadership

The most powerful security force under the jurisdiction of the PLA is undoubtedly the Central Guard Bureau. The Central Guard Bureau is under the dual leadership of the PLA General Staff Department and the Central General Office. Although the personnel of the Central Guard Bureau receive the credentials of party membership and assignments from the Central General Office, day-to-day operations, such as political education, promotion and demotion issues, and logistics and supplies, are received from the PLA General Staff Department. Like the CGB, most of the CCP's security apparatuses were under dual civilian and military leadership. Technically, the Central Guard Bureau has more than just dual leadership: it is also known as the Ninth Bureau of the Ministry of Public Security and as such receives technical guidance from the Ministry of Public Security.[71] Although the CGB is organizationally required to accept

---

[68] See Zhang Yaoci, *Zhang Yaoci huiyi Mao Zedong*, pp. 1–3.
[69] See *Wu Jicheng huiyilu*, p. 388.
[70] Ibid., pp. 388–9.
[71] *Summary of the Meeting on Adjusting Guard Apparatus and Improving the Work of Security Guard*, Central General Office Document, no. 20 (1979).

leadership from all three organizations – the CCP General Office, the MPS, and the PLA General Staff Department, it often only follows the command of the paramount leader such as Mao, Deng Xiaoping, or Jiang Zemin.[72] Considering its leading role in security detail for top leaders, it does not have local branches but is authorized to command the Central Guard Regiment.

However, the CGB was not put under the dual leadership of the CGO and the PLA General Chief Staff until October 1969. When the Central Guard Bureau was created through the merger of the Department of Administration (*xingzheng chu*) and the Department of Guard (*jingwei chu*) of the Central General Office and was named the Ninth Bureau of the MPS in 1953,[73] it was mainly responsible for guarding five main secretaries – Mao, Liu Shaoqi, Zhou Enlai, Zhu De, and Chen Yun – as well as the members of the Politburo and the Central Secretariat with residences in Zhongnanhai. The foundation of the Central Guard Bureau was the Guard Department of the Eighth Bureau, which consisted of several departments such as security guard, health care, and supplies.[74] By April 1964, the Central Guard Bureau was enlarged when it absorbed the Eighth Bureau of the MPS.[75] Through the creation of the Second Security Department (*jingwei erchu*), the merger expanded the Central Guard Bureau's power from guarding only the top CCP leaders at the levels of the Politburo Standing Committee to guarding the general high-ranking officials who had been previously guarded by the Eighth Bureau of the MPS.

Under its dual leadership, the Central Guard Regiment received tasks from the Central Guard Bureau but was subordinate to the PLA.[76] The CGB has been associated with the PLA since October 1969, when the Central Guard Regiment, a PLA unit organizationally subordinate to the PLA General Staff Department but that received commands from the CGB, was officially absorbed into the Central Guard Bureau.[77] The reorganized Central Guard Bureau also became a military unit that received dual leadership from the CCP General Staff Department and the Central General Office. The merged Central Guard Bureau was renamed the Central Guard Department and was granted the military rank of the army corps (*jun*) given its subordination to the PLA General Staff Department.[78] It was not until 1979, when Deng Xiaoping regained control over the PLA, that the PLA General Staff Department was granted main

---

[72] In the Mao era, Mao directly commanded Wang Dongxing for his security needs; none of the three organizations were allowed to ask Wang for Mao's whereabouts. Under Deng Xiaoping and Jiang Zeming, the CGB chief received the command only from the paramount leader, even though the three organizations had administrative responsibilities over the CGB such as recruitment, logistics, supplies, education, and training.

[73] *Hongqiang tonghua*, pp. 175–6.

[74] See *Wu Jicheng huiyilu*, p. 93

[75] Ibid., pp. 94–5.

[76] *Hongqiang tonghua*, pp. 176–7.

[77] *Wu Jicheng huiyilu*, p. 155.

[78] Ibid., pp. 155–6.

authority over the Central Guard Bureau; it was officially renamed the Guard Bureau of the CCP General Staff Department (*zong canmou bu jingwei ju*) at that time. Although the Central Guard Regiment officially became a subordinate unit of the Central Guard Bureau – mainly a civilian organization under dual civilian and military leadership – it remained a military unit; its personnel were active-duty service members.

In the CCP's history, the dual leadership over the Central Guard Bureau has reflected less on improved organizational efficiency, operational and combat effectiveness, organizational cohesiveness, discipline, and high morale than on its role in serving the power politics in the top leadership. In the 1950s and early 1960s, the Central Guard Bureau was under the dual leadership of both the CGO and the MPS: the CGO took charge of its daily administration and the MPS provided professional guidance.[79] The dual leadership hardly functioned well, as the paramount leader monopolized control over the CGB. The Cultural Revolution paralyzed the MPS, and Mao no longer allowed the MPS to lead the central elite security forces or to involve the central security services. Because of the close working relationship between the CGB and the MPS, the party leadership distrusted the CGB and even planned to abolish its two guard departments and incorporate them into the Central Guard Regiment, which was under the jurisdiction of the PLA, led by Lin Biao.[80] In October 1969, both the CGB and the CGR merged, and the newly established Central Guard Department of the CGO fell under the dual leadership of the Central General Office and the CCP's General Staff Department.[81] Although the CGB was still known as the Ninth Bureau of the MPS, the MPS was no longer authorized to lead the CGB.

In 1979, the PLA's General Chief of Staff Deng Xiaoping authorized the PLA General Staff Department to take full control of the CGB in acting against Wang Dongxing and his followers. Deng Xiaoping separated the Second Guard Department from the CGB and returned it to the jurisdiction of the Eighth Bureau of the MPS. Under the leadership of Jiang Zemin, the dual leadership of the CGO and the PLA General Staff Department was further strengthened, and the CGO ensured the party's control over the CGB and assigned tasks, whereas the PLA General Staff Department took charge of personnel appointments and promotions and provided logistical support. In the eras of Deng Xiaoping and Jiang Zemin, the MPS no longer had authority over the CGB, and the Ninth Bureau was only a titular organization. Compared with the MPS before the Cultural Revolution, in which Wang Dongxing was a vice minister, no CGB official has been appointed vice minister of the MPS in the post-Mao era. It was not until 1995 that the CGB was organizationally expanded and that there were increasing requests for the CGB coordinate with the MPS

[79] *Hongqiang tonghua*, pp. 175–6.
[80] See *Wu Jicheng huiyilu*, p. 132.
[81] Ibid., pp. 155–6.

(especially the Eighth Bureau) to protect top leaders. The role of the Ninth Bureau of the MPS was again emphasized. However, the Ninth Bureau was closer to the Operations Department or Command and Coordination Center of the CGB, a subordinate unit of the CGB, than to the whole CGB. Because the CGB did not have local branches nationwide, only in the capital, the CGB's leading role in coordinating security became significant when top leaders and foreign leaders were outside Beijing, where the local branches of the Eighth Bureau of the MPS were ordered to receive orders from the CGB. In the post-Deng era, the paramount leaders have taken aggressive approaches to control the CGB: Jiang Zemin monopolized his control over the CGB through his trusted follower You Xigui, and Hu Jintao relied on Ling Jihua, director of the CGO, to command and control the CGB. In both eras, the role of the PLA General Staff Department in leading the CGB has increasingly become symbolic.

The Central Security Services and the Role of Wang Dongxing

To gain in-depth comprehension of the CCP's central security apparatuses and services, a detailed and careful examination of Wang Dongxing's role can help us further understand the features, mechanisms, and operating principles of the central security apparatuses as well as their important role in leadership politics. Although Mao established the Red Army and the elite security forces in the Jiangxi base areas, he lost control over the Red Army and the elite security forces from 1931 to 1934, after the returned students gradually dominated the party leadership in the Jiangxi base areas. Once Mao had established control over the Red Army at the Zunyi Conference in January 1935, he began to focus on personally controlling the top-level CCP security forces and enabling local party organizations to take the lead of local security apparatuses. Mao's power was further consolidated after the Yan'an rectification of the 1940s, because by then his indisputable decision-making authority regarding the security apparatus had been accepted by party leaders. Beginning in April 1947, when Wang Dongxing was appointed Mao's chief bodyguard by the Social Affairs Department (SAD), Mao began to cultivate Wang's personal loyalty.[82] As part of his strategy to reward Wang for his loyalties, when the CCP leadership moved to Beijing in April 1949 and the top leaders' residences were in the northern suburbs of Beijing, Mao authorized Wang Dongxing to lead the elite security services for both the CCP's and the CMC's top leaders.[83] Thus, with Mao's support and the still-nascent organizational systems of the CCP security

---

[82] According to Shi Zhe, it was by his recommendation that Wang Dongxing was appointed to head Mao's security and become Mao's chief bodyguard. See Shi Zhe, *Mao Zedong de fanyi: Shi Zhe yanzhong de gaoceng renwu* [Interpreter of Mao Zedong: The high-level figures in the eyes of Shi Zhe], p. 43.
[83] See *Wu Jicheng huiyilu*, pp. 31–2.

apparatus, Wang Dongxing became closely linked with the CCP top security apparatus, as Mao had intended.

Contrary to most security officials in elite CCP ranks, Wang Dongxing did not have a strong background in the central security agencies or the military. Having joined the Red Army in 1932, he was mainly engaged in the Rear Service, where he was appointed political commissar of the Second Field Hospital of the Red Army in 1936 and political commissar of the Bethune International Peace General Hospital in 1937. It was not until April 1947 that Wang was appointed Mao's chief bodyguard, after Li Kenong, head of the SAD, ordered Wang Dongxing to accompany Zhou Enlai to northern Shaanxi after Zhou helped Ye Jianying and Yang Shangkun establish the Central Rear Area Working Committee in northwestern Shanxi.[84] As the personal *guanxi* and trust between Mao and Wang grew after Wang's appointment, Mao gradually felt comfortable enough to involve Wang in both his personal security and his family issues.

Among those who served Mao, Wang Dongxing was among those promoted most quickly. In 1947, Wang was Ye Zilong's assistant;[85] by May 1948 he had been promoted to the level of deputy director for the Administrative Office of the Central Secretariat, which was the same position held by Ye Zilong. The speed and nature of this promotion points to Mao's attempts to cultivate Wang's personal loyalty. At the same time, while in Yan'an, Mao approached Chen Long, director of the Third Office of the SAD and one of the most prestigious chief security guards, with the intent of persuading Chen to serve him as well. Mao focused on Wang Dongxing after Chen Long rejected Mao's offer and requested to be transferred to northern Manchuria as the director of the local SAD branch and the director of public security in Shenyang, near Chen's hometown.[86] In 1955, when the CCP awarded honors to its military

---

[84] See Ye Zilong, *Ye Zilong huiyilu* [Memoirs of Ye Zilong], p. 97; *Wu Jicheng huiyilu*, p. 25.

[85] Li Yinqiao, "Wogei Maozhuxi dang weishi" [I was Chairman Mao's guard], in Sun Mingshan (ed.), *Lishi shunjian* [An instant in history] (Beijing: Qunzhong chubanshe, 2004), vol. 3, p. 186; Wang Dongxing was deputy chief of staff to Ye Zilong, chief of staff of administration of the Central Front Commission, the leading body headed by Ren Biao that was created in April 1947 to serve Mao. See Ye Zilong, *Ye Zilong huiyilu*, pp. 97–8.

[86] In Yan'an, Chen Long served in the CCP Social Department and led the CCP security forces against spies and assassins sent by both the Nationalist government and Japanese armies. In 1946 when Mao went to Chongqing for peace negotiations with the Nationalist government, Chen Long was Mao's chief bodyguard who successfully executed Mao's security duty. After returning from Chongqing, Mao tried to keep Chen Long as his chief bodyguard. Chen denied Mao's offer, asking to be transferred to Manchuria, where communists and Nationalists were fighting for dominance. Later, Mao offered to transfer Chen to Beijing again in 1949 and 1954. Chen refused in all cases, because he was concerned about getting along with Jiang Qing. See Ma Xianglin and Xu Yan, "Baohu Mao zhuxi Chongqing tanpan – ji 'hujia de Zhao Zilong' Chen Long" [The protection of Chairman Mao in the Chongqing negotiations – "Zhao Zilong escorted the emperor" – Chen Long], in *Beijing qingnian bao* [Beijing youth daily], October 27, 2001.

personnel, among the 802 major generalships granted, only Wang Dongxing was not granted a military position. On December 21, 1955, Wang Dongxing was appointed a vice minister of public security and served as Mao's representative to the Ministry of Public Security while continuing to serve as Mao's chief bodyguard in Zhongnanhai. In summary, Mao's desire both to personally control the security forces and to establish additional personal security forces outside the institutionalized apparatus supports the idea that Mao wanted an individual with whom he had close ties to directly control the central security apparatuses.

However, Wang's control of the central security apparatus was weakened after the security forces that guarded Zhongnanhai and the high-ranking leaders who lived there merged with the Chinese People's Public Security Forces (CPPSF) in 1949. The merger was a fait accompli and brought Zhongnanhai's security forces under the direction of Luo Ruiqing, with whom Mao did not have strong personal loyalty because of Luo's lack of personal and career contacts, even though Luo had historically had close ties with Mao's faction. Thus, in May 1953, Mao separated the Central Guard Regiment (CGR) from the CPPSF, reorganizing it to become an independent armed security force for the specific purpose of guarding top party leaders. Zhang Yaoci, Wang's longtime associate, was appointed to head the newly reorganized Central Guard Regiment. Despite its organizational affiliation to the PLA, the Central Guard Regiment received orders from Wang Dongxing, who was both director of the Central Guard Bureau under the CGO and director of the Ninth Bureau under the Ministry of Public Security. In actuality, because the Central Guard Bureau and the Ninth Bureau were the exact same organization, but with different names, Wang Dongxing held one position but two titles. One of the compelling explanations for the CGB to have two names contributes to the political compromise in the party leadership: the party bureaucracy needed to institutionalize the security apparatuses and their services while Mao attempted to establish a personal security force that helped him monitor the bureaucracy as well as his associates. The central mission of the CGB was to lead the Central Guard Regiment to protect the five greater secretaries, the high-ranking leaders and agencies in Zhongnanhai, the Mount Yuquan, and the New Six Buildings (*xin liu suo*).[87]

During the Cultural Revolution, the Central Guard Bureau became Mao's personal security force, helping him to minimize the influence of his political opponents, to prevent ranking leaders from solidifying political alliances, to ensure the security and loyalty of the leadership through careful monitoring, to contain the army units that were viewed as threats to Maoist radicals, and to command the PLA units against possible rebellions from followers of the army leaders. The reason the Central Guard Bureau played such a powerful and important role in the security apparatuses can be partially

---

[87] Zhang Yaoci, *Zhang Yaoci huiyi Mao Zedong*, p. 2.

attributed to Mao's monopoly on decision making after the collapse of the Yan'an Roundtable. Mao moved strategically to use the security apparatus, including the Central Guard Bureau, as a tool to ensure that his policies were executed and that his personal preferences were imposed on other ranking leaders.

The Cultural Revolution was the apex of Mao's personal control over the Central Guard Bureau and the security apparatus as a whole. Specifically, Mao used two approaches during the Cultural Revolution to achieve absolute control over the security apparatus. First, he established a centralized and cohesive security force that received orders directly and exclusively from Mao. Of course, Mao could not hold all the positions in the security apparatus himself, so as director of the CGO and the Central Guard Bureau, Wang Dongxing was the vehicle for Mao's orders and he pulled the strings in the security apparatus. Wang was very effective in ensuring Mao's personal security and the security of other high-ranking leaders, whom Mao relied on for the assault against the party bureaucracy and the frontline leaders.

A good example of Wang's role in following Mao's directives and protecting the top leaders was the mass riots of 1967 and 1968. From late 1967 to early 1968, mass violence spread throughout China, and the PLA had to suppress the radical mass rebels. Mao viewed this period as "unusual times" and therefore ordered Wang Dongxing to "heighten vigilance."[88] Mao ordered Wang to protect the security of the twelve key leaders – Mao, Lin Biao, Zhou Enlai, Chen Boda, Kang Sheng, Jiang Qing, Xie Fuzhi, Ye Qun, Yang Chengwu, Wu Faxian, Li Zuopeng, and Qiu Huizuo. Only these twelve leaders were exempt from checking in on entering and exiting Zhongnanhai, the People's Hall, Diaoyutai, and the Jingxi Hotel. Mao also ordered Wang Dongxing to equip the front and back guards with vehicles and to allocate armed guards to members of the Politburo Standing Committee (Jiang Qing was added to the list later) whenever they left their residences.[89]

These and other important activities relating to security were usually carried out through the combined efforts of the Central General Office, Central Guard Bureau, Unit 8341, and the Beijing Garrison Command. Occasionally, the PLA units were ordered to assist the security apparatus. Such a situation occurred on September 13, 1971, after Lin Biao attempted to flee to the Soviet Union and the 38th Army Corps was ordered to cooperate with the security forces. Moreover, the security apparatus was not simply Mao's personal security forces; they were also Mao's personal special forces that were sent to propagandize his ideas and enact his policies. This was the case in the security forces' involvement in the Six Factories and Two Universities campaign (*liuchang erxiao*). The security apparatus also worked to stop violent mass conflicts when Mao decided that the mass rebels had become out of control.

---

[88] See *Wu Jicheng huiyilu*, p. 142.
[89] Ibid., p. 142.

The security forces also helped Mao maintain control over high-ranking leaders and over important buildings and utilities. During the Cultural Revolution, the jurisdiction of the security apparatus covered the entire area from the Jingxi Hotel to Mount Yuquan, and from the People's Hall to Diaoyutai. Many of these locations had not been not guarded by the security apparatus before the Cultural Revolution. For instance, Diaoyutai was taken over by the Central Guard Bureau in November 1966, when the Cultural Revolution Group (CRG) established its headquarters there. When Diaoyutai was established, it was managed by the Foreign Ministry under the professional guidance of the Eighth Bureau of the Ministry of Public Security; in addition, the Chinese People's Public Security Forces (CPPSF) sent a company to work as the compound's external guards. Beginning in November 1966, the Central Guard Bureau supplied internal guards in Diaoyutai, and Unit 8341 supplied external guards (outside the buildings and at the entrance of the compound).[90] However, before Diaoyutai was officially taken over by the Central Guard Bureau, the People's Hall had already been handed over to the CGB and Unit 8341.[91] Wang's power further increased when he took control of the special case groups, which had been established to investigate suspicious activities of high-ranking leaders. These groups were frequently guilty of performing torture and other forms of maltreatment,[92] and they often decided whether suspected cadres would continue to be tortured or would be set free.[93]

The security forces also helped Mao obtain information outside Zhongnanhai. During the Cultural Revolution, Mao increasingly relied on the security forces for information by sending security personnel to engage in on-site investigations of many different CCP, PLA, and government organizations. Mao even dispatched security force officers as personal representatives to the local party and PLA units to gather information that would inform his decision making. For example, in 1969, once the border conflict between China and the Soviet Union became Mao's primary concern, Mao did not merely rely on the CMC (led by Lin Biao at the time) for intelligence; in April 1970, Mao sent Wang Dongxing to northeastern China, where Wang personally inspected the PLA's defense and preparedness for war with the Soviet Union. Wang traveled from Changchun to Heilongjiang and from Heilongjiang to Liaoning, carefully

---

[90] Ibid., pp. 117–19.

[91] Ibid., p. 117.

[92] Frederick C. Teiwes and Warren Sun, *The Tragedy of Lin Biao: Riding the Tiger during the Cultural Revolution*, p. 22.

[93] Wang Dongxing and Xie Fuzhi were assigned to take charge of the First and Third Offices, respectively. Huang Yongsheng and Wu Faxian headed the Second Office. See Zhu Yuanshi et al., *Wu De koushu: Shinian fengyu wangshi – Wozai Beijing gongzuo de yixie jingli* [Wu De's oral history: A ten-year hardship past – Some experiences from when I worked in Beijing], p. 175.

checking the grain, fodder, and ammunition depots; tunnels; antiaircraft forti-fications; and militia training bases.[94]

Through Wang Dongxing, Mao personally controlled all security appara-tuses within the party, government, and the PLA. By the Ninth Party Congress, held in April 1969, Wang had become an alternate member of the Politburo and represented the Chairman in controlling the Central General Office, Unit 8341, the Bureau of Central Health, the Bureau of Central Archives, and the Beijing Garrison Command. Considering Wang's control of the intelligence apparatus, the security forces, the welfare of high-ranking leaders, and the armed forces in Beijing, to a certain extent, Wang had considerably more power than Lin Biao or Zhou Enlai, whom Wang closely monitored. Evidence shows that Lin Biao's every action was monitored by the Central Guard Bureau and the Central Gen-eral Office, headed by Wang Dongxing.[95] A prime example of this monitoring is the system of secret telephones employed by the high-ranking leaders. These telephones, known as red phones, provided a direct line of communication among top leaders and were impervious to security breaches from the outside. However, they were not impervious to monitoring from the inside. According to Li Wenpu, Lin Biao's secretary in charge of Lin's security, all Lin's "secret telephones" were installed, and wiretapped, by the CGO. This explains why both Lin Biao and Zhou Enlai were extremely careful when dealing with Wang Dongxing.[96]

During the Cultural Revolution, Mao strategized to gain direct control of the PLA leaders. His first move was to control the security guards of the high-ranking PLA leaders. Before the Cultural Revolution, the security of army leaders was the responsibility of the Guard Department of the CMC Gen-eral Office. Beginning in August 1966, the Central General Office assigned guards to the PLA leadership in an attempt to gain control of security details and therefore to manipulate the PLA leadership. According to Zhang Yun-sheng, one of Lin Biao's secretaries, Lin's security, before the Cultural Revo-lution, was managed by the Guard Department of the CMC General Office. After August 1966, the Central Guard Bureau sent guards from Unit 8341 to "strengthen" security to guard Lin Biao. Thus, Lin's security was managed by both the Guard Department of the CMC General Office and the Central Guard Bureau. Ye Qun, Lin Biao's wife, tried to lessen the CGB and Unit 8341's involvement in Lin's security detail by secretly ordering Lin's previous

---

[94] Chen Xilian, *Chen Xilian huiyilu* [Memoirs of Chen Xilian], p. 451.

[95] According to Li Wenpu, Lin Biao's chief bodyguard, the two encrypted telephones in Lin Biao's residence were installed and administered by the CGO and the communication section of the PLA General Staff Department. See Li Wenpu, "Lin Biao weishizhang Li Wenpu bude bushuo" [Lin Biao's chief bodyguard Li Wenpu has to say], in *Zhonghua ernu* [Journal of Chinese people], no. 2, (1999), pp. 10–21.

[96] For example, one day Wang Dongxing visited Ye Qun. Because of the accent of Lin Biao's guard, Ye mistook Wang Dongxing for someone else. After Wang left, Ye fled into a rage and the guard was later fired. See *Maojiawan jishi*, pp. 118–20.

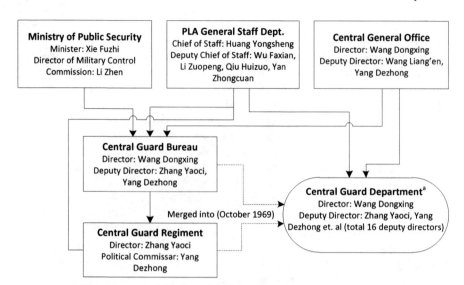

FIGURE 3.2. The Merger of Civil and Military Security Apparatuses, October 1969.
Source: Lingdao jigou yange, pp. 1086, 1102; *Wu Jicheng huiyilu*, p. 155.
[a] After October 1969, the Central Guard Bureau was renamed as the Central Guard Department of the Central General Office.

guards and secretaries to keep distance from those guards sent by the Central Guard Bureau.[97]

Mao's second move, which has been discussed before, was to merge Unit 8341 with the Central Guard Bureau of the CGO. Historically, Unit 8341 had been a subordinate unit of the PLA General Staff Department, even though Wang Dongxing had been the de facto chief of Unit 8341 since its establishment in 1953. Still, Mao thought it necessary to merge Unit 8341 into the Central Guard Bureau.[98] Even considering Wang's role as de facto chief of Unit 8341, the merger of the Central Guard Bureau and Unit 8341 in October 1969 was a notable step in Mao's strengthening control of the central security apparatus (Figure 3.2). Wang Dongxing was appointed commander of the new Guard Department of the Central General Office (*zhongyang bangongting jingwei chu*).[99] In the background of the merger, tensions surrounding the Sino-Soviet border were rising, Lin Biao's dominance in the PLA and influence in the party leadership was increasing, and conflict between Lin's faction and the Central Cultural Revolution Group (CRG) was developing.[100]

[97] Ibid., pp. 32, 243–6.
[98] See *Wu Jicheng huiyilu*, p. 155.
[99] Ibid., pp. 155–6.
[100] See Gao Wenqian, *Wannian Zhou Enlai* [Zhou Enlai's later years] (New York: Mirror Books, 2003), pp. 258–90.

After the merger, when it was necessary for the Central Guard Bureau to collaborate with other units, such as the Beijing Garrison Command, the Beijing Bureau of Public Security, local offices of the Bureau of Public Security, and PLA units, all directives originated with the Central Guard Department. The merger was successful in catalyzing Mao's efficient control of the security forces. By centralizing authority over the security forces into Wang Dongxing's hands, Mao was able to ensure his personal security and effectively monitor other high-ranking leaders. Wang Dongxing was the only person who handled Mao's personal security, such as assigning security guards, planning travel, scheduling meetings and activities, and knowing his whereabouts. Despite that local security forces contributed their services to Mao's security detail during his travels, the Central Guard Department always led Mao's personal security duties, including security for rail travel, which was conducted in specialized trains created specifically for Mao. The Central Guard Department's monopoly over Mao's security detail was such that local security forces were not even permitted to be in close proximity of Mao; they were allowed to guard only relevant roads and bridges.[101]

By 1971, after Lin Biao's death, Wang Dongxing had become a powerful figure in the CCP leadership – Wang not only completely controlled the security apparatus but also led the special case groups of investigation, which were assigned to investigate cases of suspected treason among high-ranking leaders. After Lin Biao was killed in an airplane crash, a new special case group was established to replace the three offices that had been created to investigate disgraced or imprisoned high-ranking leaders; Wang Dongxing was appointed to head all three offices.[102] To a certain extent, Wang held power over the disgraced high-ranking leaders and had the authority to decide on their sentencing, particularly whether it would involve torture or maltreatment. Although Mao ensured his own security and achieved complete control over other ranking leaders by relying on Wang Dongxing, Wang retained autonomy in much high-level decision making regarding security matters through his association with the Chairman. Mao promoted Wang as a member of the Politburo in 1973, and Wang became vice chairman of the CCP Central Committee in 1977 (Figure 3.3).

Wang Dongxing lost his power during the Third Plenum, in December 1978, when Deng Xiaoping emerged victorious from the power struggle and unveiled his vision of economic reform. The Third Plenum also set the stage for further victories for veteran leaders following the reorganization of the security apparatuses and services and the removal of Wang Dongxing. One of these victories was that key followers and subordinates of Wang Dongxing were dismissed or transferred. Those who served Wang Dongxing but were

---

[101] See Shu Yun, "Huimou 1971: Zaitan 'wuqiyi gongcheng' zhimi" [Recall 1971: Reevaluate the myth of Project 571], in *Shidai wenxue* [Times literature], no. 4 (2004), p. 21.
[102] See *Wu De koushu*, p. 175.

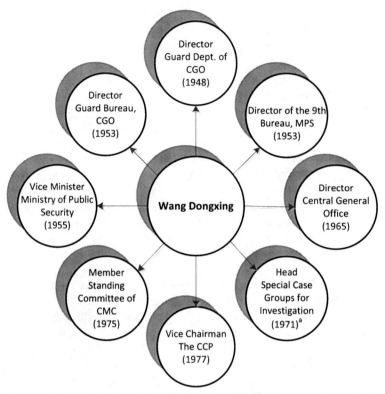

FIGURE 3.3. The Evolution of Wang Dongxing's Power and Authority, 1948–77.
Source: *Lingdao jigou yange*, pp. 976, 1101–2; Zhang Yaoci, *Zhang Yaoci huiyi Mao Zedong*, pp. 1–2.

[a] The special case groups were created to investigate high-ranking leaders under suspicion. In the early Cultural Revolution, Wang Dongxing, Huang Yongsheng and Wu Fashian, and Xie Fuzhi were assigned to take charge of the First, Second, and Third Offices, respectively. After Lin Biao died, the Second Office was abolished, and the First Office and Second Office were combined, with Wang Dongxing appointed head of the combined office. See *Wu De koushu*, p. 175.

not charged with having made "mistakes" were asked to leave Beijing and were transferred to local military units, where they were appointed to symbolic positions such as deputy commander of a military district, as in the case of Wu Jicheng, deputy director of the CGB, who was transferred to be one of the eight deputy commanders in the Anhui Military District. In addition, they were also ordered to retire early and were not allowed to return to Beijing, where their families lived. According to "Document no. 1," issued by the State Council and the Central Military Commission in 1982, the age of retirement for an army corps–level official was sixty years, but he or she would be allowed to stay in that position if necessary. However, Wu Jicheng was ordered to retire when he was only fifty-five years old and was not allowed to return to Beijing, where his family lived, until 1993, eleven years after he retired.[103] The stories of these individuals' careers and their historical connections show that, clearly, the purges and transfers of Wang's followers and other leading figures in the Central Guard Bureau were intended to eliminate Wang Dongxing's influence in the top security apparatus and to ensure the dominance of the veteran leaders in the leadership of the CGB and Unit 8341.

The Central Guard Bureau in the Post-Mao Era

In the leadership politics of the post-Mao CCP, the elite security apparatuses have continued to play an important role in guarding and protecting high-ranking leaders; they also have a crucial, often decisive, role in leadership politics. Because of the CGB's importance, control of the CGB became significant when the power struggle between veterans, led by Deng Xiaoping and Chen Yun; and the Two Whatevers faction headed by Hua Guofeng, Mao's designated successor, took place following the arrest of the Gang of Four. The veterans ultimately defeated the Two Whatevers faction and successfully controlled the central security apparatuses through three initiatives. First, the veteran leaders ordered the PLA to take control of the central security forces. Under Deng Xiaoping's leadership, the CCP's General Staff Department was responsible for logistics, training, supplies, and appointments and promotions of personnel of the central security forces, and it had a monopoly on assignments, which was previously the responsibility of the Central General Office. Although the CGO and the MPS provided day-to-day administration and professional guidance, respectively, the PLA General Staff Department had authority over the Central Guard Bureau in political control, appointments and promotions, and logistical supplies.[104] Second, Deng took another key initiative to undermine the powerful influence of the CGB, headed by Wang Dongxing and Wang's trusted followers, by resuming the Eighth Bureau of the MPS and ordering the CGB to return a large amount of security responsibilities to the Eighth Bureau.[105] Third, the veteran leaders dismissed Wang Dongxing as head of the central security apparatuses and purged a large number of his followers (Table 3.1).

The Central General Office gradually resumed its power in the dual leadership of the Central Guard Bureau after Jiang Zemin became head of the CCP. In the post-Deng era, the Central Guard Bureau has remained a powerful and special military unit in the PLA. In 1995, it was reportedly upgraded from the level of army corps to the deputy military region (*fu da junqu*). This rank is

---

[103] *Wu Jicheng huiyilu*, pp. 438–42.

[104] See *Summary of the Meeting on Adjusting Guard Apparatus and Improving the Work of Security Guard*, in Central General Office Document, no. 20 (1979).

[105] Zhang Qihou, "Zhonggong jianzheng wushi nian gong'an bu fazhan yange" [Development and evolution of MPS in the CCP fifty-year nation building], in Zhongguo dalu wenti yanjiu suo (ed.), *Zhonggong jianzheng wushi nian* [CCP fifty-year nation building], (Taipei: Zhengzhong shuju gufen youyan gongsi, 2001), p. 62.

TABLE 3.1. *Leadership Changes in the CGB and the CGR, 1979–1980*

Officials	Positions in 1979	Positions in 1980
Wang Dongxing	Director of the Central General Office, director of Guard Department of the Central General Office	
Zhang Yaoci	Deputy director of the Central General Office, associate director of Central Guard Bureau, commander of the CGR	Deputy chief of staff, Chengdu Military Region
Wu Jianhua	Deputy director of Central Guard Bureau, political commissar of the CGR	Deputy director of the Political Department, Shaanxi Provincial Military District
Wu Jicheng	Deputy director of Central Guard Bureau	Deputy commander, Anhui Provincial Military District
Mao Weizhong	Deputy director of Central Guard Bureau	
Li Zhao	Deputy director of Central Guard Bureau, deputy commander of the CGR	Deputy commander, Shangdong Provincial Military District
Di Fucai	Deputy director of Central Guard Bureau, deputy political commissar of the CGR	Deputy commander, Hubei Provincial Military District

Source: Wu Jicheng huiyilu, pp. 420–1, 438–9, 442.

much higher than that of other second-tier departments, such as the Second and Third Departments of the PLA General Staff Department, and its directors have been either lieutenant generals or senior generals – for example, Yang Dezhong and You Xigui. Because leadership security involves other security organizations such as the MPS and the Beijing Garrison Command, the Central Guard Bureau, as the institution in charge of security of top leaders, is authorized to command and coordinate other security apparatuses.

Although the general trend of CCP politics in the post-Deng era can be characterized as increasingly institutionalized, and Chinese civil-military relations as more professionalized, personalistic politics continue to play an important role in the central security apparatus. Whereas Deng Xiaoping relied mainly on Yang Dezhong to ensure control over the Central Guard Bureau, Jiang Zemin gained control over the elite security apparatus through Zeng Qinghong and You Xigui. After Jiang was appointed party chief, he gradually established his dominance over the security forces. This was a multistep process that involved consolidating control over the Central Guard Bureau in the hands of a close and loyal follower, much as Mao and Deng had done in previous eras.

In this consolidation of power, Zeng Qinghong formally replaced Wen Jiabao as director of the Central General Office in the Fourteenth Party Congress, which legitimized Zeng as the commanding officer of the security apparatus responsible for Zhongnanhai security. Second, Jiang manipulated Yang Dezhong so that he would have to leave his position as head of the CGB. Before serving Jiang, Yang Dezhong had served Zhou Enlai, Deng Xiaoping, Hu Yaobang, and Zhao Ziyang, but never Jiang – because the two had never worked closely together, they had never established a personal relationship. Therefore, Jiang supported his followers in taking control of the CGB, gradually ousting Yang as the head, by transferring You Xigui, Jiang's chief bodyguard, to be deputy director of the CGB. It was a multistage process, and Jiang had to bestow many benefits on Yang Dezhong to gain his favor and manipulate him into taking a career path that would be beneficial to both men. To begin, during Jiang's first visit to the United States, he took Yang with him in the position of special assistant to the PRC chairman. In 1994, Jiang promoted Yang to senior general, a military rank for which Yang was not yet qualified, then encouraged him to retire early with this honorable rank. Yang accepted Jiang's offer and retired, after which, in early 1996, Jiang formerly appointed You Xigui as the new head of the CGB.

Third, by appointing You Xigui director of the Central Guard Bureau after Yang Dezhong retired, Jiang was able to have direct and effective control over both civilian and military leaders. Moreover, to ensure You's absolute loyalty and to further You's dominance in the security forces, Jiang promoted You to major general in 1995, lieutenant general in 1997, and senior general in 2004. The promotions were a win-win situation for Jiang. Given his historically weak ties with the army, Jiang's promotions of Yang and You, as well as of a large number of other PLA officers, fit into his larger strategy of gaining favor to cultivate loyalty and authority. His moves to rectify his weak links with the PLA required him to manipulate politics within the PLA leadership, which involved winning PLA generals' favor by freely granting salary increases and promotions, as he had done with Yang and You. As an indication of Jiang's generosity with prestigious rewards for PLA leaders, since 1993, he has held seven ceremonies for conferring medals to PLA members, promoting more than 530 army officers to the rank of major general, lieutenant general, and general. Of these promotions, seventy-three were generals.

Under Hu Jintao's leadership, the party's control over military and security agencies has been increasingly based on the authority of institutions; formalized methods of interactions; and an emphasis on rule, law, and regulations. Unlike his predecessors, who relied on personal ties and loyalty to control key security apparatuses, Hu seems to have a comfortable dominance only in the Central General Office, which is headed by his trusted follower Ling Jihua. Nothing indicates that Hu has gained power over the top security forces, such as the Central Guard Bureau, the Central Guard Regiment, and the Guard Bureau of the CMC General Office. Although General You Xigui's retirement opened a space for Hu to consolidate his power by appointing a longtime follower, Hu failed to have Yan Min, deputy director of the CGB and Hu's chief body guard,[106] appointed as head of the CGB.[107] According to official news in January 2006 from the Jiangsu Province Public Relations Association, Yan's official title before being ordered to retire was "chief bodyguard of the CCP General Secretary and the PRC Chairman."[108]

Perhaps to keep You Xigui as chief of the security forces, Jiang took two initiatives related to retirement and ranking before he handed over the position of CMC chairman to Hu Jintao in September 2004. First, Jiang used the case of Yang Dezhong as a precedent to justify that the CGB chief could be a person with the rank of senior general; therefore the age limit for the director of the CGB could be extended to sixty-five years, with a possible additional five-year extension if necessary. According to Xu Ping, a senior colonel in the PLA, an expert on PLA military rank, and a faculty member of the PLA Logistical and Command Institute, there is a de facto five-year extension for generals at the level of military region and above, if the general serves in central PLA departments rather than the local military regions.[109] Second, Jiang promoted You Xigui to senior general in June 2004, three months before You's sixty-fifth birthday, thus allowing You to qualify as a senior member of the PLA leadership and justifying his continuation as security chief of the party and army leadership.[110] Yan was sixty-one years old when You Xigui retired in 2007, which put Yan at a disadvantage in competing with other CGB deputy directors, such as Cao Qing, who was six years his junior.[111] Because of the change in retirement policy, the promotion of You to general, and Yan's relative old age, Yan was not promoted to direct the CGB, which affected Hu's ability to consolidate power over the security forces. Although the security apparatus has become increasingly professionalized in the post-Deng era, the legacy of personalistic politics still affects the leadership today, as evidenced by the politics surrounding the director of the CGB.

Since the Cultural Revolution, the directors of the Central Guard Bureau have always been the chief bodyguards or trusted loyalists of the paramount leaders, as with Mao Zedong and Wang Dongxing, Deng Xiaoping and Yang Dezhong, and Jiang Zemin and You Xigui. Because this pattern of leadership

---

[106] Cheng Li, "The New Military Elite: Generational Profile and Contradictory Trends," in David Michael Finkelstein (ed.), *Civil-Military Relations in Today's China: Swimming in a New Sea*, p. 68.

[107] Hu Jintao and Yan Min had more than just professional ties. Both were born in Taizhou, Jiangsu, and had studied at Taizhou Middle School, from which Hu graduated in 1959 and Yan graduated in 1964.

[108] See Jiangsu Province Public Relations Association, *Dangdai junjie* [Contemporary military arena], http://www.jspra.gov.cn/hycfo.asp?uid=764 (accessed July 7, 2008).

[109] Xu Ping, interview, in *Xinwen huike ting* [Room for news interview], CCTV, August 3, 2006.

[110] See "Zhongyang junwei longzhong juxing shangjiang junxian jingxian yishi" [The CMC solemnly held the ceremony for promoting PLA and PAP generals], in *Jiefangjun bao* [PLA daily], June 21, 2004.

[111] Yan was born in 1946 and Cao in 1952.

for the CGB seemed so established, Western media predicted that Yan Min, the chief bodyguard of Hu Jintao, would replace You Xigui after his retirement.[112] Unexpectedly, Yan Min lost the position to Cao Qing.[113] There has been very little information about Cao in official media outlets, except for his age and then positions as alternate member of the Central Committee and director of the CGB.[114] As Cao has climbed the ladder, so to speak, in the Central Guard Bureau and the Central Guard Regiment, his résumé indicates that his career success is due to promotion by his longtime superiors, with You Xigui being the most influential. You Xigui served the Central Guard Regiment since 1958, beginning as a health-care specialist; in 1995, he was promoted to director of the CGB and served in that capacity until his retirement in 2007. When Cao Qing was promoted to deputy director of the CGB in May 2006, it was a clear sign that Cao would succeed You Xigui to take charge of the Central Guard Bureau after You retired. Perhaps Hu realized his limited personal influence on the central security apparatuses and thus paid great attention to his control over the Central General Office, through which Hu exerts his control over the central security apparatuses.

[112] See *Reuters*, January 12, 2006.

[113] A local official media source has identified that Yan Min was no longer the deputy director of the Guard Bureau as the retired Yan was invited to attend the opening ceremony of the China Wetland Ecotourism Festival, held in Jiangyan, Jiangsu, on April 6, 2006 (Yan was referred to as former deputy director of the Guard Bureau in the news). See "Shoujie zhongguo shidi shengtai luyoujie ji 2006 zhongguo jiangyan/qinzhang huichuan jie shengda kaimu" [Grand opening ceremony of first China wetland ecotourism festival and Jiangyan-Qinzhang boat competition], http://www.qintong.gov.cn/include/show.asp?id=1260 (accessed June 3, 2008).

[114] On the official Web site of the National People's Congress, Cao Qing was listed as a PLA delegate and educated at Zhongnanhai Amateur University (*Zhongnanhai yeyu daxue*), a school designed specifically for training employees of the Central General Office system, which organizationally includes the Central Guard Bureau. Thus, from his career path and educational background, it is evident that Cao's career has been closely tied with the Central Guard Bureau. See "Daibiao xinxi" [Information of representatives], in *Zhongguo renda wang* [NPC online], http://www.npc.gov.cn/delegate/viewDelegate.action?dbid=200811294407 (accessed June 4, 2008).

4

Elite Security Force

Central Guard Regiment

As the elite security force of the CCP, historically the Central Guard Regiment has played a paramount role in China's elite politics. This chapter addresses the historical context in which the Central Guard Regiment emerged, evolved, and developed, which dates back to the communist Soviet Republic in the Jiangxi base areas during the 1930s. In the base areas, the paramilitary policing units were used to pacify base areas, secure party conferences and key meetings, guard party and army leaders, and implement intraparty purges. In early 1930, when the returned students infiltrated the base areas, the organizational structure of CCP security forces experienced a decisive shift toward the Soviet NKVD model – that of highly centralized leadership characterized by vertical command. The CCP security forces gradually became powerful paramilitary units controlled directly by the State Political Security Bureau. These paramilitary security units used terror as their dominant military strategy, undertaking a number of brutal operations against other Red Army and party units, especially involving intraparty purges. The rise of Mao after the Zunyi Conference in January 1935 signified an important change of the security apparatuses, as they abandoned the Soviet-style vertical command system and emphasized the party's control and dual leadership based on the principle of mutual surveillance.

Professionalism of the CCP security apparatus had been an overriding goal of the party elite in the early 1950s. With the establishment of the "new" People's Republic, the legacy of leadership consensus created by the Yan'an Roundtable became the guiding principle for elite decision making.[1] With

---

[1] For example, Frederick C. Teiwes argues that there existed overall unity in the CCP's top leadership in the early 1950s, even though leadership cleavages and tensions did play a role in elite politics. See Frederick C. Teiwes, *Politics at Mao's Court: Gao Gang and Party Factionalism in the Early 1950s.*

Mao's power firmly consolidated and virtually indisputable to all, however, it was in his political interest to maintain the position of the party's sole and final decision maker in order to push his political and economic programs. One of Mao's major political moves during the 1950s and the early 1960s was to undermine the institutionalization of the CCP security apparatus to achieve personal control over the central security apparatus and to achieve allegiance from other ranking leaders. His personal control of the security apparatus became particularly significant when Mao planned his assault on the party bureaucracy in the mid-1960s.

Thus, this chapter investigates the inherent flaws in the development of the security forces in Mao's era, the greatest of which was Mao's unilateral control over the elite security forces, such as the Central Guard Bureau and the Central Guard Regiment, whereas other Party and state security agencies such as the Ministry of Public Security and the People's Armed Police Forces were pushed toward institutionalization. Mao developed powerful personal security forces to guarantee his continued dominance within CCP leadership, and he manipulated and deployed those security forces to ensure the loyalty of high-ranking leaders, to minimize the influence of his political opponents, to prevent ranking leaders from solidifying political alliances, to ensure the loyalty of other leaders through surveillance and protection, to contain army leaders considered potential threats, and to perform a leading role in commanding PLA units against possible rebellions from followers of the army leaders. Mao's monopoly of decision making following the collapse of the Yan'an Roundtable led to the CCP security apparatus becoming a behemoth in elite politics, particularly in the Cultural Revolution, when Mao used the Central Guard Regiment as a personal tool not only to guard, watch, punish, arrest, and imprison high-ranking leaders but also to ensure the execution of his policies and programs. This two-track control over the security forces not only undermined party bureaucracy authority but also proved problematic for promoting the principles of collective leadership inherited. In addition, the chapter delineates the relationship between the security apparatus and other leading party organizations, specifically the party bureaucracy and the PLA. The chapter also discusses the evolution of the Central Guard Regiment from an agency subordinate to the party, government, and PLA to superior armed forces controlled directly by Mao.

Also outlined in this chapter is the interplay between the Central Guard Regiment and elite politics in the post-Mao era. Post-Mao leaders paid great attention to the Central Guard Regiment, although they maintained varied relationships with the organization. Although Deng Xiaoping did not have a personal security force like Mao did, Deng established and developed a powerful network based on personal connections to control the central security apparatus. Unlike Mao, who depended heavily on Wang Dongxing for his control over the Central Guard Bureau and Unit 8341, Deng's control over the central security apparatus was achieved through direct and personal interactions with a number of security officials trusted by the veteran leaders, especially former generals of the Second Field Army, led by Liu Bocheng and Deng Xiaoping himself. Although Jiang Zemin relied heavily on the security apparatus to ensure his authority and security by transferring his close followers to lead the security apparatuses, including the Central Guard Regiment, Hu Jintao has strived to control the Central Guard Regiment through his dominance over the Central General Office, to which the CGR is subordinate. As professionalization of Chinese civil-military relations increasingly plays an important role in elite politics, Chinese politics in the post-Deng era can be characterized as increasingly institutionalized. Nonetheless, personal ties, loyalty, personal influence, and informal methods of control continue to play a critical role in the organization and operation of the security apparatuses given their vital role in the political survival and dominance of top leaders.

From Central Guard Brigade to Central Guard Regiment

The Special Service Team (*tewu dui*) of the General Front Committee was established in Jiangxi in October 1930 as the first military unit employed to guard top leaders. Its primary tasks were to guard the top leaders of the Red Army General Front Committee (*zong qiandi weiyuanhui* or *zong qianwei*) – Mao Zedong and Zhu De. It was expanded in December 1930 and named the Special Service Brigade (*tewu dadui*), with more than three hundred armed personnel under the leadership of Gu Bo, general secretary of the General Front Committee and a trusted follower of Mao.[2] Beginning in April 1931, the central delegation, controlled by returned students, gradually dominated the leadership of the Jiangxi base area, and Mao lost his power in the Gangnan Conference of November 1931. The CCP Central Bureau of the Jiangxi Soviet elected Zhou Enlai as its general secretary and dismissed Mao as general political commissar of the First Front Army. In June 1931, the Political Security Department (PSD) was established, and Wang Jiaxiang, a returned student from Moscow, was appointed its head. The Special Services Brigade was renamed the Brigade of State Political Security (*guojia zhengzhi baowei dadui*, BSPS) under the jurisdiction of the PSD, and was commanded directly by Wang Jiaxiang.[3] With Mao's dismissal from the leadership and ascent to the symbolic post as chairman of the newly established Soviet Republic of China, leadership was able to reform the security apparatuses and forces. The reorganization took place immediately after the Gangnan Conference: the PSD was reorganized as the State Political Security Bureau (SPSB), with its functions significantly expanded, on the basis of the Soviet vertical chain of command (Figure 4.1). The Brigade of State Political Security was increased by more than four hundred personnel and was commanded by Deng Fa, head of the SPSB. Deng Fa, a former leading

[2] Wu Lie, *Zhengrong suiyue*, pp. 32–3, 43–4.
[3] Ibid., pp. 67–8.

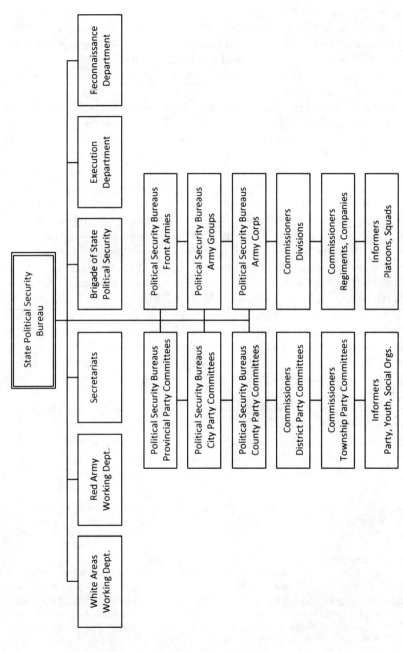

FIGURE 4.1. Command Structure of State Political Security Bureau, November 1931. *Source*: Wu Lie, *Zhengrong suiyue*, p. 90; Ouyang Yi, *Ouyang Yi huiyilu*, pp. 125–7; *Gong'an shigao*, pp. 27–31.

figure of the CCP labor movement in Guangzhou and Hong Kong, had been transferred in the summer of 1931 by the CCP's central leadership located in Shanghai to assume the leadership of the SPSB.[4]

As a powerful organization with executive powers to conduct surveillance, investigation, and arrests of suspected party members, army officers, and soldiers, the SPSB aimed to penetrate and achieve control over every level of the CCP organization and Red Army. It did so by any means possible, including military operations, torture, and execution of suspected traitors. Because of the nature of its work, the SPSB often operated in secrecy to maintain security against internal and external threats. The power of the SPSB and its subordinated security departments and commissioners was unlimited and went unchecked because "the security apparatus at all levels only received vertical commands, such that the local governments had no authority to change the decisions or orders."[5]

By the end of 1933, the size of the Brigade of State Political Security had doubled in response to the increasing need to provide security to the leadership. A large number of high-ranking party leaders flooded into the Jiangxi base areas – some were transferred, and some fled from Nationalist suppression as Chiang Kai-shek successfully shrank CCP bases in urban eras. This led to the establishment of the Second Brigade of State Political Security, led by Zhuo Xiong, in the winter of 1933.[6] Although Zhuo was mainly in charge of escorting party leaders who traveled to Jiangxi base areas from Guomindang-controlled areas, the Second Brigade was created to guarantee leaders' personal security after they arrived at the Jiangxi Soviet.[7] In July 1934 when the Political Security Regiment (*zhengzhi baowei tuan*, PSR) was established to guard top leaders, the two Brigades of State Political Security were further reorganized into three battalions.[8]

A significant change in the CCP security forces occurred after the Zunyi Conference in January 1935, when Mao was acknowledged the party's de facto leader. The combined factors of the CCP's near extermination and the absence of Moscow's interference allowed Mao to attack certain policies with

---

[4] Ibid., pp. 90–1.

[5] "Zhonghua suweiai gongheguo guojia zhengzhi baoweiju jouzhi" [Historical site of the State Political Security Bureau of the Chinese Soviet Republic], in *Ruijin shi renmin zhengfu* [The people's government of Ruijin City] online, http://www.ruijin.gov.cn/Affairs/showAffairs.asp?PKId=2463 (accessed November 23, 2008).

[6] Wu Lie, *Zhengrong suiyue*, p. 101.

[7] Zhuo Xiong successfully escorted many important party leaders, such as Chen Yun and Bo Gu, who left Shanghai for the Jiangxi base areas. The most challenging task, according to Zhuo Xiong, was the assignment to escort Otto Braun, whom the Comintern sent to the Jiangxi Soviet as its adviser. See Han Jingchun, "Tabian qingshan ren weilao – ji yuan guojia minzhengbu fubuzhang Zhuo Xiong" [Crossing the blue hills adds nothing to one's years – A story about former Vice Minister of the Civil Affairs Zhuo Xiong), in *Laoyou* [Old friends], no. 3 (2005), pp. 4–6.

[8] Wu Lie, *Zhengrong suiyue*, p. 114.

which he disagreed and consequently to gain favor in the party. He used the policies as a scapegoat for the failure of the Jiangxi Soviet and the forced retreat of the Long March. He also convinced leadership that the Red Army would be unable to evade the Nationalists if the dogmatists continued to use theoretical knowledge, refusing his "correct" strategy, which was based on real-world application. Mao's strategy consisted mainly of the Red Army's guerrilla warfare against the better-equipped and significantly larger Nationalist armies. In the aftermath of the Zunyi Conference, Mao stressed the reorganization of the CCP security forces and slowly moved to take over leadership from the returned students who dominated the party's leadership. For example, the Political Security Regiment was abolished, and only one battalion of its three survived from Mao's reorganization. The newly established Security Brigade (*baowei dadui*) of the State Political Security Bureau resulted from the merger of this battalion and a special service team. The other two battalions were absorbed into the combat forces of the First Army Group and the Third Army Group. Wang Shoudao, one of Mao's trusted followers and a Hunan native who was Mao's student in the Guangzhou Peasant Movement Institute in 1925, had served Mao since November 1933, entering the leadership of the SPSB through the Execution Department. The Security Brigade was institutionally placed under the authority of the Operating Cell of the Execution Department.[9]

After Mao arrived in northern Shaanxi, he worked to consolidate his power. A significant reorganization of the elite security force was conducted in 1938, and the newly established Central Guard Training Brigade (*zhongyang jing-wei jiaodao dadui*, CGTB) was a large expansion of the elite security force, which included four detachments, a cavalry team, and a training team.[10] Wang Shoudao, general secretary of the CCP Central Secretariat, was in fact Mao's representative in controlling the security forces, so in reality the power was in Mao's hands. In fact, according to Li Weihan, director of the CCP Organizational Department during the Long March, Wang Shoudao had been assigned to lead the CCP security forces since November 1935, shortly after the CCP arrived in northern Shaanxi.[11] Besides the Central Guard Training Brigade's responsibilities guarding top leaders, it also had obligations to train security personnel and escort leaders from one base to the next. For example, the CGTB trained security personnel to guard CCP agencies in GMD-controlled areas, such as Xi'an, Wuhan, Guilin, Lanzhou, Nanjing, and Chongqing. In addition,

---

[9] Wang Shoudao, *Wang Shoudao huiyilu* [Memoirs of Wang Shoudao], p. 166; *Renmin zhengxie bao* [Chinese People's Political Consultative Conference daily], May 12, 2006; Wu Lie, *Zhengrong suiyue*, pp. 131–2; *Lingdao jigou yange*, p. 328.

[10] Wu Lie, *Zhengrong suiyue*, pp. 184–6.

[11] Li Weihan recalls that Wang Shoudao, as director of Security Guard of the Red Army, joined the powerful five-member Commission of Party Affairs in rehabilitating Liu Zhidan and Gao Gang, leaders of the CCP's northern Shaanxi base areas, who were purged in the campaign for suppressing counterrevolutionaries. See Li Weihan, *Huiyi yu yanjiu* [Recollection and research], vol. 1, p. 372.

escorting top officials was incredibly important, and so the CGTB would be responsible for escort logistics – mostly to and from places within China. For example, high-ranking leaders such as Zhou Enlai and Peng Dehuai were escorted to Xi'an and Liu Shaoqi to the New Fourth Army in Eastern China.[12]

What was perhaps the most important move by Mao was also a major departure from the Soviet model of security for elite officials. He aimed to undermine the influence of the SPSB on the security force and put the security force – then known as the Central Guard Training Brigade – under the joint leadership of the General Staff Department, the CCP Central General Office, and the Social Affairs Department (SAD). In October 1942, the Central Guard Training Brigade expanded from approximately seven hundred personnel to more than one thousand personnel when it absorbed the Guard Battalion of the Central Military Commission. At the same time, it was renamed the Central Guard Regiment and assigned mainly to guard CCP top leaders, including Mao, Zhou Enlai, Zhu De, Ye Jianying, Liu Shaoqi, Chen Yun, Peng Zhen, Ren Bishi, Li Fuchun, and Wang Jiaxiang. Although the Central Guard Regiment received commands from the General Staff Department, the Central General Office, and the SAD, organizationally it was subordinate to the Central Revolutionary Military Committee, of which Mao was chairman.[13] Compared with approaches of previous leaders, Mao's method of control over the security forces emphasized horizontal communications of the organizations involved. In theory power was shared horizontally, but in reality Mao's authority over the security forces was evident.

The CCP's leaders before Mao had employed ruthless struggles and terror in dealing with intraparty disagreement and conflict, a Soviet-style method of achieving discipline. But this was not Mao's only choice after he successfully helped the CCP escape the pursuit of the Nationalists and establish a strong base area in Yan'an. To a certain extent, he had been viewed by many party members as the embodiment of the revolutionary victory and the correct line. They therefore voluntarily submitted themselves to Mao's leadership. Although Mao, a savvy political leader, continued to use coercive approaches to ensure the compliance of party members and colleagues, he much preferred persuasion to win voluntary compliance and loyalty from his associates and party members. Thus, in Yan'an Mao was no longer a romantic idealist, as he had been in Hunan during his youth. Instead, he was a pragmatic strategist who could employ the theories flexibly to reality on the basis of political circumstances. One of Mao's favorite strategies was the mass line, a powerful mechanism "to facilitate communication and create policy consensus between hierarchical levels."[14] As Frederick C. Teiwes points out, the emphasis of the revolutionary masses "had been largely subordinated to shrewd realism during

[12] See Wu Lie, *Zhengrong suiyue*, pp. 184–9, 197.
[13] Ibid., pp. 207–9.
[14] Lowell Dittmer, *Liu Shaoqi and the Chinese Cultural Revolution*, rev. ed., p. 245.

the actual struggle with the Japanese and GMD," and "the founding principle of Mao's revolutionary policy was to attempt only what was possible, to mobilize the masses behind achievable objectives while avoiding reckless adventures in a context where the CCP was the weaker force."[15] Mao's success in gaining support from the majority of party members after the Zunyi Conference, according to Brantly Womack, derived greatly from "the basic characteristic of Mao's own pattern of development and the main trait of his political thinking" regarding "the interaction of theory and practice with the goal of effective revolutionary action."[16]

Another strategy Mao relied on in Yan'an was democratic centralism, an organizational principle used by Leninist political parties that emphasized equal participation from all members of the organization. By promoting the mass line and democratic centralism, Mao successfully achieved cohesion among party leadership as well as general party unity. In the 1940s, although Mao was granted the authority to make all final decisions, he never abused this privilege and was careful not to give others the impression that he was imposing his ideas on them.[17] According to Shi Zhe, Mao's Russian interpreter in Yan'an who was often asked by Mao to take minutes of the Politburo meetings, it was "extremely" difficult to take minutes in the Politburo meetings because Mao's approach followed the principles characterized by the Chinese proverbs "everyone must have their say" (*geshu jijian*) and "pool knowledge" (*jisi guangyi*). Shi Zhe indicates:

He [Mao] often did not limit the topics for discussions. Instead, he let everyone voice his/her opinions freely. No matter who talked, he patiently listened, never interrupting. As a result, the atmosphere in the meetings was very lively. People liked to open their minds and air their own views.[18]

The Yan'an leadership consensus model for decision making was promoted as a party norm for decision making at all levels of the CCP. This led to a significant change in decision making in the CCP's armed units. Beginning in September 1942, the too-powerful authorities of political commissars had been gradually undermined, and the military commanders had been allowed to share the decision making involving combat operations.[19] The system of the

---

[15] Frederick C. Teiwes, "Politics at the 'Core': The Political Circumstances of Mao Zedong, Deng Xiaoping and Jiang Zemin," in *China Information*, vol. 15, no. 1 (2001), p. 7.

[16] Brantly Womack, *The Foundations of Mao Zedong's Political Thought, 1917–1935*, p. 188.

[17] Wang Nianyi, "'Wenge' mantan" [Informal Discussion of the "Cultural Revolution"], in *Ershiyi shiji* [Twenty-first century], no. 97 (2006), pp. 36–54.

[18] *Shi Zhe huiyilu*, p. 237.

[19] Although the political commissar's authority in making the final decision had been increasingly criticized, the decision to abolish that authority was triggered by an incident in which both the commander and the political commissar of a CCP military subdistrict (division level) in Hebei were killed in a Japanese military campaign in June 1942. One of the key reasons for this tragedy was that the political commissar refused to take the advice of the commander. The decision issued by the Central Revolutionary Military Committee even authorized commanders

commissar's singular responsibility was introduced in early 1930s, which gave the political commissar the final say when the commissar and the commander had disputes related to decision making.[20] Although appointing civilian commissars to lead the army was a way to consolidate the party's control over the military, it "was as much motivated by factional consideration as by ideological worry."[21] The Central Revolutionary Military Committee gradually required all decisions by commanders and political commissars in the armed units to be consensus based. This was a major departure; previously, a political commissar had full authority over CCP armed units. The Soviet-style model of a single authority figure for armed forces, instituted by the CCP under the Soviet-trained Returned Students, was replaced by the model of collective leadership. Thus, the organizational philosophy of having security forces report to multiple leaderships resulted from a strong emphasis on collectivism and an absence of monopoly over decision making. This horizontal power sharing over the security forces reduced the fears of party members, thus persuading them to trust in the new cohesive leadership and ultimately follow Mao's lead.

It should be noted that Mao's effort to reduce the power of political commissars derived from his strategy to undermine the influence of the returned students. This helps explain why the system of commander responsibility had been in place for eight years (from 1937 to 1945).[22] As a professional political commissar, Mao understood the importance of the role of political commissar in promoting the principle of "the Party's command over the gun." After Mao ensured his dominance in the party leadership, the role of political commissars was increasingly emphasized. This legacy was carried on even by leaders after Deng. Thus, political commissar "are at least as important, if not more important than combat commanders in rank and in influence," and political commissars play a far more important role than combat commanders in managing PLA affairs.[23] You Ji has observed that there are three reasons that the myth about the importance and influence of political commissars has been perpetuated for so long and is so widely held:

The first reason is institutional.... [S]*huangzhangzhi* (parallel rank of military commander and political commissar, or "the double-heads system") is exercised in the PLA to assure equality of authority for both commanders and commissars. The second reason is

to make the final decision if combat operations were involved. However, this power had been monopolized by political commissars in the past. See Lu Zhengcao, *Lu Zhengcao huiyilu* [Memoirs of Lu Zhengcao], pp. 238–42.

[20] Kang Shijian, *Zhongguo renmin jiefangjun dangwei zhi* [The party committee system in the PLA], pp. 31–7.

[21] You Ji, "Sorting Out the Myths about Political Commissars," in Nan Li (ed.), *Chinese Civil-Military Relations: The Transformation of the People's Liberation Army*, p. 92.

[22] You Ji, "Unravelling the Myths about Political Commissars," in David Michael Finkelstein (ed.), *Civil-Military Relations in Today's China: Swimming in a New Sea*, p. 157.

[23] You Ji, "Unravelling the Myths about Political Commissars," in David Michael Finkelstein (ed.), *Civil-Military Relations in Today's China: Swimming in a New Sea*, p. 155.

that commissars are responsible for important tasks such as internal security, personnel management (i.e., officer selection and promotion), legal and discipline matters, and liaising with parallel civilian party and government officers. The third reason for this myth is that the CCP has long defined the PLA as a military organization that carries out political missions. At times, the party has placed more emphasis on political missions as opposed to military tasks.[24]

As one of the three systems on which the CCP relies to command the gun (the other two being the party committee system and the military's system of political departments), the system of political commissars has contributed to institutionalized party control over the PLA, and political commissars have been the instrument of the party's control over the military.[25]

In September 1945, the CCP moved its capital from Yan'an, Shaanxi, to Chengde, Hebei. At this time the Central Guard Regiment was divided into two parts. One stayed in Yan'an to guard the top leaders; the other, led by Wu Lie, was dispatched to Chengde to prepare the location for the CCP's leadership. The Japanese surrender provided an opportunity for the CCP to control Manchuria, thus allowing the CCP to use Chengde as a temporary capital, in order to later take Beijing as its capital (Chengde's location was strategically ideal, as it was a northern suburb and hours from Beijing). Thus, the Advance Central Guard Regiment was established to guard high-ranking leaders sent to Chengde. The regiment combined one-third of the Central Guard Regiment personnel with more than one hundred officers from the Northwest Public Security School. The rest of the Central Guard Regiment remained in Yan'an and formed what would later be known as Unit 8341,[26] the famous guard regiment. Contrary to the CCP's expectations, the intense competition for dominance in Manchuria between the communists and the Nationalists in the winter of 1945 made it impossible for the CCP to establish its temporary capital in Chengde. The Advance Central Guard Regiment was ordered to move from Chengde to Manchuria, where its personnel were absorbed into local communist armed forces.[27] In other words, the breakout of civil war in late 1945 forced the CCP to have its capital in Manchuria instead. The group, led by Wu Lie, was sent to Manchuria, where it joined the PLA Northeast Army (later renamed the Fourth Field Army), headed by Lin Biao.[28]

Development toward Professionalism in the Early 1950s

The professionalism of the CCP security forces began in July 1949, when the Central Military Commission (CMC) established the Chinese People's Public Security Forces (*zhongguo renmin gong'an budui*) to command nationwide

[24] Ibid.
[25] You Ji, "Sorting Out the Myths about Political Commissars," p. 80.
[26] See Wu Lie, *Zhengrong suiyue*, pp. 248–51, 266–7.
[27] Ibid., pp. 248–56.
[28] Ibid.

armed security forces, including the Central Column of the Chinese People's Public Security Forces, to which the Central Guard Regiment was subordinate.[29] The CCP leadership came to a consensus that the PLA should be divided into two parts after the establishment of the PRC: the Defense Army for national defense and the Chinese People's Public Security Forces (CPPSF) for maintaining domestic order. PLA Commander in Chief Zhu De declared the mission of the CPPSF to "ensure that 475 million people can live and work in peace and contentment, which the enemy would not dare to sabotage."[30] Personnel of the leadership organ of the CPPSF mainly were personnel transferred from the PLA 20th Army Group (originally subordinate to the North China Field Army), in addition to some officers from the North China Military Region and the CMC.[31] Considering the position of Luo Ruiqing as commander of the CPPSF, director of the Political Department of the North China Field Army, and director of the Political Department of the North China Military Region, Luo's dominance in the CPPSF was evident. According to Zhu De, there was no need to establish other security forces, such as gendarmerie or garrison armies, because the CPPSF took charge of all security issues nationwide.[32] Zhou Enlai further clarified its function on October 30, 1949, as a special military force that commanded all local armed units nationwide to "maintain local public order, deter the activities of the enemy and ensure the country's border defense."[33] In April 1950 the Politburo approved the division of the army into the Defense Army and the CPPSF.

By 1953, the CPPSF had been named as PLA Public Security Forces that had developed into an armed unit with 590,000 personnel – larger than both the former First Field Army and the former Second Field Army. From January to May 1950, Luo Ruiqing, commander of the CPPSF, first reorganized the local security forces to better command the nationwide security forces. The reorganization of Beijing's security forces began in August 1949, when the CMC approved the establishment of the Central Column of the CPPSF, specifically to ensure the security of the CCP leadership and the capital. Thus, it was in charge of security issues related to the party, armies, governmental agencies, and high-ranking leaders. The Central Column included two divisions: the 1st Division that was reorganized by the Independent 207th Division, and the 2nd Division, an enlarged division based on the Central Guard Regiment (CGR). The integration of CCP security forces into the PLA was officially stipulated in

[29] See Shu Yun, "Xin zhongguo diyiren gongan buzhang Luo Ruiqing" [First public security minister Luo Ruiqing], in *Dangshi bolan* [General review of the Chinese Communist Party], no. 4 (2004), p. 18.
[30] *Luo Ruiqing zhuan*, pp. 283–4.
[31] Yang Jingming, "Wo he Zhao Guowei" [I and Zhao Guowei], in Sun Mingshan (ed.), *Lishi Shunjian* [An instant in history] (Beijing: Qunzhong chubanshe, 2004), vol. 3, p. 592.
[32] *Luo Ruiqing zhuan*, pp. 283–4.
[33] Ibid., p. 284.

the Common Guiding Principles of the Chinese People's Political Consultative Conference in September 1949.[34]

A significant development in the institutionalization process of the CCP security forces was that the Central Guard Regiment was put under the administration of the Central Column of the CPPSF (Figure 4.2). The CGR had been an independent security force that was assigned to guard CCP leadership since October 1942. During the Chinese civil war the CGR was entrusted with major responsibilities involving security of the CCP Central Committee and the PLA headquarters. Although the CGR was subordinate to the General Staff Department and the Social Affairs Department, Mao had tried to control the CGR directly through various channels. This included Wang Dongxing, a deputy chief of staff of the team headquarters directly under the CCP Central Committee (*zhongyang zhishudui*) and head of the Guard Department under the CCP Central Secretariat. In the late 1940s, when Mao stayed in Shaanxi to escape the pursuit of the nationalist armies while commanding the CCP armed forces nationwide against the nationalist troops, Wang Dongxing became Mao's chief bodyguard. As head of the Guard Bureau under the CCP Central Secretariat who represented the party in commanding the CGR, Wang had direct control over the CGR, led by Liu Huishan and Zhang Tinzhen, through his personal involvement in the CGR's administration and strategic maneuvers. In March 1949, when the CCP Central Committee and PLA headquarters moved from Xibaipo of Hebei to Beijing, the CGR was the key armed force in guarding and escorting both. Considering the increased scope and complexities of security responsibilities after the CCP moved to Beijing, the Central Military Commission ordered the Independent 207th Division to join the CGR in guarding both the CCP leaders and the newly established capital. As a large number of security forces were assigned to guard the CCP leadership and Beijing, Luo Ruiqing immediately became an important and powerful party leader, given his control of the CCP security forces.

When the Government Administrative Council headed by Zhou Enlai was established, Luo was assigned to head the Ministry of Public Security, a department whose personnel consisted of the Northern Bureau of the SAD combined with some additional members from the headquarters of the SAD. Over the next several years, the Ministry of Public Security recruited its lower- and middle-level officials mainly from the North China Complementing and Training Corps, the North China Military and Political University, and the North China Revolutionary University – all of which were tied to the former North China Field Army, headed by Nie Rongzhen.[35] Wu Lie, former leader of the

---

[34] See Qian Jiang, "Jianguo chuqi de jiefangjun zong canmoubu" [The PLA General Staff Department in the early PRC], in *Dangshi bolan* [General review of the Chinese Communist Party], no. 7 (2003), p. 17; *Luo Ruiqing zhuan*, p. 287.

[35] See Wang Zhongfang, "Gonganbu shi zenyang chengli de" [How was the MPS established?], in Xu Weiwei and Chang Yulan (eds.), *Lishi Shunjian* [An instant in history], pp. 8–10.

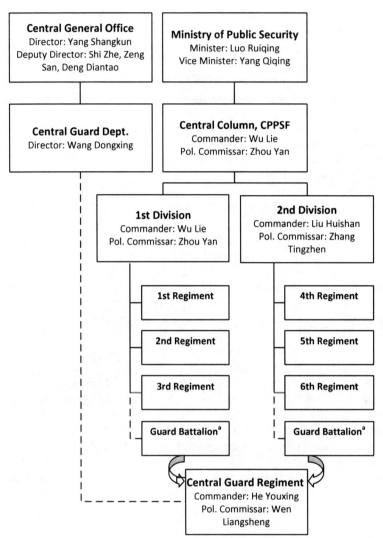

FIGURE 4.2. The CCP Security Apparatus Guarding Ranking Leaders, November 1949.
[a] The Central Guard Regiment was established in November 1949. It consisted of a
guard battalion from the First Division and a guard battalion from the Second Division, the Central Column of the CPPSF, and it absorbed a battalion (*dadui*) from the
Public Security Department of the CCP's Northern China Bureau (see Li Jianjun and Ji
Hongjian, *Shenmi de "8341*," p. 53). *Source: Lingdao jigou yange*, pp. 906, 919, 936,
939; Wu Lie, *Zhengrong suiyue*, pp. 329, 332–3; *Wu Jicheng huiyilu*, p. 93; Li Junting
and Yang Jinhe, *Zhongguo wuzhuang liliang tonglan, 1949–1989* [Overall elucidation
of China's armed forces, 1949–1989], p. 53.

Independent 207th Division and former leading figure of the CGR during the 1940s, was appointed commander of the Central Column of the CPPSF.

Wu Lie was the regimental commander and political commissar of the Central Guard Regiment from 1945 to 1947. Near the end of the Chinese civil war, Wu was appointed as a division commander of the 133rd Division under the 45th Army Corps of the Fourth Field Army led by Lin Biao. When the 160th Division of the Fourth Field Army was dispatched to guard the central leadership and Beijing, Wu Lie was transferred to lead it, which was later renamed as the Independent 207th Division. Although the Independent 207th Division was organizationally subordinate to the North China Military Region, it received tasks from the SAD and the Ministry of Public Security.[36] The redeployment of the Independent 207th Division in Beijing might have contributed to the establishment of a professional security force led by the experienced and respected senior guard Wu Lie. The predecessor to the 207th Division was the 160th Division, with most of its soldiers from the Fourth Field Army, led by Lin Biao.[37]

Two interesting developments occurred in the evolution of the elite security forces during the later 1940s and the early 1950s. First, immediately after the CCP leadership moved to Beijing in early 1949, Mao attempted to control the security apparatus through Wang Dongxing. Wang made executive decisions about issues such as the division of the guarding areas, the deployment of armed forces guarding Beijing, and the maintenance of public order in Beijing. The organizations that Wang coordinated included the Independent 207th Division, the CGR, the Social Affairs Department, and the Beijing Bureau of Public Security.[38] As demonstrated by the evidence here, Mao's grand strategy in the early 1950s to dominate the CCP security forces was to rely on the North China Military Region and the Fourth Field Army. Moreover, these armies share a commonality: they were both derived from Mao's faction that included the First Army Group and the First Front Army from the late 1920s to the early 1930s. Mao knew that relying on his faction was the best way to ensure his long-term dominance over the CCP security forces. Second, the Central Guard Regiment was expanded and reorganized as the Second Division of the Central Column under the Chinese People's Public Security Forces in September 1949.[39] This new arrangement placed all security forces (including the CGR) squarely under the control of the CPPSF, headed by Luo Ruiqing. Consequently, this change of hands organizationally removed the CGR from Wang Dongxing's jurisdiction. This implies a tendency toward the professionalism of the CCP security forces that was pushed by the collective leadership but not necessarily favored by Mao. Arguably, the establishment of the Central Guard Regiment

---

[36] Wu Lie, *Zhengrong suiyue*, pp. 320–2.
[37] *Wu Jicheng huiyilu*, p. 31.
[38] Ibid., pp. 31–2.
[39] Ibid., pp. 32–3.

in 1953 was an effort initiated by Mao to regain control over the elite security force.

The Reorganization of the Central Guard Regiment

Although the new Central Guard Regiment (later renamed Unit 8341) was created to guard the "Five Leading Secretaries,"[40] it was more Mao's attempt to establish an armed unit over which he had direct control. When it was created in 1953, it had one thousand personnel, and its jurisdictional area included the residents of the five leading secretaries, such as Zhongnanhai and Mount Yuquan. During the Cultural Revolution, it reached eight thousand personnel and extended its domain to include Tiananmen Square, the People's Hall, Diaoyutai, Beidaihe, Changping Farm, Beijing Botanical Gardens, Huayuan Village, and East Guanfang.[41] The decision by Nie Rongzhen and Luo Ruiqing in the spring of 1950 to integrate the CGR into the CPPSF, an effort to promote the professionalism of China's security forces, drew Mao's displeasure and severely cost both Nie Rongzhen and Luo Ruiqing.[42] When Mao realized that the impetus for the decision came from Nie and Luo, two of the most powerful leaders of the former North China Field Army, and that the integration was approved by the PLA Acting Chief of Staff Nie Rongzhen, Mao became indignant. As a result, Mao's relationship with Nie was sour throughout the 1950s. According to Zhang Zhen, director of operations under the PLA General Staff Department (also vice chairman of the CMC in the 1990s), Mao blamed Nie for ordering all to "block" Mao's access to certain PLA documents during a CMC meeting on July 24, 1952. In the meeting, Mao threatened Nie with "organizational adjustment," a polite expression for dismissal.[43] Nie probably realized that he was in danger of receiving Mao's retribution and decided that he was better off with self-critique, so that perhaps later Mao would look favorably on him. He resigned in late 1952, noting health problems as the reason. He had been appointed to head the PLA General Staff Department for only three years, quite a short tenure.

Mao continually punished Nie following his resignation from the PLA General Staff Department throughout the 1950s. According to Mao's senior secretary Ye Zilong, in the early 1950s Nie always attended Politburo meetings as a representative of the PLA. In the mid- and late 1950s, he was rarely invited

[40] Feng Lizhong, "Wosuo zhidaode 8341 budui" [What I know about Unit 8341], in *Baixing shenghuo* [Ordinary people's life], vol. 7 (2009), pp. 53–4.

[41] Ibid.

[42] Mao was infuriated when informed in the spring of 1950 that the Second Division had been integrated into the CPPSF. Mao questioned, "Who authorized to let this division be integrated into the CPPSF? Why did I have no idea?" See (Luo) Diandian, *Feifan de niandai* [Those extraordinary years], p. 147

[43] Zhang Zhen, *Zhang Zhen huiyilu* [Memoirs of Zhang Zhen], vol. 1, pp. 507–8.

to attend. Several times when Ye included Marshal Nie Rongzhen on the list of Politburo meeting attendees, Mao would remove Nie's name after Ye sent it to him for approval.[44] It was only in 1959 at the Lushan plenum when Peng Dehuai was purged that Mao began to pay attention to Nie again. On September 26, 1959, the Central Military Commission (CMC) was reorganized, with Lin Biao, He Long, and Nie Rongzhen as vice chairmen.[45] As with Nie Rongzhen, Mao was similarly unhappy with Luo Ruiqing's involvement in integrating the CGR into the CPPSF. As a result, Luo's power was greatly undermined after the Chairman approved both the CPPSF and the local military regimes sharing the responsibilities for control of local security forces. It should be noted that Mao intended not only to undermine the influence of Luo but also to reject the Soviet model, in which the security force was independent of, not subordinate to, local party committees. Mao's conflict with both the PLA Chief of Staff Nie Rongzhen and head of the CCP and PLA security Luo Ruiqing immediately after the establishment of the PRC confirms the extent of Mao's concern over the leadership's control of the armed security forces.

Because the merger of the CGR into the CPPSF was a fait accompli, Luo Ruiqing became even more powerful through his control of the CPPSF and the Ministry of Public Security. These security forces grew in power by guarding and watching high-ranking leaders. These developments caused the Chairman to begin to control Luo Ruiqing's amassing of power. In the summer of 1950, Mao blamed Luo for failing to report to him on Luo's work and ordered Luo to send all future reports to him directly.[46] Even though the CCP's Chinese People's Public Security Forces was only a department of the CMC, and the Ministry of Public Security a department of the Government Administration Council, the MPS and the CPPSF were required to report to and receive instructions from the Chairman directly. According to Luo Ruiqing's daughter, Luo sent 280 working reports directly to Mao between 1950 and 1956.[47]

Mao's direct control and monitoring of Luo Ruiqing also indicates his intention at the time to undermine Zhou Enlai's influence over the CCP security apparatus. Security and intelligence had been the source of power for Zhou Enlai since the end of the 1920s. In the Jiangxi Soviet, Li Kenong and Qian Zhuangfei, two of Zhou's trusted followers, controlled the security forces in the leadership, despite that fact that Deng Fa was also a leading figure in charge of the CCP security.[48] Even after Mao took control of the CCP following the

---

[44] Wang Fan, *Zhiqingzhe shuo* [Talks from insiders], vol. 1, p. 391.

[45] The CMC was reorganized on September 26, 1959, a month after Peng Dehuai was dismissed. See *Lingdao jigou yange*, p. 1046.

[46] See *Luo Ruiqing zhuan*, pp. 263–4; (Luo) Diandian, *Feifan de niandai*, p. 147.

[47] See (Luo) Diandian, *Feifan de niandai*, p. 148.

[48] Li Kenong had been director of the Political Security Bureau and the person who directly controlled the Special Services Team, the organ that took charge of the security of the CCP's leadership since 1933; Junshi kexueyuan junshi tushuguan [Military Library of the CCP Military

Zunyi Conference of January 1935, Zhou remained strongly influential on security and intelligence matters. In the 1940s, the Social Affairs Department, headed first by Kang Sheng and then by Li Kenong, had been responsible for intelligence on and security of the CCP's top leaders. Mao had made a consistent effort to undermine the influence of Zhou Enlai and Zhou's top associates in charge of the security apparatuses since becoming the de facto party chief at the Zunyi Conference. As Teweis and Sun have observed from the results of the Seventh Party Congress, there was the low standing of the security apparatus as a whole (the leading security agency became only a subordinate unit of the SAD after the SAD was established and many security responsibilities had been absorbed into the Central General Office and local public security organizations) and the key figures in the CCP security apparatuses such as Deng Fa, Li Kenong, and Pan Hannian failed to attain even alternate Central Committee members.[49] It seems reasonable that Mao's effort in the early period of the Yan'an rectification to rely entirely on Kang Sheng, with whom Mao had never established career and personal ties, to control the CCP security and intelligence was a strategy to undermine Zhou Enlai's dominance over security and intelligence. For Mao, Kang Sheng was valuable for him; he strove not only to contain the influence of Zhou Enlai and Zhou's followers but also "to consolidate the power he had won at the Zunyi conference."[50] In August 1949, the SAD was abolished and its personnel merged into either the newly established Ministry of Public Security of the PRC or the Intelligence Department of the PLA General Staff Department.[51] To undermine Zhou Enlai's influence on the security apparatus, Mao appointed Luo Ruiqing instead of Li Kenong to lead the PLA security forces and the Ministry of Public Security. This showed flagrant disrespect to Li, as he had been chief of the CCP security and intelligence apparatuses since 1947. Some party historians point out that Zhou Enlai also tried to persuade Luo to take the position offered by Mao, despite Luo's insistence that Li Kenong was more experienced and a supervisor of Luo's. No doubt Luo would be wary of the promotion, because in the summer of 1932 when Li assumed the head of the State Political Security Bureau of the CCP Revolutionary Military Commission, Luo was the director of the SPSB branch in the First Army Group. Indeed, it is clear that Zhou took Mao's concerns to heart; he knew that retaining his influence

---

Academy], *Zhongguo renmin jiefangjun zuzhi yange he geji lingdao chengyuan minglu* [The PLA organizational evolution and the list of leadership members at different levels] (Beijing: Junshi kexue chubanshe, 1990), pp. 13–19; Wu Jixue, *Hongqiang huiyi* [Memory within Red Wall], vol. 1, pp. 179–80.

[49] Frederick C. Teiwes and Warren Sun, *The Formation of the Maoist Leadership: From the Return of Wang Ming to the Seventh Party Congress*, p. 58.

[50] Roderick MacFarquhar, *The Origins of the Cultural Revolution: The Coming of the Cataclysm, 1961–1966*, p. 291.

[51] See *Luo Ruiqing zhuan*, p. 247

over the security forces could cause him to lose his career, or worse, in the future.[52]

Zhou Enlai, of course, understood Mao's intentions when Mao cut Zhou's ties with the security forces and excluded Li Kenong from top security agencies. Mao needed to undermine their authority in order to dominate the security apparatus. In the late 1940s, before the PRC was established, the CCP began to defeat the Nationalists city by city, and in doing so, it gradually took over governance of the country. During this time, the Social Affairs Department (SAD), headed by Li Kenong, played a leading role in sending party cadres to establish political authority and to ensure the nationwide implementation of public order. The SAD, headed by Li, took a leading role in organizing local public security agencies; consequently, the organizations of these agencies were based on that of the local SAD.[53] However, Li was assigned to head the Intelligence Department of the PLA General Staff Department, a post that was far less significant in terms of its rank and importance than that of the Ministry of Public Security and the CPPSF. While the Intelligence Department was only a subordinate unit of the PLA General Staff Department, the CPPSF received command directly from the Central Military Commission (CMC). Similarly, the Ministry of Public Security (MPS) was a branch of the Government Administration Council from 1949 to 1950. In 1955, Li Kenong failed to be promoted to senior general; however, his former subordinate Luo Ruiqing was, as was Xu Guangda, one of Li's subordinates in Yan'an.[54]

As mentioned before, Wang Dongxing was appointed by the SAD as Mao's chief bodyguard in April 1947. With this new avenue for cultivating loyalty in the security apparatus, Mao paid particular attention to engendering a personal relationship with Wang and authorized Wang Dongxing to lead security services for both CCP and CMC top leaders when the CCP leadership moved to Beijing.[55] Mao made a significant move in May 1953 to separate the Central Guard Regiment from the PLA Public Security Forces (the CPPSF was named the PLA Public Security Forces in September 1950). He planned for it to be reorganized as an independent armed security force with the specific assignment of guarding top party leaders. Despite its formal authority over the Central Guard Regiment (CGR), the PLA was responsible only for providing

---

[52] See Shu Yun, "Mao Zedong de da jingweiyuan Luo Ruiqing" [Mao Zedong's chief guard Luo Ruiqing], in *Hainei yu haiwai* [At home and overseas], no. 9 (1997), p. 5; *Lingdao jigou yange*, pp. 241–3.

[53] Liu Yong, "Beijing shi gong'an jun chengli jishi" [True account of founding the Beijing Bureau of Public Security], in Xu Weiwei and Chang Yulan (eds.), *Lishi shunjian* [An instant in history], pp. 28–38.

[54] When Li Kenong was acting director of the Central Intelligence Department, Xu was only one of the division heads of the CID under Li's leadership. See *Li Yimin huiyilu*, pp. 106–7.

[55] See *Wu Jicheng huiyilu*, pp. 31–2.

logistical support and recruitment assistance. It neither had authority in commanding the CGR nor was involved in detailed operations and decision making of the unit.[56] Except the Chairman, no one had the authority to appoint the leadership of the CGR, nor was anyone allowed to ask for details of its daily operations, even the minister of defense and the PLA general chief of staff.[57] When it came down to it, the CGR was required to remain loyal only to Mao. Moreover, Mao had strict requirements as to who could be CGR personnel, including a pristine background check and a family history in which at least the most recent three generations were poor or lower-middle-class peasants.[58] Thus, the reorganization of the CGR enabled Mao to have direct control of the security forces guarding top leaders, an extension of his relationship with Wang Dongxing.

While the CGR was not commanded by the Chinese police forces and the Central Guard Bureau was a subordinate agency of the MPS in name only, the Chinese police forces were pushed toward institutionalization and the party bureaucracy effectively exerted its political control over the MPS. This helps explain why China has never developed into a police state, as Andrew Nathan observes:

In a police state, the political police become a separate organization, more powerful than the regular police, the military, or the party organization. They operate without legal restriction, serve as the primary pillar of the regime, and have direct access to the leader. One thinks of Stalin's KGB, Hitler's SS, the Iranian Savak, Saddam Hussein's Mukhabarat, or the former South Korean Central Intelligence Agency. China had no similar organization. The Party never lost political control over the Ministry of Public Security, and its minister never ranked among the top figures of the regime.[59]

Because of the party's control over the Chinese police forces, it was almost impossible for Mao to have effective personal control over those agencies. It is not surprising that the police forces and agencies would become Mao's first targets before he launched the Cultural Revolution to assault the party bureaucracy on the eve of the Cultural Revolution.

The accession of the Central Guard Regiment to the Beijing Garrison Command in January 1959 was an interesting moment for this department.[60] This was during a period when tensions between Mao and Defense Minister Peng Dehuai had become public knowledge in the CCP leadership. In a speech

---

[56] *Hongqiang tonghua*, pp. 176–7.
[57] Feng Lizhong, "Wosuo zhidaode 8341 budui," pp. 53–4.
[58] Ibid., pp. 53–4.
[59] Andrew J. Nathan, *China's Transition*, p. 45.
[60] See Li Jianjun and Ji Hongjian, "Shenmi de '8341,'" in *Junshi lishi* [Military history], no. 3 (2004), p. 53.

during the 1959 Shanghai Conference, Mao openly attacked Peng: "Peng Dehuai hates me to death."[61] The tumultuous relationship between Mao and Peng may have begun as early as 1953, when Peng was involved in the Gao Gang affair,[62] which refers to leadership conflicts that resulted from initiatives of influential military leaders such as Lin Biao, Peng Dehuai, and Gao Gang to attack Liu Shaoqi and Zhou Enlai, two influential civilian leaders. Peng complained that Mao disliked him and claimed that the two had become estranged since the Gao Gang affair. It is unclear why the Defense Ministry, led by Peng, put Mao's de facto personal security force, the CGR, under the Beijing Garrison Command, but it can be speculated that doing so was partially related to Peng and Mao's estrangement. The transfer of the CGR two years later from the jurisdiction of the Beijing Garrison Command to the PLA General Staff Department (headed by Luo Ruiqing)[63] is a reason to believe that Peng was attempting to cut ties between Mao and the CGR. This speculation is supported by another event in which Wang Dongxing attempted to "rectify and strengthen" The CGR after Peng Dehuai was purged at the 1959 Lushan plenum and the Beijing Garrison Command no longer had authority over commanding the CGR.[64] Peng had been popular as an outspoken army leader who had the courage to confront and challenge the Chairman.[65] Thus, it can be inferred that, because of his displeasure with Mao's use of the CGR as his personal security force, Peng was intent on causing trouble for the Chairman.[66] Because the Beijing Garrison Command, like the PLA General Staff Department, provided only logistical support to the CGR, Peng's ploys to influence the unit had little impact on Mao's control of it, even though Peng attempt to influence the CGR through personnel appointments. Peng's actions were nonetheless a challenge to Mao.

After Peng Dehui was dismissed during the 1959 Lushan plenum, the Central Guard Regiment was again made subordinate in 1960 to the PLA General Staff Department headed by the newly appointed General Chief of Staff Luo Ruiqing.[67] At this point, Mao allowed the Beijing Garrison Command and the PLA General Staff Department to command the Central Guard Regiment while

---

[61] See Li Rui, *Lushan huiyi shilu* [True record of the Lushan conference], p. 95.

[62] Roderick MacFarquhar, *The Origins of the Cultural Revolution: The Coming of the Cataclysm, 1961–1966*, p. 163.

[63] See Li Jianjun and Ji Hongjian, "Shenmi de '8341,'" p. 53.

[64] Li Zhisui describes that Wang Dongxing used the campaign against Peng Dehuai to regain control over Unit 8341 because most of the cadres in the unit had been appointed while Peng Dehaui was in power. See Li Zhisui, *Mao Zedong siren yisheng huiyilu*, p. 330.

[65] Joseph Fewsmith, *Dilemmas of Reform in China: Political Conflict and Economic Debate*, p. 24.

[66] In 1958, Peng Dehuai told his wife Fu Anxiu about his determination to fight with Mao. Peng said: "Mao Zedong attacked me and I also attacked him. He could attack me; why could I not be allowed to attack him?" *Zhonggong wenhua dageming zhongyao wenjian huibian*, p. 425.

[67] See Li Jianjun and Ji Hongjian, "Shenmi de '8341,'" p. 53.

giving Wang Dongxing permission to first study in the Central Party School and then work in Jiangxi. Wang Dongxing was a deputy governor in Jiangxi for two and half years. This demonstrates how the Chairman did not pay great attention to amassing unilateral control of the Central Guard Regiment, probably because his dominance was already evident. Mao's intention to increase personal control over security forces and intelligence may have been triggered by the setback resulting from the economic disaster of the Great Leap Forward, which caused doubt to run rampant within party leadership about his ability to handle the economy.

Development toward a Personal Security Force in the Early 1960s

In the 1950s, Mao was confident in his collectivist triumph and his implementation of political and economic polices to industrialize and modernize the Chinese economy, and so he enjoyed increased prestige within the party and among the general public. This elevated public reputation was fueled by the rapid and relatively peaceful collectivization and transformation of the social fabric, which had not been accompanied by massive unrest.[68] By the mid-1950s, Mao had dramatically reduced the number of his personal guards. Despite this fact, he was successful in nurturing and controlling a small but efficient personal security force through Wang Dongxing. This security force helped him maintain his vigilant watch over party, government, and PLA security forces.[69] Rather than simply relying on the Central Guard Bureau and the Central Guard Regiment for protection, Mao often used the security guards to conduct investigations into how the general public would react to new collectivization and Great Leap Forward policies. In 1955, Mao ordered the Central General Office and the Central Guard Regiment to choose his guards from the PLA units nationwide. He ordered that the guards were to be chosen from each prefecture of the twenty-six provinces, in addition to the Guangxi Autonomous Region and five major cities – Tianjin, Shanghai, Guangzhou, Chongqing, and Wuhan. Mao then asked his guards to return to their hometowns in rotation and conduct investigations of public opinion.[70] Mao's irrational anxiety surrounding his personal security force likely began in the late 1950s during the chaos of the Great Leap Forward. The failing economy undermined party cohesion and Mao's reputation.[71] As Mao became more closely identified with the Great Leap Forward, its failure discredited the legitimacy of his charismatic leadership and vision.[72]

---

[68] Roderick MacFarquhar, *The Origins of the Cultural Revolution: The Coming of the Cataclysm 1961–1966*, p. 466.
[69] See Li Zhisui, *Mao Zedong siren yisheng huiyilu*, p. 191.
[70] See Zhang Yaoci, *Zhang Yaoci huiyi Mao Zedong*, pp. 47–52.
[71] Li Zhisui, *Mao Zedong siren yisheng huiyilu*, pp. 221, 223.
[72] Lowell Dittmer, *Liu Shaoqi and the Chinese Cultural Revolution*, p. 52.

The first half of the 1960s was difficult for Mao, as he became increasingly paranoid about his subordinate guard groups. The Central General Office, led by Yang Shangkun, took a more active role in the control of the Central Guard Bureau and Unit 8341. Wang Jingxian, deputy director of the Central Guard Bureau, was appointed Mao's chief bodyguard in the absence of Wang Dongxing. Wang Dongxing was replaced as director of the Central Guard Bureau by Luo Daorang and later by Lai Zhulie, two of Wang's former associates.[73] Mao's reprimanding of Wang – he exiled him to Jiangxi – left Mao without a chief bodyguard.[74] Later developments indicate that Mao was not satisfied with any of Wang Dongxing's three associates who were considered for the position. It is unclear why in September 1960 Mao urgently recalled Wang Dongxing to Beijing and then, several months later, fired Wang Jingxian, but it may have been related to Mao's decision to strengthen his personal security.

Mao's feelings of paranoia involving the Central General Office had another source, the culmination of which resulted in the so-called bugging incident. Beginning in 1956, Central General Office clerks began using tape recorders at party conferences to keep more accurate records than stenographers. Soon enough, many smaller meetings and private discussions were being recorded, too. Discovering that his conversations were bugged and whereabouts monitored made him feel particularly vulnerable to other high-ranking leaders. Mao was aware that some members of his entourage were following party orders to record all his speeches and conversations outside of Beijing. According to Ye Zilong, Mao had clearly demonstrated his strong objection to recording his talks at the Hangzhou Conference in November 1959. From that point forth, the Confidential Department no longer sent personnel to record the Chairman's speeches and conversations when touring. However, in 1961 Mao was recorded flirting with a female attendant, which not only made him furious but also made him all the more wary of his subordinates. It seems strange that the Confidential Department would be recording Mao if it had agreed to terminate such actions. But Ye Zilong claimed that he had Mao's permission to record Mao's conversations during the tour to Shanghai in 1960. Ye expressed his motives as simply wanting to have the conversations in the party archives.[75] Looking back, it is impossible to decipher Ye's motives or know whether Mao was right to be suspicious. What is clear is that the bugging incident aggravated Mao's already-heightened suspicions of insubordination within his entourage, including suspicion of those whom Mao had previously trusted, such as Ye

---

[73] *Hongqiang tonghua*, pp. 178–9.

[74] Mao's dissatisfaction with Wang Dongxing came mainly from Wang's effort to seek support from the frontline leaders in guaranteeing Mao's security. Wang reported to Liu Shaoqi on Mao's insistence to swim in the Yangzi River and cooperated with Luo Ruiqing to provide the information that might persuade Mao to not swim in the river.

[75] Wang Shoufu, "Mao Zedong de jiyao mishu jian shenghuo mishu – Ye Zilong" [Mao Zedong's confidential and personal secretary – Ye Zilong], in *Mishu zhiyou* [Secretary's companion], no. 6 (2003), p. 43.

Zilong. Mao ended up firing many of those in his entourage who were found guilty in the bugging incident. It is difficult to know whether he actually gave them permission to record his conversations or whether they were guilty of betraying his trust. But as with many personnel and policy changes throughout Mao's career, it could be just another tactic he employed to purge those he distrusted in order to reorganize the central security forces. In fact, Mao used several tactics to ensure his control of the elite security forces and to reinforce the loyalty of those who served him.

First, Mao purged or transferred those he distrusted or who established close ties with other high-ranking leaders. In September 1960, the Chairman transferred Wang Dongxing back to Beijing and ordered him to launch the rectification campaign within the Central Guard Bureau and the Central Guard Regiment, which not only dismissed officials accused of corruption but also removed many others simply to strengthen Wang Dongxing's control. For example, Wu Zhenying and Kang Yimin, deputy directors of the Office of Confidential Secretaries and the former confidential secretaries of Liu Shaoqi and Zhou Enlai, respectively, were accused of "committing severe mistakes" with their involvement in the bugging incident. Whether these two committed actual punishable crimes is undetermined.[76]

Second, Mao strengthened his direct control of the Central General Office when, in September 1964, he sent Yang Shangkun to Shaanxi for the Socialist Education Movement. Yang's role in the bugging incident was covered up, and as MacFarquhar points out, Mao "apparently always suspected him of masterminding the operation."[77] Although during Yang's absence his duties were officially assigned to Deng Xiaoping, Peng Zhen, and Li Fuchun, Mao authorized Wang Dongxing to take control over the Central General Office. Third, Mao made an effort to establish his dominance over the national security apparatus by appointing Wang Dongxing to lead the reorganized Ninth Bureau of the MPS, which merged with the Eighth Bureau of the MPS in April 1964. Some officials who were transferred were given no other reason than "personal issues" for their dismissal. This was the case for Wang Jingxian, who was considered an "inflexible" person with whom Jiang Qing had irreconcilable differences.[78]

By January 1965, Mao had decided to dismiss Liu Shaoqi as a prelude to an assault on the party bureaucracy.[79] Liu was accused of being a revisionist and

---

[76] Ibid.

[77] Roderick MacFarquhar, *The Origins of the Cultural Revolution: The Coming of the Cataclysm, 1961–1966*, p. 447.

[78] *Hongqiang tonghua*, p. 30.

[79] According to Chen Boda, one night in January 1965, Chen was suddenly woken by Mao after Chen had taken sleeping bills and slept deeply. Chen was shocked that Mao had decided to dismiss Liu Shaoqi. Mao asked Chen to write down what Mao said and to take the lead in drawing up a central document based on those notes. This document was the well-known

the number one power-holder within the party who attempted to restore capitalism while pretending to uphold socialism.[80] Mao attempted to rely mainly on the army and security forces for support and assistance. Although Mao had little fear of direct opposition from the army against him, he was unsure whether the army would support him in an attack on the party bureaucracy. In particular, Mao was unsure about the response he would receive from those who led the PLA, such as He Long and Luo Ruiqing. Their long-standing working relations and camaraderie with the party bureaucracy under Liu Shaoqi, Zhou Enlai, Deng Xiaoping, and Peng Zhen led Mao to question the origins of their loyalty. In September 1959, after Peng Dehuai was dismissed at the 1959 Lushan plenum, Mao reorganized the CMC. He appointed Lin Biao, He Long, and Nie Rongzhen as the PLA's vice chairman. Mao arranged this to serve two purposes. The first purpose was to ensure the dominance of his faction in PLA leadership, because both Lin Biao and Nie Rongzhen were his longtime subordinates from the First Army Group and the First Front Army. The second purpose was to create competition between Lin Biao and He Long. Knowing full well that they harbored a tense relationship that extended back to Yan'an in the 1940s,[81] Mao strategically chose He Long as a PLA vice chairman over the higher-ranked officials Chen Yi, Liu Bocheng, Xu Xiangqian, and Ye Jianying. He Long ranked fifth on the list of granted marshals, and Liu Bocheng ranked fourth, but granting him the position worked in Mao's favor.[82]

Lin Biao withdrew from the PLA leadership in the summer of 1962 claiming health reasons. There is evidence, however, that Lin's withdrawal had more to do with his conflict with Mao than with health issues. Although Mao was impressed with Lin's use of Mao's thought in military rule and his reign as minister of defense,[83] Mao was disappointed in Lin's unwillingness to work with other leaders. This included generals who had cut their teeth on the same mountaintops as Lin, as well as Mao's trusted followers like Tan Zhen, Luo Ruiqing, Xiao Jingguang, and Luo Ronghuan, with whom Lin had not

---

"Twenty-Three Articles." Edgar Snow confirmed with Mao in December 1970 that his decision to dismiss Liu Shaoqi came in January 1965. See Ye Yonglie, *Chen Boda zhuan* [A biography of Chen Boda], vol. 2, pp. 376–83; Edgar Snow, *The Long Revolution*, p. 17.

[80] For a detailed analysis on the conflict between Liu Shaoqi and Mao, see Lowell Dittmer, *Liu Shaoqi and the Chinese Cultural Revolution*, rev. ed., pp. 175–227.

[81] See "Dangdai zhongguo renwu zhuanji" congshu bianjibu (ed.), *He Long zhuan* [A biography of He Long], p. 608; the personal conflict between He's wife, Xue Ming, and Lin's wife, Ye Qun, during the Yan'an era also fueled tensions between He Long and Lin Biao. See Quan Yanci, *Longkun – He Long yu Xue Ming* [The stranded dragon – He Long and Xue Ming], pp. 177–9.

[82] On the basis of the list of marshals published in 1955, Liu Bocheng ranked fourth, whereas He Long ranked fifth and Nie Rongzhen ninth; Chen Yi and Xu Xiangqian ranked sixth and eighth, respectively. Obviously, the appointment as CMC vice chairmen did not exactly follow rank.

[83] Kenneth Lieberthal, "The Great Leap Forward and the Split in the Yan'an Leadership, 1958–65," in Roderick MacFarquhar (ed.), *The Politics of China, 1949–1989*, pp. 126–7.

established close ties. Failure to garner Mao's support against Luo Ronghuan, together with Mao's criticism of him at the party conference, caused Lin to consider another retreat in the fall of 1962. This time he requested sick leave. An indicator of the antagonistic relationship between Luo and Lin is that after Lin Biao replaced Peng Dehuai as defense minister in September 1959, Luo told Mao that He Long should have been appointed to the position instead of Lin. Tension between Luo and Lin intensified after Lin removed Tan Zhen from office in October 1960 at a CMC meeting to which Luo was not invited. Tan had been a close associate of Luo's when Luo was the head of the PLA General Political Department in the early 1950s. In 1956, Luo even nominated Tan to replace him for when Luo would be on leave for health problems. Thus, after the CMC meeting, Luo was disgruntled that Lin attacked Tan without informing him in advance and refused to invite Luo. In November 1960 the conflict became public after Lin's return to power. Luo suggested to the Central Secretariat (shujichu) that local army units should care about the work of local party organs, report to local party organs the needs of the public, and report problems in implementing central directives put in place by local party organizations. It was unclear why Luo directly reported the PLA issues to General Secretary Deng Xiaoping instead of Lin Biao, because according to command structure, the suggestion should have gone to Lin. Lin assumed that Luo's actions were intended to subvert him.[84] Like Chen Yun, Lin had a reputation for using sick rest for political survival. He used this tactic in 1950, when he drew Mao's ire by refusing to lead Chinese troops to Korea, and in 1954, when he was involved in the Gao Gang affair. At both times he cited health reasons to duck out of the political arena. When Lin was in good favor politically, however, his health always seemed to be in good condition. After Mao voted Lin to be the CCP's vice chairman and nominated him as a member of the Politburo Standing Committee in 1958, Lin immediately announced that his "health has greatly improved."[85] After Lin asked for sick leave in summer 1962, Mao approved it and appointed He Long to oversee the day-to-day administration of the PLA. Although Mao stressed that important issues still were to be reported to Lin Biao, he announced that He Long would be responsible for major PLA administrative duties.[86]

Unlike Lin Biao, who had established a powerful backing, He Long had a much smaller military faction in the CCP. His factional politics and military base were gradually weakened in 1936 after the Second Front Army, which he led, joined forces with Mao's First Front Army. To fulfill his duties as the head of the PLA, he sought support from Luo Ruiqing. Under He's leadership, Luo was given more authority in exchange for Luo's cooperation. To contend with

[84] See Luo Ronghuan zhan, pp. 587–605; Huang Yao and Zhang Mingzhe, Luo Ruiqing zhuan, pp. 440–2.
[85] See Quan Yanci, He Long yu Lin Biao zhimi [Mystery of He Long and Lin Biao], pp. 80–2.
[86] See Luo Ruiqing zhuan, p. 447.

Lin's powerful influence in the army leadership and solidify his authority during Lin's sick leave, He Long had to establish close relationships with members of the party bureaucracy by allowing their involvement in PLA politics. Thus, He Long established good relations with Liu Shaoqi, Zhou Enlai, Deng Xiaoping, and Peng Zhen. For instance, in 1964, He ordered the PLA Political Institute to invite Liu, Deng, and Peng to give talks. He also publicly praised Liu Shaoqi as the commander in chief of the Socialist Education Movement. He Long's son He Pengfei reportedly proposed to Liu's daughter Liu Tao. He Long and Peng Zhen developed a close personal relationship, and Peng promoted Xue Ming, He's wife, from the rank of cadre number 13 to cadre number 9.[87] He Long often forwarded PLA documents to Peng Zhen and reported the PLA's work to Peng.[88]

When Mao planned to assault the party bureaucracy, he had to choose someone from the army leadership who did not have close ties with the party bureaucracy. Even though it was very unlikely that He Long would use the PLA against Mao, given his unquestionable loyalty to Mao, he was not a dependable source for executing the assault. Ultimately, He Long's limited power and influence in the PLA made it such that he was not someone whom Mao could rely on for support once he launched the assault. For Mao, the ten PLA Marshals each had his disadvantages: Zhu De was old; Peng Dehuai was dismissed; He Long had tied himself to the party bureaucracy; he had deemed both Liu Bocheng and Xu Xiangqian as untrustworthy; Chen Yi had not been in the army since the PRC was established; Nie Rongzhen fell short of Mao's expectations when he took over the PLA during the early 1950s; and Ye Jianying was neither powerful nor influential enough to handle the army because he lacked a strong factional base. If health was not a major issue, Mao regarded Lin Biao as the best option for ensuring the PLA's support. Thus, Mao made efforts to remove those in the military who were close to the party bureaucracy, and he assisted in the removal of opposition that might interfere with Lin's leadership. The purge of the PLA General Chief of Staff Luo Ruiqing and the attacks on He Long were examples of these tactics. When Luo Ruiqing became Mao's target, Mao had to first manipulate the CCP security apparatus, over which Luo had powerful influence, before it was possible to launch a campaign against ranking leaders.

Reorganizing the Security Apparatus on the Eve of the Cultural Revolution

From 1965 to 1966, Mao was anxious as he constructed his plans against the party bureaucracy. Many high-ranking leaders and members of Mao's

[87] The rank of cadres in the CCP and the PRC under Mao was divided into twenty-five scales. The lower the number was, the higher the rank was.

[88] See Ding Wang, *Zhonggong wenhua dageming ziliao huibian*, vol. 1, pp. 658–60.

entourage sensed his paranoia. Mao suspected that he was becoming a target for a coup launched by his associates. In Shanghai in April 1966, Jiang Qing complained to General Liu Zhijian that "the security of Chairman Mao is not guaranteed in Hangzhou" so that Xu Shiyou, Commander of the Nanjing Military Regime, was ordered by the PLA General Staff to strengthen Mao's security.[89] Mao suspected that his swimming pool was poisoned and that his illness was likewise caused by poison.[90] The Chairman made many mysterious movements and felt increasingly insecure. According to former deputy director of Central Guard Bureau Wu Jicheng, early one spring morning in 1965, the Chairman, without informing any of his associates and guard units, asked to leave his residence at Mount Yuquan. He brought only a guard and a driver to go with him and drove to the airport located in the suburbs of western Beijing, where the 34th Division of the Air Force was stationed. The division was assigned specifically to serve the Politburo members' travel needs and was controlled by Hu Ping, one of Lin Biao's trusted followers.[91] Mao called the officers and soldiers together and gave them a lecture, and that was all. Mao's action of secretly traveling to the airport for a lecture was considered strange behavior. According to Wu Jicheng, Mao's guard since 1950, Mao had never traveled without informing the guard unit and relevant party organizations.[92] Mao's paranoia and unusual, mysterious acts explain several decisions he made during 1965 and 1966. For example, Mao dismissed Yang Shangkun to ensure his control of the security apparatus. In doing so, Mao was attempting to alleviate his exposure to the party bureaucracy. To ensure the success of his assault against the party bureaucracy, Mao had to rely largely on the PLA and the security forces, which were relatively immune to the influence of the party bureaucracy. To accomplish the assault and bring down the bureaucracy, Mao took three measures to secure his advantage. First, Mao persuaded Lin Biao to assist in his assault against the party bureaucracy. Mao needed Lin not only because of his prestige in the party leadership and his influence over the PLA but also because of his role as a vanguard in attacking Mao's political rivals. Second, Mao secured Beijing by relying heavily on the former North China Field Army, which dominated the Beijing Military Region and the Beijing Garrison Command. Beijing would become the battleground of the Cultural Revolution. Third, Mao strengthened his control over the Central General Office and Unit 8341.

In 1966, Mao changed his residence more than ten times, perhaps to prevent assassination. Publicity of the big-character poster (handwritten, wall-mounted

[89] Huang Yifan, "Dongluan zhichu – Liu Zhijian zai 'wenge' chuqi de jingli he zaoyu" [Beginning of turbulence – Experience and lot of Liu Zhijian in the early "Cultural Revolution"], in Li Yong and Wen Lequn (eds.), 'Wenhua da geming' fengyun renwu fangtan lu [Collected interviews of the people of the moment in the "Cultural Revolution"], p. 4.

[90] See Li Zhisui, Mao Zedong siren yisheng huiyilu, p. 428

[91] See He Tingyi, Wo shuxi de lingxiu he jiangshuai [The leaders and army generals with whom I am familiar], pp. 36–7.

[92] See Wu Jicheng huiyilu, p. 101.

political posters that attacked the party and government authorities at all levels except Mao) written by Nie Yuanzi of Beijing University on June 1 fueled the student movement in Beijing.[93] Liu Shaoqi and Deng Xiaoping flew from Beijing to Hangzhou in an attempt to convince Mao to return to Beijing. Mao told Liu and Deng that he would not return to Beijing, but he refused to reveal his travel plans.[94] Three days after Liu and Deng left Hangzhou for Beijing, Mao suddenly asked Wang Dongxing and Zhang Yaoci to arrange his travel to Shaoshan, in Hunan, Mao's birthplace. While there, Mao lived in seclusion, censoring all information related to his stay. This decision is in stark difference to Mao's previous visit to Shaoshan. In 1959, Mao met more than three thousand villagers in three days in the area. This time he did not want anyone to know that he was in Shaoshan, although several people saw him when his car passed by, and they then spread the news to the entire village. As a result, Mao ordered the local Bureau of Public Security to announce: "Chairman Mao is currently in Beijing. The man seen in the vehicle was Li Qiang, the head of the Department of Public Security of Hunan Province."[95] This story is evidence that Mao truly did not want anyone to know where he was and what he was doing.

To ensure his personal security and the successful launch of the Cultural Revolution after his return to Beijing, Mao reorganized the party, governmental, and military organizations in Beijing. Mao's first move in April 1966 was to take control of Beijing's media outlets by appointing Wang Shouren, chief of staff of the 63rd Army Corps under the Beijing Military Region, as acting director of the Central Broadcasting Bureau. He then ordered Wang in May 14 to control the Beijing Broadcasting Station while Peng Zhen was targeted at the Politburo Standing Committee conference. For Mao, targeting Peng Zhen was crucial for his attack against other key party leaders. First, as the first party secretary of the Beijing Party Committee, Peng was symbolically a central figure and officially responsible for Beijing, the dominant arena for Mao's assault on the party bureaucracy. Second, as party secretary of the Political and Legal Commission of the State Council, Peng had been a leading figure in charge of public security and intelligence,[96] and he had established a long, close working

---

[93] In the Cultural Revolution, big-character posters were one of the most important means for the Red Guards and the mass organizations to participate in politics and were used as weapons of criticism among the Chinese.

[94] Ma Shexiang, "Mao Zedong zai Shaoshan 'Dishui dong'" [Mao Zedong at the "Dishui Hole" of Shaozhan], in *Hubei wenshi* [Hubei literature and history], vol. 4 (2000), pp. 2–3.

[95] Ibid., pp. 6–7.

[96] The Political and Legal Commission of the State Council was established in October 1949, and Dong Biwu was appointed to lead the commission, which was responsible for the Ministry of Internal Affairs, the Ministry of Public Security, the Ministry of Justice, the Commission of Legislative Affairs, and the State Ethnic Affairs Commission, and for guiding the Supreme Court, the Supreme Procuratorate, and the People's Supervision Commission. Peng Zhen was appointed acting director after Dong Biwu took sick leave in July 1954. Peng since became the de facto commission chief. In June 1958, Peng was appointed head of the newly established

relationship with Luo Ruiqing, dating back to 1949.[97] As acting secretary of the Central Secretariat, Peng Zhen represented the party leadership's involvement and management of public security.[98] Immediately after the May 16 notice passed in the Politburo Standing Committee conference, the Beijing Security Working Group, led by Marshal Ye Jianying, was established to reorganize the Beijing Municipal Party Committee, the Beijing Garrison Command, and the Beijing Bureau of Public Security.

Mao's first move to secure Beijing was to reorganize the Beijing Municipal Party Committee, headed by Peng Zhen. Eventually, Peng was dismissed during the Politburo Standing Committee conference in Hangzhou between April 19 and April 24, 1966.[99] Li Xuefeng and Wu De were appointed to lead the new Beijing Municipal Party Committee. The CCP's North China Bureau, headed by Li Xuefeng, sent a work team to the Beijing Municipal Party Committee. Many members of the Beijing Municipal Party were purged during this time.[100] Mao's second move was to reorganize the Ministry of Public Security. Because of Mao's role as instigator of the Cultural Revolution, constraints on the police system became significant for him to be able to promote the mass rebellion. Otherwise, as Lynn White indicates, "Public security forces might, in their normal fashion, have prevented political expression by frustrated groups and individuals at that time" and "might have kept political violence focused on its usual pre-1966 targets."[101] Thus, Mao tried to ensure that the MPS did not act against the Cultural Revolution. Following the dismissal of former public security minister Luo Ruiqing and Beijing's mayor Peng Zhen, a large-scale campaign to purge their followers was launched by the Beijing Bureau of Public Security. By May 1966, Feng Jiping and Xin Xiangsheng, the former and then-current director of the Beijing Bureau of Public Security, respectively, and thirty-two department heads of the Beijing Bureau of Public Security had been dismissed.[102] In late May and early June 1966, Xu Zirong and Ling Yun,

CCP Political and Legal Group and formally took charge of the party's legal and security issues. See "Dong Biwu nianpu" bianji zu, *Dong Biwu nianpu* [Chronicle of Dong Biwu], pp. 348, 440, 482–3.

[97] Li Haiwen and Wang Yanling, *Shiji duihua – yi xinzhongguo fazhi dianjiren Peng Zhen* [Centurial dialogue – Reminiscing with the founder of the PRC law and legal systems Peng Zhen], p. 53.

[98] Ibid., p. 96.

[99] See Li Xuefeng, "Wo suo zhidao de 'wenge' fadong neiqing" [The inside story that I know about how the "Cultural Revolution" was launched], in Zhang Hua and Su Caiqing (eds.), *Huishou "wenge"* [Recollection of the "Cultural Revolution"], pp. 608–9.

[100] *Wu De koushu*, p. 5.

[101] Lynn T. White III, *Policies of Chaos: The Organizational Causes of Violence in China's Cultural Revolution*, p. 309.

[102] See Cai Mingzhong, "Liu Chuanxin, wei 'siren bang' xunzang de gong'an juzhang" [Liu Chuanxin – Director of public security who sacrificed his life for the Gang of Four], in *Yanhuang chunqiu* [Spring and autumn in China], no. 1 (1994), p. 82.

both vice ministers of public security, were purged.[103] In August 1966, Mao targeted frontline leaders and gave the party leadership no choice but to accept Liu Shaoqi's dismissal at the Eleventh Plenum. By then, Mao had successfully taken control over both the Ministry of Public Security and the Beijing Bureau of Public Security.

Mao appointed Minister of Public Security Xie Fuzhi to reorganize the Beijing Bureau of Public Security after it had become the target for "eliminating the pernicious influence of Luo Ruiqing." The Beijing Bureau of Public Security was accused as "a tool for the counterrevolutionary revisionist clique headed by Peng Zhen and Liu Ren that instigates bourgeoisie dictatorship."[104] Thus, on May 12, 1966, Xie Fuzhi sent a work group with forty-four personnel, led by Li Zhao, to take over the party's leadership of the bureau, and by June 20 Xie Fuzhi had transferred 313 party cadres to control the bureau at all levels.[105] The Beijing Bureau of Public Security was under military control in February 1967 and Mou Lishan, deputy commander of the 38th Army Corps, was appointed director of the Military Control Committee.[106] To ensure Mao's control of Beijing, in May 1966 the Beijing Security Working Group, led by Ye Jianying, was ordered to implement reorganizations of the Beijing Municipal City Party Committee, the Beijing Garrison Command, and the Beijing Bureau of Public Security (Table 4.1).[107] A large-scale purge was launched in the Beijing Bureau of Public Security to "eradicate the influence" of the "Peng Zhen anti-party clique" in early 1967; it resulted in 10 leadership members and 117 department leaders being dismissed or arrested.[108]

Mao's third move to secure Beijing was to strengthen the Beijing Garrison Command. Mao paralyzed the Ministry of Public Security through large-scale purges in an effort to eliminate the influence of Luo Ruiqing and Luo's former subordinates at different levels of the MPS, he needed to find other armed forces to guard Beijing during the Cultural Revolution. The Beijing Garrison Command (BGC) was an ideal candidate. In June 1966, the BGC was expanded by adding two divisions. Unlike its status in the past, when the BGC was

---

[103] Tao Sijun, *Gongan baowei gongzuo de zhuoyue lingdaoren: Xu Zirong* [The outstanding leader in the work of public security and security guard: Xu Zirong], pp. 204–9.

[104] Liu Guangren, Zhao Yimin, and Yu Xingqiang, *Feng Jiping zhuan: Jingdu gongan juzhang* [A biography of Feng Jiping: Director of public security in the capital], p. 334.

[105] Ibid., p. 328.

[106] Gong'an bu he Beijing weishuqu [Ministry of Public Security and Beijing Garrison Command], "Guanyu jieguan Beijing shi gong'an ju de bugao" [Announcement for taking over Beijing Bureau of Public Security], in Ding Wang, ed., *Zhonggong wenhua dageming ziliao huibian*, vol. 5 (Hong Kong: Minbao yuekanshe, 1970), p. 21.

[107] See "Gonganbu, Beijing weishuqu silingbu bugao, February 11, 1967" [Announcement of Ministry of Public Security and Beijing Garrison Command headquarters, February 11, 1967], in Ding Wang (ed.), *Zhonggong wenhua dageming ziliao huibian*, vol. 5, p. 21; Cai Mingzhong, "Liu Chuanxin, wei 'siren bang' xunzang de gong'an juzhang," p. 82.

[108] Liu Guangren, Zhao Yimin, and Yu Xingqiang, *Feng Jiping zhuan: Jingdu gongan juzhang*, p. 334.

TABLE 4.1. *Leadership Changes in Beijing, May 1966*

Beijing Security Working Group
Director, Ye Jianying; deputy directors, Yang Chengwu and Xie Fuzhi; members,
Zheng Weishan and Fu Chongbi

Organizations	Leadership, January 1966	Leadership, May 1966
Beijing Municipal City Party Committee	First party secretary: Peng Zhen Second party secretary: Liu Ren Secretaries: Zheng Tianxiang, Wan Li, Chen Peng, Deng Tuo, Chen Kehan, Feng Jiping, Zhao Fan, and Jia Tingsan	First party secretary: Li Xuefeng Second party secretary: Wu De Secretaries: Guo Yingqiu, Gao Yangwen, Ma Li, Wan Li, Chen Kehan, and Zhao Fan
Beijing Garrison Command	Commander: Li Jiayi First political commissar: Liu Ren Second political commissar: Liu Shaowen	Commander: Fu Chongbi Political commissars: Xie Fuzhi, Li Xuefeng, and Huang Zuozheng
Beijing Bureau of Public Security[a]	Director: Xin Xiangsheng Deputy directors: Lu Zhan, Min Buying, Yan Tang, Li Yiping, and Zhang Lie	Director: Li Zhao Deputy directors: Liu Jianfu, Cheng Cheng, and Ma Xingwu

[a] Military control was imposed in February 1967, and the Beijing Bureau of Public Security was headed by Mou Lishan (director) and Liu Chuanxin and Wang Gengyin (deputy directors).
Source: Lingdao jigou yange, pp. 1054, 1014; Liao Hansheng, *Liao Hansheng huiyilu* [Memoirs of Liao Hansheng], pp. 246–8; Fu Chongbi, *Fu Chongbi huiyilu* [Memoirs of Fu Chongbi], pp. 178–80; see also Li Xuefeng, "Wo suo zhidao de 'wenge' fadong neiqing" [The inside story that I know about how the Cultural Revolution was launched], pp. 612–13.

subordinate to the Beijing Military Region, it was authorized to report directly to the Politburo.[109] Interestingly, when the Beijing Garrison Command (BGC) was put under the direct command of the Politburo, Zhou Enlai was assigned to command the BGC units. Deng Xiaoping was second in line to Zhou, with executive authority in Zhou's absence.[110] One might speculate that the Politburo, dominated by frontline leaders such as Liu Shaoqi and Deng Xiaoping, might have attempted to put the Beijing Garrison Command under the jurisdiction of Politburo members instead of Mao so that the collective leadership would still be able to limit the damage by the Chairman.

Mao's fourth move to control the security forces in preparation for the Cultural Revolution was to abolish the Chinese People's Public Security Forces (the PAP was renamed the CPPSF in January 1963). Before launching his

[109] Zhonggong zhongyang wenxian yanjiushi, *Zhou Enlai nianpu, 1949–1976* [Chronicle of Zhou Enlai, 1949–1976] (Beijing: Zhongyang wenxian chubanshe, 1997), vol. 3, p. 31.
[110] Ibid., p. 33.

assault against the party bureaucracy, Mao had reorganized security forces in the PLA. After Luo Ruiqing was dismissed in December 1965, the Chinese People's Public Security Forces (CPPSF) were abolished in spring 1966, and the Beijing Garrison Command was reassigned a leading role guarding Beijing.[111] Although Xie Fuzhi had replaced Luo as the commander of the CPPSF, the base of the CPPSF comprised Luo's subordinates. Mao was not interested in running the risk of having the CPPSF's loyal to Luo; therefore, in February 1966, he ordered the Central Secretariat to work to abolish the CPPSF;[112] this happened on June 7, 1966. The Beijing unit of the CPPSF was absorbed into the Beijing Garrison Command, and all other units of the CCP's CPPSF were merged with the PLA such as military regimes, military districts, military subdistricts or garrison commands, and People's Armed Forces Departments (at the county level).[113] The CPPSF were originally designed to safeguard public order, which it had accomplished during its operation. In the end, Mao's rationale for not keeping the public security forces around was twofold. First, he distrusted the armed police forces' willingness to discipline the mass movement and help purge high-ranking leaders. Second, he viewed the forces as the deadly threat to his political campaign against the party bureaucracy because of its ties with Luo Ruiqing.

The foregoing evidence demonstrates that Mao relied mainly on three different armed forces and the party agency to ensure his security and guarantee his approaching assault – the Cultural Revolution – against the party bureaucracy: the CMC, led by Lin Biao and administrated by Ye Jianying; the Central General Office, the Central Guard Bureau, and Unit 8341, headed by Wang Dongxing; and the Beijing Garrison Command, commanded by Fu Chongbi. The Central Guard Bureau, controlled directly by Mao, was responsible for Mao's security and was authorized to command both Unit 8341 and the Beijing Garrison Command. The CGB gave orders to arrest, imprison, and sometimes protect high-ranking leaders. Unit 8341, according to Frederic Wakeman, "acted as the secret service of the central government," which "gathered intelligence on other Chinese leaders, arrested and imprisoned Mao's foes."[114] For example, Unit 8341 and the Beijing Garrison Command imprisoned Liu Shaoqi, Deng Xiaoping, Peng Zhen, and Luo Ruiqing in their residences. Zhu De, Chen Yi, more than thirty provincial leaders, and noncommunist celebrities such as Song Qingling and Zhang Zhizhong were protected by the Beijing Garrison Command in Beijing. Mao also relied heavily on Unit 8341 and the Beijing Garrison Command to contain mass rebels and prevent

---

[111] Liao Hansheng, *Liao Hansheng huiyilu* [Memoirs of Liao Hansheng], pp. 246–9.

[112] 'Dangdai zhongguo' congshu bianji weiyuanhui, *Zhongguo renmin jiefangjun* [Chinese People's Liberation Army; hereafter, *Zhongguo renmin jiefangjun*], vol. 2, p. 297.

[113] Li Junting and Yang Jinhe, *Zhongguo wuzhuang liliang tonglan, 1949–1989*, p. 56.

[114] Frederic Wakeman Jr., "Models of Historical Change: The Chinese State and Society, 1839–1989," in Kenneth Lieberthal (ed.), *Perspectives on Modern China: Four Anniversaries*, pp. 91–2.

violence when factional rebels were out of control. Such a situation occurred when Mao sent Unit 8341 to regain control of major universities in Beijing, such as Beijing University and Qinghua University.[115] The PLA's role from 1965 to 1966 was symbolic in nature, as Mao sought to demonstrate to the party bureaucracy that a solidified PLA leadership, led by Lin Biao, supported him and was willing to intervene in the event of conflict between Mao and the party bureaucracy. From Mao's perspective, Lin's significance was not the extent to which he controlled the PLA but his position as a vanguard representative of the PLA, willing to attack other party leaders such as Liu Shaoqi, Deng Xiaoping, Peng Zhen, and Lu Dingyi.

Leadership Security and Politics in the Zhongnanhai

When Mao was dissatisfied with or distrusted those who served him and attempted to punish them, he did so under the guise of sending them to the countryside for the purpose of social investigation or obtaining grassroots experience, as in the cases of the transfers of Wang Jingxian (1955), Shi Zhe (1957), Ye Zilong (1960), and Li Yinqiao (1960), as well as the various demotions of Wang Dongxing (1956–1959). Although Mao was quick to demote or transfer his subordinates whenever he questioned their loyalty, he also never hesitated to support them when they needed it. Mao's generosity included providing financial aid to those whose families were financially troubled, helping them find spouses and establish families, and helping them find gainful employment if they were transferred from Zhongnanhai. To cultivate absolute loyalty, every year before 1969 Mao would meet with Unit 8341's new recruits. None of the armed units in the PLA ever received this honor. In addition, Mao often personally taught the officers and soldiers of Unit 8341 by giving lectures and correcting homework.[116]

In Zhongnanhai, each team of Unit 8341 guarded the top leaders they were assigned to and ensured the security of their residences and the surrounding areas. Within Zhongnanhai, the residence and surrounding areas of each top leader were classified as section A, B, or C, on the basis of security priority (Figure 4.3). Without special permission, those at a lower security level could not enter a higher-ranked level, but those of a higher-ranked level could enter a lower-ranked level. For example, those with section C designations were not allowed to enter sections A or B and those with section B designations were not allowed to enter section A, but those with section A designations could freely

---

[115] See *Wu De koushu*, p. 59.
[116] See Li Jianjun and Ji Hongjian, "Shenmi de '8341,'" pp. 53–4; Quan Yanchi, *Lingxiu lei* [Tears of leaders], pp. 67–8; Qi Li, *Mao Zedong wannian shenghuo jishi* [Record of events of Mao Zedong's later life], pp. 151–4; Shui Jing, *Teshu de jiaowang – shengwei diyi shuji furen de huiyi* [Unusual communications – recollections of a provincial party first secretary's wife] (Beijing: Zhongyang wenxian chubanshe, 2005), pp. 35–7.

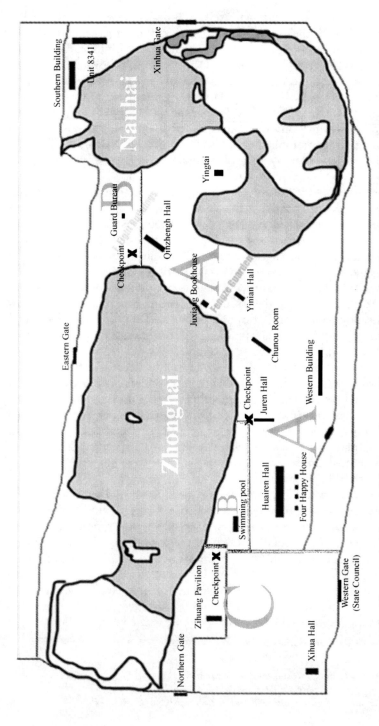

FIGURE 4.3. The Zhongnanhai in the Mid-1950s. *Source:* Zhang Baochang and Zhang Shixian, "Zhongnanhai neibu dianying" [Internal films in Zhongnanhai], pp. 67–71; Chen Xiaonong, *Chen Boda zuibou koushu huiyi* [Chen Boda's last dictation recollection], pp. 203–9; Wang Fan, "Zhongnanhai lide gongchengshi (zhong)" [Engineer within the Zhongnanhai, party 2], pp. 37–42; *Hongqiang tonghua*, pp. 185–6, 201, 203, 207.

enter sections B and C, and those with section B designations were allowed to enter section C. During the 1950s, section A covered the offices and residences of the three top leaders – Mao Zedong, Liu Shaoqi, and Zhu De. Certain key agencies of party leadership, such as the Office of Political Secretaries of the Central Secretariat and the Confidential Office of the Central General Office, were in section A as well.[117] Among the top organizations of the party, the state, and the PLA, the CCP Central Propaganda Department and the CMC were located in section B and the State Council was located in section C. In addition, the restrictions applied to soldiers and officers of Unit 8341 – they were not allowed to enter sections other than those they were assigned to guard.[118]

Security became a major task for both the Central Guard Bureau and Unit 8341 when Mao traveled outside Beijing. For example, Mao visited Hangzhou more than forty times after December 1953. Usually, he visited two or three times per year, but some years he visited up to five times.[119] Because Mao had little confidence in airplane safety, he traveled by trains instead. He had trains designed specifically for his travel; each was identically outfitted with fourteen compartments, including bedrooms, meeting rooms, dining rooms, and luggage rooms. Mao usually stayed in the middle three compartments, which were his bedroom, meeting room, and bathroom. Because all stations operated under orders to give priority to Mao's trains, he traveled without ever having to stop. Naturally, when Mao's train passed a station, all other trains were ordered to stop to allow the train's passage. However, this became a huge security problem during the Cultural Revolution. To provide security against potential threats, Mao's train ended up traveling with two other identical trains in front and behind it. These trains were equipped with more than one hundred armed personnel in full battle gear from Unit 8341.[120] Each member of the Central Guard Bureau and Unit 8341 was assigned to guard a specific position or to receive a specific task on the train during travel. They were not allowed to enter any places where they were not assigned.

Among the security guards, there were armed guards and unarmed guards. The unarmed guards not only were responsible for protecting high-ranking leaders but also provided assistance in everyday tasks. Among the armed guards, there were only a small number of them who served in the internal guard squads (*neiwei ban*), in which the guards had access to high-ranking leaders. Group 1 of the internal guard squads was specifically assigned to serve Mao. He generally had four unarmed bodyguards and an armed Internal Guard Squad with a dozen armed soldiers. Wherever Mao went, both the unarmed bodyguards and the Internal Guard Squad were assigned to go with him. The

[117] *Hongqiang tonghua*, p. 45.
[118] Ibid., 45; Feng Lizhong, "Wosuo zhidaode 8341 budui," pp. 53–4.
[119] Wang Fang, *Wang Fang huiyilu* [Memoirs of Wang Fang], pp. 137, 171.
[120] Ye Yonglie, *Mao Zedong de mishumen* [Mao Zedong's secretaries], p. 357.

Internal Guard Squad functioned as gatekeepers who gave guests permission to see Mao on the basis of the list decided on by Wang Dongxing. According to Zhang Muqi, one of Mao's guards who served Mao in the 1950s, the Internal Guard Squad had a list with the names of fourteen people who were allowed to see Mao directly, without prior notification. The guards would stop anyone who wanted to see the Chairman if his or her name was not on the list, and the person was allowed to see Mao only after Mao's approval.[121]

Control of the security apparatus in the CCP leadership depended largely on loyalties between leaders of the security apparatus and their trusted subordinates. When individual guards were sent to guard ranking leaders, it was intended for them to ensure the security of the guarded leader while simultaneously observing the leaders' activities. The higher a top leader's rank was, the greater the possibility that he or she was being spied on by the guards. For example, Lin Biao was guarded by Group 2, headed by Zhang Hong, deputy commander of Unit 8341.[122] Although Group 2 was assigned to guard Lin Biao, it received orders only from Wang Dongxing and Zhang Yaoci, which enabled Mao to control Group 2 directly, spying on Lin Biao through Wang and Zhang.[123]

Not only were top leaders' movements observed and assessed by the party; there were also strict regulations ensuring party control over individual guards. Guards were tightly watched by party organizations as well as their colleagues. Even aspects of their private lives, such as marriage, were investigated and approved by party organizations.[124] Nonetheless, guards often developed personal relationships with and loyalties to the leaders they guarded. This personal loyalty between guards and high-ranking leaders became a major concern when the alliance of Hua Guofeng, Ye Jianying, and Wang Dongxing arrested the Gang of Four. In the course of arrests, Wang Dongxing ordered the separation of the gang and their guards when the gang was called to Zhongnanhai for meetings. After the gang was arrested, all of their guards, secretaries, and nurses were immediately sent to a secret place to attend a so-called learning group. Oftentimes, when guards developed loyalties to their leaders, the guards were willing to protect the leaders at all costs, even against the security forces for which they worked, as in the case of Ye Jianying and his guards. When Wang Dongxing's associates separated the gang's guards from the Gang, Mou Naichuan and Ma Xijin, Ye's guards, were also asked to join the guards of the radical leaders to avoid suspicion. Mou and Ma misperceived that Ye might be arrested, and so they tried to take action against Wang's associates. Wang Dongxing and his associates had considered the repercussions of separating the gang from their guards, yet they had not considered the repercussions of

---

[121] Quan Yanchi, *Lingxiu lei*, pp. 54–62.
[122] Feng Lizhong, "Wosuo zhidaode 8341 budui," p. 53.
[123] Ibid.
[124] *Wu Jicheng huiyilu*, pp. 59–60.

the ploy to trick the gang's guards by including Ye's guards in the group. In the end, even though they took some precautions, guard loyalties still ended up making some trouble for them.[125]

During the Cultural Revolution, Mao heavily relied on both the Central Guard Bureau and Unit 8341 for his security and his communication with the outside. Mao personally set up several models of protocol for controlling mass movements during the Cultural Revolution with the goal of applying them to the entire country and the models detailed how to control the chaos when civil war broke out among the mass rebels, the Red Guard, and the PLA units. These models included the Beijing General Knitting Factory, the Beijing Xinhua Printing Factory, the Beijing Chemical Industry, the Beijing Lumber Mill in the northern suburb, the Beijing Two-Seven Rolling Stock Plant, the Beijing Nankuo Rolling Stock Machinery Plant, Qinghua University, and Beijing University. These were known as the six factories and two universities. To ensure order and help achieve unity of leadership after the mass rebels' violent power struggles, Mao stationed Unit 8341 in the six model factories and two model universities. As a result, an interesting phenomenon occurred. During the Cultural Revolution, Unit 8341 became one of the most recognized names in Chinese society, representing authority, justice, power, and legitimacy through its representation of Chairman Mao. Wherever Unit 8341 was sent, mass rebels rarely dared to cause trouble; on the contrary, they were willing to cooperate with Unit 8341. It soon became clear that places where Unit 8341 was stationed were always the safest; Zhou Enlai therefore sent both the central and provincial party leaders to hide wherever Unit 8341 was stationed to escape the persecution of the mass rebels.[126]

The Central Guard Bureau and Unit 8341, as Mao's personal security forces, were powerful armed units. They were so prestigious that their officials had become the subjects of attention and envy among other high-ranking leaders during the Cultural Revolution. Most of the requests or appeals that high-ranking leaders or disgraced veterans sent to Mao went through the Central Guard Bureau and Unit 8341. Even Lin Biao, the most powerful leader, second to Mao during the Cultural Revolution, strove to cultivate good relationships with officers of the Central Guard Bureau and Unit 8341. When Lin Biao died after his failed attempt to flee to the Soviet Union, the Politburo launched a campaign to purge his followers. Substantial evidence shows Ye Qun and Lin Biao's efforts to establish and cultivate close relationships with members of the Zhongnanhai security forces. Almost all the key leaders of the Central Guard Bureau and Unit 8341, had established or continued personal ties, though to different degrees, with the Lin Biao group. Some of them, such as Wang Dongxing, had cooperated with Lin, even supported him in the debate over the state chairmanship issue. Some received Ye Qun's "help" in sending their

---

[125] Ibid., pp. 394–5.
[126] Tong Xiaopeng, *Fengyu sishi nian* [Forty years of wind and rain], vol. 2, pp. 440–1.

children to join the PLA; others had been engaged in "abnormal" contacts with the members of the Lin Biao clique.[127]

After the 1970 Lushan plenum, where the debate over the state chairmanship triggered the Mao-Lin conflict, Mao launched a rectification campaign in both the Central Guard Bureau and Unit 8341. As almost everyone was vulnerable, the dominant sentiment in the rectification campaign was to stay out of trouble and please Mao by offering self-criticism, even though they did not do anything wrong. Even Wang Dongxing and Zhang Yaoci, Mao's chief bodyguards, wrote letters to Mao criticizing themselves. Originally, the Politburo asked Wang Dongxing to hand over his authority to Ji Dengkui; but later Mao changed his mind and kept Wang as his chief bodyguard. The crisis caused by the 1970 Lushan plenum was over once Mao accepted the leaders of his security apparatuses self-criticism; however, its impact continued to trouble leaders of the Zhongnanhai security forces. Sixteen months after Lin Biao died, Wang Liang'en, acting director of the Central General Office, was targeted as "a person who gathered information for Lin Biao" and later committed suicide. At the 1970 Lushan plenum, Wang Liang'en published the "Sixth Bulletin of the North China Group," a document that included Wang Dongxing's speech and was later called a counterrevolutionary bulletin by Mao. Wang Dongxing's speech, which supported Lin Biao's initiative to keep the chairmanship in the constitution, caused Wang Dongxing great troubles. Facing severe criticism from Mao, Wang Dongxing claimed that Wang Liang'en did not confirm with him when he published Wang's speech and that parts of the article were embellished.[128]

Elite Security Apparatus under Post-Mao Leadership

The challenges Mao brought for the institutionalization of the CCP security apparatus corresponded with his effort to dominate CCP leadership and to secure his absolute power in the party, government, and the PLA. Mao relied mainly on individuals such as Wang Dongxing, Zhou Enlai, Yang Chengwu, Fu Chongbi, and Wu Zhong, rather than the party, government, or PLA institutions, for his control of the security apparatus. The security apparatuses of Zhongnanhai, the Central Guard Bureau, and Unit 8341, were institutionally subordinate to the Central General Office, the Ministry of Public Security, and the PLA General Staff Department, but none of these organizations had real authority to command the CGB or Unit 8341. Although both Yang Shangkun and Luo Ruiqing were the immediate superiors of Wang Dongxing before the Cultural Revolution, neither of them had real power in directing his actions, given Wang's close relationship with Mao. Similarly, both the Beijing Garrison Command and the 38th Army Corps were subordinate to the Beijing Military

---

[127] *Wu Jicheng huiyilu*, p. 312; Zhang Yaoci, *Zhang Yaoci huiyi Mao Zedong*, pp. 119–27.
[128] *Wu Jicheng huiyilu*, pp. 301–9.

Region. However, after Mao placed elite-level security duties under their jurisdiction, the Beijing Military Region no longer had authority over them.

Leaders after Mao also paid much attention to the security forces. Although
Deng Xiaoping did not have a personal security force like Mao, Deng established and developed a powerful network based on personal *guanxi* to control
the security apparatus. Deng's control over the security apparatuses became
an indispensable source of his undisputable position as the core of the party,
a position defined by Fewsmith as "something more than simply first among
equals."[129] Unlike Mao, who depended heavily on Wang Dongxing for his
control over the Central Guard Bureau and Unit 8341, Deng's control over the
security apparatus was achieved through direct and personal interactions with
trusted followers and former subordinates. His followers included Yang Dezhi
and Yang Yong, who were in charge of the PLA General Staff Department; Pan
Yan, who was in charge of the Beijing Garrison Command; Zhao Cangbi and
Yu Sang, who were in charge of the Ministry of Public Security; Qing Jiwei,
who was in charge of the Beijing Military Region; Yang Dezhong, who was in
charge of the Central Guard Bureau; and Sun Yong, who was in charge of Unit
8341 (Figure 4.4).[130]

As deputy general chief of staff, Yang Yong represented the general chief of
staff, Deng Xiaoping, in controlling the General Staff Department, to which
the security forces were subordinate since Deng Xiaoping returned to office
in 1977. In April 1979, operations of the CMC General Office and the General Office of the General Staff Department resumed. Both offices jointly provided security guards for the PLA's high-ranking leaders and important organizations during the Cultural Revolution. Over the years, the CMC General
Office became gradually less significant, and the General Office of the General
Staff Department gradually came to control the PLA security apparatus. This
approach was viewed as Deng Xiaoping's attempt to weaken Marshal Ye Jianying's control over PLA security forces. Once Wang Dongxing was removed in
December 1978, Deng Xiaoping immediately appointed Yang Dezhong to control both the Central Guard Bureau and the Central Guard Regiment. The key
factors that led Deng to employ Yang contributed to Yang's close ties with
Zhou Enlai, his experience in both the Central Guard Bureau and Unit 8341,
and Yang's innocence in Mao's campaigns against Deng Xiaoping in 1976.
Mao's ambivalence about Yang's loyalties kept Yang on the fringes of elite
politics during the Cultural Revolution but ended up making him a good candidate for leading the CGB and CGR in the post-Mao era. Historically, Yang's
close personal ties with Zhou Enlai kept Yang from gaining Mao's complete
trust.

---

[129] Joseph Fewsmith, *China since Tiananmen: The Politics of Transition*, p. 7.
[130] In 1977, when Wang Dongxing was still in charge of the security apparatus and services, the
Central Guard Regiment was reorganized into the Central Guard Division, led by Commander
Zhang Shuizhi and Political Commissar Wu Jianhua. After Mao died, Unit 8341 was changed
to Unit 57003, and it was later renamed Unit 61889. See *Wu Jicheng huiyilu*, pp. 420–1.

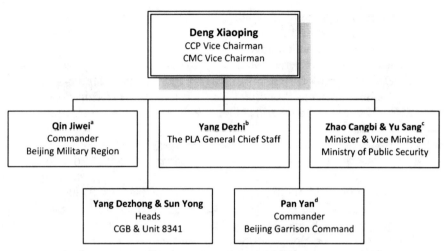

FIGURE 4.4. The CCP Security Apparatus, May 1980. *Source: Lingdao jigou yange*, pp. 1137, 1163, 1167–8; He Shangchun, "Wode lao lingdao Pan Yan tongzhi" [Comrade Pan Yan – The past superior of mine], p. 225. "Shi Xiaoli, Yang Yong zai zongcan de rizi li" [Yang Yong in the years of the PLA General Staff Department], vol. 4, pp. 3–8. [a]Qin Jiwei was Deng's subordinate from 1938 to 1953. [b]Deng handed over his position as the PLA's general chief of staff to Yang Dezhi on March 2, 1980. Yang was the commander of the First Column of the Shanxi-Hebei-Shandong-Henan Military Region, led by Liu Bocheng and Deng Xiaoping during the civil war against the Nationalists in the 1940s. Deng initially chose Yang Yong, deputy general chief of staff and another veteran of the Shanxi-Hebei-Shandong-Henan Military Region, to take charge as general chief of staff. As Yang Yong had been diagnosed with cancer since 1978, Deng chose Yang Dezhi as general chief of staff. [c]Both Zhao Cangbi and Yu Sang were appointed to lead the Bureau of Public Security of the CCP's Southwest Bureau, headed by Deng, during the end of 1940s and early 1950s. [d]Like Yang Yong, Pan Yan also served in the Shanxi-Hebei-Shandong-Henan Military Region under Deng's leadership from 1943 to 1953.

Yang was appointed as Wang Dongxing's top associate during the Cultural Revolution, thus making his position similar to that of Zhang Yaoci, but he wasn't given responsibilities involving Mao's security. At the time, Wang Dongxing had overall responsibility for the security apparatuses in Zhongnanhai and personally managed issues of Mao's security; Zhang Yaoci was specifically in charge of Unit 8341, guarding and serving Mao; and Yang was assigned to manage the dispatchment of bodyguards for other high-ranking leaders and other less significant tasks, such as preparing leadership conferences and making arrangements for personnel to support the left-wing rebels (*zhi zuo*) in the six factories and two universities (*liuchang erxiao*) revolutionary model.[131] In addition, the personal tension between Wang and Yang also lent to Yang's insignificant role in Zhongnanhai security forces, and it particularly

---

[131] Ibid., pp. 113, 162, 315.

contributed to Yang's exile from Beijing to Shaanxi in 1973.[132] In November 1973, Yang was unexpectedly demoted and transferred to Shaanxi, where he was appointed political commissar of a local military subdistrict (*jun fengqu*). This transfer took place when Mao targeted Zhou Enlai for Zhou's "right capitulation" in foreign policy toward the United States.[133] Mao also trussed Marshal Ye Jianying with Zhou Enlai as his targets for the so-called revisionist line. With Zhou deemed a threat to the party by Mao, Yang Dezhong was also deemed a threat, as the possibility of him turning against Mao and cooperating with the PLA was too great to keep him around.[134]

Because of Yang's transfer to Shaanxi, Yang was not involved in the suppression of the Tiananmen Incident in April 1976, which triggered the purges of Deng Xiaoping. The main actor involved in the Tiananmen Incident was Wang Dongxing: he was commanding the Beijing Garrison Command against the students at Tiananmen. After the fall of the Gang of Four, unlike other members of the leadership from the Central General Office, Yang refused to ally with Hua Guofeng and Wang Dongxing. He instead helped Deng take control of the Zhongnanhai security forces. Yang was reportedly highly influenced by Deng Yingchao, Zhou Enlai's wife, who coached him in his political positioning and alliances. Her mentoring helped him keep distance with Deng's opponents improved Yang's relationship with Deng Xiaoping and other party veterans as well. To become closer to Deng, Yang offered Deng significant support through his alliance with the veteran leaders against his former supervisor Wang Dongxing. As a result of Yang's history avoiding assisting Deng's opponents and supporting Deng throughout the years, Yang gradually developed strong loyalties to Deng.

Yang's loyalty to Deng Xiaoping is also seen in Yang's unconditional obedience to Deng's orders against CCP general secretaries Hu Yaobang and Zhao Ziyang in the 1980s. The central security forces had been used by veteran leaders to ensure that the appointed party chiefs stayed on the course defined by the veteran leaders, even though the veteran leaders' strategy for reconstructing the official ideology was ambiguous and the central core of the Chinese political

---

[132] Ibid., pp. 315–20.
[133] Zhou was blamed for "committing mistakes" during Zhou's conversation with Henry Kissinger in the Sino-U.S. negotiation in November 1973. Zhou was criticized for "promising the U.S. for the Sino-U.S. military cooperation and accepting the protection under Washington's nuclear umbrella without consulting Mao because Zhou "was terrified to nuclear weapon." See Gao Wenqian. Wannian Zhou Enlai [Zhou Enlai's later years] (New York: Mirror Books, 2003), pp. 463–4.
[134] Yang's relationship with Wang Dongxing became estranged after Mao dismissed Yang following Mao's initiative against Zhou Enlai in the winter of 1973 and the spring of 1974. Mao blamed Zhou for "giving incorrect statements" when Zhou had diplomatic negotiations with Henry Kissinger in November 1973 and "yielded to the United States." Mao ordered the Politburo to criticize Zhou Enlai and Marshal Ye Jianying. See *Wu Jicheng huiyilu*, pp. 316–17.

system was itself in crisis.[135] In the mid- to late 1980s, Deng instructed Yang to monitor the former party general secretary Hu Yaobang after Hu was dismissed, and he instructed him to place another party general secretary, Zhao Ziyang, under house arrest after Zhao was dismissed, both of which Yang did.[136] In Yang's fourteen years of service to Deng, the position immediately superior to Yang's – the director of the Central General Office – had changed hands six times (Yao Yilin, Hu Qili, Qiao Shi, Wang Zhaoguo, Wen Jiabao, and Zeng Qinghong), but Yang never left the office. In effect, none of the supervisors had abiding authority to command Yang, who was considered highly loyal to Deng,[137] and Deng was able to maintain control of the Zhongnanhai security apparatuses. Although Mao relied mainly on the security apparatus and adversarial interactions between army factions to ensure his own security and dominance during his reign, Deng exerted direct control over both the security apparatus and the PLA. Mao's prestige and charisma, which created a personality cult framing him as the undisputable leader of the CCP, guaranteed the obedience of the PLA during his reign.[138] Because of the circumstances of the revolution, Mao did not have to continuously strive for loyalty from the PLA – but PLA loyalty would never come that easily for any future leader. With a political death sentence from Mao, Deng faced an uphill battle to gain legitimacy within the PLA and the party. Thus, the direct and tangible support that Deng garnered from the PLA can be viewed as highly significant in reinforcing his legitimacy and authority in the party leadership.

Deng relied on Yang Dezhong for direct control over the security forces, particularly the Central Guard Bureau; in addition, he appointed his chief bodyguard Sun Yong to lead the Central Guard Regiment.[139] The strategy that Deng used to control the security forces was to appoint the influential veterans of the Central Guard Bureau and the Central Guard Regiment who did not ally with Wang Dongxing during the Cultural Revolution. As was Yang Dezhong, Sun Yong was a senior guard who joined the Eighth Route Army in August 1938 when he was twelve years old. In the late 1940s, when the Guard Department under the Central General Office was located in Xibeipo, Hebei, Sun was one of Mao's bodyguards. He often was assigned the task

---

[135] Gordon White, *Riding the Tiger: The Politics of Economic Reform in Post-Mao China*, pp. 157, 170.

[136] According to Zhao Ziyang, he had been put under house arrest by the Central Guard Bureau since June 1989. See Zhao Ziyang, *Gaige licheng* [Journey in the course of reform], p. 77.

[137] M. D. Swaine, *The Military and Political Succession in China: Leadership, Institutions, Beliefs*, p. 87.

[138] Despite Lin Biao's dominance in the PLA leadership and the powerful influence from Lin's trusted followers at the local levels during the Cultural Revolution, Lin was unable to launch a military coup against Mao.

[139] For example, Sun Yong was Deng's chief bodyguard when Deng visited local governments. See "Xiaoping zai Yantai de rizi" [Xiaoping in Yantai], in *Shenghuo zhoubao* [Life weekly], August 19, 2004.

of guarding Jiang Qing. In the early 1950s, both Sun Yong and Li Yinqiao were promoted to deputy chief bodyguards; Sun was in charge of the armed guards (*wuzhuang jingwei*), and Li was in charge of the inner guard (*neiwei* or *shenghuo weishi*).[140] Both Li Yinqiao and Sun Yong became important figures in serving Mao and ensuring his security in the early 1950s. Beginning in the mid-1950s, Sun became a deputy director and later director of a department under the Guard Department. Although little material is available on Sun Yong's career in the Cultural Revolution, several memoirs written by his colleagues in the Central General Office reveal Sun's fate in the Cultural Revolution. Sun was sent to the Study Class of the Central General Office in Jiangxi, after it relocated from Beijing in January 1969. The class, according to Wang Dongxing's associate Tong Xiaopeng, was created by Wang Dongxing to exile those subordinates and their families who "were not suitable or were no longer needed in Zhongnanhai."[141] According to Wu Jicheng, several members of the leadership of Group 1 of the Central Guard Bureau (the team that served Mao) were sent, under Mao's order, to the study class in the spring of 1968.

Apparently, these officers attempted to seize power from Wang Dongxing after they were inspired by the Shanghai revolutionary movement, launched by radicals, to seize power from the CCP's Shanghai Party Committee. After Wang reported the incident to Mao, Mao decisively removed those officers, stating, "They are dangerous because they are armed."[142] Although Wu Jicheng did not mention the names of those guards removed from Group 1, it is reasonable to speculate that, as the director of Group 1, Sun Yong might have been among them. This is also supported by the evidence that, starting in 1968, Sun's name no longer appeared in the ranks of the leadership of the Central Guard Bureau.[143] Perhaps Wang Dongxing took into consideration that punishment for revolution in a climate in which "rebellion is justifiable"[144] sends a conflicting message, or perhaps he just wanted to give Sun a break. In any respect, Sun was not treated as many of the other officers in the Central General Office who committed "mistakes." Wang might simply have categorized Sun as one who was not trusted by the proletarian headquarters and therefore was not suitable for working in Zhongnanhai. Later, however, Sun was redeemed. He

---

[140] Li Yinqiao replaced Wang Dongxing as chief bodyguard in 1955 when Wang no longer concurrently held the position as Mao's chief bodyguard. See Li Yinqiao, "Wogei Mao zhuxi dang weishi" [I was a guard of Chairman Mao], in Sun Mingshan (ed.), *Lishi shunjian* [An instant in history], vol. 3, p. 254; Li Jiaji and Yang Qingwang, *Lingxiu shenbian shisan nian – Mao Zedong weishi Li Jiaji fangtan lu* [Thirty years at the site of the leader – Interview with Mao Zedong's guard Li Jiaji], vol. 1, p. 31; Quan Yanchi, *Zouxia shentan de Mao Zedong* [Mao Zedong stepping down from altar], pp. 142–3.

[141] Tong Xiaopeng, *Shaoxiao lijia laoda hui – Tong Xiaopeng huiyilu*, p. 550.

[142] *Wu Jicheng huiyilu*, p. 112.

[143] Ibid., pp. 95, 420–1.

[144] See Wang Nianyi, *Da dongluan de niandai* [China 1949–1989: the years of great turmoil] (Xinxiang: Henan renmin chubanshe, 1990), p. 51.

was appointed as a member of the leadership in the May 7 Cadre School, and in 1978 he was made deputy principal of the school.[145] Finally, in December 1978 veteran leaders appointed Sun to lead Unit 8341 in the Third Plenum of the Eleventh Party Congress.[146]

As Deng historically had little influence on the Central Guard Bureau and the Central Guard Regiment, pursuing the support of the security apparatus became one of his primary objectives after he returned to his posts as vice premier and general chief of staff of the PLA. Before Deng returned to his posts, Deng reportedly asked Wang Zhen to lobby Wang Dongxing for Wang's support for Deng's return and a possible political alliance between the two. Given Wang's role in helping Deng when he was in political exile, Deng may have really hoped to cultivate a good relationship and political alliance with Wang. Wang helped Deng by allowing him access to Mao, sending Deng's paralytic son to one of the best hospitals in China, providing accommodation for Deng when he was exiled to Jiangxi, and arranging for two of Deng's daughters to attend universities.[147] Unfortunately, Wang Dongxing turned down Deng's offer, instead offering the snarky remark that Deng "should stay at home and hug his grandchildren," adding that he "would be better off not involved in politics."[148]

Wang Dongxing's denial of support was a great blow to Deng, and it made it difficult for him to challenge Hua Guofeng. As a result, Deng had three approaches to gain control over the security apparatus. First, Deng and other veteran leaders rehabilitated the case of Yang Shangkun, former director of the Central General Office, before the Third Plenum in December 1978. Perhaps in the hope of not provoking Wang Dongxing, Yang did not resume his position as director of the Central General Office on December 10, 1978. Instead, he was appointed deputy party secretary and mayor of Guangzhou. Then, during the Third Plenum, Wang Dongxing was asked to hand over control of the Central General Office, the Central Guard Bureau, and the Central Guard Division (the Central Guard Regiment was upgraded as the Central Guard Division in 1977) or Unit 8341. At the same time, Yao Yilin, Yang Dezhong, and Sun Yong were appointed to take charge of the Central General Office, the Central Guard Bureau, and Unit 8341, respectively. Still, Yang Shangkun was personally assigned by Deng Xiaoping to play a leading role in reorganizing the CCP security apparatus. It was not until late January 1979 that Yang completed the reorganization of the Central General Office, after which he took office in Guangdong.[149]

[145] Ibid., p. 436.
[146] Chang Feng, *Ganxiao jishi* [Recorded stories of the Cadres School], http://www. thegreatwall.com.cn/phpbbs/index.php?id=82013&forumid=4 (accessed January 13, 2010); *Wu Jicheng huiyilu*, p. 436.
[147] *Deng Xiaoping "Wenge" suiyue*, pp. 119, 122, 222.
[148] *Singtaonet*, January 23, 2007.
[149] *Yang Shangkun huiyilu*, pp. 353–4.

Second, senior veterans in the Third Plenum decided to create a party agency for handling the party's day-to-day affairs. In effect, this agency served to divide Wang Dongxing's power and undermine his influence. Because of the challenges involved in resuming the Central Secretariat, a party organization that was created to handle the party's day-to-day affairs before the Cultural Revolution, veteran leaders appointed Hu Yaobang, Hu Qiaomu, and Yao Yilin to be in charge of the new agency. Hu Yaobang was appointed secretary-general, and Hu Qiaomu and Yao Yilin were appointed as deputy secretary-generals.[150] Obviously, veteran leaders, headed by Deng Xiaoping and Chen Yun, strategically gave Wang Dongxing a symbolic position as a party vice chairman in exchange for his handing over of the security apparatus and forces. In addition, the separation of the Central Guard Bureau and Unit 8341 from the Central General Office not only weakened the influence of Wang Dongxing and his key followers, such as Zhang Yaoci and Li Xin, but also consolidated Deng Xiaoping's control over the armed security forces. Once everything in the Third Plenum was said and done, Deng Xiaoping had direct authority over the PLA General Staff Department, which solely commanded the CCP security forces.

Third, veteran leaders launched large-scale purges in the Central General Office, the Central Guard Bureau, and Unit 8341. The purges essentially targeted Wang Dongxing's followers and those who played active roles in the Cultural Revolution. The veteran leaders strategized to reinstate Cultural Revolution victims in office while removing Cultural Revolution beneficiaries from office within the security apparatus and forces. For example, both Yang Dezhong and Sun Yong, prestigious senior guards in Zhongnanhai later exiled by Wang Dongxing, were appointed to head the Central Guard Bureau and Unit 8341, respectively. They were also charged with leading the campaign against Wang's followers and others who were active in the Cultural Revolution. For Deng and the veteran leaders, the key strategy toward the armed security forces was to cultivate loyalty from Yang Dezhong and Sun Yong to consolidate control over the security forces. Promoting the two men, in part, helped achieve this goal. In December 1978, Yang was authorized to lead Zhongnanhai's security forces; in 1982 he was promoted to membership in the Central Party Committee. Likewise, in late 1978 Sun was appointed to lead Unit 8341 and to become Deng's chief bodyguard. When Deng Xiaoping resumed military ranks in 1988, both Yang and Sun were granted higher military ranks. Yang was promoted to lieutenant general, and Sun was promoted to major general. Sun was further promoted to lieutenant general in 1991.

As the professionalization of Chinese civil-military relations as well as the civil-security apparatus increasingly plays an important role in elite politics, the trend of CCP politics during the post-Deng era can be characterized as

---

[150] Jin Chongji and Chen Qun, *Chen Yun zhuan* [A biography of Chen Yun], vol. 2, p. 1495.

increasingly institutionalized. The reform and openness that aim to modernize China soften and fade communist ideology, replacing it with the growth of commercialism, profits, and a socialist system with market features. The Chinese military, to which the Central Guard Regiment is subordinate, is required to both improve its technical war-fighting capability and improve its officer corps so that it is better equipped to compete with advancing international standards.

However, personal ties, loyalty, personal influence, and informal methods of control continue to play a critical role in the security apparatus, because control thereof directly affects the political survival and advantages of top leaders. For example, Jiang Zemin had neither military experience himself nor historical ties with the PLA and the security forces. For Jiang, the conditions to become a paramount leader like Mao or Deng – the prestige, revolutionary achievement, and strong networks of loyal military followers – were missing. Although he attempted to draw in the army's support for his leadership by increasing the military budget and promoting senior military commanders,[151] Jiang nonetheless relied heavily on the security apparatus to establish his authority and ensure his security. Jiang took three steps to establish his control over the security apparatus. First, Jiang transferred his close secretary Jia Tingan and close associate Zeng Qinghong from Shanghai to Beijing. Jiang appointed Jia deputy director of the CMC General Office and Zeng deputy director of the Central General Office in an effort to control the security forces that guarded both civilian and military ranking leaders.[152] Jia had served Jiang since the late 1970s, and in 1994 Jia was awarded the rank of a major general despite his limited military experience.[153] It has become an unwritten rule in the leadership that a high-ranking leader is often allowed to bring his or her secretaries and guards with him or her when transferred or promoted. In 1973, When Mao called Deng Xiaoping to return to Beijing after more than three years of exile in Jiangxi, Deng was allowed to bring his former secretary Wang Ruilin and guard Zhang Baozhong with him. Wang Ruilin had been Deng's secretary since 1952, and Zhang Baozhong had served Deng as an indoor staff member between 1954 and 1960 and as a bodyguard since 1960. Chen Pixian, former Shanghai first party secretary, was rehabilitated in November 1976 and appointed a deputy party secretary in Yunnan; Chen was given the option of either bringing his former secretaries and bodyguards with him or accepting the secretaries and

[151] Joseph Fewsmith, "Reaction, Resurgence, and Succession: Chinese Politics since Tiananmen," in Roderick MacFarquhar (ed.), *The Politics of China: The Eras of Mao and Deng*, p. 518.
[152] According to an interview, although Zeng was formally appointed to the CCP General Office in October 1992, he had taken the job from Wen Jiabao three years earlier to strengthen the CCP General Office role as communication center for Jiang Zemin.
[153] Tai Ming Cheung, "The Influence of the Gun: China's Central Military Commission and Its Relationship with the Military, Party, and State Decision-Making Systems," in David M. Lampton (ed.), *The Making of Chinese Foreign and Security Policy in the Era of Reform, 1978–2000*, p. 68.

bodyguards assigned to him by the Central Guard Bureau.[154] Second, Jiang arranged for Zeng Qinghong to gradually take control of the Central General Office. After Wen Jiabao was replaced by Zeng Qinghong in the Fourteenth Party Congress as director of the General Office, Zeng became the commanding officer of the security apparatus that guarded Zhongnanhai. Third, Jiang promoted Yang Dezhong as a full general to exchange Yang's retirement, a successful move that enabled Jiang to appoint You Xigui, Jiang's chief bodyguard, to take charge of the elite security apparatuses.[155]

---

[154] Chen Xiaojin, *Wode "wenge" suiyue* [The years of my life in the Cultural Revolution], pp. 435–6.
[155] Bruce Gilley, *Tiger on the Brink: Jiang Zemin and China's New Elite*, p. 215.

5

Armed Police and Their Historical Role in CCP Politics

This chapter chronicles the evolution of the CCP's armed police and describes the historical context that allowed them to emerge and develop as a crucial security force in CCP politics. The CCP established the armed police forces after the civil war against the Nationalists had already been won. The armed police resulted from a consensus among the CCP leadership to modernize China's military. Among leaders, there was the understanding that having an armed police would enable the People's Liberation Army (PLA) to professionalize along the lines of the Soviet model, but for the paramount leader, the armed police represented the possibility of weakening powerful local military generals and centralizing China's armed forces. Although the party's leadership was still unquestioned, the increased professionalism of the armed police undermined arbitrary interference from the party to a certain degree. An issue that continues to surface for the armed police is the enduring debate about whether they should follow a vertical chain of command.

In the original organizational structure of the People's Armed Police (PAP), the PLA was in charge of the security forces at the provincial level and above, and the Ministry of Public Security led the security forces below the provincial level. It was under this dual system of public security and military leadership that the MPS managed professional police work, public security, and operational duties, and the Central Military Commission (CMC) was responsible for corps-building activities and logistics and supplies. However, on the eve of the Cultural Revolution the system disintegrated because the armed police forces were completely enmeshed with local PLA units. The forces were renamed the People's Armed Police in June 1982, when party leadership decided to integrate all guarding duties and security responsibilities that had formerly been under the PLA's jurisdiction into the Military of Public Security. In March 1995, the PAP it was institutionally removed from the MPS, to be housed under the dual command of the State Council and the CMC.

This chapter examines the political and social climate under which the armed police were created, reorganized, abolished, and enhanced throughout the history of the People's Republic of China. Similar to the PLA in the late 1950s, the armed police became the target of criticism, because the Soviet format they were based on was viewed as inefficient, rigid, routine, and formal, and unit functions were deemed redundant. As a result, the model was increasingly challenged. The beginning of the Great Leap Forward in early 1958 triggered a veritable avalanche of decentralization, sending power cascading to local party committees. One effect of decentralization was the reorganization and return of the armed police forces to the jurisdiction of local public security offices. Units of the armed police personnel were subordinate to local bureaus of public security, which were under the leadership of local party committees. The change from local control over the armed police forces to a dual public security–military leadership system occurred while China was suffering the severe consequences of the Great Leap Forward.

It is important to note, however, that the reorganized armed police forces were not put under equal authority of the MPS and the PLA. Although the MPS and its local organs provided professional guidance for the armed police forces, the PLA played a vital role in its construction, personnel allotments, finances, political control, education and training, supply, and personnel turnover. The expansion of local power became one of Mao's key political moves – he directed local armed forces to replace local party organs during the Cultural Revolution. Indeed, it could be argued that Mao's initiative to let local military regions control the abolished armed police centered on disabling the ability of the central bureaucracy to use force directly against him after he launched the Cultural Revolution. But the abolishment of the armed police created greater problems for Mao, given their inability to curtail violence and to restore social order during the Cultural Revolution. With the armed police forces defunct, Mao had to rely on ordinary PLA units, which were not properly trained, to deal with citizens in restoring social order. Lack of direct control over the armed police forces also impeded Mao's ability to execute personal security plans and hindered emergency responses to threats to high-ranking leaders. In the capital city, for example, Mao underestimated the scale of the mass violence and thus was unable to control it by relying on only Unit 8341 and the Beijing Garrison Command. In particular, the abolishment of the armed police forces limited Mao's ability to control local party and military leaders. Because of their deep involvement with local politics, the armed police units allied with certain mass rebels against others, sometimes even against the PLA's local units. In some regions, the personnel or leaders of some armed police units were split because of their alliances with different factions of the Red Guards and the revolutionary mass organizations.

Perhaps no CCP organization has had as malleable an existence as the People's Armed Police (PAP). Since its inception, the group's name has been changed several times to reflect the various ways that the party elite has

TABLE 5.1. *Historical Evolution of China's Armed Police, 1949–2012*

From	To	Name	Jurisdiction
August 1949	December 1949	Central Column of the Chinese People's Public Security Forces (*zhongguo renmin gong'an zhongyang zongdui*)	MPS
December 1949	September 1950	Chinese People's Public Security Forces (CPPSF, *zhongguo renmin gong'an budui*)	MPS and CMC
September 1950	July 1955	PLA Public Security Forces (PLAPSF, *zhongguo renmin jiefangjun gong'an budui*)	CMC
May 1955	August 1957	PLA Public Security Army (PLAPSA, *zhongguo renmin jiefangjun gong'an jun*)	CMC
August 1957	August 1958	PLA Public Security Forces (PLAPSF, *zhongguo renmin jiefangjun gong'an budui*)	CMC
August 1958	January 1963	People's Armed Police (PAP, *renmin wuzhuang jingcha*)	Dual command by MPS and CMC
January 1963	June 1966	Chinese People's Public Security Forces (CPPSF, *zhongguo renmin gong'an budui*)	Dual command by MPS and CMC
July 1966	June 1982	"Independent" units of the PLA after the CPPSF was abolished and integrated into local PLA units	Local PLA command
June 1982	April 2012	Chinese People's Armed Police Force or People's Amed Police (PAP, *zhongguo renmin wuzhuang jingcha budui*)	Dual command by MPS and CMC

Year

Source: "Dangdai zhongguo" congshu bianji weiyuanhui ["Contemporary China" Series Editing Committee], *Zhongguo renmin jiefangjun* [The People's Liberation Army] (Beijing: Dangdai zhongguo chubanshe, 1994), vol. 2, pp. 292–7; Wang Jianying, *Zhongguo gongchandang zuzhishi ziliao huibian: lingdao jigou yange he chengyuan minglu* [A collection of reference materials about the CCP organization history: The evolution of the leadership structure and the list of its members] (Beijing: Zhonggong zhongyang dangxiao chubanshe, 1995), pp. 939, 994, 1052, 1106, 1221.

perceived its mission. The Chinese People's Public Security Forces, PLA Public Security Forces, PLA Public Security Army, and the People's Armed Police have all referred to this organization at some point in its existence (Table 5.1). The PAP's organizational affiliations within the party have changed eight times in five different incarnations. The PAP and its predecessors have always been subordinate to either the PLA (under the auspices of the Central Military

Committee) or the Ministry of Public Security. Fittingly, even the PAP's place in this command structure has been complicated and confused, as the PAP was traditionally under the dual jurisdiction of the PLA and the Ministry of Public Security.

Chinese People's Public Security Forces, 1949–1950

In Yan'an during the 1940s, Mao defined his vision of the future system of the CCP armed forces (*junzhi*). Military pressure from the Japanese, the Guomindang (GMD), and rogue communists forged Mao's idea of a tripartite military: field armies, local armed forces, and militia and/or military reserve forces. The local armed forces, as Mao explained to Peng Zhen, would be the armed police.[1] These three parts of the CCP military would eventually become the foundation for the PRC's armed forces after the CCP's government takeover in 1949.[2]

In late 1949, shortly after the formation of the PRC, the first steps toward a unified and efficient public security group run by the party became apparent. On August 31, 1949, the Central Military Commission ordered the Central Column of the Chinese People's Public Security Forces to be organized under the jurisdiction of the Ministry of Public Security. Its duties included guarding the CCP Central Committee and the central government, as well as ensuring social order in Beijing. By May 1950, the major battles against the Nationalist armies had ended, and the PLA was divided into two parts, the Defense Forces (*guofang jun*) and the Public Security Forces (*gong'an jun*). The Chinese People's Public Security Forces (CPPSF) accounted for 4.5 percent of the reorganized former PLA troops and comprised twenty-two divisions.[3] Within the divisions, those stationed in Beijing fell under the direct leadership of the CPPSF headquarters. Other divisions fell under the dual leadership of the headquarters of the CPPSF in Beijing and the local military regions where they were stationed (similarly, railway divisions were under the dual jurisdictions of both CPPSF headquarters and the Ministry of Railway, which was under the jurisdiction of the State Council).[4]

---

[1] This system of the CCP armed forces had been introduced by Peng Zhen in the *Xinhua Daily* in 1942 under Mao's direct guidance. According to Peng, Mao told him that the CCP's armed forces must consist of field armies, local armed forces, and militia in which local armed forces were the armed police. See Li Haiwen and Wang Yanling, *Shiji duihua – yi xinzhongguo fazhi dianjiren Peng Zhen* [Centurial dialogue – Reminiscing about the founder of the PRC law and legal system, Peng Zhen] (Beijing: Qunzhong chubanshe, 2002), p. 74.

[2] *Xinhua*, July 10, 2007.

[3] See 'Dangdai zhongguo' congshu bianji weiyuanhui ["Contemporary China" Series Editing Committee], *Zhongguo renmin jiefangjun* [The People's Liberation Army] (Beijing: Dangdai zhongguo chubanshe, 1994), vol. 2, pp. 292–3.

[4] Ibid., pp. 293–4.

Although local CPPSF units were put under the direct control of the PLA military regions, CPPSF headquarters was still obligated to advise local armed police forces on issues of professional administration, training, and political education. By April 1950, the estimated number of CPPSF personnel nation-wide reached 240,000.[5] In May 1950, the CPPSF was authorized to establish branches in the South-Central, Eastern, Northeastern, Northwestern, and Southwestern military commands, and it sent armed police to these branches for the protection of the railway, border control, and administration.[6] The establishment of an armed police force arose from the objective to professionalize the military force in line with the Soviet model. Thus, the armed police resulted from a consensus among CCP leadership to modernize China's military. However, professionalization based on the Soviet model was not the sole goal of the modernization plan; it also fit Mao's strategy to weaken the powerful local military generals and centralize the power of China's armed forces. In April 1950, the CMC abolished the headquarters of five field armies (*yezhan jun*) and the PLA army groups (*bingtuan*) as they planned to merge the PLA units into local military regions and special military groups (*tezhong bing*), such as the air force, navy, armored forces, and engineering corps.[7]

Obviously, the main distinction between the two forces was that the field army corps, the essential combat forces of the PLA directly under the jurisdiction of military regions, were much better equipped and had stronger combat forces than the local army corps, mainly the local garrison and guard troops headed by the military districts, and they were usually referred to as independent units (e.g., independent divisions, independent regiments, independent battalions).[8] When the Chinese People's Public Security Forces was established in 1949, the local military districts were ordered to relinquish their independent units to the CPPSF. These changes met overwhelming resistance from both local military regions and some localities, which complained that the only duties left to local military regions were to control the local militia. Some generals in the local military regions complained that the transfer of the independent divisions significantly weakened the local military regions and districts, with

---

[5] Tao Siju, *Xinzhongguo diyiren gongan buzhang: Luo Ruiqing* [The first public security minister of the new China: Luo Ruiqing] (Beijing: Qunzhong chubanshe, 1997), p. 157.
[6] See 'Dangdai zhongguo' congshu bianji weiyuanhui, *Zhongguo renmin jiefangjun*, vol. 2, pp. 293–4.
[7] Ibid., p. 6.
[8] In the 1940s civil war, a large number of independent units merged to replace the communist field army corps in taking charge of the social order in the base areas and the regions where the CCP had taken over from the GMD after the field army corps were sent to the major battleground against the Nationalist Army. The independent units mainly derived from local army forces, the militia, and insurgent GMD army units. After the founding of the PRC, most of the independent units were reorganized as the Independent Division and were put under the jurisdiction of the military districts. See Dongfang He, *Zhang Aiping zhuan* [A biography of Zhang Aiping] (Beijing: Renmin chubanshe, 2000), p. 627.

the fundamental problem being that "military district commanders now have no soldiers to command!"[9] Local army leaders also questioned the necessity of establishing the CPPSF, because the CPPSF's duties overlapped with those of the local military regions and districts.[10]

People's Liberation Army Public Security Forces, 1950–1955

Beginning in 1950, the CPPSF was ordered to reorganize the existing armed police of the CCP and PLA at the provincial and municipal levels across the nation. These organizations included the Political Guard Teams (*zhengzhi baowei dui*), which were led by the bureaus of public security, local security forces, and PLA army corps.[11] The CPPSF was renamed the People's Liberation Army Public Security Forces (PLAPSF) in September 1950. In September and October 1950, the headquarters of the PLAPSF and its leading organs in local military regions and the Railway Ministry were established.[12] The entire PLA was reorganized into two parts: the Defense Forces (*guofang jun*) and the Public Security Forces (*gong'an jun*). The Public Security Forces became responsible for "eradicating the remnants of enemy forces, maintaining social order, and safeguarding the country's constructions," and the Defense Force served to "fight against foreign invasion and strengthen national defense."[13]

The PLAPSF was established to fill a previously unfulfilled niche in the PLAPSF. At first it consisted of twenty divisions and three regiments, with a total of about 188,800 personnel.[14] This was a relatively small number of soldiers, compared with the 5.2 million personnel in the PLA ground forces in 1950.[15] The low number of the PLAPSF units stemmed from a debate within the party as to where the public security forces would be placed within the reorganized security structure. Ultimately, this likely shrank the leadership of the PLAPSF. In addition, around 360,000 personnel were absorbed into the local public security forces, the border defense security force, and the prison guard remained as the Chinese People's Public Security Forces, under the jurisdiction of the MPS (Figure 5.1). This system of public security, which was divided into civilian and military public security forces, was

---

[9] Ibid., p. 628.
[10] Ibid., pp. 627–9.
[11] Yang Jingming, "Wo he Zhao Guowei" [Zhao Guowei and I], in Sun Mingshan (ed.), *Lishi shunjian* [An instant in history], vol. 3, p. 591·
[12] See "Dangdai zhongguo" congshu bianji weiyuanhui, *Zhongguo renmin jiefangjun*, vol. 2, p. 294.
[13] See Liu Han and Huang Yao, *Luo Ruiqing zhuan* [A biography of Luo Ruiqing] (Beijing: Dangdai zhongguo chubanshe, 1995), p. 284.
[14] See "Dangdai zhongguo" congshu bianji weiyuanhui, *Zhongguo renmin jiefangjun*, vol. 2, pp. 294–5.
[15] Ibid., p. 6.

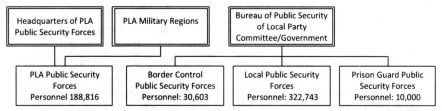

FIGURE 5.1. *People's Liberation Army Public Security Forces, September 1950*
Source: "Dangdai zhongguo" congshu bianji weiyuanhui, *Zhongguo renmin jiefangjun*, vol. 2, pp. 292–7; Wu Lie, *Zhengrong suiyue*, pp. 348–9.

later criticized as lacking "the unified organizational format, smooth leadership relationships, and effective management." This resulted in the incorporation of the civilian public security force into the military system in the spring of 1952, which expanded the PLAPSF from 188,000 to 538,000 personnel. The reorganized PLAPSF was under the dual leadership of the CMC and the MPS.[16]

After the CCP's takeover in 1949, there was a growing trend in the PLA to push for professionalism in the armed forces. The PLA was critically aware of its history as a guerrilla force and was tactically insecure with respect to its ability to project real power throughout the country. The PLA leadership was reminded of the military realities on the ground during the conflict with the Japanese and the Guomindang, and many saw a real need to reinforce the established strategy of attrition-based warfare with more modern machinery, armaments, and training. This tendency was further encouraged after China confronted the well-equipped, well-trained American troops in Korea, and after the PLA invited Soviet advisers to assist in developing China's military modernization.[17]

The Soviets viewed the PLA's military development as subpar, which further exacerbated leading generals' insecurities. Although tension between party control and limited military autonomy had always existed in the PLA, striving toward professionalism has played a major role in its evolution since the 1950s. During Marshal Peng Dehuai's tenure as minister of defense, professionalization became one of the army's greatest priorities.[18] Thus, embarrassment and the requisite self-adjustment were predictable responses to the Soviet visit. As were other leading government and army organs, the Ministry of Public Security and the PLAPSF were urged to follow the Soviet system. Specifically, this model emphasized a vertical chain of command based on professionalism and

---

[16] Ibid., pp. 294–5.
[17] Stalin sent many Soviet advisers to China soon after Liu Shaoqi visited Moscow in the fall of 1949. See Nie Rongzhen, *Nie Rongzhen huiyilu* [Memoirs of Nie Rongzhen], vol. 3 (Beijing: Jiefangjun chubanshe, 1984), pp. 729–30.
[18] David Shambaugh, *Modernizing China's Military: Progress Problems, and Prospects*, p. 17.

independence from party committees.[19] The Soviet system certainly echoed the ideas of most party leaders to transfer the public security forces and apparatus from party control to state control.[20] Although the party's leadership was still unquestionable, the increase in PLA professionalism did, to a certain degree, undermine arbitrary interference from the party. In contrast to the contemporary party line, evidence suggests that Mao was one leader who disagreed with the idea of transferring the security forces from party control to state control. Although no published material is available on the detailed debate on the issue among party leadership, Mao's rejection of the transfer can be seen in three cases.

One telling example of Mao's disagreement was his criticism of Luo Ruiqing, who followed the governmental organizational hierarchy and reported his work to Zhou Enlai instead of Mao. In September 1950, Mao ordered Luo to report to him directly and warned Luo by writing a note in one of Luo's reports: "the work of public security must be put under the absolute control of party committees at different levels; otherwise, it is dangerous."[21] By the same token, Mao was not happy when Luo followed the party hierarchical structure to report his work to Peng Zhen, a member of the Central Secretariat who was assigned to head China's legal system, including the MPS.[22] Mao's message to the party leadership was clear: he would control the security forces and apparatus himself, under the auspices of the party.

The second example of Mao's displeasure with the leadership transfer occurred in the spring of 1950 and regarded a decision by the PLA leadership, led by Nie Rongzhen (acting general chief of staff), to merge the Central Guard Regiment with the CPPSF. On the surface, Mao blamed the PLA leadership by claiming that they had made the decision without his knowledge or consent.[23] However, he was more likely unhappy about the merger because it undermined his direct control of the Central Guard Regiment. Much of Mao's power had been tied up in his ability to control high-ranking leaders, including those of the CGR. Thus, the reassignment of the CGR to another jurisdiction would have been a great threat to Mao's political primacy. The other significant factor in turning Mao against this decision was his concern with the

[19] Liu Han and Huang Yao, *Luo Ruiqing zhuan*, p. 297.
[20] This led to a decision by the party leadership in October 1949 to abolish the CCP Social Affairs Department, the leading party organ in charge of public security, in an effort to transfer its function to the state. See Tao Siju, *Xinzhongguo diyiren gongan buzhang: Luo Ruiqing* [The first public security minister of the new China: Luo Ruiqing] (Beijing: Qunzhong chubanshe, 1997), pp. 9–10.
[21] See Liu Han and Huang Yao, *Luo Ruiqing zhuan* [A biography of Luo Ruiqing], p. 264.
[22] Peng Zhen was assigned by the Central Secretariat to take charge of the MPS; he also led the Politics and Law Committee of the State Council, and Luo was his assistant in charge of the general office. See Li Haiwen and Wang Yanling, *Shiji duihua – yi xinzhongguo fazhi dianjiren Peng Zhen*, p. 53.
[23] (Luo) Diandian, *Feifan de niandai* [Those extraordinary years], pp. 146–7.

armed police force becoming too powerful. In this way, he probably viewed the possibility of the merger as a kind of pincer movement,[24] both relieving him of personal clout and empowering potential enemies against his rule. Here again we see the Chairman's infamous political instincts (or paranoia) coming into play to shape the CCP's structure.

The third example of Mao's support of party control, rather than state control, over the armed security forces is the jurisdiction of the PLAPSF local units. There was debate over whether they should be subordinate solely to the headquarters of the CPPSF and PLAPSF in Beijing or whether they should fall under the dual leadership of CCPSF and PLAPSF headquarters and the local party and military regions. The vertical relationships between the headquarters of the CPPSF and PLAPSF and its local units were based on guiding principles that had been borrowed from the Soviet Union in the early 1950s. Party consensus supported the process of the PLA's modernization and professionalization that encompassed this vertical hierarchy, so many leaders assumed that the CPPSF and PLAPSF would be incorporated into the established bureaucracy. The split between the Chairman and the party on this issue demonstrates that Mao was one of the few who opposed establishing a vertical chain of command for the armed security forces.

Unfortunately, there is little detailed published material available on the debate among the leadership. Information provided by Diandian, daughter of Luo Ruiqing, revealed that the true leadership debate over the CPPSF did not concern whether control of the local units would originate from upper-level CPPSF organizations or from a dual leadership of the CPPSF and local military regions. Instead, according to Diandian, "there were some divergences in opinion between the Chairman and other comrade including [my] father about the question of the jurisdiction of the public security forces; some decisions were not made in accordance with the original intention of the Chairman."[25]

Several important implications follow from these three examples. First, Mao clearly did not want the party's role in controlling the PLA and the armed security forces to be weakened, because of the potential mutual reciprocity of the relationship: the party's involvement gave more clout to the army leadership, and likewise, having control over the armed security forces gave the party more legitimacy. Mao's uncompromising position on the jurisdiction of the CPPSF and PLAPSF local units was, according to Luo Ruiqing, based on the fundamental concept that "the work of public security must be put under the leadership of the party committees at all levels."[26] The party's absolute control over the armed security forces is evident in the required percentage of party members with positions in the CPPSF and PLAPSF: personnel were required

---

[24] A military maneuver that attacks both flanks of an enemy forces with the aim of attaining complete encirclement.

[25] Ibid., p. 147.

[26] Ibid., p. 148.

to be carefully screened, including a strict background check, and at least 80 percent of officers and soldiers were required to be party members.[27] This politically motivated personnel emphasis provided a tough challenge for CPPSF and PLAPSF recruitment, because half of the CPPSF and PLAPSF units in some regions (e.g., Henan) had not established party branches, which resulted in a low percentage of party members (e.g., 10 percent).[28]

In the early history of the PLAPSF, the priority, as dictated by the leadership, evolved into establishing party branches at all company levels and strengthening party committees in all units. The progress in achieving this priority explains the increasing numbers of party members in the PLAPSF between 1952 and 1954. For example, in 1952, party organizations of the PLAPSF recruited 17,800 new party members, a 24.8 percent increase over 1951. Although there was a slight increase in 1953 (3 percent), the scale of the increase jumped dramatically in the following year to 40.1 percent.[29] To strengthen party control of all PLAPSF units, PLAPSF leaders established regulations to evaluate officers annually using a rubric of moral conduct, style of work, background checks, and social connections (e.g., overseas relationships).[30]

Another implication of the internal leadership schism was Mao's concern that vertical organization of the security forces would not accommodate party committee supervision. He feared that the PLAPSF could be manipulated by ambitious high-ranking leaders and would become a powerful, independent organ that would endanger the legitimacy of party leadership. Mao was particularly distressed by the possibility that the PLAPSF would become an all-powerful armed organization resembling the Soviet secret police (the most powerful and feared institution throughout the Stalinist period), headed by Lavrenty Pavlovich Beria (1899–1953). Interestingly, Mao did not follow Stalin's example in his considerable reliance on the secret police; rather, he relied on his personal prestige and charisma combined with his effective control over the security apparatus to maintain and enhance his power.

The revolutionary peasant victory over the GMD gave Mao great confidence in his role as spokesman for the common people. He continued to cite this victory throughout his career as his primary tool to rectify issues with the

[27] This was the expectation proposed by Liu Shaoqi; in practice, it was reduced to 60 percent for new recruits to the CPPSF. For existing personnel, the percentage of party members was much lower than new recruits; the percentage of party members in the CPPSF in late 1952 was only 24.8 percent. See Wu Lie, *Zhengrong suiyue* [The eventful times] (Beijing: Zhongyang wenxian chubanshe, 1999), p. 351; Shu Ping and Xiao Mingxing, "Luo Ruiqing dajiang yu zhongguo renmin gongan budui de zujian" [Senior general Luo Ruiqing and the establishment of the Chinese People's Public Security Force of China], in *Wenshi chunqiu* [Chronicle of literature and history], no. 7 (2005), p. 6; Liu Han and Huang Yao, *Luo Ruiqing zhuan*, p. 285; Yang Jingming, "Wo he Zhao Guowei," pp. 593–4.
[28] See Yang Jingming, "Wo he Zhao Guowei," p. 591.
[29] Ibid., pp. 593–4.
[30] Li Yimin, *Li Yimin huiyilu* [Memoirs of Li Yimin] (Changsha: Hunan renmin chubanshe, 1996), p. 171.

general population. Mao was convinced that smashing old ideas and reshaping Chinese society successfully relied on mass movements more than on the Soviet model of secret police. For example, when Mao decided to assault the party establishment and bureaucracy during the Cultural Revolution, he mobilized the general population rather than the secret police to achieve his goal. Compared with Stalin's terror against his associates, Mao preferred coercive persuasion in dealing with intraparty conflicts. In Frederick Teiwes's analysis of Mao's rectification campaign, he examines Mao's blend of coercion and persuasion to achieve control:

> Coercion is a source of vulnerability as well as potential strength. On the positive side, coercive methods are essential both to provide the environmental control which facilitates persuasive efforts, and to create conditions for far-reaching change. But while this was clearly recognized by Mao's injunction to "give the patient a fright," the thrust of rectification doctrine warns against excessive harshness. Similarly, out behavioral analysis of "coercive persuasion" shows coercion will be counterproductive if used to excess, especially when genuine attitudinal change, high morale and creative leadership are major goals. The traditional persuasive approach, then, is firmly rooted in the actual constraints of the disciplinary process.[31]

Compared with Mao's "selective and surgical rather than arbitrary" approach to dealing with individuals, in which he calculated decisively and intentionally who, when, and how to attack, Stalin's methods were based on "unpredictability and arbitrariness in striking someone regardless of whether he obeys the state's commands." Stalin's secret police "involved a far higher purge rate, harsher sanctions including frequent use of capital punishment, secret police administration, and a cynical disregard for reform and education."[32]

Mao had been received as the indisputable party leader since he established his dominance during the Yan'an rectification in the mid-1940s. The personality cult around him grew throughout the entire party and the masses after the PRC was established in 1949. Mao had been deemed "the all-knowing, all-wise leader who led the party through 'storm and stress,' overcoming every sort of difficulty to achieve final victory in 1949."[33] Stuart R. Schram and Nancy J. Hodes also point out, "Mao Zedong's thought was written into the Party statutes as the guide to all work, and Mao was hailed as the greatest theoretical genius in China's history for his achievement in creating such a remarkable doctrine."[34] As Mao felt increasingly confident in his ability to control party leadership and achieve the compliance of the party and the population, he did not need to rely on secret police and terror to maintain his dominance. That

---

[31] Frederick C. Teiwes, *Politics and Purges in China: Rectification and the Decline of Party Norms, 1950–1965*, 2nd ed., p. 45.

[32] Ibid., pp. 25–6.

[33] David Graff and Robin Higham, *A Military History of China*, p. 245.

[34] Stuart R. Schram and Nancy Jane Hodes, *Mao's Road to Power: Revolutionary Writings 1912–1949*, xix.

being said, nor did Mao underestimate the importance of maintaining control over the armed forces – if force was deemed necessary, they would provide critical support. In addition, Mao would have felt threatened if someone who controlled the security apparatus and the secret police developed more authority than his own, especially someone with whom Mao had not established personal loyalty.

Third, the CPPSF was established during a large-scale reorganization of the PLA. By May 1950, PLA disarmament had been fully initiated, and by 1951, 1.4 million armed PLA personnel were ordered demobilized.[35] In January 1952, the CMC decided to further reduce the total number of PLA personnel by an additional 45.6 percent, and more than half the ground forces (55.7 percent) were disarmed.[36] The reduction of the PLA forces begs the question of why Mao did not allow the armed police to become an independent armed force without any local party supervision. In addition, scholars have asked why Mao allowed only a small number of armed police into the force in the first place.

The headquarters of the CPPSF and PLAPSF shared joint responsibility with the PLA military regions to control 200,000 personnel, whereas the local public security forces numbered 322,000. The reorganization was clearly designed to return some power to local police forces while ensuring that the large central security apparatus remained intact. It is possible that Mao was attempting to give more jurisdiction over the public security forces to local party and government organizations, in the hope that doing so would engender more efficient law enforcement operations. Enhancing local power decreased the chance of centralized military power becoming a threat to the party, and it aligned with the imperative of streamlining and reducing the central intelligence and security organ to prevent a bloated, overpowered group.

Although this system clearly defined the duties of the armed police force and the civil police force so that they could efficiently respond to public security issues, a serious flaw in the system was its confusing organizational structure, the unclear responsibilities of the involved leading organs, and inadequate oversight and discipline of local public security forces. Thus, in early 1952 the CMC decided to reorganize the public security forces so that all forces, including the Internal Guard Corps (*neiwei budui*), the Border Defense Corps (*bianfang budui*), and local public security forces, were merged into one organization, known as the PLA Public Security Forces. The PLAPSF was no longer divided into a regular public security force and a local public security force; rather, it was wholly incorporated into the PLA. Its units were organized into unified system of divisions (*shi*), regiments (*tuan*), general detachments (*zongdui*), battalions (*dadui*), and companies (*zhongdui*).

---

[35] Nie Rongzhen, *Nie Rongzhen huiyilu*, vol. 3, pp. 721–2.
[36] See 'Dangdai zhongguo' congshu bianji weiyuanhui, *Zhongguo renmin jiefangjun*, vol. 2, p. 7.

The reorganized PLAPSF, with 538,000 personnel, was still under the control of PLAPSF headquarters and the PLA military regions and districts. Perhaps the most important result of this reorganization was the strengthening of party control over the public security forces. Party control was reinforced through the implementation of three approaches. First, party leaders of all local bureau of public security were automatically placed under the command of the political commissars of the PLAPSF units. Second, PLA units were the locus of power within the party; each PLAPSF unit was led by its own party committee. The party committee of PLAPSF units at the prefecture and county levels were under leadership of its corresponding party committee. Third, all PLAPSF units under the level of the PLA military regions, though officially under the leadership of the upper-level PLAPSF units, received supplementary supervision and leadership from local military districts or subdistricts, even though these organizations were at the same military level as the PLAPSF units they were supervising.[37]

The PLA Public Security Army, 1955–1957

In May 1955, the PLAPSF was renamed the PLA Public Security Army (*gong'an jun*) and formally fell under the control of the PLA's five main armies (Ground Army, Navy, Air Force, Air Defense Army, and Public Security Army). The most significant change resulting from this reorganization was the party's decision to move the former PLAPSF units at the prefectural and county levels under the control of local governments. This was primarily an effort to establish a more effective armed civil police. This entire process occurred during a full CMC reorganization, which was intended to steer the PLA toward military professionalism and modernization. The first step the CMC took was to reorganize the theaters of operation (*zhanqu*) in February 1955. The changes focused on decreasing the number of military regions from four to three (Figure 5.2).

In 1950, the military regions of the PLA were divided into four levels: Level 1 military regions (*yiji junqu*), which were established to match the six CCP Regional Central Bureaus; Level 2 military regions (*erji junqu*), which represented Level 1 military regions at the provincial level; and Level 3 military regions (*sanji junqu*), which were assigned to oversee specific areas in each provincial and military subdistrict (*jun fenqu*). This layout transformed the PLA from being solely a field army to a new systematic defense army in which military regions were set up in accordance with the strategic needs of the country. The four levels were established in correspondence with party authorities at different levels. Level 1–3 military regions corresponded to local central

37 Li Junting and Yang Jinhe, *Zhongguo wuzhuang liliang tonglan, 1949–1989* [Overall elucidation of China's armed forces, 1949–1989] (Beijing: Renmin chubanshe, 1992), pp. 54–5; 'Dangdai zhongguo' congshu bianji weiyuanhui, *Zhongguo renmin jiefangjun*, vol. 2, p. 295.

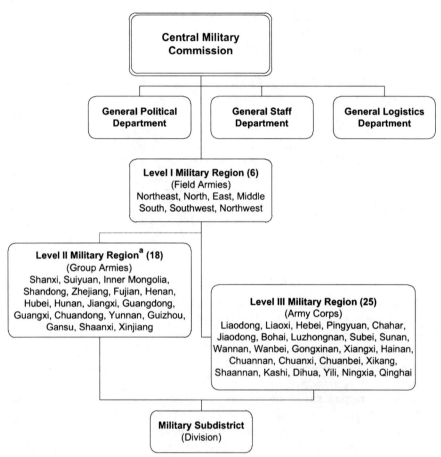

FIGURE 5.2. *PLA Military Regions, April 1950 Source*: Wang Jianying, *Zhongguo gongchandang zuzhishi ziliao huibian: lingdao jigou yange he chengyuan minglu*, pp. 871–80; Li Junting and Yang Jinhe, *Zhongguo wuzhuang liliang tonglan* [Overall elucidation of China's armed forces, 1949–1989] (Beijing: Renmin chubanshe, 1992), pp. 20–1.
a Four military commands (*junshi bu*) – Jilin, Songjiang, Heilongjiang, and Rehe in the Northeast – were not named as military regions (*jun qu*) but were equivalent to Level 3 military regions.

bureaus of the CCP (*zhongyang ju*), branches of local central bureaus of the CCP (*zhongyang fenju*), and provincial party committees, respectively.[38]

Although commanders in Level 2 military regions (i.e., group armies) held higher military rank than their counterparts in Level 3 military regions

[38] 'Dangdai zhongguo renwu zhuanji' congshu bianjibu, *Zhongguo renmin jiefangjun*, vol. 1, pp. 362–3.

(i.e., army corps), there were few differences in terms of their function and responsibilities. The Public Security Army (PSA) personnel were also ranked at different levels, which were equivalent to those of the military regions. The PSA units (i.e., garrison commands) at the municipal level (e.g., Beijing, Tianjin, Shanghai, and Chongqing) had the same status as Level 2 military regions; as such, they were under the jurisdiction of Level 1 military regions. Garrison commands in most large and midsize cities (e.g., Guangzhou, Harbin) were usually at the divisional or regimental level in the command chain. This was not always the case, as some garrison commands (e.g., Hangzhou) were at the battalion level. The variation of PSA units nationwide and the lack of a standardized system (as demonstrated by the incongruous levels of garrison commands located at the city level) indicate the PSA's dependence on party authorities and local PLA units (formed only after the civil war broke out). The reorganization of the PLA military regions took place after the four-level system of regions was established in 1950. Before this large-scale reorganization was implemented in 1955, from October 1950 to December 1954 there were numerous efforts to regularize the structure of military regions (see Table 5.2). This reorganization was initiated to make the system more streamlined and efficient, and it was executed by combining Level 2 and 3 military regions; the product was only three military regions, not four – large military regions (*da junqu*), military districts (*sheng junqu*), and military subdistricts (*jun fenqu*).

The reorganization of the military regions, under the auspices of the increased professionalism and modernization of China's armed forces, provided perfect conditions for the leading local PLA organizations to take control of local PSA units. Although local PSA units at the provincial level were absorbed into reorganized local military regions, PSA units at the prefectural and county levels were returned to the jurisdiction of local bureaus of public security. The personnel of PSA units at the prefectural and county levels were ordered to be demobilized and officially transferred from the PLA to public security organizations.[39]

The PLA Public Security Forces, 1957–1958

After taking suggestions from Soviet advisers, the CMC leadership decided to adopt a system of eight departments for both the CMC and the expanded military regions in an effort to professionalize, modernize, and standardize the PLA.[40] Along with the four large systems of conscription, salary, rank,

---

[39] See "Dangdai zhongguo" congshu bianji weiyuanhui ["Contemporary China" Series Editing Committee], *Zhongguo renmin jiefangjun*, vol. 2, p. 296.

[40] The process to establish the departments began in 1954. There were eight departments: General Staff, General Political, General Logistic, General Training Supervision, General Cadres, Armed Force Supervision, General Ordinance, and Financial Affairs. See 'Dangdai zhongguo renwu zhuanji' congshu bianjibu, *Peng Dehuai zhuan* [A biography of Peng Dehuai] (Beijing: Dangdai zhongguo chubanshe, 1993), p. 498.

TABLE 5.2. *Reorganization of PLA Military Regions, October 1950–December 1954*

Month/Year	Abolished MR	Newly Established or Existing Military Region	Note
11/1951	Kashi	Nanjiang	
12/1951		Xizhuang	Newly established
01/1952	Wannan, Wanbei	Anhui	Merged
04/1952	Xiangxi	Hunan	Absorbed
06/1952	Huanan	Middle South	Absorbed
06/1952		Yuezhong, Yuexi, Yuedong, Yuebei	Newly established
08/1952	Bohai, Luzhongnan	Shangdong	Absorbed
09/1952	Jiaodong	–	Abolished
10/1952	Chuanbei, Chuannan, Chuandong, Chuanxi	Sichuan	Merged
10/1952	Yili	–	Abolished
11/1952	Sunan, Subei	Jiangsu	Merged
11/1952	Dihua	–	Abolished
12/1952	Chahar	Hebei	Absorbed
06/1954	Ningxia	Gansu	Absorbed
08/1954	Liaodong, Liaoxi	Liaoning	Merged
08/1954	Songjiang, Helongjian	Helongjian	Merged

Source: Wang Jianying, *Zhongguo gongchandang zuzhishi ziliao huibian: Lingdao jigou yange he chengyuan minglu*, pp. 940–56, 995–9.
Note: Sichuan Military Region, Jiangsu Military Region, and Anhui Military Region were established in 1952 to replace the Chuanxi, Chuandong, Chuannan, Chuanbei, Sunan, Subei, Wannan, and Wanbei military regions. In 1952, the Xiangxi, Yili, Dihua, and Kashi Military Regions were consolidated into the Nanjiang Military Region.

and medal, the PLA had adopted the model of the Soviet army to structure its own defense force. Although the CMC, led by Peng Dehuai, pushed for modernization following the Soviet model, there were also debates among PLA leaders over how the PLA might keep its traditions of partisan warfare while still moving forward with the Soviet model. These conversations often became quite heated between traditionalist PLA generals and reformist Soviet advisers who demanded that the PLA adhere to the Soviet model.[41] A key debate concerned the Soviet idea of the single responsibility of combat commanders, in which

[41] See 'Dangdai zhongguo renwu zhuanji' congshu bianjibu, *Peng Dehuai zhuan*, 540–50; Liu Han and Huang Yao, *Luo Ronghuan zhuan*, pp. 526–32; Li Jing, *Rujiang Xiao Hua* [Scholarly general Xiao Hua] (Beijing: Jiefangjun wenyi chubanshe, 1998), pp. 552–4.

field commanders took charge of military units, and the officers in charge of political affairs (e.g., political commissars, directors of political departments) played subordinate roles in the chain of combat command.

From 1953 to 1954, two significant approaches were taken by the CMC to bring the single-responsibility system to the forefront, after the position of director of political departments was abolished at the regimental level in early 1953. This was a significant departure from the PLA tradition, in which the party played an unchallengeable leading role. The Political Department, as John Gittings observes, is "an integral part of the army's structure" and "is regarded as the senior of the various departments (Rear Services, Cadres, etc.) which comprise a unit's general staff headquarters." Most important, the Political Department "carries out the policy decisions of the party committee, and is responsible for the detailed implementation of measures intended to educate the rank and file of the army."[42] The second move by Peng and the CMC was to revise the "Order of the Internal Affairs" in April 1953. This forced the dismissal of political officers at the levels of battalion and company command, an obvious step to reduce the influence of the party on PLA grassroots units.[43]

It is notable that that the single-responsibility system confronted strong resistance from the PLA political officers, primarily because of the complaint that the move would result in the party's failure to maintain control over the armed forces. The party exercised control over the PLA through a hierarchy of party committees, political officers, political departments, and party members (a hierarchy that exactly paralleled the military chain of command), which ensured subservience and loyalty of the armed forces when it came to executing commands from the party.[44] Thus, without this system in place, it seemed to the PLA's political officers that the entire traditional chain of command would be lost. The threat of potential collapse generated friction between groups advocating professionalism and political reform, and conflict between the factions emerged at all levels of the PLA, because high-command directives were still conveyed to lower PLA levels through the party committees, thus causing the lower-level organizations to receive contradictory information.[45] Many PLA generals were extremely resistant to the single-responsibility system because they believed that it undermined the importance of the political work that had been essential for CCP combat forces. It was this strong resistance from "most of the PLA cadres," especially those engaged in political work, that led Peng Dehuai to give up the legislation to promote professionalization in the public security forces.[46]

---

[42] John Gittings, *The Role of the Chinese Army*, p. 107.

[43] 'Dangdai zhongguo renwu zhuanji' congshu bianjibu, *Peng Dehuai zhuan*, pp. 543–4.

[44] Ellis Joffe, *Party and Army: Professionalism and Political Control in the Chinese Officer Corps, 1949–1964*, p. 58.

[45] Ibid., p. 58.

[46] 'Dangdai zhongguo renwu zhuanji' congshu bianjibu, *Peng Dehuai zhuan*, p. 544.

Thus, the Soviet single-responsibility system was so short lived because it met with strong resistance from PLA leadership. Between December 1953 and January 1954, the conference Party High-Ranking Cadres in the Military System was held in Beijing, with Defense Minister Peng Dehuai presiding.[47] On the agenda was to reach a consensus among PLA leaders on the single-responsibility system. This conference passed the "Regulations of PLA Political Work," which abandoned the single-responsibility system and resumed the party's control over the PLA at all levels. In addition, the CMC decided to resume the old system on the basis of the principle of "individual responsibility of the leaders under the collective leadership of the Party committee" (*dangwei jiti lingdao xiade shouzhang fengong fuzezhi*).[48]

After the CMC gave up the single-responsibility system, the Soviet model faced criticism and challenges. There was also increasing criticism of excessive reliance on Soviet practices. The year 1956 signaled the turning point in the PLA's attitude toward learning from the Soviet Union and its military advisers. Before 1956, the PLA implemented Soviet theories to ensure that the Soviet experience was properly imitated and adapted in the PLA. This copycat strategy was, of course, pushed heavily by Soviet advisers. After 1956, however, the emphasis was placed on learning with "analysis and criticism" (*you fenxi you pipan*) regarding Soviet ideas.[49] This was partially caused by an increasing conflict between the Soviet model and the CCP's traditional military system. Mao encouraged the conflict by challenging Soviet leadership in spreading the international communist movement and by rethinking China's road to industrialization and modernization.

Moreover, many PLA generals had complained that an organizational system modeled on the Soviet system was inefficient; they claimed that units' functions often overlapped because the system was too rigid, routine, and formal. In April 1956, Mao's "On Ten Relations" was published; it stressed that learning from foreign models should be done "with analysis and criticism" and that foreign experience "should not be followed blindly, copied mechanically or taken unselectively."[50] This increasing political climate pitted against the Soviet model triggered the antidogmatism campaign in the summer of 1958,

---

[47] Most sources only mention the debate without describing the details; however, other sources give some clues about the contentious issues and debates in the PLA leadership. One such source was Marshal Luo Ronghuan, director of the General Political Department, who not only opposed the Soviet model of the single-responsibility system but also directly confronted Soviet advisers about the issue. In addition, this conference came after Luo had convinced Peng Dehuai to support the opposition against the Soviet single-responsibility system in the summer of 1953. See Liu Han and Huang Yao, *Luo Ronghuan zhuan*, pp. 528–32.

[48] See Liu Han and Huang Yao, *Luo Ronghuan zhuan*, pp. 528–9; 'Dangdai zhongguo renwu zhuanji' congshu bianjibu, *Peng Dehuai zhuan*, p. 544.

[49] 'Dangdai zhongguo renwu zhuanji' congshu bianjibu, *Peng Dehuai zhuan*, p. 544.

[50] Mao Zedong, *Mao Zedong wenji* [Collected Works of Mao Zedong], vol. 7 (Beijing: Renmin chubanshe, 1999), pp. 41–2.

which emphasized the PLA's traditions and attacked adoption of the Soviet model.

Between 1957 and 1958, the eight departments of the CMC, which were established in 1954 when the PLA had followed the advice of Soviet advisers, were abolished, and the CMC resumed the division of labor through three departments: the General Staff Department, the General Political Department, and the General Logistics Department.[51] Similarly, the PLA's "five major armies" were reduced to three, and the Public Security Army's unit designation was abolished in September 1957. The headquarters of the Public Security Army saw large-scale reorganization as well. It merged into the Garrison Department (*jingbei bu*) under the General Staff Department, led at the time by Li Tianhuan. The General Staff Department was responsible for the inner guards nationwide, the armed public security forces, and professional guidance to armed forces relating to border control.[52] As for the reorganization of the armed services (*junzhong*), the PLA Public Security Army was one of two major armed forces targeted for reorganization.[53] Beginning in 1955, a debate emerged over whether the Public Security Army was necessary because the MPS had similar functions to both PLA border control units, who were under local military districts, and the PLA units of internal guards, controlled by the local military regions. As indicated by General Zhang Aiping, deputy chief of staff, establishing the Public Security Army was not only unnecessary but also created conflicts between the Public Security Army and other PLA units, such as local military districts, units of internal guards under dual leadership of the local military regions and the headquarters of the Public Security Army in Beijing, and even PLA army corps.[54]

In August 1957, the name of the PLA Public Security Army was changed back to the PLA Public Security Forces, and the leadership of the former PLA Public Security Army was removed. The PLAPSF was reorganized under the auspices of the Guard Department of the PLA General Staff. The Guard Department became the de facto headquarters of the PLA Public Security Forces. The PLAPSF reorganization should be understood as one aspect of the sweeping, massive PLA cuts at the time. As a result of this reorganization, the leadership of local branches of the PLA Public Security Army was removed, and local public security forces were integrated into local military area commands. For most local military commands, the public security forces were put under the jurisdiction of the Operations Department or the Intelligence Department. Some local military commands, such as Shenyang, Beijing, Jinan, and Lanzhou, put the

---

[51] "Dangdai zhongguo renwu zhuanji" congshu bianjibu, *Peng Dehuai zhuan*, p. 498.
[52] Li Junting and Yang Jinhe, *Zhongguo Wuzhuang liliang tonglan, 1949–1989*, p. 55.
[53] The air defense army was also ordered to merge with the air force. See 'Dangdai zhongguo renwu zhuanji' congshu bianji bu, *Zhongguo renmin jiefangjun*, vol. 2, pp. 278–9.
[54] Dongfeng He, *Zhang Aiping zhuan*, p. 696.

public security forces under command of the guard or garrison departments of their military commands.

From People's Armed Police to People's Public Security Forces, 1958–1966

In August 1958, the PAP was established by diverting some duties from the PLA Public Security Forces, which led the armed forces to conduct border control and to guard prisons, railways, and factories. The remainder of PLAPSF duties – such as guarding high-ranking central and provincial leaders; maintaining social order; guarding important bridges, railways, and military factories; and guarding coastal cities – remained with the PLA. Although the People's Armed Police was organizationally subordinate to the Ministry of Public Security, its de facto chain of command came from both the MPS and the CMC. Local units of the PLA Public Security Forces, however, were abolished and taken over by local military regions or military districts, as was the case in Hubei, where the units of the PLA Public Security Forces were taken over by the Hubei Military District in May 1957. This initiative was perhaps part of the effort of the Great Leap Forward to diverge from the standard Soviet planning model and to promote the decentralization of industry, the fiscal system, and agricultural and political decisions in communes.

The tendency of civilian control over the armed police units related to security and prisoner guards was also promoted during the Great Leap Forward. When the People's Armed Police was established in August 1958, local military regions and districts handed over their units in charge of watching prisoners and guarding important government buildings to local public security organs, which were then organized as the local People's Armed Police.[55] For example, before January 1959, the Guangdong Military District commanded all public security forces, which included eight public security regiments. When the PAP was established in January 1959, the Guangdong Military District handed over the public security forces to the Guangzhou PAP, which was under the authority of the Guangzhou Bureau of Public Security.[56] Thus, civilian control over the armed police had become a prominent feature of the Great Leap Forward, as the local units of the armed police were ordered to be demobilized and integrated into the civilian system of the Ministry of Public Security.

---

[55] "Wuhan shi difang zhi bianzuan weiyuanhui bangongshi" [Office of Compilation Committee of Wuhan city local annals], in *Wuhan jiefang he xin zhongguo shiqi* [Liberation of Wuhan and the era of new China), http://www.whfz.gov.cn/Article_Print.asp?ArticleID=6 (accessed August 12, 2009).

[56] Guangzhou shi difang zhi bianzuan weiyuanhui [Compiling Commission of the Local History and Annals of Guangzhou City], *Guangzhou shizhi: junshi juan* [Annals of Guangzhou city: Military annals] (Guangzhou: Guangzhou chubanshe, 1995), vol. 13, pp. 81, 84.

The Great Leap Forward in early 1958 concentrated power in the local party committees. It was in this climate that the People's Armed Police was reorganized and returned to the jurisdiction of local public security offices. These units of newly established PAP personnel were subordinate to local bureau of public security, under the leadership of local party committees. The Garrison Department under the CCP General Staff Department was merged with the Ministry of Public Security's Sixteenth Bureau to form the MPS's Fourth Bureau, responsible for providing professional guidance to the PAP. Because this system was organized along local leadership, provincial and local bureaus of public security formed their own armed police units, which were in charge of internal guard units, as well as guarding prisons, most factories, ports, schools, and even borders. Eventually, the MPS leadership in Beijing provided only professional guidance to the local armed police, and the PLA maintained control over only the internal guard units responsible for central and provincial bodyguard duty, disaster relief, important factories and bridges, sensitive ports, and international borders.[57]

In November 1961, the Politburo decided to put the PAP under a dual public security – military leadership system in which the CMC took charge of all corps-building activities and the MPS was responsible for providing guidance and leadership on police work as well as public security duties and operations. This partial recentralization and remilitarization of the forces was a response to the disaster of the Great Leap Forward.[58] Because the PAP was subordinate to the MPS, Public Security Minister Xie Fuzhi was appointed both commander and political commissar of the PAP. This organizational structure became the model for the armed police forces when Deng Xiaoping launched initiatives for military modernization in the reform era and reestablished the People's Armed Police in April 1983.

The change from local control over the PAP to a dual public security–military leadership system occurred when China was suffering from the severe consequences of the Great Leap Forward. The massive famine and economic crisis that killed tens of millions of people during the Great Leap Forward, coupled with natural disasters, left China in the throes of social unrest and famine. Attempts by local party cadres to meet unrealistic production goals alienated both peasants and workers alike. The results were food shortages, shortages of raw materials for industries, and a widespread decline in the people's morale and trust in the party. As the economic crisis deepened, with the explosion of social unrest came endemic abuses from unaccountable local officials and an acute drop in the government's ability to carry out social justice. Issues such as organized robbery and disturbances in both urban and

[57] Li Junting and Yang Jinhe, *Zhongguo Wuzhuang liliang tonglan, 1949–1989*, pp. 55–6.
[58] Murray Scot Tanner, "The Institutional Lessons of Disaster: Reorganizing the People's Armed Police after Tiananmen," in James C. Mulvenon and Andrew N.D. Yang (eds.), *The People's Liberation Army Organization*, p. 595.

rural China became uncontrollable social problems, especially in rural areas, where famine threatened the lives of millions of people.[59] Facing this large-scale social unrest, bureaus of public security and PAP units controlled by local party and government authorities not only were powerless in maintaining social order but also created more tension between the populace and the regime. This is because local bureaus of public security and PAP units often abused their power, which included imposing harsh punishments on small-time criminals (e.g., sending those who committed robbery to labor camps or concentration camps), unlawfully reading personal letters and other violations of human rights, illegal detainments, and obtaining confessions by compulsion.[60]

The CCP leadership realized the problem and ordered the MPS to stop the local bureaus of public security and the PAP units from committing crimes. They did this by issuing the MPS document "Notice about Sincere Investigation on the Violation of Law and Discipline of Local Public Security Cadres."[61] Sources show that placing the PAP under a dual public security–military jurisdiction served to discipline it and rebuild the people's trust. Strengthening leadership and discipline was significant to achieving this goal. At the same time, the disaster of the Great Leap Forward compelled the leadership to push for a partial recentralization and remilitarization of the forces. According to General Wu Lie, deputy commander of the PAP, the dual public security–military leadership system served to strengthen the party's control; to guarantee education, training, and better management of the public security cadres; and to strengthen the organizational infrastructure. Dual leadership also made it easier for the PLA to coordinate logistics, to recruit and transfer personnel, and to accomplish duties requiring cooperation between the MPS and the PLA.[62] Ensuring strict political control was a central motivation for the CCP leadership to put the armed police under the PLA's jurisdiction. Since the early days of the communist army, political control had been used creatively as a means to disseminate propaganda and raise army morale.[63] After the PAP was put under the dual leadership system, all its personnel were transferred from civilian to active duty, and its units were reorganized under a much more disciplined military system.[64]

---

[59] Tao Siju, *Gong'an baowei gongzuo de zhuoyue lingdaoren Xu Zhirong zhuan* [A biography of Xu Zhirong – The outstanding leader of guard and public security] (Beijing: Qunchong chubanshe, 1997), p. 149.

[60] Ibid., pp. 162–75.

[61] Ibid., p. 162.

[62] Wu Lie, *Zhengrong suiyue*, p. 416.

[63] Gittings, *The Role of the Chinese Army*, p. 101.

[64] Office of Wuhan City Annals, *Wuhan jiefang he xin zhongguo shiqi* [Liberation of Wuhan and the era of new China], http://www.whfz.gov.cn/Article_Print.asp?ArticleID=6 (accessed October 3, 2009).

It is important to note that command over the reorganized PAP was not distributed equally between the MPS and the PLA. Although the MPS and its local organs provided only professional guidance to the PAP, the PLA played a vital role in its construction, human resources, finances, political control, education, training, and supply. According to the "Regulation on Several Issues about the Dual Leadership System Implemented in the People's Armed Police," issued by the PLA Department of the General Chief of Staff, the General Political Department, the General Logistics Department, and the Ministry of Public Security on December 18, 1961, the PAP "is under the leadership of the CMC and the PLA Department of the General Chief of Staff, the General Political Department, and the General Logistics Department," and "receives leadership from the MPS when it carries out tasks related to public security and the professional work of public security."[65] In addition, according to the regulation, the provincial PAP General Corps "is mainly under the leadership of the PLA headquarters of the PAP," whereas "the provincial PAP General Corps receives leadership from local bureaus of public security in terms of the employment of the PAP units and the professional guidance regarding public security." The regulation also noted that party committees of lower-level local PAP units received leadership from party committees at the next-highest levels instead of the party committees of local public security organs, as they had in the past.[66] In the spring of 1963, the PAP was renamed the Chinese People's Public Security Forces, although its leadership and organizational system did not change.[67]

Merger with the People's Liberation Army, 1966–1982

The dismissal of Luo Ruiqing, the PLA general chief of staff and former public security minister, in December 1965 did not herald good news for the MPS or the armed police, given the organizations' long-standing ties with him. Several key leaders of the MPS were dismissed, and the Chinese People's Public Security Forces (*zhongguo renmin gong'an budui*) was ordered abolished. The leading organs of the CPPSF were merged with the administrative organs of the PLA Artillery Army, which were specifically in charge of the missile units, to form the headquarters of the newly established PLA's Second Artillery in June 1966. Mao personally ordered the reorganization of the MPS and the abolishment of the CPPSF in February 1966.[68] As a result, the armed police units were absorbed by a variety of competing local military units, including military regions (*da junqu*), provincial military districts (*sheng junqu*), and

[65] Wu Lie, *Zhengrong suiyue*, pp. 417–8.
[66] Ibid., p. 418.
[67] Li Junting and Yang Jinhe, *Zhongguo wuzhuang liliang tonglan, 1949–1989*, p. 56.
[68] 'Dangdai zhongguo renwu zhuanji' congshu bianjibu, *Zhongguo renmin jiefangjun*, vol. 2, p. 297; Wu Lie, *Zhenrong suiyue*, pp. 442–4.

local garrison commands (*jingbei qu*).[69] It can be speculated that abolishing the armed police and merging them with local military units served Mao's overall strategy to weaken the party bureaucracy, which was controlled by the frontline leaders, and strengthen local forces, in order to ensure his own dominance. In fact, Mao had been in close contact with local leaders, even to the point of being directly involved in decision making at the local party level, because of his reluctance to relinquish power in 1962.[70] Mao also reinforced the CPPSF's decentralization when, in 1964, he pushed the program of the three-fronts construction, which was based on war preparation against foreign invasion.

In the early 1960s, intraparty conflict grew as a result of Mao's increasing dissatisfaction with the frontline leaders who "adopted policies that Mao regarded as unnecessary or unacceptable" – "Mao became increasingly frustrated by his inability to bend the bureaucracy to his will."[71] Starting in mid-1964, Mao seriously considered the possibility that China would be attacked by either the United States or the Soviet Union and would be forced to engage India's or Taiwan's nationalist armies. The relationship with the Soviets was perhaps the most complex one. The political division between the Soviet Union and China was triggered in 1959 after Nikita S. Khrushchev opened talks with the United States in pursuit of his policy of "peaceful coexistence." To put pressure on the CCP for China's compliance, the Soviets withdrew economic assistance and technical advice in August 1960. Mao was convinced that Stalin's successors were attempting to control China, threatening China's national interests. An intense exchange of insults lasted over several years and the conflict spread across all fronts of Sino-Soviet relations, beginning with the Soviets organizing more than forty international communist parties to isolate and attack China openly, after which the Chinese accused Soviet leader Khrushchev of modern revisionism and the betrayal of Marxist-Leninist ideals. The split increased Mao's concern over Soviet invasion. As Mongolia sided with the Soviets, Mao had been growing cautious of Mongolia's political and military alliance with the Soviet Union, which later led to a treaty in January 1966.[72] Given the presence of significant Soviet land forces in Mongolia,

---

[69] For example, the General Detachment of Public Security (*gong'an zongdui*) in Beijing was taken over by the Beijing Garrison Command. See Beijing dang'an ju, *Zhongguo gongchandang Beijing shi zuzhi shi ziliao, 1921–1987* [Materials of the organizational history of the CCP Beijing Municipal City, 1921–1987] (Beijing: Renmin chubanshe, 1992), pp. 778, 784–5.

[70] After the Seven Thousand Cadre conference in 1962, it was clear that few among the party leaders trusted Mao to create government policy, and Mao reluctantly handed over his power in making national economic policy to the frontline leadership, led by Liu Shaoqi.

[71] Roderick MacFarquhar, John Fairbank, and Denis Twitchett, *The Cambridge History of China: The People's Republic*, part 2, *Revolutions within the Chinese Revolution, 1966–1982*, pp. 113–4.

[72] The treaty between the Soviet Union and Mongolia called for a strong Soviet military presence in Mongolia and fifty-three divisions of Soviet troops stationed on the eastern Soviet borders in 1967.

the Soviet-Mongolia military alliance made China vulnerable to a possible blitzkrieg-type military attack on northern China to capture Beijing.

But as equally threatening as the attack on China's northern border was the U.S. involvement in the Vietnam War on the southern border. Soon after John F. Kennedy became president in 1961, he sharply increased military and economic aid to South Vietnam to help Diem defeat the growing insurgency. Between 1961 and 1964, the army ranks increased from about 850,000 to nearly 1 million. A carefully calculated air campaign was launched, because the U.S. government, then with President Johnson at the helm, believed it to be the most effective means of exerting pressure against North Vietnam and the least likely to provoke intervention by China. In early 1965, U.S. military strength in South Vietnam exceeded fifty thousand troops.[73] Even more real for China was the border dispute with India, which broke out into conflict in 1962. The Sino-Indian border conflict lasted six weeks and ended when China declared a cease-fire after driving Indian forces back behind Chinese claim lines. Although China achieved the strategic objectives it had set forth, a permanent shadow had been cast over Sino-Indian relations, giving rise in India to a sentiment of retaliation. Talks between the two countries began in late 1963, but to date no agreement has been reached concerning the border.[74]

The foregoing factors played an important role in shaping Mao's development of his three-fronts initiative, despite the fact that he initially did not intend to change the unbalanced distribution of Chinese industry.[75] At that point, most industrial activity was concentrated in coastal cities and in northern China. In a central work conference in May 1964, Mao formerly proposed the three-fronts initiative,[76] in doing so, he silenced those such as Liu Shaoqi, Chen Yun, and Deng Xiaoping, who viewed economic recovery and agricultural development, not heavy industry and defense – as the nation's priority.[77]

[73] See Vincent H. Demma, "The U.S. Army in Vietnam," in *American Military History: Army Historical Series* (Washington, DC: U.S. Army Center of Military History, 1989), ch. 28, http://www.ibiblio(6:indentry o:id="5.439")(/6:indentry).org/pub/academic/history/marshall/military/vietnam/short.history/chap_28.txt (accessed August 10, 2010).

[74] Chen Donglin, "Xiaoyan miman de xibu kaifa (1) – liushi niandai sanxian jianshe juece shimo" [Gun smoke clouded the air over the opening of the west: Part 1, The beginning and end of decision making about construction of the three-fronts project during the 1960s], in *Dangshi bolan* [General review of CCP history], no. 1 (2001), pp. 8–9.

[75] According to Mao, China needed to establish the three fronts to defend foreign invasion because war was inevitable. See Zhongyang wenxian yanjiu shi, *Jianguo yilai Mao Zedong wengao* [Mao Zedong's manuscripts since the founding of the state], (Beijing: Zhongyang wenxian chubanshe, 1996), vol. 11, pp. 120, 196–7.

[76] A key project installed by China to strengthen China's defense by moving many strategic manufacturing plants from the coastal region to inland to avoid possible attacks from the sea, and by allocating a large portion of the nation's investment to the west and inland areas.

[77] Chen Donglin, "Xiaoyan miman de xibu kaifa (2) – liushi niandai sanxian jianshe juece shimo" [Gun smoke clouded the air over the opening of the west: Part 2, The beginning and end of decision making about construction of the three-fronts project during the 1960s], in *Dangshi bolan* [General review of CCP history], no. 2 (2001), pp. 24–5.

To convince the CCP leadership to accept the initiative, Mao pledged to donate his own salary to build an industrial base in southwestern Sichuan, which was one of the key projects of the initiative.[78] The international climate furthered Mao's resolve to adjust priorities for the third five-year plan from agriculture, light industry, and heavy industry to heavy industry, light industry, and agriculture. Moreover, the three-fronts initiative took up 42 percent of China's total investment in the 1965 outline proposed by the State Planning Commission. Mao was convinced that establishing three fronts both nationally and provincially would be integral to China's national security interests, in large part because of possible attacks from foreign countries.[79]

The Gulf of Tonkin incident occurred when North Vietnamese torpedo boats attacked the U.S. destroyer *Maddox* in the Gulf of Tonkin off the coast of Vietnam on August 2 and August 4, 1964.[80] The incident resulted in the Tonkin Gulf Resolution, which allowed President Johnson to take "all necessary steps" to protect the forces of the United States and its allies, which involved committing major U.S. forces to the war in Vietnam. Strong evidence indicates that Mao took the Gulf of Tonkin incident as a sign of serious U.S. military initiatives in Asia.[81] Meanwhile, Sino-Soviet relations further deteriorated as a result of increasing tension from the ideological confrontation that Mao perceived as a sign for an all-around Sino-Soviet split,[82] and Sino-India border issues went unresolved despite a return to the negotiation table. Thus, Mao spent most of 1965 urging high-ranking party and army leaders to "prepare for war" (*beizhan*).[83] To accelerate the process of building the three fronts, Mao disabled the State Planning Commission, headed by Li Fuchun, and appointed Yu Qiuli, the petroleum minister who successfully led the Daqing petroleum campaign, to head the newly created National Economic Supreme Command. The body's mission was to lead the development of the three fronts.

---

[78] Bo Yibo, *Ruogan zhongda juece yu shijian de huigu* [Reflections on certain major decisions and events], vol. 2, pp. 1197–8, 1200–1201.

[79] Before the Gulf of Tonkin incident, Mao had planned to spend the summer inspecting the Yellow River valley, especially the origin of the Yellow River. He had arranged to ride a horse from the confluence of the Yellow River and the sea to the river's head. To do so, Mao had practiced riding a horse during his stay on Beidaihe beach. After the incident, he announced that he had to give up his travel plans because "the war [was] going to come." See Zhangyang wenxian chubanshe, *Jianguo yilai Mao Zedong wengao*, vol. 11, p. 120; Peng Xianzhi and Jin Congji, *Mao Zedong zhuan, 1949–1976* [A biography of Mao Zedong, 1949–1976] (Beijing: Zhongyang wenxian chubanshe, 2003), vol. 2, p. 1349.

[80] A popular claim suggests that President Johnson deliberately triggered the Vietnam War by orchestrating the Gulf of Tonkin incident and duping the U.S. Congress. Several recent scholars have further supported this claim. See Sedgwick Tourison, *Secret Army, Secret War: Washington's Tragic Spy Operation in North Vietnam*; Edwin Moise, *Tonkin Gulf and the Escalation of the Vietnam War*.

[81] Peng Xianzhi and Jin Congji, *Mao Zedong zhuan (1949–1976)*, vol. 2, p. 1391.

[82] Ibid., pp. 1295–7.

[83] Ibid., p. 1391.

To minimize the vulnerability of China's industries to air attacks, Mao moved a considerable number of key industries into the remote interior, away from key cities that were vulnerable to invasion. In addition, most the military was moved to the three-fronts hinterland, known as Big Three Fronts. The complete three fronts also included Little Three Fronts (*xiao sanxian*), the less developed areas of the provinces, municipalities, and autonomous regions where local governments independently developed their own military industries, militia, armies, and even armed police. Without a doubt, the three-fronts initiative brought with it marked decentralization, which granted tremendous power to local party and army leaders.

This plan of decentralization did not merely serve the purpose of preparing for war; it also served to facilitate Mao's regaining of control over the decision making regarding the national economy. To a degree, it also created other political forces against the frontline leaders, with whom Mao was increasingly at odds. As previously mentioned, the Seven Thousand Cadres Conference at the beginning of 1962 signified Mao's declining reputation, caused by many high-ranking party leaders' overwhelming distrust of Mao's ability to lead the national economy. As Liu Yuan and He Jiadong have indicated, "many comrades in the Party were afraid of Mao's direct involvement in economy while they had to accept his leadership unconditionally."[84] After Mao had abdicated his power to frontline leaders so they could begin the process of economic recovery, the leadership conflict was exacerbated as the inner party leadership further fractured on economic and social issues. They could not agree on approaches to promote economic recovery or on the anticorruption campaign known as the four cleanups, a mass campaign launched as part of the Socialist Education Movement in early 1960s to remove bourgeois influence from politics, ideology, organization and the economy.

The conflict between Mao and the frontline leaders, led by Liu Shaoqi, finally reached a breaking point during an expanded Politburo conference in December 1964. At the conference, Liu Shaoqi openly clashed with Mao, a shocking occurrence considering that open arguments were not looked on favorably by the party, especially those from a subordinate to a leader, as with Liu and Mao (even though Liu was a frontline leader).[85] Mao made high demands of local leaders in their development of little-three-fronts campaigns throughout 1965, insofar as to openly urge local leaders to prepare for rebellion against the center if frontline leaders came to dominate party leadership. Mao told local leaders that he deemed frontline leaders "modern revisionists."[86] On October 10, 1965, when Mao spoke with local first

---

[84] Liu Yuan and He Jiadong, "'Siqing' yituan" [Doubt about the four-cleanup campaign], in Wang Guangmei, Liu Yuan, et al. (eds.), *Nisuo bu zhidao de Liu Shaoqi* [Liu Shaoqi, whom you don't know], p. 96.

[85] See Peng Xianzhi and Jin Congji, *Mao Zedong zhuan (1949–1976)*, vol. 2, pp. 1366–71.

[86] Ibid., pp. 1394–5, 1406–8.

party secretaries at a central working conference, he mentioned the possibility of war and an intraparty military coup for which they should prepare. He further declared, "If revisionists appear in the Center, you must rebel; every province has its own 'Three Fronts,' so of course [the provinces] are capable of rebelling!"[87] In November 1965, Mao visited Shandong, Anhui, Jiangsu, and Shanghai to push provincial leaders to build the little three fronts.[88] Thus, the expansion of local power and decentralization became one of Mao's key political moves after 1965 – in remarkable Maoist-era politics, second only to when local armed forces ousted and replaced local party organs during the Cultural Revolution.

The move toward decentralization reached its apex in the Cultural Revolution during the period 1966–1976. In this mass movement initiated by Mao to strengthen his position and reduce elitism in social and cultural institutions, which turned into social and economic chaos and political purges, Mao had to rely on powerful local army generals to defend China against possible foreign invasion and to maintain domestic social order, which included the daunting task of disciplining mass rebels. As a result, local army leaders became influential political forces in the PLA and party leadership. For example, before 1966 there were no local army leaders who were also CMC members, but by July 1969 around 53 percent of CMC members came from local military regions (see Table 5.3). In fact, after more than a decade of emphasis on decentralization, local leaders had become too influential among the leadership, even by Mao's standards. In December 1973, Mao switched the commanders of eight military regions, to weaken the influence of powerful local military leaders.

It could be argued that giving jurisdiction over the abolished armed police to local military regions was one of Mao's many tactics to prevent the central bureaucracy from using force against him after he launched the Cultural Revolution. Contrary to his expectations, the abolishment of the armed police, which before the Cultural Revolution had been under central leadership command, created innumerable problems for Mao. Without guidance and the combined effort from the party bureaucracy and the Central Military Commission, the armed police were unable to curtail the violence after the mass movement grew out of control. Moreover, the abolishment of the armed police forces limited Mao's ability to control local party and military leaders. To restore social order, Mao had to rely on regular PLA units, which were not properly trained to deal with citizens. Lack of direct control over the armed police forces also created problems for central leadership, which could not respond to the immediate threats against high-ranking leaders when the mass

[87] Peng Xianzhi and Jin Congji, *Mao Zedong zhuan (1949–1976)*, vol. 2, pp. 1394–5.
[88] *Yijiu liuwu nian zhongguo shehui beijing ziliao* [Background materials of Chinese society in November 1965], http://www.ndcnc.gov.cn/datalib/2002/NewPRCBackground/DL/DL-165351 (accessed August 13, 2009).

TABLE 5.3. *The PLA Central Military Commission, April 1966 and June 1969*

PLA leadership	May 1966	July 1969
Chairman and vice chairmen	Mao Zedong, Lin Biao, He Long, Nie Rongzhen	Mao Zedong, Lin Biao, Liu Bocheng, Chen Yi, Xu Xiangqian, Nie Rongzhen, Ye Jianying
Standing Committee Members	Mao Zedong, Lin Biao, He Long, Nie Rongzhen, Zhu De, Liu Bocheng, Chen Yi, Deng Xiaoping, Xu Xiangqian, Ye Jianying	n/a
Military department		
General Staff Department	Yang Chengwu	Huang Yongsheng, Peng Shaohui, Ye Qun, Li Tianyou, Wen Yucheng
General Political Department	Xiao Hua	Xiao Hua
General Logistics Department	Qiu Huizuo	Qiu Huizuo, Zhang Chiming
Navy	Xiao Jingguang, Su Zhenhua	Xiao Jingguang, Li Zuopeng
Air Force	Wu Faxian, Yu Lijin	Wu Faxian, Wang Huiqiou
Engineering Corps	Chen Shiju, Tan Furen	Chen Shiju
Railway Corps	Li Shouxuan, Lu Zhengcao, Cui Tianmin	Liu Xianquan, Song Weishi
Armored Forces	Xu Guangda, Huang Zhiyong	Huang Zhiyong
Commission of Defense, Science, and Technology	Nie Rongzhen	Nie Rongzhen, Wang Bingzhang
Academy of Military Science	Su Yu, Wang Shusheng	Ye Jianying, Su Yu, Wang Shusheng
Military region		
Beijing	Yang Yong, Li Xuefeng, Liao Hansheng	Zheng Weishan, Li Xuefeng, Chen Xianrui, Liu Geping, Xie Fuzhi
Shenyang	Chen Xilian, Song Renqiang	Chen Xilian, Zeng Shaoshan, Pan Fusheng
Jinan	Yang Dezhi, Tan Qilong, Yuan Shengping	Yang Dezhi, Wang Xiaoyu, Yuan Shengping
Nanjing	Xu Shiyou, Xiao Wangdong, Jiang Hua, Li Baohua, Du Ping	Xu Shiyou, Zhang Chunqiao, Du Ping
Fuzhou	Han Xianchu, Ye Fei, Liu Peishan, Yang Shangkui	Han Xianchu, Pi Dingjun

(continued)

TABLE 5.3 *(continued)*

PLA leadership	May 1966	July 1969
Guangzhou	Huang Yongsheng, Tao Zhu, Liu Xingyuan	*Ding Sheng, Wei Guoqing, Liu Xingyuan*, Kong Shiquan
Wuhan	Chen Zaidao, Wang Renzhong, Zhong Hanhua	*Zeng Siyu, Liu Feng*
Kunming	Qin Jiwei, Yan Hongyan, Li Chengfang	Qin Jiwei, Li Chengfang, *Tan Furen*
Chengdu	Huang Xinting, Li Jingquan, Liao Zhigao, Guo Linxiang, Gan Weihan	*Liang Xingchu*, Liao Zhigao, Guo Linxiang, Gan Weihan, *Zhang Guohua*
Nanzhou	Zhang Dazhi, Liu Lantao, Xian Henhan	*Zhang Dazhi, Xian Henhan*
Xinjiang	Wang Enmao	You Shujin, *Wang Enmao*, Cao Siming

Source: Wang Jianying, *Zhongguo gongchandang zuzhishi ziliao huibian: lingdao jigou yange he chengyuan minglu*, pp. 1046, 1100–1114; Zhonggong zhongyang zuzhi bu, et al., *Zhongguo gongchandang zuzhi shi ziliao*, Appendix 2, pp. 163–268.
Note: Names in italics are those generals who were the CMC members.

violence grew out of control. Even in the capital city, Beijing, where Maoist radicals took full control of the political situation, the violent conflict among the Red Guard and mass rebels was still the obvious feature, especially in the early Cultural Revolution. Mao's contingency plan to discipline the masses was based on his assumption that Unit 8341 and the Beijing Garrison Command, the two security forces under his direct control, would be able to handle the movement if it went awry. In reality, Mao grossly underestimated the scale of the mass violence, which the two forces were not equipped to handle alone.

After Lin Biao's attempt to flee to the Soviet Union and tragic death, Mao was immediately informed that a group of Lin's trusted followers in Shanghai, Hangzhou, and Nanjing allegedly were plotting to kill him. Had the armed police continued to be under the dual jurisdiction of the MPS and CMC, Mao could have called on them to arrest Lin's followers. However, because the armed police forces has been disbanded and absorbed by local PLA units, there was no option of recourse for the center. Instead, Mao had to rely on Xu Shiyou, commander of the Nanjing Military Region, to arrest Lin's followers, even though Mao was not sure about Xu's position on the matter.[89] The year

[89] Three days after Lin Biao died, Xu was secretly called to Beijing, where he received the order to arrest Lin's trusted followers, who were allegedly involved in the plot against Mao. Perhaps for reasons of safety or secrecy, Mao ordered Xu to take an ordinary train instead of an airplane, which might easily expose his moves. In Beijing, Xu was ordered to arrest four key features who were allegedly involved in the plot: Jiang Tengjiao (acting director of Political

1967 was the first in which Mao relied on the PLA to restore social order, but it was not the last. At that time, to put an end the chaos, local army leaders were ordered to take over local governments. This was a monumental transfer of power; consequently, the threat that these increasingly powerful local army leaders posed for the top leadership caused Mao increasing distress. The local army leaders included figures such as Chen Xilian (commander of the Shenyang Military Region), Han Xianchu (commander of the Fuzhou Military Region), and Xu Shiyou (commander of the Nanjing Military Region). These three in particular had established unchallenged power in their jurisdictions. In the Nanjing Military Region, for example, General Xu Shiyou controlled four army corps, three provincial military districts (Jiangsu, Zhejiang, and Anhui), and two garrison commands (Shanghai and Nanjing).[90] When the Nanjing Military Region was ordered to arrest Lin Biao's followers in Shanghai, the Shanghai Garrison Command cooperated with Xiao Yongyin, acting commander of the Nanjing Military Region, to arrest Wang Weiguo and Chen Liyun.[91] In hindsight, dismantling the armed police under the Center's control made it difficult to control local army leaders, who dominated local armed forces and the abolished armed police.

After Mao ordered the abolition of the Chinese People's Public Security Forces (CPPSF) and split it into numerous independent PLA divisions, regiments, battalions, companies, and squadrons at the county and city levels at the onset of the Cultural Revolution, the more established CPPSF units were subordinated to PLA provincial military commands or local garrison regions. Deep distrust in both the CPPSF and the MPS caused Mao to rely on the mass movement to assault the party bureaucracy. Although Mao wrote large-character posters (*dazi bao*) to mobilize the Red Guard, he was not prepared to let the Red Guard lead the Cultural Revolution. Immediately after the Cultural Revolution began, it became apparent that the abolishment of the public security forces was a disastrous political move – the enthusiasm of the Red Guard was aroused and maintained only by uncontrollable violence. The subsequent backlash from local PLA units served only to aggravate the chaotic situation. If, instead, armed police units under the leadership of local military regions had been called forth to deal with the Red Guard, the state probably would have been more successful in suppressing the violence. Thus, it is a fair assessment to say that Mao was responsible for the violence nationwide, not only because

---

Department, Air Force), Wang Weiguo (political commissar of the 4th Army Corps of the Air Force), Chen Liyun (political commissar of the 5th Army Corps of the Air Force), and Zhou Jianping (acting commander of the air force of the Nanjing Military Region). See Leng Meng, *Baizhan jiangxing: Zai Liu Bocheng, Deng Xiaoping, Xu Xiangqian huixia* [Star of generals who experienced hundred battles: Under the leadership of Liu Bocheng, Deng Xiaoping, and Xu Xiangqian] (Beijing: Jiefangjun wenyi chubanshe, 1997), pp. 309–10.

[90] Li Wenqing, *Jinkan Xu Shiyou – 1967–1985* [A close observation on Xue Zhiyou: 1967–1985] (Beijing: Jiefangjun chubanshe, 2002), p. 50.

[91] Ibid., pp. 223–8.

he disbanded the CPPSF but also because he protected the Red Guard from potential backlash from local PLA units and the party seniors who were the objects of the Red Guard's violence.

After even Mao deemed that the mass movement had progressed too far, he employed the PLA to end the violence. Because the merged armed police fell under the leadership of the provincial military districts and municipal garrison commands, local army leaders became the indisputable authorities, by virtue of their control over the army, security forces, and resources. With that authority bestowed on them, the leaders established relatively independent factional bases derived from their historical ties, thus consolidating their power even more. In the province of Fujian, for example, army officials comprised more than two-thirds of the heads of county-level Revolutionary Committees.[92] Local PLA units were not always the answer for resolving the violence, however; sometimes the PLA units themselves were involved in inciting violence. In such situations special measures had to be taken. One such situation in Wuhan found resolution only when Mao visited Wuhan to help make peace between the various mass organizations and their respective PLA units. In Wuhan, the Wuhan Military Region, headed by Commander Chen Zaidao, supported the conservative mass organization known as the Million Heroes, which aimed to defend the military region and the majority of veteran cadres,[93] and Chen was responsible for the Wuhan workers' open challenging of the central authorities in 1967.[94]

Mao had sensed that disciplining the PLA units would not be easy, given the military factionalism that had developed. His leadership conflict with Lin Biao further encouraged him to reduce the PLA's influence over army leaders. Beginning in August 1972, Mao attempted to weaken the PLA's influence by withdrawing army representatives from Revolutionary Committees at all levels and by ending the three supports–two militaries campaign (*sanzhi liangjun*). Ending the campaign was an effort to stop the PLA's further involvement in the local politics.[95] Immediately after the 1970 Lushan plenum, when Mao and Lin's leadership conflict became public, Mao assaulted the army leadership in the Beijing Military Region, a strategy aimed to catalyze the reorganization of the Beijing Military Region, with the ultimate goal of ensuring Mao's security before he targeted Lin Biao. Mao called the Huabei (North China) Conference to "expunge the influence of Chen Boda" and to criticize the leaders of the Beijing Military Region – Commander Zheng Weishan, First

---

[92] Tan Qilong, *Tan Qilong huiyilu* [Memoirs of Tan Qilong] (Beijing: Zhonggong dangshi chubanshe, 2003), p. 666.

[93] Harry Harding, "The Chinese State in Crisis, 1966–9," in Roderick MacFarquhar (ed.), *The Politics of China: The Eras of Mao and Deng*, p. 213.

[94] Hong Yung Lee, *From Revolutionary Cadres to Party Technocrats in Socialist China*, p. 131.

[95] This refers to the PLA's involvement in the Cultural Revolution; it sent PLA units to support the left-wing mass organizations; to help industry and agriculture; to impose military control over some localities, departments, and units; and to give military training to students.

Political Commissar Li Xuefeng, and Political Commissar Chen Xianrui. The Huabei Conference lasted for more than a month (from December 22, 1971, to January 26, 1972); Zheng Weishan and Li Xuefeng were dismissed immediately after the conference.[96] Mao had charged the leaders of the Beijing Military Region with building alliances with Lin Biao and Chen Boda at the Lushan plenum, thus prompting their subsequent dismissals. Their dismissals were significant, considering the importance of the Beijing Military Region in ensuring Mao's security, especially after Mao had decided to dismiss his previously loyal follower Lin Biao.

Mao's withdrawal of army representatives from local governments primarily stemmed from his goal of eliminating Lin Biao's influence and rebuilding a trustworthy PLA from the bottom up. This did not gain Mao supporters in the party, however, because the Cultural Revolution was instigated by Lin Biao and Lin's faction, at Mao's behest, but also at the cost of other army leaders and factions. Thus, the Mao-Lin conflict severely undermined Mao's reputation and furthermore raised an overwhelming amount of doubt about the Cultural Revolution. This loss of faith explains Mao's attempts in early 1972 to assuage tensions with senior army generals and restore their trust in him. Examples of these attempts include Mao's public statement on November 14, 1971, to redress the February Adverse Current, an event in February 1967 during which governmental and army veterans cooperated to challenge the radicals; the participation in Marshal Chen Yi's funeral on January 10, 1972; the decision to "liberate" Su Zhenhua, former political commissar of the navy in March 1972; the remarks on a letter written by Yang Junsheng, daughter of Yang Chengwu, about the redress of Yang Chengwu and Liao Hansheng's case in March 1972; the decision to reemploy Deng Xiaoping in August 1972; and the order to redress Marshal He Long's case in February 1973.[97]

According to the *Mao Zedong zhuan*, written by Peng Xianzhi and Jin Chongji, Mao seemed to disappear completely from the political arena in the year following Lin Biao's death, supposedly because of severe health problems, which partially resulted from the Lin Biao affair. Over the course of the year, Mao attended no important meetings and gave no speeches. The greatest evidence of his continued involvement in politics is a few remarks noted in several documents; all the remarks concerned the rehabilitation of senior high-ranking leaders.[98] Perhaps Mao's most vital move to rebuild the PLA generals' trust was his decision to rehabilitate 175 high-ranking generals in December 1972. The generals were pardoned for their "crimes" against the "proletariat

---

[96] Tao Zhuwen, "Lishi xuanwuo zhongde Chen Xianrui" [Chen Xianrui in the historical eddy], in *Dangshi bolan* [General review of CCP history], no. 8 (2001), p. 16.

[97] Peng Xianzhi and Jin Congji, *Mao Zedong zhuan (1949–1976)*, vol. 2, pp. 1608, 1612, 1619, 1621. Wang Nianyi, "Guanyu helong yuanan de yixie Ziliao," in *Dangshi yuanjiu ziliao*, no. 4 (1979), p. 11.

[98] Peng Xianzhi and Jin Congji, *Mao Zedong zhuan (1949–1976)*, vol. 2, pp. 1618–19.

headquarters" and absolved of their various sentences of suspension, work in labor camps, or imprisonment – they then were reinstated to their former PLA leadership posts within sixteen months.[99] Returning the rehabilitated army generals to their posts after Lin Biao's death was an important aspect of Mao's reorganization of the PLA, but not the only aspect. He also rebuilt his control over the PLA by undermining military factionalism and weakening the influence of local army leaders. Mao was increasingly concerned with the influence of these local military leaders on both local politics and leadership politics in Beijing. He particularly bore a grudge about the local military leaders' support of the Lin Biao faction as evidenced by their motions against the radicals in the 1970 Lushan plenum.

By 1973, Mao had switched his focus to other powerful local army leaders after having dismissed the Beijing Military Region leaders. Mao believed that the increasing power and influence of the local army leaders weakened central and local government control over local military leaders. In many military regions, powerful army generals – usually commanders – dominated local military units, such that other leaders, such as political commissars, were leaders only in name. This was the case in the Nanjing, Fuzhou, and Shenyang military regions. On December 12, 1973, Mao bemoaned the overly powerful local army commanders:

It is not good if one stays in the same place for too long. One will be slippery if one stays for too long. In several military regions, nobody heeds the words of the political commissars. Only the commanders make final decisions.[100]

Beginning in late 1973, Mao went about removing power from the local military leaders. An important political move was to reemploy Deng Xiaoping, a prestigious and influential military leader during the Sino-Japanese War and the Civil War. Mao needed someone with Deng's credentials to help him reorganize the PLA, especially when Mao was planning to transfer the commanders of eight military regions. The transfers were significant because local military leaders not only would lose control over their former military domain but also would no longer be allowed to head local party organizations and governments.[101]

Like other PLA units, the armed police forces were an important part of military politics. This is in part because of their merger with the PLA and their subsequent responsibilities as "independent" PLA units that guarded army leaders during the Cultural Revolution. The historical importance of the armed police

99 Zhang Shude, "Mao Zedong wei 175 jiangjun pingfan de qianqian houhou" [Before and after Mao Zedong rehabilitated 175 generals], in Dangshi bolan [General review of CCP history], no.3 (2001), pp. 11–17.
100 Peng Xianzhi and Jin Congji, Mao Zedong zhuan (1949–1976), vol. 2, p. 1672.
101 Li Qi, Zhou Enlai nianpu: 1949–1976 [Chronicle of Zhou Enlai: 1949–1976], vol. 3 (Beijing: Zhonggong zhongyang wenxian nianjiuzhi, 1997), p. 637.

also derives from their deep involvement in local politics, given their role in maintaining political and social order, in protecting governmental organizations, and in guarding local civilian leaders. When the former Chinese People's Security Forces were abolished and its units reallocated to provincial military districts, they became key armed forces for military districts to use against mass rebels and the Red Guard during the Cultural Revolution. After the PLA took over local civilian governments during the Cultural Revolution, the armed police forces were the main army units assigned to support the leftist mass organizations (*zhi zuo*). They did so by stationing personnel in civilian organizations such as factories and institutions of higher education. A better-known clash in which the armed forces represented the PLA in dealing with mass rebels and the Red Guard was the Zhao Yongfu incident, in Qinghai, on February 23, 1967. Under the order of Zhao Yongfu, deputy commander of the Qinghai Military District, the PLA Qinghai Independent Division (the Qinghai Public Security Corps before the PLA merger) killed 169 civilians and injured 168.[102] In Sichuan, the Independent Division of the Chengdu Military Region (the Sichuan Public Security Corps before the PLA merger) was ordered to maintain social stability and detain criminals. It is speculated that hostility between the Independent Division and the mass organizations motivated the murder of Du Ling, commander of the Independent Division.[103]

Because of the armed police forces' deep involvement in local politics, leaders and officers in some units allied themselves with different, sometimes rival mass organizations, thereby complicating the involvement of the forces' role in politics. Some even allied with local mass organizations pitted against local PLA units. For example, leaders of the Shanghai Garrison Command split into two factions: one followed its organizational superior, the PLA Nanjing Military Region, and the other supported the Maoist radicals in rebellion against the PLA Nanjing Military Region.[104] This deep involvement of independent divisions or the armed police units of the local military districts in the Cultural Revolution may well have been Deng's reason for abolishing them in his campaign to reduce and reorganize the armed forces in 1980, along with the

---

[102] Wen Yu, *Zhongguo zuohuo* [China's left disaster] (Beijing: Chaohua chubanshe, 1993), p. 435.

[103] Du Ling was assassinated on January 22, 1968, in his car while returning to the headquarters of his army unit after he participated in a regiment party committee meeting. See Wang Shaoyong and Jiang Lugan, "Huohong de nianhua, zhandou de yisheng – Du Ling zhuanlue" [Flaming years and fighting throughout the entire life – Outline of a biography of Du Ling], in Zhonggong Jiangyou shiwei dangshi yanjiushi [Research Office of the CCP Party History of Jiangyou Party Committee] (ed.), *Jiangyou dangshi yanjiu huibian* [Research compilation of Jiangyou party history] (Chengdu: Sichuan renmin chubanshe, 1991), http://zzb.jy.gov.cn/jybmwz/78841580781305856/20100126/226142.html (accessed October 24, 2009).

[104] See Zhou Chunlin, *Zhou Chunlin huiyilu* [Memoirs of Zhou Chunlin] (Beijing: Zhonggong dangshi chubanshe, 2005), 544–68.

other reforms he enacted to promote the modernization of the military.[105] The abolishment of the independent divisions of local military districts occurred before major military reforms, such as the downsizing of 1 million military personnel in the mid-1980s. All independent divisions were cut at that time, although some personnel were absorbed into the new People's Armed Police, which was established in April 1983. The independent divisions saw the first effects of Deng's grand reform program that was intended to downsize the PLA; mitigate the PLA's overpoliticized nature; and transform the PLA into a modern, mobile, high-tech power capable of mounting operations beyond China's national borders.

[105] See *Jiefangjun bao* [The PLA daily], December 22, 2008; Li Junting and Yang Jinhe, *Zhongguo wuzhuang liliang tonglan, 1949–1989*, p. 90.

6

People's Armed Police in the Reform Era

This chapter examines the evolution of the People's Armed Police, particularly its emergence in its current organizational form, and traces its rise in the politics of reform. China's armed police forces have experienced a tremendous vicissitude of political upheaval, beginning with their abolishment during the Cultural Revolution,[1] followed by their absorption into the PLA and their becoming the early target for the military reform launched by Deng Xiaoping to downsize the PLA in 1980.[2] The current People's Armed Police (PAP) was established in April 1983 and has maintained substantial growth and has increased its political influence through the absorption of many demobilized PLA troops and its upgrade of military rank from deputy military region to chief military region. Since its establishment, the PAP has become one of the most important internal security and law enforcement forces of the PRC.

Among the PRC's three armed force branches (the PLA, the PAP, and the militia and reserve forces), official media in 2009 reported the PAP's numbers at 680,000,[3] but it is estimated that PAP personnel number between 1.5 million and 2.3 million.[4] During wartime, the PAP is under military command to carry out missions involving battlefield security, anti-infiltration, and protection of coastal territories. In peacetime, the PAP performs a wide variety of security duties, including maintaining domestic order, guarding key government buildings (including party and state organizations, foreign embassies, and

---

[1] "Dangdai zhongguo renwu zhuanji" congshu bianjibu, *Zhongguo renmin jiefangjun* (Beijing: Dangdai zhongguo chubanshe, 1994), vol. 2, p. 297; Wu Lie, *Zhenrong suiyue* [The eventful times] (Beijing: Zhongyang wenxian chubanshe, 1999), pp. 442–4.

[2] Li Junting and Yang Jinhe, *Zhongguo wuzhuang liliang tonglan, 1949–1989* [Overall elucidation of China's armed forces, 1949–1989] (Beijing: Renmin chubanshe, 1992), p. 90.

[3] See *Dongfang zaobao* [Eastern morning news], August 28, 2009.

[4] Karl DeRouen Jr. and Paul Bellamy, *International Security and the United States: An Encyclopedia*, p. 152; National Geographic Society, *National Geographic Atlas of China*, p. 70.

consulates), providing security details to senior party and government officials, guarding and execution duties in civilian prisons, patrolling borders, securing natural resource locations that contain rare mineral deposits, protecting forests and water sources, securing power sources (including nuclear power plants), and enforcing laws. Thus, the PAP is often viewed as a national police force and a defensive paramilitary ground force.

In recent years, the PAP has improved its efficiency by integrating manpower, facilities, and technology. Since the 1990s, Chinese leaders have sought to make the paramilitary PAP more capable of responding to emergencies and serving as the leading force in major cases of protest or civil unrest. The post-Deng leaders Jiang Zemin and Hu Jintao have poured funding and other resources into the PAP in an attempt to produce a disciplined, loyal, and ideologically committed armed police force. Salient changes in the PAP implemented by post-Deng leaders include strengthening the PLA's leadership of the PAP, guaranteeing direct and continuous financial support from the State Council (1995), creating an additional fourteen PLA mobile divisions in the PAP, upgrading the PAP's military rank from deputy military region to chief military region (1996), and increasing its influence through establishing the independent PAP Party Committee (2005).[5] According to the *Huanqiu ribao*, in 2006 the government increased salaries of PAP personnel, such that the salaries of soldiers doubled; in 2009 the government gave a 50 percent salary increase to PAP officials and soldiers.[6] Although the PAP personnel have received the same raises as their counterparts in the PLA, they have also enjoyed additional cash allowances from local governments.[7]

The establishment of the PAP symbolized a change in the leadership's focus from China's security in the international environment to development of the domestic economy. Current policy departs from Mao's strategic positioning, in which military construction, recruitment, and disposition of PLA units were all to prepare for impending war with other nations. After Deng Xiaoping returned to power in 1977, he launched economic reform throughout China's industries and implemented further modernizations in China to ensure that the economy was prioritized over the army. Between 1978 and 1982, Deng launched three campaigns to reduce, reorganize, and restructure Chinese armed forces, specifically targeting the inefficient and overstaffed organs of the PLA, as well as the improvement of morale and leadership cohesion. Deng made further changes to the PLA, such as the 1985 disarmament, to reduce personnel by an

---

[5] The PAP party committee (*dangwei hui*) was established in June 2005. In the past, the PAP did not have an independent Party Committee. This effort served to enhance its influence in the party leadership and strengthen the party's control over the PAP. See *Jiefangjun bao*, June 23, 2005.

[6] *Huanqiu shibao* [Global times], March 25, 2009.

[7] *South China Morning Post*, March 24, 2009.

additional 1 million troops and to merge certain military organizations; the objective of these changes was to raise the combat power of the PLA and improve its efficiency. To gain support from party and army leaders, Deng projected his understanding of China's position in the international arena to justify his decision. Without a doubt, the establishment of the PAP marked a significant shift of China's focus from concern about international threats to concentration on domestic stability, a shift that heralded the advent of China's four modernizations.

This chapter illustrates the development of the PAP since it was created in 1983 and discusses the political drivers and social trends that have led to its increasing role in Chinese politics. The rise of the PAP was also triggered by a strong appeal among party leaders to strengthen the security duties of the armed police in order to maintain domestic order, guard key government buildings, provide personal protection to government officials, provide guard duty in civilian prisons, secure China's borders, and protect important state industries and resources, all of which had been severely undermined during the Cultural Revolution. As increasing crime, mass rural migration, rising urban unemployment, and soaring ethnic discontent put pressure on the regime, the leadership deemed the establishment of the PAP as not only necessary but also essential to the grand campaign launched by Deng Xiaoping.

This chapter also assesses the mechanisms, outcomes, and implications of the rise of the PAP. The PAP is currently under the dual leadership of the State Council and the CMC, whereby the State Council is responsible for the PAP's tasks and operations, authorizing the size and number of the PAP's subordinate organizations and the numbers of their personnel, providing financial and material support, and ensuring logistical supply for the PAP; institutionally, the PAP is subordinate to the CMC. The PLA increasingly plays an important role in the PAP's organizational development; its influence over the PAP became evident after the 1989 student demonstration in Tiananmen Square. The PAP's change from deputy military region to chief military region in December 1996 supported the PAP's appeal to fall under military jurisdiction because it was no longer organizationally subordinate to the Ministry of Public Security. Although the MPS, representing the State Council, continually provides professional guidance to the PAP, the transfer of the PAP's command system from under the MPS to the military not only strengthened the military function of the PAP but also provided more discipline for the armed police.

Toward Transition: From Mao Zedong to Deng Xiaoping

The establishment of the PAP in April 1983 symbolized a significant change in the leadership's focus from national defense to domestic economic development. During the early 1960s, China felt that its borders were unsecure, given tensions with its neighbors. The Sino-Soviet ideological dispute deepened and brewed hostility in the 1960s as a result of major ideological, military, and economic conflict between the Soviet Union and China. Moscow withdrew all advisers from China and refused to honor agreements to provide nuclear weapons technology to China, and it began to support India in the long-standing India-China border dispute. The Sino-Soviet border dispute was deemed a threat by leadership when Moscow increased its military capacity along the shared border with China and Mongolia.

It became imperative for China's national defense to keep a large PLA force, develop nuclear weapons technology, and launch the so-called three-fronts initiative to prepare against possible foreign invasion.[8] Soviet aggression and dominance played a large role in the sudden development of China's defense sector. The Soviet-led Warsaw Pact invasion of Czechoslovakia in 1968 illustrated a reassertion of communist influence after the Prague Spring reforms strayed from communist bloc policy of tight controls of citizens' rights. The Soviet Union's marked aggression toward other satellite nations and the armed clashes on the Sino-Soviet border in 1969 spurred Mao to improve national defense. Since the early 1960s, the PLA had been on combat-ready alert, guided by the principle of preparing for a war that would "break out early (*zao da*), be of a large scale (*da da*), and involve nuclear weapons (*da he zhanzheng*)."[9] Thus, the construction, recruitment, and disposition of PLA units maintained a high level of military preparedness, superseding political efforts in other sectors, such as economic, agricultural, and industrial development. The PAP's emergence highlights the fundamental differences between Mao's and Deng's leadership.

After Deng Xiaoping returned to the power center in 1977, he firmly rooted his politics in economic reform, prioritizing it over military development. Deng "reaffirmed the primacy of the new economic imperative over all other policies" and emphasized an "independent" stance vis-à-vis both superpowers,[10] a clear indication that China would not side with either against the other but rather would focus on its attention to economic development and modernization. Deng's initiatives can be summarized into three major areas: domestic economic construction, national unification, and the maintenance of world peace, especially for a peaceful environment for China's development. Namely, political struggle and world revolution were no longer in vogue, China's relations with the West needed to improve, great efforts needed to be made to achieve national unification (e.g., the return of Hong Kong), and a favorable international environment for China's industrialization and modernization needed to

---

[8] The Third Front program was an initiative to move the military and other key state enterprises from large or coastal cities to cities in provinces farther inland.

[9] 'Dangdai Zhongguo' congshu bianjibu, *Zhongguo renmin jiefangjun*, vol. 1, pp. 238, 296.

[10] Kay Möller, "Diplomatic Relations and Mutual Strategic Perceptions: China and the European Union," in Richard L. Edmonds (ed.), *China and Europe since 1978: A European Perspective*, p. 13.

be promoted.[11] Since Deng launched economic reforms and initiated China's peace-and-development line in the 1980s, China has become one of the biggest beneficiaries of the post–Cold War reduction in interstate violence due to its increasing economic ties with the major international powers and its neighbors and its growing influence in world affairs.[12]

In his book *Selected Works of Deng Xiaoping*, Deng summarizes his policies of reforming China's military: "our military must submit to the overall priority of the development of our nation."[13] Deng had been an advocate for restraining military growth even before he rose to paramount leader. He and Marshal Ye Jianying had begun a disarmament process in 1975, but the efforts were discontinued in 1976, when Deng was dismissed for the second time.[14] The disarmaments were a policy response to the problems incurred by the ballooning PLA, which was further overstaffed as a result of the campaign of three supports and two militaries during the Cultural Revolution.[15] During this campaign, whenever a group of PLA officers was sent out to "support the Left," a new group of PLA officers would be promoted. Once the campaigns ended, all PLA officers were ordered to return to their original units, which resulted in a huge surplus of officers. Although the disarmament was terminated in 1976, Deng resumed the policies when he assumed power again in 1977. The disarmament signaled the beginning of a series of reforms implemented by Deng to streamline and mechanize the military apparatus while simultaneously lifting the country out of poverty and ensuring domestic security.

Between 1978 and 1982, Deng launched three campaigns to reduce and reorganize the armed forces; he targeted problems that prevented efficiency, such as overstaffed organizations, low morale, and lack of a cohesive leadership.[16] Deng announced that the CCP's motivation to restructure the PLA was to "raise the army's combat capacity and improve its administrative efficiency."

[11] Lau Siu-kai, "Pragmatic Calculations of National Interest: China's Hong Kong Policy, 1949–1997," in Suisheng Zhao (ed.), *Chinese Foreign Policy: Pragmatism and Strategic Behavior*, p. 98.

[12] Quansheng Zhao and Guoli Liu, "China Rising: Theoretical Understanding and Global Response," in Quansheng Zhao and Guoli Liu (ed.), *Managing the China Challenge: Global Perspectives*, p. 10.

[13] Deng Xiaoping, *Deng Xiaoping wenxuan* [Selected works of Deng Xiaoping], vol. 3 (Beijing: Renmin chubanshe, 1993), p. 100.

[14] Devised in September 1975, the initial plan for PLA disarmament was to disarm 26.2 percent of total personnel. In the year before its termination, the PLA achieved 13.6 percent disarmament. This ended when the campaign Anti-Right Reverse Wind was launched against Deng Xiaoping. See Han Huaizhi, *Dangdai zhongguo jundui de junshi gongzuo* [Contemporary Chinese army's military work], vol. 2, pp. 14–15.

[15] The campaign of three supports and two militaries refers to "the three supports of supporting industry, supporting agriculture, and supporting the broad masses of the Left and the two militaries of military control, political and military training." Mao launched the campaign to send PLA officers to support the "leftist" mass organizations and to take control of the civilian organizations.

[16] 'Dangdai Zhongguo' congshu bianjibu, *Zhongguo renmin jiefangjun*, vol. 1, pp. 299–300.

According to Deng, "[the CCP is] reducing military personnel so that allotted funds can be invested in new equipment; this is our guiding principle [for disarmament]."[17] The three campaigns to restructure the PLA successfully shrank it from 6.6 million personnel to 4.2 million; the defense budget was reduced from 17.37 percent of the national budget in 1979 to 10.63 percent in 1984.[18] Only a few military units were merged or reorganized according to plan.[19] More important, the three campaigns were not able to mitigate the most crucial problem of the PLA: the many aging leaders at all levels.

Deng made further changes to the PLA to raise combat capacity and improve administrative efficiency, such as the disarmament in 1985, which reduced personnel by an additional 1 million troops and merged military organizations. To gain support from the party and army leadership, Deng appealed to them by arguing that, because of a lack of enemies and adversarial relationships, China had little to fear and less to defend against than during the height of the Cold War. He pointed to China's relative peace with the international community, including the major superpowers at the time, the United States and the Soviet Union. He was confident that neither country would go to war with each other despite their respective large nuclear arsenals, and he drove home the idea that restructuring was essential to the military's advancement. In addition, the rise of developing countries and the emergence of the nonallied movement changed the dynamics of the international political system that had been promoting world peace. China benefited from the culture of peace in that it was able to devote itself completely to the socialist modernization program.[20] The principle of China's foreign policy in the late 1970s and 1980s was to promote a peaceful environment for China's industrialization and modernization and to develop harmonious relations with countries that would foster China's economic development. Although Sino-U.S. relations experienced a honeymoon in the early 1980s, China also began to see the Soviet Union as less of a threat. Sino-Soviet consultations on normalizing relations resumed in 1982 and were held twice yearly, although certain foreign affairs still managed to alarm China with respect to Soviet aggression, particularly the Soviet invasion of Afghanistan.

[17] Liu Huaqing, *Liu Huaqing huiyilu* [Memoirs of Liu Huaqing] (Beijing: Jiefangjun chubanshe, 2004), pp. 402–3.

[18] Zhang Xingxing, "Zhongguo jundui da caijun yu xin shiqi jingji jianshe" [Great disarmament of China's army and economic development in the new era], in *Dangdai zhongguo shi yanjiu* [Research of contemporary Chinese history], vol. 13, no. 1 (January 2006), p. 22.

[19] Three significant mergers or reorganizations were carried out between 1980 and 1983. The Defense Science and Industry Commission was created by merging the Defense Science Commission, the Defense Industry Office, and the CMC Science and Equipment Office. The leadership organs of the PLA Artillery, the PLA Armored Forces, and the PLA Engineering Corps merged into the Business Office of the PLA General Staff Department. The PLA Railway Corps and the PLA Construction and Engineering Corps merged into the Railway Ministry and local construction companies, respectively. See Liu Huaqing, *Liu Huaqing huiyilu*, p. 403.

[20] 'Dangdai Zhongguo' Congshu bianjibu, *Zhongguo renmin jiefangjun*, vol. 1, pp. 296–9.

As the Cold War between the United States and the Soviet Union posed little direct threat to China, China adjusted its foreign policy to develop relations with both superpowers while not currying favor with either side. China strove to create favorable conditions by assuming a passive attitude toward international relations; nurturing this peaceful international environment helped ensure the success of its reforms. Deng Xiaoping did not believe that other nations were threats to China, yet he never disarmed the PLA so much so that it was helpless to defend the country. China needed to resolve the issues of people being demobilized as a result of the large-scale disarmament and of how to maintain domestic security for the long road of reforms ahead. The solution lay in the establishment of the People's Armed Police.

Emergence of the People's Armed Police

The creation of the People's Armed Police (PAP) was driven by a number of forces that served to achieve both short- and long-term reform-oriented goals. The emergence of the PAP allowed the PLA to focus on defense against external enemies.[21] The PAP's rise was a salient part of Deng Xiaoping's economic reforms, which focused on China's industrialization and military modernization. As Murray Scot Tanner indicates:

From a military perspective, the PAP's reformation reflected Deng's desire to streamline and rectify a bloated PLA that was involved in far too many aspects of government and society. From the public security perspective, this move must be seen as part of a much broader effort to reorganize, civilianize, and professionalize internal security, intelligence, and legal coercion.[22]

The establishment of the PAP marked a significant shift of China's focus from international threats to domestic stability, the precondition for China's four areas of modernization – agriculture, industry, science and technology, and national defense. Unlike Mao, Deng Xiaoping did not believe that another world war would happen soon or that China was facing imminent danger from possible foreign invasions. Deng had no doubt that China would experience a relatively peaceful time in which it could concentrate on infrastructure and industrial and military development.[23] Not only would a strong armed police force play a vital role in maintaining social order; it would also absorb a large

---

[21] Paul H. B. Godwin, "The PLA Faces the Twenty-First Century: Reflections on Technology, Doctrine, Strategy, and Operations," in James R. Lilley and David Shambaugh, *China's Military Faces the Future*, p. 47.

[22] Murray Scot Tanner, "The Institutional Lessons of Disaster: Reorganizing the People's Armed Police after Tiananmen" in James C. Mulvenon and Andrew N. D. Yang (eds.), *The People's Liberation Army Organization*, p. 596.

[23] Deng was convinced that there was a favorable environment in international affairs that overrode the possibility of a world war. See Deng Xiaoping, *Deng Xiaoping wenxuan*, vol. 3, pp. 104–5.

number of personnel demobilized from the PLA. The creation of the PAP and its absorption of the PLA's demobilized personnel downsized not only the PLA but also the PLA's budget. On the surface, having separate budgets for the PAP and the PLA promoted an image of demilitarization. The State Council provided the PAP's budget, but this was not the only source of the PAP's funding – it also received revenue from some operations, such as the Communications Corps, the Hydropower Corps, mining, and agriculture, as well as administrative fines and fees.

The establishment of the PAP was also triggered by a strong appeal from party leadership to strengthen the security duties of armed police. During the Cultural Revolution, many duties were sorely neglected, such as maintaining domestic order, guarding key government buildings, providing security details to government officials, providing guard duty in civilian prisons, patrolling borders, and protecting state industries and resources. Another reason to establish the PAP was the need to establish a special armed force trained to prevent and manage airplane hijackings in the late 1970s and early 1980s. In October 1981, the CCP Central Committee, the State of Council, and the CMC gave a joint order to the Ministry of Public Security (MPS) to organize an antihijacking armed police force. Realizing its inability to do so, the MPS had to ask the PLA General Staff Department for help. The department appointed a PLA unit to execute missions against the increasing hijackings in China.[24] The first counter-aircraft-hijacking special force was created in July 1982 in response to growing threats of domestic and international terrorism targeting civil aviation flights.

To the CCP leadership, another significant advantage for the PAP is its mobility. The PAP units have been deployed in cities as well as in "unstable" areas, where they become the vanguards in taking part in large-scale antiriot exercises and in suppressing popular resistance and separatist insurgencies.[25] In addition to its role in various special operations (e.g., security duty for government buildings, utilities, and prisons; border control; hijacking first response; terrorist first response; hostage rescue; other high-risk missions), party leaders expected the PAP to be able to quell a large-scale urban disturbance and to shoulder the burden of nationwide internal security.[26] These special teams are highly trained; can scale buildings and rappel from helicopters; and are armed with a variety of special weapons, including crossbows for silent operations.[27]

---

[24] Li Gang et al., "Shenqie huainian Zhao Cangbi tongzhi" [Deeply think of comrade Zhao Cangbi], in Yu Sang, *Zhao Cangbi zhuanlue ji jinian wenji* [A brief biography of Zhao Cangbi and collected works commemorating Zhao Cangbi], p. 143.

[25] Børge Bakken, "State Capacity and Social Control in China," in Kjeld Erik Brødsgaard and Susan Young (eds.), *State Capacity in East Asia: Japan, Taiwan, China, and Vietnam*, p. 195.

[26] David Shambaugh, *Modernizing China's Military*, p. 171.

[27] Richard D. Fisher, *China's Military Modernization: Building for Regional and Global Reach*, p. 34.

Rising crime rates, mass rural-urban migration, increasing urban unemployment, and soaring ethnic discontent put the pressure on the regime;[28] thus, the establishment of the PAP not only was necessary to house demobilized PLA officers but also was essential to facilitate the campaigns against increasing crimes in the early 1980s and to mitigate the growing social unrest in China. The campaign against crime was known as "merciless punishment" (*yanda*), which successfully cracked down on seventy thousand instances of organized crime, even though it was launched in August 1983 and only lasted for three months, closing immediately after the PAP was founded.[29]

The establishment of the PAP served to reinforce central authority at a time when military factionalism based on locality was rising. Deng appointed his former subordinates and trusted followers to lead the PAP and to ensure his control over the PAP. On January 25 1983, the PAP leadership was formally established under the supervision of Zhao Cangbi, political commissar, and Li Gang, former acting commander of the Beijing Garrison Command and newly appointed commander of the PAP.[30] In the PAP leadership, Zhao Cangbi was head of the Party Committee, and Commander Li Gang was appointed as Zhao's assistant.[31] Since 1948, Zhao Cangbi's career had been tied closely to Deng Xiaoping's, as Zhao had been transferred to serve Deng Xiaoping in the Central Social Affairs Department (SAD). Deng Xiaoping relied on Zhao Cangbi to reorganize the security forces and to control both the PAP and the MPS. In April 1983, Liu Fuzhi was transferred from the Department of Law to the Ministry of Public Security, replacing Zhao Cangbi as public security minister.[32] Liu was Deng's secretary in 1938 and had been one of Deng's closest assistants in charge of the security forces when Deng led the 129th Division and later the Second Field Army in the 1940s.

Features and Functions of the PAP

It should be noted that the PAP personnel, or units, are not military police as are the garrison commands, but rather are paramilitary police.[33] The PAP has been organizationally located under the State Council, although the PLA is responsible for the management, command, training, and political work of its officers. For duties related to public security, however, the PAP receives orders

[28] Tai Ming Cheung, "Guarding China's Domestic Front Line: The People's Armed Police and China's Stability," *China Quarterly* (1996), p. 525.

[29] Liu Fuzhi, "'Yanda' jiushi zhuanzheng" ["Strike Hard" is dictatorship], in Sun Mingshan (ed.), *Lishi shunjian* [An instant in history] (Beijing: Qunzhong chubanshe, 2001), vol. 2, pp. 3–17.

[30] Yu Sang, "Zhao Cangbi tongzhi zhuanlue" [A brief biography of Zhao Cangbi], in Yu Sang (ed.), *Zhao Cangbi zhuanlue ji jinian wenji*, pp. 109–11.

[31] Ibid., pp. 110–1.

[32] Liu Fuzhi, "'Yanda' jiushi zhuanzheng," p. 5.

[33] Dennis J. Blasko, *The Chinese Army Today: Tradition and Transformation for the 21st Century*, p. 23.

from the Ministry of Public Security.[34] It is incorrect to identify the PAP as part
of the PLA, because the PLA is not expected to be actively involved in controlling domestic unrest on a routine or recurring basis; it is deployed only if the
civilian Ministry of Public Security police and paramilitary PAP fail to maintain
domestic stability.[35] To a certain extent, the PAP's partial separation from the
PLA creates a system of checks and balances for the armed forces that benefit
civilian leadership and China's political stability overall. Akin to conventional
police forces, the PAP is also funded by central and local governments. The PAP
is organized as the military is, with ranks, uniforms, organizational structure,
and training that mirror those of the PLA; conventional police do not use military rank to structure their chain of command.[36] Similar to conventional police,
some of the PAP units, such as Border Defense, Firefighting, and Guard Corps,
are controlled directly by the MPS and "have full police powers to enforce
the law, including criminal investigation, detention, arrest, and execution of
administrative coercive and punitive sanctions."[37]

Specifically, the disarmament merged the duties of PLA units responsible
for domestic defense duties and the duties of the MPS and local bureaus of
public security to form the new PAP. Former duties of the PLA included security detail for leading party and government departments and the armed and
border defense police; duties previously of the MPS and local bureaus of public security were the fire brigades. According to official media, the total PAP
force spans forty-five divisions and is deployed in all twenty-two provinces,
five autonomous regions, and four centrally administered cities.[38] The Internal
Guard Corps (IGC) is the largest force of the PAP and comprises provincial
and municipal general corps, mobile divisions, and units directly subordinate
to the PAP general headquarters in Beijing.[39]

There are three groups that make up the PAP (Figure 6.1). The first
group is the Internal Guard Corps, which includes fourteen mobile divisions
and thirty-one provincial and municipal internal security general corps, the
Xinjiang Production and Construction Corps, and military colleges and special
units (e.g., reconnaissance, special services, artillery, chemical defense) that are

[34] *Xinhua*, December 29, 2006.
[35] Blasko, *The Chinese Army Today: Tradition and Transformation for the 21st Century*,
pp. 176–7.
[36] Ivan Y. Sun and Yuning Wu, "The Role of the People's Armed Police in Chinese Policing,"
Asian Criminology, vol. 4, no. 2 (2009), p. 120.
[37] Except the MPS-led active service troops within the PAP, such as the Border Defense, Firefighting, and Guard Corps, other PAP units do not have the power to impose sanctions (e.g., arrest
and detain). See C. Gao, B. Chiu, H. Tsai, and Y. Su, *Zhongguo renmin wuzhuang jingcha de
jiegou* [An analysis of the Chinese People's Armed Police] (Taipei, Taiwan: Yang-Chih Book
Co., 2003); and Ivan Y. Sun and Yuning Wu, "The Role of the People's Armed Police in Chinese
Policing," p. 122.
[38] See *Dongfang zaobao* [Eastern morning news], August 28, 2009.
[39] Ivan Y. Sun and Yuning Wu, "The Role of the People's Armed Police in Chinese Policing," p.
117.

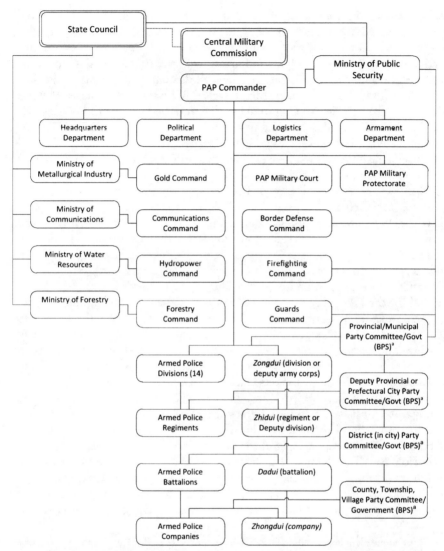

FIGURE 6.1. *Organizational Structure of the PAP. Source*: Zhongguo renmin gongan shigao bianxie xiaozu, *Zhongguo renmin gongan shigao* [Draft of Chinese People's public security history], internal publication, pp. 413–14; "Junshi zhidu" [Military system], *Xinhua*, http://news.xinhuanet.com/ziliao/2003–08/22/content_1039434_3.htm (accessed April 2, 2009).

[a] Local bureau of public security led by local party committees or governments represent local party committees and governments to take charge of administration duties and coordination with local PAP units.

directly under the command of the PAP general headquarters.[40] The second group is related to management of four capital constructional units – the Gold, Hydropower, Communications, and Forestry Corps. The PAP shares administrative responsibilities of the second group with the professional departments of the State Council administration. The professional departments of the State Council include the Ministry of Metallurgical Industry, the Ministry of Water Resources, the Ministry of Communications, and the Ministry of Forestry. The third group consists of the three units traditionally under MPS jurisdiction: the Border Defense, Firefighting, and Guard Corps.

The establishment of the PAP enabled the party-state to better manage local armed police and specialized security units from the PLA and the MPS, such as the PLA's Gold, Water and Electric Power, and Communications units, and the MPS's Border Defense Corps, Forestry Police Corps and Firefighting Corps. To drive the professionalism and standardization of the PAP, in 1993 the CCP leadership adopted a ranking system that the MPS had proposed in 1956 but that had never been implemented.[41] Currently, the PAP is organized into eight subunit corps: Internal Guards, Border Defense, Firefighting, Guard, Hydropower, Gold, Communications, and Forestry. The Internal Guards Corps is the largest subunit of the PAP, playing a key role in maintaining social stability and frequently assisting law enforcement. The Guard Corps includes the Immediate Action Unit (IAU), which combats terrorism and performs antiattack, antihijacking, and antiexplosion duties. Traditionally, the PAP has been involved in numerous relief operations in response to natural disasters, such as floods, snowstorms, hurricanes, earthquakes, and forest fires.[42]

The Internal Guard Corps (*neiwei budui*) is the major force of the PAP and mainly consists of two parts: units organized in fourteen mobile divisions and located around the country and thirty-one general corps at the level of deputy corps or division located in the provinces, autonomous regions, and municipalities. The thirty-one general corps are responsible for security duty of important political and economic facilities and government buildings at all levels (including party and state organizations, foreign embassies, and consulates), municipal armed patrol, security duty for senior government officials,

[40] *Jinhua xinwen* [Jinhua news] online, December 14, 2004, http://www.jhnews.com.cn/gb/content/2004-12/fourteen/content_3572fourteen.htm (accessed July 2008).

[41] On October 10, 1956, the State Council passed a proposal sent by the MPS about the establishment of police ranks, with implementation to begin in 1957. Although the proposed police ranking system had a structure similar to the military ranks adopted in 1955, the proposal did not allow for the ranks of senior general (*da jiang*) or general (*shang jiang*), as the military did. In other words, the highest police rank possible was that of lieutenant general (*zhong jiang*). However, when the proposal was sent to the Politburo for approval, Mao turned it down. See Da Xing'an Ling diqu xingshu gong'an ju, "Zhonghua renmin gongheguo renmin jingcha jingxian jibie jianshi" [Brief history of the levels of police ranks in PRC People's Police), *Beiji gong'an* [North Pole Public Security] online, http://ga.dxal.hl.cn/Article_Show.asp?ArticleID=643 (accessed December 24, 2009).

[42] Blasko, *The Chinese Army Today: Tradition and Transformation for the 21st Century*, p. 175.

and security duty of public corporations and major public events. Some units of the Internal Guard Corps perform guard duties in civilian prisons and provide state executioners. The Internal Guard Corps is also assigned with providing aid for national economic infrastructural construction and emergency as well as lead aid and assistance work when natural disasters occur. The mobile units in the Internal Guard Corps are mainly responsible for dealing with terrorism, violent crime, riots, and public security threats. Besides the fourteen mobile divisions, each of the thirty-one general corps also has its own mobile unit, which are usually better equipped than other PAP units. These independent mobile units are viewed as daggers or fists of the PAP general corps and are used specifically to respond to emergency incidents (*tufa shijian*). For example, the Third Regiment (*zhidui*) of the PAP Hunan General Corps is the only mobile unit of the PAP Hunan General Corps, and it plays the first responder role in emergencies, natural disasters, or severe mass incidents.[43]

Because mobile units are responsible for dealing with large-scale protests and social unrest, among their ranks are engineering and chemical defense troops that employ artillery such as mortars and recoilless rifle cannon. Other units responsible for security detail and guarding duties are equipped with small arms and nonlethal weapons. Some units are even equipped with helicopters and armored vehicles. Because of the demanding nature of their duties, when not engaged in emergency operations, mobile units receive full-time training to increase combat effectiveness. Mobile divisions of the PAP general corps located in the provinces, autonomous regions, and municipalities are nominally under the jurisdiction of their supervising general corps, authorization granted by the PAP general headquarters in Beijing. However, the fourteen independent mobile divisions are controlled directly by the PAP general headquarters in Beijing. It is reasonable to speculate that the general corps located in the provinces, autonomous regions, and municipalities play a supportive role to the fourteen independent mobile divisions, with limited assistance in providing military training, political education, and logistical supplies. For example, the PAP general corps in Jiangsu was authorized to manage all PAP units in its jurisdiction on behalf of the PAP general headquarters in Beijing, including the PAP mobile divisions Unit 8690 in Yixing and Unit 8720 in Wuxi, the PAP Command College on the Nanjing campus, and the PAP 5302 Factory. In reality, the PAP provincial general corps in Jiangsu has no authority to deploy or officer appointments of these units; instead, they receive command directly from the PAP general headquarters in Beijing.

Compared to the thirty-one general corps, the fourteen mobile divisions are stronger combat forces with higher cohesion, patriotism, physical fitness, training, equipment, and skills because the PAP absorbed them directly from

[43] *Xiaoxiang chenbao* [Xiaoxiang morning news], August 2, 2004.

the PLA infantry; the fourteen mobile divisions also enjoy more resources from post-Deng leaders. Although these mobile divisions receive antiterrorism and antiriot training, they are otherwise trained under the same standards as PLA units. Although they may not be the best PLA units, they command the strength of the PLA infantry through the use of camouflage, concealment, and deception, as well as efficient operations and communication procedures. In addition, officials in the mobile divisions have more opportunities to be promoted than officials in the PAP general corps; many general corps commanders and political commissars were transferred or promoted from the fourteen mobile divisions. This has occurred in the PAP units in Fujian, Shandong, Henan, Guangxi, Xinjiang, Jiangxi, Anhui, Liaoning, Hubei, Guizhou, Tibet, Ningxia, Shanxi, Shandong, Shaanxi, Henan, Zhejiang, Yunnan, and Qinghai.

Except for the fourteen mobile divisions that are organized by military hierarchy such as divisions, regiments, battalions, companies, and platoons, each corps under the PAP general headquarters is organized as the (1) *zongdui* (general corps or detachment), which are subordinate headquarters at the levels of deputy army corps or division and are located in provinces, autonomous regions, and municipalities; (2) *zhidui*, which are at the level of regiment located in provinces, prefectures, or specifically designated cities; (3) *dadui*, which are at the level of battalion located in the districts of the important cities; and (4) *zhongdui*, which are at the level of company located in counties, townships, and villages.

Both the PAP mobile divisions and detachments that are stationed in provinces, autonomous regions, and municipalities directly under the central government have similar functions in terms of tasks and responsibilities. Neither is assigned routine patrols or conventional police duties; instead, each is directed to maintain military preparedness through intensive training to deal with large-scale riots, social disorder, emergency rescue, and disaster relief. Although other armed forces such as the PLA and the militia also participate in operations to quell social unrest, these mobile divisions and detachments as well as their subordinate units lead the efforts. They also carry out a wide variety of law enforcement duties, including preventive patrolling. The PAP mobile divisions and detachments' primary function is preparedness in the event of an emergency or mass incident. In contrast to the PAP mobile divisions and detachments, conventional police are assigned duties of routine maintenance of social order, are responsible for handling small-scale street-level nonorganized crime and may play a supportive role in assisting the PAP with large-scale protests and mass incidents.

Unlike the fourteen mobile divisions that receive orders only from the PAP general headquarters in Beijing (although local party or government organizations may be authorized to co-lead the mobile divisions when the mobile divisions operate in the areas under their jurisdiction), the detachments follow orders of local party and government leadership while receiving command from the PAP leadership. Unlike the detachments that are mainly responsible for maintaining social order in their jurisdiction, mobile divisions are dispatched anywhere they are needed. During the 2008 Beijing Olympic Games, officials and soldiers from a mobile division were sent to Beijing to maintain social order.[44] In rescue efforts after the devastating earthquake of May 2008 in Wenchuan, Sichuan, the PAP mobile divisions comprised part of the first responding forces, leading search-and-rescue missions.[45]

Dilemma of Dual Leadership

The People's Armed Police receives the professional guidance from the MPS, yet it is under dual leadership of the MPS's parent organization, the State Council, and the CMC (Figure 6.2). The MPS and State Council are responsible for command and operations of the PAP, authorizing the size and number of subordinate organizations, assigning tasks, providing financial and material support, and ensuring logistical supply. Professional guidance is provided to the PAP by the State Council through granting MPS officials appointments as first political commissars throughout all levels and branches of the PAP. The CMC handles the PAP's organizational structure, leadership, operations, training, and political education.[46] In other words, although the PAP receives command and guidance from the MPS about active service duties such as guard, border patrol, and firefighting duties, operationally it is controlled by the CMC. The transfer of the PAP's command system from under the MPS, a fundamentally police organization, to the CMC, a military organization, served to strengthen the military functions of the PAP and further discipline the armed police.

The dilemmas of dual leadership, though touching all aspects of administration, also have a real impact on the PAP's missions in the field. The necessity of frequent and timely PAP deployment to quell incidents of domestic unrest, and the difficulty of handling emergency responses perfectly has made relations between civilian law enforcement units and PAP units less cooperative than would be ideal. Whenever local civilian authorities confront mass incidents and it is determined to be necessary to deploy PAP units, local authorities need to ask permission from the PLA first. Herein lies a potentially devastating logistical issue of dual leadership, because it often means that responses are not decisive or fast enough. Party leadership took matters into their own hands in August 2009 when they passed the People's Armed Police Law, which clarified responsibilities of the State Council and the PLA. More important, the law

[44] *Fazhi ribao* [Legal system daily], July 24 2008.
[45] *Zhongguo qingnian bao* [China youth daily], May 15, 2008.
[46] "Guanyu tiaozheng zhongguo renmin wuzhuang jingcha budui lingdao guanli tizhi de jueding" [Decision about adjusting the PAP's leadership system of administration], in *Guowuyuan, zhongyang junweihui wenjian* [State Council and the CMC Document], no. 5, 1995.

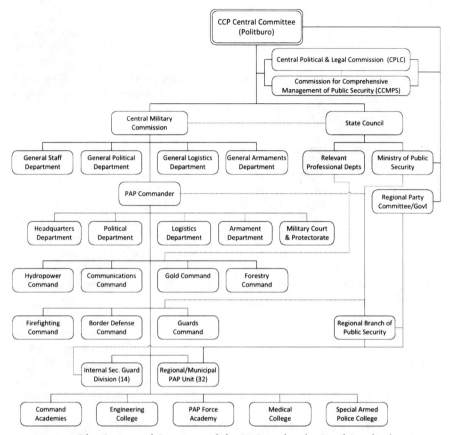

FIGURE 6.2. *The Command Structure of the PAP under the Dual Leadership System.* *Source*: Zhongguo renmin gongan shigao bianxie xiaozu, *Zhongguo renmin gongan shigao*, pp. 413–14; "Junshi zhidu" [Military system], *Xinhua*, http://news.xinhuanet.com/ziliao/2003–08/22/content_1039434-3.htm (accessed April 2, 2009).

reinforced the ability of the State Council to "entrust tasks to the PAP" and "command the PAP."[47] Last, the law implied that civilian authorities led by the State Council could deploy PAP units before they reported the incident to the PLA.

The MPS's advisory relationship with the PAP is largely symbolic, as the CMC has decision-making powers over the most prominent aspects of the PAP's work. Except for the Border Defense Corps, Firefighting Corps, and Guard Corps, with their 230,000-personnel units around the country, the CMC is responsible for appointing and promoting all officials and for ensuring political control. Essentially, the Border Defense Corps, Firefighting Corps, and

---

[47] *Dongfang zaobao* [Eastern morning news], August 28, 2009.

Guard Corps are controlled by the MPS but are nominally subordinate to the PAP, the logic behind which is not quite clear. Perhaps the most salient reason is that these three corps have traditionally functioned as part of the MPS's local police force. The Firefighting Corps and Guard Corps are subordinated to local MPS organizations (bureaus of public security, whereas the Border Defense Corps receive command directly from the MPS. Because of these historical ties, party leadership has deemed it ideal for the MPS to remain in control of these three subunits.

The PAP is integral to the state system of domestic security and policing, in coordination with public security units among others, but its second role as part of the military allows it to fill niches in battlefield security, anti-infiltration, and wartime coast guarding. For example, China sent the armed police units to North Korea during the Korean War, where they took charge of security in areas previously controlled by Chinese armies. Its duties then included maintaining social order, monitoring enemy airplanes, escorting military supply and materials, guarding roads and transportation, executing bandits and spies, guarding government buildings and facilities, and guarding prisons.[48] Since the 1990s, PAP units have been assigned to participate in more peacekeeping missions abroad, such as the UN peacekeeping missions in East Timor, Liberia, Bosnia and Herzegovina, Haiti, and Afghanistan.[49]

Besides a dual State Council–CMC leadership system, the PAP also receives guidance from the party's top legal and public security advisory organs, including the Central Political and Legal Commission (*zhongyang zhengfa weiyuanhui*, CPLC) and the Commission for Comprehensive Management of Public Security (*shehui zhi'an zonghe zhili weiyuanhui*, CCMPS). The CPLC functions as the general chief of staff of the party committees and represents the party in overseeing the country's intelligence, law enforcement, judicial, and to a lesser extent, lawmaking systems. The CPLC was established in January 1980 to separate the duties of the government and the party. Under the leadership of Hu Yaobang and Zhao Ziyang in the mid- and late 1980s, there was a tendency to reduce party intervention in the legal system to promote the independence of the legal organs – the courts, public security, and procuratorate. Dual supervision and restrictions were a part of the effort to guarantee justice. Thus, the CPLC was abolished in May 1988 and the Central Political and Legal Group, a much small organization with the limited functions, replaced the CPLC.[50] Perhaps in response to the 1989 Tiananmen incident, the CPLC was restored in March 1990 so the party could resume its supervision over the legal system.

[48] See Huang Yao and Zhang Mingzhe, *Luo Ruiqing zhuan* [A biography of Luo Ruiqing] (Beijing: Dangdai zhongguo chubanshe, 1996), pp. 293–4.
[49] Ivan Y. Sun and Yuning Wu, "The Role of the People's Armed Police in Chinese Policing," p. 125.
[50] Zhonggong zhongyang zuzhi bu [CCP Organization Department] et al., *Zhongguo gongchandang zuzhi shi ziliao* [Reference materials of the history of the CCP organizations) (Beijing: Zhonggong dangshi chubanshe, 2000), vol. 7, part 1, pp. 238.

The CPLC established branches at the county level and above, creating a large bureaucracy of around thirty thousand personnel nationwide.[51]

Like the CPLC, the CCMPS is a standing body in charge of the state security apparatus underneath the Central Party Committee and the State Council. Its primary function is to coordinate official activities in the field of public order and security from anticrime campaigns to monitoring dissident initiatives, the joint effort among the CPLC, MPS, Supreme Court, Justice Ministry, Supreme People's Procuratorate, Ministry of State Security as well as the armed forces and many government departments, has become the prominent feature of this principal party organ. Like the CCMPS at the central level in which Zhou Yongkang is head of both the CPLC and CCMPS, many local CPLC and CCMPS branches are led by the same persons who usually are the members of the standing committees of local party organizations as the cases in Beijing, Tianjin, Jiangsu, Zhejiang and Ningxia. In some provinces or cities such as Shanghai, Yunnan, Shanxi, the positions of the CCMPS leaders are symbolically taken by the acting party secretaries while the CPLC heads, who are the standing committee members of the local party organs and head of local MPS branches, actually run both local CPLC and CCMSS branches. Because the CPLC plays a leading role in the CCMPS, the operating organ (*bangong shi*) of the CCMPS is merged with the administrative office of the CPLC (*heshu bangong*).[52]

The PAP fits into a larger picture of policing in China and is one of three categories of police groups: social order and control police (public security police and state security police), criminal justice police (prison guards and judicial police), and the armed police, the last of which is the PAP (Figure 6.3). State security police are located under the Ministry of State Security and are engaged in counterespionage work, ensuring state security, and maintaining social and political stability. The criminal justice police include the judicial police in courts, in procuratorial-prosecutorial systems and in prisons as guards and is led by the Ministry of Justice. Public security police, in contrast, are located under the Ministry of Public Security and are responsible for internal security, social control, and basic police functions such as maintaining law and order, investigating common criminal cases, managing traffic control, monitoring citizens' political attitudes, conducting background investigations and the census, executing civil registrations, patrolling government buildings, and carrying out occasional government and party development activities.

---

[51] Ibid., p. 238; Li Ming, "Dangwei zhengfawei zhineng jiqi zhengfa gongzuo" [Functions of party committee and political and legal commission as well as the political and legal work] in *Jiangdushi renmin zhengfu* [Government of Jiangdu City], http://www.jiangdu.gov.cn/xwzx/info.asp?id=25500 (accessed August 20, 2009).

[52] Zhonggong zhongyang zuzhi bu et al., *Zhongguo gongchandang zuzhi shi ziliao*, vol. 7, part 1, p. 238.

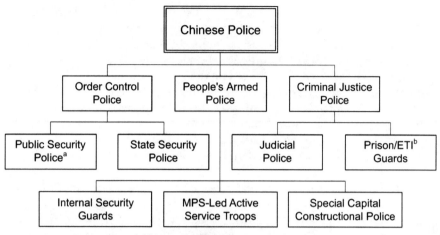

FIGURE 6.3. *Categories of Chinese Police Forces.*
[a] Public security police covers most responsibilities of the MPS, such as maintaining order and registering households. Local bureaus of public security led by local Party committees or governments represent local Party Committees and governments to take charge of administration duties and coordination with local PAP units.
[b] ETI stands for the education through labor.

Before 1996, the PAP was a subordinate armed unit of the MPS, such that MPS ministers' names were listed before PAP commanders' names on PAP documents, a sign of the absolute leadership of the MPS. The PAP functioned as a regular police force primarily to maintain public order and protect public security; however, it was treated as a special force for its capacity to carry out police tasks with military features.[53] The large supervisory role of the MPS explains why some members of the PAP leadership publicly complained that "the PAP was grandson to the MPS's grandfather."[54] In the words of General Zhou Yushu, PAP commander between January 1990 and December 1992, the PAP was "the armed force led by the Party and the state, not the armed force of the MPS!"[55] In addition, because many PAP personnel were demobilized or transferred PLA officers or soldiers, critiques of the PAP compared it to the PLA. Throughout the 1980s, the PAP was viewed as having poor management and low morale as a result of it having poorer training and discipline than the PLA, as well as the MPS's failure to provide similar benefits as the PLA became an additional source of unpopularity of MPS authority over the PAP.

[53] Yang Yize, "Shilun wujing budui de tedian" [A discussion of the characteristics of the armed police force], in *Wujing xueyuan xuebao* [Academic journal of the Chinese People's Armed Police College], no. 1 (1997), pp. 55–8.
[54] See Tian Bingxin, "Zhou Yushu: Zaozao baoxiao dasheng ti" [Zhou Yushu: Announce the dawn daily and crow loudly], in *Hainan jingji bao* [Hainan economic daily], December 12, 2005.
[55] Ibid.

Questioning about the PAP's status was not limited to a few officials' or soldiers' opinions; in fact, there had been a long-standing debate in the 1980s about what the PAP's central mission should be – guarding duties (*zhiqin*) or handling emergencies (*chutu*). Although the question was framed in terms of its central mission, the issue really hinged on the question whether the PAP should be controlled by the MPS or whether it should be independent. A compromise was reached in September 1992 by which the central mission of the PAP was defined as guarding duties and handling emergencies. Thereafter, part of the PAP units continued to carry out guard duties, and part of the PAP units became mobile units, focusing on handling emergencies such as mass incidents and terrorist attacks.[56]

The reevaluation of the PAP's role in early 1995 was a huge victory for those in the camp who believed the PAP should not be subordinate to the MPS. In fact, the PLA played an increasingly important role in the PAP's organizational development, and the PLA's influence over the PAP had become evident after the 1989 Tiananmen incident.[57] The PAP's upgrade from the level of lieutenant (*fu*) military region to chief (*zheng*) military region in December 1996 supported the PAP's appeal to be no longer institutionally subordinate to the MPS. In what seems like a compromise, the party leadership ordered the PLA to become an additional supervisory organ for the PAP, which led to the current setup of CMC control of personnel, cadre management, organizational discipline, training, and political work of the PAP, although the State Council assigns tasks and manages the PAP on a daily basis through the MPS. Although the culture, internal structure, and training of the PAP mirror the PLA, the tendency of the PAP is to develop similarly to the professional departments under the State Council because of financial, structural, and operational realities. The dual leadership creates a fragmented command structure with widely varying standards for professionalism, encourages competing institutional loyalties, and inhibits coordination and communication across corps.[58] As Tanner has pointed out, the dual leadership of the PAP created significant organizational tension among the PLA, the PAP, and local MPS officials.[59]

The PAP and Local Politics

Considering the nature of the PAP and its involvement in local security and politics, party leadership has shown increasing concern about the PAP units'

---

[56] Ibid.
[57] Murray Scot Tanner, "The Institutional Lessons of Disaster: Reorganizing China's People's Armed Police after Tiananmen," p. 632.
[58] Tai Ming Cheung, "Guarding China's Domestic Front Line: The People's Armed Police and China's Stability," p. 528.
[59] Murray Scot Tanner, "The Institutional Lessons of Disaster: Reorganizing China's People's Armed Police after Tiananmen," pp. 587–635.

close ties with society's "undesirables." It is understood that certain populations with whom the PAP typically associates could corrupt it and undermine
its ideological loyalties as well as its role as guardian of the regime. The PAP
units are not evenly distributed across the country but rather are concentrated
in urban and wealthy areas in addition to more volatile regions with dense
minority group populations, because of the policy that requires local governments to subsidize local PAP units.[60] The fundamental difference between the
PAP and the PLA is that the PAP can be employed by local party leadership
and governments to supplement public security efforts.

Local public security organs, to which PAP units are formally subordinate,
can also affect the dimensions of PAP unit involvement in local politics by virtue
of their participation in the governmental decision-making process and their
membership in party committees of the local PAP units. Heads of local public
security organizations concurrently hold the title of first political commissars of
their counterpart PAP units. Because local party and government leaders have
been granted power over local PAP units, they have decision-making authority
regarding a local PAP unit's deployment, funding, logistics, and appointments.
According to a State Council document issued in 2002, local governments were
responsible for providing logistical supplies for armed forces located in their
jurisdiction, including the PLA and PAP units. These logistical supplies included
food, barracks, vehicles, health care, cloth, gas, and other services.[61] According
to the Ministry of Finance, local authorities are gradually bearing more of
the costs for PAP expenditures. From 1996 to 2003, the local share of PAP
expenditure costs rose 7.5 percent – from 2.5 percent to 10 percent.[62] Aside
from nonflexible operational expenditures, the PAP receives extrabudgetary
allocations from local party authorities and governments depending on the
cost of operations for mass incidents; it also receives contingency funds for use
during crises and natural disasters.[63] In addition, the PAP units benefit from
the contributions of land or goods, instead of money, from local authorities.
Clearly, despite the efforts of the PLA and the PAP general headquarters to
control local PAP units, local leaders and branches of the MPS have increasingly
consolidated their power over local PAP units.

Although local PAP units are reliant on the financial support of local party
and government organizations, some PAP units depend more on this support
than others, as in the case of the PAP Firefighting Corps, whose budget largely
comes from local financial resources. As a result, their budgets are largely

---

[60] Ivan Y. Sun and Yuning Wu, "The Role of the People's Armed Police in Chinese Policing,"
p. 118.

[61] State Council document, no. 20 (2002); see also *Xinhuanet*, September 30, 2002.

[62] Shaoguang Wang, "China's Expenditure for the People's Armed Police and Militia," in Nan Li
(ed.), *Chinese Civil-Military Relations: The Transformation of the People's Liberation Army*,
p. 153.

[63] Tai Ming Cheung, "Guarding China's Domestic Front Line: The People's Armed Police and
China's Stability," p. 534.

affected by the state of the local economy and their degree of importance according to local leaders. It is commonplace in western China, where local economies are often underdeveloped, that local governments are unable to support the PAP Firefighting Corps, thus threatening the existence of the corps.[64] For those PAP units that receive funding from local government and party organizations, financial support does not come without its costs. In return for sustaining the PAP's livelihood, local PAP units give unconditional help to their benefactors. Consequently, PAP units' involvement in violent incidents under the orders of local party and governments has markedly increased in recent years. Local PAP units are deployed frequently against angry farmers, unemployed workers, miners, and separatist groups. The aforementioned case of local PAP units firing into a mob of protesters in Shanwei, Guangdong, was ordered by local party leaders. The use of one's local police forces, including PAP units as personal tools against annoying civil disturbances, critical dissidents, and other potentially politically damaging groups, has become common among local leaders. According to the *Banyue Tan*, the mouthpiece of the CCP Propaganda Department, the misuse of the police forces including the PAP has become one of the three "deep origins" that have triggered the large-scale and violent "mass incidents," such as the incidents in Ci'an of Guizhou, Fugu of Shaanxi, and Menglian of Yunnan in 2008.[65] The misuse of PAP units by local leaders indicates the lack of control that the central government and PAP general headquarters have over local PAP units.

When PAP forces confront sudden incidents of mass violence and disorder, in reality, they tend to follow the unilateral orders from local officials rather than from a joint command given by the local party officials and the upper-level PAP units and upper-level PLA organizations. On December 6, 2005, for example, PAP forces subdued a mass uprising in Shanwei, Guangdong, by opening fire at a mob of explosive-lobbing protesters, killing at least twenty people. In this case, local officials had given orders to fire live rounds when the protests did not comply with the call to stand down. Another case was the riot triggered by a girl's death in Guizhou Province on June 28, 2008, that partially contributed to excess employment of the PAP by the local officials. The PAP has been criticized for becoming a tool of local officials who are in collusion with local mobsters to the detriment of socially disadvantaged groups. Another problem of the PAP in practice is the difficulty of ensuring lower-level PAP unit compliance with upper-level PAP units regarding quick and effective

---

[64] Chen Zhiwen, *Jiaqiang xiaofang teqing duiwu jianshe, shiying miehuo qiangxian xuyao* [Strengthen the construction of the fire control special services squad, adapt to the needs of fire control and emergency response], http://www.fire.hc360.com/daquan/2004wlb/yxlw/thesis_2 .htm (accessed September 23, 2009).

[65] "Qunti xing shijian tufa, wei jicheng zhizheng qiaoxiang jingzhong" [Rising emergent mass incidents that alarm the grassroots administration], *Banyue tan* [Biweekly conversation], August 13, 2008.

mass incident response. Although upper-level units see the need for lower-level incident reports and stand by for orders in every situation, even mass incidents, in reality, given the PAP's current structure, waiting for a response from general headquarters in Beijing. These examples demonstrate how the organizational and administrative issues of the PAP and its supervisory organs have an affect on the ability of the PAP to carry out its missions, particularly those related to mass incident response and coordination.

After Deng Xiaoping launched economic reforms, CCP leadership was convinced that the PLA was an armed force solely to be used to defend the country. Local party and governments were not allowed to deploy the PLA, because the regime was concerned that the lag time in requesting PLA troops from Beijing to quell local uprisings would be problematic for local party and government organizations. Thus, the creation of the PAP helped local party and government organizations quickly and effectively suppress mass incidents. In establishing the PAP, Central leadership addressed the obvious issue of local leaders consolidating loyalty among local PAP troops to overthrow the party-state. Although local PAP units are strong enough to impose social stability on riots or protests, they are by no means trained well enough in combat or equipped well enough to threaten the PLA. It can be speculated that party leadership never expected ties between local PAP units and local civilian leaders to become such an obstacle for effective control. The prevalence of these ties has brought the central authority's attention more closely to the role of the PAP. In August 2009, central leadership took action and enacted new laws to redefine the bounds of both local and PAP authority. The legislation makes it so that county-level local leaders can no longer request the PAP to handle disorders.[66] These efforts are aimed to prevent low-level government officials from enlisting the PAP in clear abuses of power.

The Role of the PAP in Maintaining Social Stability

Although China's market reforms have led to a boon in economic choice and China is enjoying its best period of economic growth, these things have brought about corruption, social inequality, urban-rural conflict, pollution, environmental damage, and unemployment that have become the sources for the ever-widening and sometimes violent social unrest. The CCP is right to be worried about social stability. China's crime rate has increased more than 10 percent yearly since 1988.[67] The ballooning crime rate indicates growing tensions between citizens and the regime (Table 6.1 and Figure 6.4). According to

[66] *Xinhua*, August 27, 2009.
[67] Bai Jianjun, "Cong zhongguo fanzuilu shuju kan zuiyin, zuixing, yu xingfa de guanxi" [Relations among the sources of offenses, crime, and punishment from the data of China's crime rate], *Zhongguo shehui kexue* [Chinese social science], no. 2 (2010), p. 144.

TABLE 6.1. *China's Crime Rate (1000), 1978–2009*

Year	1978	1979	1980	1981	1982	1983	1984	1985	1986	1987	1988	1989	1990	1991	1992	1993
No. of cases	530	594	750	890	749	611	514	542	547	570	828	1,972	2,217	2,366	1,583	1,617
Year	1994	1995	1996	1997	1998	1999	2000	2001	2002	2003	2004	2005	2006	2007	2008[1]	2009
No. of cases	1,661	1,621	1,601	1,614	1,986	2,249	3,637	4,458	4,337	4,394	4,718	4,648	4,653	4,746	4,770	5,300

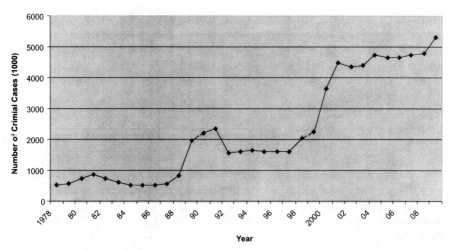

FIGURE 6.4. *China's Crime Rate, 1978–2009. Source*: Zhongguo falu nianjianshe [China Law Yearbook Press], *Zhongguo falu nianjian, 1987–2005* [China law yearbook, 1987–2005] (Beijing: Zhongguo falu chubanshe); Gong'an bu [Ministry of Public Security], "Gong'an bu zhaokai xinwen fabuhui tongbao 2006 nian shehui zhi'an xingshi ji zhenpo ming'an gongzuo qingkuang" [Ministry of Public Security calls a news conference to report the situation of social order and the work of resolving the homicide cases], *MPS*, February 6, 2007, http://www.mps .gov.cn/cenweb/brjlCenweb/jsp/common/article.jsp?infoid=ABC000000000000037722 (accessed September 3, 2009); *Xinhua*, January 30, 2008; *Zhongguo xinwenshe* [China news service], February 25, 2010.

ᵃ There has been no official figure provided. However, the official media indicate that there had been an estimated 10 percent increase from 2008 to 2009, on the basis of data collected between January 2009 and October 2009. See *Zhongguo xinwenshe* [China news service], February 25, 2010.

Chen Jiping, deputy director of the CCMPS, there had been 5.34 million cases between January and November in 2010, a 7.5 percent increase compared with the same time in 2009.[68]

The CCP has also become increasingly concerned in recent years over problems stemming from the country's rapid economic growth. Mass incidents, which include protests, riots, strikes, roadblocks and petitioning, are triggered by many diverse issues: frustration over official corruption, failure of the rule of law, anger over a growing gap between the rich and the poor, and an inadequate social security system. These mass incidents involving violent clashes between state authorities and aggrieved citizens have been fueled by the issues such as growing inequalities, harsh treatment, low wages, wage arrears, extremely long hours of work, environmental disasters, land requisitions, resettlement

[68] "Chen Jiping: 2011 nian shehui hexie wending xin bushu" [Chen Jiping: New arrangement of social harmony and stability in 2011], *Liaowang*, vol. 8 (2011), p. 36.

TABLE 6.2. *China's Mass Incidents (1000 cases), 1993–2009*

Year	1993	1994	1995[a]	1996[a]	1997	1998	1999	2000	2001[b]
No. of cases	8.7	10	11	12.1	15.93	25	32	50	53
Year	2002[b]	2003	2004	2005	2006	2007[a]	2008[a]	2009[a]	
No. of cases	55	58	74	87	90	92	95	100	

[a] The exact official figures are not available; however, the data here are based on estimates from the official media.
[b] The data are based on my estimates.

of migrants, disposition of collectively owned assets, product and food safety scandals, mining deaths, and so on.[69] Since 1993, according to Hu Lianhe, Hu Angang, and Wang Lei, the mass incidents have increased dramatically, as there was 10 percent growth rate in 1995 and 1996 and a 25.5 percent average annual growth rate from 1997 to 2004.[70] The official publications have indicated a steady increase of the mass incidents from 1993 to 2010 in China (Table 6.2 and Figure 6.5).

However, some scholars and government officials question the data published by authorities and believe that the actual numbers are much higher. For example, Zhu Lijia, director of the Teaching and Research Office under the National Public Administration Institute, believes that the cases of the mass incidents doubled from 2006 to 2010. Some were even convinced that the cases of mass incidents in 2010 reached 180,000.[71] Yu Jianrong, director of the Research Center on Social Problems under the Agricultural Institute of China Social Science Academy, summarizes that there are five types of mass incidents – protection of rights, vent of anger on society, riots, social conflicts, the organized crimes.[72]

The PAP was created to lead the vanguard of nation internal security, especially in situations of deteriorating social order. However, the PAP had been inefficient in first several years of its birth, in particular, its role in responding to the 1989 Tiananmen student demonstration.[73] Thus, "PLA responsibility

[69] Mark W. Frazier, *Socialist Insecurity: Pensions and the Politics of Uneven Development in China*, p. 1; Ching Kwan Lee, "Pathways of Labor Activism," in Elizabeth J. Perry and Mark Selden (eds.), *Chinese Society: Change, Conflict and Resistance*, 3rd ed., pp. 54, 65.

[70] See Hu Lianhe, Hu Angang, and Wang Lei, "Yingxiang shehui wending de shehui maodun bianhua taishi de shizheng fenxi" [Empirical analysis of change and trend of social contradictions that affect social stability], *Shehui kexue zhanxian* [Front line of social science], vol. 4, pp. 175–85.

[71] Sun Liping, "Quanli shikong daozhi shehui shixu" [Out-off-control power results in social disorder], *Nanfang nongcun bao* [Nanfang country daily], March 1, 2011.

[72] Yu Jianrong, "Dangqian woguo quntixing shijian de zhuyao leixing jiqi jiben tezheng" [Major types and basic features of current mass incidents in China], *Zhongguo zhengfa daxie xuebao* [Journal of China University of Political Science and Law], vol. 6 (2009), p. 115.

[73] Paul H. B. Godwin, "Party-Military Relations," in Merle Goldman and Roderick MacFarquhar (eds.), *The Paradox of China's Post-Mao Reforms*, p. 82.

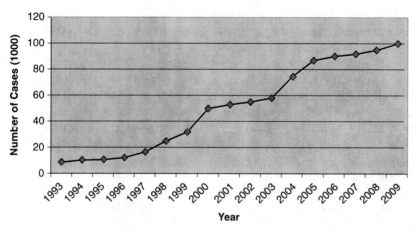

FIGURE 6.5. *China's Mass Incidents, 1993–2009. Source:* Tian Xiaowei, "Ruhe tigao zhengfu yingdui qunti xing shijian de nengli" [How to enhance the ability of the government in response to mass incidents?], in *Harbin shiwei dangxiao xuebao* [The journal of Harbin Party Committee School], vol. 63, no. 3 (May 2009), p. 48; *Yangcheng wanbao*, February 27, 2010; Zhao Qinxuan, "'Qunti xing shijian' de beihou shi shenme suqiu?" [What is the appeal behind "mass incidents"?], *Minzhu yu kexue* [Democracy and science], no. 5 (2005), p. 61; Song Weiqiang, "Kangzheng zhengzhi shiye zhongde nongmin qunti xing shijian" [Perspective of contention in the rural mass incidents], *Zhongguo nongcun yanjiu wang* [Chinese rural studies online], May 18, 2006; Lu Mei and Wang Wanling, "Qunti xing shijian yingdui zhongde zhengzhi sixiang gongzuo tansuo" [Exploration of political and ideological work in response to mass incidents], in *Jingji yanjiu daokan* [Economic research guide], vol. 6 (2011), p. 215.

for the lethal suppression of the Tiananmen protesters was the direct result of the failure of the People's Armed Police (PAP) to control the massive demonstrations in and around Tiananmen Square in the spring of 1989."[74] Over the years CCP leadership has become reluctant to employ the PLA for nonmilitary internal security duties. After the use of the PLA in quashing the "democratic movement" in Tiananmen Square in 1989 severely damaged the PLA's image, the CCP made the great effort to upgrade the PAP and deemed the PAP as the main force to be mobilized in any large-scale domestic upheaval.[75] Thus, the PAP was vastly strengthened after the Tiananmen incident "to create a new internal army to fight large-scale political movements, such as the pro-democracy protesters of 1989, that might again rise against the CCP."[76] After the Tiananmen Square incident, the PAP's importance was emphasized

[74] Ibid., p. 82.
[75] The PAP was viewed as ineffectiveness in 1989 Tiananmen incident due to a lack of riot-control training and appropriate equipment. See Paul H. B. Godwin, "Party-Military Relations," p. 82.
[76] Richard D. Fisher, *China's Military Modernization: Building for Regional and Global Reach,* p. 34.

through a series of reforms and reorganizations that aimed to improve its capacity and effectiveness in responding to social disorder and political unrest.[77] As the PLA has been traditionally viewed as the people's army, deploying the PLA in mass incidents would call into question the CCP's legitimacy. Since its founding in April 1983, the PAP has been used by the regime as the vanguard against a rising crime rate that has become one of the most serious challenges to the central government. Over the past twenty years, China has seen an explosion of social unrest, including growing waves of demonstrations and uprisings caused by urban unemployment, rural instability, and ethnic minority separatist movements, a rapidly growing violent crime rate (e.g., murder, rape, armed robbery), trafficking of illegal drugs and armaments, and the organization of small, private or quasi-legal armies and security forces.

A recent development of the PAP is the establishment of a number of elite special police units (SPUs) to carry out high-risk missions such as counterterrorism, antihijacking, hostage rescuing, and engaging heavily armed criminals. The SPUs are organizationally subordinate to the PAP and receive leadership from the internal guard (*neiwei*) or the security guard (*jingwei*) divisions. Their members were dispatched to guard the Chinese embassies in war-torn regions such as Iraq and Afghanistan. The SPU's membership is competitive; recruits are selected from active PAP service personnel. The training SPU units undergo is rigorous and involves the best weaponry. In January 2001, China's key cities were required to establish an antiriot squad of no less than three hundred members for municipalities or two hundred members for province capitals; the antiriot squads were equipped with armored cars or personnel carriers and sophisticated small arms.[78] The Snow Leopard Strike Force (*xuebao tuji budui*) is another elite unit of PAP special forces. This force attended the joint exercise with Russian special forces for an antiterrorist drill in Moscow from September 4 to September 6, 2007.

The PAP has played an important role in three anticrime campaigns that have taken place since the early 1980s. Collectively named Strike Hard, the nationwide anticrime campaign deals with outbreaks of crime and works to lower increased crime rates. Under Mao, harsher, quicker and more effective measures against crime became a part of the political campaign to construct a new China. Although both legislative and judicial bodies have been emphasized since economic reforms, Deng Xiaoping echoed Mao in the belief that a crackdown against crime would be much more efficient if China employed a Maoist-style political campaign rather than exercised the rule of law. This approach of using campaign against increasing crime rates has been inherited by Hu Jintao, but in a different way. Because crime control campaigns such as severity and swiftness (*yanda*) has not significantly deterred crime rates, Hu has

---

[77] M. Tanner, "The Institutional Lessons of Disaster: Reorganizing China's People's Armed Police after Tiananmen," pp. 587–635.

[78] "China to Enhance Anti-Riot Police Force," *Xinhua* online, January 27, 2001.

appealed to "build a harmonious society" to prevent crimes. The harmonious society, according to Hu, is a society with "democracy, rule of law, fairness, justice, trustfulness, friendship, full of vitality, stability, order, and harmony between human being and nature."[79]

In particular, Hu's emphasis on prevention rather than punishment in how the armed forces deal with mass incidents starkly deviates from his predecessors. To implement Hu's ideas of building a harmonious world, the PAP will play an important role in overseeing the population and deterring mass violence, much more than the PLA. Even if the PLA could be used against mass riots in the future, the PAP has consistently filled the niche as the vanguards of dealing with mass violence, such as during the summer 1989 demonstration in Tiananmen Square in which the PAP was ordered to remove the angry students and clear barricades "at all cost" before the PLA units marched in Beijing.[80] An effective prevention of mass violence requires deployment of a large police force, including the PAP. China continues to pour more resources into the PAP; the government announced in November 2006 that it deployed more police than ever before in rural regions and built more than thirty thousand police stations in rural regions.[81]

To build such a harmonious society, according to Hu, it is necessary to "balance the interests of different social groups to avoid conflicts and to make sure people live a safe and happy life in a politically stable country." In other words, Hu not only questions the effectiveness of the Strike Hard Campaign based on severity and swiftness but also imposes his own guidelines to change people's minds and resolve the growing social conflicts. Clearly, Hu is attempting to use a "soft" approach that is comparable with his "theory of the three harmonies," which replaces the traditional capital punishment methods employed by the CCP to deter crime. Hu's idea was later explained by Luo Gan in the Party journal *Seeking Truth* (*qiushi*):

When [we] deal with criminal cases, [we] cannot only employ methods of punishment to frighten criminals; rather, [we] must strive to transform them into new people who no longer are adversarial to society. When [we] mediate civil and business disputes, [we] must seek the way to end appeals and lawsuits through administrative, economic, and educational approaches while relying on the legal system for adjudication. When [we] deal with mass incidents, [we] should not be satisfied by temporary pacification. Rather, [we] must pay great attention to working for the masses and relieving their essential concerns. When [we] maintain public order, [we] should not depend only on punishment to make people comply; rather, [we] must try to encourage the masses to

---

[79] Quoted from Luo Gan, "Zhengfa jiguan zai goujian hexie shehui zhong danfu zhongda lishi shiming de zhengzhi zeren" [Political and law organizations undertake political responsibilities of historical importance in constructing a harmonious society], in *Qiushi* [Truth seeking] (March 2007), p. 3.

[80] Wang Fang, *Wang Fang huiyilu* [Memoirs of Wang Fang] (Zhejiang renmin chubanshe, 2005), p. 371.

[81] "China Extends Police Presence in Countryside," *Xinhua*, November 7, 2006.

wholeheartedly abide by public order of their own accord and reduce their need for antagonism.[82]

Without a doubt, the regime's move toward the pursuit of a harmonious society has signaled a shift in China's focus from singularly promoting economic growth to solving worsening social tension.

The harmonious society motto proposed by Hu Jintao is code for conforming to the requirements of the party-state, as Hu believes that the CCP needs to establish "a fine-tuned management system" and has "the capacity of dealing with serious problems."[83] On October 11, 2006, when the Sixth Plenary Session of the Sixteenth Party Central Committee was held in Beijing, Hu's idea to build a harmonious society was formally accepted by party leadership. A party document entitled "Resolution of the CCP Central Committee on Major Issues Regarding the Building of a Harmonious Socialist Society" was issued. This document admitted "the number and scope of mass incidents have become the most egregious problem that seriously threatens social stability," and that the act of preventing and properly handling mass incidents is a major challenge to the government.[84]

The PAP and Post-Deng Leadership Politics

As civilian control of the military is weakly institutionalized in China, the personal allegiances of top generals to the quasi-official position of paramount leaders are still crucial.[85] Unlike Mao and Deng who enjoyed their achievement in the revolutionary struggle, long-standing ties to the military leaders, and strong personal charisma, Jiang and Hu have no military record, no military experience, no particular familiarity with military affairs, and no connections in the armed forces. Thus, both Jiang and Hu could not rely on the unconditional support of the PLA as a matter of course in all circumstances.[86] Besides their effort to promote many army officers and grant generous benefits, they strove to cultivate good relations with the army generals. For Jiang, gaining the support of the armed forces was much trickier, because when he was put in power after the Tiananmen Square incident in 1989, he had no military experience or backing, which made it impossible for the veteran PLA generals to accept him as the PLA's commander in chief.

[82] Luo Gan, "Zhengfa jiguan zai goujian hexie shehui zhong danfu zhongda lishi shiming de zhengzhi zeren," p. 4.
[83] *Renmin ribao* [People's daily], February 20, 2005.
[84] "China Strives to Prevent, Handle Mass Incidents," *Xinhua*, December 9, 2006.
[85] Andrew Scobell, "China's Evolving Civil-Military Relations: Creeping *Guojiahua*," in Nan Li (ed.), *Chinese Civil Military Relations: The Transformation of the People's Liberation Army*, p. 34.
[86] Ellis Joffe, "The Chinese Army in Domestic Politics: factors and Phases," in Nan Li (ed.), *Chinese Civil Military Relations: The Transformation of the People's Liberation Army*, p. 15.

When Jiang became chairman of the Central Military Commission in November 1989, he made sure that his support of the PAP was obvious and grandiose. Only three years after he was appointed as the CCP general secretary, the annual budgets for the PAP increased from $1.1 billion in 1989 to $1.6 in 1992, a rate of 45 percent.[87] In addition to developing ties with influential army generals, Jiang devoted time to building relationships with lower-level army officials. In two years of his appointment as CMC chairman, he visited almost every military region, spent considerable time with a number of PAP units, and even attended important PAP meetings. Despite the budget increases, visits, promotions, and lavish benefits packages he showered on generals and officials of all levels, Jiang did not feel confident in his ties to the PLA. Jiang carefully built his power base within the leadership and successfully maintained legitimacy in 1992, three years after his initial appointment, when Deng traveled to the southern provinces to push for risky policies advocating the continuation and expansion of reforms. Without Deng's support or permission, it would have been impossible for Jiang to execute many initiatives in the 1990s that served to strengthen his legitimacy: he removed the Yang brothers in 1992, continued to restructure the PLA in April 1992, appointed his former bodyguard Ba Zhongtan as PAP commander in December 1992, appointed his follower Zeng Qinghong to lead the Central General Office in 1993, imprisoned his formidable rival and Beijing Party chief Chen Xitong in 1995, and elevated many of his supporters from positions in the Shanghai municipal government to high central government positions in the early 1990s.

One of Jiang's important moves in controlling the PAP was the transfers of the PAP commander Zhou Yushu and appointed Ba Zhongtan, one of Jiang's followers, to take charge of the PAP. The PAP had been traditionally controlled by the Beijing Military Region and most of its leadership members had been historically tied to the Beijing Military Region. While Yang Baibing was the political commissar of the Beijing Military Region (Beijing MR), PAP Commander Zhou Yushu was the Commander of the 24th Group Army under the Beijing MR and Political Commissar Xu Shouzeng served as deputy director of the Beijing MR Political Department. The 24th Group Army led by Zhou Yushu was one of the key army units the Yang brothers relied on for the suppression of the student demonstrations in June 1989. After suppressing the 1989 demonstrations, the CMC reorganized the PAP and on January 12, 1990, Yang Baibing, the CMC general secretary, played an important role in Zhou's appointment as the PAP commander and Xu as the PAP political commissar.[88] The PLA's purges and reorganization after the 1989 student demonstration undoubtedly provided the Yang brothers with a great opportunity to control

---

[87] Shuanwen Yang, "Wujing budui 'zhifa quan' chutan" [A preliminary exploration on the "law enforcement power" of the armed police], in *Wujing gongcheng xueyuan xuebao* [Journal of Engineering College of Armed Police Force], vol. 20, no. 1 (2004), pp. 39–40.

[88] See Tian Bingxin, "Zhou Yushu: Zaozao baoxiao dasheng ti," December 12, 2005.

China's armed forces and police. However, the dominance of the Yang brothers in the CMC leadership disgruntled the PLA generals who were not politically tied to the Yang brothers. This discontent sowed the seeds of a joint effort by many influential PLA generals and senior high-ranking leaders against the Yang brothers in 1992.

The Yang brothers' fall out of favor provided Jiang the opportunity to reorganize the leadership of the PAP. After the Yang brothers were dismissed, both PAP Commander Zhou Yushu and Political Commissar Xu Shouzeng were removed in late 1992 because of their personal ties with Yang Baibing. Thus, removing Zhou and Xu helped Jiang solidify his power over the PAP. Moreover, the retired Ba Zhongtan's appointment to take charge of the PAP brought Jiang more security in his position and built on Deng's efforts to solidify Jiang's authority in the military and armed forces leadership.[89] Ba commanded the PLA's Shanghai garrison in the mid-1980s when Jiang was the city's mayor, party secretary, and the first political commissar of the garrison. With Ba's willingness to throw the weight of the PAP behind Jiang, Jiang reciprocally strengthened the PAP, and even attempted to turn it into a personal armed force. This political move ensured his personal security while creating somewhat of a counterweight to the PLA, although it may be more accurate to identify the PAP's function vis-à-vis Jiang's legitimacy as a deterrent to disobedient generals to consolidate their own military power.

Although the PAP is unable to compete against the PLA because of its lack of firepower and training, a powerful PAP was considered helpful by the leadership for Jiang to keep the PLA in check, especially when divisions within PLA leadership led to rival factions that were willing to resort to violence. Historically, pitting military factions against one another has proved helpful to the incumbent party leadership, so much so that manipulating competing PLA military factions is viewed as a classical leadership strategy in the CCP. For example, during the Cultural Revolution when Lin Biao's faction dominated PLA leadership, Mao promoted many generals from the former Fourth Front Army to provide counterbalance to Lin's influence in the army. Mao also used the 20th Army Corps in Zhejiang to watch the Nanjing Military Region led by powerful General Xu Shiyou and used the air force units in Wuhan to contain the Wuhan Military Region, led by General Chen Zaidao. The realist perspective that drives these political stratagems are understood to be advantageous by many in the party leadership, such that Jiang's moves to strengthen and gain allegiance from the PAP would be applauded by his supporters in the PLA.

However, Jiang was severely embarrassed by public criticism of the PAP leadership led by his former bodyguard Ba Zhongtan because of the PAP's

---

[89] When Ba was appointed PAP commander in 1992, he had technically not been serving for twelve years, having retired as the former commander of the Shanghai Garrison Command in June 1990.

weak role in responding to the deteriorating social order and increasing crime. In particular, the public expressed anger over a case where a PAP bodyguard murdered a leading member of the National People's Congress, Li Peiyao, in February 1996. At the time, the regime had been under pressure to improve law enforcement, especially several unsolved cases related to weapons robbery and the murder of armed police personnel. For example, the 1996 Bai Baoshan case in Beijing involved fifteen deaths, including civilians and armed forces personnel from both the PLA and the PAP. It was listed by the MPS as the most serious case in 1996 and one of the most violent crimes in 1997.[90] Under pressure from the party and the public, Jiang had to discipline the PAP and dismiss several leaders, including PAP Commander Ba Zhongtan, Political Commissar Zhang Shutian, Beijing PAP Commander Meng Zhende, and Beijing PAP Political Commissar Zhang Shiyuan. In February 1996, Ba Zhongtan was replaced by Yang Guoping, vice president of the PLA National Defense University, who had close ties with Zhang Wannian. Yang had served as chief of staff of the Jinan Military Region, and Zhang was commander of the Jinan Military Region from 1990 to 1992. As Jiang was attempting to cultivate Zhang as his key follower in PLA leadership, and Zhang had been appointed as the CMC vice chairman in December 1995, Yang's appointment as the PAP chief was an ideal choice for Jiang to continue his dominance over the PAP. The later developments in the Jiang-Zhang relationship proved that Jiang successfully cultivated Zhang as one of Jiang's leading followers. In a leadership conference of the Sixteenth Party Congress, on December 13, 2002, Zhang led a group of PLA generals to submit to the Standing Committee of the Congress Presidium meeting a motion proposing the extension of Jiang's term as chairman of the CMC.[91]

The PAP's support has been crucial to CCP top leaders in many ways. It has ensured proper control over high-ranking leaders, deterred disobedient army generals, and safeguarded social order and political stability of the party. Both Mao Zedong and Deng Xiaoping were able to use their prestige and their factional dominance to control the PLA as well as the armed police forces, but this cannot be the case for all paramount leaders. Without military background and strong personal ties with PLA and PAP leaders, both Jiang Zemin and Hu Jintao have had to rely on their ability to use resources and incentives to cultivate followers in the ranks of the armed forces, the PAP in particular. For the PAP, this meant increasing personnel, improving military equipment, and raising officer salaries. In addition, Jiang was able to win the support of PAP top leaders by generously awarding promotions. Between December 1993 and August 1995, more than forty senior commanders and political commissars were promoted to the rank of major-general or higher. In addition, Jiang pushed for increases in military spending beginning in the early 1990s. Although there

---

[90] *Fazhi zaobao* [Legal system morning news], May 29, 2006.
[91] *Zhengming* [Liberal monthly], December 2002.

were instrumental reasons for increasing military spending, such as the acceleration of China's real gross domestic product growth, Deng's passing, and concerns over the Taiwan issue, it served to strengthen Jiang's relationship with the PLA and reward it for its loyalty.[92] Thus, strengthening the PAP was an important initiative taken by Deng and Jiang to help solidify Jiang's power. Under Jiang Zemin's leadership, the PAP received sizable increases in funding from central and local authorities, and its workload expanded greatly so that it would be able to deal with the growing public disorder. At the Fifteenth Party Congress in September 1997, both the PAP commander and the political commissar became members of the Central Committee.

Furthermore, the command system of the People's Armed Police was transferred from the Ministry of Public Security to a dual command system of the State Council and MPS and the CMC, a system under which the PAP receives better training and financial support. Being integrated into the military system strengthened its military function; in recent years, the PAP has been equipped with advanced weaponry, such as wheeled armored vehicles, command vehicles, patrol cars, and more. In addition, air-patrol units such as the flyboat and helicopter units have been activated with mobile and long-range disposition capabilities in the field. Its contingencies have capabilities far better than those of public security police. Jiang's strategy to strengthen the PAP and cultivate its loyalty has had a marked positive impact on his authority in CCP leadership, because of his lack of prestige and credibility with PLA leaders when he first came to office. In addition, because the PAP is responsible for guarding high-ranking leaders, Jiang was able to monitor many leaders' activities through his control of the PAP. Furthermore, absorbing PLA units into the PAP after PLA disarmament enabled Jiang to improve China's image in the international community by reducing its armed force and won support from the demobilized PLA personnel, who regarded employment in the PAP positively. Moreover, deploying the PAP to maintain domestic social order prevented the PLA from sullying its image by being involved in suppressing mass incidents.

The current leadership, lead by Hu Jintao, continues in the footsteps of predecessors by cultivating personal loyalties in the military and armed forces. Evidence shows that Hu Jintao, like Jiang, uses promotion, officer salary increases, retirement benefits, and advances in equipment to gain the PAP's support. The financial support that Hu provides the PLA is staggering – for example, in 2008, the PLA was awarded a budget of $57.23 billion, a 17.6 percent increase over 2007.[93] Moreover, although Jiang promoted on average about twenty-four

---

[92] Michael D. Swaine, "Civil-Military Relations and Domestic Power and Policies," paper presented at the conference "Chinese Leadership, Politics, and Policy," November 2, 2005, p. 5.
[93] Many Western scholars believe that the actual expenditure of China's armed forces is up to three times the official budget. See Willy Lam, "China Flaunts Growing Naval Capabilities," in *China Brief*, vol. 9, no. 1, January 12, 2009.

PLA generals a year, Hu Jintao promoted thirty-four generals per year in 2005 and 2006, after he took charge of the CMC in September 2004. Clearly, Hu has realized that his power and even political survival relies greatly on effective authority over the armed forces. Thus, Hu's initiatives mirror Jiang's in that their benefits are usually twofold: they benefit the armed forces, which in turn helps him consolidate power. Compared with ex-president Jiang Zemin, who was unprepared to become commander in chief when he did, Hu had already established a strong base among party and army leaders before he took charge of China's armed forces. Thus, Hu's aggressive steps to consolidate his power immediately after he took over leadership from Jiang Zemin were no surprise.

In the future, the current regime anticipates more challenges to its authority from disaffected peasants, workers, and ethnic-based separatists in Tibet and Xinjiang. Though like his predecessors Hu continues to heavily rely on the PAP to quell social disorder and ensure social stability, he is unique in his policies and campaigns in that he emphasizes the imperative of preventing public discontent and mass incidents before they start. A few initiatives have been put into practice to ensure that this happens. For one, CCP authorities have appealed to grassroots cadres to improve public relations with their constituency by personal defusing and periodically meeting petitioners.[94] Another initiative focuses on "winning the 'people's welfare' by safeguarding national security and ensuring sociopolitical stability under new conditions." To do this, the party-state is establishing local "leading groups," headed by municipal party secretaries, and "social stability offices" to coordinate the efforts of party organizations, financial support, the armed police, and local public security branches to prevent flare-ups of dissent and instability. As China's leaders are obsessed with social stability, the prevention of large-scale unrest has become the central task of the regime, thus allowing the CCP to continue in power.[95] Without a doubt, the PAP will be expected to play an increasingly important role not only in preventing large-scale mass incidents but also in suppressing domestic unrest if it develops into large-scale mass violence.

---

[94] See *Asia Times*, August 6, 2008.
[95] Susan L. Shirk, *China: Fragile Superpower*, pp. 53–4.

7

Garrison Commands

The People's Liberation Army (PLA) has established garrison commands in most major cities, key coastal defense locations, and important strategic military sites. In China, garrison duties are frequently assigned to operational PLA units or other headquarter units stationed in the area, as an additional duty of the local commander. The prime function of garrison duties in the PLA units are to guard military facilities and to maintain order among the troops when they are outside military barracks on pass, leave, or official duties, similar to the role of military police in other armies.[1] The garrison commands are structurally subordinate to local military districts; however, they are simultaneously subject to the leadership of local party committees. They not only guard cities and strategic military locations but also are responsible for militia and reserve forces, conscription, and the mobilization of military services. The garrison commands are police agencies that operate in major cities to maintain national security.

Among all garrison commands established in major cities, the Beijing Garrison Command was undoubtedly the most important one because of its rank (*jun*, army corps). Its importance in guarding Beijing and its historical involvement in leadership politics also lends to its status as the most important garrison unit. The garrison commands are responsible for event security, security of facilities, and supervision of discipline and military order in the garrison. These functions are carried out in cooperation with local PLA units and the People's Armed Police. Since the mid-2000s, garrison commands have been established in almost all major cities, and the CCP has been making preparations for garrisons to have an enhanced security roles. This includes garrison commands' responsibility as the military organ of provincial capital cities and major cities

---

[1] Dennis J. Blasko, *The Chinese Army Today: Tradition and Transformation for the 21st Century*, pp. 36–7.

to command local PLA units and the defense reserve forces. Garrison commands are highly regarded by Hu Jintao's leadership as an important armed force aimed to promote "a harmonious society."[2] This is a result of their role in coordinating between civilians and all PLA units stationed in cities (e.g., ground forces, air force, navy, PAP) and their leading role in administrating and disciplining PLA units stationed in the cities.

This chapter provides an overview of the evolution of China's garrison commands, highlighting the factors that influenced the development of garrison commands as well as their role in Chinese politics. Although a few garrison commands were created to maintain political and social order in the communist-controlled areas during the early communist revolution, a large number of garrison commands were transferred from the communist combat forces to guard the cities after the CCP captured cities from the nationalist government during late 1940s civil war. During the Cultural Revolution, garrison commands expanded greatly when they were expected to contain the chaotic mass movements and to play a leading role in guarding cities. This occurred after the PLA army corps was ordered to hand over garrison duties to garrison commands during the emerging Sino-Soviet border conflict, which required the PLA army corps to prepare for possible the Soviet invasion.

Under Deng Xiaoping's leadership in the 1980s, there was a gradual decline of garrison command influence on Chinese politics. This was achieved through two approaches: (1) most garrison commands were replaced by, merged with, or renamed as PLA military subdistricts, and (2) the People's Armed Forces Departments (PAFDs) or the corresponding PLA military subdistricts were handed over to local party committees and governments.[3] Before the 1980s, the People's Armed Forces Departments at the county level were part of the overall military organization, although they were subordinate to county party committees as well.[4] Since Jiang Zemin was appointed party chief in 1989, garrison commands have experienced unprecedented expansion and have played an important role in coordinating the relationship between civilians and PLA units stationed in cities (e.g., ground forces, air force, navy, PAP) as well as in managing and disciplining those PLA units. There has been an enhanced role of garrison commands in the post-Deng eras. Besides their role in maintaining social order and assisting local civilian authorities in effectively controlling society, garrison commands are the police agencies of major cities that maintain national security through providing guarding duties (e.g., of cities and strategic military locations), commanding militia and reserve forces (including

---

[2] *Renmin ribao* (People's daily), February 20, 2005.

[3] PAFDs were the grassroots organizations of China's armed forces at the levels of county, township, district, or city. They were mainly responsible for commanding and training militia and for conducting conscription work for the PLA.

[4] Zhiyue Bo, "The PLA and the Provinces: Military District and Local Issues," in David Michael Finkelstein and Kristen Gunness (eds.), *Civil-Military Relations in Today's China: Swimming in A New Sea*, p. 121.

conscription and mobilization of military services), and playing a leading role in disciplining PLA units stationed in cities and mediating disputes or conflicts between military units/servicemen and civilian organizations/individuals.

Compared with the People's Armed Police units, garrison commands play more of a leading role in coordinating the relationship between civilians and PLA units stationed in cities. The increase in the size, scale, and power of garrison commands has had a profound impact on civilian control over the military, given the authority that garrison commands have over PLA units. It should be noted, however, that civilian control of military districts, military subdistricts, garrison commands, and the PAFDs will remain limited as long as the authority to make personnel appointments and salary decisions remains in the hands of the PLA. Limited civilian control also reflects a lack of local party or government leader influence on local garrison command officers as a result of less developed personal ties and patron-client relationships more than it does the power of institutional authorities.

This chapter traces the changing nature of garrison commands in the reform era nurtured by the increasing institutionalization of China's political system, including the increasingly important role of garrison commands in maintaining social and political order, their new role as the leading organ for commanding the army reserve, their growing role in helping local authorities in controlling the armed forces stationed locally, mediating conflict between civilian and military organizations, and their increasing influence in the central leadership due to their increasing size in the urban areas due to the expansion of cities caused by China's urbanization. Since Jiang Zemin became chairman of the CMC in November 1989, garrison commands have been emphasized as leading organs in maintaining social order and in commanding local militia and reserve forces. The rising importance and influence of garrison commands reflect a greater need for armed forces to maintain social order and control massive unrest and for facilitating and strengthening national defense in important cities.[5]

Historical Evolution of Garrison Commands

The earliest appearance of the CCP garrison command can be traced to the early 1930s, when the Red Army established garrison commands in Jianning, Nichuan, and Taining to guard Jiangxi base areas. In northern Shaanxi base areas, the Suide Garrison Command was created in 1938 to guard the Shaanxi-Gansu-Ningxia border base areas. In 1942, five garrison commands under the Shanxi-Suiyuan Joint Defense Headquarters, headed by General He Long, were set up to ensure the security of the base areas. In Yan'an, the capital city of the CCP, party leadership established the Yan'an Garrison Command, which was divided into three geographical regions – east, south, and north.

[5] *Xinhuanet*, December 29, 2003.

Wang Zhen, commander of the 359th Brigade, was appointed its commander.[6] During the 1940s civil war, the PLA renamed its combat units as garrison headquarters (*jingbei siling bu*) and assigned them to guard the midsize and larger cities it had taken over from Nationalist command, as in the cases of Shijiazhuang, Baoding, Xuzhou, and Tianjin. While the garrison headquarters guarded the newly established governments and maintained social order, most of their assignments involved coordinating with local public security organs and following orders to arrest, detain, imprison, and execute the regime's enemies.[7] It should be noted, however, that garrison headquarters usually led several garrison commands, as in the case of Wuhan, where Wuhan Garrison Headquarters was in charge of five garrison commands.[8]

After the PRC was established, the CCP established garrison commands in some important cities and strategic positions for China's defense such as borders, ports, and nuclear test sites. The garrison commands not only guarded the cities but also served as the primary representatives of the PLA units in the cities. Local party committees and governments relied on garrison commands to communicate and interact with PLA local units. The garrison commands were also responsible for maintaining social order, protecting the region's security, guarding key public facilities, responding to emergencies (including riots, insurgencies, and other mass incidents), and conducting disaster-relief and rescue operations. Because they were receiving orders from both military regions and local party committees, the garrison commanders were usually also appointed as leaders of local party committees.[9] In some places, army generals of the PLA army corps were concurrently in charge of garrison commands; therefore, the PLA local army corps assumed many of the same duties as those of the garrison commands.[10]

Ji You has indicated that garrison forces traditionally comprise two major parts: independent divisions (*duli shi*) under the command of the PLA provincial military district and garrison divisions (*shoubei shi*) that assume the tasks of border security, protection of major military bases such as naval ports,

[6] Wu Lie, *Zhengrong suiyue* [The eventful times], pp. 208–9.

[7] Tao Dazhao, *Jiang zhi meng: Cong tiedao youjidui zou chulai de Zheng Ti jiangjun* [Dream from a general: General Zheng Ti who came from the Railway Guerrilla Force] (Beijing: Jiefangjun chubanshe, 2005), p. 249.

[8] Wuhan shi difangzhi bianzuan weiyuanhui [Compiling Commission of Wuhan Local Annals], *Wuhan shizhi: Junshi zhi* [Annals of Wuhan: Military annals] (Wuhan: Wuhan University Press, 1989), p. 18.

[9] For example, both the commander and the political commissar of the Beijing Garrison Command are members of the Beijing Party Committee's Standing Committee, and a Beijing party secretary is its first political commissar. Fang Zhu, "Political Work in the Military from the Viewpoint of the Beijing Garrison Command," in Carol Lee Hamrin and Suisheng Zhao (eds.), *Decision-Making in Deng's China: Perspectives from Insiders*, p. 122.

[10] For example, Fu Chongbi and Huang Zuozheng, commander and political commissar, respectively, of the PLA's Sixty-Third Army Corps, stationed in Shijiazhuang, were concurrently commander and political commissar of the city garrison command. *Fu Chongbi huiyilu*, p. 168.

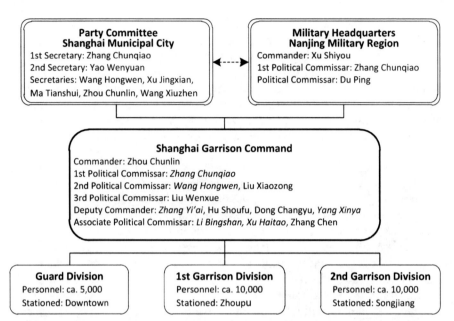

FIGURE 7.1 *Affiliation of Shanghai Garrison Command, 1970–1974. Source: Lingdao jigou yange*, pp. 1083, 1109; *Zhou Chunlin huiyilu* [Memoirs of Zhou Chunlin], pp. 530–4, 546–50; Leng Meng, *Baizhan jiangxing: zai Liu Bocheng, Deng Xiaoping, Xu Xiangqian huixia* [Star of generals who experienced hundred battles: Under the leadership of Liu Bocheng, Deng Xiaoping, and Xu Xiangqian], p. 313.
Note: Leaders who were politically tied with the radical Maoists and who dominated the Shanghai Municipal Party Committee are in italics.

and defense of other strategically important areas.[11] Oftentimes, garrison commands absorbed military units from abolished armed police or PLA Public Security Forces.[12] During the Cultural Revolution, however, the armed police in Shanghai were absorbed into the Shanghai Garrison Command under the dual leadership of the Nanjing Military Region and the Shanghai Municipal Party Committee, controlled by Maoist radicals (Figure 7.1). This dual leadership of the local military regions and local party organizations was certainly the major source of the deep involvement of the garrison commands and the abolished armed police in mass conflicts and violence, particularly when they were controlled mainly by the heavy-handed Maoist radicals rather than the

---

[11] Ji You, *The Armed Forces of China*, p. 50.
[12] For example, the abolished armed police in Hubei during 1966 reorganized as a PLA independent division, including three regiments, two detachments at the prefectural level, and six brigades at the prefectural or city level. This division was subordinate to the Hubei Military District and assigned to the garrisons of Hubei. See Hubei sheng di fang zhi bian zuan wei yuan hui, *Hubei sheng zhi: Junshi* [Annals of Hubei Province: Military] (Wuhan: Hubei renmin chubanshe, 1996).

disadvantaged army generals who were suffering the persecution of the mass rebels.

Thus, there was a trend of increasing power and responsibilities for garrison commands after PLA Public Security Forces were abolished during the Cultural Revolution. Although the abolished armed police in Shanghai were reorganized into the Guard Division of the Shanghai Garrison Command, the reorganized Guard Division was still assigned to guard downtown Shanghai, as its predecessors had done in the past. It proved the most crucial armed force for the security of the newly established municipal party committee, which was dominated by radicals who had played the role of vanguard in the Cultural Revolution. Unlike other two divisions of the Shanghai Garrison Command, which were assigned to Shanghai but stationed far from the city, the Guard Division was primarily in charge of maintaining social order within the city. There was very little change in the division's duties and functions from before the abolition of the armed police and their absorption into the Guard Division. The Guard Division, with more than five thousand personnel, was still headed by Li Renzhai, former commander of the Shanghai General Corps of Chinese People's Public Security Forces. Because the garrison command units were assigned to not only protect the local leaders but also to support the Red Guards and the radical mass organizations, they were often confused by conflicting goals when the Red Guards and the radical mass organizations assaulted and persecuted some local leaders. Thus, the nature of their duties often pushed them into the controversy of local politics and they were often compelled to be deeply involved in local conflicts with the Red Guards, the radical mass organizations, or even other PLA units. This involvement also contributed to the paralyzed and conflicting dual leadership of local party committees and the PLA.[13]

In the Shanghai Garrison Command during the Cultural Revolution, there were clear factions among its three garrison divisions. One division – Garrison Division – allied with the local party committee, and the other two divisions allied with the Nanjing Military Region. Similarly, the division leadership also split into the different factions. Zhang Yi'ai and Yang Xinya (deputy commanders), Li Binshan (associate political commissar), and Li Renzhai (commander of the Garrison Division), allied with the Shanghai party leaders, headed by Zhang Chunqiao. This put them in opposition to the other division leaders, headed by Zhou Chunlin, commander of the Shanghai Garrison Command.[14] Another instance of the development of such factions was the well-known

---

[13] For example, in Shanghai, Zhang Chunqiao was first party secretary and first political commissar of the Shanghai Garrison Command. He deeply influenced local civilian leaders in cases involving the Shanghai Garrison Command. Garrison commands not only were directly involved in mass factional strife but also dealt with tension in their own units. Almost all garrison commands, to different degrees, were involved in local politics, given their close ties to or working relationships with either the PLA or local leaders. The Shanghai Garrison Command is a quintessential example of garrison involvement and factions in local politics.

[14] See *Zhou Chunlin huiyilu* [Memoirs of Zhou Chunlin], p. 547.

Wuhan Incident in July 1967. With support from the Wuhan Military Region, headed by Commander Chen Zaidao, the Independent Division of the Hubei Military District (its predecessor was the Hubei General Corps of Chinese People's Public Security Forces and it became a garrison troop after the Chinese People's Public Security Forces were abolished in June 1966), kidnapped and interned Wang Li, an important figure in the Cultural Revolution Group (CRG) headed by Mao's wife Jiang Qing. This incident was later denounced as a military rebellion against Mao, and the key figures of the Wuhan Military Region and the Independent Division of the Hubei Military District were dismissed and arrested, including Chen Zaidao (commander of the Wuhan Military Region), Zhong Hanhua (political commissar of the Wuhan Military Region), Niu Huailong (commander of the Independent Division), and Cai Bingchen (political commissar of the Independent Division). A similar occurrence in Qinghai – known as the February 23 Incident, in 1967 – illustrates the same pattern as in Wuhan. In this instance, the Independent Division supported by Zhao Yongfu, deputy commander of the Qinghai Military District, retaliated against the radical mass rebels. The incident resulted in a massacre of civilian protesters who had occupied a newspaper office in the provincial capital of Qinghai Province.[15] Thus, both the garrison commands and the abolished armed police had been deeply involved in local politics during the Cultural Revolution.

When the mass movement and the rebellion of the Red Guard became out of control during the Cultural Revolution, and with many garrison commands deeply entrenched in local politics, the duties of the garrison commands in many cities were taken over by the PLA. Putting the PLA in command was an attempt by Mao to control the chaos.[16] This was part of what seemed a consistent effort by the CCP leadership to separate the garrison commands from the mass movements, thereby containing the zeal of the garrison commands. From 1974 to 1975, Deng Xiaoping was put in control of the PLA; he subsequently launched his campaign to rectify the PLA. Deng took a much more radical approach to cut the PLA's ties with local leaders in cases where the garrison commands or military subdistricts were deeply seated in local politics. The exchange of the military posts for two garrison troops was an example of Deng's new radical approach in Zhejiang in 1975: two military subdistricts and their subordinate People's Armed Forces Departments (PAFDs) were required to exchange troops with their counterparts in Anhui because of their active roles in local politics.[17]

[15] Wang Zhongfang, *Lian yu* [Purgatory], pp. 24–5.
[16] In Hengyang of Hunan, for example, the military subdistrict was ordered to assume the responsibilities of the garrison command from the end of 1966 until the end of 1969. See *Zhongguo renmin jiefangjun hengyang jingbeiqu* [The PLA Hengyang Garrison Command], *Hengyang Yellow*, http://www.hyo734.com/zf/f21-31.htm (accessed August 9, 2010).
[17] *Liao Hansheng huiyilu*, p. 360.

A large number of garrison commands were created after November 1969, when Mao urged China to prepare for war as a result of the emerging Sino-Soviet border conflict. As Mao contemplated mobilizing the PLA army corps to prepare the CCP for a quick response to the possible Soviet attack, the PLA army corps were ordered to hand over their garrison duties to local armed forces, including the garrison commands and the military subdistricts. The Central Military Commission (CMC) required that garrison commands be established in the most important cities so as to assume a leading role in China's domestic security. For those cities with no garrison command, the CMC ordered the transformation of the military subdistricts or the People's Armed Forces Department into garrison commands, or required at the very least that the provincial military regions jointly take on the duties of the garrison commands.[18]

Garrison Commands in the Reform Era

Under Deng Xiaoping's leadership in the 1980s, there was a gradual dissipation in the garrison commands' influence in the Chinese political arena. The garrison commands were ordered to hand over their duties regarding internal security to local bureaus of public security, as in Beijing, where the Beijing Garrison Command turned over the maintenance of the capital's internal security to the Bureau of Public Security, which operated under the civilian Ministry of Public Security.[19] Throughout the 1980s, PLA military subdistricts functioned similarly to the garrison commands, as in Jinan, in Shangdong, where PLA military subdistricts were ordered to take over responsibilities of the garrison commands.[20] Since the early 1990s, after Jiang Zemin became the CCP's chairman, there has been a tendency to emphasize the importance of garrison commands, especially in major cities. This is the case with the Hengyang Military Subdistrict, which was renamed the Hengyang Garrison Command in November 1992 – this command essentially took charge of twelve People's Armed Forces Departments (*renmin wuzhuang bu*, PAFDs) in twelve counties.[21] Historically, the PAFDs had been party organs at the village, township, and county levels used to mobilize local civilians and local militia to support PLA operations, and they were the backbone of logistic and personnel

---

[18] On the CMC directive issued on November 15, 1969, "Guanyu chengshi gaishe jingbeiqu wenti de jueding" [Decision on the Issue regarding the Reestablishment of Garrison Commands in Cities], see Yu Ruxin, "1969: Duisu zhanbei zhongde junwei banshizu, Lin Biao yu Mao Zedong" [1969: The CMC Administrative Group, Lin Biao, and Mao Zedong during the war preparation against the Soviet Union], in Ding Kaiwen (ed.), *Bainian Lin Biao* [The centennial of Lin Biao], p. 337.

[19] Ellis Joffe, *The Chinese Army after Mao*, p. 153.

[20] *Jinan ribao*, September 30, 2004.

[21] *Zhongguo renmin jienfangjun hengyang jingbeiqu*, http://www.hyo734.com/zf/f21-31.htm (accessed August 9, 2010).

support to operations in the locales where the PLA was operating.[22] Although the PAFD is an element in the military chain of command, it has representatives in the local party committee as well as local civilian authorities, and it is responsible for commanding militia units, civil defense agencies, defense education offices, and joint military and civilian command centers.[23] The garrison commands' role in controlling and leading the PAFDs implied the increasing importance of the garrison commands in ensuring the PLA's support to local civilian party leadership.

There has been a tendency in the post-Deng era for garrison commands to develop close ties with local party leaders. As local garrison commands are under the dual leadership of the local military regions and local party committees, it is not surprising that these relationships exist. It is reasonable to speculate that there is a tendency for garrison commands or military subdistricts to develop close relationships with local leaders, given close contact or even local leaders' deliberate cultivation of personal relationships. This helps explain why the leaders of garrison commands and military subdistricts were often dismissed, transferred, or ordered to retire when local leaders were dismissed.[24]

The responsibilities of garrison commands in the post-Mao era have included the following:

- *Protect cities*: Send garrison troops to protect the cities; handle violations involving personnel of the armed units stationed in the same areas; enforce disciplinary measures and give due punishment to those involved; resolve civilian-military disputes; protect local mass gatherings, conferences, and meetings; help local public security maintain social orders.
- *Conscription and special care*: Take responsibility for meeting the recruitment quota of new soldiers and ensure sufficient performance; provide special care to family members of both active and deceased military service members.
- *Militia reserve service*: Recruit and register personnel from the militia for reserve service. The militia reserve service cooperates with PLA units and

[22] James C. Mulvenon and Andrew N. D. Yang (eds.), *The People's Liberation Army as Organization: Reference Volume v1.0*, p. 189.
[23] James D. Seymour and Richard Anderson, *New Ghosts, Old Ghosts: Prisons and Labor Reform Camps in China*, p. 52; Jonathan D. Pollack, "Short-Range Ballistic Missile Capabilities," in Steve Yui-Sang Tsang (ed.), *If China Attacks Taiwan: Military Strategy, Politics and Economics*, p. 139.
[24] For example, Chen Liangyu concurrently held the position of Shanghai party secretary and first party secretary of the Shanghai Garrison Command. When the central leadership decided to arrest Chen Liangyu, Dai Changyou, political commissar of the Shanghai Garrison Command, was also replaced. This move made by the CCP leadership might be the effort to gain control over the Shanghai Garrison Command and prevent a possible revolt from the Shanghai Garrison Command due to the close ties between its leaders and Shanghai party chief Chen Liangyu. See *Wenhui bao* [Wenhui daily], December 6, 2006.

local public security organizations to maintain social order; train the militia in peacetime and call the militia to active service in wartime.

- *Administrative oversight and command*: Organize the militia, especially by assembling important militia units, including units to defend against enemy aircraft and terrorism and units responsible for handling mass incidents; train the militia by dispatching personnel to militia units or by systematically sending militia members to the training campus; organize the militia to participate in local political and economic activities.
- *Community services*: Establish good relationships with civilians by participating in and contributing to local issues (e.g., city sanitation), protecting the environment, supporting education and charities, donating food, clothes, and computers to the poor, helping the elderly and children, and providing unpaid community service to local public organizations and businesses; importantly, provide disaster-relief and community services; oversee university student military training.

Excluding the responsibility of garrison commands to guard cities, there are few differences between garrison commands and military subdistricts. Military subdistricts are organizationally subordinate to provincial military districts, and they are the working bodies of local party committees' military departments. One difference is that military subdistricts were established in accordance with civilian administrative areas (a military subdistrict was created in every prefecture-level city), but garrison commands were set up only in certain cities, those deemed important strategic locations. Both garrison commands and military subdistricts are under the dual leadership of the PLA military districts (or PLA military regions, as in the case of municipalities directly under control of the central government, such as Beijing, Shanghai, Tianjin, and Chongqing) and local party committees, and both are responsible for leading People's Armed Forces Departments.

Since 1999, the People's Armed Forces Departments have expanded to include the levels of township (*xiang or zheng*) and streets (*jie dao*), and these are referred to as Grassroots People's Armed Forces Departments (*jiceng renmin wuzhuang bu*). The township level of the People's Armed Forces Departments serves to "strengthen the building of militia and reserve forces" in an effort to "complete the system of defense mobilization."[25] In addition, some garrison commands and PLA military subdistricts, including the garrison commands in Yantai, Zhoushan, Shantou, and Sanya, control a certain number of PLA units, especially those that encompass strategically important cities. In some cities, however, garrison commands and military subdistricts have the same functions, as in Chongqing. The Chongqing military subdistrict was

---

[25] Document issued by the CCP General Office, General Office of State Council, and PLA General Office, (1999) No. 24.

renamed the Garrison Command in November 1969 and changed back to Military Subdistrict in June 1983. It was renamed Garrison Command again in March 1984 and has remained the Garrison Command since.

Since Hu Jintao took charge of the CMC in 2004, he has masterminded a series of changes in the military, focusing on the transformation of the military's organization. Reforming the current system, in Hu's own words, involves "concentrating on establishing and perfecting the joint-combat commanding system, the joint training system, and the integrated joint logistics system."[26] To achieve these goals, the PLA adopted a few measures to promote more effective and efficient army units and personnel, and to improve its armed forces, with more advanced weaponry and technology. In 2004 the PLA demobilized its two hundred thousand personnel, mainly from the ground forces and noncombat units. It abolished the system of local-level commands in the air force and navy, albeit temporarily preserving the obsolete and rigid military-region command structure. Also, the PLA has approved funds to improve the informatics and digitization of military operations as well as to develop and purchase hardware. Another area of reform is that the PLA has employed civilians to replace noncommissioned officers and compulsory service members in noncombat duties, as cooks, typists, telephone operators, movie projectionists, announcers, drivers, repair people, and paramedics.[27] Noncommissioned officers (*shi guan*) are those with a rank below that of warrant officer; they are invaluable to the PLA, as they constitute half of all PLA soldiers. They consist of volunteer active service members who were hired by the PLA as core technical personnel after their compulsory service, and people recruited from either military or civilian universities. They have become the backbone for ensuring that the PLA becomes more technically advanced and complex in order to achieve its goal of modernizing the military.[28] The recruitment of noncommissioned officers from nonmilitary organizations began in 2003 and has gradually become more common in the PLA.[29] The PLA demobilized 170,000 officers in 2006, and 70,000 officer posts were filled by noncommissioned officers. So far seventy different job titles that PLA officers previously held have been taken over by noncommissioned officers.[30]

In recent years, PLA scholars from the Academy of Military Sciences and the National Defense University who have been trained or educated in industrialized Western countries have increasingly criticized the traditional military region, which is based on the Soviet model imported during the 1950s: the Central Military Commission, general departments, military regions and districts, and configuration of services (ground forces, navy, air force, PAP, and second

[26] *Xinhua*, March 12, 2007.
[27] *Renmin ribao*, February 17, 2006.
[28] *Xinhuanet*, June 29, 2007.
[29] *Urumqi wanbao* [Urumqi evening news], January 24, 2007.
[30] *Xinhuanet*, June 29, 2007; *Jiefangjun bao*, July 10, 2007.

artillery).[31] The criticism has raised a debate over whether the existing military region headquarters should be abolished, or reduced to so-called theaters or "war zones" that centralize command and control of forces spread over a large-scale regional battle theater, for the PLA to improve its command system.[32] In the existing system, the functions of the military regions overlap not only with those of the General Staff Department but also with those of provincial military and group armies. Organizational reform has become an integral part of military modernization, and the PLA recognizes that it needs to restructure so as to improve its efficiency. Moreover, restructuring military organizations will spur the development of regional military capacity and promote the efficiency at the military subdistrict and garrison levels, which include militia, reserve, paramilitary, and other law enforcement forces. Active-duty PLA forces will gradually shrink in size as the PLA comes to emphasize technological quality and advanced weaponry. This could mean a significant increase in regional force personnel, because the personnel affected by reductions in active-duty forces are expected to find their way into the PAP, garrison commands, and PLA reserves.

In April 2007, the PLA officially introduced a theater-level joint logistics system in the Jinan Military Region, a step toward establishing a fully integrated joint logistics system to support its joint operations capabilities. The separate services of the PLA have maintained separate logistical infrastructures since the 1950s. As part of the effort to support the joint-combat commanding system and the integrated joint logistics system, PLA garrison commands would certainly play an important role in ensuring the security of local regions and enhancing the capacities of the integrated joint logistics system, especially if the PLA considers abolishing its archaic military-region command structure in the future.

Since 2004 the CMC has strove to establish garrison commands for all provincial capital cities and other important cities. This is evidence that the PLA is advancing toward enhancing the role of its garrison commands even further. Garrison commands have been established in many major cities such as Nanjing, Taiyuan, Kunming, Chengdu, Jinan, and Urumqi, or the existing military subdistricts have been ordered to change their names from military subdistricts to garrison commands. According to official media, garrison commands will gradually be established in all capital cities as part of comprehensive military reform. The crux of this reform is to expand the role of military organs in provincial capital cities such that in the future the organs will command PLA units and defense reserve forces.[33] Most important, enhancing the role of local garrison commands aims to strengthen party

[31] David L. Shambaugh, *Modernizing China's Military Progress, Problems, and Prospects* (Berkeley and Los Angeles, CA: University of California Press, 2002), p. 109.

[32] Ibid., p. 65

[33] *Nanjing ribao* [Nanjing daily], January 8, 2004.

control over the local armed forces. According to state-run media, with more control over the garrison commands, the CCP can achieve "the adherence of the party's leading role in the direction of ideology, the construction of thought, the organizations and commands, and the decision making on important issues."[34]

Compared with the People's Armed Police (PAP) units, garrison commands play more of a leadership role in coordinating the relationship between civilians and the PLA units. The CMC named the garrison commands the leading organs of the PLA local units and all other local military units. No matter what their ranks are, all units "must receive the leadership of the garrison commands in the aspects of garrison."[35] Thus, garrison commands are the PLA's prime coordinators in representing local PLA units to the populace at large. This includes negotiating with civilians, protecting the PLA units' interests, and facilitating good civil-military relations. At the same time, garrison commands are the local authority of the CMC in administrating and disciplining PLA units stationed in the cities. In addition to its responsibilities mentioned above, its role in disciplining PLA units and functioning as the law enforcement of the CMC has been enhanced. According to the Temporary Regulations of PLA Garrison Duties issued by the CMC in 1992, garrison duties in disciplining PLA units and functioning as the law enforcement of the CMC include five aspects:

1. Safeguarding military conduct and discipline
2. Ensuring the safety of military vehicles
3. Administering coming and going military personnel
4. Fulfilling the duties of security guards and the protection of cities
5. Organizing and coordinating PLA units in cities to participate in local gatherings, carry out disaster relief, and assist local authorities in maintaining social order.[36]

This declaration of garrison duties was further revised and issued by the CMC in October 1997 to describe the responsibilities and leading roles of garrison commands and the punishments of military personnel they are authorized to give.[37] In some cities such as Guangzhou, where there are a large number of PLA units (ground forces, air force, navy, and PAP) stationed, the garrison commands are expected to "bridge the PLA and local civilians."[38] They are

---

34 *Nanjing ribao* [Nanjing daily], January 22, 2007.
35 *Temporary Regulations of PLA Garrison Duties*, issued by CCP General Staff Department, General Political Department, and General Logistics Department and approved by the CMC on January 18, 1992.
36 Ibid.
37 *Regulations of PLA Garrison Duties*, issued by the CMC on October 7, 1997, CMC Document No. 58 (1997).
38 *Guangzhou ribao* [Guangzhou daily], October 18, 2002.

authorized not only to protect the interests of the PLA units but also to discipline armed personnel. A joint committee, including the garrison commands and the PLA units stationed in Guangzhou, was established for this purpose.[39] The primary administrative duties of garrison commands include carrying out inspection of the military personnel and military vehicles under their jurisdiction and resolving civil-military disputes such as the disputes of economic interests, conflicts regarding business interactions, and traffic accidents.[40]

Arguably, allowing the functionally overlapping garrison commands and other military security forces to operate in the same cities is problematic. Historically, garrison duties have been frequently assigned to operational PLA units or the local headquarters of PLA services (e.g., navy and air forces) stationed in the areas. The overlapping responsibilities and lack of communications as a result of the different military or civilian organizations to which they are subordinate not only wastes resources but also creates confusion and even conflict. During the Cultural Revolution, the violence in most cities was mainly fueled by PLA units that aligned with different rebel groups.[41] When responsibilities overlap, the potential for conflict between garrison commands and other military units is great.

In contrast, it is possible the competing security forces might benefit the central leadership as it strives to create checks and balances among local party committees, PLA units, and garrison commands. Currently, however, central leadership simply tends to ensure the party's control over the armed security forces. Local party control over garrison commands in which party chiefs take the positions as the first party secretaries of garrison commands was organizationally designed so that the party is able to dominate the decision making of garrison commands. Despite the structural guarantee of local party control over the armed security forces, the positions of local party leaders in the PLA were more symbolic than substantial, as local leaders were not authorized to appoint officers of garrison commands or provide them with salaries (even though garrison commands increasingly relied on local party committees and local governments for funding for operations and activities). Liao Hansheng was political commissar of the Nanjing Military Region between 1975 and 1979 and the first political commissar of the Shenyang Military Region between 1980 and 1983; as such, he has some insight to the relationship between garrison commands

---

[39] *Guangzhou ribao* [Guangzhou daily], October 18, 2002.

[40] Office of Double Support in Southern District of Qingdao City, "Qingdaoshi nanshiqu yufang he chuli junjingmin jiufen gongzuo yijian" [Suggestion on Prevention and Handling of Military/Police – Civilian Disputes in Southern District of Qingdao City], in the website of Party Committee of Southern District of Qingdao City, http://www.qdsn.gov.cn/n16/n1870882/n5989741/n5990076/5990327.html (accessed on March 22, 2012).

[41] In Shanghai during the Cultural Revolution, for example, the Fourth Army Corps of the Air Force supported the radical rebels against the Shanghai Garrison Command. It even sent security units to protect the radical-controlled Shanghai Party Committee, a job that was supposed to be executed by the Shanghai Garrison Command. See *Zhou Chunlin huiyilu*, p. 536.

and local party leadership. He has commented that the direct orders given by local leaders to the garrison commands "were to not conform to the stipulated organizational relations in which garrison commands are subordinated to and receive commands from PLA military regions."[42] In addition, PLA officials have traditionally cared about the qualification and prestige (*zhi li*) and historical background (*zhi ge*) of their leaders, not just their positions. Classic examples of top leaders who did not carry much clout were Wang Hongwen, vice chairman of the CMC, and Zhang Chunqiao, director of the PLA General Political Department, political commissar of the Nanjing Military Region and first political commissar of the Shanghai Garrison Command. Despite holding powerful positions in the PLA, few PLA units took these men seriously, which explains why Zhang always complained that he was only a titular (*gua ming*) political commissar, with whom people would "ask only for a signature but never tell anything."[43] However, the increasing trend toward institutionalization in the post-Deng PLA has given local civilian leaders increasing control over local security forces, including garrison commands.

Institutional Guarantee of Civilian Control over the Military

Despite the difficulties that local civilian leaders face in effectively commanding military units such as garrison commands and military subdistricts, the CCP has set up at least four institutional arrangements to ensure civilian control over the military. First, the dual leadership of the local party committee and the upper-level military organizations is designed to guarantee the party's control over the military. For example, military districts are organizations constructed by the PLA as its provincial administrative bodies and are under the command of its military regions (*da junqu*). However, according to the white papers released in 2006 by the CCP that define China's military goals over the coming fifty years, military districts also serve as military departments of party committees in charge of military work and as governmental agencies for military service at the provincial level. Similarly, military subdistricts (*jun fenqu*) and garrison commands are organizations set up by the PLA in prefectures (prefectures include prefecture-level cities and autonomous prefectures)[44] and serve as military departments of party committees in charge of military work and as governmental agencies for military service at the level of the prefecture while they are under the command of military districts. This dual leadership is also applied to the People's Armed Forces Departments at the county level. The People's Armed Forces Departments receive commands from military

---

[42] *Liao Hansheng huiyilu*, p. 381.

[43] *Zhou Chunlin huiyilu*, p. 544.

[44] Whereas China has a total of five provincial-level autonomous governments called "autonomous regions," it has thirty minority autonomous prefecture in regions under ethnic autonomy and mostly located outside autonomous regions.

subdistricts or garrison commands, and they serve as departments of local party committees in charge of military work and as governmental agencies for military service at the county level (the PAFD chiefs are also the members of local party committees).[45]

Second, one of the leading figures in each local military unit (commander or political commissar) at the level of the military district, garrison command, military subdistrict, or the People's Armed Forces Department must be a member of the local party standing committee.[46] The participation of these figures in local party committees facilitates smooth communication between the military and the party organizations. It also provides opportunities for local party leaders to become familiar with military leaders and affairs, to understand the concerns of local military units, and to cultivate personal relationships with military leaders. Third, a leader of each local military unit at the level of the military district, garrison command, military subdistrict, or People's Armed Forces Department must also be a member of the party committee in the upper-level military units. As a leadership member of the upper-level military unit, a local army leader is able to play a crucial role as a bridge between the local party committee and the upper-level army unit, and it coordinates the development of constructive civil-military relations.[47]

Fourth, the dual leadership system has been used by the CCP to control the militia and reserve forces. The militia and reserve forces at prefecture level received the leadership of prefecture Party committee and garrison command or PLA military subdistrict. The militia and reserve forces at the county level received the leadership of the county Party committee and the People's Armed Forces Department. Here, the garrison command, military subdistrict, or People's Armed Forces Department functions as the day-to-day administrative body of the People's Armed Forces Commission (PAFCs, *renmin wuzhuang weiyuanhui*), the leading party organs in charge of militia at different levels across the country.[48] There has been a tendency to emphasize the role of

---

[45] PRC Government, 2006 *White Papers*.
[46] "Dangguan wuzhuang yuanze yongfang guangmang – Xiezai zhongguo gongchandang jiandang bashi zhounian zhiji" [The principle of party control over armed forces shines forth everywhere – Writing during the eighty-year birthday of the CCP], *Zhongguo minbing* [Chinese militia], no. 7 (2001), pp. 4–9.
[47] Ibid.
[48] The PAFCs were initially created in 1940, when the CCP needed a committee to strengthen its control over the militia; the system was later extended nationwide in 1952. At the central level, the PAFC consists of the leading figures of the State Planning Commission, the State Sports Commission, the Ministry of Public Security, the Financial Ministry, the Ministry of Civil Affairs, the Ministry of Education, the Ministry of Agriculture and Forest, the General Labor Union, the National Women's Association, the Communist Youth League, the PLA's General Staff Department, the PLA's General Political Department, and the PLA's General Logistics Department. Generally speaking, the director of the central PAFC is a CMC vice chairman, and the central PAFC's day-to-day administrative body is the Mobilization Department (*dongyuan*

PAFCs in urban areas, where they not only are involved in the administration of the militia and reserve forces in general but also directly command the core (*jigan*) militia, the emergency-response teams of the militia, and the units of militia that specifically consist of temporary migrants who are assigned to maintain social order in the areas where a large number of temporary migrants live and work.[49] The dual leadership of the PAFCs creates an interesting power dynamic between the PLA and the party, especially considering that the local party is obligated to allocate finances and resources to the PAFCs' budgets. Nonetheless, having local party leaders in control of the PAFCs facilitates party leaders' command of local militia and reserve forces. As garrison commands replace military subdistricts in municipalities, provincial capitals and autonomous regions, and so-called strategic cities, and function as the day-to-day administrative body of the PAFCs and local National Defense Mobilization Commissions (NDMCs) by leading the militia and reserve forces, the garrison commands will play an increasing role in the evolution of China's civil-military relations.

Rise of Garrison Commands in the New Millennium

Since Jiang Zemin became chairman of the CMC in November 1989, the importance of the garrison commands has been increasingly emphasized, given their role in maintaining social order and in leading local militia and reserve forces. The PLA's reserve forces have undergone a transformation no less significant than that of its counterpart, China's active-duty PLA. The reserve force, which is incorporated into the PLA's order of battle, receives military training in peacetime according to relevant regulations and helps maintain social order in accordance with the law. In wartime, it may be called into active duty in pursuance of a state mobilization order. As Blasko points out, a larger reserve force would be able to assist with many of the disaster relief and community service missions that the PLA, PAP, and militia are often called to perform.[50] More important, the PLA reserve is becoming increasingly professional. Units

---

bu), under the CCP General Staff Department. See Li Junting and Yang Jinhe, *Zhongguo wuzhuang liliang tonglan, 1949–1989*, pp. 70–1.

[49] In China, migrant workers differ from urban workers in that they are only allowed to work in urban cities as temporary migrant workers. An estimated 100 million temporary migrant workers have left the countryside to enter towns and cities in search of nonagricultural jobs. Because of the lack of effective management and guidance, they have increasingly become a severe social problem for the regime to maintain social stability. See Alvin Y. So, "The State and Labor Insurgency in Post-socialist China: Implication for Development," in Joseph Y.S. Cheng (ed.), *Challenges and Policy Programmes of China's New Leadership* (Hong Kong: City University of Hong Kong Press, 2007), p. 139; *Zhongguo guofang bao* [China national defense daily], November 30, 2006.

[50] Dennis Blasko, "A New PLA Force Structure," in James C. Mulvenon and Richard H. Yang (eds.), *The People's Liberation Army in the Information Age*, p. 269.

assigned from the navy, the air force, the Second Artillery Force, and professional arms of the ground force account for 78 percent of the entire reserve force.[51]

At the local level of the PLA's operational organization structure, local garrison command units are assigned to mobilize, organize, train, and equip local reserve forces to complement regular PLA forces during wartime and to provide aid to local and regional organizations in times of natural disaster. For example, the Changsha Garrison Command organized ten professional and technical units to perform maintenance of road and bridges in addition to making emergency repairs to buildings and other structures. It also performed maintenance on antinuclear and antibiological weapons, as well as satellite communication.[52] The Chongqing Garrison Command established the first Militia Internet War Special Unit in 2000.[53]

China's reserve force was created in 1955, when China established its first conscription law. By January 1956, ten divisions of reserve forces had been established. They were abolished in 1957 with the PLA disarmament. The reserve force resumed in the early 1980s under Deng Xiaoping's leadership. The CCP's decision to resume its reserve force was an attempt both to reduce military spending and to build up a system for rapid mobilization.[54] In the 1990s, a large number of garrison commands were established under Jiang Zemin's leadership, an effort that has continued into the twenty-first century. This is exemplified by the establishment of new garrison commands in Jinan, Zhengzhou, Urumqi, and Hangzhou in 2004.[55] A significant change took place in 2003 and 2004, when the CCP established garrison commands in the capital cities of all provinces and autonomous regions, and gave them responsibilities typical of military subdistricts (*jun fenqu*), including authority over PLA agencies in charge of the People's Armed Forces Departments, military services, and local reserve forces.

Historically, the evolution of garrison commands has been related to the interchange of names between PLA military subdistricts and garrison commands in the process of merging and detaching units of the armed police (the name of the same organization was changed from garrison command to military subdistrict or from military subdistrict to garrison command several times). The case of the Guangzhou Garrison Command (GGC) is a typical example of this evolution (Table 7.1). As Table 7.1 indicates, the predecessor of the Guangzhou Garrison Command was the Guangzhou Military Subdistrict

---

[51] *Jiefangjun bao* [The PLA daily], November 21, 2008.

[52] *Jiefangjun bao*, March 14, 2005.

[53] *Xinhua*, August 29, 2000.

[54] See 'Dangdai zhongguo' congshu bianji weiyuanhui (ed.), *Zhongguo renmin jiefangjun* [Chinese People's Liberation Army] (Beijing: Dangdai zhongguo chubanshe, 1994), vol. 1, pp. 726–36.

[55] See *Jinan ribao* [Jinan daily], September 9, 2004; *Hongzhou ribao* [Hongzhou daily], December 12, 2004; *Urumqi wanbao* [Urumqi evening news], October 28, 2004, and *Henan ribao* [Henan daily], November 17, 2004.

TABLE 7.1. *Evolution of Guangzhou Garrison Command*

Year	Name[a]	Rank	Subordinated units
1960	Guangzhou Military Subdistrict	Division	People's Armed Forces Departments in 2 counties and 7 districts of Guangzhou city
1965	Guangzhou Military Subdistrict	Division	People's Armed Forces Departments in 2 counties and 5 districts of Guangzhou city; 3 professional systems of Guangzhou city, the Independent 13th Battalion of the Guangdong Military District
1966	Guangzhou Military Subdistrict and Guangzhou Garrison Command	Division	People's Armed Forces Departments in 2 counties and 5 districts of Guangzhou city; 3 professional systems (Industrial/ Transportation, Finance/Trade, and culture/education) of Guangzhou city; the independent 7th, 8th, and 9th Regiments (the Independent 13th Battalion was transferred)
1967	Guangzhou Garrison Command	Army Corps	People's Armed Forces Departments in 2 counties, 5 districts, and 3 professional systems of Guangzhou city; the independent 7th, 8th, and 9th regiments
1970	Guangzhou Garrison Command[b]	Army Corps	People's Armed Forces Departments in 2 counties, 5 districts, and 3 professional systems of Guangzhou city; the independent 1st, 2nd, and 3rd regiments (the Independent 7th, the 9th Regiment, and the 376th Regiment of PLA Unit 0952 were transferred)
1976	Guangzhou Garrison Command	Division	People's Armed Forces Departments in 6 counties and 6 districts; the Independent 1st, 2nd, 3rd Regiments
1983	Guangzhou Garrison Command[c]	Division	People's Armed Forces Departments in 8 counties, 6 districts, and 1 professional system (industrial and transportation) in Guangzhou city
1986	Guangzhou Military Subdistrict	Division	People's Armed Forces Departments in 8 counties, 8 districts, and 1 professional system (industrial and transportation) in Guangzhou city
1992–current	Guangzhou Garrison Command	Division	People's Armed Forces Departments in 8 counties, 8 districts, and 1 professional system (industrial and transportation) of Guangzhou city

Source: Guangzhou shi difang zhi bianzuan weiyuanhui [Compiling Commission of the Local History and Annals of Guangzhou City], *Guangzhou shizhi: junshi juan* [Annals of Guangzhou city: Military Annals] (Guangzhou: Guangzhou chubanshe, 1995), vol. 13, pp. 102–14.

[a] The PLA has been divided into several large military regions (*da jun qu*). Within each MR there are military districts (*jun qu*), beneath which are military subdistricts (*jun fen qu*).

[b] The predecessors of the independent 1st, 2nd, and 3rd regiments were the 3rd and 5th regiments of the General Corps of the Public Security of Guangzhong Province, respectively.

[c] The Independent 1st and 3rd Regiments and the 3rd Battalion of the Independent 2nd Regiment were handed over to the Guangdong General Corps of People's Armed Police. At the same time, rest of the 2nd Regiment was abolished.

(GMS), which belonged under the authority of the PLA Guangdong Military District, which was established in October 1960. The GGC was established by the merger of the People's Armed Forces Department of Guangzhou and the headquarters of the Third Regiment of the Guangdong Military District. Historically, the military subdistrict of the Guangdong Military District fell under the dual leadership of the CCP Guangdong Military District and the Party Committee of Guangzhou.

The evolution of the Guangzhou Garrison Command is indicative of the overall evolution of garrison commands. First, the history of the Guangzhou Garrison Command exemplifies the history of name changes between the military subdistrict and the garrison command. Because military subdistricts and garrison commands have similar responsibilities, the garrison command was able to take over military subdistricts without too much effort. Still, the garrison command placed more emphasis on guarding the city and maintaining social order than on administering the militia and reserve forces. Also, the garrison commands were usually the units that absorbed the abolished armed police or the Chinese People's Public Security Forces. The Guangzhou Garrison Command exemplified this in 1966, when it absorbed the CPPSF and subsequently handed over the forces to the People's Armed Police (PAP) when it was established in 1982.

The third theme seen in the garrison command's evolution is the changing size of the military subdistrict or garrison command, which has resulted from changing features of top leadership politics. When Mao realized that he was losing control over the violent mass movement in early 1967 after he launched the Cultural Revolution, he increased the size of the garrison command and expanded its influence to ensure social order. He did so by upgrading it from the division level to the army corps level, thus giving garrison commands direct command over PLA combat units. However, in the early 1980s, when Deng Xiaoping attempted to reduce the size of the PLA and terminate its involvement in civilian politics, the Guangzhou Garrison Command was renamed the Guangzhou Military Subdistrict and no longer commanded the garrison units. Instead, it was assigned to control the People's Armed Forces Departments, specifically to command the militia and reserve forces.[56]

An important implication of establishing the garrison commands in major cities is the importance of their leading roles in coordinating relationships and resolving conflicts between local governments and local PLA units. Garrison commands as the military departments of local party committees (each local party committee organizationally has a military department) are viewed by the official media as the staff officers (*can mou*) and assistants (*zhu shou*) of local party committees and governments.[57] Garrison commands are required to

---

[56] Guangzhou shi difang zhi bianzuan weiyuanhui [Compiling Commission of the Local History and Annals of Guangzhou City], *Guangzhou shizhi: Junshi juan* [Annals of Guangzhou city: Military annals] (Guangzhou: Guangzhou chubanshe, 1995), vol. 13, p. 112.

[57] *Nanjing ribao* [Nanjing daily], May 24, 2011.

"play an important role in coordinating the disputes and legal cases concerning the PLA units" and to function as "the bridges linking the PLA and civilians."[58] In fact, the effort made by the CCP leadership and the CMC to discipline the military units and to authorize garrison commands to reinforce regulations has been derived from increasing concerns from both the CCP leadership and the CMC regarding the negative images of the PLA since the reform. Since Deng Xiaoping launched economic reforms, PLA units have been engaged in commercial activities (secretly, as commercial activities were not allowed after 1997)[59] and have used their privileges to conduct illegal activities such as gang fighting, organized smuggling, and renting military vehicles and license plates to civilian businesses and individuals for profit. Numerous civilian organizations and individuals have used the military vehicles and license plates for further illegal activity, which undoubtedly has blemished the reputation of the PLA.[60]

As local representatives of the Central Military Commission in disciplining PLA units, garrison commands have increasingly played a significant role against the illegal activities and discipline violation of the PLA units and personnel. In recent years, garrison commands have cracked down on the illegal activities in an effort to rebuild a positive image of the PLA. For example, a joint garrison and traffic guard team was established in the spring of 2009 to scrutinize the disciplinary violations of the military personnel in Guangzhou. The Guangzhou Garrison Command led 120 military personnel assigned to the joint guard team, which included members of the local units of the PLA ground forces, the navy, the air force, and the PAP.[61] When the PLA's image was damaged when some PLA units in Guangzhou conducted commercial services using the PLA's privileges in which PLA's business activities were treated as nonprofit services (this implies that PLA units did not pay tax to local government), the Guangzhou Garrison Command was authorized to coordinate an investigation and administer appropriate remediation to the PLA units involved.[62]

There are at least three implications for the rising number of garrison commands. First, there is an increasing need for the armed forces to maintain social order and crack down on the increasing mass unrest against local authorities.

---

[58] Supreme Court and PLA Political Department, *Guanyu renzhen chuli shejun jiufen he anjian qieshi weihu guofeng liyi he junren junshu hefa quanyi de yijian* [Suggestions on carefully handling disputes and cases concerning the PLA and earnestly safeguarding the interest of national defense and the legal rights of military personnel and the relatives of military personnel], Supreme Court Document No. 31 (2001).

[59] Many PLA units have continued to conduct commercial activities even after the CMC banned the PLA's commercial activities in 1997. See Zhao Hua, "Zuohao budui bu jingshang wenti qingli jiancha gongzuo de jidian renshi" [Some understandings about handling well with the liquidation and examination for putting an end to the army's noncommercial activities], in *Wujing houqing* [Logistics of the People's Armed Police], no. 3 (2002), p. 62.

[60] See *Jiefangjun bao* [The PLA daily], October 17, 1997, and December 31, 2000.

[61] See *Guangzhou ribao* [Guangzhou daily], February 28, 2009.

[62] *Dayang* online, July 30, 2007.

Second, the establishment of the garrison commands in the capital cities of provinces and autonomous regions "facilitates and strengthens the mobilization and construction of national defense in the important cities."[63] Third, the establishment of more garrison commands reduces the local governments' reliance on the PAP. Garrison commands can manage small-scale and middle-scale mass unrest, leaving large-scale incidents to local PAP units. Unlike military subdistricts, according to the official media, the new role of the garrison commands includes the city garrison, which assists local government in maintaining social stability and participates in disaster-relief operations.[64]

Arguably, the increased role of the garrison commands implies that the militia and reserve forces will become important for reestablishing domestic social stability following an increasing number of mass incidents. According to the Master Emergency Response Plan for Emergent Public Events in Guangzhou, issued by the General Office of the Government of Guangzhou, the Guangzhou Garrison Command, the PAP Guangzhou Detachment (*zhi dui*), and the militia and reserve forces are the "core (*gu gan*) and vanguard force" in emergent events.[65] Certainly, the employment of the militia and reserve forces instead of the PLA or PAP alone helps reduce tension between the army and civilians. Fourth, as the CCP increasingly stresses the party's role in controlling the army (*dang guan jundui*) and as the party chiefs of local party committees are the first secretaries of the party committee of the garrison commands,[66] the establishment of and emphasis on garrison commands enable the local party committee to respond to emergencies quickly and to directly command and employ the armed forces to confine increasing social unrest and mass incidents.

In cities where no garrison commands are established, local military subdistricts are usually assigned garrison duties. According to the "Notice on Assigning Some Military Subdistricts for Garrison Duties," issued by the Beijing Military Region, only some military subdistricts are chosen by the Beijing Military Region and approved by the PLA General Staff Department to implement garrison duties.[67] For those military subdistricts that are chosen to implement garrison duties, a garrison and duty platoon (*jingbei jiucha pai*) is set up for each military subdistrict specifically in charge of the garrison duties, including

[63] *Xinhuanet*, December 29, 2003.

[64] Ibid.

[65] Yingji guanli bangongshi of the Guangdong renmin zhengfu [Emergency Management Office of the People's Government of Guangdong Province], *Guangzhou shi tufa gonggong shijian zongti yingji yu'an* [Master emergency response plan for emergent public events in Guangzhou], http://www.gdemo.gov.cn/yasz/yjya/gdsya/200712/t20071206_36843_11.htm (accessed March 27, 2009).

[66] For example, Xi Jinping and Zhang Gaoli were concurrently the first secretaries of the party committees of the Shanghai Garrison Command and of the Tianjin Garrison Command, respectively, when they were the party chiefs of those cities. See *Jiefang ribao* [Liberation daily], July 17, 2007; *Tianjin ribao* [Tianjin daily], April 23, 2008.

[67] See Beijing Military Region Document No. 58 (2006).

investigation and discipline of military personnel and vehicles committing violations, temporary security guard, and assistance in the maintenance of social order.[68]

Beijing Garrison Command in the Early 1960s

The Beijing Garrison Command (BGC), under the Beijing Military Region, was established in January 1959, when the Beijing Military Region no longer held responsibilities as the Beijing-Tianjin Garrison Command. Its history can be traced back to early 1949, when the headquarters of the Beijing-Tianjin Garrison Command was established in the North China Military Region (predecessor of the Beijing Military Region). Its purpose was to guard Beijing, one of the most important cities in China, and Tianjin, one of the most important commercial cities in China, given its geographical location as a port city close to the capital. In January 1959, the CMC replaced the headquarters of the Beijing-Tianjin Garrison Command with two separate military units: the BGC (*Beijing weishu qu*) and the Tianjin Garrison Command (*Tianjin jingbei qu*).[69] Thus, the BGC was historically tied to the North China Military Region and North China Field Army, headed by Nie Rongzhen. When the BGC was established, it included the following divisions and bureaus: the Capital Guard Division (led by division commander Liu Huishan and political commissar Deng Bo), Central Guard Regiment (led by regiment commander Zhang Yaoci and political commissar Yang Dezhong), a martial music regiment, a battalion guard of honor, seventeen bureaus of military service at the district and county levels, and a hospital.[70] Organizationally, the BGC was subordinate to the Beijing Military Region, but it fell under the dual leadership of the Beijing Military Region and the Beijing Municipal Party Committee, with professional guidance from the PLA General Staff Department (see Figure 7.2). Its primary duties included the following:

- *Security guard*: Guarding the party, the government, the army leaders, the leaders of the eight "democratic" parties, important mass organizations controlled by the CCP, foreign diplomats, diplomatic envoys and corps, and attendees at important meetings and gatherings.
- *Public security*: Maintaining public order in the capital and guarding important roads, bridges, and mass gatherings.
- *Parade and flags or weapons carried by the honor guard*: Training the personnel for parades and sending guards of honor.

---

[68] For example, the garrison and duty platoons in Weihai of Shandong and Leshan and Mianyang of Sichuan are the core armed forces controlled by the Weihan Military Subdistrict and the Sichuan Military District, respectively. See *Jiefangjun bao* [The PLA daily], April 4, 2001.

[69] Wu Lie, *Zhengrong suiyue*, pp. 391–2.

[70] Ibid., p. 394.

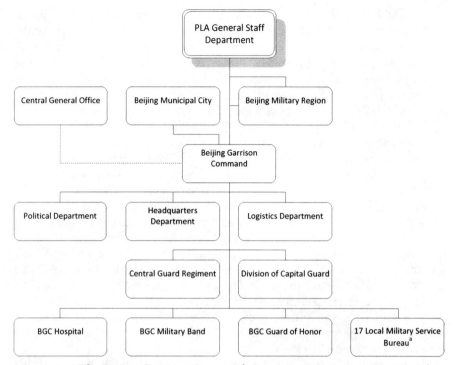

FIGURE 7.2. *The Beijing Garrison Command, January 1959. Source*: Wu Lie, *Zhengrong suiyue*, pp. 391–5.
ᵃ The BGC took charge of the Military Service Bureau of seventeen Beijing districts and counties.

- *Training and providing guidance to local militia*: Providing political education to and military training of the militia organizations in seventeen Beijing districts and counties.[71]

As a guard division subordinate to the Beijing Military Region, the 1950s and early 1960s saw the BGC in charge of guarding the party, the government and leading army organizations, and the residences of the high-ranking leaders (except for a few top leaders, such as Mao Zedong, Liu Shaoqi, Zhou Enlai, and Politburo members). These high-ranking leaders instead fell under the security umbrella of the Central Guard Regiment (CGR), which was directly controlled by the Central Guard Bureau, even though the CGR was institutionally put under the jurisdiction of the BGC between January 1959 and March 1961.

Still, the BGC had quite a few varying responsibilities. Different personages and circumstances required different security measures. The most obvious form of security was witnessed in government agencies. Here, armed guards

[71] Ibid., pp. 391–7.

were publicly positioned to ensure security and to provide a public image as the shield that protects the state and its people and show national pride. However, guarding the residences of high-ranking party members and leading governmental figures required a different strategy. To ensure security in such situations, armed guards with hidden weapons were secreted in either inner houses or half-public sentry boxes. For residences of prominent nonparty figures (e.g., democratic parties, minorities) and important nongovernmental organizations, the BGC executed security measures by setting up guard boxes with plainclothes security guards or by disguising security guards as dispatchers who served the residents.[72] In addition, the BGC was responsible for guiding the work of the militia in Beijing and its suburban counties. Despite the number of responsibilities the BGC directed, it still became a major target for budgetary and personnel reductions in early 1960s.[73] A major reason for its budgetary and personnel reductions might be the loss of its organizational authority over the Central Guard Regiment (Unit 8341) as well as its duties in guarding high-ranking leaders. In March 1961, the Central Guard Regiment was no longer subordinated to the BGC, but instead was directly under the authority of the PLA's General Staff Department.[74] The BGC was left only to control of the militia in the eighteen counties surrounding Beijing. In March 1963, the PLA General Staff Department informed the Beijing Military Region and the BGC that the duties of guarding Beijing were to be taken over by the Chinese People's Public Security Forces (CPPSF).

It was not until December 1965, when Luo Ruiqing, the PLA general chief of staff, was dismissed and the CPPSF abolished, that the BGC was reassigned a leading role guarding Beijing.[75] An important step in securing Beijing for the BGC was its enlargement by two divisions, which were added in June 1966. Before this point, it had consisted of only one division and one regiment. The two divisions were chosen from the Beijing Military Region: the 189th Division of the 63rd Army Corps and the 70th Division of the 24th Army Corps. Particularly notable was the 70th Division of the 24th Army Corps, one of the most mechanized divisions in China. After the enlargement, the BGC contained more than one hundred thousand personnel and was authorized to command the 112th Division, 196th Division, and 193rd Division around Beijing if necessary.[76]

Despite being a unit subordinate to the Beijing Military Region, the BGC did not receive commands from the Beijing Military Region; rather, it was directly controlled by party leadership, mainly by Zhou Enlai. To ensure the BGC's loyalty to the Chairman, the leadership was reorganized such that Fu Chongbi

[72] Ibid., p. 403.
[73] Liao Hansheng, *Liao Hansheng huiyilu*, p. 246.
[74] Beijing shi difang zhi bianzuan weiyuanhui [Compiling Commission of Local Annals of Beijing Municipal City], *Beijing zhi, junshi juan, junshi zhi* [Military annals, volume of military, annals of Beijing] (Beijing: Beijing chubanshe, 2002), p. 515.
[75] Liao Hansheng, *Liao Hansheng huiyilu*, pp. 246–9.
[76] See Fu Chongbi, *Fu Chongbi huiyilu*, pp. 179–181.

replaced Commander Li Jiayi who was only appointed as the BGC commander in July 1965. Fu was a general from the former North China Field Army led by Nie Rongzhen. Li was originally from the Fourth Front Army, headed by Zhang Guotao during the late 1920s and early 1930s, and was assigned to join the East China Field Army and the Third Field Army in the 1940s civil war against the Nationalists. Mao had never viewed the generals from the Fourth Front Army as a military faction associated with him, and Mao was concerned about Li's ability to work with and gain the trust of generals from the former North China Field Army, despite the fact that the 24th Army Corps, to which he was appointed chief of staff, had been under the jurisdiction of the Beijing Military Region since 1955, when the 24th Army Corps returned from Korea.[77] As did Unit 8341, the BGC became a major force on which Mao relied to secure Beijing.

Beijing Garrison Command in the Cultural Revolution

Before launching the Cultural Revolution in the summer of 1966, Mao reorganized the PLA to ensure the support of the army. The reorganization included the dismissal of the PLA's general chief of staff, Luo Ruiqing, in December 1965; the abolishment of the Chinese People's Public Security Forces in June 1966; and the reorganization of the Beijing Garrison Command in the summer of 1966. In addition, Mao strove to win the support of the PLA units that guarded Beijing and the areas around Beijing. One of Mao's strategies to control Beijing included his effort to approach Marshal Nie Rongzhen for support; Nie had established powerful influence over the army units in and around Beijing because he was former commander of the North China Field Army (predecessor of the Beijing Military Region), and Nie's former subordinates controlled most of the key positions in the Beijing Military Region. As mentioned in Chapter 4, throughout the 1950s, the relationship between Mao and Nie Rongzhen was effectively estranged, partially because of Nie's powerful influence on the North China Military Region and partially because of Mao's dissatisfaction with Nie. When Nie was the PLA's acting chief of staff in the early 1950s, he integrated the Central Guard Regiment into the Chinese People's Public Security Forces without Mao's consent, and he ordered the PLA General Staff Department to send incomplete and only important military information to Mao in order to relieve Mao of the more insignificant duties of routine administration.[78] Mao viewed this as an attempt by Nie to "blockade" him, and he thus threatened to dismiss Nie (or to make an "organizational adjustment," in Mao's own

---

[77] "Xinghuo Liaoyuan" bianjibu, *Zhongguo renmin jiefangjun jiangshuai minglu* [PLA list of generals and marshals], vol. 2, p. 477.

[78] Mao was infuriated when informed in the spring of 1950 that the CGR had been integrated with the Chinese People's Public Security Forces. Mao also blamed Nie, who gave an order to block his to access to the PLA documents. See [Luo] Diandian, *Feifan de niandai* [Those extraordinary years], p. 147; Zhang Zhen, *Zhang Zhen huiyilu* [Memoirs of Zhang Zhen] (Beijing: Jiefangjun chubanshe, 2003), vol. 1, pp. 507–8.

words).[79] Nie was eventually forced to resign, citing health problems, and he kept a low profile throughout the entire 1950s. The appointments of Yang Yong and Liao Hansheng to take charge of the Beijing Military Region were a significant move by Mao to undermine Nie's influence on the armed forces in and around Beijing, as Yang and Liao were not historically tied to the North China Field Army faction. Regardless of his scheming against Nie during this time, Mao approached Nie on the eve of the Cultural Revolution to curry favor with him against the party bureaucracy, particularly the PLA leaders who had built strong working relationships with the frontline leaders such as Luo Ruiqing and Marshal He Long.

The Beijing Garrison Command was one of the most active military units and one of the armed forces on which Mao depended to ensure his personal security, as well as to maintain social order in the capital during the Cultural Revolution. To ensure his absolute control over the PLA and to prevent any uprising against him, Mao issued an order that any military dispatch of the BGC that included more than two companies must be reported to him for approval. According to the order, issued on January 10, 1968, all tasks, disposition, dispatches, and temporary services of the BGC and of the militia in Beijing must be reported to the PLA General Staff Department and approved by both Mao and Lin Biao. The BGC could act independently if the military dispatch requested less than a platoon's worth of personnel, but if the personnel requested ranged from two platoons to two companies, it needed to gain approval from the PLA General Staff Department.[80] Even Defense Minister Lin Biao, who represented Mao in controlling the PLA, tried to avoid dispatching PLA units without Mao's approval.[81] However, because the BGC's responsibilities were so extensive, it was impossible for Mao to approve every dispatch. Although Zhou Enlai and Ye Jianying were authorized to command the BGC to dispatch units, in practice, Commander Fu Chongbi was a key figure in determining the terms and size of BGC deployments.

One of Mao's key strategies on the eve of the Culture Revolution was to ensure the support of the PLA through military factionalism. He mainly relied on the First Army Group and First Front Army faction, which he had established at Jinggang Mountain of Jiangxi (Jiangxi base area) during the summer of 1928. Both Lin Biao and Nie Rongzhen were key figures in this faction. Thus, Mao depended highly on them to ensure his dominance in the PLA. This helps explain why Mao picked Fu Chongbi to lead the BGC. After Mao planned to

[79] See Zhang Zhen, *Zhang Zhen huiyilu*, vol. 1, pp. 506–9.
[80] See Yu Ruxin, "1969: Duisu zhanbei zhongde juwei banshizu, Lin Biao yu Mao Zedong" [1969: The CMC Administrative Group, Lin Biao, and Mao Zedong during the war preparation against the Soviet Union], p. 313.
[81] After receiving Xiao Hua's suggestion to send a PLA company to help a local commune to gather wheat, Lin forwarded the suggestion to Mao for approval. See Zhang Yunsheng, *Maojiawan jishi: Lin Biao mishu huiyilu* [True account of Maojiawan: The memoirs of Lin Biao's secretary], pp. 300–2.

assault the party bureaucracy by launching the Cultural Revolution, the PLA's support was significant enough to overpower party veterans, who were led by Liu Shaoqi and Deng Xiaoping.

The factions were deep and multifarious, so although systematic opposition from the PLA generals was unlikely, Mao was concerned that military factionalism triggered by the conflict among party leadership might weaken the army's support of him. Much of the conflict surrounded the relationship between Lin Biao and other CMC leaders, such as He Long and Luo Ruoqing. He Long had been estranged from Lin Biao since the 1940s in Yan'an, and he had taken charge of the CMC after Lin was on sick leave in 1962. Therefore, supporting Lin against He had become an important strategy for Mao to ensure his dominance over the PLA. Luo Ruiqing, PLA general chief of staff who was organizationally in charge of Unit 8341 and had strong influence over the security apparatus because of his role as former public security minister and former commander of the Chinese People's Public Security Forces,[82] was also a target of Mao's assault. Luo had become increasingly close to He Long, which increased tension between Luo and two leading figures in Mao's faction, Lin Biao and Nie Rongzhen.

Historically, Luo Ruiqing's career had been tied to the factions led by both Lin Biao and Nie Rongzhen. Early on, Luo was a key figure in the security forces in the First Front Army, headed by Lin Biao, in the Jiangxi base area, and later, during the civil war, he was deputy political commissar in the North China Field Army, led by Nie Rongzhen. Conflict between Luo and Lin began with Luo's closeness to He Long and Lin's discontent with what he considered Luo's arbitrary work style. This trait of Luo's effectively prevented Lin from assuming his dominance in the PLA's decision making. Conflict between Luo and Nie began with Luo's position of supporting He Long against Nie in the long-standing institutional conflict between the Defense Industry Commission and the Defense Science Commission, of which He and Nie were, respectively, heads. As a result of Luo's lack of support, he was blamed of "denying the great achievements made by the Defense Science Commission led directly by Comrade Nie Rongzhen" and of "deciding to abolish the military representatives in the Defense Science Commission without the permission of Comrade Nie Rongzhen."[83] Considering these political rifts, Mao's decision to abandon He Long and Luo Ruiqing in favor of Lin and Nie, two of three vice chairmen of the CMC, makes sense: the support of their factions, which consisted of the former Fourth Field Army and the former North China Field

---

[82] On March 1, 1961, the Central Guard Regiment (Unit 8341) was removed from the BGC and put directly under the authority of the PLA General Staff Department. See Beijing shi difang zhi bianzuan weiyuanhui, *Beijing zhi, junshi juan, junshi zhi* (Beijing: Beijing chubanshe, 2002), p. 515.

[83] See Zhonggong zhongyang, "Guanyu Luo Ruiqing cuowu wenti baogao de pishi" [Instructions about the report regarding Luo Ruiqing's errors], in *Zhonggong wenhua dageming zhongyao wenjian huibian*, p. 28.

Army, was necessary for Mao to dominate the PLA leadership and secure Beijing.[84]

Later developments reveal Mao's strategy even more clearly. Mao pushed Lin Biao to play an active role in leading the CMC, and he relied on the generals of the former North China Field Army to protect Beijing. By February 1967, the generals of the former North China Field Army controlled the PLA General Staff Department (Yang Chengwu), the Beijing Military Region (Zheng Weishan), and the BGC (Fu Chongbi). In June 1966, the BGC was reorganized from one division and one regiment to three divisions and one regiment, and it was authorized to take over the suburbs of Beijing. Thus, the newly added 4th Division of the BGC, previously the 189th Division of the 63rd Army Corps before the reorganization, was stationed in the Changxingdian, the Jinghe, and the Nanyuan suburbs under the command of the BGC.[85] If needed, the BGC was also authorized to command the 112th Division of the 38th Army Corps in Gaobeidian of Beijing, the 198th Division in Tianjin, and the 193rd Division in Xuanhua of Hebei.[86] On top of all this, the BGC was upgraded from the rank of army corps (*jun*) to army groups (*bingtuan*).

The rise of the BGC in the Cultural Revolution derived from Mao's attempt to rely on the armed forces to ensure order in Beijing, the center of the Cultural Revolution. Mao knew that the BGC would play a crucial role in ensuring social stability in the capital, and so he never allowed mass rebels or the Red Guard to catalyze a mass movement within the BGC. The so-called four greats – speaking freely, airing views fully, holding great debates, and writing big-character posters (handwritten political posters expressing criticisms and complaints) – were not allowed in the BGC either.[87] The power of the BGC was further enhanced after it was ordered to take over the Beijing Bureau of Public Security in February 1967.[88] Although Mao asked Zhou Enlai to take charge of the BGC directly, Mao was often personally involved in its activities.[89] Mao's effort to control the BGC was based on his attempts to directly control, often through Zhou Enlai, Commander Fu Chongbi. In other words, Mao's control

---

[84] The three vice chairmen of the CMC elected in September 1959 were Lin Biao, He Long, and Nie Rongzhen. In January 1966, four vice chairmen of the CMC, Chen Yi, Liu Bocheng, Xu Xiangqian, and Ye Jianying, were added to the PLA leadership. See Wang Jianying, *Zhongguo gongchandang zuzhishi ziliao huibian: Lingdao jigou yange he chengyuan minglu*, p. 1046.

[85] Fu Chongbi, *Fu Chongbi huiyilu*, p. 178.

[86] Ibid., pp. 179–80.

[87] See Zhu Yuanshi et al., *Wu De koushu: shinian fengyu wangshi – Wozai Beijing gongzuo de yixie jingli* [Wu De's dictating: Past events with ten-year hardship – Some experiences when I worked in Beijing] (Beijing: Dangdai zhongguo chubanshe, 2004), p. 23.

[88] "Zhonghua renmin gongheguo gong'an bu, Beijing weishuqu silingbu bugao (February, 11, 1967)," in Song Yongyi (ed.), *Zhongguo wenhua dageming wenku* [Chinese Cultural Revolution database], part 1, February 11, 1967.

[89] For example, Mao made recruitment decisions for the BGC and often personally called in leaders of the BGC for information. See Fu Chongbi, *Fu Chongbi huiyilu*, pp. 181, 198–200, 204.

over the BGC was mainly achieved by commanding Fu Chongbi directly and exclusively, whereas other leaders of the BGC were not allowed to ask about what was going on with the BGC's activities.[90]

Following Mao's mobilization of the Red Guard and the mass "rebels," bureaucracy and party leaders at all levels became targets of violence. Mao gave permission to the Cultural Revolution Group (CRG), the radical intellectuals headed by Mao's wife Jiang Qing, to use the BGC to detain and persecute "capitalistic roaders" at all levels of the government. At the same time, Mao ordered Zhou Enlai to use the BGC to protect high-ranking leaders who Mao might need in the future. The duties assigned to the BGC were, by nature, confrontational with those of the CRG and even with those of Mao. Their primary objective was still to protect high-ranking officials by taking defensive actions against mass rebels. Veteran leaders increasingly resisted, which inevitably led to confrontation between the PLA and the CRG. Many army leaders allied with senior civilian leaders, openly challenged the CRG in and after the incident of February 1967. The PLA-CRG conflict became Mao's primary concern throughout the entire Cultural Revolution.

Furthermore, Mao felt vulnerable to the possibility of resistance from top army leaders following the Wuhan incident during the summer of 1967. The dismissal of general chief of staff Yang Chengwu and the BGC commander Fu Chongbi was the result of an allied effort among Mao, Lin Biao, and the CRG. Yang and Fu were dismissed to prevent senior army leaders from rebelling by undermining the influence of the former North China Field Army faction, which controlled the Beijing areas, considering the increasing resistance from the PLA old marshals, including Marshal Nie Rongzhen, against the Maoist radicals. The personal ties of Yang and Fu with the PLA veterans, particularly with old marshals, played a crucial role in their dismissals. Despite the CRG's attack on army veterans and Mao's discontent with the old marshals, which arose with the Huairen Hall incident of February 1967, both Yang Chengwu and Fu Chongbi remained loyal to the old marshals, especially to their former superior, Nie Rongzhen.[91] As the BGC commander, Fu Chongbi had to provide

---

[90] Wu De, for example, never knew how decisions were made, despite his position as political commissar of the BGC. At one point, Wu was chased by mass rebels, but he the BGC commander Fu Chongbi did not allow him to stay in Qingwang Mansion, the headquarters of the BGC, in order to escape the persecution of the mass rebels. After Fu Chongbi was dismissed, Wu was utterly clueless as to what had happened in the BGC. See Zhu Yuanshi et al., *Wu De koushu: Shinian fengyu wangshi – Wozai Beijing gongzuo de yixie jingli*, pp. 45, 53–5.

[91] For example, despite Lin Biao's warning, after February 1967 Yang continued to send party documents to Ye Jianying. While refusing to leak anything to Lin Biao, Yang passed on to the old marshals Mao's comments from his trip to southern China in the summer of 1967. See Yang Chengwu, *Yang Chengwu jiangjun zishu* [The autobiographical notes of General Yang Chengwu], pp. 301–4, 312; Zhang Zishen, *Zhanjiang yu tongshuai – Yang Chengwu zai Mao Zedong huixia de sishiba nian* [Combat general and commander – Yang Chengwu's forty-eight years under Mao Zedong's leadership] (Shenyang: Liaoning renmin chubanshe, 2000), pp. 354–61.

protection, often under the directive of Zhou Enlai, for veteran comrades who had been framed by the CRG. Zhou Enlai ordered Fu to rescue Peng Zhen, who had been kidnapped by the Red Guard, and to protect Luo Ruiqing and Chen Yi. He also protected many high-ranking provincial leaders and army generals from being harmed by radical mass organizations.[92] After the 1967 Wuhan Incident, Fu hid the principal, Wuhan Military Region Commander Chen Zaidao, in a dark elevator to escape the persecution of the CRG and the rebels. In addition, Fu was the primary informant for the old marshals when the CRG organized a series of attacks against them after they hid, during February 1967, in the Western Hills (*xishan*) in the west of Beijing.[93] More important, Fu's control of the BGC aggravated Mao's concerns that the tension between Mao and the old marshals developed as a result of Fu's long-standing personal loyalty to Nie Rongzhen. In fact, the close ties between Fu and the old marshals heightened the vigilance of both Mao and Lin Biao.[94] Mao was particularly concerned about the safety of the Cultural Revolution Group, which the BGC was guarding. Mao's concerns played a vital role in the dismissal of Yang Chengwu and Fu Chongbi who were charged with "conspiring to assault the CRG with armed forces" in the Diaoyutai, the headquarters and residence of the CRG, in February 1968.[95]

In early 1967 the chaotic mass movement began to spin even further out of control, and the old marshals gradually became the target of the Red Guard and the radical mass rebels. The only armed force on which the old marshals could rely for their safety was the BGC. To protect the PLA's high-ranking generals, the BGC took quite a few measures. It sent a regiment to guard PLA 302 Hospital, which specifically served high-ranking PLA leaders; it increased the guards from two to three battalions in the Western Hills (the location of the CMC and the residences of the PLA senior leaders); and it hid more than thirty provincial party leaders and government ministers in its military barracks.[96] It should be noted, however, that the BGC protected only those who were attacked by the Red Guard and mass rebels but who had not yet been targeted by the Cultural Revolution Group. Once the CRG targeted a high-ranking leader, the BGC had to follow the orders of the CRG to jail the

[92] Fu Chongbi, *Fu Chongbi huiyilu*, pp. 188–9, 192–5.

[93] Despite the CRG's warnings and even Lin Biao's orders not to contact the old marshals when they were assaulted by the rebels, Fu Chongbi secretly provided information to the old marshals and continually made efforts to protect them. See Fu Chongbi, *Fu Chongbi huiyilu*, pp. 196–7.

[94] For example, Lin realized that Fu still had close ties with the old marshals even after the old marshals were under attack; Lin warned Fu not to visit or call the old marshals. See Fu Chongbi, *Fu Chongbi huiyilu*, p. 196.

[95] In February 1968, the CRG ordered Fu Chongbi to search the manuscripts of Lu Xun, one of the most prominent writers in the 1930s and 1940s. However, Jiang Qing and Kang Sheng did not know that the manuscripts were stored in the secret office of the CRG in the Diaoyutai. When Fu went to the Diaoyutai to search the manuscripts, Jiang Qing viewed Fu's act as "an armed assault against the CRG." See *Fu Chongbi huiyilu*, pp. 215–9.

[96] Ibid., pp. 195–7.

CRG's identified enemies.[97] The importance of the BGC is also illustrated by its role providing supplemental guards for top leaders. As Fu Chongbi has indicated, even Lin Biao's residence and the Diaoyutai were guarded by the BGC.[98] Because the Central Guard Bureau and Unit 8341 were responsible for providing security services for the top leaders, it is reasonable to speculate that the range of guarding the top leaders expanded as the political chaos affected the security of top leaders.

Like Wang Dongxing, who selectively cultivated trusted followers from his subordinates to maintain the cohesion of the Central Guard Bureau and Unit 8341, Commander Fu Chongbi carefully nurtured the loyalty of some of his subordinates. Fu always assigned important tasks to his trusted followers, especially to former subordinates from the 63rd Army Corps, of which he was commander between 1950 and 1966.[99] Considering Fu's powerful influence and possible resistance from the BGC, Fu may have been completely in the dark about his dismissal before he was called to go to the People's Hall to "receive directives from central leaders." Fu was sent to Shenyang immediately after his "transfer" was announced at the People's Hall.[100] In 1974, Fu returned to Beijing, no longer the BGC commander; nor did he hold any other position at the BGC. Nonetheless, most leaders of the two divisions remained close with Fu, and so he was able to maintain his influence on both the Second Guard and the Fourth Guard Divisions.[101]

By February 1967, the tension between the radicals supported by Mao and the old marshals had become evident. This tension ultimately triggered a conflict on February 16, 1967, between a group of party and army veterans and the radicals. Mao had already begun to distrust the faction of the former North China Field Army, which included Nie Rongzhen, CMC leaders, and old marshals. In addition, he was concerned about the possibility of collective resistance from the old marshals and the PLA's senior leaders. All these factors pushed Mao to reconsider his control over the BGC. The tension between Lin Biao and Yang Chengwu further fueled Mao's determination to purge the faction of the former North China Field Army. The purges of this faction seem

[97] For example, the CRG ordered the BGC to imprison Peng Zhen, Peng Dehuai, and Huang Kecheng.
[98] Ibid., pp. 212–13, 216–17.
[99] For example, he often gave important assignments to Third Political Commissar Huang Zuozheng and Associate Political Commissar Zhou Shuqing, both of whom were transferred from the 63rd Army Corps. More important, Fu had powerful influence over two of the three divisions in the BGC – the 2nd and 4th Guard Divisions. Both divisions originated in the North China Field Army, whereas the predecessor of the 4th Guard Division was the 189th Division of the 63rd Army Corps. The 189th Division was led by Fu Chongbi before he was transferred to lead the BGC.
[100] Fu was told that he would be transferred to Shenyang Military Region to be deputy commander. After the announcement, he was immediately sent to Shenyan, where he was imprisoned for more than six years.
[101] See Fu Chongbi, *Fu Chongbi huiyilu*, p. 250.

to have been planned in November 1967, when Wen Yucheng, one of Lin Biao's trusted followers, was promoted to deputy chief of staff in charge of the Combat Department. The dismissal of Yang Chengwu was anticipated, because he had been responsible for the Combat Department under the General Staff Department for more than ten years.[102]

Fu Chongbi was dismissed in March 1968, and Wen Yucheng, deputy chief of staff, was appointed to take charge concurrently of the BGC. Huang Yongsheng, another close, trusted follower of Lin Biao, was also promoted to take charge of the PLA General Staff Department. By this point, it had become clear that Mao seemed to have very limited choices for ensuring the loyalty of the PLA, and relying greatly on Lin Biao and his followers was the best option. Wen Yucheng was an important figure in the BGC at the time, as he represented Lin Biao in many executive powers. Being commander of the BGC had some undesirable effects, such as making Wen a target for the CRG, especially Jiang Qing, because the CRG wanted more political leverage, especially with the PLA. The power struggle for dominance in the Ninth Party Congress between Lin's group and the CRG intensified. For one, Lin Biao and Ye Qun suspected that Wen was shifting from Lin's group to the CRG, which was political sui- cide for Wen, especially considering that switching one's political leader is an unforgivable act in Chinese political culture. Wen Yucheng was requested to convey a letter written by Li Bida, the secretary of Huang Yongsheng, to Jiang Qing. This letter claimed that Ye Qun and Huang Yongsheng had engaged in activities against Jiang Qing. After six months of mental struggle, Wen decided to give the letter to Lin Biao rather than Jiang Qing. Wen was exposed by Li Bida, who had sent similar letters to the one in question to Jiang Qing. Upon hearing the news, Jiang was outraged and swore that she would kill Wen. Later, Wen not only failed to get into the Politburo; in June 1970, he was demoted and transferred to the Chengdu Military Region as a deputy commander.[103] After Lin Biao's death, Jiang Qing forced Zhou Enlai to order Wen's imprisonment in October 1971.[104]

Mao increased his vigilance against Lin Biao's dominance in the PLA pre- dominantly by fostering competing military factions to contain Lin. These com- peting factions included the former Fourth Front Army, led by Xu Xiangqian,

[102] Chen Hong, "Yang Chengwu yanzhong de 'Yang, Yu, Fu' shijian" ["The Yang, Yu, Fu affairs" in the eyes of Yang Chengwu], in *Yanhuang chunqiu* [Spring and autumn in China], no. 6 (2000), pp. 7–8.

[103] Although Wen kept his loyalty to Lin Biao, he tried to straddle Lin Biao's group and the radicals, led by Jiang Qing. However, Wu Faxian believes that Wen switched his support from Jiang Qing to Lin Biao because Wen failed to become a member of the Central Committee in the Ninth Party Congress during April 1969 and thus was convinced that Jiang Qing was not capable of helping him. See Wu Faxian, *Suiyue jiannan – Wu Faxian huiyilu* [Difficult years – The memoirs of Wu Faxian] (Hong Kong: Beixing chubanshe, 2006), vol. 2, pp. 734, 747; Zhang Yunsheng, *Maojiawan jishi* [True account of Maojiawan: The memoirs of Lin Biao's secretary] (Beijing: Chunqiu chubanshe, 1988), pp. 215–20.

[104] See Tao Zhuwen, "Wen Yucheng chenfu lu" [Rise and fall of Wen Yucheng], in *Dangshi tiandi* [Field of party history], no. 10 (2000), p. 18.

and the Second Field Army, headed by Liu Bocheng and Deng Xiaoping. Mao relied on his personal contacts with generals from local military regions, such as Xu Shiyou, Chen Xilian, Li Desheng, Pi Dingjun, and Wu Zhong, all of whom served in the former Fourth Front Army and the Second Field Army. The BGC's commander Wu Zhong and political commissar Yang Junsheng served in the Fourth Front Army, led by Zhang Guotao, before 1938, and then in the 129th Division of the Second Field Army led by Liu Bocheng and Deng Xiaoping during the Sino-Japanese War, and finally in the Civil War in the 1940s. Thus, Wu and Yang had no personal ties with either Lin Biao's faction or the North China Field Army faction.

Before Wu Zhong was promoted from deputy commander to commander of the BGC, Lin Biao appointed Wen Yucheng, one of Lin's longtime followers, to take charge of the BGC. This appointment occurred after Fu Chongbi was dismissed and after several of Fu's close associates had been dismissed because of their close ties with Fu, and given the growing dominance of Lin Biao's group in the PLA.[105] Wu Zhong was the commander of the 40th Army Corps before he was promoted to deputy commander of the BGC in April 1968.[106] The appointment of Wu Zhong can be viewed as a significant move by the Chairman to contain the increasing dominance of Lin Biao's faction in the PLA. A similar move of Mao's was to protect Xu Shiyou, commander of the Nanjing Military Region. He promoted Xu to the Politburo in April 1969 and moved Li Desheng, commander of the 12th Army Corps, to the Administrative Office of the CMC (*junwei banshichu*), which Lin's followers had controlled. In April 1970 Mao promoted Li to director of the CCP General Political Department.[107]

As Lin's group dominated the PLA leadership after Yang and Fu were dismissed, Mao expended much energy to facilitate the BGC's gaining of a larger government roles, undoubtedly in an effort to contain the PLA, which then was controlled by Lin Biao. Lin's dominance over the PLA and influence among party leadership put him in a dangerous position with respect to Mao's increasing vigilance. Lin's dominance, compounded by the lack of checks and balances on his power among the PLA leadership, encouraged his arbitrary military decisions and fueled Ye Qun's burning ambitions to consolidate Lin's position as Mao's successor. It is no surprise, then, that Lin's dominance of the PLA, along with his powerful influence in the party leadership after the withdrawal of the old marshals, was a key reason for Mao's discontentment with him. It is not surprising that the BGC became Mao's key armed force against Lin's group once the conflict intensified between Mao and Lin.

---

[105] Fu Chongbi, *Fu Chongbi huiyilu*, 252.
[106] Qu Aiguo, *Baizhan jiangxing – Wu Zhong* [Star of generals who experienced a hundred battles – Wu Zhong] (Beijing: Jiefangjun wenyi chubanshe, 2000), pp. 362–4.
[107] Li Wenqing, *Jinkan Xu Shiyou – 1967–1985* [A close observation on Xue Shiyou – 1967–1985] (Beijing: Jiefangjun wenyi chubanshe, 2002), pp. 81–3, 152; Xue Qingchao, "Angshou yu gaofeng yu digu zhijian – Li Desheng danren zhonggong zhongyang fuzhuxi qianhou (1)" [Strut between peak and valley – Before and after Li Desheng became a vice chairman of the CCP Central Committee, part 1], in *Lingdao kexue*, no. 11 (2002), pp. 32–3.

The BGC undoubtedly became an important weapon that Mao attempted to use against Lin Biao. To ensure his absolute control of the BGC, Mao ordered the BGC to receive commands directly only from Zhou Enlai rather than from his superiors: the General Staff Department and the Office of the CMC, controlled by Lin's followers and the Beijing Military Region. The leadership conflict that ended in Lin Biao's death in an airplane crash on September 13, 1971, proved the great extent to which Mao relied on the BGC for his security. Under Mao's orders, ten divisions were maneuvered to guard Beijing under the leadership of the BGC.[108] Fewer than three hours after Lin's airplane took off from Beidaihe, the BGC was ordered to take control of Beijing. This included taking over Beijing's five airports; searching for evidence regarding Lin's "crime"; sending additional troops to guard Zhongnanhai and the People's Hall; and controlling media outlets, such as the Xinhua News Agency, the *People's Daily*, the Central Radio Station, and the Beijing Telegram Tower.[109] More important, the BGC was authorized to command an additional six divisions dispatched from the Beijing Military Region, which expanded its control to cover the prefecture of Nankou, the Capital Airport, and the prefecture of Baoding in Hebei.[110]

Furthermore, the BGC was ordered to stop the military maneuver or dispatchment from any military authority in the capital. This led to an incident in which the BGC disarmed an army unit of the air force that was searching for Lin Biao's followers, originally dispatched by Li Desheng, commander of the Beijing Military Region.[111] Following Mao's orders, the BGC imprisoned influential followers of Lin Biao who were in the PLA leadership, including Huang Yongsheng, Wu Faxian, Li Zuopeng, Qiu Huizuo, and twenty other high-ranking PLA generals.[112] After Lin Biao's death, Wu Zhong became the de facto commander of all PLA units in Beijing. However, despite the fact that Mao depended on the BGC for securing Beijing more than other military units after the death of Lin Biao, he still did not completely trust the BGC; therefore, he put strict limits on leaders in terms of their power over maneuvers and the organization of their military units. According to the stipulations on the authority of calling on the BGC, the leaders of the BGC were allowed only to move or use a maximum of one squad. Although the use of a platoon had to be approved by the PLA's chief of staff, the use of a company had to be approved by Mao himself.[113]

[108] Zhu Yuanshi et al., *Wu De koushu: shinian fengyu wangshi – Wozai Beijing gongzuo de yixie jingli*, p. 141.
[109] Ibid., pp. 141–2; Qu Aiguo, *Baizhan jiangxing – Wu Zhong*, pp. 373–5.
[110] Zhu Yuanshi et al., *Wu De koushu: shinian fengyu wangshi – Wozai Beijing gongzuo de yixie jingli*, p. 141.
[111] Qu Aiguo, *Baizhan jiangxing – Wu Zhong*, pp. 379–81.
[112] Ibid., pp. 385–8.
[113] See "Wu Zhong zhuihuailu" bianxie zhu, *Wu Zhong zhuihuailu* [Memoirs that bring Wu Zhong to mind], p. 213; Lin Jiajie, "Wenge zhong de Beijing weishuqu silingyuan Wu Zhong"

Before Lin's death, Mao had tried to reduce the possible influence of the Beijing Military Region on the BGC, a result of their organizational affiliations. The Beijing Military Region had been the immediate superior of the BGC, and the commander and political commissar of the BGC was concurrently the deputy commander and associate political commissar of the Beijing Military Region. When Commander Wu Zhong and Political Commissar Chen Junsheng were appointed to take charge of the BGC, by convention the Beijing Military Region appointed them as deputy commander and associate political commissar of the Beijing Military Region, respectively. Surprisingly, Mao rejected this idea; according to Wu Zhong, Mao "did not want the BGC to have any working relationship with the Beijing Military Region," even though the BGC was organizationally subordinate to the Beijing Military Region.[114] Mao's reasons were many: he refused to see the BGC controlled by the PLA leadership, which Lin dominated, or by the powerful Beijing Military Region. As Wu Zhong recalled:

Organizationally, the BGC was subordinate to the Beijing Military Region. To build an intimate relationship between the Beijing Military Region and the BGC, Comrade Zheng Weishan therefore made the suggestion [to appoint Wu Zhong and Yang Junsheng as a deputy commander and a deputy political commissar of the Beijing Military Region, respectively]. However, the Chairman [Mao] rejected it. This rejection reflected his careful consideration. The grand old Chairman didn't allow any working relations between the BGC and the Beijing Military Region and wanted to make sure that the BGC was absolutely controlled directly by the Center and the CMC.[115]

The BGC played an increasingly important role in elite politics, as it was fully authorized to guard many high-ranking leaders, key government buildings, and the offices of the official media.

After Mao died on September 9, 1976, Hua Guofeng, the previous prime minister of the People's Republic of China (preceded by Zhou Enlai) and first vice chairman of the CCP, assumed the position of chairman of the Communist Party and the CMC from Mao, at Mao's behest. Mao's death set the stage for a power struggle between the Gang of Four and the comparatively moderate faction in the CCP leadership. Specifically, Hua Guofeng, Marshal Ye Jianying, and Wang Dongxing were the vanguard faction set to oust the Gang of Four. They relied heavily on three units of the CCP's elite security forces – the Central Guard Bureau, Unit 8341, and the BGC. When the alliance of Hua Guofeng, Ye Jianying, and Wang Dongxing discussed details of the arrest the Gang of Four, Marshal Ye Jianying was particularly concerned about possible action (i.e., entering Beijing in support of the Maoist radicals) by the 6th Armored Division, which was stationed in Changping, a county well-known as northern gate of Beijing. The BGC was responsible for overseeing the Sixth Armored Division

[Commander Wu Zhong of Beijing Garrison Command in the Cultural Revolution], in *Sichuan dangshi* [Party history of Sichuan], no. 4 (1994), p. 19.

[114] Qu Aiguo, *Baizhan jiangxing – Wu Zhong*, p. 366.

[115] Ibid., p. 366.

through its two armored divisions, so the BGC's support was fundamental to the trio's plan.[116]

As such, the three men proceeded to build their alliance, becoming a formidable power. Wang controlled Unit 8341, whereas Hua had to lobby the BGC for its support against the Gang of Four. Hua went about his work thoroughly and delicately: he asked General Su Zhenhua, a Politburo member and political commissar of the navy, to convince Wu Zhong's ally that Hua and Wang needed the support of the BGC. As de facto commander of all PLA units in Beijing, Wu Zhong could pledge the BGC's allegiance to any singular cause. As Wu Zhong's superior since 1947, General Su Zhenhua had the leverage to convince Wu Zhong's ally. Hua also ordered Wu De, mayor of Beijing Municipal City and first political commissar of the BGC, to lobby the support of Wu Zhong directly, as he was also in a position to influence Wu Zhong.[117] Under Wu De's arrangement, Hua met secretly with Wu Zhong; in that meeting, he secured the support of the BGC against the Gang of Four.[118] Not only did the BGC consent to assisting in the arrest of the Gang of Four; Wu also pledged the BGC's support for both the Central Guard Bureau and Unit 8341 if the arrests failed or if there were setbacks.[119] When Hua, Wang, and Ye finally decided to take military action against the Gang of Four and their followers, the Central Guard Regiment and the BGC were the key armed forces they used against the radicals. The Central Guard Regiment was assigned to arrest the radicals' leaders, and the BGC was responsible for imprisoning their followers and taking over the media.[120] In the end, the BGC was at the vanguard when it came to securing the arrests of the Gang of Four, which illustrates the instrumental influence of this military organization.

Beijing Garrison Command in the Post-Mao Era

After Deng Xiaoping was restored to his position in the CCP in July 1977, his first priority was to control the PLA and the security forces before challenging Hua Guofeng for the dominance of the CCP leadership. Luo Ruiqing was appointed general secretary of the CMC in August 1977, immediately after Deng Xiaoping took control over the PLA.[121] The Beijing Garrison Command also became a key security force that Deng strove to control. The available evidence suggests that the leadership of the BGC was reorganized in September

---

[116] Zhu Yuanshi et al., *Wu De koushu: Shinian fengyu wangshi – Wozai Beijing gongzuo de yixie jingli*, pp. 242–3; Qu Aiguo, *Baizhan jiangxing – Wu Zhong*, pp. 423–4.

[117] Qu Aiguo, *Baizhan jiangxing – Wu Zhong*, pp. 421–3.

[118] Zhu Yuanshi et al., *Wu De koushu: shinian fengyu wangshi – Wozai Beijing gongzuo de yixie jingli*, pp. 243–5.

[119] Ibid., p. 247.

[120] Qu Aiguo, *Baizhan jiangxing – Wu Zhong*, p. 425.

[121] Shu Yun, *Dajiang Luo Ruiqing* [Senior General Luo Ruiqing] (Beijing: Jiefangjun chubanshe, 1998), p. 402.

1977, when Commander Wu Zhong was replaced by Fu Chongbi, BGC commander until March 1968. Wu Zhong was accused of being a follower of the Gang of Four because of his active role in suppressing the mass demonstration in Tiananmen Square against radicals in April 1976. Deng Xiaoping was particularly critical of Wu Zhong and his work, especially when Wu was in charge of the BGC during the Cultural Revolution.[122] Ousting Wu Zhong from the BGC leadership might seem a counterintuitive move for Deng, but Deng had his reasons.

However, Deng should have kept Wu Zhong in control of the BGC while he was competing with Hua Guofeng for power. Wu had historical ties with the Second Field Army and with Deng. Wu's career began when his local guerrilla force was integrated into the Shanxi-Hebei-Shandong-Henan Military Region (the predecessor of the Second Field Army), led by Deng Xiaoping, in October 1945. In the late 1940s and 1950s, Wu had been known as one of the most talented junior officials in the Second Field Army, and because of that, he gradually attracted Deng's attention. In June 1947 Wu was promoted to commander of the Twentieth Brigade of the Zhongyuan Military Region, and in January 1949 he was promoted to commander of the Fifty-Second Division of the Second Field Army, under the leadership of Liu Bocheng and Deng Xiaoping. In June 1950, Wu was appointed to lead the advanced troops of the Second Field Army to Tibet for the CCP's military action against the Tibetan government. After Wu successfully commanded the PLA units at the northern front against the Tibetan troops and subsequently occupied Changdu, in Tibet, he was given the opportunity to study in the Nanjing Military Institute.

Following his education, he gradually became a rising star in the PLA's program of military modernization. Wu became commander of PLA's first machinery division in May 1955, and three months later – two months before his thirty-fourth birthday – he became major general (the youngest general of the 1,044 who became generals in 1955). Wu had been commander of the 40th Army Corps, but he was transferred to the BGC in 1968.[123] More important, Wu Zhong had never had political ties with either Lin Biao's group or the Gang of Four; rather, he played a vanguard role against both groups, despite the fact that he had been a beneficiary of the Cultural Revolution. From any perspective, Deng should have kept Wu Zhong in the post rather than dismiss him: Deng needed the BGC's support (and Wu Zhong's support) to compete for the dominance in the party leadership with Hua Guofeng. Deng's dismissal of Wu is still highly debated to this day.

Evidence shows that after Deng had been "rehabilitated" and returned to power in 1975, Deng and Wu had a good relationship. Deng's return had the backdrop of the economic decline and political chaos, brought by Mao's Cultural Revolution policies, which led party leaders to favor Deng. Wu supported

---

[122] Fu Chongbi, *Fu Chongbi huiyilu*, p. 255.
[123] Qu Aiguo, *Baizhan jiangxing – Wu Zhong*, pp. 118, 206, 288–9, 294–326, 328–9.

Deng's program of the PLA's readjustment (*zheng dun*), and as an initiative to back Deng, he reorganized five party committees at the regiment level and 104 party branches at the company level in the BGC. The readjustment program that Deng and other seniors were advocating called for economic modernization on the basis of emphasizing profits, putting experts in command, continuing to rehabilitate the veterans who were dismissed in the Cultural Revolution, improving military efficiency and combat forces, and expanding foreign trade and even some preliminary foreign investment. By the summer of 1975, opposition from the Maoist radicals against Deng and other revisionists had intensified. At that point, Deng viewed Wu Zhong as a trusted follower: he ordered Chen Xilian to call on Wu Zhong to "strengthen the work of security and guard in particular" against the Gang of Four. Chen Xilian was commander of the Beijing Military Region and general of the former Second Field Army; he also was a longtime trusted subordinate of Deng Xiaoping. Chen Xilian conveyed Deng's words to Wu Zhong:

Right now the battle within the Center is very intense. As you know, there is an issue of the "Shanghai Gang." You must be prepared and strengthen the work of security and guard in particular.[124]

Understanding Deng's concern, Wu immediately discussed Deng's directives with his associates in charge of security in the BGC, and he strengthened his control over the BGC's armed security forces.[125] However, Wu also passed Deng's words to Liu Chuanxin, director of Beijing Bureau of Public Security and a trusted friend of his.[126]

Liu Chuanxin was associate political commissar of the 27th Army Corps before he was transferred to the military-controlled Beijing Bureau of Public Security as a PLA representative in February 1967. According to an official publication, Liu was favored by radical leaders such as Kang Sheng, Jiang Qing, and Xie Fuzhi, given his role as a vanguard against party veterans. As a result, he was quickly promoted to take over Beijing Bureau of Public Security.[127] Perhaps motivated by his political orientation, Liu reported Deng's "conspiracy" to the Gang of Four, and it became an important piece of evidence against Deng when the radicals targeted him in late 1975 and early 1976.[128]

It is unclear how much of a role Deng's alleged conspiracy to organize security forces against the Gang of Four played in Mao's dismissal of Deng. Mao was cautious of Deng and had gradually taken away his leadership responsibilities, but only in December 1975 did he finally dismiss Deng. After December

---

[124] Ibid., p. 417.
[125] Ibid., p. 417.
[126] Ibid., pp. 417–18.
[127] See Cai Mingzhong, "Liu Chuanxin, wei 'siren bang' xunzang de gong'an juzhang" [Director of public security who sacrificed his life for the Gang of Four], in *Yanhuang chunqiu* [Spring and autumn in China], no. 1 (1994), p. 82.
[128] Qu Aiguo, *Baizhan jiangxing – Wu Zhong*, pp. 417–18.

1975, Deng was temporarily kept in his position and was still in charge of many important events. At the same time, though, he was asked to receive criticism and to make self-criticisms in Politburo meetings. On January 21, 1976, Mao announced that Deng no longer was in charge of day-to-day administration, only of foreign affairs. In late February 1976, Mao called many "known before-hand" meetings among high-ranking leaders (the informal meetings initiated by Mao to lobby support from the high-ranking leaders against Deng) and formally launched the campaign of anti-right deviationist wind against Deng Xiaoping.[129] According to Wu De, upon realizing that Mao was considering his dismissal, Deng's first response was to voluntarily retire from his most "sensitive" positions in the PLA.[130] These positions, of course, included his control over security forces. Deng was fully aware of his imminent losses once Mao confronted him, so his strategy was to concede these losses and withdraw his authority over security forces before the Chairman could do so. In adopting this strategy, Deng actually had the advantage of potentially relieving Mao's suspicion of him, thus mitigating his long-term losses.

Wu Zhong's divulgence of Deng's words had a huge impact on Wu's career and on Deng's view on Wu. Veteran leaders denounced Wu as a follower of the Gang of Four, thus rendering him an untrustworthy associate.[131] More costly for Wu was his damaged relationship with Deng Xiaoping. He regretted his action, and he recognized it as a grave mistake, given the blow it dealt to Deng. Available evidence illustrates that Wu was an active supporter of Deng, and he probably had not smeared Deng's name intentionally or had not fully understood the consequences of his actions. After Deng returned to office in 1974, he had been active in supporting Deng and Deng's programs. In 1976, after Mao dismissed Deng for the second time, Wu persisted in resisting the BGC's campaign against Deng.[132] According to Wu De, Wu Zhong's discontent with the Gang of Four was predominately caused by the 1975 campaign launched against Deng Xiaoping after Wu Zhong was an unwitting informant. These events affected Wu Zhong, and therefore became a key factor in his vanguard role against the Gang of Four in October 1976.[133] Although his loyalty toward Deng was unquestionable, he had lost all credibility in Deng's eyes when he divulged Deng's plan.

As a result, once Deng was in power, Wu relinquished all of his duties. After he was put under investigation, he was transferred to the Guangzhou Military Region, where he took a symbolic position as one of several deputy

---

[129] See Peng Xianzhi and Jin Chongji, *Mao Zedong zhuan (1949–1976)* [A biography of Mao Zedong] (Beijing: Zhongyang wenxian chubanshe, 2003), vol. 2, pp. 1765–6.

[130] See Zhu Yuanshi et al., *Wu De koushu: Shinian fengyu wangshi – Wozai Beijing gongzuo de yixie jingli*, p. 195.

[131] Qu Aiguo, *Baizhan jiangxing – Wu Zhong*, pp. 418–19.

[132] Ibid., pp. 416–18.

[133] See Zhu Yuanshi et al., *Wu De koushu: Shinian fengyu wangshi – Wozai Beijing gongzuo de yixie jingli*, p. 243.

commanders. Wu was dismissed in January 1979, but he left his position as a deputy commander of the Guangzhou Military Region in January 1980. He spent more than eight years under party-ordered parole, and in September 1987 he was ordered to retire at the age of sixty-seven.[134] Wu's treatment was obviously related to his perceived unfaithfulness: although there were plenty of cases similar to his, those offenders were treated better than he was. For example, Chen Xilian and Li Desheng, commander of the Beijing Military Region and commander of the Shenyang Military Region, respectively, were also both trusted subordinates of Deng's from his tenure with the Second Field Army, and they later were beneficiaries of the Cultural Revolution. Because of their leading positions in the Cultural Revolution, both Chen and Li were suspected of having been involved in persecuting military and party veterans, as well as in carrying out radical initiatives. Nonetheless, Deng immediately protected them after he returned to power, especially in regards to shielding them from potential purges.[135] Furthermore, when Deng launched the campaign to root out the followers of the Gang of Four in Shenyang Military Region, he urged campaigners to "hunt out all the persons and facts"[136] On the contrary, Deng prevented Li Desheng from becoming a target, even though he should have been one due to his role as the beneficiary of the Cultural Revolution and his inevitable cooperation with the radical Maoists during the periods when he was in charge of the Anhui Revolutionary Committee and the PLA General Political Department during the Cultural Revolution. Deng did so by personally interfering with the process of the campaign by informing Gan Weihan, second political commissar of Shenyang Military Region, "Comrade Li Desheng is clean and has no involvement with the Gang of Four."[137] Unlike Wu Zhong, whom Deng dismissed and forced to retire, both Chen and Li were allowed to keep their posts, and later they even enjoyed the prestige of being inducted into the Party Consultant Committee, where they served until it was abolished in 1992. In 1985, to ensure that Li would be honored as a full general upon his retirement and therefore be bestowed with the highest PLA honor, Deng appointed sixty-nine-year-old Li political commissar of the National Defense College, a position that would qualify Li as a full general three years later, when the PLA resumed his program to adopt military ranks.[138]

[134] Qu Aiguo, *Baizhan jiangxing – Wu Zhong*, pp. 431–9, 449–52.
[135] For example, Deng called Chen to his residence, told Chen the accusations the leadership had against him, and advised him on how to mitigate the damages while assuring Chen of his support. Chen Xilian, *Chen Xilian huiyilu* [Memoirs of Chen Xilian], pp. 495–6.
[136] *Deng Xiaoping nianpu, 1975–1997*, vol. 1, p. 251.
[137] Xue Qingchao, "Angshou yu gaofeng yu digu zhijian – Li Desheng danren zhonggong zhongyang fuzhuxi qianhou" (3) (Strut between peak and valley – Before and after Li Desheng became vice chairman of the CCP Central Committee, part 3), in *Lingdao kexue*, no. 15 (2002), p. 35.
[138] Chen Xilian, *Chen Xilian huiyilu*, pp. 486–7; Li Desheng, *Li Desheng huiyilu* [Memoirs of Li Desheng], pp. 514–16.

TABLE 7.2. *Beijing Garrison Command, August and September 1977*

Position	August 1977	September 1977
Commander	Wu Zhong	Fu Chongbi
First political commissar	Wu De	Wu De
Second political commissar	n/a	Wu Lie
Political commissar	Yang Junsheng, Huang Zuozheng, Liu Shaowen	Yang Junsheng, Huang Zuozheng, Liu Shaowen
First deputy commander	n/a	Li Zhongxuan
Deputy commander	Li Zhongqi, Pan Yongti, Zeng Shaodong, Liu Guangpu	Li Zhongqi, Pan Yongti, Zeng Shaodong, Liu Guangpu
Associate political commissar	Zhou Pingguang, Chen Jie, Wang Yizhi	Zhou Pingguang, Chen Jie, Wang Yizhi

Source: Beijingshi difangzhi bianzuan weiyuanhui, *Beijing zhi* [Annals of Beijing] (Beijing: Beijing chubanshe, 2002), vol. 30, 131–5; Wu Lie, *Zhengrong suiyue*, pp. 478–81.

Besides the move that appointed Fu Chongbi to take charge of the BGC, two other significant initiatives by the CMC, led by Deng Xiaoping, demonstrate Deng's deftness at assuming control over the BGC (Table 7.2). These were the transfers of Wu Lie, political commissar of the Wuhan Military Region, and Li Zhongxuan, deputy director of the Second Department (*er bu*), under the PLA General Staff Department. Wu Lie (who was the commander of BGC in January 1959 and December 1961) and Li Zhongxuan were appointed to second political commissar and first deputy commander of the BGC, respectively, two positions that had been vacant since the early 1970s.[139] Moreover, Deng's decision to take control of the BGC signified the critical role of the BGC in elite politics. By the winter of 1977, the BGC comprised twenty-three regiments with more than 63,800 armed personnel – overall, a significant armed force very useful for dominating CCP leadership.[140] Deng's adroit strategy to control the BGC was a great boon to his securing of the leadership after the Cultural Revolution.

The final significant move by Deng Xiaoping to control the BGC was his effort to redefine the assignments and responsibilities of the BGC. The BGC's role was redefined so that it was returned to the jurisdiction of the PLA. With the BGC once again falling under the jurisdiction of the PLA General Staff Department, it was directly in Deng's control, as he was general chief

[139] Beijingshi defangzhi bianzuan weiyuanhui [Compiling Commission of Beijing Local Annals], *Beijingzhi* [Annals of Beijing] (Beijing: Beijing chubanshe, 2002), vol. 30, pp. 131–5.
[140] Wu Lie, *Zhengrong suiyue*, pp. 482–3.

of staff of the PLA. The security forces, including the Beijing Garrison Command, became a crucial power base in supporting the veteran leaders' initiative to delegitimize Hua Guofeng and the so-called two whatevers.[141] Joseph Fewsmith has observed that the process of delegitimizing Hua Guofeng and legitimizing Deng Xiaoping "illuminates the interconnections between formal position, informal politics, political issues, and ideology."[142] The formal institutional support and the informal maneuver of the security apparatuses and the influential leading security figures (both incumbents and those dismissed in the Cultural Revolution), such as Luo Ruiqing, Yang Shangkun, and Fu Chongbi, became an important political force on which the veteran leaders relied in moving against Hua Guofeng. Although Deng possessed enormous political assets, as Maurice Meisner points out, Hua Guofeng was burdened with significant political liabilities, including the lack of a real power base in the bureaucracy and any significant popular support in society at large.[143] After Deng Xiaoping achieved his dominance in the CCP leadership, he realized that a powerful security force that overrode the Beijing Military Region and the party security services not only was unhealthy but also could be potentially harmful to the security of the party leadership. In January 1978, the BGC was reorganized as a subordinate unit of the Beijing Military Region. As such the Beijing Military Region was responsible for commanding the BGC regarding "party and political affairs, appointments and promotions, combat command, training, organization and equipment, administration, logistics, recruitment and demobilization, and militia."[144]

In addition to its compliance with the authority of the Beijing Military Region, the BGC was also under the command of the PLA General Staff Department and the CCP Central General Office. According to the Regulation of Leadership and Commanding Relations of the BGC and Its Limited Authority in Making or Approving Its Dispatchment, issued on January 23, 1978, the General Staff Department commanded the BGC in its security guard duties, even though the BGC was organizationally subordinate to the Beijing Military Region. Except for its responsibilities in guarding the residences of the CCP chairman and the central leaders, as dictated by the CCP General Office, the BGC received all commands from the PLA General Staff Department. In February 1983, the BGC was significantly reduced; it handed over its 2nd Guard Division and three regiments in charge of internal security to the Beijing Bureau of Public Security. In 1985, the BGC was ordered to send its 4th Division back to the 63rd Army Corps and resume its previous name

---

[141] Two whatevers were Mao's followers who attempted to uphold "whatever policy decisions Mao Zedong had made and whatever instructions he had given." The core members of this faction included Hua Guofeng, Wang Dongxing, Chen Xilian, and Wu De.

[142] Joseph Fewsmith, *Elite Politics in Contemporary China*, p. 40.

[143] Maurice J. Meisner, *Mao's China and After: A History of the People's Republic*, p. 432.

[144] See Fu Chongbi, *Fu Chongbi huiyilu*, p. 252.

as the 189th Division.[145] Deng Xiaoping was determined to reduce the BGC's jurisdiction, even though the large-scale reduction of personnel in the BGC brought about internal resistance. The resistance from BGC personnel resulted in a drawn-out handover that took more than two years because of "the obstruction and difficulties caused by a cleavage of opinions from leadership members."[146] In the post-Deng era, the BGC, the Central Guard Regiment, and the General Beijing Corps of the People's Armed Police have been required to cooperate in guarding Beijing while they are watchdogs for the other security forces, supervising each other to prevent any one organization from becoming a threat to the party leadership.

---

[145] Wei Yingyi, "Shengsheng huainian Pan Yan tongzhi" [Deeply think of Comrade Pan Yan], in He Ting (ed.), *Pan Yan jiangjun jinian wenji* [Collected works in commemorating General Pan Yan], pp. 222–3.

[146] Liang Bing, *He Zhengwen jiangjun* [General He Zhengwen] (Beijing: Zuojia chubanshe, 2004), pp. 334–5.

8

CCP Intelligence Agencies and Services in the Revolutionary Era

A study of China's intelligence services is beyond the scope of this work. But insofar as elite politics is concerned, intelligence collection and protection provided by the intelligence services has evolved into an integral part of the conceptualization of security issues and leadership decision making, and it is a significant source of power and influence in China's elite politics.

This chapter assesses the importance of CCP intelligence organizations and services in the Chinese communist revolution as well as the crucial role they played in party leadership politics at the time. The CCP intelligence organizations were created in response to the Nationalist government's assault against the communists in 1927. Although CCP security forces were created after the Guomindang (GMD) attack, including some communist terrorist groups engaging in assassinations (such as the "Red Brigade" – an assassination corps that liquidated traitors and killed the GMD agents), they did not function well because of the lack of intelligence and information. Most problematic for the security agencies were the communist turncoats, who were sent back to the CCP as spies for Nationalist intelligence organizations. This led to the establishment in April 1928 of the Intelligence Cell of the Special Services Division, which engaged in espionage and antiespionage activities. The Intelligence Cell enabled the CCP leadership to uncover information related to GMD agents and movements. The establishment of the Intelligence Cell not only enabled the Red Brigade to increase the accuracy and focus of its operations but also uncovered information about enemy initiatives. The cell also was able to protect the CCP and its armed forces in the base areas against attacks. An important task of the Intelligence Cell was to establish an antiespionage network to access classified information of both the GMD intelligence organizations and the Shanghai Municipal Police, which governed the Shanghai International Settlement and worked in coordination with GMD intelligence.

The Central Committee's Special Services Division (SSD, or Teke) was created in November 1927, but was severely damaged by the GMD intelligence organization after Gu Shunzhang, one of the Teke's leading figures, was captured and then defected to the GMD in April 1931. It was reorganized in June 1931 to strengthen the party's control over the CCP top security and intelligence apparatuses and to respond decisively to the successful assaults of the GMD intelligence organizations, which paralyzed the CCP's underground activities in GMD-controlled areas. Compared with the Teke in Shanghai, where the party headquarters was located, CCP intelligence in the base areas developed differently and was merged with the all-powerful and greatly feared security apparatus in the communist base areas, the Political Security Department – which was later renamed the State Political Security Bureau (SPSB). Established to guard CCP leading figures and organizations in base areas, the Political Security Department provided intelligence to directly ensure leaders' security. It was controlled by the Party Central Committee but received dual leadership from the party and from the Soviet government in the base areas. The organizational structure and operations of CCP intelligence and security services were highly influenced by the Soviet experience: the NKVD was not subject to party control or restricted by law – instead, it was Stalin's personal instrument to root out enemies of his regime. The security and intelligence apparatuses in the base areas helped propagate the so-called extension of counterrevolutionary campaigns that wreaked havoc in the communist base areas during the 1930s.

The rise and fall of the State Political Security Bureau also reflected the power struggle in elite leadership politics. Mao took advantage of the SPSB's inactivity during the Long March as a result of the disappearance of the CCP Soviet government established in Jiangxi. He stopped the operation of the central security forces controlled by the SPSB and sent a large number of SPSB personnel to grassroots army units to weaken the influence of the CCP security and intelligence services, which Zhou Enlai controlled. When the CCP established its base area in the Shaanxi-Gansu-Ningxia border areas, the SPSB was abolished, and the responsibilities of the former SPSB local branches were assigned to the newly created Security Section, which was subordinate to the Political Department of local armed units. In the early Sino-Japanese War, the Security Section of each military unit was put under the authority of the Political Department and no longer enjoyed the same powerful and influential status as its predecessors.

The Social Affairs Department (SAD) was created in 1941 as an institutional guarantee of Mao's control over the intelligence and security apparatuses. By the time the Central Committee's Intelligence Department was established in July 1941, Mao had consolidated his leadership in the CCP and had secured his dominance in the security and intelligence apparatuses, despite Zhou Enlai's continued influence, which resulted from the profound intelligence network he had cultivated across the nation since the 1920s. The intelligence apparatuses became the vanguard and instrument of Mao's rectification campaign (1941–1944), which sought ideological unity, propped up Mao's loyal followers in the CCP's leadership, and purged his political enemies. However, Mao's most important political in gaining control over CCP intelligence in the 1940s was gaining Zhou Enlai's compliance and cooperation. This strategic move was a great boon for CCP intelligence services, as it allowed the organizations to recruit a large number of CCP agents, including defectors from the Nationalists; to conduct espionage in enemy-controlled areas; to establish a network of telecommunications linking major cities and parts of the countryside and the Nationalist command; and to develop an intelligence network that gained GMD top secrets. These intelligence efforts helped the CCP launch successful military campaigns against Nationalist armies and guarantee the safety of party leaders and organizations.

Establishment of the Special Services Division

It is important to recognize the nature of the beginnings of CCP intelligence. The CCP's first intelligence organization was established to govern a movement rather than a nation. The CCP's leading security service, the Work Section of Special Affairs (*tewu gongzuo chu*), was created in May 1927, under the CCP Central Military Department, to protect top leadership from increasing threats from the ruling GMD.[1] As with the security and intelligence services, before 1925 the CCP had never established an agency in charge of its military affairs, because early leaders of the Chinese communist movement did not intend to rely on an armed force to pursue dominance over the GMD. It was not until January 1925 when the CCP Fourth Party Congress decided to establish the CCP Central Military Department, which was formally established in June 1925 with Zhang Guotao, head of the Central Labor Department, as its director.[2] Besides its responsibility over military affairs, the Central Military Department was assigned to intelligence. Although the CCP had not prepared to build up armed forces until more than three years after its founding, it had experienced some activities related to military affairs and had established its own military organizations. Before the CCP leadership established the Central Military Department, its regional branch in Guangzhou – the CCP Guangdong Regional Commission (*zhonggong guangdong quwei*) – had established its own military department headed by Zhou Enlai and Nie Rongzhen.[3] According to the CCP leadership, headed by Chen Duxiu, however, the establishment of the Central Military Department was only a symbolic gesture to support the northern expedition that had been launched by nationalist armies, rather than an effort to mobilize CCP armed forces to vie

[1] Jeffrey T. Richelson, *A Century of Spies*, p. 24; *Gong'an shigao*, p. 12.
[2] Zhang Guotao, *Wode huiyi* [My reminiscence], vol. 2, p. 407.
[3] Ibid., p. 448.

for power. Arif Dirlik has observed that the important figures in the early communist movement had been greatly influenced by the anarchism that was embedded in the antiparty, antibureaucracy, and antidictatorship culture, and thus they sought to achieve the Cultural Revolution – not simply a revolution of ideas but a revolution affecting the ethical basis of society.[4] Organizing CCP members to become an armed force to pursue for power was hardly attractive for most leaders. Although the growing conflict between the CCP and the GMD had gradually undermined the united front, and the spread of the anti-CCP movement nationwide had threatened the survival of the CCP by 1926, pushing Chen Duxiu to emphasize "develop[ing] the CCP's own organization and unit[ing] with the masses of workers and peasants against the GMD Right,"[5] the establishment and development of a CCP armed force was still not considered.

Despite the CCP's successful mobilization of workers and peasants, Zhang Guotao believed that the CCP was not ready to develop into a military commanding headquarters during the united front with the nationalists in the 1920s.[6] Mainly relying on the united front for the CCP's survival and growth,[7] the CCP leadership, headed by Chen Duxiu, believed that the CCP needed to play a supportive role to the Nationalist Party and army against the warlords. Specifically, Chen Duxiu emphasized that the CCP should "not establish its own armed forces," instead limiting its efforts to organizing self-defense armed units comprising workers and peasants.[8] In the CCP-GMD united front against the warlords, Chen Duxiu attempted to push the independent development of the CCP. However, Chen ruled out any CCP initiative to develop its own armed force; rather, he paid great attention to the mobilization of workers and peasants, particularly to the effort to mobilize the peasant movement and use peasant associations to undercut warlords' power in the countryside and to provide a social basis for the left-wing GMD.[9] Compared with the GMD, the CCP was unable to compete in terms of military strength; the CCP's little success in conducting warfare against its enemies largely resulted from the lack of telegraphic communication equipment and intelligence.[10]

Consequently, when CCP leadership decided to establish the Central Military Department, the leadership also made a concerted effort to strengthen its intelligence and security services. In 1925, the CCP sent Gu Shunzhang and Lu Liu of the Shanghai General Labor Union and Chen Geng, former graduate of the Whampoa (Huangpu) Military Academy in Guangzhou (and one of Zhou Enlai's trusted followers), to study secret services in the Soviet

[4] Arif Dirlik, *The Origins of Chinese Communism*, pp. 83–5, 93–4, 271.
[5] See Hans J. Van de Ven, *War and Nationalism in China, 1925–1945*, p. 111.
[6] Zhang Guotao, *Wode huiyi*, vol. 2, p. 403.
[7] Ibid., pp. 403–4.
[8] Li Weihan, *Huiyi yu yanjiu* [Recollection and research], vol. 1, pp. 80–3.
[9] Hans J. Van de Ven, *War and Nationalism in China, 1925–1945*, pp. 111–12.
[10] Zhang Guotao, *Wode huiyi*, vol. 2, p. 536.

Union.[11] With strong ties to secret societies, Gu had been an influential leader of the labor movement in Shanghai and was even selected by CCP leaders to be the bodyguard of Mikhail Markovich Borodin, the Soviet adviser since 1923.[12] In 1925 the Central Military Department was renamed the Central Military Commission (CMC), and shortly thereafter, in November 1926, it was concurrently the Shanghai District Military Commission. At that time Zhou Enlai replaced Zhang Guotao as head of the CMC. According to Zheng Chaolin, a leading figure from the early Chinese communist movement, the establishment of the Central Military Commission (CMC) in 1925 was an effort to respond to the increasing needs of the armed "uprising" against the warlords.[13]

Perhaps to avoid the impression that the CCP was organizing its own armed forces while its members still joined the Nationalist Party under the banner of the united front, the CMC's organization and personnel were secret to both nonparty members and to most party members. Among the three key organizations of Chinese communist movements – the Chinese Communist Party, the party's CMC, and the Communist Youth League – the CMC was only institution that did not publicize even to the party members.[14] According to Marshal Nie Rongzhen, the Central Military Commission was not a military body but an administrative office that dealt primarily with statistics related to military affairs, data collection, and assignments of its military personnel.[15] In other words, during the early communist movement, the Central Military Commission was not authorized to command armed forces; rather, it was engaged only in organizational work that required it to liaise with the communist armed forces. Only after November 1931, when the CMC was reorganized in the Jiangxi base areas, did it develop into a powerful leading body that commanded the communist armed forces across the country.[16]

At least two factors contributed to the underdevelopment of the CCP Military Department and Central Military Commission. First, in the early period of the movement, the CCP lacked personnel with military expertise. Although Moscow became the major site of training CCP leaders, the training programs focused primarily on communist ideology and theory. This is exemplified by the curricula of the universities many Chinese communists attended, including the University of the Toilers of the East, the Moscow Sun Yat-sen University, and the Moscow East University. In these universities, the curricula focused on

[11] Hao Zaijin, _Zhongguo mimi zhan – Zhonggong qingbao he baowei gongzuo jishi_ [China's secret war – A true account of China's intelligence and security guard], p. 31.
[12] Wang Binbin, "Jiaru Gu Shunzhang meiyou beibu" [If Gu Shunzhang had not been captured], in _Tongzhou gongjin_ [In the same boat], no. 4 (2008`), p. 41.
[13] Zheng Chaolin, _Zheng Chaolin huiyilu – 1919–1931_ [Memoirs of Zheng Chaolin, 1919–1931], pp. 112–13.
[14] Ibid., p. 112.
[15] _Nie Rongzhen huiyilu_, vol. 1, p. 43.
[16] Ibid., p. 57.

history of the Soviet Communist Party, Soviet revolutionary history, international revolutionary history, the history of labor movements, and the history of political economy.[17] When Stalin and the Comintern helped Sun Yat-sen establish the Whampoa Military Academy in Guangzhou, they needed to train the first group of instructors. Thus, some of the students at the University of the Toilers of the East were assigned to military training at Soviet military schools, such as the Red Army Academy in Moscow. The first group of twenty-three students from the CCP to study at the Red Army Academy included Nie Rongzhen, Ye Ting, Xiong Xiong, Fan Yi, and Yan Changyi.[18] When the trained students returned to China in July 1925, they became the primary personnel of the CCP Central Military Department and its local branches.[19] Clearly, then, as Zhang Guotao has pointed out, the CCP Central Military Department and its local branches were not well staffed from the outset, which resulted in the delay of the CCP Military Department's establishment.[20]

The second factor that contributed to the underdevelopment of the Central Military Commission related to the inherent mission of the CCP. Because the central objective of the CCP under Chen Duxiu's leadership was to mobilize workers and peasants to peacefully take over the government, establishing armed forces not only departed from party guidelines but also was pernicious to the CCP's legitimacy. This explains why some high-ranking leaders such as Mao, "who despised not only the worker movement but also any movement not related to 'the barrel of a gun,' were not favored [by Chen Duxiu] and thus were only assigned insignificant jobs in the early period of the Chinese communist movement."[21] On the basis of his personal experiences, Nie Rongzhen felt that Chen Duxiu was uninterested in the work of the CCP Military Department and its branches when Nie reported his work to Chen.[22] The establishment of the CMC, albeit in secret, was the product of a compromise in CCP leadership, with the dominant group headed by Chen Duxiu leading the opposition. These communist purists, so to speak, thought of the burgeoning CMC as a violent, armed "adventure" that might turn the CCP into a "bandit" party.[23] As to be expected with such a negative reception, the Central Military Department had never been taken seriously since its inception in the summer of 1925. According to Zhang Guotao, during the period of his leadership all he did was send a few

---

[17] Ibid., p. 37.
[18] Ibid., pp. 38–9.
[19] Ibid., p. 41.
[20] Zhang Guotao, *Wode huiyi*, vol. 2, pp. 536–7.
[21] Zheng Chaolin, *Zheng Chaolin huiyilu – 1919–1931*, p. 228.
[22] Nie met with Chen Duxiu twice, and both times Chen was not interested in listening to his ideas on the CCP's military. The first meeting happened when Nie returned from Moscow and was appointed by Chen to teach at the Huangpu Military School in September 1925; the second time was when Nie served as the head of the Hubei Military Commission and reported his work to Chen in 1927. See *Nie Rongzhen huiyilu*, vol. 1, pp. 42–3, 54.
[23] Zheng Chaolin, *Zheng Chaolin huiyilu – 1919–1931*, pp. 230–1.

comrades with military affairs knowledge to mobilize workers and peasants for cooperation with the Northern Expedition Army.[24]

In May 1927, the Politburo assigned Zhou Enlai to preside as director of the Central Military Department.[25] In response to the brutal yet successful assault launched by the Nationalists against the communists in the spring of 1927, the CCP leadership finally established security and intelligence organizations to ensure the security of leading party organs and top leaders. Thus, intelligence and espionage efforts were provoked by the nationalist attack. When CCP central leadership was forced to move from Shanghai to Wuhan to escape the nationalists' massacre, the Work Section of Special Affairs (*tewu gongzuo chu*) of the Central Military Department was established to protect top CCP leaders. They did this through espionage and counterespionage, specifically by spying on the Nationalist movements and preventing security breaches caused by nationalist intelligence organizations or communist turncoats. The Work Section of Special Affairs' tenure was short lived, as it was abolished only three months after CCP leadership moved back to Shanghai in August 1927. Nonetheless, it was important in building institutional knowledge about intelligence and security services, evidenced by the Central Military Department's involvement in the execution of a British spy who had attempted to assassinate members of the Soviet Advising Delegation and in the assignment to escort the Soviet adviser Mikhail Markovich Borodin to return to Moscow. It was this knowledge and experience that set the stage for the birth of the Special Services Division (*zhongyang teke*, or Teke) in November 1927.[26]

When the Central Committee's Special Work Commission (*zhongyang tebie gongzuo weiyuanhui*), headed by Xiang Zhongfa (general secretary), Zhou Enlai (member of the Politburo Standing Committee and director of the CCP Central Organization Department), and Gu Shunzhang (alternative member of the Politburo), was established to head the CCP's intelligence and secret services in November 1928, the Teke was put directly under its leadership.[27] In the Special Work Commission, Zhou Enlai had executive decision-making authority, Gu Shunzhang managed the day-to-day administration, whereas Xiang Zhongfa was only a symbolic and titular figure because of his position as CCP general secretary.[28] When the Teke was established in November 1927, it included three operational cells: General Affairs (*zongwu*) was responsible for the protection and safety of party leadership, Operations (*xingdong*) was responsible for the execution of enemies and communist defectors who were threats to security, and Internal Communication (*jiaotong*) was responsible for

[24] Zhang Guotao, *Wode huiyi*, vol. 2, p. 536.
[25] *Lingdao jigou yange*, p. 28.
[26] *Gong'an shigao*, p. 12; Hao Zaijin, *Zhongguo mimi zhan – Zhonggong qingbao he baowei gongzuo jishi*, p. 28.
[27] *Gong'an shigao*, p. 13; *Chen Yun zhuan*, vol. 1, pp. 105–6.
[28] *Nie Rongzhen huiyilu*, vol. 1, p. 118.

the establishment and operation of the telecommunication network. Operation Cell was also known as the Red Brigade and was specifically trained for assassination operations. The Teke's functions soon expanded to encompass emergency situations, given the increasing rate of arrest and defection among CCP members. The first few years after the nationalist betrayal, CCP leaders and organs were busy simply trying to escape the grasp of the Nationalist secret police. Thus, a large amount of the CCP's resources were devoted to establishing an antiespionage network at the very center of the GMD secret service. This financial allocation was not supported by all leaders, and it is illustrated by Xiang Ying's complaint that "most of CCP spending was tied up in intelligence," to the point that other aspects of the CCP's work, such as organizing workers and peasants, were severely ignored.[29] In addition, Zhou Enlai became increasingly influential with his leadership of the intelligence and security services and the Central Military Department of the CCP. Zhou's role in commanding the intelligence and military was the key factor for Stalin's high regard of Zhou and Stalin's endorsement for Zhou's enduring presence and influence in the CCP leadership.[30] Both Stalin and the Comintern had expected that Zhou would take over leadership of the CCP.[31]

The Teke, headed by Zhou Enlai, with Gu Shunzhang running operations, recruited mostly workers in Shanghai who had played an important role in the labor movement.[32] Under Zhou the Teke developed into a formidable intelligence and security organization with operations covering the CCP's Yangtze Bureau in Wuhan, the Northern Bureau in Beijing and Tianjin, and the Southern Bureau in Hong Kong, in addition to Shanghai.[33] The General Affairs Division, established immediately after the CCP moved from Wuhan to Shanghai, was responsible for purchasing equipment and materials, renting houses and offices for party leaders and organizations, rescuing arrested and jailed high-ranking party leaders, managing the remains of communists executed by the Nationalist government, and comforting the bereaved families of those

---

[29] Zhang Guotao, *Wode huiyi*, vol. 2, p. 766.

[30] Zhou Enlai was invited to give a speech at the Sixteenth Party Congress of the Soviet Union in Moscow in April 1930. According to Zhang Guotao, the invitation "was the first time that the CCP had received special treatment," and it was even more of an anomaly because "delegates from other communist countries had rarely received this kind of honor." Zhang believes that Zhou's leading role in the CCP leadership's intelligence and military apparatuses combined with his political skills were the source of Stalin's and the Comintern's political favor. See Zhang Guotao, *Wode huiyi*, vol. 2, p. 844.

[31] According to Zhang Guotao, both Stalin and the Comintern had showed their enthusiasm for Zhou's leading role in the CCP during Zhou's Moscow visit, even opening hoping for Zhou to "take over leadership responsibilities of the CCP." However, Zhou refused to become the CCP chief instead continually supporting either Li Lishan or Qu Qiubai to be the CCP chief while he remained backstage. See Zhang Guotao, *Wode huiyi*, vol. 2, p. 845.

[32] Zhongguo renmin gong'an shigao bianxie xiaozu, *Zhongguo renmin gongan shigao*, p. 12; *Chen Geng tongzhi zai Shanghai*, p. 10.

[33] *Chen Geng tongzhi zai Shanghai*, p. 6.

dead. The Red Brigade (Operations Cell) was responsible for assassinating nationalist agents, punishing communist deflectors, protecting and rescuing high-ranking leaders, and guarding leading organizations and important meetings. The objective of the Red Brigade's work was deterring crimes involving security breaches as much as it was dealing with nationalist agents and communist turncoats. According to Nie Rongzhen, one of the leading figures in the Teke in 1930, eliminating CCP deflectors was one of the most important tasks of the Teke because "traitors posed the most danger to the Party in enemy-controlled areas."[34] The Red Brigade successfully executed several communist turncoats who betrayed the party, resulting in the deaths of several important party leaders. By late 1929, the Red Brigade had increased its ranks to forty members and was equipped with variety of weapons, including pistols, revolvers, Mauser pistols, and grenades.[35] The Red Brigade was also ordered to assassinate Chiang Kai-shek in December 1930, when Chiang was launching the bandit suppression campaign against the Red Army in Jiangxi base areas.[36]

Despite the active role of the Red Brigade in protecting the CCP leaders and punishing those who betrayed the party, it could not effectively identify the most dangerous enemies and deal with hidden communist turncoats who were sent back to spy on the party by Nationalist intelligence organizations. This led to the establishment of the Intelligence Cell in April 1928, which engaged in espionage (by sending agents to the important nationalist organizations) and antiespionage intelligence activities, led by Chen Geng.[37] The Intelligence Cell enabled CCP leadership to uncover GMD agents and movements working in opposition to communist interests. Often the Teke could gain counterintelligence information and prevent nationalist movements before Nationalist intelligence organizations could arrest communist leaders and destroy their organizations.[38]

Intelligence Cell of the Special Services Division

Before the Intelligence Cell was created in April 1928, the CCP had engaged in some intelligence activities to protect important organizations and leaders. When the CCP was incapable of defending itself against the GMD's attack, the CCP established an intelligence organization to protect CCP leaders by preempting Nationalist assassinations.[39] In May 1927, a temporary special service agency focusing on intelligence and espionage was established under the leadership of the Central Military Commission, led by Zhou Enlai.[40] The

[34] *Nie Rongzhen huiyilu*, vol. 1, p. 119.
[35] *Chen Geng tongzhi zai Shanghai*, p. 15.
[36] Frederic E. Wakeman, *Policing Shanghai, 1927–1937*, p. 151.
[37] *Chen Geng tongzhi zai Shanghai*, pp. 10–11.
[38] Ibid., pp. 21–2.
[39] Ibid., pp. 21, 44–6.
[40] Ibid., pp. 10–11.

Intelligence Cell was soon established to "collect information, be aware of enemies' moves, and fight against enemy intelligence organizations"; it supplemented the Red Brigade's work by providing the eyes and ears to increase accuracy of the Red Brigade's operations.[41] More important, the Intelligence Cell could move to protect the CCP and sabotage enemy plans.

An important task of the Intelligence Cell was establishing an antiespionage network that enabled the CCP to access top classified information about both GMD intelligence organizations and the Shanghai Municipal Police that governed the Shanghai International Settlement.[42] According to the Central Circular (No. 25) issued on December 31, 1927, CCP leadership decided to send one or two agents to leading GMD organizations to engage in intelligence or counterintelligence to prevent imprisonment of communist leaders.[43] One of the major goals of the CCP was to infiltrate the Investigation Division (*diaocha ke*) of the GMD's Central Organizational Department, controlled by the powerful CC Clique.[44] The CC Clique, or Central Club Clique, was one of the most powerful political factions in the GMD. It supported Chiang Kai-shek and represented traditionalists, zealous anticommunists, and the landlord interest. The clique was controlled by two brothers, Chen Guofu and Chen Lifu, who were close associates of Chiang Kai-shek before his rise to power. As an immensely powerful institution, the CC Clique controlled appointments and promotions; held the largest block of votes in the Central Executive Committee; and dominated intelligence, trade, banking, the military, education, and propaganda.

The CCP Teke Intelligence Cell, led by Chen Geng, began sending agents such as Qian Zhuangfei, Li Kenong, and Hu Di to leading organizations of the GMD in late 1929.[45] The Intelligence Cell led by Chen Geng cultivated a network of agents within the anticommunist forces.[46] Qian Zhuangfei joined the Nationalist Party in 1925 and, with the help of Chen Geng, enrolled in training sponsored by the Shanghai Telecommunication Administration in the summer of 1928. After graduating, Qian was hired as secretary of the Shanghai Telecommunication Administration and quickly became a trusted subordinate of Xu Enzeng, director of the Shanghai Telecommunication Administration and cousin of Chen Lifu. Qian won Xu Enzeng's trust and advanced to become Xu's confidential secretary, charged with the day-to-day administration of Xu's office. When the Investigation Division of the GMD Central Organization Department was established in February 1928 as the GMD secret service and was placed under the GMD Central Organizational

---

[41] Ibid., p. 21.

[42] Ibid., p. 22.

[43] Ibid., p. 34.

[44] The GMD Organizational Department, established in February 1928, was the GMD's secret service headed by Chen Lifu.

[45] *Chen Geng tongzhi zai Shanghai*, p. 34.

[46] John Byron and Robert Pack, *The Claws of the Dragon: Kang Sheng – The Evil Genius Behind Mao and His Legacy of Terror in People's China*, p. 97.

Department, Chen Lifu appointed Xu Enzeng to head the Central Organizational Department in Nanjing. In December 1929, Li Kenong was also sent by the Intelligence Cell to the Shanghai Telecommunication Administration, where Qian was assigned to establish local branches of GMD intelligence services and organize the espionage network nationwide.[47] In fact, Qian had become the second most-powerful figure, next to Xu Enzeng, in the Investigation Division, especially after the organization moved from Dingjiaqiao, where most of the GMD central party agencies were located, to 5 Zhongshan Donglu, a hidden location they believed to be an ideal secret operations base for GMD intelligence in Nanjing.[48]

As Xu's confidential secretary and a trusted subordinate, Qian was able to access top-secret telegrams and letters sent to the Investigation Division. All telegrams, reports, and confidential intelligence sent to Xu Enzong were directed to Qian first and handled by him personally. Taking advantage of being a trusted confidential secretary of Xu Enzeng, Qian provided CCP leadership with confidential information involving the GMD's first and second strategic plans – the well-known encirclement campaigns – to encircle the Red Army in the Jiangxi base areas. When the GMD's Investigation Division created a special double-agent organization for expanding its intelligence sources, Qian became its de facto director. After Qian and Li Kenong gained Xu Enzeng's secret code required to read extremely confidential intelligence, the CCP not only had the GMD's espionage activities at its fingertips but also had access to top-secret information from GMD leadership.

In Shanghai, the Intelligence Cell successfully established an espionage network not only in the GMD's top intelligence organizations but also in the headquarters of the GMD Shanghai Garrison Command and the headquarters of the Shanghai International Settlement Police.[49] The CCP successfully controlled top intelligence organizations of the GMD through Qian Zhuangfei and the GMD's leading intelligence organizations in Shanghai through Li Kenong.[50] The Intelligence Cell relied particularly on Li, Qian, and Hu – known as the CCP's top-three outstanding undercover agents – for gaining a large volume of GMD top-secret intelligence. This intelligence network was abolished, and its members left the Nationalist intelligence agencies after Gu Shunzhang, an

[47] *Chen Geng tongzhi zai Shanghai*, pp. 37–8.
[48] Ibid., p. 39.
[49] Ibid., p. 77.
[50] When Li Kenong was informed that Xu Enzeng planned to establish local intelligence branches as auxiliary organizations of the Investigation Division in several important cities, Li reported this information to the Intelligence Cell of the Teke. Under instructions of the Intelligence Cell Li approached Xu and offered his "help." Xu authorized Li to establish the intelligence branches under the cover of news agencies in Nanjing and Tianjin that were actually controlled by the CCP. Hu Di, one of the greatest CCP agents, along with Qian Zhuangfei and Li Kenong, was sent to take control of the Great War News Agency in Tianjin. See *Chen Geng tongzhi zai Shanghai*, pp. 39–40, 77.

alternative member of the Politburo and director of the Teke's Operation Cell, was captured in April 1931 by GMD intelligence services, confessing much information about the Teke.[51]

One of the most successful moves of the Intelligence Cell was the recruitment of Yang Dengying, the founder and leader of the GMD secrets and espionage agency in Shanghai. Since May 1928, Yang had become an agent of the CCP under the leadership of Chen Geng, director of the Intelligence Cell. Yang provided a large amount of information and intelligence to the CCP. In particular, he prevented the GMD from arresting numerous CCP members.[52] Yang especially became an important intelligence source after he was promoted as special commissioner of the GMD Investigation Division in Shanghai.[53] Yang's liaison office, where he stored all the intelligence and information, was de facto property of the Intelligence Cell. To make sure he was not a double agent for the GMD, Yang was monitored by his body guard, a CCP agent sent by the Intelligence Cell.[54] Under the leadership of the Intelligence Cell, Yang helped the CCP significantly by providing important information about CCP defectors, assisting the CCP in dispatching them, arranging CCP covert operations in the GMD central apparatus, helping the CCP purchase weapons, and rescuing high-ranking CCP leaders from the GMD.[55] For example, Yang helped the CCP execute Huang Dihong, a communist turncoat who planned to betray Zhou Enlai to the GMD in April 1930, and Bai Xin, general secretary of the CCP Central Military Commission (CMC) who leaked information that led to the arrest and death of Peng Pai (the CMC chairman and Politburo member) and Yang Yin (the alternative Politburo member and CMC member).[56] Under Yang Dengying's assistance, in the winter of 1930 the Teke was able to rescue Guan Xiangying, who was imprisoned by the GMD in October 1928, and Ren Bishi, who was imprisoned in September 1929.[57]

Political Security Department and State Political Security Bureau

The capture of Gu Shunzhang and his defection was a major blow to CCP intelligence organizations and brought about heavy losses for the intelligence network of the CCP due to Gu's important role in the Teke. As an alternative member of the Politburo who was in charge of CCP intelligence and was a leading figure of the Teke, Gu was responsible for security of top party leaders and was familiar with operations of the CCP intelligence services. Gu's knowledge included secrets relating to the communications of top leaders as

[51] *Chen Geng tongzhi zai Shanghai*, pp. 80–86.
[52] Ibid., pp. 23–32.
[53] Ibid., p. 28.
[54] Ibid., pp. 26–7, 29.
[55] Ibid., pp. 30–1, 44–5.
[56] Ibid., pp. 30–1, 45–6, 53–65.
[57] Ibid., pp. 30–1, 44–9, 51–2.

well as the locations and places of important CCP organizations and leaders.[58] Gu's betrayal paralyzed the Teke because many Teke members and agents were exposed, especially Qian, Li, and Hu, whom Zhou Enlai referred to as the three outstanding figures of CCP intelligence organizations. These agents were transferred to the Jiangxi base areas to escape the GMD's pursuit. Gu's betrayal "fundamentally destroyed" the espionage network that the CCP established in its enemies' organizations and in Zhou Enlai's own words, "was a vital strike" to the CCP.[59]

The Special Services Division was reorganized in June 1931 to strengthen the party's control over the Teke. Although Zhou Enlai continued to lead the organization, Chen Yun, Kang Sheng, Pan Hannian, and Kuang Hui'an were also appointed to its leadership. Chen Yun succeeded Zhou after Zhou was transferred to the Jiangxi base areas in December 1931. When the Internal Communication Cell of the Teke was abolished, the General Affairs Cell, Intelligence Cell, and Operations Cell were reorganized and headed by Chen Yun, Kang Sheng, and Pan Hannian, respectively. Some significant changes were made to the Teke's operations to strengthen the safety of CCP agents assigned to work in GMD-controlled areas. These changes included the requirements that each agent in the Teke must have an alias of a professional role such as journalist, businessperson, or teacher, and that communication among agents "was strictly limited to one-on-one or one-on-two contact" to mitigate the damage inflicted by turncoats.[60]

More important, the Teke became much more efficient after the reorganization, particularly under the leadership of Kang Sheng and Pan Hannian. After Chen Yun left the Teke to take charge of the CCP labor union in 1932, Kang Shen, director of the Red Brigade, was appointed to lead the Teke.[61] Under Kang Sheng's leadership, the Teke reorganized the Red Brigade and recruited its members from the base areas who were skillful in fighting, shooting, bombing, and assassination. According to Xu Enzeng, head of the Investigation Division of the GMD Central Organization Department, the Red Brigade, led by Kang Sheng, launched many successful operations against the GMD intelligence organizations and assassinated several of his important assistants and many communist turncoats.[62] Receiving commands directly from CCP top leadership, the Teke operated as an independent party agency and did not establish any working relationship with other party organizations. The communications among the members of the Teke were based on linear principles and operations in which the communications among the

---

[58] *Chen Yun zhuan*, vol. 1, p. 103.
[59] Ibid., vol. 1, p. 105; *Ouyang Yi huiyilu*, p. 152.
[60] *Chen Yun zhuan*, vol. 1, pp. 106–7.
[61] Ibid., pp. 105–7.
[62] Xu Enzeng, "Wohe gongchandang zhandou de huiyi" [Recollections of my battle against communists], in Xu Enzeng et al. (eds.), *Xishuo zhongtong juntong* [Detailed discussions on the Central Investigation Department and the Military Statistics Bureau], pp. 176–80.

Teke members were restrictedly limited to two or three members.[63] This system enabled the Teke to remain an efficient and powerful intelligence organization and created the difficulties for the GMD intelligence to hunt down the Teke's members. The Teke's success forced the GMD intelligence to change the conventional strategies that relied on the communist turncoats or the destructions of the party organizations for the capture of the Teke members. The GMD intelligence organizations directly sent their agents to infiltrate the Teke, which ultimately led to the arrests of the twenty-eight members of the Red Brigade in June 1934 and perhaps the CCP's decision to abolish the Teke in September 1935.[64]

It should be noted that the abolishment of the Teke was also derived from the growing anticommunist alliance between the Shanghai Public Security Bureau and the French and International Settlement police forces that made the CCP difficult continually stay in Shanghai. As Frederic Wakeman points out, there was the public's perception of an increased threat to law and order posed by the communists and the killings of Gu Shanzhang's family ordered by Zhou Enlai to retaliate Gu's defection and its grisly aftermath aroused popular horror and dismay and a great public indignation.[65] The communists continually suffered the damage caused by its former security chief Gu Shunzhang through whom the GMD intelligence routinely sent the photographs taken of the people seized during the raid and was able to accurately target the hidden communist cadres.[66] Although the CCP continually sent its best agents to join the Teke, especially the Red Brigade in response to the continual capture of Teke's personnel, the GMD intelligence organizations were very successful in attacking the Teke. For example, among a total of thirty-five members of the CCP Red Brigade, seven of them were GMD undercover agents. This led to the successful raid conducted by the GMD intelligence organizations against the Red Brigade in June 1934. As a result, all twenty-eight members of the Red Brigade were arrested, which included its chief Kuang Hui'an.[67] Needless to say, the intensive and successful campaign conducted by the GMD against the Chinese communists played the important role in the abolishment of the Teke.

Compared with the Teke in Shanghai, the CCP intelligence in the Jiangxi base areas developed differently; it merged with the CCP security apparatus under the Political Security Department (*zhengzhi baowei chu*) of the Central Bureau of the Jiangxi Soviet base area (*suqu zhongyang ju*). The Political Security Department was established in January 1931 and Wang Jiaxiang, director

[63] *Chen Yun zhuan*, vol. 1, p. 107.
[64] Xu Enzeng, "Wohe gongchandang zhandou de huiyi," pp. 180–4.
[65] Frederic E. Wakeman, *Policing Shanghai, 1927–1937*, p. 157; Xu Enzeng, "Wohe gongchandang zhandou de huiyi," pp. 183–4.
[66] Frederic E. Wakeman, *Policing Shanghai, 1927–1937*, pp. 154–9.
[67] Xu Enzeng, "Wohe gongcandang zhandou de huiyi," pp. 181–4.

of the Political Department of the Central Military Commission, was appointed as its director concurrent to his Political Department position.[68] Established to provide intelligence and guarding duties for ensuring the security of CCP leading figures and organizations in the Jiangxi base areas, the Political Security Department provided intelligence that ensured their security and was directly controlled by the Party Central Committee, receiving duo leadership from the party leadership and the Jiangxi Soviet government.[69] Three subordinate agencies operated under the jurisdiction of the Political Security Department: the Investigation Cell (*zhencha ke*), the Preinterrogation Cell (*yushen ke*), and the Operations Cell (*zhixing ke*). As Li Kenong, Qian Zhuangfei, and Hu Di led the Operations Cell, the Investigation Cell and the Preinterrogation Cell, respectively,[70] the legacy and knowledge of the Teke remained strong in the department.

After Zhou Enlai, chairman of the Central Military Commission, was transferred from Shanghai to the Jiangxi base areas, he became the secretary of the CCP Jiangxi Central Bureau in December 1931. By that point Zhou had become the de facto leader, controlling CCP intelligence in the Jiangxi base area. In fact, Zhou's influence on the intelligence in the Jiangxi base area became so prevalent that as early as 1931 intelligence organizations in the Jiangxi base area only used the cipher created by Zhou, called *Haomi* – "cipher of Zhou Enlai" – to communicate within both the base area and the temporary center in Shanghai.[71] Zhou's control over the CCP intelligence in the Jiangxi base areas was reinforced by the role of Zhou's wife, Deng Yingchao, who had been appointed general secretary of the CCP Jiangxi Soviet base areas and secretary of the Politburo in May 1932. The general secretary of the CCP Jiangxi base areas oversaw the secret transportation routes between the GMD-controlled areas and the CCP Jiangxi base areas, communications between the Jiangxi base areas and the CCP central leadership in Shanghai, and the confidential party documents and materials.[72] Even in October 1935 after the CCP arrived in northern Shaanxi following the Long March, Deng Yingchao continued as the director of the CCP Confidential Cell and retained control over CCP secrets.[73] Thus, Zhou's dominance in the CCP intelligence apparatus remained through the establishment of the CCP base area in northern Shaanxi during the

---

[68] Deng Fa was appointed director of the Political Security Department after Wang Jiaxiang headed it for eight months. See Zhongguo renmin gong'an shigao bianxie xiaozu, *Zhongguo renmin gong'an shigao*, pp. 26–7.

[69] Ouyang Yi, *Ouyang Yi huiyilu*, pp. 123–4.

[70] Ibid., pp. 124–5; Li Yimeng, *Li Yimeng huiyilu*, p. 143.

[71] Tong Xiaopeng, *Fengyu sishi nian* [Forty years of wind and rain], vol. 1 (Beijing: Zhongyang wenxian chubanshe, 1997), p. 11.

[72] Liu Ying, *Liu Ying zishu* [The autobiographical notes of Liu Ying] (Beijing: Renmin chubanshe, 2005), p. 43.

[73] Wang Jianying, *Zhongguo gongchandang zuzhishi ziliao huibian: Lingdao jigou yange he chengyuan minglu*, p. 326.

late 1930s. For example, Zhou ordered Li Kenong to set up a secret transceiver in Xi'an and establish underground communication stations (*jiaotong zhan*) from Wayaobao, where the CCP leadership was located, to Xi'an and from Xi'an to Beiping (Beijing), Tianjin, Shanghai, Guangzhou, and Hong Kong.[74] When the Working Committee of the Central Enemy's Rear Area was created to take charge of CCP intelligence in September 1940, Zhou and Kang Sheng became director and deputy director, respectively.[75]

The Political Security Department was replaced by the State Political Security Bureau (*guojia zhengzhi baowei ju*, SPSB), which was established in November 1931, and the Political Security Department's subordinate agencies were reorganized into two departments: the Investigation Department, headed by Qian Zhuangfei, and the Operations Department, led by Li Kenong.[76] The Investigation Department had two main responsibilities. First, the department and its local branches were responsible for unearthing the enemy's espionages, investigating the espionage activities, and solving the related cases. Second, it trained and sent its agents to spy on the enemy's intelligence.[77] Agent selection was highly competitive, as candidates had to satisfy the following three requirements:

- Candidates must be loyal to the party; loyalty to the party is evaluated and approved on the basis of experience in revolutionary struggles, such as military uprisings, strikes, and guerrilla wars.
- Candidates must be party or Communist Youth League members as well as from the worker or peasant class with more than one year of involvement in the party's organizational life (*zuzhi shenghuo*). (If candidates were intellectuals, the conditions for selection were much more rigorous.)
- Candidates must have clearly demonstrated that they had the "correct" political views, a clean personal financial history, and superior organizational responsibilities. They must have strong mental faculties to withstand the uncertain political environment, material and sexual seducement, and dissension created by the enemies.[78]

The SPSB directly commanded its local branches at the provincial and county levels. Although there were no local SPSB organizations at the district and township level, the SPSB sent special representatives to handle security issues and supervise local party and government agencies. In the Red Army, the SPSB controlled its local branches at the level of front army (*fangmian jun*), army group (*juntuan*), and army corps (*jun*).

---

[74] Tong Xiaopeng, *Fengyu sishi nian*, vol. 1, p. 26.
[75] Wang Jianying, *Zhongguo gongchandang zuzhishi ziliao huibian: Lingdao jigou yange he chengyuan minglu*, p. 549.
[76] Ouyang Yi, *Ouyang Yi huiyilu* [Memoirs of Ouyang Yi], p. 126.
[77] *Gong'an shigao*, p. 33.
[78] Ibid., p. 34.

The SPSB branches were established in the headquarters of all army groups within the Jiangxi base area (First, Third, Fifth, Seventh, and Ninth Army Groups), whereas the special representatives (*tepai yuan*) of the SPSB were sent to the division, regiment, and battalion level.[79] In the Red Army, SPSB local branches enjoyed the same military rank as staff departments (*canmou bu*) and political departments (*zhengzhi bu*), and its leading figures automatically became members of the party's standing committees as chief of staffs or directors of political departments did. For example, Ouyang Yi, a high-ranking officer of the SPSB, was sent to the Fifth Army Group as the chief of the Political Security Bureau. Although he was one of the five leading members (the five being the commander, political commissar, chief of staff, director of the Political Department, and the director of the Political Security Bureau), he was authorized to monitor and indict anyone in the army units, including the commander of the army group; he was the only officer who received all accusations of the army group. His immense power was due to his monopoly of information and intelligence sources.[80] Special representatives were sent to take charge of security and intelligence at the division, regiment, and battalion levels, whereas a hidden network of informers (*wangyuan*) masquerading as agents or supervisors was secretly developed at the company, platoon, and squad levels.[81] The hidden network of informers was secretly recruited by special representatives of SPSB local branches and kept single-line communications with the special representatives. They were secretly posted to army units with orders to identify anticommunists and counterrevolutionaries.[82]

The State Political Security Bureau (SPSB) remained an independent and powerful organization within the CCP throughout most of the 1930s. The SPSB hierarchy did involve the party, as local branches of the SPSB were subordinate to local party and governmental organizations, and their leaders were standing committee members of local party and governmental organizations. However, the all-powerful intelligence and security service of the CCP during the *sufan* (literally, "suppressing the counterrevolutionaries") period functioned only under the vertical hierarchical authority that flowed down from the headquarters of the SPSB.[83] According to Li Yimeng, director of the Operations Department of the SPSB in the Jiangxi base area during the early 1930s, the SPSB became an "extremely independent organization based on vertical hierarchy over which neither local party committees nor Political Departments in the army had authority." This confirms that despite the organizational hierarchy that placed SPSB local branches in the Red Army subordinate to an army unit's

[79] *Yang Qiqing zhuan*, p. 42.
[80] *Ouyang Yi huiyilu*, pp. 140–4.
[81] Ibid., pp. 125–6.
[82] *Yang Qiqing zhuan*, p. 42.
[83] *Ouyang Yi huiyilu*, pp. 125–7.

Political Department, in reality the Political Department was not authorized to command them.[84]

The Political Security Department and State Political Security Bureau remained one of most powerful and fearful CCP institutions in the early 1930s, especially in 1931, when the CCP launched anti-counterrevolutionary campaigns in communist base areas. Powerful party leaders, such as Zhang Guotao (secretary of the CCP Hubei-Henan-Anhui Bureau and political commissar of the Fourth Front Army) and Xia Xi (secretary of the CCP Human-Hubei Bureau) relied on DPS and SPSB local branches to launch large-scale purges and terror campaigns in the base areas, in order to consolidate power and suppress political dissent. The CCP's security and intelligence agencies that formed in the early 1930s grew into vast networks, allowing party leaders in the base areas to establish absolute authority in base areas. The SPSB branches were in charge of investigating counterrevolutionary activities and were responsible for imprisoning and executing anyone considered an enemy of the Red Army. The functions and operations of the CCP security and intelligence services during the 1930s essentially copied the Soviet model and were heavily influenced by the experience of the Soviet security and intelligence organizations that employed terror to consolidate Stalin's power and push Stalin's political, economic, and social policy and programs.

Under the pretext of combating terrorism, Stalin enhanced the power of his security services, which were all based on vertical power. Relying on the secret police, Stalin expanded his influence over mass media and political life, sending a large number of politically untrustworthy people into exile, placing questionable individuals under strict surveillance, and keeping potential rivals in long-term pretrial detention for demonstrating "intent" to commit terrorist crimes. The secret police acquired vast punitive powers and was renamed the People's Commissariat for Internal Affairs (NKVD) in 1934. No longer subject to party control or restricted by law, the NKVD became Stalin's instrument for use against the party and the country during the Great Terror of the 1930s. The Soviet experience significantly influenced the organizational structure and operation of CCP intelligence and security services and was one of the primary causes of the so-called extension of counterrevolutionary campaigns that spread throughout communist base areas during the 1930s.

Although many high-ranking leaders viewed the DPS and SPSB with repugnance and spoke out against its excesses, top leaders viewed its continued existence as crucial to the survival of the Red Army. When the CCP established its base area in the Shaanxi-Gansu-Ningxia border areas, the SPSB no longer existed; instead, the responsibilities of the former local branches of the SPSB were assigned to the newly created Security Section, which was subordinate to the Political Department of local armed units, similar to the Organizational Section and the Propaganda Section under the Political Department of an army

---

[84] *Li Yimeng huiyilu*, p. 159.

unit.[85] In the early period of the Sino-Japanese War, the Security Section of each military unit was put under the authority of the Political Department, no longer enjoying the same status that the Political and Staff Departments had in the early 1930s. It thus became much less powerful and influential than its predecessor.[86]

CCP Intelligence under Two Politburos

In the early 1930s, the desperate failure of the CCP in GMD-controlled areas and defections of several leading figures, including Gu Shunzhang, Xiang Zhongfa, and later Lu Futan, had severe repercussions. Many leaders left locations commanded by the GMD and the CCP leadership moved from Shanghai to the communist base areas. This was a forced transfer of leading figures in charge of CCP intelligence, such as Zhou Enlai, Chen Yun, Kang Sheng, Li Kenong, Qian Zhuangfei, Hu Di, and Pan Hannian, because of the severely paralyzing exposure of the organizations to the GMD. In the Jiangxi base areas, intelligence was merged with the State Political Security Bureau. Intelligence officers had to give up working in their field of expertise to perform security for party organizations and leading figures, thus largely limiting their access to information and intelligence from the GMD. Even the three outstanding figures – Li Kenong, Qian Zhuangfei, and Hu Di – had to deal primarily with routine security issues such as case investigations and the interrogation of suspected GMD spies. According to Li Yimeng, Qian Zhuangfei and Hu Di were "very vacant" in the State Political Security Bureau because "there were very few important cases" and "very few issues relating to interrogations."[87]

Before the CCP was forced to retreat from the Jiangxi base areas during the Long March, Qian Zhuangfei was appointed deputy director of the Second Bureau of the Central Military Commission in charge of decoding the telegrams of the Nationalist armies.[88] The Work Department of the GMD-Controlled Areas was created in the fall of 1933 to head the underground activities, including intelligence collection and espionage, in GMD-controlled regions. Chen Yun, former head of the Special Services Division (Teke), was appointed to lead the Work Department, but the organization was incapable of commanding the intelligence organizations nationwide; thus, it limited its responsibilities to the regions near the Jiangxi base areas.[89] Because of the intensive and desperate nature of the Long March, the CCP intelligence and espionage organizations almost discontinued their own communications and were no longer active in GMD-controlled territory. In July 1936, the Nationalist

[85] Ibid., p. 159.
[86] *Ouyang Yi huiyilu*, p. 141.
[87] *Li Yimeng huiyilu*, pp. 142–4.
[88] Yao Yize and Chen Yuhong, *Li Kenong chuanqi* [Legend of Li Kenong], p. 230.
[89] *Chen Yun zhuan*, vol. 1, pp. 145–6.

Army Work Department, headed by Zhou Enlai, was created to pursue political and military alliances with the nationalist Northeast Army and the Northwest Army.[90] After the Long March, CCP intelligence organizations once again resumed their activities in GMD-controlled areas, with Zhou Enlai continuing to play an important role in the development of CCP intelligence and espionage services throughout the 1930s and 1940s.

In the late 1930s, partially as a result of Zhou Enlai's role as an instrument of the Soviet-trained returned students to weaken Mao's influence over the CCP and the Red Army in the Jiangxi base areas during the early 1930s, Mao's relationship with Zhou Enlai was complicated by feelings of distrust. Although Zhou's influence on the CCP intelligence was apparent, Mao had taken steady steps since the Zunyi conference in January 1935 to control the intelligence services and monopolize access to the party's top secrets and leaders' communications. Mao transferred Deng Fa, director of the State Political Security Bureau (SPSB), who was trusted by both Zhou Enlai and the returned students, to take some insignificant responsibilities temporarily, such as the position as political commissar of the Third Column, a post to ensure the safety of the CCP's central organs, sick cadres, elders, and female party members during the Long March.[91] Because the State Political Security Bureau was no longer active following the fall of the Soviet government in Jiangxi base areas during the Long March, Mao took the initiative to dismember the SPSB and sent a large number of SPSB personnel to grassroots army units to weaken the influence of the CCP security and intelligence services, which Zhou Enlai controlled. Although the remaining personnel stayed under the leadership of the SPSB after the Long March, the SPSB was no longer a paramount organization under the jurisdiction of the top leadership. Rather, the headquarters of the SPSB was under the authority of the Central Political Department,[92] and each SPSB local branch was subordinate to the Political Department of a local Red Army unit, which was treated as the same rank as the SPSB organization before its demotion.[93] In October 1935, Mao formally appointed Wang Shoudao, his long-term trusted follower, to take charge of the SPSB.[94]

---

[90] *Lingdao jigou yange*, p. 326.

[91] In September 1935, Deng Fa was appointed political commissar of the Third Column of the Shaanxi-Gansu Branch. Deng Fa was sent to manage the preparation of food for the units of the CCP and the Red Army. In April 1936, he was sent to Moscow as a member of the CCP delegation. See *Zhou Enlai nianpu, 1898–1949*, pp. 293, 306.

[92] The name of the CCP Political Department had never been seen in any party document. However, it was mentioned in the Politburo conference held on November 3, 1935, and it was deemed one of the five key party central departments (Military, Organization, Political, Labor Union, and Communist Youth) immediately after the CCP arrived at northern Shaanxi following the Long March. Wang Jiaxiang was appointed to take charge of the CCP Political Department. See *Lingdao jigou yange*, p. 327; *Zuzhi shi ziliao*, vol. 2, part 1, p. 87.

[93] See *Li Yimeng huiyilu*, p. 159.

[94] Wang Shoudao was appointed to take charge of the SPSB in October 1935. However, the decision made at the Politburo conference between March 20 and March 27, 1936, indicated that the director of the SPSB must be a member of the Politburo Standing Committee, and

Wang's personal ties with Mao are traceable to the early 1920s, when Wang attended Xiuye Middle School in Changsha, Hunan; Mao had taught a history course there between April and December 1919.[95] In May 1926, Wang attended the Guangzhou Peasant Movement Institute, the original site of communist training, which Mao and Zhou Enlai founded in the 1920s.[96] In 1933, Wang was dismissed by the Temporary Center from his position as party secretary of the CCP's Hunan-Jiangxi Province when the anti–Luo Ming line campaign was launched. The campaign was an effort by the returned students to purge Mao's followers and undermine his influence, and Wang's dismissal was a direct result of that campaign.[97] However, Mao protected Wang Shoudao by transferring him to Ruijin, the capital of the Jiangxi base areas, and by appointing Wang as his assistant to conduct site investigations and research in the areas of Xingguo and Ruijin. Wang was later appointed general secretary of the Central Organizational Bureau and director of the Operations Cell of the State Political Security Bureau.[98] After the CCP arrived in northern Shaanxi, Wang was assigned to take charge of the CCP security forces and was appointed director of the Central Secretary Office, whereby he took control of confidential materials and communications of the top leadership.[99] When Ren Bishi became CCP general secretary (*mishu zhang*), the Central Secretary Office merged with the administrative body of the Central Secretariat, thus putting the Central Secretary Office directly under the leadership of Ren Bishi.[100]

Once the CCP established its bases in northern Shaanxi, Mao replaced Zhou Enlai as head of the communist army by becoming chairman of the

---

Wang Shoudao could play only a supporting role in leading the SPSB. Although Bo Gu was assigned director of the SPSB on April 5, 1936, Wang Shoudao was de facto leader of the SPSB. See *Zuzhi shi ziliao*, vol. 2, part 1, p. 87; Wang Jianying, *Zhonggong zhongyang jiguan lishi yanbian kaoshi* [Textual research of historical evolution of CCP central organizations], pp. 324-7.

[95] *Renmin ribao* [People's daily], September 9, 1996; *Changsha wanbao* [Changsha evening news], November 9, 2003.

[96] *Renmin ribao* [People's daily], September 9, 1996.

[97] *Yang Shangkun huiyilu*, pp. 78-80.

[98] *Renmin ribao* [People's daily], September 9, 1996.

[99] After the CCP arrived at northern Shaanxi, Wang was assigned to lead the Confidential Division of the CCP Secretary Department, the Confidential Division of the Central Military Commission, and the confidential agency of the State Political Security Bureau. See Fei Yundong and Yu Kuihua, *Zhonggong mishu gongzuo jianshi, 1921–1949* [Brief history of the work of the CCP secretary, 1921–1949], pp. 186-7; *Lingdao jigou yange*, p. 426.

[100] Deng Xiaoping was general secretary of the CCP Secretary Department (*mishu chu*) in January 1935 and was transferred to director of Propaganda Department under the Political Department of the First Army Group in the summer of 1935. After Deng Xiaoping was transferred, no general secretary of the CCP Secretary Department had been appointed until June 1937, when Wang Shoudao was assigned to the position. See [Deng] Maomao, *Wode fuqin Deng Xiaoping* [My father Deng Xiaoping], pp. 353-4, 360; *Zuzhi shi ziliao*, vol. 2, pp. 87, 89; *Ren Bishi zhuan*, pp. 561-2.

Soviet Northwest Revolutionary Military Commission (formerly the Chinese Revolutionary Military Commission); Zhou was one of its vice chairmen. Zhou was sent to supervise negotiations with the GMD Northeast Army and Northwest Army. Such a political alliance was significant to the CCP's survival, because of the prior encirclement that Chiang Kai-shek initiated against the communist army and because the Nationalists nearly annihilated the Red Army during the Long March. Although Zhou demonstrated compliance with Mao's request, he refused to offer Mao complete political support. In Zhou's own words, during the Yan'an rectification, on November 15, 1943, it was because he "did not have enough confidence in Mao's leadership at that time."[101] More important, as Gao Wenqian points out, Zhou still considered the Comintern's authority superior to Mao's leadership, even though Mao's dominance in the CCP leadership was evident.[102]

During the CCP's internal ideological debates during the period of the second united front, Zhou played a leading role, allied with Wang Ming and backed by the Comintern, in challenging Mao's policy toward the united front. At the expanded Politburo conference held in Luochuan between August 22 and August 24, 1937, Zhou led the majority of CCP leadership members to challenge Mao's emphasis on the CCP's political and military independence during its cooperation with the Nationalists.[103] Although Mao insisted that the CCP's military strategy rely on guerrilla warfare rather than positional or mobile warfare that would put the communist army in direct confrontation with the powerful Japanese army,[104] Zhou supported mobile warfare in combination with guerrilla warfare. Zhou believed that the party's reputation would be severely damaged and that the Chinese people would view the CCP as cowardly if the communist army always avoided direct confrontation with the enemy to preserve its own strength.[105] When Wang Ming returned to China from Moscow in November 1937, Zhou became an important supporter of his. At the December Politburo conference, Zhou echoed Wang Ming, who saw Mao's views on the united front as "over-emphasizing the CCP's independence, thereby weakening the united front."[106]

---

[101] "Zhou Enlai zai zhongyang zhengzhi ju huiyi shangde fayan tigang" [Outline of Zhou Enlai's speech at the CCP Politburo conference], November 15, 1943 (manuscript). Quote from Gao Wenqian, *Wannian Zhou Enlai* [Zhou Enlai's later years], p. 65.

[102] Gao Wenqian, *Wannian Zhou Enlai*, p. 65.

[103] Zhang Guotao, *Wode huiyi* [My reminiscence], vol. 3, pp. 1296–9.

[104] David Ernest Apter and Tony Saich, *Revolutionary Discourse in Mao's Republic*, p. 57.

[105] A. Titov, "Kangri zhanzheng chuqi zhonggong lingdao neibu liangtiao luxian de douzheng, 1937–1939" [Two line struggle within the CCP leadership in the early period of the Anti-Japanese War, 1937–1939], in Xu Zhengming and Xu Junji (trans. and eds.), *Gongchan guoji yu zhongguo geming – Sulian xuezhe lunwen xuanyi* [Comintern and Chinese Revolution – Selected and translated work of the Soviet scholars], p. 350; Zhang Guotao, *Wode huiyi*, vol. 3, pp. 1298–9.

[106] Jue Shi, "Zhou Enlai yu kangzhan chuqi de changjiang ju" [Zhou Enlai and the Yangtze Bureau in the early period of the Sino-Japanese War], in *Zhonggong dangshi yanjiu* [Research of the CCP history], no. 2 (1988), pp. 9–17; *Zhou Enlai nianpu, 1898–1949*, p. 393.

In October 1937, the CCP leadership called the Politburo Conference in Regards to the Southern Twelve Provinces, at which a decision was made to establish the CCP Yangtze Bureau in Wuhan. This bureau was to lead the communist organizations and the New Fourth Army in southern China, to manage negotiations with the Nationalist government, and to expand the communist influence in GMD-controlled areas. Its media outlets for garnering followers were the *Xinhua ribao* (*The New China Daily*, the CCP's central organizational newspaper) and the *Qunzhong* (*The Masses*, the CCP's journal).[107] As the Yangtze Bureau consisted of five Politburo members (Wang Ming, Zhou Enlai, Bo Gu, Xiang Ying, and Kai Feng),[108] it was called the Second Politburo, in relation to the Politburo in Yan'an, which was considered the first Politburo. The Second Politburo significantly influenced the CCP's policy making and decision making.[109] In the Yangtze Bureau, Zhou Enlai cooperated with Wang Ming to facilitate the CCP's support for the united front with the Nationalists and to pursue a constructive relationship with the Nationalist government. To achieve its goals, the Yangtze Bureau (under the leadership of Wang Ming and Zhou Enlai) confronted Mao about his views, especially on prioritizing the CCP's security and development. Mao urged the CCP to engage in an independent guerrilla warfare and to instigate an all-out expansion of communist power in rural areas behind Japanese lines. For example, the Yangtze Bureau urged the CCP to "cooperate honestly" with the GMD, which referred to practices such as first receiving approval from the Nationalist government before establishing CCP local governments.[110]

Unlike his colleagues in the Yangtze Bureau, Mao was cautious of the CCP's cooperation with the GMD and discouraged individual party members from joining the Nationalist government. The Yangtze Bureau, however, not only allowed but also encouraged individual party members to join the GMD government, such as Zhou Enlai, who became the deputy director of the Political Department of the Military Commission under the Nationalist government even though Mao indicated his discontent (Mao refused to reply to the Yangtze Bureau's request for his approval).[111] The Yangtze Bureau also refused to publish Mao's article "In Regards to Sustained and Protracted Warfare" in the CCP newspaper *New China Daily*. Mao's "sustained and protracted warfare," according to Wang Ming, was merely to be passive, anticipating the outbreak of war between Japan and the Soviet Union.[112]

---

[107] Tong Xiaopeng, *Fengyu sishi nian*, vol. 1, pp. 129–36.

[108] Kai Feng was transferred to the Yangtze Bureau in March 1938. See Wang Jianying, *Zhonggong zhongyang jiguan lishi yanbian kaoshi*, pp. 394–5.

[109] Otto Braun (Li De), *Zhongguo jishi*, pp. 282.

[110] The Yangtze Bureau sent a telegram to Yan'an and disagreed that a CCP local government imposed the result of its election on the GMD government. See *Zhou Enlai nianpu, 1898–1949*, pp. 398, 402.

[111] Ibid., pp. 399, 401, 406.

[112] "Wang Ming jufa 'lunchi jiuzhan' qianhou" [Before and after Wang Ming rejected to publish "sustained and protracted warfare"], in *Laonian shenghuo bao* [Senior lives], July 2, 2010.

Also, when the Yangtze Bureau proposed a Politburo conference to "discuss the severe problems in CCP-GMD relations," Mao refused to give his endorsement, causing Wang Ming, Zhou Enlai, and Bo Gu to telegram their proposals to other Politburo members, such as Ren Bishi, Zhu De, Peng Dehuai, and Kai Feng, to press Mao to accept the proposal of the Yangtze Bureau.[113] Facing a challenge from Wang Ming during this period, Mao was in a disadvantageous position; he complained, "My orders cannot reach out of my cave residence" in Yan'an.[114] Wang Ming, Zhou Enlai, and Bo Gu insisted that "the current strategic focus was defending Wuhan" and that all possible strength should be used to achieve that objective. Mao, in contrast, asked the Yangtze Bureau to prioritize developing CCP organizations and armed forces in the countryside and to avoid direct confrontation with the Japanese when they attacked Wuhan, the temporary capital of the Nationalist government.[115]

Zhou's cooperation with Wang Ming undoubtedly deteriorated Zhou's relationship with Mao, who had steadily established his dominance in the CCP leadership. In March 1943, Mao excluded Zhou Enlai from the reorganized Central Secretariat and monopolized decision-making power as Chairman of the Politburo and chairman of the Central Secretariat. After Zhou returned to Yan'an in August 1943, Mao dealt him an immediate blow by criticizing Zhou for "breaking the Party's rules" for having negotiated with the Nationalist general Hu Zongnan in Xi'an.[116] Zhou became the target of the rectification campaign that Mao had orchestrated to seek ideological unity, to purge opponents from the party's leadership, to claim the CCP's independence from Moscow's control, and to further strengthen his dominance in the party. Like other high-ranking leaders who had been associated with Wang, such as Zhang Wentian, Bo Gu, Wang Jiaxiang, Zhou had to subject himself to self-criticism and to criticism from others. Mao blisteringly attacked Zhou, accusing him of lacking principles and of being a pushover for whichever group was in power. In particular, Zhou made a self-criticism about his role in supporting the returned students in Jiangxi and his backing of Wang Ming in the Yangtze Bureau.[117]

Despite the setback of Zhou's career caused by Mao's attacks, Zhou continued to develop the CCP's intelligence network in GMD-controlled areas. During the second united front, from 1937 to 1946, the CCP intelligence and secret

---

[113] *Zhou Enlai nianpu, 1898–1949*, pp. 403–4.
[114] Li Weihan, *Huiyi yu yanjiu*, vol. 1, pp. 442–3.
[115] Tong Xiaopeng, *Fengyu sishi nian*, vol. 1, pp. 167–72.
[116] During the summer of 1943 in Xi'an, Zhou realized that the Nationalist armies had not moved to prepare for a military campaign against the CCP in Yan'an. Zhou was concerned that the mass demonstrations organized by the CCP against the GMD might provoke the Nationalist government. Zhou therefore asked Yan'an to defer publication of the mass demonstration to not give the nationalist armies an excuse to attack Yan'an. Mao criticized Zhou for "failing to show strength and resilience to GMD pressure out of fear for personal safety." See Gao Wenqian, *Wannian Zhou Enlai*, pp. 75–6.
[117] Gao Wenqian, *Wannian Zhou Enlai*, pp. 76–80.

services, led by Zhou Enlai, became much more active; ties among old agents were restored and new ones created. The services obtained counterintelligence and strategic data connected with the war effort. When Zhou Enlai and Wang Ming co-led the Yangtze Bureau in December 1937, Zhou took Li Kenong with him, who was appointed general secretary of the Yangtze Bureau in charge of intelligence, confidential materials, and communications.[118] Under Zhou Enlai's leadership, Li Kenong developed an effective intelligence network in the GMD-controlled areas and resumed secret contacts with many Nationalist high-ranking leaders and social eminent persons and celebrities such as famous politicians, business leaders, movie stars, journalists, and professors. For example, Li resumed contact with Xie Hegeng, an undercover CCP agent who had infiltrated the GMD's Guangxi troops in 1934; established himself as a ranking colonel; and become the private secretary of General Bai Chongxi, deputy commander of Guangxi troops.[119]

October 1938 saw the Yangtze Bureau abolished and the CCP Southern Bureau replace it to manage the party organizations and intelligence apparatus in southern China. In the Southern Bureau located in Chongqing, Zhou developed an effective intelligence and espionage network that included a large espionage organization led by Pan Hannian, an intelligence apparatus headed by Liu Shaowen (director of the Southern Bureau's Information Department) and Liu Xiao (party secretary of the CCP Jiangsu Province and a leadership member of the Southern Bureau). The intelligence network headed by Pan Hannian was by far one of the most successful intelligence and espionage organizations in the CCP. Pan sent Yuan Shu, a top agent in the intelligence network, to infiltrate five different organizations: the Japanese consul, the Green-Red Secret Society, the intelligence headquarters of the Wang Jingwei puppet regime in Nanjing, the Shanghai branch office of the GMD Bureau of Investigation and Statistics, and the GMD Military Statistics Bureau (led by General Dai Li).[120]

Under Zhou's leadership, a high-level intelligence network headed by Wang Shijian was established to link Xi'an, Beiping (Beijing), Shenyang, and Lanzhou. The so-called three most distinguished intelligence workers of the party of the late 1930s and 1940s, Xiong Xianghui, Chen Zhongjing, and Shen Jian, came from this intelligence network.[121] In fact, one of the most important

---

[118] Yao Yize and Chen Yuhong, *Li Kenong chuanqi*, p. 171.

[119] Ibid., pp. 176–9.

[120] Liu Yong, "Zhongguo qingbao shi shang de 'wuchong jiandie'" [The "pentahedral agent" in Chinese intelligence history], in *Lianzheng liaowang* [Honesty outlook], No. 2 (2005), pp. 52–3.

[121] These three were named as such to liken them to the top three intelligence officials of the late 1920s and early 1930s, Quan Zhuangfei, Li Kenong, and Hu Di. Zhou Enlai had named Qian Zhuangfei, Li Kenong, and Hu Di the early three most distinguished intelligence workers, and Xiong, Chen, and Shen the later three most distinguished intelligence workers. See Xiong Xianghui, *Wode qingbao yu waijiao shengya* [My intelligence and diplomatic careers], p. 66.

and successful moves by Zhou Enlai in his intelligence career was to infiltrate Xiong Xianghui in the Nationalist army during the spring of 1937. Xiong Xianghui later became the confidential secretary of General Hu Zongnan, commander in chief of the important Eighth War Zone headquartered in Xi'an. General Hu was also among the most powerful Nationalist generals and a trusted follower of Chiang Kai-shek. Xiong sent a large number of high-level secrets to the CCP when Hu led the Nationalist military's campaign against the CCP in Yan'an.[122] Like Xiong Xianghui, both Chen Zhongjing and Shen Jian were deeply concealed in Hu Zongnan's army and won Hu's trust. Both later became high-ranking officials of the Youth League of the Three Principles of the People, a powerful organization created in March 1938 and later dominated by the GMD Central Club Clique, led by Chen Lifu and Chen Guofu. The intelligence network led by Wang Shijian also received a large volume of top-secret information from the CCP agent Dai Zhongrong, who was undercover as deputy director of the Confidential Office in the headquarters of General Fu Zongnan. The information he divulged included the detailed composition of the Nationalist armies during Chiang Kai-shek's campaign against Yan'an.[123]

After the Japanese armies occupied Wuhan and Guangzhou and the Nationalist government moved its capital to Chongqing, in November 1938 the Southern Bureau, led by Zhou Enlai, set up an agency (*banshi chu*) in Guilin, Guangxi. This agency continued to develop underground party organizations and to lead the CCP's intelligence and espionage activities in eastern China, southern China, Hong Kong, and abroad.[124] As its director, Li Kenong sent CCP agents to hide in GMD organizations, as in the case of Zhou Kechuan, who took a leadership position in the Youth League of the Three Principles (*sanqing tuan*), and Yang Dongchun, who headed a school that trained GMD officials in Guangxi.[125] A communist espionage ring successfully hid in the Telecommunications Department (*dianxun chu*) of the Juntong (the GMD Military Commission's Bureau of Investigation and Statistics) until February 1942, when Dai Li uncovered it. This ring operated directly under General Ye Jianying in Chongqing, and all the Telecommunications Department's information made its way to Zhou Enlai's compound in Chongqing.[126] Zhang Kexia and He Jifeng, two CCP spies who were double agents and high-ranking Nationalist generals, received orders directly from Zhou Enlai and Li Kenong. They later led twenty-three thousand Nationalist army officials and soldiers to surrender

---

[122] Xiong Xianghui, *Wode qingbao yu waijiao shengya*, pp. 1–60.

[123] Luo Qingchang, "Duidi yingbi douzheng de zhiyin" [An intimate friend in the underground struggle against enemies], in Zhonggong Heilongjiang shengwei dangshi yanjiu shi (ed.), *Huiyi Ouyang Qin* [Recalling Ouyang Qin], p. 35; Xiong Xianghui, *Wode qingbao yu waijiao shengya*, p. 46.

[124] Yao Yize and Chen Yuhong, *Li Kenong chuanqi*, pp. 205–6, 209.

[125] Ibid., pp. 209–12.

[126] Frederic E. Wakeman Jr., *Spymaster: Dai Li and the Chinese Secret Service*, p. 373.

to the communist armies in November 1948.[127] In 1937, Zhou Enlai courted and succeeded in landing Yan Baohang, a top adviser to the Nationalist general Zhang Xueliang, as a CCP spy under Zhou's direct leadership. Yan was a celebrity who had access to many high-ranking nationalist officials, including Chiang Kai-shek, Chiang's wife Madam Chiang, Sun Ke, and Yu Youren. Among his best work was when Yan reported to Zhou the exact date Nazi Germany would attack the Soviet Union one and one-half months before the attack; this enabled Stalin to prepare defensively against the German invasion.[128] In addition, Zhou and his assistant Li Kenong organized and developed a telecommunications network that linked Yan'an, Chongqing, Shanghai, Hong Kong, the Eighth Route Army, the New Fourth Army, Guangxi, Hunan, Jiangxi, and Southeast Asia.[129]

In the CCP Southern Bureau, Zhou Enlai was personally involved in the concealment of the CCP agent Shen Anna in the GMD's top organizations. As a stenographer who had access to the GMD leaders' top secrets, Shen Anna had attended all the important GMD leadership conferences and standing committee meetings, and so, from January 1939, was able to provide a large number of GMD top secrets to the CCP. Another successful top-secret spy under the personal direction of Zhou Enlai was Li Qiang. According to a recent official publication, in 1943 the Southern Bureau sent Li Qiang to hide in the GMD's Sichuan Provincial Special Commission, the GMD's leading intelligence and espionage organization in Sichuan, and the Chengdu Branch of the GMD Bureau of Investigation and Statistics (*zhongtong*). Li Qiang assumed two positions, secretary for the Chengdu Branch of the GMD Central Statistics and senior secretary (*zhuren ganshi*) for the GMD Sichuan Provincial Special Commission; he later became the deputy commander of the Nationalist Forty-Fifth Army Corps. Only Zhou Enlai and Dong Biwu (not the Central Committee's Social Affairs Department – the headquarters of the CCP intelligence and security services) knew Li's real identity.[130]

Mao's effort to gain control over CCP intelligence, which was traditionally Zhou Enlai's domain, began in early 1938, when Kang Sheng returned from Moscow. Historians and leading experts generally purport that Kang Sheng

---

[127] In addition, Zhang Kexia was deputy commander of the GMD's Thirty-Third Army Group, and He Jifeng was commander of the GMD's Seventy-Seventh Army Corps. As Zhou Enlai and Li Kenong directly command them, Zhang and He did not even know each other's real identities. See Yao Yize and Chen Yuhong, *Li Kenong chuanqi*, p. 263.

[128] Wang Lianjie, "Qingbao zhanxian shang de wuming yingxiong – Yan Baohang" [The unknown hero of the intelligence front – Yan Baohang], in *Guangming ribao* [Guangming daily], August 13, 2008; "Yan Baohong de sanfeng zhongyao qingbao" [Three important intelligence materials of Yan Baohong], in *Wenhui bao* [Wenhui daily], December 10, 2008.

[129] See Li Dingyuan, "Kaiguo shangjiang renmin gongchen" [The colonel general who is one of China's founding fathers], in *Chaohu chenkan* [Chaohu morning journal], part 1, September 7, 2009.

[130] *Chongqing wanbao* [Chongqing evening news], April 26, 2009.

unilaterally initiated a strategic relationship with Mao. On the contrary, lesser-known research contends that Mao took the same steps to engender a relationship with Kang Sheng. When Mao and Kang met in Yan'an in December 1938, both carefully evaluated the possibility of developing a political alliance; however, they had never worked together and thus had no reciprocal personal ties or loyalty. In addition, when Kang Sheng accompanied Wang Ming to return to China from Moscow, he believed that Wang Ming was the Comintern representative whom Stalin firmly supported; thus, he did not break ties with Wang to align with Mao, even though his intention to establish a good relationship with Mao was evident. According to Sima Lu, when Kang Sheng accompanied Wang Ming to give a speech to the training class for CCP agents in the spring of 1938, Kang led the students in shouting, "Long live our Party's talented leader Wang Ming!" an indication that showed his support of Wang Ming.[131]

There are at least three reasons Mao would have liked Kang Sheng to be an associate. First, during Kang's stay in Moscow, Kang was deputy director of the CCP's delegation to the Comintern in the summer of 1933 and was elected alternative member of Comintern leadership in August 1935.[132] Consequently, Kang's presence in the top leadership would facilitate the Comintern's endorsement of Mao's leadership of the CCP. Kang was considered influential among the CCP leadership, and he had ties with the Comintern, whereas Mao was competing with inside party rivals such as Zhang Guotao and Wang Ming. Second, Kang had been a follower of Wang Ming and Wang's primary associate when Wang and Kang were director and deputy director, respectively, of the CCP's delegation to the Comintern from 1933 to 1937. A political alliance between Mao and Kang would significantly divide Wang's camp.

Third, Kang was one of the few high-ranking leaders who had received comprehensive security and intelligence training in the Soviet Union. Kang's former "red terror" experiences in Shanghai and with the NKVD and KGB would help Mao wipe out his political enemies and further consolidate his power. Born to a rich landowner, Kang Sheng joined the party in 1925 and had been present for some of the milestones of the CCP's early years, including the CCP's protests against the British and Japanese in 1925, urban revolts in 1926 and 1927, and the GMD's unexpected and devastating attack against the communists in April 1927.[133] Kang participated in the unsuccessful Shanghai workers' uprising in 1927, managing to escape the subsequent massacre of communists ordered by Chiang Kai-shek. Kang had risen to prominence in the CCP by the late 1920s and early 1930s, when he was director of the Organization Department of the

[131] Sima Lu, *Zhonggong lish de jianzheng: Sima Lu huiyilu* [Witness of CCP history: Memoirs of Sima Lu], p. 86.

[132] *Lingdao jigou yange he chengyuan minglu*, p. 361.

[133] Jeffrey T. Richelson, *A Century of Spies*, p. 241.

CCP's Jiangsu Province, director of the CCP's Central Organization Department, and director of the CCP's Labor Department. In the early 1930s, Kang was assigned to head the CCP intelligence and espionage services at the Teke. In 1934 he was selected as a Politburo member at the fifth plenum of the CCP's Sixth Party Congress held in Moscow.[134] Between 1933 and 1937, Kang Sheng became deputy director of the CCP's delegation to the Comintern and received training in Soviet security and intelligence techniques.

Although Kang was symbolically named director of the CCP's Labor Movement Commission in January 1938, Mao soon appointed him head of the newly established Central Security Commission (CSC, *zhongyang baowei weiyuanhui*), a party agency in charge of the CCP's intelligence and security; this shifted Zhang Hao, the previous director, to lead the Central Commission in Charge of Enemy-Controlled Areas.[135] When a large number of young intellectuals flooded into Yan'an, the situation was a double-edged sword for the CCP. On the one hand, there was increased pressure to boost intelligence and security, given the potential penetration by enemy spies; on the other hand, the CCP enjoyed increased recruitment. The CSC secretly trained the young intellectuals as agents, or informers (*wangyuan*), and sent agents to spy on the young intellectuals, as in the case of Xiao Bin, a young middle school student who was named an informer during her studies at the Chinese People's Anti-Japanese Military and Political College in 1938. In 1949 she became the wife of Yang Qiqing, vice minister of the PRC's Ministry of Public Security.[136] According to a current official publication, Jiang Qing, a Shanghai actress who later became Mao's wife, was also an informer, developed by the CSC to spy at the Yan'an Luxun Arts Institute under the cover of a political instructor (*zhidao yuan*).[137]

Kang offered significant support to Mao in March 1938, when the Politburo discussed Mao's proposal to have Wang Ming return to the Yangtze Bureau instead of staying in Yan'an. Mao proposed this initiative to weaken Wang's power and ultimately lead to Wang's dismissal. Although the proposal was ultimately rejected by most leaders, Mao viewed Kang's support as a signal of a potential political alliance against Wang Ming and his followers. Mao was also extremely grateful for Kang's role as a matchmaker for Mao and Jiang Qing, and later for Kang's verdict regarding the accusations against Jiang Qing, when CCP intelligence officers accused her of being a traitor to the party during her underground activities in Shanghai. In addition, party leadership had received unfavorable reports from Yang Fan and Wang Shiying, two leading CCP intelligence agents. The reports suggested that Jiang

[134] *Gong'an shigao*, p. 191.
[135] Ibid., p. 427.
[136] Xiao Bin, "Wohe Yang Qiqing" [Yang Qiqing and I], in Zhu Chunlin (ed.), *Lishi shunjian* [An instant in history], p. 435.
[137] Du Chao, "Diaocha Jiang Qing de ren – Xu Jianguo de beiju" [A person who investigated Jiang Qing – The tragedy of Xu Jianguo], p. 33.

had "personal taints," a more egregious "taint" being that her sexual activity reflected the activity of a "public bus" while she lived in Shanghai. Many leaders insisted that Jiang was not marriage material and disapproved of Mao's union with her.[138]

The CCP's intelligence and security activities in the late 1930s moved away from heavy security initiatives and focused on intelligence to negotiate and cooperate with the Nationalist Northeast Army, led by General Zhang Xueliang, and the Nationalist Northwest Army, headed by General Yang Hucheng, against the GMD's campaign to encircle and suppress the CCP base areas in northern Shaanxi. The Xi'an Incident, in which Generals Zhang Xueliang and Yang Hucheng kidnapped Chiang Kai-shek, eventually catalyzed the second united front between the CCP and the GMD. During this period, there was an emphasis on collectivism, harmony among the leadership, and tolerance toward those with different views in the CCP leadership. Hence, the CCP intelligence and security services were developed to lead the subversive fight against the GMD in GMD-controlled areas, not as pawns in intraparty power struggles, which they later became.

CCP Intelligence under the Social Affairs Department

The creation of the Central Committee's Social Affairs Department (SAD) was another initiative of Mao's to monopolize access to confidential information and to control the security apparatus, in order to consolidate his power. Following the Central Committee's sixth plenum in 1938, the CCP security and intelligence organizations were reorganized. The State Political Security Bureau was abolished and the Social Affairs Department (SAD) was established in October 1939. From the beginning, the SAD was the chief security organization created to lead the intelligence and espionage apparatuses of the CCP against both the Nationalists and the Japanese; it operated under the direction of the Politburo. Specifically, the SAD served both internal and external security functions, including security of party leaders and agencies; surveillance of party, government, and military organizations; and espionage operations against the Nationalists and the Japanese. Although the CCP's security in Yan'an was the responsibility of the Security Guard Regiment (*bao'an tuan*) of the CCP Shaanxi-Gansu-Ningxia Border Area Government (also known as the Social Affairs Department of the CCP Northwestern Bureau), the SAD concentrated on intelligence, espionage, and counterespionage services.[139]

According to the Decision on the Establishment of the Social Affairs Department, issued by the Central Secretariat on February 18, 1939, the following describes the SAD's mission:

[138] Liu Ying, *Liu Ying zishu* [The autobiographical notes of Liu Ying], p. 123.
[139] Hao Zaijin, *Zhongguo mimi zhan – Zhonggong qingbao he baowei gongzuo jishi*, p. 103.

1. Working systematically against enemy spies and preventing them from infiltrating the party organizations so that the party's tasks can be successfully implemented and party organizations can be protected.

2. Dispatching the CCP agents and the communist sympathizers to penetrate into enemy organizations through their operation inside the enemy's agencies to protect the party.

3. Collecting intelligence regarding the enemy's activities through which the CCP members can heighten their vigilance.

4. Managing the CCP secret agents to ensure the implementation of the party's secret work.

5. Recruiting, selecting, and training personnel to work for the SAD.[140]

In addition, the SAD provided intelligence to the Soviet Intelligence Group stationed in Yan'an;[141] they were specifically instructed to provide information on the Japanese military, because Stalin had become increasingly concerned about possible Japanese military attacks against the Soviet Union.

Soon enough, intelligence became the primary focus for the SAD, and security constituted a small portion of the SAD's responsibilities. In part, this was because the SAD did not have its own police forces in Yan'an, even though it was authorized to co-command the police forces of the Guard and Security Office (bao'an chu) of the Shaanxi-Gansu-Ningxia Border Areas Government.[142] When the SAD planned to imprison GMD spies in Yan'an, it turned to the Guard and Security Office of the Shaanxi-Gansu-Ningxia Border Areas Government for help. An example is the case of the rectification campaign, during which Kang Sheng asked the Guard and Security Office to arrest 260 suspected GMD spies to prevent them from contacting a GMD delegate during his visit to Yan'an.[143] When the Central Guard Regiment was created to guard the CCP's top leaders and organizations in October 1942, the SAD was one of the three organizations (the others being the General Staff Department of the Communist armed forces and the Central General Office) authorized to command the Central Guard Regiment.[144] Besides the SAD's major emphasis on intelligence and espionage, it was responsible for training security and intelligence personnel in its Northwest Public School in Yan'an, a school for the secret services. After receiving training, the security personnel were sent to the CCP organizations and armed units where they were assigned to take

---

[140] Zhongguo renmin gong'an shigao bianxie xiaozu, *Zhongguo renmin gong'an shigao*, p. 80.

[141] See *Shi Zhe huiyilu*, p. 219.

[142] The Guard and Security Office of the Shaanxi-Gansu-Ningxia Border Areas Government was headed by Zhou Xing and assigned to take charge of the security of the base areas. See *Lingdao jigou yange*, p. 558.

[143] *Shi Zhe huiyilu*, pp. 249–50.

[144] Wu Lie, *Zhengrong suiyue*, pp. 207–9.

charge of intelligence and security services.[145] The SAD was authorized to lead the Department of Eliminating Traitors, Spies, and Trotskyites, the leading security and intelligence organization, which had been established in 1937 to take charge of the security and intelligence in the communist armed forces. Unlike the early State Political Security Bureau (SPSB), which operated with a vertical chain of command, the Department of Eliminating Traitors, Spies, and Trotskyites was under dual leadership of the SAD local branch and the party committee of local army units.[146]

Although the SAD was created to ensure Mao's control over the intelligence and security apparatuses, Mao took two initiatives to make the organization more efficient and powerful. The first initiative was appointing Kang Sheng as its director, as he was a prominent expert in security and intelligence services. Mao and Kang's strategic relationship played an important role in Kang's rise in Yan'an, and Kang benefited greatly from his close ties to Jiang Qing, as he had served as matchmaker for Mao and Jiang. Kang was appointed to take charge of the CCP's internal security operation, and as Mao's favored security chief, he enjoyed close ties with Mao. More important, Mao intended to replace Zhou Enlai with Kang Sheng to control the intelligence and security services in the CCP and in the GMD-controlled areas. Mao encouraged Kang to establish control over the CCP intelligence services through his role in leading the SAD's organizational development and personnel appointments.

For example, many of the top agents Zhou Enlai arranged to infiltrate GMD leadership organizations were to receive orders from and report to Kang Sheng.[147] Kang was a driving force behind the Yan'an rectification, a movement that began as an ideological education campaign but evolved into a large-scale witch hunt for spies and "fifth columnists," referring to internal subversives who turned to the motivating forces behind the treasonable activities of a larger group such as the party from within. It eventually became recognized as a vicious campaign of physical and psychological persecution of real or imagined dissidents. Kang was an acknowledged expert in sinister practices and a key figure in Mao's inner circle, deeply implicated in the Yan'an rectification. In doing so, he helped Mao solidify power and boost the Mao cult. Kang's career reached its apex in the spring of 1943, when the composition of the party's ruling elite was brought into line with the new political reality that the rectification campaign had produced. Mao's dominance in the leadership was established when he became Chairman of the Politburo, where he was granted executive authority such as veto power over the secretariat.

Despite Kang's powerful role in the Yan'an rectification, Mao was cautious of his increasing influence in top leadership and of his dominance over the security and intelligence services. Thus, he employed at least four strategies

[145] Mu Fengyun, Zoujin yinbi zhanxian [Getting close to the underground front], pp. 387–8.
[146] Yang Qiqing zhuan, p. 150.
[147] Xiong Xianghui, Wode qingbao yu waijiao shengya, p. 64.

to limit Kang's power. First, Mao did not allow the SAD to establish a vertical chain of command over its branches. Instead, local branches were under the dual leadership of local party committees and the SAD. In the communist armed forces, local SAD branches were controlled by the party committee of the local military unit; the SAD provided only professional guidance. Second, Mao appointed Li Kenong, a longtime trusted assistant of Zhou Enlai, deputy director of the SAD. Mao divided authority over the security and intelligence apparatuses so that Li led the intelligence services and Kang managed the rectification, investigation, and screening of suspected CCP officials. Although Mao did not completely trust Li Kenong because of Li's personal and career ties with Zhou Enlai, limiting Li's access to top secrets relating to elite politics (e.g., initiatives and strategies against Wang Ming and the returned students), Mao nonetheless highly regarded Li and his intelligence expertise. Li was particularly familiar with the CCP's intelligence and espionage network in GMD- and Japanese-occupied areas. Li's role directing the SAD was further strengthened after Zhou Enlai returned to Yan'an and demonstrated his compliance with Mao's leadership in 1943. When the expansion of the rectification and the investigation of CCP officials caused overwhelming resentment from CCP members, Mao abandoned Kang and appointed Li Kenong to take charge of "correcting the errors," redress the cases, and rehabilitate the CCP cadres who were framed and persecuted during the Yan'an rectification.[148]

The third strategy Mao used to limit Kang Sheng's power was to exclude Kang's access to the CCP's top secrets by reorganizing the Central Committee's Confidential Cell (*zhongyang jiyao ke*) in March 1943. He did so by merging the Intelligence Department with the SAD and placing both directly under the jurisdiction of the Central Secretariat (which he headed), but Mao also removed the units in charge of confidential documents and materials from the SAD and the Central Military Commission and absorbed them into the Confidential Cell.[149] Mao's fourth strategy was to never grant Kang access to the CCP-Comintern communication system, despite Kang's role as the head of the CCP intelligence. In 1940, when telegraphic communication between the CCP and the Comintern resumed, Mao monopolized communication with the Comintern by maintaining direct contact with the "Intelligence Group of the Soviet Army" in Yan'an and the CCP Communication Bureau (*zhonggong zhongyang jiaotong ju*). The CCP Communication Bureau was an agency publicly known as the CCP Agricultural Work Department or the Agricultural Commission (*nongwei*), headed by Wu Defeng under the direct leadership of Ren Bishi. While the Intelligence Group of the Soviet Army forwarded Mao's messages and reports relating to important issues regarding CCP strategy, policy, and

---

[148] Li Dingyuan, "Kaiguo shangjiang renmin gongchen," in *Chaohu chenkan*, part 1, September 7, 2009.
[149] *Ren Bishi zhuan*, pp. 607–8.

decisions directly to Stalin, the Agricultural Commission mainly sent the Comintern telegraphs that related to intelligence. Although Ren Bishi and Shi Zhe were personally involved in translating and transmitting Mao's messages, all the telegraphs from both channels were handled by Mao personally and archived in his office.[150] According to Shi Zhe, Mao did share some information from the telegraphs with some of his associates, based on his personal preference, but he never passed on any telegraph to other leaders.[151]

During the Yan'an rectification, Kang repeated many of the horrors of the Great Terror in which Kang had enthusiastically participated while visiting Moscow a few years earlier. Kang operated as Mao's "pistol" and orchestrated the rescue campaign that involved forced confession and the enactment of false guilt, an event that served to consolidate Mao's power.[152] Rectification had never been intended as a gentle and benign process, but the struggle was not only against Wang Ming, the returned students, and the ideas they represented; it ultimately was against all party members and cadres reluctant to accept Mao's hegemony. Zhou Enlai was accused of representing empiricism, of being "the accomplice of dogmatism," and of "usurping the highest leadership of the Party and the army." Expulsion from the party was offered as a possible punishment.[153] Zhou was forced to receive criticism from other party members and to engage in self-criticism. In addition to the rectification campaign (*zhengfeng*) that served "to purify the thoughts of Party members," a cadre screening movement was launched to "purify Party organizations" by "weeding out spies and bad elements." This cadre-screening movement was instigated on the pretext that growth of the party's membership had allowed Chiang Kai-shek's intelligence services to infiltrate secret agencies.

Eventually, Kang was compelled to shoulder the blame for the excesses of the rectification campaign as a result of the fierce resistance from the opposition. Mao loathed Kang for his position of supremacy within the movement and for his role in executing and overseeing the Stalinist "red terror." Another factor that caused Kang to lose power was the Comintern's pressure on Mao. The Comintern was deeply concerned about Mao's motives to launch the rectification campaign against the returning students and repeatedly asked him to cease the campaign. In addition, the Comintern resented Kang Sheng because of his role in the campaign.[154] Kang was demoted to CCP chief in Shandong and was appointed a deputy general secretary of the East China Bureau of the CCP in the 1940s civil war, a relatively low position in comparison to

[150] *Shi Zhe huiyilu*, p. 201.
[151] Ibid., p. 203.
[152] David Ernest Apter and Tony Saich, *Revolutionary Discourse in Mao's Republic*, p. 25.
[153] Gao Wenqian, *Wannian Zhou Enlai*, p. 77.
[154] Shi Zhe, *Zai lishi juren shenbian: Shi Zhe huiyilu*, pp. 205–6; Zheng Hou'an (trans.), "Dimitrov zhi Mao Zedong de handian" [Telegrams that Georgi Dimitrov Mikhailov sent to Mao Zedong], *Guowai zhongguo jindaishi yanjiu* [Foreign research of contemporary Chinese history], no. 13 (1989), pp. 2–3.

his previous posts. Kang's reputation further suffered as a result of his radical approach to the land reform movement, in which a large number of landlords were killed. Kang's invisibility during the first years of the PRC contributed primarily to Mao's aloofness toward Kang, which may have been a factor in Kang's long illness in early 1950s.

Mao's second move was to transfer Li Kenong from the CCP Southern Bureau (where Li worked as Zhou Enlai's chief assistant) to Yan'an as deputy director of the SAD and later as director, after Kang was transferred to Shandong. Li Kenong, born in Chao County, Anhui, entered the CCP in 1926. Under the direct orders of Zhou Enlai, Li joined a GMD intelligence agency in Shanghai in 1929 where Li supervised Hu Di and Qian Zhuangfei; the latter was planted in the Nationalist intelligence agency, with headquarters at Nanjing. Gu Shunzhang's surrender and confession ended Li Kenong's ability to continue as a CCP agent, so he was sent to the Jiangxi base area, where he became a leader in the State Political Security Bureau. In the second GMD-CCP united front during the Sino-Japanese war in the late 1930s and early 1940s, Li was appointed head of the Eighth Route Army offices in Shanghai, Nanjing, and Guilin. Later, when Li became general secretary of the CCP's Yangtze Bureau and a key assistant to Zhou Enlai, his primary responsibilities included leading CCP intelligence activities in Nationalist-controlled areas. Although Mao created the SAD in October 1939 to administer CCP intelligence, the early SAD had little authority because of its limited access to intelligence from the GMD and the Japanese-controlled areas. Although Zhou Enlai was dispatched to the CCP Yangtze Bureau in December 1937, he retained dominance in CCP intelligence in the GMD- and Japanese-controlled areas, making it difficult for the SAD to gain access to information about those areas. The Politburo meeting on August 7, 1940, further consolidated Zhou's power over CCP intelligence in GMD-controlled areas, given Zhou's authority over all party organizations in those areas.[155]

The transfer of Li Kenong from Chongqing to Yan'an and the appointment of Li as deputy director and later director of the SAD was undoubtedly one of the most important and successful moves Mao made to control the CCP intelligence services, given Li's profound experience in the CCP intelligence organizations in both headquarters and enemy-controlled areas. As Zhou's long-term assistant and instrument for controlling the intelligence services in GMD-controlled areas, Li's transfer from the Southern Bureau to Yan'an gave Mao access to the CCP intelligence network in GMD-controlled areas and helped Mao weaken Zhou Enlai's dominance in the CCP intelligence organizations. According to an official publication, Li was "personally" (*qinzi*) called and nominated by Mao to be transferred from the CCP Southern Bureau to Yan'an as deputy director of the SAD; it was said that Mao personally gave a

---

[155] *Zhou Enlai nianpu, 1898–1949*, pp. 461–2.

warm reception to Li and his family when they arrived in Yan'an.[156] Besides Li's role as deputy director of the SAD, Li was also appointed as deputy director of the Central Committee's Intelligence Department (ID), an organization whose staff and administration partially overlapped with those of the SAD. Li became the de facto director of the ID after Kang was engrossed in the rectification campaign, because of his position as deputy director of the Central Study Commission (of which Mao was director). With the authority granted to him as deputy director, Kang headed the Central Commission for Inspecting Party and non-Party Cadres, and thereby had full autonomy to investigate, torture, dismiss, and kill suspected party and nonparty members.[157] Li replaced Kang Sheng as head of the ID and director of the SAD after Kang was forced to end the highly unpopular campaigns.

Although the Intelligence Department was created in July 1941 and the CMC intelligence organizations merged into it two months later, the ID and the SAD were "the same organization with two different names" (yitao jigou, liangge paizi). The ID's origins lay in Mao's preparations for the rectification campaign. On July 7, 1941, the Central Committee's Investigation and Research Commission (IRC), to which the ID was subordinate, was created to promote a unifying ideological education for party members. The education involved the study of Mao's writings and a drive toward "an organizational unity based on common will, action, and discipline" (Figure 8.1).[158] Mao attempted to establish both an "absolute ideological supremacy in matters of revolutionary strategy and military tactics – realms where the efficacy of his ideas had already been put into practice" – and "credentials as an orthodox and creative Marxist philosopher, perhaps to justify (or obscure) his departure from Marxist orthodoxies in so many other areas."[159]

As the IRC's director, Mao took charge of the IRC and concurrently headed the Office of Political Research, one of its three subordinate departments. The intelligence organizations of the communist army were integrated into the ID under the authority of the Investigation and Research Commission.[160] Because Mao created the Intelligence Department to control the entire intelligence organizations in the CCP, the Intelligence Department was the CCP's leading intelligence organization, combining both the intelligence organizations of the SAD and the CMC. As one of the IRC's three subordinate organizations, the ID was institutionally controlled by Mao and became an important source for Mao's power base. The transfer of Li Kenong from Chongqing to Yan'an

---

[156] Yao Yize and Chen Yuhong, Li Kenong chuanqi, pp. 234–5.

[157] Ibid., p. 236; Lingdao jigou yange, p. 552.

[158] Lingdao jigou yange, pp. 549–50; Ren Bishi zhuan, pp. 560–2. In the Ren Bishi zhuan, however, the Central Investigation and Research Commission (zhongyang diaocha yanjiu weiyuanhui) is described as the Central Investigation and Research Bureau (zhongyang diaocha yanjiu ju).

[159] Maurice J. Meisner, Mao Zedong: A Political and Intellectual Portrait, p. 94.

[160] Lingdao jigou yange he chengyuan minglu, p. 550.

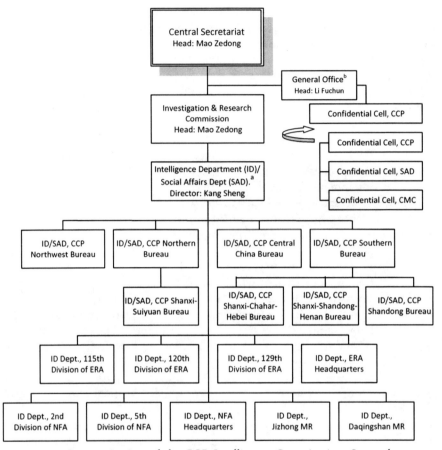

FIGURE 8.1. *Reorganization of the CCP Intelligence Organization, September 1942.*
Source: Wang Jianying, *Zhonggong zhongyang jiguan lishi yanbian kaoshi, 1921–
1949*, pp. 399–426. *Note*: ERA = Eighth Route Army, NFA = New Fourth Army, and
MR = Military Region.

[a] On September 20, 1942, the intelligence services of the Central Military Commission
(the Second Bureau and two divisions of the Third Bureau – the Second and Third Divisions) were merged with the newly established Intelligence Department of the Central
Committee. See *Zhonggong zhongyang jiguan lishi yanbian kaoshi, 1921–1949*, p. 432.
[b] On April 4, 1942, the Central Committee's Confidential Bureau was created to lead
all confidential agencies, including the CCP's Confidential Cell, the CMC's Confidential
Cell, and the Confidential Cell of the Social Affairs Department. However, the Confidential Bureau was abolished on April 18, and the central committee's Confidential
Cell was created to absorb all CCP leading confidential organizations, including the
CCP's Confidential Cell, the CMC's Confidential Cell, and the SAD's Confidential Cell.
See *Zuzhi shi*, vol. 3, part 1, p. 55; Wang Jianying, *Zhonggong zhongyang jiguan lishi
yanbian kaoshi, 1921–1949*, p. 409.

was a significant move by Mao to integrate intelligence services in the enemy-controlled areas into the IRC. It signified the compliance of Zhou Enlai and Li Kenong with Mao's leadership, thus further consolidating Mao's control over the CCP intelligence organizations. In return, Mao provided both Zhou and Li with jurisdiction over the CCP intelligence services. When Li Kenong replaced Kang Sheng as director of the Intelligence Department in October 1946, Li had arrived, so to speak, finally establishing his dominance in the CCP's intelligence organizations.[161]

The power of the ID increased in 1941 with the beginning of an all-out intelligence campaign directed at the Japanese; the previous high level of operations against the GMD continued. The ID underwent a massive change in terms of its operational methods because of the need to expand its information resources. It was assigned to lead the CCP's struggle against enemy intelligence services and to collect information about the movements and activities of Japanese troops, puppet armies, traitors, and GMD armies. On August 1, 1941, the Central Committee issued the Decision on Investigation and Research, which called for moving away from an overreliance on subjective evaluations of enemy intentions to emphasize instead objective investigations. The decision called for increasing investigation and research into domestic and international history, environment, and events; it mandated that the Central Committee set up a research organization to gather and study all available resources.[162] The intelligence gathering was to include information on the international and domestic political, economic, and cultural situation, as well as social relations in enemy, friendly, and CCP territories.[163] Published information was mainly obtained from magazines, newspapers, and broadcasts, all of which publicized information about the war situation and the military authorities of the enemy such as the organizational system and hierarchy of the enemy's armed forces.

Another strategy of Mao's to control CCP intelligence was to control the entirety of the CCP's confidential agencies and communist armies by merging the CMC Confidential Cell (*zhongyang junwei jiyao chu*) and the SAD Confidential Cell (*zhongyang shehui bu jiyao chu*) into the Central Committee's Confidential Cell.[164] The reorganization of the CCP's confidential agencies enabled Mao to undermine the influence of Zhou Enlai, who had dominated CCP intelligence and confidential agencies since the late 1920s. As a result, more than half the personnel from the three confidential agencies were cut – from more than two hundred to ninety-nine – and the reorganized Confidential Cell became a party agency specifically serving the Central Secretariat, headed

---

[161] See interview with Liu Jingfang, professor of the Central Party School, in *Beijing ribao* [Beijing daily], April 27, 2009.

[162] *Ouyang Yi huiyilu*, pp. 123–4.

[163] Jeffrey T. Richelson, *A Century of Spies*, p. 242.

[164] *Zuzhi shi*, vol. 5, p. 55; Wang Jianying, *Zhonggong zhongyang jiguan lishi yanbian kaoshi, 1921–1949*, pp. 409, 429.

by Mao.[165] Thus, the reorganization of the Confidential Cell enabled Mao to control the confidential organizations through the Office of the Central Secretariat, the administrative body of the Central Secretariat. Mao's efforts to control the CCP intelligence and confidential agencies were an integral part of his overall consolidation of power. Mao's reorganization of those organizations took place two months before the Agricultural Commission was to be abolished. The Agricultural Commission was a party agency created to take over control of the transceiver linking Mao directly and exclusively with Stalin and the Comintern; it was abolished when the Comintern was dissolved in May 1943.[166] However, when the Central Confidential Cell replaced the Agricultural Commission, Mao continued to be monopolize access to the Soviet Union and Stalin.[167] From this it is evident that Mao's control over the Central Confidential Cell significantly helped him manipulate information to achieve his political goals.

Unlike the SPSB, which retained a segmented structure and reported along a vertical chain of command, the activities of the SAD and ID were governed by a complex two-tiered system that linked territorial party committees horizontally with SAD and ID organizations at each level of the administration. Among the most significant changes in the intelligence services after the SAD and ID were established was the focus of intelligence collection. In the past, intelligence collection had concentrated on top-secret enemy information to protect high-ranking CCP leaders and important party and army organizations. After the SAD and ID were established, however, intelligence collection was expanded to include both secret and published information, and the SAD and ID were responsible for collecting, classifying, and analyzing the information.

Mao issued the party document "Decision of the CCP Central Committee on Investigation and Research" in August 1941, which established the parameters for the scale, scope, and procedures for intelligence collection. For example, the scope of media collection for the SAD and ID was newspapers, journals, and books related to politics, military, economics, culture, society, and class relations that included information related to the CCP, its enemies, and allies. The intelligence also included biographies of notable people, including landlords and business owners with property valued at more than fifty thousand *yuan*, officials of the GMD armed forces, Japanese occupation authorities, puppet armed forces personnel, allied armed forces personnel at the rank of regiment and above, civilian officials in enemy-controlled and ally-controlled areas at the county level and above, enemy party leaders, puppet leaders and allies at the

---

[165] Fei Yundong and Yu Kuihua, *Zhonggong mishu gongzuo jianshi, 1921–1949*, pp. 206, 209.
[166] *Shi Zhe huiyilu*, p. 201.
[167] According to Shi Zhe, all documents and materials regarding Mao's communications with the Comintern were handed over to the Central Confidential Bureau when the transceiver of the Agricultural Commission was no longer used after the Comintern was abolished. See *Shi Zhe huiyilu*, p. 201.

rank of county and above, celebrities, scholars, journalists, cult leaders, religious leaders, gangsters, bandits, famous prostitutes, and foreigners in China. Mao requested a biography ranging from several hundred to several thousand Chinese characters for each of these figures.[168] In addition, the SAD and ID were also responsible for collecting and analyzing the information and data that helped leaders in their decision making.[169]

CCP Intelligence and Espionage Services in the Civil War

Compared with the GMD, whose poor intelligence compounded the Nationalists' difficulties, the CCP's intelligence and espionage services developed successfully throughout the 1940s. Although the rectification campaign launched by Mao caused overwhelming anger and resistance, as a result of the so-called red terror employed by Kang Sheng, the campaign allowed the CCP to establish strong ideological control over its members. Kang's campaigns against GMD special agents, grotesque though they may have been, made it impossible for the agents to penetrate even low-level communist units. The CCP developed a telecommunications network that linked major cities and large areas in the countryside; moreover, the Nationalist command was infiltrated by communist undercover agents and sympathizers at almost every level. Chiang Kai-shek's assistant chief of staff, General Liu Fei, to all outward appearances was a typical GMD career soldier, but in reality he was an undercover communist agent. Another undercover communist was Guo Rugui, head of the GMD's War Planning Board. In the major battles at the close of the Civil War, the communist commanders knew in advance every Nationalist move, thus allowing the CCP to steadily encroach on GMD-controlled regions and cities.

The SAD and ID provided CCP leaders with reports on the international political climate and on major events and issues taking place outside of China. Another primary task of the CCP's intelligence organizations was to trade with the Japanese to gain much-needed supplies for the communist troops and rear areas, such as medicine. In the Civil War during the late 1940s, the SAD and ID strengthened control and guidance over its four primary intelligence networks in the Northeast China, North China, Shanghai, and Nanjing.[170] Many of the CCP's intelligence activities were initiated by the Southern Bureau, headed by Pan Hannian, which included recruiting agents from Nationalist intelligence agencies and developing the espionage network in enemies' armies, including the Japanese puppet armies. Because of their contact with the enemies, including the Japanese, many communist agents and cadres were

---

[168] Mao Zedong, "Zhonggong zhongyang guanyu diaocha yanjiu de jueding" [Decision of the CCP Center on Investigation and Research], in *Mao Zedong wenji* [Collected works of Mao Zedong], vol. 2, p. 360.

[169] Yao Yize and Chen Yuhong, *Li Kenong chuanqi*, pp. 237–8.

[170] *Beijing ribao* [Beijing daily], April 27, 2009.

imprisoned and convicted to serve long jail sentences when Pan was arrested in
1955.

The CCP also established another important intelligence network in
Nanjing. Headed by Wu Kejian, this network provided a large volume of
invaluable GMD confidential materials for the CCP's so-called three great
campaigns against the GMD armies, the PLA's move to cross the Yangtze
River, and the CCP's victory over Shanghai. In particular, one of its agents,
Shen An'na, sent GMD secrets to the CCP by virtue of her role as confidential
stenographer to Chiang Kai-shek.[171] The PLA's triumph over the Nationalist Army in the well-known Liaoning-Shenyang campaign of 1947 benefited
greatly from the SAD and ID undercover agents who infiltrated key organizations in the headquarters of the GMD's Suppression Forces in the Northeast,
including the Departments of Combat, Staff, and Logistics. In addition, Zhao
Wei, chief of staff of all majors in the Staff Division of the GMD's Northeast
Security Headquarters and in charge of its Confidential Office, provided a large
number of confidential intelligence to the CCP.[172] Beginning in 1948, the SAD
and ID was assigned by the Politburo to instigate defection in the Nationalist
Army to expedite the defeat of the GMD.[173]

During the Civil War in the 1940s, the CCP intelligence organizations paid
particular attention to the following three aspects. First, CCP intelligence organizations strove to send their agents to the GMD's top-level organizations
and to recruit agents from those organizations. Second, emphasis was placed
on instigating the defection of important figures in the GMD. Third, CCP
intelligence organizations increasingly emphasized the safety of their agents,
requiring agents in Nationalist-controlled areas to have well-established covers
as journalists, businesspeople, teachers, or government employees.[174] During
the Civil War, CCP intelligence organizations undertook the tasks of decoding
and deciphering GMD messages, sending CCP agents to conduct intelligence
and counterintelligence in GMD-controlled cities before invading them, and
ensuring public security in CCP-controlled cities.[175] With undercover agents
planted in GMD armies, CCP intelligence agencies successfully gained GMD
top secrets, sometimes even before GMD army commanders could use them
on the battlefield.

Although Mao tightly controlled the SAD and ID, Zhou Enlai continued to
play an important role in leading the intelligence and espionage services during
the civil war in the late 1940s. Many of the CCP top agents were associated
with him to some extent, as in the case of Xiong Xianghui, one of the "vacant

[171] Ibid.
[172] Li Dingyuan, "Kaiguo shangjiang renmin gongchen," in *Chaohu chenkan*, part 2, September
14, 2009.
[173] Ibid.
[174] *Gong'an shigao*, p. 150.
[175] Ibid., pp. 147–52.

pieces" that Zhou had laid off in 1937,[176] who later became an important source of GMD top secrets. As a confidential secretary and trusted subordinate of Hu Zongnan, Xiong Xianghui reported to the CCP Hu's plan to invade Yan'an by revealing detailed military maneuvers and planned deployments against communist armies. From the intelligence provided by Xiong, as Zhou Enlai pointed out, "Chairman Mao knew the military orders issued by Chiang Kai-shek before they ever made it to Chiang's army commander."[177] Even after Zhou Enlai was appointed acting general chief of staff of the CMC in August 1947, he remained responsible for leading the intelligence and espionage services in both the party and the armies, even during the period when the intelligence apparatus moved away from Zhou and stayed with the Central Real Area Work Commission (*zhongyang houfang gongzuo weiyuanhui*), led by Ye Jianying, a party organization that provided intelligence and logistics to Mao who was commanding the communist armed forces nationwide against the Nationalist Army.[178] For example, when one of the CCP's top espionage groups – the Wang Shijian Intelligence Group – was destroyed between September and October 1947 by GMD intelligence organizations, Zhou led the initiative to protect the intelligence network and rescue the agents. He ordered Li Kenong to initiate damage control, including informing Yang Shangkun and Li Weihan to break off communication with the captured group and propose to the GMD intelligence organizations the possible exchange of captured spies.[179]

---

[176] When Zhou arranged for Xiong to infiltrate the Nationalist Army, he ordered Xiong not to contact any CCP organization or member and not to expose his identity to anyone. Zhou prepared for a long time not to call Xiong for duties. Xiong's identity was only known by Zhou and two of Zhou's associates. See Xiong Xianghui, *Wode qingbao yu waijiao shengya*, pp. 8–10.

[177] Xiong Xianghui, *Wode qingbao yu waijiao shengya*, p. 68.

[178] Since April 1947, the major agencies of the party and the Central Military Commission moved to northwestern Shanxi, whereas the CCP Central Column (*zhongyang zongdui*), headed by Mao, Zhou Enlai, and Ren Bishi, led a small group to stay in northern Shaanxi to preoccupy the fifteen brigades of GMD troops in northern Shaanxi, which would benefit the CCP's maneuvering on other fronts. Although the primary intelligence agencies stayed with the CCP Central Real Area Work Commission, led by Ye Jianying, they reported to the CCP Central Column regularly. See *Yang Shangkun huiyilu*, p. 334; "Ye Jianying zhuan" bianxiezu, *Ye Jianying zhuan* [A biography of Ye Jianying], pp. 379–82.

[179] Sun Guoda, "Zhen Jiemin and Mao Renfeng ceng kuangwang di shengchen 'gaokua le zhonggong banbi tianxia'" [Zhen Jiemin and Mao Renfeng arrogantly claim that the GMD "destroyed half of the CCP-controlled regions"], in *Beijing ribao* [Beijing daily], August 31, 2009; Xiong Xianghui, *Wode qingbao yu waijiao shengya*, pp. 65–7.

9

The Intelligence Apparatus and Services under the People's Republic of China

This chapter probes the evolution of the CCP's intelligence apparatus by pinpointing causes and explaining the adaptation of its functions during the elite leadership changes in the era of the PRC. Although Chinese intelligence services are not directly engaged in the activities of elite security, as are China's police and security agencies, they maintain close relationships with the security services. As China's main domestic and international intelligence organization, the Ministry of State Security (MSS) is responsible for counterespionage work, ensuring state security, maintaining social and political stability, surveilling and monitoring political dissidents and ethical and religious separatists, safeguarding economic development, and encouraging Chinese citizens to be loyal to the state.

As China's largest and most active state intelligence agency, domestic intelligence is a large portion of its work, including collecting domestic intelligence and monitoring unlawful domestic activities and persons, such as corrupt government officials and political dissidents. In addition to domestic intelligence, the MSS is responsible for foreign intelligence and counterintelligence operations. Officers of the MSS are basically secret police; they do not wear uniforms when performing their duties, and their responsibilities are primarily covert. This chapter also examines the origins and the considerable role of military intelligence organizations, and it identifies the mechanisms and characteristics of military intelligence in party politics.

The mission of the MSS is to protect national interests and guarantee the CCP's rule through human, signal, remote, electronic, and communications intelligence in its operations. Because counterespionage is a primary function of the MSS, it is also responsible for monitoring foreign businesspeople; tourists; diplomats; employees of embassies and foreign companies; and Chinese citizens who have interacted with foreigners in the past, including relatives who live abroad. Another important task is intelligence collection regarding Chinese citizens (in China or abroad) and significant political events. The duties of intelligence collection often overlap with the Bureau of Domestic Security under the Ministry of Public Security. The MSS's establishment marked a large-scale reorganization of the security and intelligence apparatuses, including the CCP Central Investigation Department (CID) and the Bureau of Political Security (BPS) under the Ministry of Public Security (MPS). Both the Central Investigation Department and the Ministry of Public Security trace their institutional origins to the Social Affairs Department (SAD).

Establishment of the Central Investigation Department

The Social Affairs Department was abolished in August 1949, and its internal security and domestic counterintelligence departments were merged with the Ministry of Public Security, led by Luo Ruiqing. Its foreign intelligence departments were reorganized into the Liaison Department, under the General Intelligence Department of the CMC. The Liaison Department was headed by Li Kenong and later Zou Dapeng, after Li took leave because of health problems. The Liaison Department received dual command from the Central General Office and the PLA General Staff Department.[1] The General Staff Department is the most important department; through it the CMC ensures overall command and operational control of PLA units. As the PLA's operational headquarters, the General Staff Department involves administration and other routine command jobs, administers military buildup and oversees quality of the services, supervises all theater operations, and controls the nation's combat forces at and above the corps level and its air and naval units at the division level.[2] In March 1955, the Liaison Department of the CMC was renamed the Central Investigation Department, a reconstituted political and military intelligence apparatus that consolidated Chinese foreign intelligence efforts in one central department. According to Yang Shangkun, director of the Central General Office, the name change mainly reflected the overwhelming opinion of the Liaison Department that expressed the desire to return to the party system instead of staying under the jurisdiction of the PLA.[3]

In the early 1950s, CCP leadership was unsure how the former SAD intelligence divisions could serve the newly established PRC, particularly because of the imposed U.S.-led embargo, which limited China's initiatives overseas. Many of the former SAD top intelligence agents were transferred to work in the Foreign Ministry, as were Xiong Xianghui and Shen Jian, two of the so-called top-three most outstanding undercover agents of the late 1930s and 1940s. Although Li Kenong was appointed director of the PLA General

---

[1] Su Weimin, "Yang Shangkun tan zai zhongyang bangongting ershi nian" [Yang Shangkun talked about his twenty years in the Central General Office], in *Bainian chao* [Hundred-year tide], no. 7 (2008), pp. 19–20.
[2] John Wilson Levis and Litai Xue, *Imagined Enemies: China Prepares for Uncertain War*, p. 117.
[3] Su Weimin, "Yang Shangkun tan zai zhongyang bangongting ershi nian," p. 20.

Intelligence Department, this position was more symbolic than substantial. Li was primarily assigned to lead day-to-day administration of the foreign ministry as its vice minister, assisting Zhou Enlai with the PRC's foreign affairs. In addition, Li led the organization of the new Foreign Ministry, including the recruitment of its personnel.[4] In July 1951, Li left the leadership of the PLA General Intelligence Department after he was involved in the joint PRC-DPRK delegation as a primary negotiator with the United States in Korea.

A significant development in China's intelligence services immediately after the founding of the People's Republic of China was the division of civilian and military intelligence following the abolishment of the Social Affairs Department (SAD). The Social Affairs Department was abolished three months before the People's Republic of China was founded. The CCP's goal was to set up two state organs to replace it – the Ministry of Public Security and the Ministry of Intelligence.[5] It is unknown why CCP leadership later decided against having a state agency solely in charge of intelligence. The abolished SAD was divided into three parts and put under the auspices of other organizations: the domestic security division was placed under the MPS, the foreign intelligence and information division was merged with the General Administration of Intelligence under the Government Administration Council (the predecessor of the State Council), and the other divisions were absorbed into the PLA. When the Central Military Commission's General Intelligence Department was established in December 1950, the former SAD divisions absorbed into the PLA were reorganized as the Liaison Division, one of the three subordinate divisions of the General Intelligence Department (those being the Intelligence Administration Division, the Technology Division, and the Liaison Division). After the CMC's General Intelligence Department was abolished in February 1953, its subordinate divisions were put directly under the authority of the PLA's General Staff Department. Among them, the Intelligence Administration Division and the Liaison Division became the Intelligence Department and the Liaison Department of the PLA's General Staff Department, respectively. In March 1955, the Liaison Department of the General Staff department was renamed the Central Investigation Department, a reconstituted political and military intelligence apparatus that consolidated Chinese foreign intelligence efforts in one central department.

The CCP intelligence, led by Li Kenong, did not play an active role in party politics. Li went to the Soviet Union to receive treatment for his severe asthma condition in early 1950, but he returned to China in June 1951, a year after

---

[4] Li Dingyuan, "Kaiguo shangjiang renmin gongchen," in *Chaohu chenkan*, part 2, September 14, 2009.
[5] Tao Siju, *Xinzhongguo diyiren gong'an buzhang: Luo Ruiqing* [The first public security minister of new China: Luo Ruiqing], p. 5.

the Korean War broke out.[6] Li was replaced by Zou Dapeng after Li was appointed leader of the joint PRC-DPRK delegation and resumed his role as a primary negotiator with the United States in July 1951, managing negotiations over the Korean War. The fact that Li's roles required him to focus on foreign affairs rather than intelligence indicates that intelligence services were declining in importance, given the CCP's limited access to foreign intelligence. The MPS, headed by Luo Ruiqing and directly monitored by Mao, had taken charge of security and intelligence services for the CCP leadership; therefore, it was less important to Mao to consolidate his power in the foreign intelligence and espionage services. It has been speculated that Mao's lack of concern for the General Administration of Intelligence (the leading government intelligence organ) and the CMC General Intelligence Department (the leading PLA intelligence organ) led to their abolishment in August 1952 and the spring of 1953, respectively.[7] Although all the responsibilities of the General Administration of Intelligence were absorbed by the Foreign Ministry,[8] the abolished CMC General Intelligence Department was handed over to the PLA General Staff Department. Moreover, many former CCP important intelligence agents were treated coldly after the abolishment of the organizations; some even became targets of the political campaigns against counterrevolutionaries because of their complicated career history as past CCP agents.[9] One of the most publicized cases was that of the Pan Hannian and Yang Fan Counterrevolutionary Clique, which involved many former intelligence agents.

Dismissals of Pan Hannian and Yang Fan

Along with the 1954 and 1955 campaigns against the Gao Gang and Rao Shushi Antiparty Clique and the Hu Feng Counterrevolutionary Clique, the 1955 dismissals of Pan Hannian and Yang Fan and their "clique" were another important political campaign launched by Mao to ensure political and

---

[6] Li Dingyuan, "Kaiguo shangjiang renmin gongchen," in *Chaohu chenkan*, part 2, September 14, 2009.

[7] The CMC General Intelligence Department (*junwei zong jingbaobu*) was established in December 1950 as an independent organization directly under the leadership of the CMC. It was abolished in February 1953 and reorganized as an agency under the PLA's General Staff Department. See Nie Junhua, "Xin zhongguo chengli chuqi zhengwu yuan de sheli yu chexiao" [Establishment and abolishment of the Government Administrative Council in the early PRC], *Dangshi bolan* [General review of the CCP history], no. 6 (2009), p. 9; *Lingdao jigou yange*, p. 936.

[8] *Zuzhi shi*, appendix 1, part 1, p. 79.

[9] For example, Pao Junnan, an important intelligence source for the Teke during the 1920s, was imprisoned in early 1950 because of his background working for the GMD and the Wang Jingwei puppet government. Xu Qiang and Li Yun, two CCP top agents in the 1930s in Shanghai, were put under investigation during the Yan'an rectification of the 1940s; they did not receive a verdict for their cases until the early 1950s. Their names were cleared only when Li Kenong personally intervened. See Li Dingyuan, "Kaiguo shangjiang renmin gongchen," in *Chaohu chenkan*, part 3, September 21, 2009.

ideological unity and conformity under his leadership. The case of Pan and Yang, as Frederick C. Teiwes points out, was "complicated and tangential" because there was "really no convincing proof of their guilt" and "no unambiguous evidence of their innocence."[10] A large amount of materials have been published in recent years, and the newly released sources shed light on the story of the Pan and Yang case.

Pan Hannian had been a major figure in the CCP intelligence services since the early 1930s, so the publicity of his and Yang's case went hand in hand with the large-scale dismissals of the CCP's intelligence organizations that began in 1955 and lasted throughout the Cultural Revolution.[11] Keith Forster has argued that the arrests of Pan and Yang were linked to a nationwide political campaign of suppressing counterrevolutionaries (*sufan*), and they "were associated (without justification) with the previous purge in 1954 of a leading East China and central official Rao Shushi.[12] Born in 1906, Pan Hannian came onto the scene of the CCP intelligence services in the early 1930s and was a major figure until 1955. Pan joined the party in 1926 and had been a propagandist official in the CCP's Department of Propaganda and director of the Propaganda Department of the CCP's Jiangsu Party Committee before he was assigned to work in the central committee's Special Services Division (Teke) in 1931. He was appointed head of the Teke's Second Division (i.e., Intelligence Cell) and was later appointed head of the third section (i.e., the Red Squads) in the early 1930s. This occurred around the time that the CCP Central Committee was forced to evacuate due to intense pressure from GMD intelligence and police in the Shanghai International Settlement and the Shanghai French Concession. When Zhou Enlai reorganized the Teke in May 1931, Pan was the third-highest-ranking figure, after Chen Yun and Kang Sheng.

Pan was ordered to leave GMD-controlled Shanghai for the Jiangxi base areas after Pan Zinian and Ding Ling, two prominent left-wing writers familiar with Pan (Pan Zinian was Pan Hannian's brother), were captured by the GMD. In Jiangxi, he was appointed CCP representative to negotiate with the Anti-Chiang Fujian People's Government, headed by General Cai Tingkai, and the Nationalist local armed forces in Guangdong, headed by General Chen Jitang. Pan participated in the Long March, which he secretly left for Moscow after he received orders from the CCP leadership to reestablish communications between the CCP and the Comintern. After Pan returned from Moscow in 1936, he became one of Zhou Enlai's key assistants in negotiating the second united

---

[10] Frederick C. Teiwes, *Politics at Mao's Court: Gao Gang and Party Factionalism in the Early 1950s*, p. 131.

[11] Wen Guang, "Pan Hannian yuan'an de qianqian houhou" [Before and after the unjust case of Pan Hannian], in Zhonggong shanghai shiwei dangshi yanjiushi (ed.), *Pan Hannian zai Shanghai*, p. 426.

[12] Keith Forster, "Localism, Central Policy, and the Provincial Purges of 1957–1958: The Case of Zhejiang," in Timothy Cheek and Tony Saich (eds.), *New Perspectives on State Socialism in China*, p. 194.

front with the GMD. During most of the Sino-Japanese War, Pan led CCP intelligence organizations in eastern China. During the Civil War, Pan was sent to Hong Kong, where he established one of the most successful CCP espionage networks.[13] After the PRC was established, Pan was made deputy mayor of Shanghai, responsible for leading public security efforts and campaigns against Nationalist agents in Shanghai.[14]

The decision to imprison Pan in 1955 was made after Mao read Pan's confession regarding his 1943 unscheduled meeting with Wang Jingwei, head of the Nanjing puppet government. This was at a time when Pan was in charge of the underground CCP intelligence and espionage organizations in eastern China. Official explanations in post-Mao publications emphasize Pan's innocence, asserting that he was actually kidnapped by Li Shiqun, an infamous intelligence chief serving Wang Jingwei for the puppet government in occupied China.[15] Although top CCP leaders encouraged Pan to employ enemies' intelligence personnel, such as Li Shiqun and Hu Junhe, in CCP intelligence gathering, Pan neither reported his meeting with Wang Jingwei to Yan'an nor informed the CCP East China Bureau about the incident.[16] Simply meeting with Wang Jingwei was not a problem, but Pan's failure to report the meeting brought about disastrous consequences. The CCP had been negotiating with Japanese armies during the Sino-Japanese War to keep the CCP alive. In fact, the CCP leadership in Yan'an ordered Zeng Shan, director of the Organization Department of the New Fourth Army, to negotiate with the Japanese armies after they proposed a cease-fire with the CCP.[17] According to Pan, he concealed information about his meeting with Wang Jingwei from the party because he was afraid of being dismissed. At that time, the CCP's East China Bureau, led by Rao Shushi, was conducting a rectification campaign against Chen Yi, whom Pan supported. Pan was also afraid of being a suspected traitor, especially after Yang Fan, head of the Security Department in the Third Cell of the New Fourth Army, was accused of being "the leader of the GMD secret service" and was subsequently placed under investigation.[18]

---

[13] Yao Yize and Chen Yuhong, *Li Kenong chuanqi*, p. 308.

[14] Wang Zhengming, "Chenyuan zhaoxue yingming yongcun" [Unjust unfounded charges are cleared, heroic name endures forever], in Zhonggong shanghai shiwei dangshi yanjiushi (ed.), *Pan Hannian zai Shanghai*, p. 405; Yi Qi, "'Pan Yang anjian' shimo" [Beginning and end of 'Pan Yang case'], in Zhonggong shanghai shiwei dangshi yanjiushi (ed.), *Pan Hannian zai Shanghai*, p. 371.

[15] *Chen Yun zhuan*, vol. 2, p. 1528.

[16] Hu Junhe was a communist turncoat who became an agent for the GMD Central Bureau of Statistics and Investigation and later the Nanjing puppet government. See Wen Guang, "Pan Hannian yuan'an de qianqian houhou," in Zhonggong shanghai shiwei dangshi yanjiushi (ed.), *Pan Hannian zai Shanghai*, p. 423.

[17] Sun Yuting, "'Daoqie zhongyang dang'an guan hexin jimi' an zhenxiang" [The truth of the case of 'Stealing the Top Secrets from the Central Archive'], pp. 189, 195.

[18] Wen Guang, "Pan Hannian yuan'an de qianqian houhou," in Zhonggong shanghai shiwei dangshi yanjiushi (ed.), *Pan Hannian zai Shanghai*, pp. 422–5.

Before Pan was arrested, Mao launched a lengthy campaign against Rao Shushi, party chief of the CCP East China Bureau, which extended to include the imprisonment of Yang Fan, deputy director of Shanghai Public Security. For Mao to create a climate against the antiparty clique, led by Gao Gang and Rao Shushi, and to overall promote his "suppressing the counterrevolutionaries" campaign in the party, Yang Fan became an ideal target. Yang had employed a large number of former GMD agents to capture GMD spies in Shanghai; thus, his work in counterintelligence could be easily manipulated to be construed in a different light in the public's eye. When the CCP took over Shanghai in 1949, Yang Fan, then director of intelligence of the CCP East China Bureau, was appointed director of public security of Shanghai Municipal City, and he was charged with the task of eradicating GMD agents and spies in Shanghai. Therefore, Yang Fan created the Intelligence Commission, which provided relevant intelligence to assist with securing the city, protecting party leaders, and arresting GMD agents. Political order in Shanghai was still volatile, and with the GMD intelligence network far from eradicated, survival of the new communist regime in Shanghai was not guaranteed.

Yang's Intelligence Commission absorbed many former GMD intelligence officers who had surrendered to the CCP. Yang Fan had appointed Hu Junhe, former agent of the GMD Central Bureau of Statistics and Investigation and later of the Nanjing puppet government, to lead the commission. However, the Ministry of Public Security in Beijing questioned the creation of the Intelligence Commission, particularly the use of the surrendered GMD agents and the appointment of Hu Junhe. As a result, an investigation was conducted against Yang Fan, who was later accused of "committing severe mistakes in his work," for "employing, harboring, and covering GMD special agents and counterrevolutionaries."[19] When the campaign against Gao Gang and Rao Shushi was launched in 1954, the case of Yang Fan was mentioned and quickly associated with Rao Shushi, who had approved the establishment of the Intelligence Commission and had endorsed employing the surrendered GMD agents. Yang's case was no longer framed as "a contradiction among the people" but as "an antagonistic conflict between our enemies and us," which resulted in Yang's arrest in December 1954. At that time Mao publicly categorized Yang as a member of the Rao Shushi Antiparty Clique. After Pan Hannian was imprisoned in April 1955, he and Yang Fan's crimes were given higher status as they were named to be leaders of their own antiparty faction: the Pan Hannian and Yang Fan Counterrevolutionary Clique.[20]

The reasons Pan Hannian and Yang Fan fell out of favor are complicated. Historically, Mao generally distrusted the CCP intelligence apparatus because

---

[19] Yi Qi, "'Pan Yang anjian' shimo," in Zhonggong shanghai shiwei dangshi yanjiushi (ed.), *Pan Hannian zai Shanghai*, pp. 370–82.

[20] Ibid., pp. 379–80.

of the historical ties of the original intelligence services with Zhou Enlai and the returned students from Moscow. However, Mao's dissatisfaction with Pan dated back to the 1930s, when Pan was a trusted follower and personal friend of Bo Gu, head of the CCP's Temporary Central Committee in Shanghai and a leading figure in the returned students faction. Bo and Pan's friendship began in 1925 and grew stronger after Bo returned to Shanghai from Moscow in September 1930. At the time Pan had been working in the CCP Propaganda Department as a general staff member, and Bo was a propaganda officer in the CCP General Labor Union. After Wang Ming took charge of the CCP in 1931, Bo recommended Pan for membership in the Special Services Division. As Pan gradually won the trust of Wang Ming, Pan was the only person authorized to be the secret liaison between Wang Ming and the CCP Temporary Central Committee, headed by Bo Gu. This was a contingency plan in the event that communication between the CCP and the Comintern was disconnected after Wang left Shanghai for Moscow to lead the CCP delegation to the Comintern.[21] In 1933 Pan was transferred to the Jiangxi base areas and subsequently participated in the Long March. In February 1935, Bo Gu and Zhou Enlai sent both Pan Hannian and Chen Yun to reestablish communication between the CCP and the Comintern, particularly to inform Stalin of the change in leadership after the Zunyi conference, in which Zhang Wentian replaced Bo Gu as head of the CCP. Pan arrived in Moscow in September 1935 and spent three months at the Intelligence Bureau of the Comintern, where he was trained in the cipher that would be used for Comintern and CCP communications.

Pan's image suffered further as a result of Pan's late return to Yan'an, which prevented the CCP leadership from communicating with the Comintern because of Pan's monopoly on the new cipher. Pan and Zhang Hao were sent back to Yan'an separately; Zhang left in October 1935, and Pan left in February 1936. Whereas Zhang Hao arrived at Yan'an on November 7, 1935, taking only one month to travel, Pan took more than five months to arrive. Meanwhile, Mao was waiting in Yan'an for Pan to return so that the CCP could resume communications with the Comintern. Pan's late return outraged Mao so much that Mao refused to see Pan personally, instead simply requiring him to transcribe the new cipher for Deng Yingchao, director of the Confidential Office of the Central Secretary Division and Zhou Enlai's wife.[22] Pan's reason for delay was an unexpected route change, from Leningrad to Greece to Hong Kong, to Leningrad to Paris to Hong Kong. Although he blamed the unfavorable political situation in Greece for the long delays, some CCP top

---

[21] Qin Fuquan, "Bo Gu yu Pan Hannian guanxi de beihou" [Behind the relationship of Bo Gu and Pan Hannian], in *Yanhuang chunqiu* [Spring and autumn in China], no. 10 (2006), pp. 20–6.

[22] Qin Fuquan, "Bo Gu yu Pan Hannian guanxi de beihou," pp. 23–5; *Lingdao jigou yange he chengyuan minglu*, p. 326.

leaders, including Pan's close friend Bo Gu, were not convinced the political situation in Greece could account for a full four months of delay.[23] Because Mao knew Pan was a trusted follower of Wang Ming, Pan's inexplicable poor behavior worsened Mao's impression of him. Mao strongly believed that Pan "could not be trusted" because "he was Wang Ming's follower," and because it seemed obvious to him that "[Pan] deemed Wang Ming's assignments more important than handing over the cipher to the Center."[24]

When the PRC was established in 1949, Pan became one of several deputy mayors in Shanghai. However, Pan's career was destroyed in April 1955, when he was accused of "secretly seeking the assistance of the Japanese secret service organs and colluding with the major traitor Wang Jingwei." Pan was immediately put in prison, where he remained until his death more than twenty years later, in 1977. There were two charges against Pan when he was arrested. The first was collusion with the enemy, and the charge cited as evidence the instance when Pan had secretly met Wang Jingwei during the Sino-Japanese War but had not reported doing so to party organizations. The second was harboring the enemy, because Pan was directly responsible for "appointing enemy agents to important positions and shielding them." The accusations brought about the conclusion that Pan was a "clandestine traitor" hidden in the party.[25]

Li Kenong led an investigation of Pan on April 29, 1955; he submitted the following conclusion to the Politburo and the Central Secretariat:

1. CCP leadership and the Central Intelligence Department issued instructions that allowed CCP agents to employ enemy agents or CCP traitors to gain useful intelligence for the party.
2. There was a formal report concerning Pan's employment of Li Shiqun (the intelligence chief of the puppet government) and Hu Junhe (a communist turncoat who became an agent of the Nationalist Central Bureau of Statistics and Investigation and later an agent of the Nanjing puppet government) to gain enemy intelligence.
3. Pan and other CCP agents in Shanghai could still avail themselves of holes in the enemy's loose control over the Shanghai International settlement before the Pacific War. Although there was the risk of Pan exposing

---

[23] Bo Gu later told Pan: "After I sent you and Chen Yun to Moscow, Mao and Zhou impatiently waited for your return. It would be beyond reproach if you returned [to Yan'an] one or two months late, given that you must find a safe route out of need for protecting the cipher and due to your position as the CCP representative of negotiations with the GMD. However, you returned nine months later than we expected. Many things happened in those nine months, and the whole time we were unable to communicate with the Executive Committee of the Comintern. Of course Mao was upset!" See Qin Fuquan, "Bo Gu yu Pan Hannian guanxi de beihou," pp. 23–5.
[24] Qin Fuquan, "Bo Gu yu Pan Hannian guanxi de beihou," pp. 24–5.
[25] Yao Yize and Chen Yuhong, *Li Kenong chuanqi*, pp. 312–13.

himself (to the enemies), there were still favorable conditions (for Pan and other CCP agents) to survive (in enemy-controlled areas).[26]

4. Before the Pacific War the intelligence that Pan provided to the CCP leadership about Japanese agents, the puppet army, negotiations between the United States and Japan, and the Soviet-German War were valuable.

5. The information provided by key agents of the intelligence network led by Pan was extremely valuable.[27]

The report provided by Li Kenong found no evidence proving the charges against Pan. Some high-ranking leaders, particularly those who had worked with Pan (such as Chen Yun and Liao Chengzhi), were never convinced that Pan Hannian was a traitor to the party.[28] According to Chen Yun, if Pan was a GMD agent, many CCP intelligence organizations, at least Pan's intelligence network, would have been destroyed. In 1981, as Chen Yun pointed out when he strived to redress Pan's case:

If Pan Hannian betrayed the Party, why were no other officials in the Shanghai Party Organizations (e.g., Liu Xiao) whom Pan knew very well arrested, and why did the Party organizations remain in tact after Pan left?[29]

Liao Chengzhi, the party chief in Hong Kong between 1938 and 1942, firmly believed that "Pan was by no means a traitor," because "no underground Party organizations with which Pan was intimately familiar, such as those in Shanghai, Guangdong, or Hong Kong, had been damaged."[30] Pan's pretrial period lasted more than eight years; there has been speculation that the delay was related to the lack of evidence proving that Pan was a traitor. In January 1963, Pan was sentenced to fifteen years in prison, having waited nearly eight years after his arrest in April 1955 for a verdict.[31]

Because Yang Fan had been implicated in aiding Rao Shushi in "employing, harboring, and protecting the identities of the counterrevolutionaries," the arrest of Pan Hannian aggravated the charges against Yang Fan. Nine days after Pan Hannian was arrested, Yang Fan was imprisoned. Like Pan, Yang's pretrial

---

[26] Although some had seen Pan and his agents' ability to evade GMD capture as a result of their collusion with the GMD, Li's report claims that, in actuality, the environment was favorable enough for CCP spies to survive without being discovered by enemy agencies. See Yao Yize and Chen Yuhong, *Li Kenong chuanqi*, p. 314.

[27] Ibid., pp. 313–14.

[28] *Chen Yun zhuan*, vol. 2, p. 1529.

[29] Ibid., pp. 1529–30.

[30] *Guojia jiguan taolun lishi wenti jueyi (chao'an) jianbao* [Bulletin of Resolution regarding the Discussions of State Organizations about Historical Issues, draft], no. 22, third group, November 5, 1980, quote from *Chen Yun zhuan*, vol. 2, pp. 1530–1.

[31] *Chen Yun zhuan*, vol. 2, p. 1528.

period lasted ten years, and he was sentenced to sixteen years in prison.[32] Similar to Mao's displeasure with Pan, Mao's dislike of Yang can be traced back to the 1940s, when Yang reported to the Politburo on Mao's unofficial wife, the "actress" Jiang Qing. Yang Fan had known Jiang Qing since the 1930s, when Yang worked undercover for the CCP as a journalist in Shanghai. In September 1938, Yang was transferred to the New Fourth Army (NFA), where he was appointed secretary of the NFA headquarters and director of the Investigation Section of the NFA's Military Court Division. When news of Mao's plan to marry Jiang Qing spread to the NFA's leadership, Xiang Ying, political commissar of the NFA, ordered Yang Fan to provide information regarding Jiang Qing's past in Shanghai. This was an attempt by Xiang Ying to pressure Mao to call off his marriage with Jiang Qing.[33] Yang Fan spoke to Jiang Qing's sexual proclivities on the Shanghai Bund, which Xiang Ying used in lobbying Mao. Xiang Ying did not waver in his position that "Jiang Qing was not an appropriate wife for Chairman Mao."[34] Furthermore, Yang Fan's disclosure implied that treachery might have been involved in a GMD arrest of Jiang Qing in 1934.[35]

Yang Fan later paid a hefty price for providing information about Jiang Qing. In 1943, Yang Fan was suddenly arrested after being called to attend a meeting at NFA headquarters in Huanghuatang, in southern Anhui. The order came directly from Kang Sheng, director of the SAD in Yan'an. Yang was accused of being a traitor and was imprisoned for ten months. Yang was ultimately released by Pan Hannian, director of Intelligence of the CCP Central China Bureau and head of Social Affairs Department under the CCP Central China Bureau, who as head of the investigation dropped the charges against Yang Fan.[36] Many high-ranking leaders who were familiar with Yang Fan, such as Chen Peixian and Wang Fang, believed that the real cause of Yang

---

[32] Yang Fan, "Wuyun sanjin xian zhonghun – daonian Pan Hannian tongzhi" [Dark clouds disappear completely – Mourning for comrade Pan Hannian], in Zhonggong shanghai shiwei dangshi yanjiushi (ed.), *Pan Hannian zai Shanghai*, pp. 395–6.

[33] According to Liu Ying, spouse of current CCP General Secretary Zhang Wentian, many senior high-ranking leaders disapproved of Mao's marriage with Jiang Qing; thus, they approached Zhang Wentian for help in swaying Mao's decision. In Liu Ying's words, they all felt "it [was] very inappropriate for Chairman Mao to marry Jiang Qing." See Liu Ying, *Liu Ying zishu* [The autobiographical notes of Liu Ying], p. 123.

[34] Chen Peixian, *Chen Peixian huiyilu – Zai 'yiyue fengbao' de zhongxin* [Memoirs of Chen Peixian – At the center of the "January Storm"], p. 15; Wang Fang, *Wang Fang huiyilu* [Memoirs of Wang Fang], pp. 202–3.

[35] Jiang Qing was arrested by the GMD police in 1934 and was released after she confessed. The reason for her release might contribute to her insignificant role in the party. Kang Sheng covered her history when Jiang went to Yan'an and gradually got close to Mao, apparently under Mao's acquiescence. See Wang Fang, *Wang Fang huiyilu*, pp. 203–4; *Zhou Enlai nianpu, 1949–1976*, vol. 3, pp. 687–8.

[36] Yang Fan, "Wuyun sanjin xian zhonghun – Daonian Pan Hannian tongzhi," pp. 396–8; *Wang Fang huiyilu*, pp. 202–3.

Fan's dismissal was not his use of captured GMD agents to implicate and capture more GMD agents but that he offended Jiang Qing.[37]

Although Jiang Qing played a role in Mao's decision to dismiss Pan Hannian and Yang Fan, Mao's deep distrust in the intelligence services and his particular distrust of the two former CCP top agents were the real factors that decided their fate. The most profound impact of Pan's case was that many former CCP agents, including those who were both professionally outstanding and loyal to the party, were implicated and purged because of their ties with Pan. This was true for Yuan Shu and Dong Jianwu, who were both arrested after Pan Hannian's dismissal.[38] Although many former subordinates of Pan Hannian and Yang Fan were not arrested, many were put under investigation, transferred out of public security, or demoted, as in the cases of Zhao Zheng, He Luo, Wang Yiwei, Gan Ge, and Tang Lu. Some agents, such as Wang Dachao, ended up committing suicide mainly because of their disappointment over the party's misunderstanding of their innocence and their long-standing dedication to the party.[39]

Central Investigation Department in Elite Politics

The Central Investigation Department (CID) was responsible for collecting information and analyzing data to provide accurate and timely foreign intelligence to the CCP leadership. The CID worked closely with the Foreign Ministry, which was convenient because Li Kenong was not only director of the CID but also a vice minister in the Foreign Ministry.[40] The importance of the CID, according to Roderick MacFarquhar and Michael Schoenhals, pertained to "counterintelligence, the collection of political intelligence, ensuring the safety of senior officials traveling abroad, and supervising visits to China by foreign dignitaries and delegations."[41] In addition, the CID was responsible for recruiting and training security personnel who were stationed at Chinese embassies and PRC intelligence agencies overseas. Li Jusheng, deputy director of the Xinhua News Agency in Hong Kong during the 1970s and early 1980s, had been both a diplomat and a professional intelligence officer before he took the position with Xinhua.[42] Another case was Wang Shuren, commercial

[37] See Chen Peixian, *Chen Peixian huiyilu – Zai 'yiyue fengbao' de zhongxin,'* pp. 14–15; *Wang Fang huiyilu*, pp. 202–3.

[38] *Chen Yun zhuan*, vol. 2, pp. 1530–3; Cheng Yi, "Yuan Shu de qingbao shengya" [Intelligence career of Yuan Shu], in *Dangshi tiandi* [Field of party history], no. 11 (2004), pp. 36–44; Li Dingyuan, "Kaiguo shangjiang renmin gongchen," in *Chaohu chenkan*, part 3, September 21, 2009.

[39] Wen Guang, "Pan Hannian yuan'an de qianqian houhou," pp. 426–31.

[40] Li Dingyuan, "Kaiguo shangjiang renmin gongchen," in *Chaohu chenkan*, part 2, September 14, 2009.

[41] Roderick MacFarquhar and Michael Schoenhals, *Mao's Last Revolution*, p. 97.

[42] Xu Jiatun, *Xu Jiatun xianggang huiyilu*, vol. 1, p. 71.

counselor at the Chinese embassy in Cambodia during the 1960s. In the 1970s, Wang was also appointed deputy director of the CID's Guangzhou branch, where he was responsible for sending CID agents to foreign countries.[43] Notably, CID agents assigned to work in Chinese embassies were most likely to receive orders not from the Foreign Ministry but from the CID. Although the CID or the Liaison Department of the CMC performed many functions that the SAD had previously fulfilled, such as maintaining the classified archives,[44] the CID became less powerful than the Ministry of Public Security in terms of intelligence and counterespionage work.

In addition to the CID's responsibilities for foreign counterintelligence activities and collecting intelligence, the CID worked with the Ministry of Public Security to ensure the safety of senior officials traveling abroad as well as foreign dignitaries and delegations visiting China, under the leadership and coordination of Yang Shangkun, director of the Central General Office.[45] Whereas the Intelligence Department of the PLA's General Staff Department, the CCP Intelligence Commission, and the CID were mainly responsible for collecting and analyzing intelligence provided by spies abroad, the MPS, led by Luo Ruiqing, led domestic counterespionage efforts, including collecting and analyzing information, investigating espionage cases, and detaining and arresting suspected spies.[46] As in the case of the well-known *Kashmir Princess* incident, in which GMD intelligence attempted to assassinate Zhou Enlai when he was scheduled to take an Air India passenger plane – the *Kashmir Princess* – to an Afro-Asian conference in Bandung, Indonesia. In this instance, Li Kenong uncovered the assassination plot and provided all necessary intelligence for CCP agents outside China to protect Zhou Enlai's trip, including details of the plot as well as the names of the GMD intelligence organizations and their members operating in Hong Kong. The GMD agents still managed to sabotage the plane, causing eight members of the CCP delegation (Zhou Enlai and Vice Premier Chen Yi were not on board) to be killed at sea.[47]

Unlike the CID, the Ministry of Public Security was mainly responsible for domestic counterintelligence investigations and operations. Its political security section was assigned to conduct counterespionage operations against foreign

43 Zhou Degao, *Wo yu zhonggong he jiangong* [My career with the CCP and the Khmer Rouge], pp. 68–9.
44 Information regarding the top CCP agents was kept within the SAD. After the SAD was abolished, the SAD handed over the materials to the CMC General Intelligence Department and later the CID, as in the case of Major A Long, a staff officer of the GMD Military Commission, who became the CCP spy in 1947 and the information about him was kept in the SAD. See Sun Zhen, "'Hu Feng anjian' de qianqian houhou" [Before and after the "Hu Feng case"], in Sun Mingshan (ed.), *Lishi shunjian*, vol. 2, p. 35.
45 Su Weimin, "Yang Shangkun tan zai zhongyang bangongting ershi nian," p. 20.
46 Li Dingyuan, "Kaiguo shangjiang renmin gongchen," in *Chaohu chenkan*, part 2, September 14, 2009.
47 Ibid. Li Dingyuan, "Kaiguo shangjiang renmin gongchen," in *Chaohu chenkan*, part 3, September 21, 2009; Xiong Xianghui, *Wode qingbao yu waijiao shengya* [My intelligence and diplomatic careers], pp. 142–53.

intelligence services and counterintelligence investigations of citizens who had established close contact with foreigners. The Division of Enemy Investigation (*dizhen chu*) of the MPS was created not to collect information and intelligence abroad but to monitor enemy communications and actions, to investigate cases, and to track enemies within China. It expanded so much that some local Public Security branches split the division into two or three bureaus.[48] Counterintelligence investigations involved interviewing people and collecting evidence to identify recruited agents and foreign espionage activities. Counterespionage operations involved recruiting agents and were designed to ultimately penetrate foreign intelligence organizations, to collect information with which to manipulate the adversary.[49]

For example, the well-known case of Ji Zhaoxiang's concealed transceiver, an alleged U.S. plot to assassinate Mao and the PRC leaders atop Tiananmen Gate by attacking them with a mortar on October 1, 1950,[50] was handled and solved by the Bureau of Political Security, under the MPS. The GMD spy Ji Zhaoxiang was sent by the GMD intelligence organizations in Taiwan to obtain information in Beijing to assassinate Mao; of supreme importance to GMD intelligence that Ji was to discover was Mao's whereabouts during his trip to Moscow in November and December 1949.[51] During Mao's trip to Moscow, the Telecommunications Division of the MPS learned from agents in Taiwan that GMD agents had orders to assassinate Mao.[52] In addition, the MPS successfully cracked down on an international espionage organization that attempted to bomb Tiananmen Square in 1950. According to the MPS, they led the investigation and prevention of this U.S. Central Intelligence Agency–supported plot that resulted in the arrests of several people of various nationalities, including Antonio Riva (Italian), Ryuichi Yamaguchi (Japanese), Zhi Wei (French), Zhe Li (Italian), Waiter Geuthmer (German), and Ma Lixin (Chinese).[53] According to international human rights groups, Antonio Riva and Ryuichi Yamaguchi were convicted of involvement in the U.S. and GMD plot to assassinate Mao and other high-ranking communist leaders. Perhaps because of the MPS's powerful intelligence capabilities, the KGB even approached the organization to propose exchanging intelligence; the CCP agreed to the exchanges, which in the past had been coordinated by the Ministry of Foreign Affairs.[54]

---

[48] Sheng Xue, '*Yuanhua an' heimu* [Unveiling the "Yuan Hua case"], pp. 100–1.

[49] Nicholas Eftimiades, *Chinese Intelligence Operations*, p. 23.

[50] Chang-Tai Hung, *Mao's New World: Political Culture in the Early People's Republic*, p. 172.

[51] Yang Qiqing, deputy minister of public security, was originally assigned to lead this intelligence-gathering case, but his duties were changed to provide a security detail for Mao on his trip to Moscow. As a result, Li Kenong was temporarily put in charge of the case. See *Yang Qiqing zhuan*, pp. 198–214.

[52] Ibid., p. 226.

[53] Ibid., pp. 255–75.

[54] Ibid., p. 396.

Since 1960, the CID has played an increasingly important role in providing information and intelligence related to foreign countries and leaders to the CCP. The Great Leap Forward, which began with great expectations in 1958, turned into an economic and human disaster for China, as well as a political debacle for Mao.[55] The aggravated tensions dominated Sino-Soviet relations after Khrushchev refused to aid China because of China's refusal to toe the new ideological line and because of a series of disputes between the two countries on foreign policy.[56] As Maurice J. Meisner has indicated, the Great Leap Forward created a legacy of bitterness and distrust between the masses and the Communist Party and further contributed to the collapse of the Sino-Soviet alliance, thus adding an increasingly precarious external situation to a grave internal economic crisis.[57] By 1960, there was a strong sentiment among party leaders that the Great Leap Forward should be abandoned, with a focus instead on improving both China's desperate socioeconomic situation and tensions in foreign relations. A debate among leaders touched on the likelihood of a world war and the possibility of peaceful coexistence with capitalist countries, as well as the degree to which China should support the national liberation movement in other countries, especially third world countries.[58] A consensus had been reached among frontline leaders, including Liu Shaoqi and Deng Xiaoping, as to the strategic goal of China's foreign policy to pursue international peace so that China would be able to focus on socialist construction at home.[59] Efforts to improve foreign relations included decreasing China's involvement in international conflicts; assisting in national liberation movements of foreign countries; and generally improving relations with the United States, the Soviet Union, and India. Although Mao's campaign against the Peng Dehuai antiparty clique at the Lushan plenum of August and September 1959 quieted dissension over the Great Leap Forward, the leadership still agreed about establishing a favorable international environment for China's economic recovery. Frontline leaders assigned the CID with preparing information and intelligence for foreign visits and CCP leaders' participation in conferences, as well as with sending many agents abroad to gather intelligence. Since the early 1970s, when the Western embargo against China was lifted, the CID has become increasingly important in progressing China's initiatives for achieving a hospitable international environment for its development.

China achieved its objective of international involvement. In 1960 alone, top leaders had visited foreign countries and attended international conferences. Zhou Enlai visited Burma, India, and Nepal in April; Deng Xiaoping led the CCP's delegation to the Sino-Soviet conference in September and the

[55] Maurice J. Meisner, *Mao's China and After: A History of the People's Republic*, p. 238.
[56] Gerald Segal, *The World Affairs Companion: The Essential One-Volume Guide to Global Issues*, p. 174.
[57] Maurice J. Meisner, *Mao's China and After: A History of the People's Republic*, pp. 238–9.
[58] Qiang Zhai, *China and the Vietnam Wars, 1950–1975*, p. 114.
[59] Chen Jian, *Mao's China and the Cold War*, p. 83.

conference of International Communist Parties and Worker's Parties in October; and Liu Shaoqi led the CCP and PRC delegation to the celebration of the
October Revolution and the conference of International Communist Parties
and Worker's Parties in Moscow from November 5 to December 9.[60] In the
early 1960s, the CCP began many initiatives and efforts to attempt to improve
its relations with foreign countries. The CID became a significant agency that
provided information and intelligence to party leaders, for them to understand
the global issues in general and the targeted countries in particular. According
to Yang Shangkun's diaries, he had scheduled several individual meetings with
leadership members of the CID, such as Kong Yuan (director of the CID), Luo
Qingchang (deputy director of the CID), and Feng Xuan (deputy director of the
CID). For example, in July 1961 alone he met with the CID's leading figures
five different days as the CCP was implementing initiatives to join the United
Nations and improve the CCP's relations with the Soviet Union.[61] The CID
continually played an important role even after Mao sent Yang Shangkun, the
key leader of the CID on behalf of the frontline leaders, to Shaanxi to attend
the Socialist Education Movement in October 1964,[62] a clear sign that Mao
was planning to dismiss Yang, and Deng Xiaoping was assigned to take over
the CID on behalf of frontline leaders.[63]

The CID also played an important role in helping the CCP's security agencies
protect CCP leaders when they visited foreign countries and in assisting the
CCP leaders in presenting a united front abroad. One mission, in April 1963,
involved sending CID senior agents to Cambodia to protect Liu Shaoqi, whom
they knew was targeted by the GMD intelligence organizations during his visit
to Cambodia.[64] With the support of undercover CID agents in Cambodia, the
CID conducted the investigation and uncovered the GMD agents, thus nipping
the plot in the bud.[65] Another CID mission was to lobby General Li Zongren,
acting president of the Nationalist government in 1949, to return to China from
Switzerland.[66] In a less conventional intelligence situation, Mao mentioned to
Zhou Enlai in spring 1975 that he wanted to release the imprisoned GMD

---

[60] *Yang Shangkun huiyilu*, p. 346.
[61] According to Yang Shangkun's diaries, on July 1, 1961, he read the intelligence involving the
initiatives by both the United States and the GMD regarding to the GMD's seat in the United
Nations. On July 3, the CCP and the Soviet Union agreed that Foreign Minister Chen Yi
would meet Soviet leaders in Moscow to discuss the international situation, including political
situations in France and Laos. See *Yang Shangkun riji* [Yang Shangkun's diaries], vol. 2,
pp. 46–55.
[62] The Socialist Education movement was launched in 1963 in response to the increasing corruption and demoralization of party cadres following the failure of the Great Leap Forward.
[63] *Yang Shangkun huiyilu*, p. 350.
[64] *Huanqiu shibao* [Global times], December 23, 2005.
[65] Zhou Degao, *Wo yu zhonggong he jiangong: chise huaren jiemi – Jiangong ruhe xingwang*, pp.
70–3.
[66] Liu Zhe, "Li Zongren huiguo de lingyi lishi jianzheng ren" [Another historical witness for Li
Zongren's return to China], in *Wenshi chunqiu* [Chronicle of literature and history], no. 4
(2001), pp. 59–60.

generals who had been captured during the 1940s civil war. Thus, the CID was assigned to work with the MPS and the CCP's Central United Front Department to confirm the list of imprisoned GMD generals.[67]

When Mao decided to launch the Cultural Revolution, it was important for him to control all the major security organizations – the PLA, the Ministry of Public Security, the CID, and the Central General Office – so that he could impose his campaign on the party leadership. In November 1965, Mao dismissed Yang Shangkun and appointed Wang Dongxing, Mao's chief bodyguard, as director of the Central General Office. Within a month, Mao dismissed Luo Ruiqing, PLA chief of staff and former public security minister, in order to consolidate Lin Biao's leadership in the army and to undermine Luo's influence in both the PLA and the MPS. The arrest of the former minister of public security triggered large-scale purges in the MPS. Although Mao successfully demoted Liu Shaoqi and attacked Deng Xiaoping during the Eleventh Plenum in August 1966, Deng's rank was not affected, and he retained his responsibilities in the party and the government, the CID included.[68]

Immediately after the Eleventh Plenum, Mao ordered an expanded Politburo conference specifically to "criticize" Liu and Deng. By that time, Liu was no longer allowed to work, so the real purpose of the conference was to target Deng. Radicals attacked Deng, forcing him to hand over his power to the Cultural Revolution Group; his positions in the Central Liaison Department and the Central Investigation Department went to Kang Sheng.[69] Kang had reluctantly left the SAD in the late 1940s as a result of his role in the Yan'an rectification campaign. Since then he had been excluded from all central decision-making power in the CCP intelligence services. Although CGO chief Yang Shangkun was assigned to control the CID, Zhou Enlai retained influence over CCP intelligence services through his direct leadership and indirect guidance of his trusted followers Li Kenong, Kong Yuan, and Zou Dapeng, who headed the CID.[70] Before Kang Sheng took over the CID, he ordered the Red Guard to attack Kong Yuan, director of the CID, forcing Kong to leave office. After Kang replaced Deng Xiaoping as leader of the CID, he accused Zou Dapeng, acting director of the CID, of being a member of the northeastern clique of counterrevolutionaries and traitors, led by Gao Chongmin. Zou and his wife underwent so much persecution from the mass rebels, as well as immense pressure from Kang Sheng, such that they committed suicide in April

---

[67] Ji Min, "Zhou Enlai chuli Taiwan wenti de zuihou zhutuo" [The last advice of Zhou Enlai on dealing with Taiwan issues], *Zongheng*, no. 1 (2002), p. 9.

[68] Deng was moved from seventh place to sixth place, and Liu was demoted from second to eighth place. See *Lingdao jigou yange*, p. 1071.

[69] *Deng Xiaoping "Wenge" suiyue*, pp. 25–7.

[70] Wang Jun, "Kang Sheng zai zhongyang shehui bu" [Kang Sheng in the Social Affairs Department], in *Bainian chao* [Hundred-year tide], no. 5 (2003), p. 28.

1967.[71] Although Kang Sheng was in charge of the CID on behalf of the party leadership, the CID was taken over by the so-called Group of Representatives for Military Control (*junguan daibiao xiaozu*), led by Unit 8341, the CMC, and the PLA Political Department following Unit 8341's military control over the Third Bureau of the CID in spring 1967.[72]

Another campaign Kang Sheng launched in February 1968 was the so-called February 4 instruction of Senior Kang, which targeted middle-level CID leaders such as Ma Ciqing, Dan Dianyuan, Xu Danlu, Liu Jinzhong, He Changqian, and Cui Jiyuan. These campaigns and movements helped Kang achieve dominance in the CID.[73] In the Cultural Revolution, the CID and its "rebel factions" became important sources of "evidence" that Maoist rebels used against senior party leaders. While Maoist radicals used bombs provided by the CID and its mass rebels against senior party leaders, China's spies overseas became increasingly vulnerable of having their identities exposed by the mass rebels, who were seeking more names of people to purge. To guard party secrets and to protect the CCP's agents abroad, Zhou Enlai prevented the mass rebels from accessing CID confidential documents and archives. Under Zhou's orders, many CID documents were transferred to the CGO, and Li Zhizhong, deputy director of the CGO, stopped the rebel factions in the CID from looting the confidential documents and archives.[74]

While Kang Sheng strived to achieve dominance in the CID, there seemed to be a unwritten agreement between him and Zhou Enlai in terms of their joint effort to control the CID. Whereas Kang needed Zhou's help to provide career professionals to run the CID operations (most capable staff were Zhou's longtime subordinates), Zhou needed Kang to ameliorate the problems Zhou faced from the Maoist radicals, headed by Jiang Qing. Luo Qingchang, a longtime trusted follower of Zhou, was deputy director of the Premier Office under the State Council in the 1950s and deputy general secretary of the State Council in the 1960s; he then was appointed to head the CID. The role of the CID was further emphasized in 1969, when the Sino-Soviet border dispute turned into a military confrontation, and Mao prepared the PRC for possible Soviet invasion. The CID was abolished and most of its activities and assets were absorbed by the Second Department (or Intelligence Department) of the PLA's General Staff Department in 1969. According to the Reorganization Plan of the General Staff Department and the General Logistic Department, issued by the CMC on June 28, 1969, three civilian agencies (the CID, the Central Meteorology Bureau, and the State Bureau of General Surveying and Mapping) were merged with the corresponding professional units of the PLA General Staff

[71] Yan Mingfu, "Wokan Kang Sheng" [My view of Kang Sheng], in *Lingdao wencui* [Literature collection of leadership], no. 8 (2005), p. 143.

[72] *Zhou Enlai nianpu – 1949–1976*, vol. 3, p. 138.

[73] Wang Jun, "Kang Sheng zai zhongyang shehui bu," p. 29.

[74] Tong Xiaopeng, *Fengyu sishi nian*, vol. 2, p. 299.

Department.[75] These mergers were largely part of China's preparation for a possible Sino-Soviet war. Sino-Soviet tensions "had been building up since the Soviet-led invasion of Czechoslovakia in August 1968 and reached open hostilities during the border clash at Zhenbao Island on the Ussuri River in March 1969."[76]

Since the early 1970s, when the Western embargo against China was released, the Intelligence Department of the GSD became increasingly important in nurturing initiatives that engender a positive international environment for China's development. By the time Sino-U.S. relations were normalized in 1971 and the PRC was admitted to the United Nations, China had gained diplomatic recognition by a number of Western countries, and it had greatly improved its economic relations across the globe. China had viewed the developing nations of Asia, Africa, and Latin America as major forces in international affairs; thus, it had sought to continually expand its influence in developing nations, and it considered itself an integral part of those forces in international affairs. The vital role of the GSD Intelligence Department in global politics, combined with Zhou Enlai's political maneuvering, elevated the department's position in the 1970s, enabling it and its agents to emerge from the Cultural Revolution relatively unscathed.

Under Zhou Enlai's initiative and Mao's approval, the GSD Intelligence Department was able to help many of Zhou's trusted followers avoid persecution by the radicals. Zhou also saw to it that many young and talented agents from China's top universities were recruited for the GSD Intelligence Department. During the Cultural Revolution, Zhou Enlai discreetly protected many CID and GSD Intelligence Department personnel by sending them to so-called cadre school, where they were immune from the humiliation, torture, and persecution of the Red Guard and the mass rebels, even though they were still required to engage in reeducation through physical labor. Unlike most party organizations and labor camps of which the mass rebels took over operations, the cadre schools of the CID were run by the leaders of existing party organizations, such as Li Zhenyuan and Wang Yantang. Both Li and Wang were former directors of CID departments and were assigned to operate the cadre school as principals and party secretaries.[77] Most senior agents tied to Zhou Enlai suffered much less at the hands of the Red Guard and the mass rebels than did other senior party cadres, who were imprisoned or exiled at the beginning of the Cultural Revolution. Following China's admission to the United Nation in 1971, many CID officials were able to return to their

---

[75] Administrative Group (*banshizu*) of the CMC, *Zhongyang junwei banshizu gongbu zong canmou bu, zong houqing bu jiguan jingjian zhengbian fang'an* [Administrative Group of the Central Military Commission announces the plan for simplifying and reorganizing the organs of the General Staff Department and the General Logistics Department); *Zhongguo renmin jiefangjun*, vol. 1, pp. 352–3, 359–60.

[76] Frederick C. Teiwes and Warren Sun, *The Tragedy of Lin Biao*, p. 111.

[77] *Renmin ribao* [People's daily], March 14, 2000; *Xinhua*, April 14, 2008.

international posts because party leadership needed them to enhance China's diplomatic relations. Because they were beneficiaries of the Cultural Revolution, many stayed loyal to Mao even though they deeply loathed the radical leaders who manipulated the Red Guard into destroying the party bureaucracy. It is not surprising that these officials of the CID and GSD Intelligence Department had the same stance as Hua Guofeng and Wang Dongxing, to "firmly [uphold] whatever policy decisions Chairman Mao made and . . . unswervingly adhere to whatever instructions Chairman Mao gave" after Mao's death in 1976.

Since President Richard Nixon's visit to China in 1972, China's foreign intelligence initiatives have improved considerably. With Kang Sheng's cooperation – especially his role in restraining radical leaders – Zhou Enlai was able to lead the GSD Intelligence Department to become a significant intelligence gathering agency for the CCP. Kang had remained a powerful influence on the Maoist radicals because of his advantage in cultivating key individuals, such as Guan Feng, Qi Benyu, and Nie Yuanzi, as well as his role in serving as a bridge between Jiang Qing and some of the radical intellectuals she brought to the fore in the early stage of the Cultural Revolution.[78] The CID and GSD Intelligence Department continued to send spies abroad, to assign military attachés to traveling leaders, and to assign agents to Chinese embassies. Kang further attempted to get closer to Zhou Enlai and the rehabilitated Deng Xiaoping, and he distanced himself from radical leaders such as Jiang Qing and Zhang Chunqiao after Mao increasingly became dissatisfied with the Gang of Four because of growing tensions between the Gang of Four and other Politburo members in 1974.[79] In return, Zhou and Zhou's trusted followers acquiesced in ignoring or even in aiding Kang in purging those whom he disliked. Although Yuan Geng, deputy director of the First Bureau of the CID, was a longtime subordinate of Luo Qingchang, director of the CID, Luo had to cooperate with Kang Sheng to send Yuan to jail when Kang accused Yuan of having a "serious problem." Yuan was arrested in the spring of 1968.[80] The Central Investigation Department was reestablished in 1973, and many agents who had been dismissed or informally cast aside during the Cultural Revolution were allowed

---

[78] Kenneth Leiberthal, "The Great Leap Forward and the Split in the Yan'an Leadership," in Roderick MacFarquhar (ed.), *The Politics of China: the Eras of Mao and Deng*, pp. 133–4.

[79] According to the official publication, Kang Sheng attempted to approach Zhou Enlai and Deng Xiaoping after Deng returned to Beijing from Jiangxi. Kang did not allow Jiang Qing to visit him when Kang was in the hospital ill, which vexed Jiang. Kang asked Wang Hairong and Tang Wensheng to convey his words to Mao that Jiang Qing and Zhang Chunqiao were traitors. See "Kang Sheng linsi qian weihe jiefa Jiang Qing?" [Why did Kang Sheng expose Jiang Qing before he died?], in *Yangzhou shibao* [Yangzhou times], April 20, 2009; [Deng] Maomao, *Wode fuqin Deng Xiaoping*, vol. 1, pp. 180–1.

[80] After the Cultural Revolution, Luo apologized to Yuan and personally led the initiative to redress Yuan's case. See Tu Qiao, *Yuan Geng zhuan: Gaige xianchang, 1978–1984* [A biography of Yuan Geng: Scene of reform, 1978–1984], pp. 59–65.

back into the organization. The CID's functions and power expanded later, when Hua Guofeng and Wang Dongxing used the department to consolidate their authority.

The CID became an important supporter of Hua Guofeng, premier of the State Council, who strived to dismantle the Gang of Four's power nexus and steer China out of the chaos of the Cultural Revolution after Mao's death. A recent official publication revealed that the 1976 alliance between Hua Guofeng and Marshal Ye Jianying was initiated by Xiong Xianghui, deputy director of the CID and one of the well-known three most distinguished intelligence agents of the party during the late 1930s and early 1940s. In April 1976, Xiong approached Ye and suggested that he ally with Hua Guofeng against the Maoist radicals.[81] Xiong was not the only one invested in these alliances. Before Xiong's efforts, Hua Guofeng had already initiated the move to gain the CID's support by cultivating personal relationships with CID leaders. For example, when Hua Guofeng discovered that Luo Qingchang, CID director, had been ill but had not been sent to the best hospital for treatment, he immediately wrote a note entreating the health minister Liu Xiangping to move Luo Qingchang to Beijing Hospital, the best health-care institution and the one that served top leaders.[82] Hua became public security minister in January 1975, and he needed all the alliances he could find. He understood the importance of the intelligence apparatus in elite politics, especially in what was at the time one of the most significant moments for succession politics in the history of the CCP. With Mao gravely ill and battling cancer, the struggle to take his place at the head of the party and government dominated elite politics.

When Deng Xiaoping returned to office and launched the political campaign against the Two Whatevers faction, led by Hua Guofeng from 1977 to 1978, the discussion of "practice as the sole criterion of truth" and Deng's emphasis on "seeking truth from facts" were particularly critical in Deng's defeat of Hua,[83] Deng did not trust the CID to be his vanguards against Hua Guofeng, and he deemed the CID a "severe disaster area";[84] many CID officials were accused of being Kang Sheng's followers and were either dismissed or exiled to small cities. When Deng finally took over party leadership in the late 1970s, he conducted a large-scale screening of all personnel and officials. To screen the CID officials abroad, he issued a CCP document ordering all CID personnel and agents assigned to embassies or consulates abroad to return to China by December 1985. The document also stated that China would in the future rely on legal covers for intelligence officers abroad, such as accredited diplomats, trade

---

[81] Xiong Lei, "1976 nian, Hua Guofeng he Ye Jianying zenyang lianshou de" [1976, how did Hua Guofeng and Ye Jianying become allies?], *Yanhuang chunqiu* [Spring and autumn in China], vol. 10 (2008), p. 4.

[82] Ibid., p. 5.

[83] Joseph Fewsmith, *Elite Politics in Contemporary China*, p. 89.

[84] Wang Jun, "Kang Sheng zai zhongyang shehui bu," pp. 28–9.

and industry figures, commercial officers, military attachés, tourists, scientists, professors, and students.[85] Perhaps the most important and profound change in the evolution of the CID took place in 1983, when it merged with the newly established Ministry of Public Security (MPS). The merger formed the new Ministry of State Security (MSS) under the State Council, and Deng was able to use this reorganization to screen intelligence agents and dismiss those whom party seniors distrusted.

Deng's approach was successful on a number of levels. First, he was able to make the CID more efficient through strategic reorganization and to reduce the risk of having foreign countries target the CID officers because of their poor covers. Second, under the guise of increasing efficiency, Deng was able to screen all intelligence agents and dismiss those whom party seniors distrusted. The newly established MSS was assigned to a wide range of missions, including political espionage and the pursuit of economic and technological intelligence. It was established as part of a large-scale reorganization of China's state apparatus, which mainly included the CID, a party organ that consolidated China's foreign intelligence efforts into one central department, and the Bureau of Political Security, which fell under the MPS. China's reform policy has required its intelligence services to play a greater role in supporting national policy objectives by targeting and exploiting the technological, economic, political, and military infrastructures of developed nations.

Ministry of State Security

In 1983, the CID and the espionage, counterintelligence operations, and security divisions of the Ministry of Public Security (MPS) were merged to form the new Ministry of State Security (MSS) under the State Council. In other words, the majority of the MPS's Bureau of Investigating Counterrevolutionaries (*dui fangeming zhencha ju*, or the First Bureau) merged with the MSS, even though many functions of the Bureau of Investigating Counterrevolutionaries remained in the MPS. Even after the MSS was established in 1983 and began to dispatch agents to foreign countries for intelligence and espionage activities, the MPS continued to send agents to conduct similar activities outside of China.[86] Since the 1990s, the First Bureau of the MPS has developed a powerful intelligence system, and many of its functions overlap with the MSS.[87] The MSS headquarters was located where the previous CID was, at No. 100 Xiyuan, a location with tight security in the western suburbs of Beijing, twenty-five kilometers west of Tiananmen Square. To date, the MSS

[85] Ding Ke, "Tegong–minyun–Falun Gong: Yige shengming de zhenshi gushi" [Secret agent – democratic movement – Falun Gong: the true story of a life], in Zhao Ming et al. (eds.), *Hongchao huangyan lu* [Record of lies in a red dynasty], p. 274.
[86] Xu Jiatun, *Xu Jiatun xianggang huiyilu*, vol. 1, pp. 52–5.
[87] Sheng Xue, *'Yuanhua an' heimu*, p. 101.

has expanded to have more than thirty departments and bureaus, seventeen of which are professional operations departments (see Figure 9.1). As described already, a key objective of merging the CID and the MPS intelligence divisions was to purge personnel whom the veteran leaders distrusted because of their connections with Maoist radicals and Kang Sheng.[88] At the same time, the merger removed from power those reluctant to cooperate with party seniors when the veteran leaders attacked Hua Guofeng or redressed the "crimes" against party seniors that had been committed before or during the Cultural Revolution.

When the Chinese intelligence community revised the mission of its predecessor to account for technological advances in intelligence, the Ministry of State Security became China's largest and most active intelligence agency in charge of foreign intelligence and counterintelligence operations. Since its inception, the MSS has been increasingly efficient and successful against foreign espionage activities targeting China. For example, the KGB sensed that its operations against China were seriously hampered by "the continuous intensification of the counter-intelligence measures in Beijing."[89] Because the MSS is responsible for collecting and assessing civilian intelligence relevant to national security issues and for conducting counterespionage against foreign countries, as well as against Taiwan, it conducts a wide variety of Taiwan-related activities such as "the analysis of domestic Taiwanese political, social, and economic developments and of international trends relevant to cross-strait relations, as well as counter-measures against Taiwan's espionage."[90] The MSS's assignments increasingly contributed to secret contacts between the GMD and the CCP, such as exchanges of letters and secret envoys during the 1980s. Moreover, both the GMD and the CCP had agreed to let the Buddhist master Nan Huaijing be the intermediary for political negotiations in 1988.[91] In addition, strict regulations were imposed to ensure the successful operation of the MSS. For example, MSS agents are required to stay loyal to the MSS, which means in practice that personnel transfers to other organizations are virtually impossible; only the Central Organization Department can issue an order for a transfer out of the MSS. If an agent must leave the MSS and the MSS has no objection to the transfer, the agent must sign an agreement to promise not leave China for at least fifteen years.[92]

---

[88] Official publications have viewed the CID as the key stronghold from which Kang Sheng dominated in the Cultural Revolution. See Wang Jun, "Kang Sheng zai zhongyang shehui bu," p. 29.

[89] Christopher M. Andrew and Vasili Mitrokhin, *The World Was Going Our Way: The KGB and Battle for the Third World*, p. 288.

[90] Michael D. Swaine, "Chinese Decision-Making Regarding Taiwan, 1979–2000," in David M. Lampton (ed.), *The Making of Chinese Foreign and Security Policy in the Era of Reform, 1978–2000*, p. 295.

[91] Chi Su, *Taiwan's Relations with Mainland China: A Tail Wagging Two Dogs*, 280.

[92] Ding Ke, "Tegong–minyun–Falun Gong: Yige shengming de zhenshi gushi," pp. 273, 285.

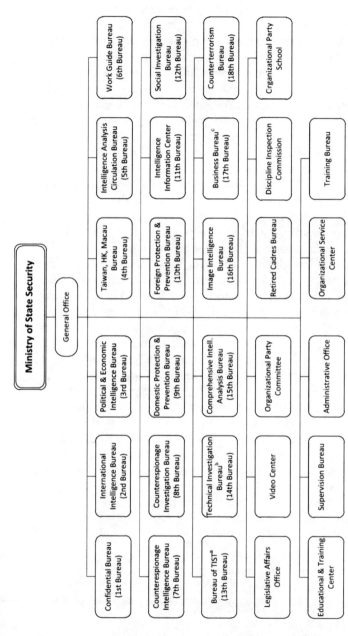

FIGURE 9.1. *Organizational Structure of the Ministry of State Security. Source:* Du Ling, *Zhonggong gong'an zhidu yanjiu* [Research on the system of the CCP public Security], p. 102; information here also comes from the various official newspapers (both national and local).

[a] The complete name of the Thirteenth Bureau is the Bureau of Technical Investigation of Science and Technology. This bureau is responsible for the management, research, and development of high technology.

[b] The Technical Investigation Bureau (the Fourteenth Bureau) is in charge of postal and telecommunications inspection.

[c] This bureau was in charge of the companies and enterprises owned by the MSS, and it was reportedly abolished in 2000.

Domestically, the MSS engages in intelligence activities such as collecting intelligence; monitoring political dissidents; and monitoring and recruiting businesspeople, researchers, and officials. Apart from professional agents, the MSS employs nonprofessional intelligence agents such as travelers, business-people, and academics, with a special emphasis on overseas students and high-tech professionals working abroad who have access to sensitive technology. In addition, the MSS employs intelligence from Chinese firms that acquire U.S. companies with desired technology or from front companies that engage in technology development and acquisition. As China's leading intelligence appa-ratus, the MSS does not merely support policy makers in their decision making; it also keeps abreast of developments in the foreign policy decision-making pro-cess, tools of economic development, and methods of political control.[93] The MSS has regional and functional offices that support its initiatives and has a main think tank, the Chinese Institute for Contemporary International Rela-tions, which not only provides intelligence collection and analysis for decision-making leaders but also sends "scholars" abroad.[94]

China's reforms have required that its intelligence services play a greater role in supporting national policy objectives by targeting and exploiting the techno-logical, economic, political, and military infrastructures of developed nations.[95] Public exposure of Chinese intelligence activities in Hong Kong, Taiwan, Japan, and the United States – activities carried out by Chinese intelligence personnel posing as business executives and diplomats – indicates the increasing num-ber of initiatives in intelligence abroad. Since 1979, China's economic reforms have enabled many Chinese citizens to travel abroad and hundred of thou-sands of Chinese businesses to establish operations in foreign countries. Under official government cover, China's intelligence organizations conduct overseas espionage activities and obtain intelligence through accredited diplomats, trade and industry figures, commercial officers, military attachés, journalists, scien-tists, and students. When Hong Kong was still a British colony, the MSS, the MPS, and the PLA all commanded intelligence organizations and conducted espionage activities on the island.[96] To avoid redundant intelligence efforts in the mid-1980s, the intelligence organizations of the MSS and the MPS in Hong Kong were merged and put under the leadership of the Xinhua Hong Kong Agency. Nonetheless, both organizations refused to hand over their top spies to the Xinhua Hong Kong Agency, instead maintaining direct control over them.[97] A testament to the professionalism of China's intelligence organizations, these

[93] Nicholas Eftimiades, *Chinese Intelligence Operations*, pp. 4, 6, 17.
[94] Richard D. Fisher, *China's Military Modernization: Building for Regional and Global Reach*, p. 37.
[95] Nicholas Eftimiades, *Chinese Intelligence Operations*, p. 6.
[96] Xu Jiatun, *Xu Jiatun xianggang huiyilu*, vol. 1, p. 53.
[97] The newly established agency that merged both the MSS and MPS in Hong Kong was called the Security Department (*bao'an bu*). See Xu Jiatun, *Xu Jiatun xianggang huiyilu*, vol. 1, pp. 54–5, 76.

organizations have been increasingly used to detect and track corrupt party and government officials, particularly under Hu Jintao's leadership.[98]

China's intelligence agencies also engage in media surveillance and participation in state censorship efforts, currently emphasizing monitoring electronic communication and the Internet. Their services monitor and infiltrate diplomatic and economic facilities of foreign countries that pursue activities in Chinese territory. They recruit agents among Chinese and foreign nationals to gather information. The MSS sends agents or personnel to party and government agencies, as well as to organizations such as the Labor and Human Ministry, the General Aviation Administration Bureau, and the publisher of *China Youth Daily*. In Beijing during the 1980s, for example, the MSS dispatched agents to control the Offices of Foreign Affairs (*waishi bangong shi*) of the official media, including the *Guangming Daily* and the *Xinhua News Agency*. According to Ding Ke, an MSS agent from 1982 to 1989, MSS agents received commands and instructions directly only from the Liaison Department of the MSS, even though their public status is employees of the news organizations. The agents then screen employees of the news organizations and handle passport applications and visas for them, and they are responsible for receiving foreign media delegations and arranging their visits in China.[99] Oftentimes, agents are dispatched to foreign countries as journalists for a certain news organization, and then they become a journalist for another news agency later on in their trip. For example, Sun Wenfang, an MSS agent, was assigned to be a Xinhua News Agency journalist in the Middle East and Western Europe, but he later was appointed to be a journalist for the *Guangming Daily* in London. After his tenure at the *Guangming Daily*, he was promoted to deputy director of the Second Bureau of the MSS.[100]

The relationship between the MSS and the police forces in China was rather complicated and at times quite strained. Western security and intelligence services have also had similar interinstitutional tension, but in China such problems were more than merely structural. As an institutionalized repressive apparatus, the MSS encompasses a range of structures from regular police to intelligence and counterintelligence services. The MSS is closely affiliated with the police and is authorized to instruct police to engage in police actions, such as taking suspects into custody and searching property. In practice, it also uses police and other divisions of the security apparatus for its own purposes. Both the MSS and the MPS have strict regulations governing internal matters, as well as a military structure of authority and obedience. They are guided

---

[98] For example, in 2001 Mu Suixin and Ma Xiangdong, mayor and deputy mayor of Shenyang, respectively, were sentenced to death after being found guilty of corruption. The case was first discovered by the MSS in Macao, where Ma Xiangdong gambled $4.8 million in public funds. See Guan Gengyin, *Shen Pan* [Trial], p. 1.

[99] Ding Ke, "Tegong–minyun–Falun Gong: Yige shengming de zhenshi gushi," pp. 275–6.

[100] Ibid., p. 278.

by their responsibility for ensuring state security and safeguarding the security, rights, and interests of citizens. Nonetheless, they historically have also played a large role in protecting the party-state's power and the interests of the nearly irremovable incumbents. The MSS and MPS were also charged with suppressing any political opposition against the party-state and with maintaining political control over society. Clearly, with these objectives, they serve an immensely political function, which the high status of the political police also indicates. Notably, however, reforms and openness during three decades have engendered a certain transparency, efficiency, and effectiveness, including depoliticized anticrime efforts, such as counterterrorism and counter-human-trafficking both domestically and abroad, as well as professional relations with counterpart services in democratic states.

Because the CCP is mainly concerned with its ability to control society so that it remains in power as long as possible, political and social stability are its priorities. As long as the CCP continues its impressive economic growth, it will be in a position to hold the party's monopoly on power. As Tony Saich points out, there has been no strong constituency that favors political change – new urban elites appear to have little interest in more democratic reform because they have benefited from rapid economic growth, private entrepreneurs enjoy beneficial connections to the party, and laid-off workers retain trust in national leaders and view the problems as purely local aberrations rather than systemic flaws. By consistently cracking down on alternatives and restricting the growth of vibrant civil society that could form the basis for a new system, according to Saich, the CCP has created the possibility that "uncivil society" might take over power.[101] As political stability has become a top priority of the party-state, intelligence organizations are required to take aggressive censorship initiatives to monitor political dissidents and antigovernment sentiments. Although monitoring practitioners of Falun Gong, political dissidents, ethnic separatists, religious extremists, and underground churches has been a high priority for the MSS, China's intelligence agencies have other missions, such as gaining commercial, technological, and military technology. Like the MPS, the MSS has a wide scope of authority in domestic intelligence activities, and that authority overlaps with the law enforcement responsibilities of the MPS. Thus, the MSS not only is involved in police functions (similar to the U.S. FBI) but also fulfills other roles, such as court hearings (akin to the role of the judiciary in Western democracies).[102]

Intelligence Organizations of the People's Liberation Army

China's intelligence organizations in the reform era are divided into civilian and military systems. The military intelligence system of the PLA engages in

---

[101] Tony Saich, "Development and Choice," in Edward Friedman and Bruce Gilley (eds.), *Asia's Giants: Comparing China and India*, p. 237.
[102] Nicholas Eftimiades, *Chinese Intelligence Operations*, p. 47.

military intelligence and counterintelligence operations; most of its work is conducted by the Intelligence Department of the General Staff Department (also called the Second Department of the General Staff Department), the Third Department of the GSD, the Fourth Department of the GSD,[103] and the Liaison Department of the General Political Department (GPD). Although civilian and military systems have different functions that result from their different specialties, they often cooperate and share resources. As one might expect of two systems with overlapping responsibilities, they are prone to competing for status, control, and authority. The military system is responsible for human intelligence collection and analysis, but it has limited targets and resources.[104] Another military agency known for intelligence collection and analysis is the Commission of Science, Technology, and Industry for National Defense, an organization in charge of research and development for military technologies and weapons systems that engages in both overt and clandestine intelligence collection.[105]

The Second Department of the GSD can be traced back to the Espionage Division of the CMC General Staff Department, established in 1931. In 1933, the Second Bureau of the CMC's GSD was created to lead intelligence services in the Red Army. In September 1941, the Second Bureau merged with the newly established Central Committee's Intelligence Department, of which Kang Sheng was director and Yie Jianying and Li Kenong were deputy directors. The creation of a comprehensive intelligence organ by merging military and party intelligence services was undoubtedly Mao's effort to control the intelligence apparatus to enhance his power. In November 1942, the Second Bureau was returned to the Central Military Commission; during the 1940s civil war, it became a subordinate unit of the GSD. In December 1950, the CMC established its General Intelligence Department, which was in charge of three subordinate departments: intelligence, technical, and liaison. After the General Intelligence Department was abolished in February 1953, the three departments were placed under the jurisdiction of the GSD. In June 1955, the Liaison Department was renamed the Central Investigation Department and was placed under the leadership of the CCP Central Secretariat.

The Second Department of the GSD is responsible for collecting military intelligence mainly through spies and military attachés at Chinese embassies abroad. It has a unique position in influencing decision making among the leadership because it "is superior to all other civilian or military organs as a source of national security and defense intelligence and military-related strategic analysis for the senior leadership."[106] Although it is responsible for

---

[103] Strictly speaking, the Fourth Department of the GSD is not a unit in charge of intelligence and counterintelligence. In recent years, it has been increasingly engaged in the collections and analysis of the intelligence and intelligence and counterintelligence activities.

[104] Nicholas Eftimiades, *Chinese Intelligence Operations*, p. 103.

[105] Ibid., p. 104.

[106] Michael D. Swaine, "Chinese Decision-Making Regarding Taiwan, 1979–2000," p. 303.

collecting and analyzing strategic political and military intelligence,[107] it also engages in information analysis and intelligence gathered from publically available sources in other countries. It provides both long- and short-term intelligence reports to PLA leaders, general departments, services and arms, and military region headquarters, key organs of the military-industrial complex, and unit commanders.[108] Although the Second Department maintains the Second Bureau, a tactical reconnaissance bureau, to foster communication among the intelligence division commands in each military region, the bulk of the Second Department's work occurs within the First Bureau. The First Bureau is responsible for military human intelligence collection and analysis, for which it conducts clandestine intelligence operations overseas through dispatched agents and in five domestic geographical divisions: Beijing, Shenyang, Shanghai, Guangzhou, and Tianjin. Each local branch of the Second Department is publicly known as an office of the local government, as in the case of the Guangzhou local branch, which is the Fourth Office of the Guangdong Provincial Government. Although each military region has its own intelligence department at the rank of division level (*shiji*), the Second Department of the GSD has the higher rank of army corps unit (*junji*).[109] Since Deng Xiaoping launched economic reforms, the Second Department has increasingly focused on military science and technological intelligence, an expertise not emphasized in the Maoist era.

The Third Department is usually called the Technical and Reconnaissance Department (*jishu zhencha bu*), or simply the Technical Department. It is responsible for collecting and processing strategic information, monitoring, conducting aviation reconnaissance, and conducting research and analysis of military information and intelligence. Like the GSD Second Department, the Third Department is also responsible for gathering and analysis of intelligence, not only on military matters but also on strategic and foreign policy issues, even though the Third Department pays great attention to gathering technical intelligence.[110] Unlike the Second Department, the Third Department is responsible for "signals and communications intelligence, monitoring diplomatic, military and international communications by foreign nationals in China."[111] It operates not only through its own monitoring stations nationwide but also through the Third Bureaus of the headquarters of the seven military regions,

[107] Richard C. Bush, *The Perils of Proximity: China-Japan Security Relations*, p. 132.
[108] Michael D. Swaine, *The Role of the Chinese Military in National Security Policymaking*, rev. ed., p. 69.
[109] Sheng Xue, '*Yuanhua an' heimu*, pp. 92–3, 96.
[110] Tai Ming Cheung, "The Influence of the Gun: China's Central Military Commission and Its Relationship with the Military, Party, and State Decision-Making Systems," in David M. Lampton (ed.), *The Making of Chinese Foreign and Security Policy in the Era of Reform, 1978–2000*, p. 80.
[111] James C. Mulvenon, "Chinese C4I Modernization: An Experiment in Open-Source Analysis," in James C. Mulvenon and Andrew N. D. Yang (eds.), *A Poverty of Riches: New Challenges and Opportunities in PLA Reresearch*, p. 204.

the air force, and the navy. Moreover, the Third Department has established a large number of monitoring stations (*jianting zhan*) in border areas and coastal cities. It has been assigned to monitor the Internet and long-distance calls, especially concerning sensitive issues such as the 1989 Tiananmen Square student demonstration and Falun Gong practitioners. In addition, the Third Department uses satellite monitoring and analysis. The Luoyang Foreign Language Institute is subordinate to the Third Department and is responsible for providing personnel to the Third Department. Unlike the General Office of the CMC, located in the Sanzuomen, both the Second and Third Departments of the GSD are located in the Western Hills (the location of the CMC and the residences of the PLA senior leaders).[112]

The Fourth Department of the GSD, better known as the Electronic Warfare Department, is responsible for all types of electronic warfare, including radar and electronic countermeasures and computer network attacks. Since its establishment in 1990, it has increasingly engaged in the collection and analysis of electronics intelligence and counterintelligence efforts.[113] Among the six departments that constituted a new Department of Specialized Arms (*bingzhong bu*) of the GSD, the Electronic Warfare Department was the only one that survived the merger in its original state (the Artillery Department, Armored Corps, Telecommunication Corps, Engineering Corps, and Ground Force Aviation merged into one new department: the Department of Specialized Arms of the GSD).[114] We can speculate that the Department of Electronic Warfare also operates ground-receiving stations and channels data to other PLA units through an intelligence support cell under a joint theater command. The rise of the Fourth Department of the GSD aids the PLA's attempt to expand its ability to conduct electronic warfare in terms of strategy and tactics. Beside the responsibilities for managing electronic warfare, defending key state and military headquarters in Beijing, and directing electronic signals intelligence operations to the division level of the PLA's army, air force, and navy, the Fourth Department is also in charge of developing electronic warfare, electronic countermeasures, and electronic counter-countermeasures.[115] Although the Fourth Department of the GSD focuses on collecting military intelligence regarding electric warfare, it has broadened its focus to include military intelligence and counterintelligence. For example, it was involved in locating the individual who revealed information about the research process of the J-10 Sky-Fighter on the Internet.[116]

[112] Ji You, *The Armed Forces of China*, p. xxi.
[113] Guo Ruihua, *Zhonggong duitai gongzuo zuzhi tixi kailun* [Outline of the organization system of CCP work toward Taiwan], p. 129; Song Wen, *Yige zhongguo jiandie de huiyi* [Recollections of a Chinese spy], p. 21.
[114] Ji You, *The Armed Forces of China*, p. 32.
[115] Richard D. Fisher Jr., "Unconventional Warfare Options," in Steve Tsang (ed.), *If China Attacks Taiwan: Military Strategy, Politics and Economics*, p. 67.
[116] Song Wen, *Yige zhongguo jiandie de huiyi*, pp. 204–5.

The Liaison Department of the GPD is responsible for overseeing the political education, ideological indoctrination, and discipline of foreign armies. Historically, among its primary tasks are disintegrating enemy armies by destroying morale and instigating rebellions among the ranks. One of its major missions is to influence political attitudes and opinions of enemy personnel (i.e., brainwashing prisoners of war). The Liaison Department is responsible for collecting and analyzing intelligence and conducting research on social, political, and demographic issues in foreign countries. For example, it dispatched agents overseas under commercial covers to collect information on Taiwan.[117] Intelligence on Taiwan is imperative, demonstrated by the fact that there is a branch in Shanghai and Guangzhou, each of which focuses mainly on Taiwanese armies.[118]

Leading figures of the GPD's Liaison Department are assigned important missions or tasks regarding Taiwan-related issues. For example, Yang Side, a major general who was appointed deputy director (in 1956) and director (in 1975) of the GPD's Liaison Department, was promoted to director of the CCP's Taiwan Office in 1985. In 1986, when Taiwan-based China Airlines pilot Wang Shi Chuen defected from Taiwan to China in a China Airlines cargo plane, Yang led a group to investigate, which included leaders of the General Aviation Administration Bureau, the Liaison Department of the GPD, and the International Division of the PRC Foreign Ministry.[119] During the 1990s, when China and Taiwan were engaged in high-level secret talks, the Liaison Department of the GPD was the leading body responsible for coordinating meetings between Zeng Qinghong (director of the CCP's Central General Office) and Su Chih-Cheng (director of President Li Tenghui's Office of Taiwan).[120] Moreover, the Liaison Departments of the GPD and of local military regions have dispatched agents outside of China, such as in Hong Kong, who continue to live undercover as employees of Chinese-funded companies or private institutions.[121] Liaison Department agents not only engage in espionage and counterespionage activities but also monitor their own agents.

The PLA intelligence apparatuses command and operate their own intelligence organizations and espionage activities outside of China.[122] The PLA's GSD had many spies in Hong Kong and Macao, and individual military regions also sent their own spies to conduct espionage activities.[123] Unlike the intelligence organizations of the MSS and the MPS, which may receive orders from

---

[117] Nicholas Eftimiades, *Chinese Intelligence Operations*, p. 103.

[118] Chen Donglong, "Zhongguo fan qingbao wang" [Chinese counterintelligence network], *NowNews*, January 18, 2004.

[119] Li Li, "*Muji taihai fengyun*" (extract), *Xinhua wenzhai* [New China digest], no. 13 (2005), pp. 64–87.

[120] See *Shanghai fazhi bao* [Shanghai legal system daily], June 6, 2008.

[121] Xu Jiatun, *Xu Jiatun xianggang huiyilu*, vol. 1, p. 54.

[122] Ibid., p. 53.

[123] Ibid., p. 54.

local party authorities (e.g., the MSS and MPS bureaus in Hong Kong),[124] the PLA intelligence organizations have remained independent, receiving commands only from the PLA. The Second, Third, Fourth Departments of the GSD divide intelligence work such that the Second Department manages special agents and the Third Department is responsible for technical reconnaissance, including monitoring and decoding; the Fourth Department focuses on the collection and analysis of the electronic intelligence. Like the MSS, the Second Department carries out and monitors the policies of the Central Military Commission and runs the daily affairs of the PLA's intelligence services. Its primary missions involve collecting and analyzing both political and military intelligence from other nations and engaging in military exchanges with foreign countries. The Second Department focuses mainly on the following areas of expertise: monitoring foreign diplomats and interests in China; conducting political surveillance of Chinese diplomats abroad; and cooperating with the MSS to collect political, economic, industrial, scientific, and technological intelligence from industrial nations, especially the United States and Europe. The Nanjing Diplomatic Institute was renamed the Institute of PLA International Relations; it specifically trains agents in necessary language and espionage skills for the Second Department.

[124] Ibid., pp. 54–5.

The PLA, Security Services, and Elite Politics

The People's Liberation Army (PLA) remains an important apparatus in the security of high-ranking CCP leaders, although there is considerable debate about how extensive its role is. This chapter delves into the security organizations of the People's Liberation Army and their role in party politics. It examines the causes, patterns, and dynamics of the PLA's involvement in party politics, with a particular focus on the role of the PLA's security organizations. The PLA, solely or jointly, commands six main security organizations: the Central Guard Bureau, the Central Guard Regiment, the Guard Bureau of the CMC General Office, the Security Department of the PLA General Political Department, the PAP, and the PLA Garrison Commands (especially the Beijing Garrison Command). For the Central Guard Regiment and the PAP, the two organizations under dual command, the PLA is responsible for recruitment, cadre management, logistics, organizational discipline, training, and political work (e.g., the organizational construction of the party and the Communist Youth League in PLA units, propaganda, the education of cadres, culture and entertainment, and mass line), and ideological education, whereas civilian leadership provides institutional support and assigns tasks.

The dual leadership system is a unique model implemented by the CCP in its control over and administration of both civilian and military organizations. The leadership system of the PAP provides an example of the dual leadership system: a local PAP unit is under the dual leadership of the PAP organ directly superior to it in the vertical chain of command and the local party and government offices at the same level of command. Dual leadership creates a complicated vertical and horizontal relationship, in which local party and government offices ensure that the line, principles, and policies of the party are upheld. They also provide logistic support and salaries, whereas the superior PAP organ provides professional guidance. Throughout the history of the People's Republic of China, the adoption of different leadership systems – vertical,

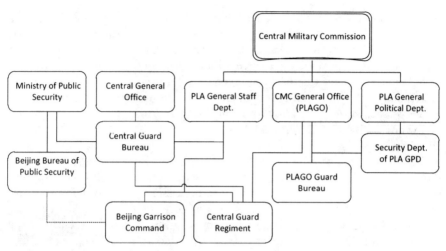

FIGURE 10.1. *Command Structure of PLA Security Apparatus, 1979–Present Day*
Source: Zhongyang bangongting, *'Guanyu tiaozheng jingwei jigou, gaijin jingwei gongzuo de huiyi jiyao' de tongzhi* [Notice about the summary of the meeting on adjusting guard apparatus and improving the work of security guard], in *Central General Office Document, No. 20* (1979).

horizontal, local, and dual – has resulted from leadership politics, which reflect both institutional tensions and conflict among party leaders. For example, a long struggle existed between the MPS and the PAP, because the MPS continually sought to control the PAP, and the PAP unceasingly strove for greater autonomy from the MPS. On the whole, dual leadership inevitably creates problems in that it fails to clarify responsibilities between the two leaderships and makes officers of armed units susceptible to the manipulation and influence of local leaders, as a result of personal ties.

There are several levels of the command structure of PLA security apparatuses in the capital (Figure 10.1). The first organ in charge of the CCP elite security forces is the Central Guard Bureau, an agency under the dual leadership of the PLA General Staff Department and the Central General Office with the professional guidance of the MPS. Although individuals with the CGB have credentials of party membership, which derive from the Central General Office, and are assigned tasks from the Central General Office, they receive commands from the PLA General Staff Department about political education, promotions or demotions, and logistics and supplies. Since Mao's era, control over the CGB has been a significant indicator of whether a paramount leader has successfully consolidated his power. The second leading security agency of the PLA is the Security Department of the PLA General Political Department (GPD), a powerful organization in charge of guarding PLA high-ranking generals, including local army ranking leaders and office buildings of local army unit headquarters. In the reform era, the

GPD's Security Department increasingly has been involved in investigating corruption cases in the PLA and enforcing discipline among army generals and their family members. It is responsible for overall security within the PLA, and it provides guidance to PLA security organizations nationwide, including assisting in the prevention, suppression, and investigation of criminal or counterrevolutionary activities; antiterrorism efforts; maintenance of security and order within the PLA; guarding of PLA leaders and important military facilities; and security inspections of public information networks.

Next in the line of important PLA security agencies is the CMC's General Office, the leading PLA administrative body that processes all CMC communications and documents, coordinates meetings, and conveys orders and directives to other subordinate organs. As far as security services are concerned, the CMC General Office is the leading organization that offers security detail for the Central Military Commission and its leaders. The CMC General Office has its own Guard Bureau, which functions similarly to the Guard Bureau of the Ministry of Public Security (Eighth Bureau of the MPS). Because the personnel of the Guard Bureau of the MPS and the Guard Bureau of the CMC General Office provide similar services, they are often mutually transferable; as such, the two Guard Bureaus have traditionally maintained a close relationship. The CMC General Office is in charge of security of high-ranking PLA generals; it provides security details for individuals and coordinates with the Beijing Garrison Command to guard leaders' residences. Because elite politics has historically played a significant role in Chinese politics, controlling the security apparatus to guard leadership members, leadership compounds, and capital cities is a crucial part of a paramount leader consolidating his power and authority.

For a paramount leader, the ability to manipulate the organization and composition of the security forces indicates his or her powerful authority necessary to exert political influence over the leadership. Deng Xiaoping consolidated his power by reorganizing the Beijing Garrison Command and the Central Guard Bureau, as well as its subordinated unit, the Central Guard Regiment, immediately after he returned to office in 1977. Jiang Zemin made similar decisive maneuvers to consolidate his power, such as expanding and modernizing the PAP and garrison commands after he became party chief. Under Jiang's leadership, group armies were no longer responsible for garrison duties, as they had been in the past. Instead, garrison commands have since been established in capital cities and strategic municipalities of all provinces and autonomous regions to take over responsibility of garrison duties. In Beijing, the Beijing Garrison Command was authorized to play a leading role in guarding the capital, commanding the reserve forces, and coordinating other PLA units in defense of the capital. The increasing size and power of both the PAP and the garrison commands and their partial separation from the PLA and the system of pluralism creates a system of checks and balances for the administration of

China's armed forces that is beneficial for China's political stability and crucial for civilian leadership.[1]

The reforms launched by Deng Xiaoping to reorganize the security services included the withdrawal of heavy involvement of the PLA's army corps and group armies in defense of the capital and increased employment of the People's Armed Police, the Beijing Garrison Command, and army reserves in the Beijing garrison. In general, since the reforms began, the army corps and group armies involved in the Beijing garrisons have been reduced, and they now have a more limited role in military politics; moreover, organizational relationships have been clarified. This chapter critically evaluates the changing roles of the PLA army corps and group armies garrisoned around the capital since the inception of the PRC; it then analyzes the rationale and impact of those changes.

Among all military regions, the Beijing Military Region historically has played the most important role in defending the capital and ensuring the security of CCP leaders. Control over the army units garrisoned in Beijing has always been crucial for gaining advantage in leadership politics. Mao exemplified his adeptness in gaining this advantage on many occasions, such as on the eve of the Cultural Revolution, when he added two divisions to the Beijing Garrison Command, and in February 1967, when he moved the 38th Army Corps from Liaoning to Baoding. These and many other efforts manipulating the PLA served to consolidate Mao's control over the capital and put pressure on other party and army leaders.

Although military factionalism and personal ties have played an important role, the PLA has strived to become modernized and professionalized since the People's Republic of China was established in 1949. Since China launched the economic reforms of 1979, there has been an increasing trend toward the institutionalization of civil-military relations. Top civilian leaders in the post-Deng era have particularly made tremendous efforts to promote military professionalism and to establish a more institutionalized and merit-based system of officer promotion and mandatory retirement. This institutionalized system has been used to achieve modernization and to prevent the emergence of military strongmen or the stagnation of the military establishment. Despite the continual prevalence of personal ties, or nepotism and favoritism in Cheng Li's words, the future of civil-military relations will be shaped by the institutional rules and norms of the modern PLA, such as age-based retirement and term limits. However, it will also be shaped by the characteristics of new PLA leaders – their professional competence, political associations, military doctrines, and worldviews.[2] The conflicting coexistence of military professionalism and

[1] Fang Zhu, "From the Viewpoint of the Beijing Garrison Command," in *Decision-Making in Deng's China: Perspectives from Insiders*, p. 122.
[2] Cheng Li, "The New Military Elite: Generational Profile and Contradictory Trends," in David M. Finkelstein and Kristen Gunness (eds.), *Civil-Military Relations in Today's China: Swimming in a New Sea*, pp. 64–8.

the prevalence of personal ties has become one of the most important features of post-Mao military politics. Thus, security services in the PLA and the PLA units that have been heavily employed for purposes of the CCP leaders' security have developed a contradictory trend that has created tension between military professionalism and political allegiance. On the one hand, the PLA security apparatus has been encouraged to become more professionally competent and better trained for the development of technology and the changing composition of their personnel. On the other hand, they are required to provide unconditional and absolute loyalty to the party leaders on the basis of the politicized criteria of appointment and promotion, as well as long-standing patron-client or leader-subordinate relations.

The Security Department under the PLA General Political Department

The Security Department of the PLA General Political Department (GPD) is responsible for "investigation and security within the PLA."[3] As a leading ideological and political administration branch, it not only politically educates the PLA soldiers, monitors officers, and maintains morale but also protects high-ranking PLA officials.[4] Although the duties of the GPD Security Department involve providing security details for high-ranking PLA officers, the department is also responsible for controlling and supervising those same officers. Managing leaders' security detail necessitates background checks of those with close relations to the leaders, such as relatives, friends, and partners. The organization that preceded the GPD Security Department was the Bureau of Armed Security (*wuzhuang baowei ju*), which was concurrently established with the Ministry of Public Security in 1949 as a subordinate bureau of the MPS. The Bureau of Armed Security (BAS) was specifically assigned to direct the security apparatus within the PLA. Beginning in April 1950, the Bureau of Armed Security operated under the dual leadership of the Ministry of Public Security and the PLA General Political Department. Soon thereafter the BAS was removed from the jurisdiction of the MPS and renamed the Security Department; it became a PLA unit reporting to the GPD only. Local branches of the GPD Security Department were established one by one in the PLA military regions, the navy, the air force, the Second Artillery Forces, the Defense Science and Engineering Commission, army groups (*bingtuan*), army corps (*jun*), divisions, and regiments.[5]

After June 1985, the political departments of local PLA units commanded the security departments (*baowei bu*) in the military regions, the navy, the air force, the Second Artillery Force, the Defense Science and Engineering Commission,

---

[3] *Zhongguo renmin jiefangjun*, vol. 1, p. 634.
[4] Yinghong Cheng, *Creating the "New Man": From Enlightenment Ideals to Socialist Realities*, p. 109.
[5] *Zhongguo renmin jiefangjun*, vol. 1, p. 635.

the Military Academy, the National Defense University, the security division (*baowei chu*) at the levels of group armies and provincial military districts, the security section (*baowei ke*) at the levels of divisions or brigades, and the security secretary (*ganshi*) at the level of regiment.[6] Local branches of the GPD Security Department are in charge of guarding local army leaders and office buildings with headquarters of local army units. For example, the GPD Security Department of the navy sent a guard company with two platoons in charge of internal and external security to guard navy headquarters. Another major duty of this department was managing and executing security detail for the top leaders of the navy.[7]

Similar to the Ministry of Public Security, the GPD Security Department has functional departments for areas such as intelligence, military police operations, security of leaders, and political and communications security. Moreover, the GPD has authority over all security responsibilities within the PLA and provides guidance to PLA security nationwide. This includes preventing, suppressing, and investigating criminal or counterrevolutionary activities; fighting terrorist activities; maintaining security and order in the PLA; providing security details for PLA leaders and important military facilities; and inspecting and monitoring public information networks. In addition to external threats, the GPD Security Department places importance on internal security and investigations, which is demonstrated by its involvement in investigations of charged PLA ranking officers. In terms of intelligence gathering, it stores many confidential files and materials related to high-ranking PLA generals, including their political blemishes and blunders. Thus, it was not surprising that, after he took charge of the day-to-day administration of the CMC, Huang Yongsheng immediately destroyed part of his files stored in the GPD Security Department. This was an especially significant accomplishment for Huang, because it enabled him to have sole access to his files during the Cultural Revolution, when a minuscule political misstep could have resulted in his execution.[8]

Guard Bureau of the CMC General Office

The CMC General Office is the nerve center that processes all CMC communications and documents, coordinates meetings, and conveys orders and directives to subordinate organs.[9] In terms of security organs, the CMC General Office is the leading organization that provides security detail for the Central Military Commission and its leaders. The CMC General Office provides secretarial, administrative, and personnel support for the CMC leadership and

[6] Ibid., p. 636.

[7] *Zai Su Zhenhua shangjiang shengbian de rizi* [The days with Colonel General Su Zhenhua], *Qingdao xinwen* [Qingdao news online], November 2, 2005.

[8] Hao Zaijin, "Shi Jinqian jiangjun he quanjun luoshi zhengce gongzuo" [General Shi Jinqian and the work of policy execution in the entire PLA], in *Da Di* [Earth], vol. 21 [*Renmin ribao* online], January 9, 2003, and vol. 22, 2002 [*Renmin ribao* online], January 15, 2003.

[9] David Shambaugh, *Modernizing China's Military: Progress, Problems, and Prospects*, p. 121.

serves as the nexus of party-army relations.[10] It carries out the CMC's activities on a daily basis, including making arrangements for CMC meetings regarding defense plans, the defense budget, other key aspects of defense policy, and dispute resolution. The CMC General Office also facilitates and supervises personal interactions among the senior members of the PLA leadership, coordinates bureaucratic interactions among the core PLA agencies and their subordinate systems, supervises daily operations of CMC departments, and coordinates and evaluates strategic research and assessments developed by the PLA bureaucracy.[11] The CMC General Office has its own Guard Bureau, which serves a similar function as the Guard Bureau of the Ministry of Public Security. Because the personnel of the Central Guard Bureau and the Guard Bureau of the CMC General Office are often mutually transferable, the two organizations have traditionally shared a close relationship. For example, Ma Xijin and Mou Naichuan, the bodyguards of Marshal Ye Jianying during the Cultural Revolution, were transferred from the Central Guard Bureau or the Guard Bureau of the Central General Office to the Guard Bureau of the CMC General Office.[12] General Li Hongfu started his career in the Guard Bureau of the CMC General Office and became the deputy director of the Central Guard Bureau in 2007.[13] The close relationship between the CMC General Office Guard Bureau and the Central Guard Bureau facilitated flexible transfers like the aforementioned.

The Central Guard Bureau provides security services to leading figures of the CMC and guards CMC agencies. The CMC General Office, established in November 1954, was concurrently known as the General Office of the Ministry of Defense. Its predecessor was the General Office of the Central Government's People's Revolutionary Committee, established in October 1949. In early 1950, the CMC General Office was also concurrently the General Office of PLA General Staff.[14] After General Chief of Staff Luo Ruiqing was dismissed and Yang Chengwu was appointed acting general chief of staff in November 1965, the CMC General Office was absorbed by the General Office of the General Staff Department. After the Gang of Four was arrested in October 1976, the CMC General Office was concurrently known as the General Office of the General Staff Department and the General Office of the Defense Ministry. Not only the General Office of the GSD concurrently served as the CMC General Office, but also its Guard Bureau as concurrently the Central Guard Bureau.[15] This

---

[10] Maryanne Kivlehan-Wise, Dean Cheng, and Ken Gause, "The 16th Party Congress and Leadership Changes in the PLA," in Andrew Scobell and Larry Wortzel (eds.), *Civil-Military Change in China Elites, Institutes, and Ideas after the 16th Party Congress*, p. 207.

[11] Michael D. Swaine, *The Role of the Chinese Military in National Security Policymaking*, p. 53.

[12] See *Wu Jicheng huiyilu*, p. 393.

[13] See *Jiefangjun bao* [PLA daily], February 25, 2003; *Jinzhou ribao* [Jinzhou daily], November 17, 2003.

[14] *Huang Kecheng zishu*, p. 238; *Zhongguo renmin jiefangjun*, vol. 1, pp. 341, 351.

[15] You Ji, "Sorting Out the Myths about Political Commissars," in Nan Li (ed.), *Chinese Civil Military Relations: The Transformation of the People's Liberation Army*, p. 91.

mechanism of one organization serving more than one superior organization facilitates the coordination of multiple organizations when the relevant organizations are involved in the tasks with the similar functions. In April 1979, the CMC General Office was separated from the General Office of the PLA General Staff Department, but it continued its role as the day-to-day administrative body of the CMC and the Defense Ministry.[16] The Guard Bureau of the CMC General Office has been under the dual leadership of the CMC General Office and the Security Department of the General Political Department, in which it is the subordinate unit of the CMC General Office and a professional agency of the Security Department of the General Political Department.[17] In addition, the CMC General Office is responsible for providing guidance to the Beijing Garrison Command for guarding important PLA personnel and facilities in Beijing. Important places included in guarding duties are the Western Hills (*xishan*) in the suburb of western Beijing, the residences of PLA marshals and top leaders, and the headquarters of the CMC command center. The CMC General Office is authorized to command the Jingxi Hotel, a military hotel of the PLA General Staff Department that provides internal services and meetings for the PLA and foreign military guests (Table 10.1).

Thus, the CMC General Office is in charge of security detail for high-ranking PLA generals; to do so, it coordinates bodyguards to serve high-ranking generals and directs the Beijing Garrison Command to guard generals' residences. However, if a PLA general would like to retain a bodyguard who served him or her before a transfer or promotion to Beijing, the general is allowed to have that bodyguard transferred. For example, Fei Sijin was transferred from the 121st Division of the 41st Army Corps, Guangzhou Military Region, to serve as a bodyguard of Huang Yongsheng, then commander of the PLA Guangzhou Military Region. He accompanied Huang to Beijing and continued as Huang's bodyguard after Huang was transferred to Beijing as the PLA's general chief of staff and promoted to member of the Politburo. However if this happens, the guards must be transferred as well to become officers of the Central Guard Bureau and receive commands from the CGB leaders. The CCP leadership recognized the PLA generals' right to choose their guards, although it was considered risky if loyalty to the general was greater than loyalty to the party. Still, it was understood that the generals and their security guards had closer bonds than high-ranking civilian leaders and their security guards, given the elevated role of loyalty (*zhong*) and righteousness (*yi*) in military culture.

Generally speaking, the CMC General Office does not continue to provide security detail for PLA leaders who become Politburo members or higher in the CCP leadership. If a PLA general is promoted out of the PLA into the

---

[16] *Zuzhi shi*, appendix 2, p. 281.
[17] See Zhongyang bangongting, '*Guanyu tiaozheng jingwei jigou, gaijin jingwei gongzuo de huiyi jiyao' de tongzhi* [Notice about the summary of the meeting on adjusting guard apparatus and improving the work of security guard], in Central General Office Document, no. 20 (1979).

382*China's Security State*

TABLE 10.1. *Comparison of Central Guard Bureau, Guard Bureau of the CMC General Office, and the GPD Security Department*

	Central Guard Bureau	Guard Bureau of CMC General Office	GPD Security Department
Organizational rank	Army Corps level	Division level	Army Corps level
Feature of organization	Administrative body and security service provider	Administrative body and security service provider	Administrative body
Affiliation	Under dual jurisdiction of both the CMC and the Central General Office; technical guidance from MPS	Under the CMC General Office; technical guidance from GPD Security Department	Under the GPD
Responsibility	Guarding top leaders at the level of four vices and two chiefs and above; commanding the Central Guard Regiment	Guarding top CMC generals and the important PLA leading organs; commanding the Beijing Garrison Command for security assignments	Mainly providing macro-level administration related to security issues and technical guidance to the PLA security units nationwide, coordinating the security apparatus and forces among the PLA security units and between the PLA security units and civilian security apparatus from different affiliations; conducting investigation, detainments, and pretrial hearings for criminal cases and political cases in the PLA

government, the Central Guard Bureau replaces the CMC General Office in providing security services to the leader. For example, before the Cultural Revolution Lin Biao's security was managed solely by the CMC General Office. In August 1966, when Lin was elected vice chairman of the CCP, the Central Guard Bureau started taking responsibility for Lin's security detail. The CGB sent Han Qingyu to guard Lin. Han was a departmental director under the CGB and deputy chief of staff of Unit 8341. Some of Lin's guards who served him before he became the only vice chairman of the CCP were also transferred from the CMC General Office to the CGB and continued to serve Lin, as in the case of Liu Jicun. Liu Jicun was transferred from the CMC General Office to guard Lin Biao in early 1966 when the PLA General Staff Department and the PLA Political Department reported to the center that Lin Biao's security needed strengthening. After Liu became Lin's guard, his title immediately changed to officer of the Central Guard Bureau from officer of the CMC General Office, as he had been before Lin's promotion.[18]

Despite the regulation that stipulates that the Central Guard Bureau would automatically take over security for PLA leaders once they become government leaders, in practice, the regulation is not strictly enforced for army generals who become party leaders. Although it is the responsibility of the CGB to administrate security services for high-ranking party leaders, more often than not, those leaders often override the CGB's decisions in choosing guards or establishing rules for the involvement of the security services in their personal lives. For example, Deng Xiaoping kept Zhang Baozhong as his guard and chief bodyguard from 1954, when Zhang served Deng as an internal guard, until Deng's death. For more than thirty years Zhang was Deng's bodyguard, when Deng was vice premier (1952–1966, 1973–1977), a Politburo member (1955–1966, 1973–1987), general party secretary (1956–1966), PLA general chief of staff (1975–1976, 1977–1980), and chairman of the CMC (1981–1989).[19]

Lin Biao's case is also a classic example. After Lin was promoted in August 1966, the CGB attempted to take over his security from the CMC General Office. This attempt was aborted at Ye Qun's objection. Ye was concerned with handing over control of Lin's security detail to the CGB because there were no personal ties between Lin and the Central Guard Bureau, headed by Wang Dongxing. Neither party would capitulate; thus, Lin's security became the joint responsibility of both the CMC General Office and the CGB, although the CGB only played a supportive role. According to Zhang Yunsheng, Ye Qun (Lin's wife) and a supporter skilled in political maneuvering, was always suspicious of the guards sent by the CGB, so she resorted to monitoring them. She conducted surveillance of the guards and attempted to exclude them from important guarding duties when she could. She also denied an offer from the

---

[18] See *Wenhui dushu zhoubao* [Wenhui reading weekly], June 3, 2005.
[19] *Xinhuanet*, August 13, 2004.

CGB to send Lin a deputy director of the bureau to lead his security.[20] The CMC General Office supported their former generals instead of siding with the CGB, and it offered temporary guards to high-ranking PLA leaders. Lin Biao accepted the offer often; thus, the CMC General Office sent temporary guards to help with Lin's security detail whenever requested.[21]

In addition to providing security details to high-ranking PLA generals, the CMC General Office is also responsible for providing them with health care. For instance, PLA generals need to gain the CMC General Office's approval before being treated at a hospital; if they are outside of Beijing, PLA generals need approval for which hospitals they are qualified to enter and whether they are allowed to travel to Beijing for treatment if their units station outside Beijing.[22] Besides its explicit duties, the CMC General Office also has certain practices that derive from their relationships with the generals they serve. For example, the CMC General Office often plays a vanguard role for newly appointed PLA leaders who attempt to change or reform the PLA. After Lin Biao's death and the abolishment of the CMC Working Group (*junwei banshi zu*), controlled by Lin Biao's followers in October 1971, Mao appointed Ye Jianying to head the CMC and lead a ten-member working conference (*bangong huiyi*) and to take charge of day-to-day administration of the PLA.[23] Consequently, the CMC General Office was instrumental to Ye in his work in reorganizing the PLA after Lin Biao's faction had dominated for more than twelve years.[24] Because the incumbent PLA director's input played a large role in the selection of the director of the CMC General Office, at any point in the General Office's tenure, the director was generally a longtime, trusted follower of the incumbent PLA leaders. For example, the personal ties between the 1965–1966 General Chief of Staff Yang Chengwu and the CMC General Office Director Lu Yang can be traced back to the 1940s, when Lu Yang was an officer of the Propaganda Department of the Jizhong Military Region and later an officer of the Third Column of the Shanxi-Chahar-Hebei Military Region, both commanded by Yang Chengwu. Still, the most prominent example of the CMC promoting former subordinates to positions for which they may not have been qualified was the appointment of Jia Ting'an. Jia became Jiang Zemin's secretary in 1982, when Jiang was deputy minister of the Electronics Industry Ministry. When Jiang Zemin became party chief in 1989, Jiang brought Jia Ting'an with

---

[20] See *Maojiawan jishi*, pp. 243–4.

[21] Ibid., p. 120.

[22] For example, Han Xianchu asked for medical treatment in Beijing when he was commander of the Nanzhou Military Region in May 1974. Because the CMC General Office denied his request, he had to stay in Nanzhou for local treatment. See Zhang Zhenglong, *Zhanjiang* [Combat general], p. 349.

[23] See *Ye Jianying zhuan*, p. 773.

[24] Ye Jianying relied mainly on the CMC General Office, the General Staff Department, the General Political Department, the General Logistic Department, and the Military Academy for his plan to reorganize the PLA. *Ye Jianying zhuan*, pp. 607–8.

him as Jiang's secretary, and he later promoted Jia to deputy director of the CMC General Office in 1994 and then director of the CMC General Office in 2003.

Sometimes there were no close personal relationships between incumbent PLA leaders and directors of the CMC General Office, but because of the correspondence of positions and the importance of the CMC General Office director to incumbent PLA leaders, it was assumed that a relationship existed. For example, when Mao launched the campaign against Lin Biao's faction following Lin's death, CMC General Office Director Xiao Jianfei was accused of being Lin's follower and was subsequently dismissed. Another case is that of Xiao Hongda, who had been director of the Ye Jianying Office when Ye Jianying was appointed to the Central South China Military Region in the 1950s. In October 1976, when Ye allied with Hua Guofeng and Wang Dongxing to arrest the Gang of Four, he took over direction of the PLA and transferred Xiao Hongda to director of the CMC General Office. At the time, Xiao was director of the General Office of the Guangdong Provincial Party Committee. In 1977 Deng Xiaoping resumed his position as PLA general chief of staff, and he began to consolidate his power in the PLA. Although he could not outright fire Ye's followers, he did go about undermining their influence in the PLA, especially targeting Xiao Hongda. In April 1979, under the guise of reorganization, the General Office of the General Staff Department separated from the General Office of the CMC; this office gradually replaced the original CMC General Office in its authority over the PLA, becoming the real power center that Deng Xiaoping relied on in commanding the PLA. Because Xiao was director of the General Office of the CMC, he no longer had the power to make high-level decisions in the PLA's security apparatus bureaucracy. More often than not, directors of the CMC General Office often became victims of power politics when the incumbent PLA leaders with whom they were associated retired or were demoted or dismissed because of their strong political or personal ties (see Table 10.2).

Leadership Security in the Capital City

As the politics of vying for power has historically played a significant role in Chinese politics, the security apparatus is crucial to any leadership that hopes for longevity. In this respect, protection of the power centers comprises a large part of a strong security network. Guarding the ruler, the leadership compound, and the capital are among the security apparatuses' toughest jobs, because doing so is the most visible duty with the most at risk if it fails. Securing the capital and guarding the ruler have been the most important mission for security forces throughout Chinese history, and security can be traced all the way back to the Qin dynasty (221–206 BC). In the Qin dynasty, security forces were assigned to one of the three components of security duties as they knew it: protecting the emperor, the imperial palace, and the capital city. Although the

TABLE 10.2. *Changes of the CMC General Office Directors Caused by Changes in the PLA Leadership*

Name	Period	Cause
Xiao Xiangrong	Jan. 1952–Nov. 1965	Accused of being a follower of General Chief Staff Luo Ruiqing, who was dismissed in November 1965
Lu Yang	Aug. 1967–Dec. 1968	Accused of being a follower of Acting General Chief Staff Yang Chengwu, who was arrested in March 1968
Xiao Jianfei	May 1969–Apr. 1971	Accused of being a follower of Lin Biao, who died in an airplane crash on September 13, 1971
Hu Wei	Oct. 1976–Feb. 1977	Accused of being a follower of the Gang of Four, who were arrested in October 1976
Xiao Hongda	Oct. 1977–Sep. 1985	A trust follower of Marshal Ye Jianying; transferred after Ye Jianying retired in September 1985

Source: *Zuzhi shi*, appendix 2, pp. 9, 281–2; *Lingdao jigou yange*, p. 1101.

Qin dynasty is not necessarily the ideal model for rule, the security apparatus developed then remained the model for later dynasties. In the Han dynasty (206 BC–AD 220), the Qin model was augmented, such that enhanced power of security forces became a notable feature. Having enhanced power meant that the security forces not only guarded the emperor, imperial palace, and capital cities but also were often sent to suppress rebels and resist foreign invasions. The idea of enhanced power grew, to the point that in the Tang dynasty (AD 618–907) the scale of the security forces developed far beyond that of the Han. In the Tang dynasty central security forces were divided into two systems to jointly manage the responsibilities for guarding the emperor, the imperial palace, and the capital cities, in addition to a special security force that was controlled by the crown prince himself. Not only were forces created specially to serve the leadership in its unique security needs, but the system of having multiple central forces was more sophisticated than any security system China had seen before.

This and other research show that security and garrison forces in the capital played a crucial role in imperial court politics. Since the Ming dynasty established Beijing as its capital in AD 1421, the security of the capital and control over the security forces guarding Beijing has been a central task of the ruler and the ruling elite. Enhancing the power and influence of its security forces greatly, the Ming dynasty established security forces as a garrison command for Beijing and as the dominant forces used to protect the entire Ming empire. The Qing empire took this concept and expanded it further. Immediately after the Manchu armies conquered China, half of the approximately two-hundred-thousand-strong Manchu Banner Army forces were stationed in Beijing to serve both as the capital's garrison and as the Qing government's main striking force. Control over a strong and capable armed force guarding the capital has been a key criterion for a ruler concerned with dominance in imperial court politics in traditional China.

After the CCP set up Beijing as the capital of the PRC, the 160th Division of the 47th Army Corps from the Fourth Field Army led by Lin Biao was dispatched to guard Beijing in January 1949. In September 1949, the fifteen-thousand-strong 160th Division (later the PLA Independent 207th Division) and the Central Garrison Regiment were reorganized as the Central Column of Chinese People's Public Security Force (*zhongguo renmin gong'an zhongyang zhongdui*) to be the major armed forces to guard the capital.[25] Because Beijing was peacefully taken over from the Nationalist armies, led by General Fu Zuoyi, the security forces faced a challenge in rooting out all the GMD spies and supporters. Still, the CCP seemed confident relying on mainly the Central Column of the Chinese People's Public Security Forces (CPPSF), with its twenty-five thousand personnel, and the 66th Army Corps in Tianjin for its security.

In 1953, when the Central Guard Regiment was reorganized, the security forces in the capital were organized into several levels of guarding duties. At the top of elite security in Beijing were the Central Guard Bureau and the Central Guard Regiment, which provided security details for the leadership compound in Zhongnanhai, for Mao, and for the top leaders in the Central Secretariat member and above. The next level of security in the capital was the PLA's Guard Division of Public Security (*gong'an jingwei shi*). It was established in November 1949 and was specifically in charge of security detail for top leaders below the level of Central Secretariat, the offices of the CCP, the CMC in Beijing, and several locations in the suburbs of Beijing. From 1950 to 1955 the Guard Division of Public Security was subordinate to the CPPSF and later the PLA Public Security Forces, and from 1955 to 1957 was subordinate to the Public Security Army. After the Public Security Army was abolished in 1957, the Guard Division of Public Security came under the direct authority of the Central Guard Bureau . In January 1959 it was renamed the Capital Guard Division (*shoudu jingwei shi*), when it was absorbed into the forces of the newly established Beijing Garrison Command.[26]

The next level security apparatus in Beijing below the previous one were the local security forces under Beijing Municipal City, which were assigned to manage security detail for government offices and buildings. The General Corps of Public Security of Beijing Municipal City (its predecessor was the Second

[25] Wu Lie, *Zhengrong suiyue*, pp. 320–2, 329–33.
[26] See Beijing shi difang zhi bianzuan weiyuanhui [Compiling commission of local annals of Beijing Municipal City], *Beijing zhi, junshi juan, junshi zhi* [Military annals, volume of military, annals of Beijing], p. 515; Wu Lie, *Zhengrong suiyue*, pp. 391–4.

Corps of the North China Infantry School) was specifically responsible for the security detail of city offices and Beijing municipal leaders, and for securing transportation for both central and local leaders in Beijing.[27] Last, beginning in 1951, there were several PLA army units assigned to guard Beijing and the satellite cities and counties around Beijing. These army corps included the 66th Army Corps (assigned in 1951), the 69th Army Corps (assigned in 1953), and the 24th Army Corps (assigned in 1955), all of which received command from the Beijing Military Region and North China Military Region. The 66th Army Corps returned to China from Korea in 1951. In 1953, the 65th Army Corps and the 69th Army Corps were stationed at Zhangjiakou and Baoding, respectively, after returning from Korea. Two years later, the 24th Army Corps also returned from Korea and was stationed in the Beijing suburb, Chengde, and Tangshan.

Since the PRC was founded in 1949, Mao wanted to ensure the absolute loyalty of the PLA, particularly the security forces and army units that guarded the capital. Mao's control over the PLA relied on his unilateral decision making for army officers' appointments. In the early 1950s, all PLA officer appointments at the level of army corps commander (*zheng jun*) and above had to be approved by Mao.[28] Mao's frustration with Acting General Chief of Staff Nie Rongzhen in the early 1950s and Defense Minister Peng Dehuai in 1959 partially derived from their initiatives to put the Central Guard Regiment under the jurisdiction of the Chinese People's Public Security Forces and the Beijing Garrison Command, respectively. This was not ideal for Mao, because maintaining the status quo would keep the Central Guard Regiment in the hands of the Central Guard Bureau, led by Mao's chief bodyguard Wang Dongxing. When Mao decided to launch the Cultural Revolution, he realized that his assault against the party establishment and bureaucracy required the PLA's support. This was particularly salient in November 1965, when Mao secretly arranged to publish criticism of the drama *Hai Rui*, written by Yao Wenyuan, which served Mao's political campaign. In Mao's own words, "To mobilize the broad masses we must expose our dark aspects in an open, comprehensive, and bottom-up way."[29] He felt the army's support as crucial for the campaign.[30] However, when Mao turned his attention to the PLA, he realized that there was a potential crisis of leadership, which had become a severe problem for the

---

[27] In 1959 when the BGC was established, the General Corps of Beijing Public Security was reorganized as the PAP Beijing Corps, subordinate to the Public Security Bureau under Beijing Municipal City. See Beijing shi difang zhi bianzuan weiyuanhui, *Beijing zhi, junshi juan, junshi zhi*, pp. 516–7.

[28] Li Jing, *Rujiang Xiao Hua* [Scholarly General Xiao Hua], p. 555.

[29] *Jianguo yilai Mao Zedong wengao* [Mao Zedong's manuscripts since the founding of the state], vol. 12, p. 220; the PLA had been long viewed as the most crucial element in Mao's power base.

[30] See Harry Harding, "The Chinese State in Crisis, 1966–9," in Roderick MacFarquhar (ed.), *The Politics of China*, p. 155.

PLA's cohesion. Mao faced the critical challenges that were ruining leadership solidarity and undermining the army's support of his political campaign.

Starting in the winter of 1965, Mao sought to solidify his leadership over PLA military factions to ensure the PLA's support for the Cultural Revolution, because the PLA had historically exerted a strong influence over the political elite.[31] During the early stages of the Cultural Revolution, there were no major military maneuvers, except for two divisions that were moved to strengthen the Beijing Garrison Command in 1966. This shows the primarily symbolic role that the PLA played in security issues during the early Cultural Revolution. Later, after Mao destroyed the civil security apparatus, he had to rely greatly on the PLA to fill the civil security apparatus's role. The PLA was assigned not only to restore and maintain social order but also to implement Mao's grand strategy against the frontline leaders. However, Mao's control over the PLA throughout the Cultural Revolution often had to rely on manipulating PLA factions. For example, Mao ordered the Beijing Garrison Command, a stronghold of the former North China Field Army, to arrest Yang Yong, commander of the Beijing Military Region in January 1967, and he ordered Wu Faxian and Li Zuopeng, key followers of the Lin Biao faction, to imprison Yang Chengwu and Fu Chongbi. When the Lin Biao group was dismissed, Mao relied on local PLA generals to arrest Lin's followers. Mao similarly ordered Xu Shiyou to disarm the 4th and 5th Army Corps of the PLA Air Force and to arrest the leaders Chen Liyun and Wang Weiguo.

During the Cultural Revolution, the Beijing Garrison Command (BGC) became extremely powerful, because it was upgraded to the rank of army group (*bingtuan*) and had more than one hundred thousand personnel. The leaders of the BGC could attend meetings that typically only leaders of military regions (*da junqu*) and military districts (*sheng junqu*) were qualified to attend. In addition, the BGC received more confidential documents from the party leadership than did the Beijing Military Region (MR), its immediate superior.[32] This seems a bit strange, considering that before the Cultural Revolution, the Beijing Military Region had played an important role in ensuring the security of the capital; many of its best units were stationed around Beijing. This was the case for the 70th Division of the 24th Army Corps in Tongxian and the north of Shunyi, the 179th Division of the 24th Army Corps in Tangshan, the 196th Division of the 66th Army Corps in Tianjin, and the 193rd Division of the 65th Army Corps in Xuanhua.[33]

---

[31] See Ellis Joffe, "The Chinese Army in Domestic Politics: Factors and Phases," in Nan Li (ed.), *Chinese Civil-Military Relations: The Transformation of the People's Liberation Army*, pp. 8–9; David Shambaugh, "The Soldier and the State in China: The Political Work System in the People's Liberation Army," *CQ*, vol. 127 (September 1991), p. 535.

[32] *Fu Chongbi huiyilu*, pp. 179–80.

[33] Ibid., p. 180; Li Yanke, Li Jianjun, and Ji Hongjian, "Jinlu xiongfeng – Jiefangjun mou jing-weishi de fazhan yange ji zhandou licheng" [Awe-inspiring crack force: The revolution and combat course of a guard division of the PLA], in *Junshi lishi* [Military history], no. 1 (2006), pp. 60–3.

Because Mao was concerned about the loyalty of the Beijing Military Region to him, he made several significant military moves to ensure his dominance in the capital, which included dismissing the commander and political commissars of the Beijing MR in January 1967, separating the BGC from the Beijing MR in the summer of 1966, and transferring the 38th Army Corps from the Shenyang MR to the Beijing MR in February 1967. The 38th Army Corps, one of the PLA's best-trained and best-equipped units and a rapid reaction force, was transferred from Tonghua, in Jilin, to Baoding, in Hebei, in 1967 to keep the dominance of the Beijing MR over other garrison organizations of Beijing under check. The transfer of the 38th Army Corps undoubtedly served to alleviate Mao's concern about a possible military rebellion against the radicals and the Cultural Revolution. Mao's concern was not unfounded, as the Beijing MR, Hebei Military District (MD), and most army corps around Beijing had been accused of being "conservatives" by the Maoist radicals because of their sympathies with local "capitalists." The violence between the radical mass organizations supported by the 38th Army Corps and the conservative mass organizations backed by the Hebei MD and the 63rd Army Corps derived partially from the conflict between the 38th Army Corps and the Beijing MR.[34] The efficacy of the 38th Army Corps' efforts against military rebellion was further strengthened after Mao upgraded it from an ordinary infantry army corps to the only motorized infantry army corps in the PLA in 1969.[35]

Throughout the Cultural Revolution, the armed forces in the entire garrison of Beijing were split into three parts that supervised one another – the Beijing Garrison Command, the Beijing MR, and the 38th Army Corps. This tendency became evident especially after Mao cut ties between the Beijing Garrison Command and its immediate superior the Beijing MR. According to Wu Zhong, deputy commander of the BGC between 1968 and 1970 and commander of the BGC between 1970 and 1979, Mao did not take many liberties with authority in the garrison organizations of Beijing. First, he never gave permission to let both the BGC commander and political commissar take concurrent positions as deputy commander and deputy political commissar of the Beijing MR, even though the previous BGC commanders and political commissars had done so before the Cultural Revolution. Nor did he authorize the Beijing MR to command the BGC. The imperial legacy of strong security in the capital continued in the Maoist era, delineated by Mao's maneuvering and tight control over the authority and jurisdiction of the various garrison organizations. The PLA

---

34 Wang Nianyi, *Da dongluan de niandai* [China 1949–1989: The years of great turmoil], p. 410; Chen Xiaonong, *Chen Boda: Zuihou koushu huiyi* [Chen Boda: Last reminiscence based on an account in Chen Boda's own words], pp. 334–5.

35 See Lujun di sanshiba jitunjun junshi bianshen weiyuanhui [Editing Commission of the Military History of the PLA 38th Group Army], *Gangtie de budui: Lujun di sanshiba jitunjun junshi* [Iron and steel army: Military history of the PLA 38th Group Army], pp. 621–2.

played a large role in the capital garrison, but only insofar as it would help Mao consolidate power.

During the reform era, the armed forces guarding Beijing gradually have reduced in size and have played a limited role in military politics. The clarity of their organizational relationships, cut during the Cultural Revolution, is gradually being restored. Deng's reforms that reorganized the security services included withdrawing the PLA's army corps' and group armies' heavy involvement in the capital garrison and increasing employment of the army reserves in the garrison of Beijing. Like the Central Guard Bureau and its subordinate unit, the Central Guard Regiment, the BGC was reorganized and its leading figures were transferred to different organizations after Deng regained power in 1978. For example, a division and a regiment of the BGC were handed over to the newly established People's Armed Police (PAP) in 1983, and the 4th Division of the BGC was returned to the 63rd Army Corps in 1985.[36]

Another effort that Deng made to contain the BGC's power was to reestablish the authority of the Beijing MR over the BGC, which Mao had expropriated from the Beijing MR in the Cultural Revolution. Thus, the BGC was again put under the authority of the Beijing MR, which was done by issuing the "Regulation about the Command and Leadership of the Beijing Garrison Command and Its Limits in Approving the Dispatch of its Units" in January 1978. This regulation indicated that the Beijing MR was the BGC's supervisor in terms of "the work of the Party, the appointments of its leadership personnel, combat and command, training, organization and equipment, administration, logistics, recruitment and demobilization, and militia related work."[37]

Another move Deng made was to change the 38th Army Corps' emphasis from garrison duties to combat duties. This move is a component of Deng's push for China's military modernization. So far, the 38th Group Army has been heralded as one of the best units in the PLA and a pioneer in the PLA's modernization, informationization or computerization, and regularization.[38] For example, in September 1982, the 38th Army Corps was established as the experimental unit for PLA group armies at the army's premier training center to test advanced military strategies and new organizations – similar to Fort Irwin, the U.S. Army's National Training Center. As the first Group Army in the PLA (it obtained group army status in middle 1980s), the 38th Group Army (GA) has risen to become one of the top group armies in the PLA, in terms of personnel size, scope of services, advanced equipment and weapons, firepower, mobility, offense and defense, readiness, joint combat, independent combat, integrated support, logistics, and digital combat. In the reform era,

---

[36] Wei Yingji, "Shengsheng huainian Pan Yan tongzhi" [Deeply think of comrade Pan Yan], in He Ting (ed.), *Pan Yan jiangjun jinian wenji* [Collected works in commemorating General Pan Yan], pp. 222–3.

[37] *Fu Chongbi huiyilu*, pp. 251–2.

[38] The 38th Army Corps was upgraded as the 38th Group Army in 1984.

the 38th GA has transitioned from a garrison unit guarding the capital to one of the most elite group armies of the PLA, leading the army in the military modernization necessary to respond to the demands of modern warfare and foreign threats.

Furthermore, under the leadership of Jiang Zemin, group armies were no longer responsible for garrison duties. Instead, garrison commands have been established in special administration cities and in provincial and autonomous region capital cities to manage garrison duties. In Beijing, the BGC was authorized to assist in leading the capital's security efforts, commanding the reserve forces, and coordinating other PLA units' garrison duties in the capital. Reflecting the overall shift of garrison command duties across the country, the BGC's responsibilities emphasize support of local civilian government to promote social stability and harmony. The BGC also operates as the military department of the local party committee; thus, it relies greatly on local party committees and governments for funding. Because the BGC now operates predominantly under the auspices of the local party committee, there is more civilian control over the BGC than ever before, an overarching trend in the post-Deng leadership.

Beijing Military Region and Security in the Capital

Among all military regions, the Beijing Military Region has played the greatest role in guarding the capital and ensuring the security of the CCP leadership. Historically, the Beijing Military Region was the power base of the North China Field Army, headed by Marshal Nie Rongzhen. It is plausible that the association with Nie is the reason that Mao targeted leaders of the Beijing MR when he attempted to undermine Nie's influence and establish his own dominance in the Beijing MR. Nie's powerful influence on the North China MR and Beijing MR and his unsatisfactory performance (according to Mao) when he was acting general chief of staff in the early 1950s were key factors in Mao's disfavor of Nie during the 1950s. Under Mao's order, Nie was not invited to attend many party and PLA leadership meetings, and he was excluded from the decision making of military maneuvers related to the Beijing MR and the Beijing Garrison Command.[39] Nie was later blamed for using his power to prevent downsizing of the North China Field Army when all other field armies were ordered to downsize immediately after the CCP seized power over the country.[40] When leaders of the Beijing MR, such as Zheng Weishan and

---

[39] For example, Ye Zilong, Mao's secretary in the 1950s, found that Mao no longer invited Nie to attend the Politburo meetings that Nie used to attend in previous years. It occurred several times that Mao would personally delete Nie's name from the leadership attendance meeting lists he would prepare. See Wang Fan et al., *Zhiqing zheshuo* [Said by insiders], vol. 1, p. 391.

[40] See Dong Baochun and Pu Suanzi, "Huabei huiyi yu Beijing junqu da gaizu (2)" [Northern China Conference and the great reorganization of Beijing Military Region, part 2], in *Dangshi buolan* [General review of the Chinese Communist Party], no. 2 (2006), p. 35.

Li Xuefeng, were attacked for their support of Lin Biao at the 1970 Lushan plenum, Jiang Qing gave a partial explanation of why Mao did not trust Nie Rongzhen in the 1950s. Jiang Qing accused the leaders of the former Northern Field Army – Nie Rongzhen, Yang Chengwu, and Zheng Weishan – of "engaging in factionalism," referring mostly to the accusation that the former generals of the North China Field Army "squeezed out and discriminated the generals from other field armies" and the instance in which the Northern Field Army refused to make personnel cuts as all other field armies had done immediately after the CCP established the PRC.[41]

Perhaps the most important move Mao made to undermine the dominance of the North China Field Army faction was in 1958, when key leadership positions of the Beijing MR were filled by generals who did not have ties to the North China Field Army faction. As mentioned in Chapter 7, in September 1958, Yang Yong, a general from the former Second Field Army, replaced Yang Chengwu, one of Nie's longtime assistants, as commander of the Beijing MR. Mao appointed Liao Hansheng, a general from the former First Field Army, as political commissar of Beijing MR, to replace Zhu Liangcai, former political commissar of the Beijing MR who had served Nie since 1938. According to official media, Zhu Liangcai asked to retire because of health reasons (*jiankang yuanyin*) in November 1958.[42] Thus, the appointments of Yang Yong and Liao Hansheng to head the Beijing Military Region were significant in undermining Nie's influence on the armed forces within and around Beijing.

In September 1959, Marshal Nie became one of three CMC vice chairmen in the reorganized CMC following the dismissal of Defense Minister Peng Dehuai.[43] However, Nie was still not allowed to be involved in important decision making regarding the Beijing MR, despite his understanding of his former subordinates. While Marshal Nie was assigned to lead the National Defense Science and Technology Commission, Marshal He Long, another CMC vice chairman, was assigned to lead the Beijing MR on behalf of the PLA leadership.[44] Marshal He Long established influence over the Beijing MR mainly by cultivating professional and personal relationships with the leading figures of the Beijing MR at the time, in particular Liao Hansheng, political commissar and He's nephew.[45] When Mao and Lin Biao decided to dismiss Marshal He Long

---

[41] Ibid., pp. 33–5.
[42] Before Liang Hansheng became political commissar of Beijing Military Region, Lai Chuanzhu, deputy director of the PLA General Cadres Department, was ordered to replace Zhu Liangcai for less than a year. See *Lingdao jigou yange*, p. 1054; *Renmin ribao* [People's daily], December 3, 2005.
[43] Ibid., pp. 1046–7.
[44] See Yin Jiamin, "'Wenge' zhong zuizao shuangshuang beizhua de Beijing junqu zhuguan" [The leading figures of Beijing Military Region who were early arrested in the "Cultural Revolution"], in *Dangshi bolan* [General review of the Chinese Communist Party], no. 4 (2008), p. 29.
[45] As the Beijing MR was close to the CMC, Yang and Liao had close contact with He Long. Liao was He's nephew and was also familiar with He Long's family, whom he often visited. See

in the early Cultural Revolution, the Beijing MR became an important military unit for the playing out of power politics. Lin Biao accused the Beijing MR of blocking information from him and openly complained in 1966 that he knew nothing about the Beijing MR, although he was aware of the happenings of other military regions. By stating this, he implied that the leaders of the Beijing MR refused to report their work to Lin and therefore refused to accept Lin's leadership.[46] Thus, the arrests of both Yang and Liao also contributed to their estrangement from Lin Biao, the key figure on whom Mao relied to control the PLA.

The dismissals of Yang and Liao occurred in January 1967 and were much greater controversies. On the eve of the Cultural Revolution, Mao decided to rely on the former North China Field Army to control Beijing, partly to solidify Lin Biao's leadership in the PLA. Although Yang Yong also served in the First Front Army, led by Mao, in the Jiangxi base areas, Yang was historically tied to the Third Army Group, headed by Peng Dehuai in the late 1920s and early 1930s, and the Shanxi-Hebei-Shandong-Henan Military Region and Second Field Army in the 1940s, led by Liu Bocheng and Deng Xiaoping. In addition, Yang was Peng Dehuai's key associate when Peng led the People's Volunteer Army (PVA) in the Korean War against the U.S. Army. Liao Hansheng was He Long's nephew and a longtime trusted follower of He Long.

Because of the strong political alliances that threatened Mao's consolidation of power, Mao did not trust the leaders of the Beijing MR when he decided to launch the Cultural Revolution. When the Beijing Security Working Group, headed by Marshal Ye Jianying, was established in May 1966 to reorganize the security forces guarding the capital, both Commander Yang Yong and Political Commissar Liao Hansheng of the Beijing MR were not the members of the Beijing Security Working Group, even though they were invited to attend the important meetings. Ironically, their subordinates Zheng Weishan and Fu Chongbi, two deputy commanders of the Beijing MR and former generals from the North China Military Region, were appointed as the members of the Beijing Security Working Group.[47] This implies that they were excluded from the decision making but needed to cooperate unconditionally with the Beijing Security Working Group – a powerful decision-making body directly under the authority of the Politburo – regarding the security and garrison of the capital city and comply with its orders.[48] In January 1967, both Liao and Yang were arrested, and Deputy Commander Zheng Weishan as well as Deputy Political Commissars Li Xuefeng and Chen Xianrui of the Beijing MR were promoted

Jiang Feng et al., *Yang Yong jiangjun zhuan* [A biography of General Yang Yong], pp. 400–2, *Liao Hansheng huiyilu*, pp. 261–3.

[46] See Jiang Feng et al., *Yang Yong jiangjun zhuan*, pp. 400–2, *Liao Hansheng huiyilu*, pp. 261–3.
[47] *Liao Hansheng huiyilu*, p. 247.
[48] This group was established on May 15, 1966, following Mao's "directive of protecting the capital." Ye Jianying was its director, and Yang Chengwu and Xie Fuzhi were appointed deputy directors, respectively. See *Zhou Enlai nianpu, 1949–1976*, vol. 3, p. 31.

as heads of the Beijing MR. Clearly, the promotion of officials with ties to the North China Field Army was no accident, as Mao felt he could trust those from his own faction better than those from others.

Although Mao eliminated a potential political threat by arresting Yang and Liao, he underestimated its impact on the PLA generals who were in charge of other military regions and military districts who had to defend themselves against the attacks of the overzealous mass rebels. Although the Beijing MR was only one of twelve expanded military regions in which both commander and political commissar were arrested, other military leaders feared becoming targets of either Mao or the radical mass rebels. At the same time, the arrests of Yang and Liao also aroused strong resistance from local military leaders against the radical mass rebels and the Central Cultural Revolution Group (CRG) in particular. To appease the angry local military region generals, Mao pretended that he knew nothing of Yang and Liao's arrests; in March 1967, he even asked the new leadership of the Beijing MR to conduct an investigation.

Nonetheless, General Chen Xianrui, second political commissar of the Beijing MR, was convinced that Mao played an important role in Yang and Liao's arrest. Chen's logic follows that if the order was not from the Chairman, no one would dare to arrest Yang, a deputy general chief of staff and the commander of a military region, and Liao, a deputy defense minister and the political commissar of a military region. According to Chen, "I think that it was clear [who arrested Yang Yong and Liao Hansheng and put them in jail]; but the 'top' (Mao) asked several times to identify who gave the order and who arrested them. Chen insisted, "If [the arrests] were a mistake, wouldn't it have been easy to release them if [Mao] simply gave the word?" Chen implies that Mao obviously tried to place the blame on others to reduce the army general's hostility toward him.[49] In addition, it is alleged that Yang had attempted to protect Peng Zhen by forwarding Peng "the synopsis of the symposium on the work of culture and arts in the PLA called by Comrade Jiang Qing that was entrusted by Comrade Lin Biao," a guide made with Mao's support, challenging the February outline that was made by Peng Zhen and even approved by frontline leaders. Before the synopsis was openly published, Mao intentionally concealed it from frontline leaders and sent it only to PLA leaders for their support. Yang secretly acquired the synopsis from Liao Hansheng and then sent it to Peng Zhen; it would be used as evidence to tie him politically with Peng Zhen.[50]

Despite his heavy reliance on the former North China Field Army to control the Beijing MR, Mao was apprehensive of allowing the former North

---

[49] See Chen Xianrui, "Liao Hansheng, Yang Yong beizhua yu sowei 'huabei shangtao zhuyi' wenti" [Liao Hansheng and Yang Yong's arrest and the issue of the so-called Northern China factionalism), in *Bai nian chao* [Hundred-year tide], no. 4 (2000), pp. 21–2.

[50] See Shi Dongbing, *Zuichu de kangzheng – Peng Zhen zai "wenhua da geming" qianxi* [The last resistance – Peng Zhen on the eve of the Cultural Revolution], pp. 253–5.

China Field Army to play such a large role in his security. He was particularly concerned about the loyalties of the generals from the former North China Field Army when, in the spring of 1967, they allied with military and civilian veterans against the CRG and the radical mass rebels. In January 1967, when the Maoist CRG confronted strong opposition from both the party's high-ranking leaders and army marshals, a rumor circulated that a military coup was under way. In particular, PLA generals nationwide showed discontent with the Cultural Revolution and the radical, CRG-supported mass organizations. At the top leadership, Mao sensed doubt and even resistance from both senior and army leaders regarding the CRG and the mass organizations. As Jiang Qing indicated in a talk on January 22, 1967, "Some people are trying to isolate Chairman Mao and Comrade Lin Biao."[51] In early 1967 Mao experienced conflict with the PLA marshals during the collective resistance against the Cultural Revolution, particularly the confrontation with PLA marshals and several senior governmental officials in the so-called "February Adverse Current," an incident Mao regarded as "an attack on the CRG as virtually an attack on him" and "the most intolerable attack on the Cultural Revolution since the movement's inception."[52]

Mao's strategy in early 1967 was to create an image that sent the message of a united central leadership supporting him. This may have been the result of leadership members pressuring Mao to in turn push the CRG to symbolically "protect" several senior party and high-ranking army leaders such as Zhou Enlai, Chen Yi, and Xiao Hua.[53] Even with this campaign, many senior army and civilian veterans became targets of the CRG and the radical mass organizations, which aggravated the already-tense atmosphere following the arrest of Commander Yang Yong and Political Commissar Liao Hansheng of the Beijing MR. When Marshal Nie Rongzhen and Marshal Xu Xiangqian, former leaders of the North China Field Army, clearly expressed their displeasure with the Cultural Revolution, Mao began to question the loyalty of the former North China Field Army officers. At this juncture, Mao urgently needed an armed force in Beijing that he could trust to secure the Cultural Revolution and prevent a military coup. Thus, the 38th Army Corps, one of the PLA top army units in the PLA with deep ties to Lin Biao, was transferred from Liaoning to Baoding, to secure Mao's safety and monitor the Beijing MR.

Although Lin Biao was pushed by the Chairman to be involved in the conflict at the outset of the Cultural Revolution, Lin's power and authority were

[51] See *Zhonggong wenhua dageming zhongyao wenjian huibian*, p. 300.
[52] Frederick C. Teiwes and Warren Sun, *The End of the Maoist Era: Chinese Politics during the Twilight of the Cultural Revolution, 1972–1976*, p. 214; Frederick C. Teiwes and Warren Sun, *The Tragedy of Lin Biao: Riding the Tiger during the Cultural Revolution, 1966–1971*, p. 149.
[53] Jiang Qing talked to the Beijing Red Guard on January 22, 1967, and "ordered" them not to target Zhou Enlai, Chen Yi, Xiao Hua, and Kang Sheng. See *Zhonggong wenhua dageming zhongyao wenjian huibian*, pp. 300–1.

limited, as Mao centralized PLA decision-making power in his own hands. Mao's intentions for the Cultural Revolution were unclear to Lin, as well as his role as Mao's successor.[54] It gradually became clear that the role of successor was a symbolic position only, to accompany Mao in greeting the Red Guard, to give speeches supporting Mao, and to speak on behalf of Mao when it was not appropriate for Mao to speak personally. According to Li Xuefeng, Peng Zhen's replacement as mayor of Beijing and party leader in June 1966, Mao gave an order at the beginning of the Cultural Revolution that no one, including Lin Biao, was allowed to move troops without his permission. Clarifying this, Mao insisted that any movement of a PLA unit, even a platoon, must first be reported to him for approval.[55] This explains why during the early Cultural Revolution, Lin carefully followed this order, and he continued to do so after mid-1967, when Mao was forced to grant him full power over the PLA. Although Mao did not allow anyone in the party leadership to dispatch PLA units without his permission, he believed that if he used the army to solve intraparty conflict, it would set a bad example, and therefore his access to that power held inherent risks.

Mao's plan in the summer of 1966 to add two divisions to the Beijing Garrison Command, effectively consolidating his control over the capital, was yet another move to protect his leadership from enemies and competitors in the party leadership. But the move of the 38th Army Corps from Liaoning to Baoding in February 1967 was particularly aggressive but decisive. Mao faced a united challenge from party veterans and old PLA marshals, presenting a perfect opportunity for a coup d'état. The 38th Army Corps replaced the 69th Army Corps to garrison Baoding, in Hebei, an important strategic place for securing Beijing. The transfer of the 69th Army Corps was a result of Mao and Lin's distrust of the corps, given its lack of historical ties with Lin. Among its three divisions, the 205th Division was an army unit from the Second Field Army, led by Liu Bocheng and Deng Xiaoping; the 207th Division came from a surrendered Nationalist army unit; and the 206th Division merged personnel from both the 205th Division and the 207th Division.[56] In addition, a month before the move of the 38th Army Corps, Mao showed concern about the ability of the 69th Army Corps to protect party leadership from mass rebels, given the 69th Army Corps' positioning. When the party committee in Hebei collapsed and party leaders had to hide to avoid persecution from the mass

---

[54] Although Lin's position as Mao's successor was established in August 1966 in the Eleventh Plenum, Lin was uncertain of Mao's intentions and his role as Mao's successor.

[55] Li Xuefeng, "Wosuo zhidao de 'wenge' fadong neiqing" [What I know about the inside story regarding the launch of the "Cultural Revolution"], in Zhang Hua and Su Caiqing (eds.), *Huishou "wenge": Zhongguo shinian "wenge" fengxi yu fansi* [Recalling the "Cultural Revolution": Analyzing and rethinking China's ten-year "Cultural Revolution"], vol. 2, p. 605.

[56] Ouyang Qing, *Baizhan jiangxing Xie Zhenhua* [Star of generals who experienced hundred battles – Xie Zhenhua], pp. 240, 257.

rebels, Commander Xie Zhenhua used the 69th Army Corps as a place of refuge for local party leaders such as Liu Zihou, party secretary of Hebei Province, and Li Ruinong, a prefecture party secretary in Hebei.[57]

Harry Harding pointed to four key developments that encouraged a group of senior party leaders from both the civilian and military spheres to launch an attack on the CRG and the concept of the Cultural Revolution during January and February 1967. The first key development was that an organizational framework was provided to restore order and discipline to the country. This organizational framework was a coalition between the directive revolutionary committees and the PLA, who were to intervene in the Cultural Revolution in support of the Left. The second key development was that Mao intervened to limit the use of force and violence by the radical mass organizations. The third key development was that the center attempted to limit the impact of the Cultural Revolution on those who were crucial to the maintenance of economic production and political order in state and military organizations. The fourth key development that caused a group of senior party leaders from both the civilian and military spheres to launch an attack on the CRG was narrowing of the scope of activities in which mass organizations were permitted to participate. Along with that narrowed scope, the central directives ordered mass organizations to stop traveling the country so that middle school students could return to school.[58]

Besides Harding's four factors, there are more direct causes that triggered the confrontation between senior leaders and the CRG during January and February 1967. The chaotic situation in late 1966 and early 1967 provoked a strong resistance to the CRG from the mass organizations, which were appealing for political order and stability. During this period, campaigns were launched by conservative mass organizations to attack the CRG, such as the campaign Bombarding Zhang Chunqiao in Shanghai. Big-character posters against the CRG in Beijing filled the streets. Soon the battle progressed from a verbal to a physical one. Violent confrontations between the radical mass organizations and the local army units escalated and resulted in tragedy, such as in Shihezi, in Xinjiang, where twenty-four people died and seventy-four were seriously wounded. In Sichuan, tens of thousands of rebels were detained by local army authorities. Similar incidences occurred in Guangdong, Inner Mongolia, Anhui, Henan, Hunan, Fujian, and Tibet.[59]

The chaos and violence were most extreme in Beijing, where leadership split and many army leaders stood united against the CRG to show their discontent with the Chairman. When the Cultural Revolution was brought to the army

---

[57] Ibid., pp. 260–1.

[58] See Harry Harding, "The Chinese State in Crisis, 1966–9," pp. 206–9.

[59] Wang Nianyi, *1949–1989 nian de Zhongguo: Dadongluan de niandai* [China 1949–1989: The years of great turmoil], pp. 202–6.

ranks, few high-ranking PLA leaders could escape being targets of the violent mass movements. The CRG encouraged soldiers to participate in revolutionary activities of "speaking freely, airing views fully, holding great debates, and writing big-character posters" to carry out the Cultural Revolution, which in many cases snowballed into physical assault against the army leaders.[60] The strong response of local army units to the rebels aggravated instability across the country. Even Mao experienced difficulty restraining local army generals, but he made it a priority to ensure that the Beijing MR was secured, because he knew a rebellious armed force in Beijing would pose a threat to the security of himself and the CRG, on which Mao relied to further the Cultural Revolution.

The Beijing MR was targeted again in December 1970, after the state chairmanship debate triggered the Mao-Lin conflict at the September Lushan plenum. By 1969, in fact, Mao had been concerned about the growing dominance of the PLA as a whole in the central and local politics. He was also concerned about the loyalty of the PLA toward him, especially the army forces around the capital. Thus, he had to use PLA units from different factions to check one another in an effort to ensure that no military faction could challenge his political power. According to Michael D. Swaine, Mao's transfer of the 27th Army Corps from the Nanjing MR to the Beijing MR in 1970 was a significant initiative to balance the armed forces in Beijing, such as the 38th Army Corps.[61] The key leaders of the Beijing MR – Commander Zheng Weishan and First Political Commissar Li Xuefeng – were blamed for plotting against the Chairman with Chen Boda and several key members of the Lin Biao faction, such as Ye Qun, Wu Faxian, Li Zuopeng, and Qiu Huizuo. "Bulletin No. Six" was the minutes of the discussions of the Northern China Group published at the Lushan plenum, which Mao viewed as a critical piece of evidence implying a challenge to his reign, because it supported Lin Biao and attacked Zhang Chunqiao. "Bulletin No. Six" expressed the view of the Northern China Group, condemning the radicals along with PLA generals from the Beijing MR for showing support for the initiatives of Lin Biao's followers against Zhang Chunqiao. Mao perceived the bulletin as high-ranking PLA generals collaborating against him, and he became particularly wary of the Beijing MR leaders, given their active role in the discussions.[62]

---

[60] See *Ye Jianying zhuan*, p. 578–9, 582–3.

[61] Michael D. Swaine, *The Military and Political Succession in China: Leadership, Institutions, Beliefs*, p. 270; On August 20, 1969, the 27th Army Corps was ordered to move to Zhangjiakou, in Hebei, and was put under the authority of the Beijing Military Region. It was moved again from Zhangjiakou to Shijiazhuang and Xingtai in March 1970. See Lujun di ershiqi jitunjun junshi bianweihui [Editing Commission of the Military History of the PLA 27th Group Army], *Zhongguo renmin jiefangjun lujun di ershiqi jituanjun junshi*, 1935.11–1998.10 [Military history of the PLA 27th Group Army, November 1935–October 1998] (1999), pp. 423–4.

[62] Dong Baocun and Pu Suanzi, "Huabei huiyi yu Beijing junqu da gaizu (1)," *Dangshi buolan*, no. 1 (2006), pp. 4–6.

The Beijing MR traditionally was an important base of the former North China Field Army faction and the former North China Field Army was inextricably linked with Lin Biao, because Lin Biao had led the Fourth Red Army from which the North China Field Army originated. Thus, Mao was very concerned about the possible military alliance against him between the Lin Biao group and the former North China Field Army faction. The Huabei (Northern China) conference, launched by Mao in December 1970 and January 1971, was his effort to attack the key leadership members of the Beijing MR – Zhen Weishan, Li Xuefeng, and Chen Xianrui – and to reorganize the Beijing MR. At the conference, Jiang Qing tied the key leaders of the Beijing MR to Nie Rongzhen, Xu Xiangqian, and Yang Chengwu, the leaders of the former North China Field Army faction, and claimed that the factionalism of the former North China Field Army "had a historical nature" (lishi xing). The Huabei conference ultimately resulted in the dismissal of Zheng Weishan and Li Xuefeng, commander and first political commissar of the Beijing MR, a significant move to undermine the influence of the former North China Field Army faction, thus easing Mao's security concerns for the time being.[63] To a certain extent, the Huabei conference was an expansion of the Yang Chengwu, Yu Lijin, and Fu Chongbi affairs, a March 1968 campaign initiated by Mao to purge the key figures of the PLA leadership and weaken the faction of the former North China Field Army.

An important development in the Beijing MR took place in the summer of 1975, when Deng Xiaoping and Ye Jianying reorganized the PLA leadership, reshuffling twenty-five key units of the PLA. With Mao's permission, Deng and Ye reorganized the leadership of the CMC departments and local military regions in August 1975. Because the proposal for personnel appointments bypassed the PLA Political Department, headed by Zhang Chunqiao, the veterans' control over the PLA was cemented, laying the foundation for the PLA's support in arresting the Gang of Four in October 1976.[64] Another impact of the reorganization was that the leadership of the Beijing MR was dominated by the former Second Field Army faction, a powerful military group headed by Liu Bocheng and Deng Xiaoping during the civil war in the 1940s. Chen Xilian and Qin Jiwei, two of Deng's most trusted subordinates from when they served Deng in the former Second Field Army, were appointed to head the Beijing MR. Chen had been commander of the Beijing MR since December 1973, when a major reshuffling of military region commanders caused him to hand over his position as commander of Shenyang MR to Li Desheng, former commander of the Beijing MR. Although this reshuffling was proposed and

[63] Chen Xianrui, "Pi Chen pi Lin qijian de Beijing junqu" [Beijing Military Region during the period of criticizing Chen Boda and Lin Biao], in Bai nian chao [Hundred-year tide], no. 5 (2000), p. 43.
[64] See Yang Zhaolin, Baizhan jiangxing – Su Zhenhua [Star of generals who experienced hundred battles – Su Zhenhua], p. 290.

TABLE 10.3. *Commanders and Political Commissars of the Beijing MR, October 1975–April 1990*

Year			
From	To	Commander	Political commissar(s)
10/1975	9/1977	Chen Xinian	Ji Dengkui, Qin Jiwei
9/1977	1/1980	Chen Xinian	Qin Jiwei
1/1980	10/1982	Qin Jiwei	Yuan Shengping
10/1982	6/1985	Qin Jiwei	Fu Chongbi
6/1985	11/1987	Qin Jiwei	**Yang Baibing**
11/1987	4/1990	Zhou Yibing	Liu Zhenhua

Sources: Zuzhi shi, pp. 178, 295.
Note: Boldface indicates generals from the 129th Division of the Eighth Route Army (January 1938–May 1945) and the Second Field Army (May 1945–November 1949), headed by Liu Bocheng and Deng Xiaoping.

executed by Deng Xiaoping, it served as a part of Mao's overall strategy to undermine the influence of powerful local PLA leaders and to reassert civilian control over local governments. Because the generals of the former Second Field Army dominated the leadership of the Beijing MR from the mid-1970s to the late 1980s (see Table 10.3), the Beijing MR would later play an important role in supporting Deng's reform programs, ensuring his dominance in the party leadership, and securing his control over the PLA.

The 38th Army Corps under Mao

Although virtually all military corps in the Beijing MR have been assigned to protect Beijing, none of them has played a more important role in guarding Beijing than the 38th Army Corps or Gourp Army (the 38th Army Corps was renamed as the 38th Group Army in middle 1980s). By the time the 38th Army Corps was transferred from Laoning to Baoding, several PLA army corps had been stationed around Beijing. These army corps included the 65th Army Corps in Zhangjiakou, the 66th Army Corps in Tianjin, and the 24th Army Corps in the Beijing suburbs of Chengde and Tangshan, all of which received commands from the Beijing MR. The unique situation of the 38th Army Corps derived not merely from its reputation as the most elite and modernized ranks of the PLA but also from its historical ties to Lin Biao.

To gain Mao's trust in early 1967, it was helpful for a PLA unit to have a connection with Lin Biao, considering his commitment to support Mao. The 38th Army Corps was a perfect match, given its historical ties to Lin Biao. Although the origins of the 38th Army Corps are strongly connected to the Fifth Red Army, led by Peng Dehuai and Teng Daiyuan in the late 1920s, and the Twenty Fifth Red Army, led by Wu Huanxian in the early 1930s, the true predecessor of the 38th Army Corps was the First Column of the Northeast

Democratic Allies and later the Fourth Field Army, commanded by Lin Biao during the civil war in the 1940s. The First Column had been known as one of the three tigers in the Fourth Field Army under Lin Biao. It played an important role in the CCP's major campaigns against the Nationalists in the Manchuria during the civil war, including the Linjiang campaign, the Battle of Siping, the campaign to defend Siping, and the Liaoning-Shenyang campaign. In the famous Beiping-Tianjin campaign, the 38th Army Corps was the main striking force, which proved a significant military move that resulted in the surrender of the Nationalist armies in Beijing. The 38th Army Corps fought in Korea as a main component of the People's Volunteer Army (PVA), particularly in the second campaign, in which its 113th Division penetrated UN lines deeply and captured Samso-ri after marching on foot for forty-five miles in fourteen hours. More important, in one instance its strong combat force prevented UN forces from joining, even though they were only slightly more than a half mile apart.[65] Because of its crucial role in the PVA's second campaign, the 38th Army Corps was honored as the Army of Long Life (*wansui jun*) by PVA Commander Peng Dehuai.[66]

By moving the 38th Army Corps from Liaoning to Hebei in February 1967, Mao intended to reduce his dependence on the former North China Field Army and to install his "spy" to monitor and contain the Beijing MR. Thus, the 38th Army Corps replaced the 69th Army Corps in Baoding, which protected the southern entrance of Beijing. The 69th Army Corps was probably chosen for replacement because the radicals had given it the reputation of "the armed force that protects local capitalist roaders" (*bao huang jun*).[67] The 69th Army Corps moved to Shanxi and replaced the 21st Army Corps after that corps was transferred to Xi'an.[68] Even if the transfer of the 38th Army Corps to Beijing was initially suggested by the PLA General Chief of Staff Yang Chengwu and approved by the Chairman,[69] Mao had successfully achieved his goal – to strike at the heart of the former North China Field Army faction.

After the 38th Army Corps moved into Baoding, it backed the radical rebels against the conservative rebels, supported by both the Hebei Military District and the Beijing MR.[70] The presence of the 38th Army Corps in the Beijing MR succeeded in inhibiting the dominance of the generals from the former

[65] See Lujun di sanshiba jitunjun junshi bianshen weiyuanhui [Editing Commission of the Military History of the PLA 38th Group Army), *Gangtie de budui: Lujun di sanshiba jitunjun junshi* [Iron and steel army: Military history of the PLA 38th Group Army), internal publication (Beijing: Jiefangjun wenyi chubanshe, 1993).

[66] Xiao Qing, "Tiexue zhujiu 'wansui jun'" [Iron blood casts the "army of long life"], in *Wenshi chunqiu* [Chronicle of literature and history], vol. 4 (2002), p. 18.

[67] Ouyang Qing, *Baizhan jiangxing – Xie Zhenhua* [Star of generals who experienced hundred battles – Xie Zhenhua], pp. 260–1.

[68] See the CMC telegram order from February 15; Quan Yanchi, *Weixing: Yang Chengwu zai yijiu liuqi* [Tour in disguise: Yang Chengwu in 1967], pp. 27–8.

[69] Ibid., pp. 27–8.

[70] Chen Xianrui, "Pi Chen pi Lin qijian de Beijing junqu," p. 45; Quan Yanchi, *Weixing: Yang Chengwu zai yijiu liuqi*, 55–6; Chen Xiaonong, *Chen Boda: zuihou koushu huiyi*, pp. 333–5.

North China Field Army. Self-assured, with Lin Biao's support and its unique status in the PLA,[71] the 38th Army Corps rarely took the leadership of the Beijing MR seriously and openly supported the radical mass rebels against the Hebei Military District, supported by the Beijing MR.[72] Perhaps General Yang wanted to avoid Mao's suspicion that he was excluding other factions from the jurisdiction of the former North China Field Army to keep its dominance in the Beijing MR; therefore, when Mao asked Yang for his opinion, he proposed relocating the 38th Army Corps from the Shenyang MR rather than an additional military unit from the Beijing MR.[73] In fact, Yang had learned his lesson in subversive influence seven months prior when the Chairman ordered the PLA chief of staff to deploy two divisions from the Beijing MR to enhance the Beijing Garrison Command. Yang Chengwu rejected Commander Yang Yong and Political Commissar Liao Hansheng's proposal to send the 70th Division from the 24th Army Corps and the 189th Division from the 63rd Army Corps to the Beijing Garrison Command. Yang Chengwu wanted to send the 193rd Division from the 65th Army Corps, an army unit from the North China Field Army, instead of the 70th Division, an army unit originated from the Third Field Army faction during the 1940s.[74]

Yang was attempting to influence the Beijing Garrison Command by establishing the dominance of the former North China Field Army faction. However, Yang Chengwu's proposal was turned down and the 70th Division, not the 193rd Division, was sent to the Beijing Garrison Command.[75] Although the commander and political commissar of the 38th Army Corps were not from Lin's factions when it was deployed to the Beijing MR, the base of the 38th Army Corps was predominately composed of Lin's former subordinates. This included deputy commanders, deputy political commissars, chiefs of staff, and most officers at the middle and lower levels. By November 1970, the commander and political commissar, neither of whom was a former subordinate of Lin, were transferred and replaced by Lin's trusted followers (Table 10.4).[76]

One of these critical transfers was that of Li Guangjun. The transfer of Commander Li Guangjun from the 38th Army Corps to the Wuhan Military Region

---

[71] Although the 38th Army Corps might have deemed Lin Biao its supporter in its conflict with the Beijing MR, Lin dealt with this issue carefully and tried to avoid direct involvement in the conflict between the corps and the Beijing MR. Ye Qun particularly was unwilling to support the corps at the cost of Maojiawan's *guanxi* with Chen Boda, who backed the Hebei Military District against the corps. See *Maojiawan jishi*, pp. 182–4.

[72] Chen Xiaonong, *Chen Boda: Zuihou koushu huiyi*, pp. 334–5.

[73] See Quan Yanchi, *Weixing: Yang Chengwu zai yijiu liuqi*, pp. 27–8.

[74] *Zhou Enlai nianpu, 1949–1976*, vol. 3, pp. 31–2; *Liao Hansheng huiyilu*, pp. 246–7.

[75] See *Zhou Enlai nianpu, 1949–1976*, vol. 3, pp. 31–2; *Liao Hansheng huiyi lu*, pp. 246–7. Obviously, Yang did not want Mao to have the impression that he only considered the army units from the former North China Field Army.

[76] See Zhang Yunsheng, *Maojiawan jishi: Lin Biao mishu huiyilu*, pp. 135–6; "38 jun liren junzhang zhengwei" [List of commanders and political commissars of the 38th Army Corps or Group Army], in *38 jun zhangyou zhijia* [Family of 38th Army Corps or Group Army personnel], http://38jun.net/thread-204872-1-1.html (accessed April 2, 2010).

TABLE 10.4. *The Leadership of the 38th Army Corps, February 1967–December 1970*

Positions	February 1967	December 1970
Commander	Li Guangjun	**Liu Haiqing**
Political commissar	Wang Meng	**Xing Ze**
Deputy commanders	**Liu Haiqing**	**Zhu Yuehua**
	Mou Lishan	**Li Lianxiu**

Sources: "38 jun liren junzhang zhengwei," in *38 jun zhangyou zhijia*. See http:// 38jun.net/thread-204872-1-1.html (accessed on April 2, 2010). This is official website sponsored and administrated by former soldiers and officials of the 38th Army Corps/Group Army.
Note: Boldface indicates generals who had been in the 38th Army Corps under the Fourth Field Army, which Lin Biao led starting during the Chinese civil war in the 1940s.

in 1968 took place when Mao was increasingly vulnerable to the collective resistance of the old marshals and local military leaders. The confrontation between the PLA leaders and the radicals, along with the collective actions taken by the PLA marshals and senior government ministers in voicing their discontent over the Cultural Revolution, deepened Mao's questioning of the PLA's loyalty to him. Thus, the transfer of Li Guangjun was probably another move to strengthen Lin's dominance in the 38th Army Corps, because Li came from the former Third Field Army and was not Lin's former subordinate.

In the Huabei conference between December 1970 and January 1971, at which Mao attempted to reorganize the Beijing MR, Jiang Qing accused Yang Chengwu and Chen Boda of collusion in squeezing Commander Li Guangjun and Political Commissar Wang Meng out of the 38th Army Corps,[77] implying that the transfer was not related Mao's overall plan to consolidate Lin's power. Still, even if General Chief of Staff Yang Chengwu had proposed the dispatch and transfer, Yang could have been trying to please Mao and Lin Biao, and had certainly perceived Mao's concern about securing the power of Lin's faction. Although Yang was dismissed six months before Li was transferred, the idea still could have originated with Yang; however, it is safe to assume that the transfer occurred at Mao's initiation. As Wang Nianyi points out, the priority of Mao's grant strategy was to ensure the stability of the Beijing MR, which further promoted stability within the PLA, which was crucial for ending the chaos in the country.[78] After Li Guangjun was transferred, Lin Biao refused to accept any nominations for generals not raised from the 38th Army Corps

[77] See Dong Baocun and Pu Suanzi, "Huabei huiyi yu Beijing junqu da gaizu (2)," p. 32.
[78] Wang Nianyi, "Yichang dayou laitou de xiaoxing wudou" [A small-scale violent struggle with strong backing], in *Bai nian chao* [Hundred-year tide], no. 1 (1999), pp. 35–9.

to ensure their loyalty.[79] After Li Guangjun was transferred, the 38th Army Corps became the only source for commanders of the corps; Liu Haiqing, Zhu Yuehua, and Li Lianxiu were successively appointed as commanders of the 38th Army Corps over the years. The overwhelming dominance of the 38th Army Corps generals was still evident even after 1968, and it remained so until 1985, when Deng Xiaoping downsized the PLA's by 1 million military personnel, and the 38th Army Corps became Deng's target for undermining Lin Biao and the influence of the Fourth Field Army in the PLA.

Although Mao depended on Lin for support more than he depended on other army generals, it is naive to believe that he would place complete trust in Lin Biao, the most powerful army leader among the PLA military factions in the early Cultural Revolution. The move of the 38th Army Corps from northeastern China to Beijing was a tactic of Mao's to employ different military factions in the capital to monitor and contain one another so that none would be able to gain absolute dominance. Another tactic Mao took to prevent the former North China Field Army from dominating was the February 1967 exclusion of Nie Rongzhen from the PLA's leadership decision making, as had occurred previously in the 1950s. Because Mao heavily relied on the Beijing Garrison Command to guard Beijing, Mao wanted to weaken the influence of Marshal Nie Rongzhen in the army leadership. So, in February 1967, despite his position as vice chairman of the CMC, Nie Rongzhen was excluded from attending expanded Politburo meetings, and Ye Jianying and Xu Xiangqian, two standing CMC committee members, were formerly invited. Mao explicitly ordered that the expanded Politburo meetings "should not inform Nie Rongzhen [as to the discussions that took place]."[80]

When PLA Chief of Staff Yang Chengwu was dismissed in March 1968, the primary charge levied was the crime of building factions, which alluded to his close relationship with Nie Rongzhen, a key army leader in February 1967 against the Maoist radicals and a figure whom Mao blamed as the "creator of multiple centers" against the Mao-led center.[81] As mentioned already, the North China Field Army was further weakened after the 1971 Lushan plenum, when Mao tied the leaders of the Beijing MR, Zheng Weishan and Li Xuefeng, to Chen Boda. Mao used Chen Boda's case as an excuse to dismiss Zheng and Li to further his goal of weakening the former North China Field Army. According to Chen Xianrui, deputy political commissar at the time and political commissar of the Beijing MR from 1961 to 1974, "Chen Boda had very little influence in the Beijing MR, but Mao Zedong overestimated it.... His harsh

[79] See *Maojiawan jishi*, pp. 135–6.
[80] See Wang Nianyi, "Guanyu 'eryue niliu' de yixie ziliao" [Some materials related to the "February adverse current"], in *Dangshi yanjiu ziliao* [Materials related to the study of party history], vol. 150 (January 20, 1990), p. 3.
[81] In explaining why Yang was dismissed, Mao charged Yang and Nie of establishing so-called multi-centers, meaning that Yang and Nie established another center in opposition to Mao's center. See Wang Nianyi, *Da dongluan de niandai*, pp. 278, 286–8.

criticism of the Beijing MR indicated his distrust of [those] leaders." Mao held firmly to his position, claiming, "the reason Chen Boda was so daring in the Lushan plenum was because the Beijing MR backed him."[82]

To ensure the 38th Army Corps's loyalty to Mao and Lin, the leadership took several important initiatives after the corps was transferred to the Beijing MR. The first initiative was to establish loyal followers of Lin as the leaders of the corps, particularly those with ties to the Fourth Field Army. As previously mentioned, Li Guangjun, commander of the 38th Army Corp, and Wang Meng, political commissar of the 38th Army Corps, were transferred in October 1968 and November 1970, respectively. In October 1968, Li Guangjun was suddenly transferred to the Wuhan MR to assume the position of deputy chief of staff. Liu Haiqing, deputy commander of the 38th Army Corps and a longtime veteran of the corps, replaced Li as commander. In November 1970, Xing Ze, deputy political commissar of the 38th Army Corps and another longtime veteran, replaced Wang Meng as political commissar. Moreover, before Xing Ze's promotion, Xing was appointed director of the Political Department of the Beijing Garrison Command, where he functioned as an informant on the activities of the generals from the North China Field Army. In his own words, he "was authorized to report to Vice Chairman Lin directly if necessary," even though his immediate superiors, not Lin Biao, were the leaders of the Beijing MR.[83] Ensuring dominance was not simply about appointing the right people, it was about rejecting the wrong people and having believable reasons for why they were not suitable. For example, Lin Biao rejected Yang Chengwu's proposal to appoint Xu Xing, a general from the former North China Field Army, to replace Li Guangjun. Lin insisted that the new commander should be a veteran of the 38th Army Corps.[84] The second initiative to ensure the 38th Army Corps's loyalty was to make it the most powerful military unit in the Beijing MR. In February 1969 it was bestowed with the equipment to make it the first motorized troop of the PLA.[85]

At the 1970 Lushan plenum, Mao and Lin's leadership conflict became apparent as the issues of state chairmanship and "genies" intensified the existing issues between the two.[86] Lin received strong support from most leaders

---

[82] See Chen Xianrui, "Liao Hansheng, Yang Yong beizhua yu suowei 'huabei shantao zhuyi' wenti," p. 23; Chen Xianrui, "Pi Chen pi Lin qijian de Beijing junqu," p. 44.

[83] This information comes from an online memoir written by Shao Hua, a veteran of the 38th Army Corps and a comrade in arms of Xing Ze. See Shao Hua, *Huiyilu – Yige ren he yige shijie* [Memoirs – One person and one world], http://www.shuku.net:8082/novels/mingjwx/shaohua/hylu/hylu12–06.html (accessed May 29, 2009); Beijing shi difang zhi bianzuan weiyuanhui], *Beijing zhi, junshi juan, junshi zhi*, p. 137.

[84] *Maojiawan jishi*, pp. 135–6.

[85] Lujun di sanshiba jun [The 38th Army Corps of the PLA], *Lujun di sanshiba jun junshi* [The military history of the 38th Army Corps], pp. 621–2.

[86] In the Lushan plenum, Lin asked the party formally to deify Mao as a transcendent "genius." However, Mao viewed Lin's initiative as a strategy for his own ends, specially, Lin's attempt to

for reestablishing the state chairmanship and for attacking Zhang Chunqiao by accusing him of "not recognizing Chairman Mao's genius." Although Lin might have lacked the enthusiasm and might have been reluctant to be Mao's successor,[87] a group involving Lin's household, particularly Lin's wife and son, and top central military officials from Lin's faction felt increasing insecurity about Lin remaining as Mao's successor, and so the foregoing initiatives served to reestablish Lin's foothold as Mao's successor and to attack those who might be Lin's competitors. Mao, in contrast, was making other political maneuvers and taking precautionary measures against Lin to ensure his position as the paramount leader, given that the military, as Mao had sensed, had garnered too much power.[88] He did not take his conventional approach of attacks and dismissals of his perceived political opponents, which was to use party conferences to rally support. Rather, he made Chen Boda a scapegoat to avoid provoking Lin. Perhaps Mao was not sure whether he could succeed if he launched a full-fledged campaign against Lin, considering Lin's popularity in the party and his dominance among PLA delegates. From August 25 to August 31, Mao spent six days in meetings with various high-ranking leaders to lobby for support against Lin. During that time, Mao worked more than twelve hours a day, returning to his residence after two or three o'clock in the morning.[89] In the end, Mao decided to target only Chen Boda, because he lacked confidence in the success of an attack against Lin.

Mao was looking for the PLA's support of his attack against Lin Biao to ensure his dominance in the leadership and to appease his ultimate concern of personal security. Although his security had been ensured previously in part by the 38th Army Corps, it could very easily change if Lin decided to betray him, given Lin's powerful influence over corps. To ensure his personal security, Mao had at least three options immediately following the Lushan plenum. One option was to rely mainly on the Beijing MR for support in his struggle with Lin Biao. A second option was to transfer another army unit to Beijing that was more loyal to him than to Lin. A third option was to draw the 38th Army Corps over to his side against Lin Biao.

---

use the issue of "genius" to rally the support from vast majority of the delegates against Zhang Chunqiao, a potential competitor for Mao's successor, who refused to view the Chairman as "genius." See Peng Xianzhi and Jin Chongji, *Mao Zedong zhuan* (1949–1976) [A biography of Mao Zedong] (Beijing: Zhongyang wenxian chubanshe, 2003), vol. 2, pp. 1572–6.

[87] Frederick C. Teiwes, "The Politics of Succession: Previous Patterns and a New Process," in John Wong and Zheng Yongnian (eds.), *China's Post-Jiang Leadership Succession: Problems and Perspectives*, pp. 30–1.

[88] Ibid., pp. 30–1.

[89] Mao usually slept in the day and worked at night. According to Zhou Fuming, one of Mao's guards, Mao usually started working at two or three o'clock in the afternoon and went to bed around seven or eight o'clock in the morning. See Qi Li, *Mao Zedong wannian shenghuo jishi* [Record of events of Mao Zedong's later years], p. 41.

The first option was not a realistic possibility, considering that leaders of the Beijing MR had allied with Lin Biao's group against the CRG at the 1970 Lushan plenum. In addition, the March 1968 dismissals of Yang Chengwu and Fu Chongbi had severely damaged Mao's relationships with the generals of the former North China Field Army, who constituted the majority of the Beijing MR generals. The second option was also difficult because Mao had purged key leaders of his own major factions as early as 1959, such as Peng Dehuai and Deng Xiaoping. He had severely weakened other army leaders from his own factions as well, such as Nie Rongzhen. It would be even more risky for Mao to use army units from other factions, such as those tied to the Second Front Army, led by He Long, or to the Fourth Front Army, headed by Xu Xiangqian. Moreover, a large-scale military move to replace the 38th Army Corps might have triggered resistance from the unit and would likely alert Lin Biao. The third option was also difficult, considering Lin's historical ties with the 38th Army Corps. Success in cultivating loyalty among the 38th Army Corps depended on Mao's ability to marginalize Lin's influence over the corps.

Mao eventually took the third option and actuated it through two steps. First, Mao inserted himself as guardian of the 38th Army Corps and allied himself against the Beijing MR, a longtime rival of the corps since its move to Beijing in February 1967, even though the corps was a subordinate unit to the Beijing MR. This also corresponded to Mao's strategy to gradually weaken the former North China Field Army faction. As conflict between the 38th Army Corps and the Beijing MR developed, Mao's stance helped win the appreciation of the unit. The Hebei Military District, an army unit that was subordinate to and bolstered by the Beijing MR, backed the conservative "rebels" against the radical rebels in Baoding, who were backed by the 38th Army Corps. As such, the two units were deeply involved in violent mass conflict. Although Mao publicly revealed his support for the 38th Army Corps after the Lushan plenum, he tried to give the impression that he had already done so, albeit through Lin and the CRG. The instance to which he referred was in March 1968 when Yang Chengwu and Fu Chongbi were dismissed, and both Lin Biao's group and the CRG charged the Beijing MR with "factionalism" and "squeezing out the 38th Army Corps."[90] Later, Mao successfully used the Huabei conference – between December 22, 1970, and January 26, 1971 – to publicize support for the 38th Army Corps by naming Chen Boda as a behind-the-scenes backer of the Beijing MR.[91]

The second step Mao took to actuate his plan to cultivate supreme loyalty among the 38th Army Corps was to create discord between the corps and

[90] See Shu Yun, *Zhongjiang Zheng Weishan pingfan de qianqian houhou* [Before and after the rehabilitation of Lieutenant General Zheng Weishan], p. 15.

[91] See Chen Xianrui, "Pi Chen pi Lin qijian de Beijing junqu," pp. 42–5; Tao Zhuwen, "Lishi xuanwo zhong de Chen Xianrui" [Chen Xianrui in the eddy of history], in *Dangshi bolan* [General review of the Chinese Communist Party], no. 8 (2001), pp. 15–16.

Lin Biao by linking Lin Biao and his followers, such as Huang Yongsheng, Wu Faxian, Li Zuopeng, and Qiu Huizuo, to Chen Boda and the Beijing MR. When Mao visited southern China in the summer of 1971 to lobby local civilian and military leaders against Lin Biao, he gave them the impression that the 38th Army Corps was a longtime victim of the alliance of Lin Biao, Chen Boda, and the Beijing MR.[92] However extensive Mao's lobbying was for the 38th Army Corps, his support of the unit did not necessarily indicate that he trusted the corps completely. Rather, he strived to prevent the corps from participating in Lin's military activities against him. From October 1970 to September 1971, Mao was preparing a political campaign against Lin Biao in which he made a great effort to appease and placate the 38th Army Corps. On September 13, 1971, hours after Lin Biao died in an airplane crash while attempting to flee to the Soviet Union, Mao ordered the Beijing Garrison Command to take control of all army units in guarding Beijing, including seizing power over the six divisions of the 38th Army Corps.[93]

The 38th Army Corps or Group Army in the Reform Era

To this day, of all the army units stationed around Beijing, the 38th Army Corps, or Group Army, is still undoubtedly the most important armed force in guarding Beijing. Because of its reputation and prestige in the PLA as well as its unique role as a PLA field army in guarding Beijing, the 38th Army Corps has always been equipped by the CMC with the best and advanced weaponry of the PLA units. The 38th Army Corps was the first PLA army converted to an group army structure, and it was the PLA's first mechanized group army. Among the PLA units, the 38th Group Army established the first PLA electronic countermeasures brigade, the first mixed antiaircraft artillery brigade, the first army aviation brigade, and the first digitized brigade. It is one of seven major PLA mechanized group armies and one of three mechanized group armies that were honored as the Central Strategic Reserves.[94]

The 38th Army Corps or Group Army has been the center of the PLA, because it has the most advanced equipment and weaponry, organizational structure, and strategic methods and systems. The Mechanized Air Defense Brigade of the 38th Army Corps or Group Army has improved in tactics and methods of defending against cruise missile attacks, and it has improved the

---

[92] See Wang Dongxing, *Wang Dongxing huiyi: Mao Zedong yu Lin Biao fangeming jituan de douzheng* [The recollections of Wang Dongxing: The struggle between Mao Zedong and Lin Biao's antirevolutionary clique], pp. 100, 118, 156.

[93] See Wu De, "Lushan huiyi he Lin Biao shijian" [Lushan plenum and Lin Biao affairs], in Zhang Hua and Su Caiqing (eds.), *Huishou "wenge"* [Recollection of the "Cultural Revolution"], p. 1036.

[94] The strategic reserve forces are controlled by the PLA leadership and are prepared to launch offensive against targets within hours. The very purpose of the strategic reserves is to deter major attacks throughout a conflict.

weapons fire-control system and detection capabilities. By the mid-1980s, the 38th Group Army had been equipped with three mechanized infantry divisions, an armored division, an artillery brigade, and an antiaircraft artillery brigade. In 1985, the reconnaissance units of the 38th Army Corps were dispatched to Laoshan along the Sino-Vietnamese border, where they successfully accomplished several important intelligence missions regarding Vietnamese armies. In addition, the 38th Group Army created the PLA's first helicopter brigade in January 1988. Moreover, more than three hundred officers from the ranks of the 38th Army Corps or Group Army have been promoted to PLA generals.

While Deng Xiaoping supported enhancing the military strength of the 38th Army Corps by providing the best equipment possible, he attempted to undermine the dominance of the former Fourth Field Army in the unit. The Chinese military, as Ellis Joffe points out, "has had a long history of factionalism that had derived from field army loyalties forged during the revolutionary period, and reinforced by cultural norms which emphasize personal bounds and patron-client relationships."[95] Historically, generals from the former Fourth Field Army maintained a consistent influence on the 38th Army Corps, such that few officers from other military factions could easily exercise the authority granted by their institutional positions in the 38th Army Corps or Group Army. Between 1949, when the 38th Army Corps came into being, and 1989, when Deng retired and handed over his position as the CMC Chairman to Jiang Zemin, a total of eleven army commanders had been appointed to command the 38th Army Corps. Among them, only three came from other military factions, and two were appointed in the 1980s after Deng Xiaoping took over the PLA.[96] Since 1985, most commanders of the 38th Army Corps have not come from the unit itself or from the former Fourth Field Army faction, but rather from outside. Between 1985 and 2006, the CMC has appointed eight commanders and seven political commissars to the unit, but only three commanders and four political commissars were promoted from the 38th Army Corps itself (Table 10.5). The effort to move away from traditional factional control over military units partially served to facilitate Deng's dominance in the PLA, particularly in the wake of Deng's modernization and discipline of the PLA and the armed forces. Promoting professionalism became the primary feature of Deng's program to modernize the PLA.

Although there have been the post-Mao leadership attempts to instigate modernization and military professionalism among the PLA, political loyalty remains a top priority for army development and officer selection, including for the 38th Army Corps or Group Army. According to Li Laizhu, deputy commander of the Beijing MR between 1985 and 1993 and commander of the Beijing MR between 1993 and 1997, the appointment of leading officers at the division level and above in the Beijing MR is strictly enforced (*yange*

---

[95] Ellis Joffe, "The Chinese Army in Domestic Politics: Factors and Phases," pp. 8–9.
[96] "38 jun liren junzhang zhengwei," in 38 *jun zhanyou zhijia*, http://38jun.net/thread-204872-1-1.html (accessed April 2, 2010).

TABLE 10.5. *Commanders and Political Commissars of the 38th Army Corp or Group Army, 1946–2005*

Commander	Political commissar
Wan Yi (1946–1947)	Wan Yi (1946–1947)
Li Tianyou (1947–1949)	Liang Biye (1948–1950)
Liang Xingchu (1949–1952)	*Liu Xiyuan* (1950–1952)
Jiang Yonghui (1952–1957)	Wu Dai (1952–1956)
Liu Xianquan (1957–1960)	**Zeng Xianghuang** (1956–1960)
Deng Yue (1960–1964)	Ren Rong (1960–1964)
Li Guangjun (1964–1968)	Yu Jingshan (1964–1966)
Liu Haiqing (1968–1972)	**Wang Meng** (1966–1970)
Zhu Yuehua (1972–1978)	Xing Ze (1970–1972)
Li Lianxiu (1978–1984)	Wang Pili (1973–1978)
Li Jijun (1985–1987)	Xing Ze (1978–1981)
Xu Qinxian (1987–1989)	Miao Jingfen (1982–1984)
Zhang Meiyuan (1989–1993)	Gao Tianzheng (1984–1988)
Liu Pixun (1993–1994)	*Wang Fuyi* (1988–1989)
Huang Xinsheng (1994–1995)	Wu Runzhong (1990–1993)
Gao Zhongxing (1995–2002)	**Shao Songgao** (1993–1996)
Li Shaojun (2002–2006)	Guan Xianxiang (1996–2001)
	Huang Jiaxiang (2001–2005)
Wang Xixin (2007–2011)	**Wu Gang** (2005–2011)
Xu Linping (2011–)	Zou Yunming (2011–)

Source: Lingdao jigou yange; Liao Gailong, *Xiandai zhongguo zhengjie yaoren zhuanlue daquan* (Large collection of important contemporary political figures in China) (Beijing: Zhongguo guangbo dianshi chubanshe, 1993); *Jiefangjun zuzhi yange;* "38 jun liren junzhang zhengwei," in *38 jun zhanyou zhijia,* see http://38jun.net/thread-204872-1-1.html (accessed on April 2, 2010).
Note: No italics or boldface indicates generals from the 38th Army Corps or Group Army. Italics indicate generals from other units of the former Fourth Field Army. Boldface indicates generals from outside the military units of former Fourth Field Army faction.

baguan) to ensure that "the political standard is the number one criterion."[97] In the reform era, post-Mao leaders have emphasized the loyalty of the 38th Group Army. Loyalty is ensured through undermining military factionalism and dominating personnel appointments, including appointing generals who have no historical ties with the 38th Group Army to command the unit. Political loyalty was further emphasized after the Tiananmen incident in June 1989, when the 38th Group Army, albeit without organized disobedience, resisted the order to impose martial law, thus resulting in the arrest of its commander Xu Qinxian. However, the indisputable position of the 38th Group Army as the PLA's most elite group army contributes to its unique role in guarding the capital and the central leadership. With an armored division, three mechanized

[97] Li Laizhu, *Zhu: Wode rensheng lu* [Refining: The road of my life], pp. 379–80.

infantry divisions, an artillery brigade, a mechanized air-defense brigade, and an aviation regiment, in addition to various support and logistical units, 38th Group Army, located in southern Beijing and its surrounding suburbs, is prepared to defend against potential threats from the north and to intervene in internal unrest in the city. Without a doubt, the 38th Group Army has played and will continue to play a pivotal role in the security of the capital city and of its paramount leaders.

The PLA in the Era of Reform and Beyond: Professionalism versus Politicization

Deng Xiaoping was not the first to pursue military modernization; it has been a driving force for the professionalism of the PLA and the security forces that the CCP has commanded since the early 1950s. The communist triumph over the Nationalists ensured that the resources and experience of the Korean War reinforced incentives for the PLA to modernize its military forces. The intensive program of modernization at both the technical and the administrative levels involved an emphasis on professionalism and a knowledge of military science, such as sophisticated weaponry. The PLA's professionalization was also driven by modeling the Soviet armies to form a modern hierarchical army. This model illustrates the PLA's effort to institute a system of rank with a differentiated pay scale and professional criteria for advancement.

Unfortunately, this model clashed with the democratic and egalitarian tradition of the PLA, which eventually caused resistance among the PLA's leadership to the Soviet model. In particular, the criticism focused on the tendency to replace traditional military doctrine of comradely relations and informality between ranks with modern Soviet doctrine, which emphasized relations based on hierarchy, discipline, and status. The debate among the PLA finally triggered the antidogmatism campaign in 1958, which was an effort to critique the excessive reliance on Soviet practices. A radical change from professionalization to the revival of political work occurred in 1959, after Lin Biao replaced Peng Dehuai as leader of the PLA. This revival intensified the army's program of political education and restored many of the military traditions that the PLA had exercised during the revolutionary period. Although professionalization was not always the number-one priority, there has never been a PLA leader who was not a proponent of military modernization. Deng Xiaoping, however, acted where others only spoke, and he transformed the PLA to the capable force that it is today.

Deng's attempt to reform the PLA started in the mid-1970s, when he viewed the PLA as a deeply troubled institution that had suffered from "bloating, laxity, conceit, extravagance, and inertia."[98] The PLA had long been poorly

---

[98] Deng Xiaoping, "The Tasks of Consolidating the Army," July 4, 1975, in *Selected Works of Deng Xiaoping*, p. 27.

trained and equipped, and to exacerbate those issues, it had become highly politicized in the Cultural Revolution for its involvement in the confrontation with the masses. Because PLA officers had permanent tenure, the PLA became overstaffed in all army units. Not only was its ratio of officers to enlisted men the highest of any major army in the world; the multitudes of revolutionary veterans were simply not competent to lead a modern military force. There was no denying the severe contradictions between Deng's policies of modernization and the general policies enacted during the Cultural Revolution. Eventually, Deng was confronted with the objections of both the radicals and the Chairman, so he was dismissed in the spring of 1976.

Once Deng took back control of the PLA in 1977 and assumed chairmanship of the Central Military Commission in 1981, his strategies to modernize the PLA included institutionalizing regulations to retire a legendary generation of revolutionary-era generals; increasing efficiency and accountability of the PLA; and recruiting a new generation of young, technically competent officers to replace hundreds of thousands of superannuated officers. Parallel to the institutionalization of the military, a comparable series of institutionalized processes have taken hold in the political sphere as well, thus complementing Deng's efforts to reestablish the PLA professionalism in the same period. With nearly a decade's effort, Deng restructured the military mainly by reducing the officer corps, cutting the military regions from eleven to seven, and improving the resource allocation system. Although Deng's primary goal in reorganizing the PLA in the early to mid-1980s was to accelerate the retirement of senior officers more than enhancing the combat strength of the armed forces, his main emphasis on reforming the armed forces was the promotion of institutionalization. This includes the reintroduction of ranks, a transition fundamental to establishing institutionalized personnel arrangements based on professional competence, merit, and technical expertise. The reintroduction of ranks also helps delineate criteria for professional development and career options later in life for PLA officers; moreover, it creates a mechanism for recruiting capable, well-educated officers who approach a military career with motivation, purpose, and long-term commitment.

Deng's military modernization restored two very critical systems: the first criteria for promotion, which emphasized professionalism, military academy training, and technical expertise; the other is ranks, which changed operational doctrine and concepts (e.g., the abandonment of the People's War Doctrine, the emphasis on military professionalism over political rectitude); facilitated collaborative operations among different arms; and improved military organization, discipline, and morale. As the preceding analysis suggests, the institutionalization of routine promotion and retirement procedures in the military seems to be affecting appointments at the top levels of the military system. The target impact of these processes is the reshaping of tactics by which the party general secretary, who serves concurrently as CMC chairman, can stack the PLA brass to his political advantage. Although the CCP's new emphasis on professionalism in the armed forces does not necessarily imply a shift toward nationalization or depoliticization of the armed forces,[99] it does facilitate the PLA's move away from the over-politicized military exercised in the 1960s.

To achieve his goals of reforming the PLA, Deng used his personal influence and prestige to ensure support from the PLA leadership and to require the senior military leadership to be accountable to him. In other words, Deng employed personalism and personal ties to ensure his dominance in the PLA leadership, insofar as he was able to instigate a more professionalized and regularized PLA. In his later years, he primarily tried to ensure that top leadership followed his reform policies and developed institutionalized systems to guarantee the continuation of the reform. In fact, Deng established the policy of the third plenum of the Eleventh Party Congress as the party's de facto constitution, and he required the party and PLA leaders to follow it unconditionally, generation after generation.[100] To ensure the continuation of his reforms, Deng strove to weaken the powerful influence of army leaders over party leadership and to strengthen civilian authority over the PLA. Throughout the 1980s, Deng gradually reduced the institutional and individual capacities for the military or its leaders to intervene in the policy process, thereby strengthening civilian control over the PLA. Early on Deng realized there was no way to guarantee his reform policy of modernization if paramount political leaders, especially those from the military, had opportunities to unilaterally dominate CCP leadership after he was gone. Deng believed "it would be unhealthy and very dangerous if the fate of a country depends on the prestige of one or two persons."[101] This helps explain why Deng wished to establish a system after his retirement that departed from personalism to instead be regulated by institutionalized mechanisms.

Although Deng was the architect who initiated and urged the PLA's institutionalization, and the attempts at doing so under his leadership did achieve several important goals – such as modernization of the PLA, discipline of the army units and officers, improved professional skills of PLA personnel, and the abolishment of lifetime tenure for PLA generals – he was not prepared to be constrained by the rules and regulations required by the PLA's institutionalization. For Deng, personal loyalty, *guanxi* (personal ties), and factional alignment remained the paramount criterion for career advancement. By virtue of his great prestige and large network of connections in the PLA – an enduring source of his political power – Deng commanded absolute military loyalty, acted as key arbitrator in policy-making disputes within the party, and retained

---

[99] PLA's "nationalization" means that the Chinese military seeks neutrality in the country's political development. The regime has emphasized the absolute loyalty of the armed forces to the Chinese Communist Party.

[100] *Deng Xiaoping nianpu, 1975–1997*, vol. 2, p. 1303.

[101] Ibid., p. 1281.

paramount power behind the scenes even as he steadily surrendered his public titles. When Deng appointed the new PLA leadership to support Jiang Zemin immediately after the Tiananmen Square incident in 1989, Deng personally decided that the deputy CMC chairman should be a senior general who had been with the former Fourth Front Army during the 1920s and 1930s, because the generals from the former Fourth Front Army took the majority of current PLA leadership,[102] more likely because that was the army generals whom Deng led in the Second Field Army during the end of 1930s and the 1940s and with which Deng had personal ties.[103] Even in 1992 – three years after Deng resigned all of his positions, he continued to be the decision maker for key posts in the CMC, such as those of vice chairman.[104]

Although Deng by no means used institutionalization to replace his personal influence and power, his policies certainly accomplished his goals of sweeping military professionalism. He enacted routine promotion and retirement procedures in the military to encourage the retirement of aging senior PLA officers and to improve PLA combat effectiveness. He launched the campaign to reorganize the PLA, cutting 1 million military personnel from the payroll in the mid-1980s. These measures and policies were accompanied by programs that commissioned new PLA officers from universities and developed a professional, noncommissioned officer corps to reform and improve the quality of training. Many civilian institutions of higher education have been entrusted with offering technological training to military officers to increase the level of military modernization.

Intrusive aspects of political control were questioned by Deng Xiaoping and his lieutenants, as they abhorred the degree to which the PLA was politicized during the Cultural Revolution as well as the resulting confusion in both the party and the army about the future of communist ideology. The PLA high command in the post-Mao era has therefore reached a loose consensus concerning general PLA development, agreeing to a balance between political control and professionalism (the consensus is considered loose because of the ongoing debate concerning which factor is more important). The increasing emphasis

---

[102] *Liu Huaqing huiyilu*, pp. 575–6.

[103] The Fourth Front Army was led by Zhang Guotao and was one of the most powerful front armies in CCP during late 1920s and early 1930s. The major part of the Fourth Front Army was reorganized into the 129th Division of the Eighth Route Army led by Liu Bocheng and Deng Xiaoping in 1938. The 129th Division (1938–45) became the foundation of the PLA Second Field Army (1945–49) and the Southwest Military Region (1949–53), which were led by Deng Xiaoping. After Deng returned to office in 1977, he had promoted into key party, government and army positions a large number of high-ranking cadres who had served in the 129th Division of the Eighth Route Army, the PLA Second Field Army, and the Southwest Military Region. In 1982, when the PLA was reorganized, most of the key positions in the PLA departments and eleven military regions were controlled by Deng's former subordinates. See Xuezhi Guo, "Dimensions of Guanxi in Chinese Elite Politics," in *The China Journal*, no. 46 (July 2001), p. 80.

[104] *Liu Huaqing huiyilu*, pp. 629–30.

on absolute PLA compliance with party leadership that came about in the later period of Jiang Zemin's tenure, in addition to the political indoctrination of the PLA that is occurring under Hu Jintao, preoccupies party leadership and seems to be an indication that the CCP is pushing for more political control over the PLA.

The organizational framework for ensuring political controls within the PLA is also being reinforced by using the traditional five-principles policy. The general outline of the policy is as follows: The first principle states that all military units must be located under the leadership of the CCP and the CMC, without exception. Any other parties or political organizations are not allowed to exist in the army, and no one is allowed to employ the army without the permission of the party and army leadership. The second principle is that PLA units at the regimental level and above must have party committees, whereas party grassroots committees should be established at the battalion level. The third principle states that political commissars are established at the regimental level and above and that they are the authorities of party and political work; leading military officers share these responsibilities with military commanders. The fourth principle states that political departments are established at the regiment level and above and are responsible for party and political work under the dual leadership of the respective next-highest political department and the party committee of the same level. The fifth principle states that party branches are established at company level so that party grassroots organizations can control every unit of the PLA. The five principles ensure organizational guarantees for party directives and decisions, but it is hard to say how the reemphasis of political control will resurrect the party's role in PLA affairs. The party, of course, played a gargantuan role in military affairs under Mao, but with the death of communist ideology worldwide, the CCP's failure in fighting rampant corruption, and the party's battle against increasing decentralization, this situation seems unlikely to arise again.

Modernization in the PLA has aimed to transform into an ever more complex and effective fighting force, pushing an accelerated program of professionalism, institutionalization, and acquisition of military equipment and technology that has largely abandoned the Maoist ideology of the people's war. This is yet another gap between doctrine and operation, one that is embodied in the relationship between the CCP and the PLA. As a result, the party's representatives have lost considerable zeal in touting the party line, because military modernization requires the PLA to promote many officers who are familiar with the imperatives of modern warfare and who demonstrate professional competence in their careers. While the PLA retains its tradition as a critical force in upholding the absolute leadership and legitimacy of the party (and its ideology) as well as unconditional party loyalty; it has also steadfastly dedicated itself to the long-term goals of professionalism and autonomy. As the party's control over the PLA has often been observed (most recently by Jiang Zemin) as the soul of the army (*jun hun*), and as the precondition (*qian ti*) to establishing a modern PLA (observed by Hu Jintao), reemphasis on political priority has dominated PLA-civilian relations in recent years. On the basis of the information available, it is reasonable to assume the CCP will continue to pursue balanced development, of contradicting goals of professionalism and politicized military involvement. Still, tension between professional and political priorities will continue to be a prominent feature in PLA politics in the foreseeable future.

Conclusion

All regimes, including modern democracies, have domestic and foreign enemies. The twentieth century saw countless examples of state action against presumed enemies: the United States' actions against suspected German and Japanese spies during World War II and political persecution against communists in the 1950s, Western Germany's actions against presumed extremist groups in the 1970s and the infiltration of East German agents throughout the Cold War, and recent antiterrorism measures undertaken by major Western democracies. Notable is that the fight against political enemies in democracies is conducted not by regular police or the military but by special police and intelligence agencies. These agencies "typically are granted wider powers and operate under less restrictive rules than their police counterparts."[1]

Contrary to Western democracies, China is governed by a monopolistic party whose leaders are not democratically elected, which means that political legitimacy is not based on popular support. As a result, the CCP has protected itself from internal and external threats by means of a strong security system. Though firmly committed to economic reform, the CCP imposes severe limitations on Chinese citizens in its effort to maintain strict political and social control, such as restricting access to information, as well as restricting freedom of expression and freedom of association when sensitive subjects are involved. The CCP believes that China is threatened by "Western hostile forces," led by the United States, and that those forces are attempting to Westernize, divide, and overthrow the CCP by supporting democracy activists, religious groups (including practitioners of *falun gong*), separatists (Tibetans, Uighurs, and Taiwan), and political dissidents.

---

[1] Paul R. Gregory, *Terror by Quota: State Security from Lenin to Stalin – An Archival Study*, p. 3.

418

Although this study has sought to provide comprehensive research on China's security and intelligence agencies from a historical perspective, its central focus is investigation of the role that security and intelligence apparatuses have played in Chinese politics by providing new evidence and by offering alternative interpretations to events throughout CCP history. Although this analysis suggests several inferences that may be drawn from the findings of the foregoing chapters, the patterns discussed in the following sections are more pronounced with respect to the important role of the CCP's security and intelligence organs and services in CCP politics.

Toward Professionalism and Institutionalization

The institutionalization of the CCP security and intelligence apparatuses has been prominent since the 1950s. Although Mao never hesitated to control the security and intelligence apparatuses, and viewed his leadership over them as among his most important responsibilities, the top party organs, such as the Politburo and the Central Secretariat, predominantly led and guided the security and intelligence apparatuses throughout the 1950s and early 1960s.[2] In the party leadership, the use of the CCP security and intelligence apparatuses in elite political conflicts was undertaken with care and caution, mostly because consensus had been a primary principle of the leadership collective. The party bureaucracy and the frontline leaders dominated the major CCP security and intelligence apparatuses, such as the MPS and the Central Investigation Department (CID). Decisions to use the security apparatus were often reached by consensus among the Politburo, the CCP secretariats, the State Council, and the Central General Office.

A significant development in the institutionalization of the CCP's security forces was the establishment of the Ministry of Public Security and the Chinese People's Public Security Forces (CPPSF). At the same time, garrison commands were created to help local civilian leaders maintain social order and political stability. In addition, the Central Guard Regiment, the security force for elite officials, was put under the administration of the Central Column of the CPPSF. The pursuit of military modernization has been the driving force for the professionalism of the PLA since the early 1950s, and thus has forged the path to institutionalized security organizations. The communist triumph over the Nationalists ensured that political and economic resources would be available, and the experience of the Korean War reinforced the incentive for the PLA to modernize its military forces. The intensive program of both technical and administrative modernization emphasized knowledge

---

[2] An excellent analysis of the development of China's institutionalization in the 1950s is conducted by Alice Miller. See Alice L. Miller, "Institutionalization and the Changing Dynamics of Chinese Leadership Politics," in Cheng Li (ed.), *China's Changing Political Landscape: Prospects for Democracy*, pp. 62–8.

of military science, specific and sophisticated weaponry, and professionalism.

The professionalization of the CCP armed forces and security forces (most of China's security forces were under the dual leadership of the Central Military Commission [CMC] and the civilian party committee) was also due to influence from the Soviet Union. Soviet armies provided a model of a modern hierarchical army, which helped the PLA institute a rank system that encompassed a differentiated pay scale and professional criteria for advancement. In the early 1950s, the CMC pushed for modernization following the Soviet model; however, there were also debates within the PLA leadership over how the PLA might keep its tradition of partisan warfare while still moving forward with borrowing from the Soviet model. These conversations often became quite heated, which is not surprising considering that the PLA leadership had to face frequent conflicts between old-school PLA generals and reformist Soviet advisers who demanded the PLA's adherence to the Soviet model. One of the key debates concerned the Soviet system of "the single responsibility of combat commanders," in which commanders in the field took full charge of their military units, and the officers in charge of political affairs (e.g., political commissars, department directors) played subordinate roles in the chain of combat command.[3] Two significant approaches were taken by the CMC (then led by Defense Minister Peng Dehuai) from 1953 to 1954 to push the system of the single responsibility of combat commanders to the forefront of debate. One approach, in early 1953, was the abolishment of the position of director of political departments at the regimental level and above. This was a significant departure from the PLA tradition, in which the party held an unchallengeable leading role at the grassroots level. The second approach, taken by Peng in April 1953, was to revise the Order of Internal Affairs. This forced the dismissal of political officers at the battalion and company levels, an obvious step toward abolishing the duties of the political officers at the grassroots PLA level.

The development toward professionalism of the Ministry of Public Security and other civilian security forces had been the major feature since the PRC was established in 1949, despite the setbacks they experienced at times. The vertical chain of command in the civilian security apparatuses was abandoned, and dual leadership by higher-level security agencies and local party committees was introduced. Professionalization had its drawbacks in the PLA, as well, as the democratic-egalitarian tradition of the PLA was significantly undermined by the vertical command system of the Soviets. This departure from communist ideals eventually catalyzed resistance within the PLA leadership to the adoption of Soviet military models. In particular, the criticism focused on the tendency to replace the traditional military doctrine of comradely relations and informality between ranks with modern Soviet doctrine that emphasized

---

[3] You Ji, "Sorting Out the Myths about Political Commissars," in Nan Li (ed.), *Chinese Civil Military Relations: The Transformation of the People's Liberation Army*, p. 89.

relations based on hierarchy, discipline, and status. In 1958 the debate within the PLA finally triggered the antidogmatism campaign, an effort to criticize excessive reliance on Soviet practices.

A radical change from professionalization to the revival of political work occurred in 1959, after Lin Biao replaced Peng Dehuai as head of the PLA, and the CMC intensified the army's program of political education and restored many of the military traditions that the PLA had exercised during the revolutionary period.[4] Professionalization also experienced a setback during Lin Biao's campaign to give prominence to politics in the early 1960s, as well as during the Cultural Revolution. The Soviet-style vertical chain of command based on professionalization was replaced by the heavy-handed control of the party committees in the security and intelligence apparatuses. Thus, the party bureaucracy exercised strong control over the security and intelligence apparatuses in the 1950s and early 1960s. The leadership conflict between Mao and other top leaders in the early 1960s put security and intelligence organizations in a cumbersome position. On the eve of the Cultural Revolution, controlling the security and intelligence organizations – including the Ministry of Public Security, the Central Investigation Department (CID), the CGO, the Central Guard Bureau, and Unit 8341 – was significant for the political survival of Mao and other top leaders. Despite Mao's long-standing effort to control the MPS and the CID, the party bureaucracy had the greater advantage in controlling and influencing these organizations.

It is possible to assess whether an organization is "institutionalized" by assessing the processes that are based on institutional rule and the degree to which officeholders are effectively bound by the responsibilities of their office. The greater the institutional rule and the more an officeholder follows that rule (and does not unilaterally institute new rules), the more institutionalized the organization is. The MPS and the CID were relatively more professionalized and institutionalized than most other CCP organizations because both highly emphasized discipline with strict enforcement of the rules and regulations. The party bureaucracy was able to reinforce its values and norms, which in turn strengthened the loyalty of both the MPS and the CID to the party as a whole. This is probably why Mao had to purge so many officials at every level and to paralyze the organizations on the eve of the Cultural Revolution. He recognized the institutionalization of the security and intelligence apparatuses, and he actively worked to dismantle them, in order to prevent the party bureaucracy from using them to stop the Cultural Revolution. After

---

[4] Defense Minister Peng Dehuai was criticized for de-emphasizing political work as the guiding principle of the PLA and transferring large numbers of political affairs officers to other posts. After Lin Biao replaced Peng as defense minister in September 1959, Lin introduced a system of indoctrination to brainwash the PLA personnel and emphasized the basic tenet of a politicized PLA – politics takes in command – and the absolute party control over China's armed forces.

China launched economic reforms in the late 1970s, institutionalization and professionalism measures followed. Not wanting to repeat previous mistakes, the CCP attempted to codify intelligence and security agencies, and statutes set out their functions and established formal arrangements for control and oversight.

The overlap of state and PLA intelligence services encouraged a competitive intelligence environment, thus leading observers to believe that the party advocates for pluralistic competition among intelligence agencies. Although the professionalization of intelligence officers and intelligence services, and the constant oversight of intelligence organizations, has gradually developed since Deng Xiaoping launched economic reforms, the organizations are still controlled by the CCP. This has politicized the security and intelligence apparatuses, which continue to reign over the political system in China, unchanged from previous eras. Unlike democratic regimes, in which depoliticization of the intelligence services is easily ensured through legal and institutional arrangements, the CCP employs the intelligence services as tools to consolidate power and to survive. However, because the professionalization of civil-military and civil-security relations has played an increasingly important role in elite politics, CCP politics during the post-Deng era have been characterized as more institutionalized.

In addition, there has been a loose separation of foreign intelligence and domestic security functions in China's intelligence services. Specifically, the Second Department of the PLA General Staff Department is in charge of foreign intelligence, focusing on foreign intelligence and espionage against rival nations. This includes monitoring foreign diplomats and foreign interests within China and conducting political surveillance of Chinese diplomats abroad. In contrast, the MPS is responsible for domestic intelligence and security services, despite the fact that it also gathers intelligence abroad. The MSS is responsible for a wide range of domestic missions (e.g., political espionage; pursuit of economic and technological intelligence; supervision of foreign executives, tourists, diplomats, and locals employed at embassies and by foreign companies), and it is also in charge of foreign intelligence and counterintelligence operations.

In elite party politics, intelligence organizations have played an important role in helping paramount leaders consolidate their power through monopolizing information and secrets. Intelligence is collected on all high-ranking party officials, but only the paramount leader and the security organizations typically have access to these confidential materials. Oftentimes, these files include evidence of corruption and crime committed by party officials and their families, especially their children – both at home and abroad. Consequently, paramount leaders can use this information as blackmail to target, intimidate, or purge political rivals. Depending on the circumstances, paramount leaders will decide whether to hide or reveal illegal activities committed by high-ranking officials and their children and to impose sanctions on them.

Of late, the MPS has worked with the MSS to increase industrial, economic, scientific, and technological espionage efforts, especially in Western nations. Economic intelligence, which is not confined to industrial and technological espionage and provides policy makers with analyses of long-term economic trends, is no longer an instrument to enhance military power; instead, it is an instrument of economic enhancement, given cutthroat international economic competition. Moreover, the CCP is keenly aware that scientific and technological intelligence are key in international security today. It is not enough to simply take a stance on nuclear weapon development for one's own country; knowledge of an adversary's nuclear capability and the likelihood of an attack are imperative to maintain political security. Therefore, monitoring the abilities and intentions of other countries is of paramount importance to international security in the nuclear age.

Security and Intelligence Organizations under Personalistic Politics

Scholarship on Chinese elite politics has achieved a broad consensus concerning the weaknesses of the CCP's institutional systems as well as the importance of informal personal connections in the Chinese political system.[5] Supporting these assertions is the relationship between the CCP security apparatus and top leaders, particularly the security apparatus's role in ensuring leaders' political power. For example, personal control of the CCP security forces played a prominent role during the leadership of Mao Zedong, Deng Xiaoping, and Jiang Zemin. Mao was rarely involved in specific administrative issues of the party, government, and army, but he never hesitated to intervene personally in issues related to foreign policy and security. Security services have always been always staffed with loyalists who can be counted on to carry out orders without question and to speak candidly with top leaders. This explains why holding a leadership position in a security service is equally powerful and risky. To do their job well, state security officers must have considerable power to gather sensitive information that could be used against dominant leaders.

The tradition of dominant leaders directly controlling the top security and intelligence agencies began in communist base areas in the late 1920s and early 1930s. In the Jiangxi base areas, Mao directly commanded the top security apparatus through Gu Bo, secretary of the General Front Committee, which was led by Mao. After the entire Party Center, headed by the returned students Bo Gu and Zhang Wentian, took control over the Jiangxi base areas, Zhou Enlai, at the time the party's chief of the Jiangxi base areas, replaced Mao

---

[5] The increasing emphasis on the importance of informal political connections can be found in various approaches, including Dittmer's model, which links historical ties of high-ranking leaders with the bases of their political power, and MacFarquhar's analysis of political alignment based on personal loyalty rather than ideological orientation or institutional interests. Also relevant are the factional models proposed by Nathan and Huang Jing.

in commanding the security and intelligence organizations. Still, the most significant change associated with the security forces took place after the Zunyi Conference in January 1935, when Mao was acknowledged as the party's de facto leader. The CCP had been on the brink of extermination, so when Moscow's interference was waning, Mao seized the opportunity to attack the policies that he blamed for the failure of the Jiangxi Soviet and the forced retreat of the Long March. Wang Shoudao, Mao's former secretary, entered the leadership of the State Political Security Bureau (SPSB) through his role in leading the Execution Department of the SPSB, and he thereafter represented Mao in his command of the SPSB.

Mao became the indisputable leader of the party when he established his dominance after the Yan'an rectification in the mid-1940s. The personality cult he cultivated grew throughout the party and the general population after the People's Republic of China (PRC) was established. Mao felt confident in his ability to control the party's leadership and enjoyed the prestige bestowed on him by achieving the compliance of the party and the population. At this stage, Mao did not need to rely on terror or secret police to maintain his dominance. Although Mao rarely employed the security and intelligence organizations as tools for carrying out political terror against party members, he never underestimated the importance of the security and intelligence apparatuses and realized the potential threat of someone from the security apparatus developing his own faction against Mao. Thus, Mao's control over the security apparatus in the late 1940s and his later control over the intelligence organizations was mainly achieved through Wang Dongxing, Mao's chief bodyguard.

Beginning in 1947, when Wang was appointed to be in charge of Mao's security, Wang had been a key figure in representing Mao by monitoring and commanding the security agencies. Wang also played a leading role in organizing the security services when the CCP moved to Beijing in 1949. When Mao put the Central Investigation Department under the authority of the Central General Office in 1955, he also appointed Wang to the supervisory role of vice minister of the MPS. Although formally Wang was not the leader of the Central Guard Regiment, Wang's de facto rule of the CGR was well known in private CCP circles.[6] Mao's intent to strengthen control of the security forces and intelligence organizations in the early 1960s might have been triggered by the setback resulting from the economic disaster of the Great Leap Forward, which caused a widespread loss of faith within the general population. During the Cultural Revolution, the Central General Office, as well as its instrument – the Central Guard Bureau and the Central Guard Regiment, played a key role by carrying out Mao's orders against firstfront leaders, targeting the veterans in particular. Both Liu Shaoqi and Deng Xiaoping were imprisoned by the

[6] *Wu Jicheng huiyilu*, pp. 155–6.

Central Guard Bureau and Unit 8341, and hence their fate was largely decided by the CGO.

During the Cultural Revolution, Mao took leadership of the security and intelligence organizations into his own hands and relied heavily on the Central Guard Bureau and Unit 8341 for his security and communication with the outside world. Mao personally set up several models for pilot mass movements to apply to the entire country in terms of how the mass movement in the Cultural Revolution should be carried out and how the chaos could be controlled when the "civil war" took place among the mass rebels, the Red Guard, and the PLA units. Like the Central General Office, both the Central Guard Bureau and Unit 8341 were incredibly powerful security apparatuses, and their officials had coveted positions during the Cultural Revolution. Most of the requests or appeals that high-ranking leaders or disgraced veterans sent to Mao went through the CGO, the Central Guard Bureau and Unit 8341, headed by Wang Dongxing.

The Central Guard Bureau and Unit 8341 helped Mao in myriad ways, such as by minimizing the influence of his political opponents, preventing ranking leaders from solidifying possible political alliances, ensuring the loyalty of the leadership through careful monitoring, containing army units that were viewed as potential threats to Maoist radicals, and occupying a leadership role in commanding PLA units against possible rebellion. Another way Mao attempted to strengthen his control over the security forces was the organizational merger of the CGR into the reorganized Guard Department, led by Wang Dongxing, in 1969. This merger significantly consolidated the power of Wang Dongxing on whom Mao depended to implement his policies and retain control.

Post-Mao leaders also paid great attention to their personal control over the security forces. Although Deng Xiaoping relied on existing loyalty networks in the PLA to obtain control over the military and security forces, he continued to build his own political influence by lobbying party leadership to restore to office old cadres who had been purged during the Cultural Revolution. By doing so, he was able to elevate his former protégés to key positions within the party. Unlike Mao, who depended heavily on Wang Dongxing to control the Central Guard Bureau and Unit 8341, Deng's control over the security apparatus was achieved through direct and personal interactions with trusted followers and veterans of the Second Field Army. This included personalities such as Yang Yong (head of the PLA General Staff Department), Pan Yan (head of the Beijing Garrison Command), Zhao Cangbi and Yu Sang (both heads of the Ministry of Public Security), and Qing Jiwei (head of the Beijing Military Region). With the assistance and recommendation of Yang Shangkun, Deng appointed Yang Dezhong and Sun Yong to lead the Central Guard Bureau and the Central Guard Division (previously Unit 8341), respectively.

Although the trend of CCP politics during the post-Deng era can be characterized as increasingly institutionalized, not to mention the growing professionalization of Chinese civil-military relations, personalistic politics in the security services continues to play an important role in elite politics. Whereas Deng Xiaoping relied mainly on Yang Dezhong for his direct control over the Central Guard Bureau, Jiang Zemin maintained control over the elite security apparatus through Zeng Qinghong, You Xigui, and Jia Ting'an. After Jiang was appointed party chief, he took gradual steps to establish his dominance over the security forces. He appointed Zeng Qinghong director of the Central General Office and transferred his own followers to work in the Central Guard Bureau, slowly replacing the power of Yang Dezhong. In addition, Jiang transferred his close secretary Jia Tingan from Shanghai to Beijing and appointed Jia deputy director of the CMC General Office. In 1994, Jiang Zemin promoted You Xigui, his trusted follower and chief bodyguard, to director of the Central Guard Bureau. Under Hu Jintao's leadership, the party's control over the military and security agencies has shifted away from blatant manipulation of personal control and has instead found more grounding in the authority of institutions; formalized methods of interactions; and an emphasis on rule, law, and regulations. Thus far, Hu Jintao has maintained distance from cultivating personal ties in security organizations such as the Central Guard Bureau, the Central Guard Regiment, and the Central Guard Bureau of the PLA General Office. In this respect, Hu has shown uncharacteristic restraint for a Chinese paramount leader, but in other ways, Hu still manages to continue the tradition of employing personalistic politics to control the security apparatus. Most notably, he has ensured a comfortable dominance of the Central General Office, headed by his trusted follower Ling Jihua, through whom Hu manages to exert considerable control over the security apparatus.

Security and Intelligence Services in the PLA

The CCP established its armed forces in opposition to the Nationalist Party following the failure of the CCP-Guomindang united front in the late 1920s. Since then, the CCP armed forces have witnessed many changes institutionally and in practice, but what unifies each era is the continued influence over the CCP security and intelligence apparatuses. From the late 1920s to the early 1930s, it was the Red Army; from the late 1930s to the early 1940s, it was the Eighth Route Army and the New Fourth Army; and from the late 1940s to the present day, it has been the People's Liberation Army. The PLA's powerful influence over security and intelligence has origins in the long tradition of joint civilian and military leadership over security and intelligence organizations.

The PLA's security and intelligence is separate from that of the CCP. The Security Department of the PLA General Political Department is an organization that is responsible for investigation and internal security within the PLA. Although its duties involve guarding and protecting high-ranking PLA officers, it is also responsible for controlling and monitoring the very same officers. In addition, the CMC General Office is the main organization of the PLA that offers security guards and protection for the Central Military Commission and its leaders. It also functions as the nerve center that processes all CMC communications and documents, coordinates meetings, and conveys orders and directives to other subordinate organs. The CMC General Office has its own Guard Bureau that functions similarly to the Guard Bureau (the Eighth Bureau) of the Ministry of Public Security. Although the Fourth Department of the PLA General Staff Department has conducted some intelligence gathering, the Second and Third Departments are the leading intelligence organizations of the PLA. The Second Department is responsible for collecting military intelligence through spies and military attachés at Chinese embassies abroad, and the Third Department is responsible for technical reconnaissance, including monitoring and decoding data and information.

The PLA shares responsibilities with the civilian party and government agencies in commanding the top security apparatus. The most powerful security force that falls under the joint jurisdictions of the PLA and the civilian party agency in guarding high-ranking leaders is the Central Guard Bureau (CGB), which is under the dual leadership of the PLA General Staff Department and the Central General Office. In addition, the Central Guard Regiment or Unit 8341 also fall under the dual authority of the Central Guard Bureau and the PLA General Staff Department. Whereas the Central Guard Regiment receives guidance from the PLA General Staff Department about political education, promotion and demotion, and logistics and supplies, it mainly receives professional assignments from the Central Guard Bureau. However, the responsibilities of dual leadership have never followed an institutional design; rather, they are the result of a combination of the elite power struggle, cooperation, and competition. Although the CGB and Unit 8341 were mainly controlled by the CCP General Office in Mao's era, the PLA completely took over command in the late 1970s and throughout the 1980s. Post-Deng leaders have shown concern over the lack of clarification of the responsibilities regarding the dual leadership of the PLA and the CCP General Office over the elite security apparatuses. Although Jiang Zemin put the elite security forces almost equally under the firm control of both the PLA and the CGO, given the authority he enjoyed in effectively commanding both the PLA and the CGO, Hu Jintao seems to rely exclusively on the CGO for his control over the elite security forces. The armed police, such as the People's Armed Police, are also commanded by the dual leadership of the PLA and the civilian party committees. While civilian leaders are primarily responsible for identifying objectives and work plans, the PLA has directly and indirectly commanded the armed police forces and remains a powerful influence in their development.

Besides the tradition of dual leadership of the CCP security apparatus, security personnel from civilian and military organizations have at times been interchangeable, if necessary. For example, the beginning of the Great Leap

Forward in early 1958 triggered a veritable avalanche of decentralization, sending power cascading down to local party committees. It was there that the People's Armed Police (PAP) were reorganized and returned to the control of local public security offices. After the PAP was put under a dual public security–military leadership system in the early 1960s, its personnel were transferred from civilians to active-duty status, and its units were reorganized under a much more disciplined military system. It is important to note, however, that the reorganized PAP was not under the equal leadership of the MPS and the PLA. Although the MPS and its local organs provided the professional guidance for the PAP, the PLA made decisions about the PAP's development, personnel allotments, finances, political control, education and training, supply, and personnel turnover.

The removal of Luo Ruiqing in December 1965 got both the MPS and the armed police into trouble, as a result of their long-standing ties with Luo Ruiqing. Several key leaders of the MPS were purged and the leadership of the MPS was reorganized after Luo was dismissed, and the Chinese People's Public Security Forces was abolished. Following its abolishment the units of its armed police were absorbed by various local military units, including military regions, military districts, and local garrison commands. Mao's abolishment and merger of the armed police relieved his concern about their loyalty and served his grand strategy to weaken the party bureaucracy. Unfortunately for the leadership, there were some repercussions of Mao's movements. Wiping out the armed police, which had been controlled directly by the party bureaucracy, effectively gave more power to local army leaders, because they had dominance over a large number of local armed forces and armed police.

Because of the dismantlement and abolishment of the major public security and armed police forces during the Cultural Revolution, Mao had to rely completely on the PLA to end the mass violence and resume social order. As the merged armed police fell under the leadership of the military districts and municipal garrison commands, local army leaders became indisputable political authorities by virtue of their control of the army, security forces, and resources. Because Mao had to rely on local army generals to defend China against possible invasion and to maintain domestic social order, the local army leaders gradually became influential political forces in both the PLA leadership and in the party leadership. Arguably, granting local military regions control over the abolished armed police disabled the central bureaucracy from using force against Mao after he launched the Cultural Revolution. But the move also created severe problems for Mao later. Without the armed police, it was almost impossible to curtail the violence after the mass movement was out of control. To restore social order, Mao had to rely on ordinary PLA units that were not trained to deal with public security and conflict mediation among mass organizations. Lack of direct control over the armed police forces also created security problems for the party leadership, which at that time was dominated by Maoist radicals. High-ranking leaders could not respond fast enough when the mass violence was out of control. Mao had underestimated the scale of the mass violence, such that Unit 8341 and the Beijing Garrison Command were not enough to quell the movement. Clearly, the abolishment of the armed police forces limited Mao's ability to control local party and military leaders.

As did other PLA units, the armed police forces (after their merger into the PLA) constituted an important part of military politics. This was in part because of their presence in the PLA and in part because of their responsibilities for guarding army leaders and civilian leaders during the Cultural Revolution. In addition, the armed police forces were deeply involved in local politics as a result of their role in maintaining political and social order, protecting governmental organizations, and guarding local civilian leaders. When Mao relocated the armed police forces to the jurisdiction of the provincial military districts, they became key armed forces against the mass rebels and the Red Guard during the Cultural Revolution. Because of their deep involvement in local politics, the personnel and leaders of some armed police units even defected, given their alliance with mass organizations working against local PLA units.

As illustrated by their complicated history, the armed police units never had a clear role in the military districts: their relocation was only part of Mao's strategy to retain power. Needless to say, leaders in the reform area were eager to see them go. The armed police units under the military districts were abolished even before 1 million personnel were downsized in the military in the mid-1980s. Because the units were part of the independent divisions, they were eliminated early on in Deng's reforms, and some of the personnel were absorbed into the newly established People's Armed Police. Deng's reforms initiated the institutionalization and professionalization of the PLA by downsizing it; depoliticizing it; and transforming it into a compact, modern, mobile, high-tech military capable of mounting operations beyond its borders.

Like the People's Armed Police, garrison commands are the important security forces in influencing local politics due to their role in maintaining social order and guarding cities. The post-Deng leaders have paid particular attention to enhancing the power of garrison commands in the security of local leaders, event security, security of facilities, control of the reserve forces and militia, and supervision of discipline and military order in the garrison. Without a doubt, the Beijing Garrison Command was the most important one because of its rank (jun, army corps) and its historical involvement in leadership politics.

The Beijing Garrison Command (BGC) was created in 1959 and organizationally received commands from both the PLA General Staff Department and the Beijing Military Region with the guidance of the Beijing Municipal Party Committee. In the Cultural Revolution, the BGC became extremely powerful as it was upgraded from the rank of army corps (*jun*) into the rank of army group (*bingtuan*), with more than one hundred thousand personnel in its ranks. The leaders of the BGC could attend meetings in which only leading figures of the military regions (*da junqu*) and the military districts (*sheng junqu*) were qualified to attend. To add to its prestige, the BGC received more confidential documents from party leadership than did the Beijing Military Region, its immediate superior. The BGC undoubtedly became an important security force in ensuring Mao's safety and an important weapon that Mao attempted to use against Lin Biao. To ensure his absolute control of the BGC, Mao ordered the organization to receive commands only from Zhou Enlai, not from the BGC's superiors in the General Staff Department, the Office of the CMC, and the Beijing Military Region. The leadership conflict between Mao and Lin proved how much Mao relied on the BGC for his security. Fewer than three hours after Lin's airplane took off from Beidaihe, the BGC was ordered to take control of Beijing, including of five airports. It was also ordered to search for evidence of Lin's "crime" in Beijing; to send additional troops to guard Zhongnanhai and the People's Hall; and to control media outlets such as the Xinhua News Agency, the headquarters of the *People's Daily*, the Central Radio Station, and the Beijing Telegram Tower. More important, the BGC was authorized to command an additional six divisions that were dispatched from the 38th Army Corps to expand its control to cover the areas of Nankou, Beijing Airport, and Baoding of Hebei. When Hua Guofeng decided to ally with Marshal Ye Jianying and Wang Dongxing against the Gang of Four in September and October 1976, two units of the security forces – Unit 8341 and the BGC – became the organizations they relied on most. The BGC also played a vanguard role in arresting the Gang of Four, and it was responsible for supporting the Central Guard Bureau and Unit 8341 if the arrests of the Gang of Four met setbacks or failed.

Military control over CCP security agencies was further enhanced after Deng returned to power in 1977. In the 1980s Deng ordered Yang Shangkun to directly control both the Central Guard Bureau and the Central Guard Regiment on Deng's behalf. Yang Shangkun could do this through his appointment as executive vice chairman of the CMC and general secretary of the CMC. Because veteran leaders wanted to avoid a second Cultural Revolution in which Mao paralyzed the party bureaucracy and created a powerful CGO in pushing his political programs and controlling the party, the CGO lost its power and became a normal party agency that dealt with daily administration and services. It became increasingly insignificant in its role assisting frontline leaders with important decisions. Instead, Deng Xiaoping and party veterans decided that the Politburo and the Central Secretariat should become more powerful. Deng let his concern show about the ability of the leaders of the third generation by keeping Zhongnanhai security forces in the PLA under his direct control. The "leaders of the third generation" refers to Hu Yaobang and Zhao Ziyang, who had to gain the confidence of veterans before they were bestowed with any power over the security apparatus. If Deng transferred control of the security forces from the PLA to the Central General Office (institutionally subordinate to the CCP General Secretary and the Politburo), then the authority to command the services would essentially be theirs. Deng's concern was further aggravated after numerous senior veterans showed dissatisfaction with Hu Yaobang in the mid-1980s. Moreover, Deng himself at one point questioned the "democratic" style of Hu's leadership, in which Hu relied primarily on collective decision making in the Politburo. Hu would consult more with the Central Secretariat (an administrative body that deals with the day-to-day affairs of the Politburo and the Politburo Standing Committee) than with the veteran leaders.

Since the economic reforms, the Central Guard Bureau has remained a powerful and special military unit in the PLA, because its rank at the deputy military region (*fu da junqu*) is higher than other second-tier departments, such as the Second Department and the Third Department of the PLA General Staff Department. In addition, its directors have been either lieutenant generals or generals, as in the case of Yang Dezhong and You Xigui. The Central General Office gradually resumed its authority over the Central Guard Bureau after Jiang Zemin took charge of the CCP. In short, a prominent feature in post-Deng elite politics has been the growing power of the CGO in the top leadership and its role in leading the security apparatus.

The Security Department of the PLA General Political Department (GPD) is responsible for investigation and internal security within the PLA. Although its duties involve guarding and protecting high-ranking PLA officers, it is also responsible for monitoring high-ranking army officers. To ensure security, it reviews the background of friends and family of high-ranking leaders. Besides the GPD Security Department in the PLA leadership in Beijing, there are the security branches in local military units controlled by political departments of local military units. The political departments of local PLA units command (1) the security departments (*baowei bu*) at all levels (military regions, navy, air force, Second Artillery Force, the Defense Science and Engineering Commission, Military Academy, National Defense University), (2) the security division (*baowei chu*) at the levels of group army and provincial military districts, (3) the security section (*baowei ke*) at the levels of divisions or brigades, and (4) the security secretary (*ganshi*) at the level of regiment. Local branches of the GPD Security Department are in charge of guarding local ranking army leaders and the headquarters of local army units. Like the Ministry of Public Security, the GPD Security Department has functional departments for areas such as intelligence, military police operations, and political and communications security. It has overall security responsibilities in the PLA and provides guidance to PLA security organizations nationwide. Its responsibilities include the prevention, suppression, and investigation of criminal or counterrevolutionary activities; antiterrorism activities; maintenance of security and order in the PLA; security detail of PLA leaders and important military facilities; and security inspection of public information networks. The GPD Security Department has been involved in investigations of PLA ranking officers charged with committing criminal activities. In addition, it stores a large number of confidential files and materials related to high-ranking PLA generals. Thus, control of the GPD Security Department is instrumental for paramount leaders to ensure their dominance in the PLA leadership.

During the reform era, armed forces guarding Beijing have experienced personnel cutbacks and a decrease in influence on military politics, alongside a renewed clarity of their organizational relationships, which changed drastically during the Cultural Revolution. The reform program launched by Deng Xiaoping that sought to reorganize PLA security forces included the withdrawal of heavy involvement of the PLA's army corps in the Beijing garrison and an increase in employment of army reserves in the Beijing garrison. Similar to the Central Guard Bureau and to its subordinate unit, the Central Guard Regiment, the Beijing Garrison Command was reorganized, and its leading figures transferred, after Deng regained power in 1978. An important move taken by Deng after he achieved dominance in the CCP leadership was to redefine the assignments and responsibilities of the BGC. Deng believed that a powerful BGC that overrode the Beijing Military Region and the party security apparatus was not only unhealthy but also a potential security risk for party leadership. In January 1978, the BGC was reorganized as a subordinate unit of the Beijing Military Region, which was responsible for commanding the BGC regarding party and political affairs, appointment and promotion, combat command, training, organization and equipment, administration, logistics, recruitment and demobilization, and militia. In addition to its compliance to the authority of the Beijing Military Region, the BGC received commands from the PLA General Staff Department and the CCP General Office. In the post-Deng era, the BGC, the Central Guard Regiment, and the General Beijing Corps of the People's Armed Police have been required to cooperate in jointly guarding Beijing. At the same time, they are not officially affiliated with one another; on the contrary, they are competing security forces that monitor one another to prevent security threats to the party leadership.

Like Deng Xiaoping, Jiang Zemin aggressively pursued control of the security and intelligence apparatuses during his tenure as party chief and the PLA's commander in chief. When Deng Xiaoping passed away in 1997, Jiang had successfully controlled the CCP General Office, the Central Guard Bureau, and the PLA General Office through his loyalists Zeng Qinghong, You Xigui, and Jia Ting'an, respectively. Under the leadership of Jiang Zemin, group armies were no longer responsible for local garrison duties. Instead, garrison commands were established in all capitals and important cities of all provinces and autonomous regions to manage garrison duties. In Beijing, the BGC was authorized to assist in guarding the capital, commanding the reserve forces and coordinating other PLA units for the Beijing garrison. Under Jiang's leadership civilian control of the BGC was enhanced. As a result, The BGC has taken an increased role in supporting the local civilian government in promoting social stability. It is also the military department of the local party committee, and it relies greatly on local party committees and governments to fund its organizational operations and activities.

The PLA has historically kept a powerful influence over and remained in control of the top CCP intelligence organizations. Since the central committee's Social Affairs Department (SAD), the leading Party and army intelligence agency, was abolished in August 1949, its intelligence sections in charge of foreign countries were reorganized into the Liaison Department under the General Intelligence Department of the CMC. Thus, instead of the SAD, the Chinese People's Public Security Forces became the primary base for providing personnel for the Ministry of Public Security. After the General Intelligence Department was abolished in February 1953, its subordinate divisions were placed under the authority of the PLA General Staff Department (GSD). As for intelligence collection outside of Mainland China, the PLA commands its own intelligence organizations and operates its own espionage activities. Both the PLA General Staff Department and some military regions have a large number of spies in Hong Kong and Macao.[7] Unlike the intelligence organizations of the Ministry of State Security (MSS) and the Ministry of Public Security (MPS), which may receive leadership guidance from local party authorities,[8] PLA intelligence organizations remain independent and received commands only from the PLA.

One of Deng's reform programs was the division of China's intelligence organizations into two systems: civilian and military. The military intelligence system engages in military intelligence and counterintelligence operations and mainly consists of the Intelligence Department of the GSD (also called the Second Department of the GSD), the Third Department of the GSD, and the Liaison Department of the General Political Department (GPD). Although civilian and military systems have different functions because of their specialties and focuses, they often cooperate and share resources. Considering that their responsibilities sometimes overlap, there is competition between the two. The Liaison Department of the GPD has responsibilities involving human intelligence collection and analysis but with limited information objectives and resources compared to those of the GSD's Second and Third Departments. Another agency involved in intelligence collection and analysis is the Commission of Science, Technology, and Industry for National Defense (COSTIND), an organization that is in charge of research and planning for military technologies and weapons systems and that engages in both overt and clandestine collection and functions.

In terms of division of labor, the Second Department of the GSD manages special agents, who are various professionals overseas and the military attachés of Chinese embassies. The Third Department is responsible for technical reconnaissance, including monitoring and decoding. Like the MSS, the Second Department is the leading organization that carries out and monitors

---

[7] Xu Jiatun, *Xu Jiatun xianggang huiyilu* [Memoirs of Xu Jiatun on Hong Kong], vol. 1 (Hong Kong: Xianggang lianhe bao youxian gongsi, 1993), p. 54.
[8] Ibid., p. 55.

the policies of the Central Military Commission (CMC) and runs the daily affairs of the PLA intelligence services. Its primary missions are related to collecting and analyzing political and military intelligence from rival nations as well as engaging in military exchanges with foreign countries. Besides its focus on monitoring foreign diplomats and foreign interests within China and conducting political surveillance of Chinese diplomats abroad, it cooperates with the MSS to pursue political, economic, industrial, scientific, and technological intelligence from the West, particularly the United States and Europe.

Dual Leadership, Civilian Rule, and Security Apparatuses

The dual leadership system is a unique model implemented by the CCP in its control over and administration of both civilian and military organizations. The PLA, solely or jointly, commands six main security organizations: the Central Guard Bureau, the Central Guard Regiment or Unit 8341, the Guard Bureau of CMC General Office, the Security Department of the CCP General Political Department, the PAP, and the PLA garrison commands nationwide, especially the Beijing Garrison Command. Although the Central Guard Bureau is under the dual authority of the Central General Office and the CMC, local PAP units and garrison commands are under the dual leadership of the upper-level PAP units or garrison commands and local party committees. The dual leadership system creates a complicated vertical and horizontal relationship in which local party and government offices ensure that the principles and policies of the party are upheld and provide logistical support and resources. The higher-level PAP units or garrison commands provide professional guidance.

The People's Armed Police, a Chinese paramilitary force under the dual leadership of the Central Military Commission and the State Council, is a typical example of how civilian leadership controls the armed police. The People's Armed Police receives professional guidance from the MPS, yet it is under the dual leadership of the MPS's parent organization, the State Council, and the CMC. The MPS and State Council are responsible for command and operations of the PAP, authorizing the size and number of subordinate organizations, assigning tasks, providing financial and material support, and ensuring logistical supplies. Police forces under the MPS are usually unarmed, in contrast to the personnel of the PAP. However, the increasing size and scale of "mass incidents" in the reform era has forced the MPS to rely more on the PAP to ensure civilian control and to maintain social order. Consequently, it has been a long struggle between the MPS, which sought continual control over the PAP, and the PAP, which desired greater autonomy from the MPS.[9] The party leadership supports civilian control over the PAP, which underscores the organizational principle of the relationship between party secretaries and their local military

[9] See Tian Bingxin, "Zhou Yushu: Zhaozhao baoxiao dasheng ti" [Zhou Yushu: Announce the dawn daily and crow loudly], in *Hainan jinji bao* [Hainan economic daily], December 12, 2005.

units. This was a result of a change that occurred in 1984, when all provincial and municipal party secretaries were asked to step down as the first political commissars of their respective local military regions while continuing to hold the office of first party secretary of their respective local military region. In contrast, the ministers of public security continued to hold both the positions of first political commissar and first party secretary in the PAP. This arrangement did not change even after 1996, when the PAP was integrated into the PLA. Although the PAP was no longer controlled by the MPS, party leadership still approved of the MPS's support of civilian control of the PAP.

It is no mistake that the security apparatuses operate under dual leadership and a complex hierarchy, as these features ensure the CCP's civilian rule over the military. Although there are cultural and philosophical roots that contribute to China's civilian rule, the convoluted structure of the CCP organizations reinforces these roots and has been crucial to ensuring the army leaders' compliance. Civilian control over the PLA is structurally guaranteed, because the security apparatus is organized with so many overlapping agencies and competing chains of command. In other words, a coup against civilian leadership is highly unlikely. In addition, there have been at least four elements that support the CCP's civilian rule: traditional political ideology, military factionalism, dual leadership, and the civilian leadership's supervision of military leaders.

Traditional political thought based on rectification of name (*zhengming*) and mandate of heaven had and continue to have deep influence on the ruling elite. Rectification of name also defines one's role in bureaucratic politics and dictates which personality attributes are prescribed for each bureaucratic position. Confucianism purports that society would be in proper order if everyone acted according to the "name" of their designated social position; the concept of rectification of name is the unparalleled value placed on certain government positions and the respect that the individuals in those positions command from their subordinates. It constitutes one of the central political-ethical doctrines in traditional Chinese political thought. The rectification of name lays the foundation for the overwhelming influence of the code of civility, by which the elite comply with generally accepted norms such as consensus, unity, and respect for seniority and institutional authority. In any case, historically, organized or unorganized political groups accused of illegitimacy were abolished because they challenged or were perceived as challenging the core leadership, and therefore they were viewed as undermining the unity of the system. Although institutional position does not necessarily determine the real power of a political leader, rectification of name has created a powerful convention among the elite to comply with the authority defined by political institutions. For a paramount leader, the mandate of heaven defines that political pursuit must be based on benevolence, and the goal of politics is to achieve harmony and promote voluntary compliance rather than coercion. For scholar-officials and the ruling elite, Chinese political tradition links the person of the nobleman directly to moral virtue, and all behaviors of the nobleman must arise from his moral obligation. Thus, there is a strong taboo against the pursuit of self-interest when one is serving the government. The ideal realm of political pursuit for a political leader, as the *Analects* defines, is to cultivate conditions in which "all stars twinkle around the moon" and "everyone wholeheartedly supports the leader as the core" rather than relying on power and coercion.

Military factionalism has been a prominent feature in Chinese politics, despite the fact that reforms have greatly undermined the strength and endurance of this phenomenon. Because political pursuit emphasizes moralistic responsibility and personal loyalty, it often becomes an effective tool for the paramount leader to control the bureaucracy and the military. It is exactly this type of factional politics that is deeply embedded in the Chinese political system. In fact, military factionalism encourages powerful and influential group armies to supervise one other, thus allowing the civilian paramount leader to become the final arbitrator over the military.

Although Chinese security forces are large and strong, they hardly pose a threat to civilian leadership, given the complex dual leadership system in which civilian authorities assign work and provide financial support to local security forces while military authorities provide guidance and supervision. This setup seems to have been created by Mao and other frontline leaders for just this purpose – to keep the coercive apparatus under party control. Mao's direct control over the Central Guard Bureau and Central Guard Regiment was a crucial component of his dominance in the CCP leadership, as the organizations would report on the movements and communications of other senior civilian or military leaders, thus giving Mao a leg up in his political maneuvering and control.

Civilian leadership cultivates the security forces so as to play an even larger role in supervising other military groups, even the PLA. To a certain extent, the PAP's partial separation from the PLA creates a system of checks and balances for the armed forces that benefit civilian leadership and China's political stability overall. Akin to conventional police forces, central and local governments also fund the PAP. The PAP's organization mirrors that of the PLA, including ranks, uniforms, organizational structure, and training, as opposed to conventional police, who do not use military rank to structure their chain of command. The security forces play, and will continue to play, an exceptionally decisive role in factional politics in PLA leadership as long as the PLA is unable to form a unified armed force against civilian leadership. In essence, it is impossible for military leaders to form a coup or to find ways to work together without involving the security forces that guard them, which would invariably tip off central party leadership. The civilian paramount leader's monopoly over the elite security forces ensures compliance of army generals to the civilian leadership because the security forces collect intelligence on high-ranking army leaders as they provide them with security detail. As a result, any move made by the army generals – individually or collectively – against the civilian paramount leader not only is risky but also is most likely impossible. In summary, China's civilian rule is guaranteed by cultural, institutional, and structural factors, and its unique and costly form of civilian control of the military has been and will continue to be a feature of Chinese politics.

Legacy, Development, and Reform in the Post-Mao Era

In the post-Mao era, there has been an increasing tendency to enhance the size and power of public security organizations and their role in carrying out the overriding mission of the regime: ensuring social order and social stability and maintaining CCP rule. Historically, public security agencies have wielded their power brutally against CCP enemies. Their work has been crucial in reinforcing the communist proletarian dictatorship and in guaranteeing the unchallengeable authority of the CCP. In addition, they have played a pivotal role in elite politics and often have the crucial forces behind intraparty conflict. In the communist revolution, they served leaders by eliminating their political rivals, consolidating their power, and ensuring their absolute control over the party and the armed forces. Millions of innocent victims perished at the hands of the security forces under the control of dominant leaders in the base areas. They have been the vanguards and the weapons used by the powerful party leaders against the internal and external enemies.

In the early 1950s, the MPS was China's principal police authority, with departments covering intelligence; police operations; prisons; and political, economic, and communications security. The MPS took the lead in domestic and criminal operations, including domestic patrol, traffic control, and detective work, as well s anticrime, antiriot, and antiterrorism functions.[10] The MPS was mainly responsible for domestic counterintelligence investigations and operations, but its political security section was assigned to conduct foreign counterespionage operations and counterintelligence investigations of citizens who had established close contact with foreigners. Since Deng Xiaoping launched economic reforms in 1979, the MPS has experienced numerous changes that followed in the wake of China's open-door policy. For example, a major change was implemented following a promulgation of the People's Police Law, which placed restrictions on police forces in conducting arrests, investigating crimes, and searching suspects. The People's Police Law has detailed provisions on functions, rights and obligations, and rewards and sanctions in regard to police officers and procurators.[11] Other changes to the law books, for example, are that a court or procuratorate warrant is required for any planned arrest, and the torture of criminals is illegal.

[10] Dennis J. Blasko, *The Chinese Army Today: Tradition and Transformation for the 21st Century*, p. 17.
[11] "The PRC People's Police Law," *Xinhua*, March 1, 1995.

Another significant organizational change for public security organizations is the increased power of local party organizations to control local branches of public security. Because social stability has been a top priority during economic reforms, compounded with the requirement that local party leaders be held responsible for maintaining social order, local branches of the MPS played a larger role in local politics. Many public security leaders at the provincial or municipal level not only were members of party standing committees but also led the party's Political and Legal Commission. Although local public security branches were under the dual leadership of upper-level public security organizations and local party committees, in certain areas the local party committees had more control over the bureaus of public security than did the upper-level public security organizations. For example, local party committees were more intricately involved in recruitment, promotions, salaries, and resource allocation of local public security branches. With power consolidated among a few people in local party and public security organizations, accountability to the Ministry of Public Security dictates and party discipline often is lost, thus making local organizations a playground for indulging the personal interests of powerful local leaders. As Murray Scot Tanner and Eric Green point out, there are many powerful incentives and opportunities for local party and public security officials to undermine both central government goals for police professionalization and social control.[12]

In light of this, CCP leadership has become increasingly concerned in recent years with the strong influence of local party organizations over local public security branches, particularly the role of some local public security organizations in the protective umbrellas of underground societies. Many of these underground societies flourish as a result of the involvement of local political leaders and the loyalty they command from the local bureaus of public security. Local party offices experience such nefarious and widespread corruption because of the political, organizational, and economic dependence of local public security branches. After realizing the overwhelming collusion between the two types of local organizations, party leadership strengthened the role of upper-level public security organizations in overseeing subordinate branches. Beginning in January 2007, all appointments for local public security chiefs must first gain the approval of the superior upper-level public security organization, a policy that prevents unilateral control of appointment and promotion by local party organizations.[13] Other initiatives by CCP leadership include reducing the dependence of local public security branches on local party organizations and emphasizing economic benefits solely at the disposal of local public security branches. Instead of punishing the branches for poor

---

[12] Murray Scot Tanner and Eric Green, "Principals and Secret Agents: Central versus Local Control over Policing and Obstacles to 'Rule of Law' in China," in Donald C. Clarke (ed.), *China's Legal System: New Developments, New Challenges*, p. 115.

[13] *Fazhi ribao* [Legal System Daily], January 24, 2007.

behavior, the CCP rewards them for good behavior and promotes morale at the same time. Since the reforms, the MPS and its local branches have suffered from public complaints regarding bureaus of public security' inability to deal with rising crime and involvement in local corruption scandals. The MPS has pinpointed insufficient pay, poor training, and low officer morale as the source of many of these issues. As a result, CCP leadership has attempted to increase pay and improve benefits for public security officers while introducing a mechanism for competition that seeks to improve the quality of public security personnel.[14]

Another prominent feature of the post-Mao era is the CCP leadership's effort to institutionalize PLA security organization standards and enhance civilian control over the military security apparatus. Even the PLA's elite security forces in the post-Deng era, the Central Guard Bureau (CGB) and the Central Guard Regiment (CGR), have increasingly complied with the institutional authority of the Central General Office. Although these organizations are couched under the PLA with joint supervision from the Central General Office (CGO), they historically have been controlled by the paramount leader and used as personal security forces. Under Mao's regime, the CGO never had complete authority over the CGB or CGR. As elite security forces, the legacies of the Central Guard Bureau and the Central Guard Regiment are inseparable from that of CCP politics, given their pivotal role in ensuring the compliance of high-ranking leaders and in intraparty leadership conflicts. One such instance was when Wang Dongxing commanded both the CGB and the CGR in October 1976 to arrest the Gang of Four and the leading Maoist radicals.[15] After the Maoist era, the CGB and the CGR experienced a more stable existence, as well as increased professionalism. As the praetorian guards of the CCP, the CGB and the CGR are responsible for providing security for top leaders, providing protection for important government sites, and escorting top foreign officials on their travels in China. Other responsibilities include supervising other security and intelligence services, such as monitoring government ministers, leaders of the armed forces, and internal security operations for potential security breaches. Both the CGB and the CGR are not only the eyes and ears of the party leadership; they are also the hand that implements, directly or indirectly, the party chief's security directives.

There has been a tendency for increasing civilian control over the military and paramilitary forces in the reform era. Although the Ministry of Public Security has delineated the role of the People's Armed Police (PAP) to maintain social order and deal with "mass incidents" in particular, local civilian leaders

---

[14] *Fazhi ribao* [Legal System Daily], March 5, 2007; *Guangzhou ribao* [Guangzhou Daily], June 29, 2002.

[15] *Wu Jicheng huiyilu*, pp. 390–7; Frederic Wakeman Jr., "Models of Historical Change: The Chinese State and Society, 1839–1989," in Kenneth Lieberthal (ed.), *Perspectives on Modern China: Four Anniversaries*, pp. 91–2.

rely on the garrison commands to ensure party dominance and maintain local social stability. Garrison duties are frequently assigned to operational PLA units stationed in an area as an additional duty of the local commander. Not only do garrison commands guard cities and strategic military locations; they are also responsible for militia and reserve forces, conscription, and mobilization of military services. Garrison commands are police agencies that operate in major cities to maintain national security. The primary duties of garrison commands also include guarding military facilities and maintaining order among troops when military personnel are outside the barracks on pass, leave, or official duties; in this sense, garrison troops function similarly to other foreign armies' military police. They are responsible for providing security for the military and for national events and facilities on the garrison premises, and for supervising military discipline and order in the garrison. They do so in cooperation with local PLA units and the People's Armed Police. Garrison commands are subordinate to local military districts, but they also receive instruction and advising from local party committees. Since the mid-2000s, garrison commands have been established in almost all major cities, after the CCP decided that enhancing the role of garrison commands would be an objective for the immediate future. The plan is to increase the responsibility of garrison commands to include commanding local PLA units and providing a defense reserve force. Garrison commands work to resolve disputes and legal cases involving PLA units, provide a link between the PLA and civilians, and act as the working bodies of local party committees' military departments. Hu Jintao's leadership has acknowledged that garrison commands are an important armed force to promote "a harmonious society,"[16] precisely because of their role mediating between civilians and PLA units and their administration and discipline of PLA units, but also because of their role facilitating "the development of uniting the army with the people,"[17] a new initiative taken by Hu Jintao to blaze a path of development with Chinese characteristics and featuring military and civilian integration.

China's intelligence organizations in the post-Mao era have become indispensible for the regime in supporting its pursuit of industrialization and modernization. Although military intelligence agencies such as the Second and Third Departments of the General Staff Department of the PLA have been crucial for gathering domestic and foreign intelligence, the mission of the central government's largest security agency, the Ministry of State Security (MSS), is to protect national interests and to guarantee CCP dominance by using human, signal, remote, electronic, and communications intelligence in its myriad operations. The MSS is responsible for a wide range of missions, including political espionage, pursuit of economic interests, and technological intelligence. The MSS carries out intelligence, counterintelligence, counterterrorism, economic crime

---

[16] *Renmin ribao* [People's daily], February 20, 2005.
[17] *Jiefangjun bao* [The PLA daily], August 4, 2009.

investigation, electronic intelligence, border control, and "social monitoring" (e.g., watching dissidents and conducting Internet surveillance). Although the MSS assigns agents to serve in Chinese embassies or consulates abroad, it favors nonprofessional intelligence agents, such as travelers, executives, and academics. It places a special emphasis on overseas Chinese students and Chinese high-tech professionals working abroad who may have access to sensitive technological material. The agents of the MSS are responsible for surveillance of foreigners conducting business, tourists, diplomats, local staff employed at embassies and foreign companies, ordinary Chinese citizens who have had contact with foreigners, and all of these targets' relatives abroad. Other tasks include collecting intelligence on Chinese citizens in China or abroad and on sensitive political events that touch on China's national interests. Thus, the MSS has played an important role in collecting intelligence related to foreign countries and leaders. Although civilian and military security agencies have different functions depending on their specialties and focuses, they often cooperate and share resources with each other. However, because responsibilities sometimes overlap, competition between the two does exist, which creates challenges and inefficiencies for the entire intelligence apparatus.

Interpretation of Perspectives and Patterns

This study has sought to provide comprehensive research on China's security and intelligence agencies from a historical perspective, and its central focus is to investigate the role that the security and intelligence apparatuses have played in Chinese politics by providing new evidence and offering alternative interpretations to consequential events throughout CCP history. From the security and intelligence perspectives, it specifies some of the broader implications for theory and research that enhance our understanding of the nature and dynamics of Chinese elite politics.

Contemporary Chinese security and intelligence agencies have deep roots in the violent organizations during the early communist movement that engaged in operations to suppress political enemies and that were instrumental in crushing "counterrevolutionaries" and dissidents. However, China has never developed a Cheka-like secret police, and terror has never been systematically used on the entire population, as with the Soviet security organizations. Overall, the application of violence in elite politics has been much more cautious than with China's Soviet counterparts. Compared with Soviet communists, the CCP leadership has placed more emphasis on collective responsibilities. In 1927, the CCP established the Central Supervision Commission to discipline members and ensure the principle of collective leadership. Early CCP leaders were convinced that CCP members still needed to be supervised, even though they were the vanguards or representatives of proletariats (there was no mechanism in the Soviet-style communism for checks and balances because the Leninist dictatorship of the proletariat was turned into a dictatorship of the party) and represented the working class.[18] There was debate among party leaders over who supervises party members – the party bureaucracy or the masses – a debate that continued even after the PRC's founding. Although most leaders, particularly the frontline leaders, emphasized the role of party institutions in enforcing discipline in and supervision of individual party members, Mao insisted that the masses would be the most effective and fundamental instrument in maintaining the party spirit and morality against corruption and the abuse of power.

In the Mao era, the CCP exercised control primarily through a series of mass campaigns of indoctrination and rectification to ensure the dependability, efficiency, and effectiveness of the bureaucracy and to curb abuses of power and bureaucratic problems. Some of the larger campaigns were those against bureaucracy and commandism (1950 and 1953, respectively) and against waste and corruption (1951–1952),[19] as well as the Great Leap Forward (1958–1961), the Social Education campaign (1962–1966), and the Cultural Revolution (1966–1976). In the post-Mao era, the political system underwent a transition from rule by a monolithic charismatic leader to rule by a collective elite group in which rival factions cooperate out of necessity but compete for policy differences, power, and influence. The regime has relied on the mechanism of structural control to maintain the CCP's legitimacy among the populace, whereas mass campaigns are reserved for disciplining party bureaucracy and government officials. The CCP relies on internal mechanisms such as party control commissions, party and state coercive disciplinary and supervisory apparatuses, internal security forces, and intelligence agencies to fight corruption. These internal mechanisms are China's alternative to a democratically elected central government in which voters hold the power to accept or dismiss government and party authorities. Control mechanisms provide officials with incentives and sanctions to engender discipline and responsibility for the public good. Combined with the CCP's economic policies in the reform period, the CCP's management of domestic security and intelligence has assisted the party in gaining popular support and maintaining relative public order.

China's economic "miracle" in transforming itself from one of the world's poorest countries to one of the world's fastest-growing economies, and now the second-largest economy, has benefited greatly from a relatively stable, committed, and devoted leadership. However, leadership based on personal ties, factional identities, and personal charisma may not continually ensure political stability in the future because of the profound changes of Chinese society

[18] Zeng Chenggui, "Lun 1927 nian zhonggong zhongyang jiancha weiyuanhui de chuangli" [On the creation of the CCP Supervision Commission in 1927], in *Xuexi yu shijian* [Studies and practices], no. 12 (2008), pp. 5–9.
[19] Commandism means a dictatorial tendency that forces the masses to carry out orders and a deviation in the implementation stage of the mass line.

and China's integration into the world economy, unless the leaders in question transfer their authority to governmental institutions. As China has not yet fully institutionalized leadership authority, internally there is no guarantor of political legitimacy, which means that internal security and intelligence are key components of the regime's survival – having a monopoly on power is the only way the party-state can maintain its authority. Thus, political reform under CCP rule is concentrated on promoting intraparty checks and balances, which includes improving the system for institutionalized control over both civilian and army cadres and strengthening supervision and discipline.

Although the CCP elite do not face the pressures of democratic electoral politics, the checks and balances among the CCP's leadership reinforce the consensus-based decision-making process; strengthen institutional norms and procedures required of a stable government; and promote a culture of compromise and tolerance, especially among high-ranking officials. Since the 1980s, implemented checks and balances have contributed to cohesiveness of elite members and political stability and have facilitated the emergence of a group of dedicated leaders. In the post-Mao era, as part of the shift toward institutionalization, leaders have been careful to use fewer draconian measures as sanctions for not observing party dictates and Chinese law. Without the former tools of the intraparty power struggles, such as exile, impoverishment, imprisonment, and execution, checks are provided through other means to prevent officials from acting out of pure self-interest or from attempting to form a power monopoly that could lead to instability.

What is notable about the intraparty system of checks and balances is that it does not pose the risk of undermining the CCP's political monopoly. Operations are based on serving the interests of society, government, and the party by continuing to implement economic reforms and limited politic reforms. This internal watchdog system is likened to an intraparty "democracy," and it is intended to facilitate the expansion of personal freedoms and social mobility, institutional pluralism and freedom, greater legal independence, tolerance of limited public space, and the emergence of grassroots democratic participation and political activism. It is much more likely that China's political institutions will become more democratic than that an autocratic dictatorship will return. In summary, the future Chinese model of political rule will not be a Singapore-style democracy that combines benevolent government and autocracy. Nor will it be an illiberal Russian democracy, in which free elections occur against the backdrop of a compromised media, an underdeveloped party system, and few checks on the presidency. Nor will the future Chinese model emulate a Japanese democracy, characterized by a strong state bureaucracy with a weak prime minister and a general lack of political competition. Although Taiwan went through a remarkably smooth and peaceful democratic transition, China will by no means replicate that struggle for accountability among political officials, in which party politics created a zero-sum game for both the ruling and the opposition parties.

With a long economic boom, social stratification, political decentralization, and the rise of the middle class, most Western scholars would be optimistic about China moving in the direction of Western-style democracy. However, although China refuses an American-style liberal democracy or Western European-style social democracy, it may fashion a system of selective democratic governance to suit its own situation – that is, a democracy with Chinese characteristics, which would emphasize community welfare over individual rights and that is neither fully democratic nor completely repressive. The CCP refuses to adopt multiparty democracy and adheres to a "democracy" based on the absolute CCP rule with the cooperation of other parties.[20] One can expect that the party's monopoly on power might be upheld for a rather long time (although increasing pressure on the regime to push political reform and pluralism has been evident). To maintain social stability and to ensure the dominance of the party, the regime has never hesitated to rely on state-sanctioned repression and sometimes human rights violations against political dissidents, ethnic separatists, and angry demonstrators, even though there is a significant decline in the frequency and severity of political repression compared with that under Mao. To reduce any instability from any source, the CCP also openly censors the free flow of information and tolerates political and judicial corruption.

Despite CCP's adherence to its absolute leadership over the state, societal pressures from the increasing middle class and a silent yet steadily growing civil society movement push the CCP to engage in political reform. There is an increasing tendency for intraparty democracy that focuses on the limited institutionalized checks and balances within the party. First, a mechanism of checks and balances is created with respect to competition among political factions that represent the interests of different socioeconomic classes and geographical regions. The intraparty democracy also means an enhanced institutionalized process of accountability and transparency, such as the mandatory retirement of high-ranking leaders and merit-based promotion, through which intraelite competition based on the principles of fairness and equality could be guaranteed. China has successfully built close diplomatic and economic relations with a wide range of countries in the developing world, and its public image in many of those countries is currently far more positive than that of other major powers. Although the regime shows a strong stand toward national security, territorial integrity, and protecting access to resources and markets, the CCP has been confident as its ruling elite have expanded efforts to emphasize social cohesion and fair distribution of wealth, in addition to their focus on socioeconomic development and growth of the gross domestic product. The CCP will remain economically liberal but with limited political liberalization.

---

[20] *Renmin ribao*, Ocrober 20, 2010.

Although China faces a large number of external challenges, such as a shaky global economy; external pressures from human rights groups; increasing complaints and conflicts regarding its currency, trade, and foreign investment policies; and territorial and maritime disputes with Japan and in the South China Sea, China's concerns are primarily domestic. In March 2011, the National People's Congress (NPC) approved a 624.4 billion yuan (US$95 billion) budget for China's effort to maintain sociopolitical stability, a 13.8 percent increase over the 2010 budget, surpassing for the first time the expenditures of the PLA.[21] The large budget combined with the tremendous efforts of the CCP enables the party to maintain very large, complex, and strong security and intelligence apparatuses. Also, it strengthens the party's coercive organs of control not only in dealing with turbulent times of domestic unrest and taking over China in the case of a crisis but also in offering more sophisticated controls over the party elite to ensure their unconditional support and cohesion among the leadership. Also supporting this idea is the fact that the military and civilian domestic security functions are interwoven in complicated ways that are different from those of most regimes – for example, the People's Armed Police reports to both the State Council and the Central Military Commission; garrison commands (which are military units) liaise with local civilian authorities, run the local militia, and hold ultimate responsibility for local security and backup; and security for the party leadership is provided by a specialized unit, the Central Guard Regiment, which is a military unit but reports directly to a central general office. Although the institutionalized formal norms and laws are established to monitor the use and abuse of power by elites, the powerful party commissions, such as the Central Discipline Inspection Commission and the Central Political and Legal Commission, supervise party cadres and impose disciplinary sanctions and legal penalties on offenders. Thus, the complex and costly internal security and intelligence system, combined with a network of pervasive and powerful supervision and disciplinary organizations, is able not only to keep the CCP in power but also to help the CCP continue its route toward socialism with Chinese characteristics.

[21] Willy Lam, "'Wei-Wen' Imperative Steals the Thunder," in *Asia Times*, March 12, 2011.

Bibliography

Adelman, R. Jonathan. "Soviet Secret Police," in Jonathan Adelman, ed., *Terror and Communist Politics: The Role of the Secret Police in Communist States*, Boulder, CO: Westview Press, 1984.

Andrew, Christopher M., and Vasili Mitrokhin. *The World Was Going Our Way: The KGB and Battle for the Third World*, New York: Basic Books, 2005.

Apter, David Ernest, and Tony Saich. *Revolutionary Discourse in Mao's Republic*, Cambridge, MA: Harvard University Press, 1994.

Averill, Stephen. "The Origin of the Futian Incident," in Hans Van De Ven, ed., *New Perspectives on the Chinese Communist Revolution*, Armonk, NY: M. E. Sharpe, 1995, pp. 79–115.

Bachman, David M. *Bureaucracy, Economy, and Leadership in China: The Institutional Origins of the Great Leap Forward*, New York: Cambridge University Press, 1991.

Bai Jianjun. "Cong zhongguo fanzuilu shuju kan zuiyin, zuixing, yu xingfa de guanxi" [Relations among the sources of offenses, crime, and punishment from the data of China's crime rate], *Zhongguo shehui kexue* [Chinese social science], no. 2, 2010, pp. 144–59.

Bakken, Børge Bakken. "State Capacity and Social Control in China," in Kjeld Erik Brødsgaard and Susan Young, eds., *State Capacity in East Asia: Japan, Taiwan, China, and Vietnam*, New York: Oxford University Press, 2000, pp. 185–202.

Baum, Richard. *Burying Mao: Chinese Politics in the Age of Deng Xiaoping*, Princeton, NJ: Princeton University Press, 1996.

Beijing dang'an ju. *Zhongguo gongchandang Beijing shi zuzhi shi ziliao, 1921–1987* [Materials of organizational history of the CCP Beijing Municipal City, 1921–1987], Beijing: Renmin chubanshe, 1992.

Beijing Military Region Document, no. 58 (2006).

Beijing shi difang zhi bianzuan weiyuanhui [Compiling commission of local annals of Beijing municipal city]. *Beijing zhi, junshi juan, junshi zhi* [Military annals, volume of military, annals of Beijing], Beijing: Beijing chubanshe, 2002.

Blasko, Dennis J. *The Chinese Army Today: Tradition and Transformation for the 21st Century*, New York: Routledge, 2006.

———. "A New PLA Force Structure," in James C. Mulvenon and Richard H. Yang, eds., *The People's Liberation Army in the Information Age*, Santa Monica, CA: RAND, 1999, pp. 258–89.

Bo Yibo. *Ruogan zhongda juece yu shijian de huigu* [Reflections on certain major decisions and events], vol. 2, Beijing: Zhonggong zhongyang dangxiao chubanshe, 1993.

Braun, Otto (Li, De). *Zhongguo jishi* [A Comintern agent in China], trans. Li Kuiliu et al., Beijing: Dongfang chubanshe, 2004.

Brugger, Bill, and Stephen Reglar. *Politics, Economy and Society in Contemporary China*, Stanford, CA: Stanford University Press, 1994.

Bush, Richard C. *The Perils of Proximity: China-Japan Security Relations*, Washington DC: Brookings Institution Press, 2010.

Byron, John, and Robert Pack. *The Claws of the Dragon: Kang Sheng – the Evil Genius behind Mao and His Legacy of Terror in People's China*, Touchstone Books, 1993.

Cai Mingzhong. "Liu Chuanxin, wei 'siren bang' xunzang de gong'an juzhang" [Liu Chuanxin – Director of bureau of public security who sacrificed his life for the 'Gang of Four'], *Yanhuang chunqiu* [Spring and autumn in China], no. 1, 1994, pp. 80–9.

Center for Chinese Research Materials. *Hongweibing ziliao, xubian 2* [Red Guard publications, supplement 2], vol. 8, Oakton, VA: Center for Chinese Research Materials, 1992.

———. *Teng Hsiao-p'ing fan-tung yen-hsing hui-pien* [Collection of excerpts of reactionary words and deeds of Deng Xiaoping], Oakton, VA: Center for Chinese Research Materials, 1990.

Chen Changjiang. *Mao Zedong zuihou shinian: jingwei duizhang de huiyi* [Mao Zedong's last ten years: Recollection of the head of security guards], Beijing: Zhongyang dangxiao chubanshe, 1998.

Chen Donglin. "Xiaoyan miman de xibu kaifa – Liushi niandai sanxian jianshe juece shimo" [Gunsmoke clouded the air over the opening of the west – The beginning and end of decision making about construction of the "three fronts" project during the 1960s], *Dangshi bolan* [General review of CCP history], no. 1, 2001, pp. 4–10, no. 2, 2001, pp. 22–6.

Chen Donglong. "Zhongguo fan qingbao wang" [Chinese counterintelligence network], in *NowNews*, January 18, 2004.

Chen Hong. "Yang Chengwu yanzhong de 'Yang, Yu, Fu' shijian" ["The Yang, Yu, Fu affairs" in the eyes of Yang Chengwu], *Yanhuang chunqiu*, no. 6, 2000, pp. 6–13.

Chen Jianfu. "Legal Institutions in the People's Republic of China," in Jianfu Chen, Yuwen Li, and Jan Michiel Otto, eds., *Implementation of Law in the People's Republic of China*, The Hague, The Netherlands: Kluwer Law International, 2002, pp. 307–21.

Chen Peixian. *Chen Peixian huiyilu – Zai 'yiyue fengbao' de zhongxin'* [Memoirs of Chen Peixian – At the center of the "January storm"], Shanghai: Shanghai renmin chubanshe, 2005.

Chen Xianrui. "Pi Chen pi Lin qijian de Beijing junqu" [Beijing Military Region during the period of criticizing Chen Boda and Lin Biao], *Bai nian chao*, no. 5, 2000, pp. 42–9.

————. "Liao Hansheng, Yang Yong beizhua yu sowei 'huabei shangtao zhuyi' wenti" [Liao Hansheng and Yang Yong's arrest and the issue of the so-called Northern China factionalism], *Bai nian chao*, no. 4, 2000, pp. 19–24.

Chen Xiaojin. *"Wenge" suiyue* [The years of my life in the "Cultural Revolution"], Beijing: Zhongyang wenxian chubanshe, 2009.

Chen Xiaonong. *Chen Boda: Zuihou koushu huiyi* [Chen Boda: Last reminiscence based on an account in Chen Boda's own words], Hong Kong: Sun Global Publishing Hong Kong Limited, 2005.

Chen Xilian. *Chen Xilian huiyilu* [Memoirs of Chen Xilian], Beijing: Jiefangjun chubanshe, 2004.

Chen Xingeng. *Chise beiju* [Red tragedy], Hong Kong: Shidai guoji chuban youxian gongsi, 2005.

Chen Zhaohong. "Jiancha jiguan paizhu lingdao tizhi gaige de sikao" [Thoughts on the reform of organizational system in the CDIC/MOS dispatched groups], Xin xi bu [New west], no. 3, 2007, pp. 60–1.

Chen Zhengren. "Huiyi Luofang huiyi" [Recollect Luofang conference], in Zhonggong Jiangxi sheng dangshi yanjiushi, ed., *Jiangxi dangshi ziliao* [Materials of Jiangxi party history], 6 (1988), pp. 258–63.

Cheng Yi. "Yuan Shu de qingbao shengya" [Intelligence career of Yuan Shu], *Dangshi tiandi* [Field of party history], no. 11, 2004, pp. 36–44.

Cheung, Tai Ming. "Guarding China's Domestic Front Line: The People's Armed Police and China's Stability," CQ, 146 (June 1996), pp. 525–47.

————. "The Influence of the Gun: China's Central Military Commission and Its Relationship with the Military, Party, and State Decision-Making Systems," in David M. Lampton, ed., *The Making of Chinese Foreign and Security Policy in the Era of Reform, 1978–2000*, Stanford, CA: Stanford University Press, 2001, pp. 61–90.

Clark, William A. *Crime and Punishment in Soviet Officialdom: Combating Corruption in the Political Elite, 1965–1990*, Armonk, NY: M. E. Sharpe, 1993.

Dai Anlin. "Futian shibian yu suqu sufan" [Futian Incident and suppression against counterrevolutionaries in the Soviet base areas], *Xiang chao* [Hunan tide], no. 6, 2007, pp. 26–30.

Dai Xiangqing. "Lun AB tuan he Futian shibian" [Comment on the AB Corps and Futian Incident], *Zhonggong dangshi yanjiu* [Research of CCP party history], no. 2, 1989, pp. 22–7.

Dai Xiangqing and Luo Huilan. *AB tuan yu Futian shibian* [AB Corps and Futian Incident], Zhengzhou: Henan renmin chubanshe, 1994.

Dammer, Harry R., and Jay Albanese. *Comparative Criminal Justice Systems*, 4th ed., Belmont, CA: Wadsworth, 2011.

"Dangdai zhongguo" congshu bianji weiyuanhui. *Zhongguo renmin jiefangjun* [The People's Liberation Army], 2 vols., Beijing: Dangdai zhongguo chubanshe, 1994.

"Dangdai zhongguo renwu zhuanji" congshu bianjibu (ed.). *He Long zhuan* [A biography of He Long], Beijing: Dangdai zhongguo chubanshe, 1993.

————. *Chen Yi zhuan* [A biography of Chen Yi], Beijing: Dangdai zhongguo chubanshe, 1991.

————. *Luo Ronghuan zhuan* [A biography of Luo Ronghuan], Beijing: Dangdai zhongguo chubanshe, 1995.

_____. *Peng Dehuai zhuan* [A biography of Peng Dehuai], Beijing: Dangdai zhongguo chubanshe, 1993.

_____. *Ye Jianying zhuan* [A biography of Ye Jianying], Beijing: Dangdai zhongguo chubanshe, 1995.

Dangguan De Bary, Wm. Theodore. *Sources of East Asian Tradition: The Modern Period*, vol. 2, New York: Columbia Universwity Press, 2008.

Deng Liqun. *Wowei Shaoqi tongzhi jiangxie hua* [I would like to make a few words for comrade Shaoqi], Beijing: Dangdai zhongguo chubanshe, 1998.

[Deng] Maomao. *Wode fuqing Deng Xiaoping "wenge" suiyue* [My father Deng Xiaoping's "Cultural Revolution" years], Beijing: Zhongyang wenxian chubanshe, 2000.

Deng Xiaoping. *Selected Works of Deng Xiaoping*, Beijing: Foreign Languages Press, 1984.

_____. *Deng Xiaoping wenxuan* [Selected works of Deng Xiaoping], vol. 3, Beijing: Renmin chubanshe, 1993.

DeRouen, Karl, Jr., and Paul Bellamy. *International Security and the United States: An Encyclopedia*, Westport, CT: Greenwood Publishing Group, 2008.

Ding Ke. "Tegong–minyun–Falun Gong: Yige shengming de zhenshi gushi" [Secret agent – Democratic movement – Falun Gong: The true story of a life), in Zhao Ming et al., eds., *Hongchao huangyan lu* [Record of lies in a red dynasty], vol. 1, Sunnyvale, CA: Boda chubanshe, 2004, pp. 272–313.

Ding Qun. *Liu Shunyuan zhuan* [A biography of Liu Shunyuan], Nanjing: Jiangsu renmin chubanshe, 1999.

Ding Wang (ed.). *Zhonggong wenhua dageming ziliao huibian* [Compilation of materials published in the Cultural Revolution], Hong Kong: Mingbao yuekan chuban, vol. 1, 1967, vol. 5, 1970.

Dirlik, Arif. *The Origins of Chinese Communism*, New York: Oxford University Press, 1989.

Dittmer, Lowell. "Leadership Change and Chinese Political Development," *CQ*, 176, December 2003, pp. 903–25.

_____. *Liu Shaoqi and the Chinese Cultural Revolution*, rev. ed., New York: M. E. Sharpe, 1998.

"Dangguan wuzhuang yuanze yongfang guangmang – xiezai zhongguo gongchandang jiandang bashi zhounian zhiji" [The principle of Party's control over armed forces shines forth everywhere – writing on the time during the eighty-year birthday of the CCP], in *Zhongguo minbing* [Chinese militia], no. 7 (2001), pp. 4–9.

Dong Baocun and Pu Suanzi. "Huabei huiyi yu Beijing junqu da gaizu" [Northern China Conference and the great reorganization of Beijing Military Region], *Dangshi buolan* [General review of the Chinese Communist Party], no. 1, 2006, pp. 4–10, no. 2, 2006, pp. 30–41.

"Dong Biwu nianpu" bianji zu, *Dong Biwu nianpu* [Chronicle of Dong Biwu], Beijing: Zhongyang wenxian chubanshe, 1991.

'Dong Biwu zhuan' zhuanxie zu, *Dong Biwu zhuan* [A biography of Dong Biwu], vol. 2, Beijing: Zhongyang wenxian chubanshe, 2006,

Dong Yufeng. "Yichang fan faxisi shencha fangshi de douzheng" [A struggle against fascist-style forms of investigation], in Sun Mingshan, ed., *Lishi shunjian* [An instant in history], vol. 2, Beijing: Qunzhong chubanshe, 2001, pp. 453–61.

Dongfang He. *Zhang Aiping zhuan* [A biography of Zhang Aiping], Beijing: Renmin chubanshe, 2000.

Dongfang zaobao [Eastern Morning News], August 28, 2009.

Du Chao. "Diaocha Jiang Qing de ren – Xu Jianguo de beiju" [A person who investigated Jiang Qing – The tragedy of Xu Jianguo], *Wenshi jinghua* [Gems of literature and history], no. 8 (2007), pp. 32–9.

Eftimiades, Nicholas. *Chinese Intelligence Operations*, Annapolis, MD: U.S. Naval Institute Press, 1994.

Esherick, Joseph W. "Collapse of the Old Order, Germination of the New: Chinese Society during the Civil War, 1945–1949," in Werner Draguhn and David S. G. Goodman, eds., *China's Communist Revolutions: Fifty Years of the People's Republic of China*, London: RoutledgeCurzon, 2002, pp. 23–49.

Fan Shuo. *Ye Jianying zai yijiu qiliu nian* [Ye Jianying in 1976], rev. ed., Beijing: Zhongyang dangxiao chubanshe, 1995.

Fei Yundong and Yu Kuihua. *Zhonggong mishu gongzuo jianshi, 1921–1949* [Brief history of the work of the CCP secretary, 1921–1949], Shenyang: Liaoning renmin chubanshe, 1992.

Feng Lizhong. "Wosuo zhidaode 8341 budui" [What I know about Unit 8341], *Baixing shenghuo* [Ordinary people's life], no. 7, 2009, pp. 53–4.

Fewsmith, Joseph. *Elite Politics in Contemporary China*, Armonk, NY: M. E. Sharpe, 2001.

———. "The New Shape of Elite Politics," *China Journal*, no. 45 (January 2001), pp. 83–93.

———. "The Sixteenth Party Congress: Implications for Understanding Chinese Politics," *China Leadership Monitor*, 5 (Winter 2003), pp. 43–53.

Finkelstein, David M. "China's National Military Strategy," in James C. Mulvenon, ed., *The People's Liberation Army in the Information Age*, Santa Monica, CA: RAND 1999, pp. 99–145.

———. "The General Staff Department of the Chinese People's Liberation Army: Organization, Roles, & Missions," in James C. Mulvenon and Andrew N. D. Yang, eds., *The People's Liberation Army as Organization: Reference Volume v1.0*, Santa Monica, CA: RAND, 2002, pp. 122–4.

Fisher, Richard D. *China's Military Modernization: Building for Regional and Global Reach*, Westport, CT: Greenwood Publishing Group, 2008.

———. "Unconventional Warfare Options," in Steve Tsang, ed., *If China Attacks Taiwan: Military Strategy, Politics and Economics*, New York: Routledge, 2006, pp. 60–79.

Forster, Keith. "Localism, Central Policy, and the Provincial Purges of 1957–1958: The Case of Zhejiang," in Timothy Cheek and Tony Saich, eds., *New Perspectives on State Socialism in China*, Armonk, NY: M. E. Sharpe, 1997, pp. 191–233.

Frazier, Mark W. *Socialist Insecurity: Pensions and the Politics of Uneven Development in China*, Ithaca, NY: Cornell University, 2010.

Fu Chongbi. *Fu Chongbi huiyilu* [Memoirs of Fu Chongbi], Beijing: Zhonggong dangshi chubanshe, 1999.

Gao, C., Chiu, B., Tsai, H., and Su, Y. *Zhongguo renmin wuzhuang jingcha de jiegou* [An analysis of the Chinese People's Armed Police], Taipei, Taiwan: Yang-Chih Book Co., 2003.

Gao Hua. *Hong taiyang shi zenyang shengqi de – Yan'an zhengfeng de lailong qumai* [How did the sun rise over Yan'an? A history of the rectification movement], Hong Kong: Chinese University of Hong Kong, 2000.

Gao Wenqian. *Wannian Zhou Enlai* [Zhou Enlai's later years], New York: Mirror Books, 2003.

Garver, John W. *Chinese-Soviet Relations, 1937–1945: The Diplomacy of Chinese Nationalism*, New York: Oxford University Press, 1988.

Gilley, Bruce. *China's Democratic Future: How It Will Happen and Where It Will Lead*, New York: Columbia University Press, 2004.

_____. *Tiger on the Brink: Jiang Zemin and China's New Elite*, Berkeley and Los Angeles: University of California Press, 1998.

Gittings, John. *The Role of the Chinese Army*, London: Oxford University Press, 1967.

Godwin, Paul H. B. "Party-Military Relations," in Merle Goldman, ed., *The Paradox of China's Post-Mao Reforms*, Cambridge, MA: Harvard University Press, 1999, pp. 76–99.

_____. "The PLA Faces the Twenty-First Century: Reflections on Technology, Doctrine, Strategy, and Operations," in James R. Lilley and David Shambaugh, eds., *China's Military Faces the Future*, Armonk, NY: M. E. Sharpe, 1999, pp. 39–63.

Gong Chu. *Gong Chu jiangjun huiyilu* [Memoirs of General Gong Chu], Hong Kong: Mingbao yuekanshe, 1978.

Graff, David, and Robin Higham. *A Military History of China*, Boulder, CO: Westview Press, 2002.

Greene, Jack R. *The Encyclopedia of Police Science*, vol. 1, New York: Routledge, 2007.

Gregory, Paul R. *Terror by Quota: State Security from Lenin to Stalin; An Archival Study*, New Haven, CT: Yale University Press, 2009.

Griffin, Patricia E. *The Chinese Communist Treatment of Counterrevolutionaries: 1924–1949*, Princeton, NJ: Princeton University Press, 1976.

Guan Gengyin. *Shen Pan* [Trial], Shanghai: Wenhui chubanshe, 2005.

Guangzhou shi difang zhi bianzuan weiyuanhui [Compiling Commission of the Local History and Annals of Guangzhou City], *Guangzhou shizhi: junshi juan* [Annals of Guangzhou city: Military annals], vol. 13, Guangzhou: Guangzhou chubanshe, 1995.

"Guanyu tiaozheng zhongguo renmin wuzhuang jingcha budui lingdao guanli tizhi de jueding" [Decision about adjusting the PAP's leadership system of administration], in Guowuyuan, zhongyang junweihui wenjian [State Council and the CMC Document], no. 5, 1995, http://www.zxtlaw.com/indexd/indexd497.htm (accessed August 15, 2009).

Guo Hongtao. *Guo Hongtao huiyilu* [Memoirs of Guo Hongtao], Beijing: Zhonggong dangshi chubanshe, 2004.

Guo Ruihua, *Zhonggong duitai gongzuo zuzhi tixi kailun* [Outline of the organization system of CCP work toward Taiwan], Taipei: Fawubu diaochaju gongdang wenti yanjiu zhongxin, 2004).

Guo Xuezhi. "Dimensions of Guanxi in Chinese Elite Politics," *China Journal*, 42 (2001), pp. 69–90.

Han Huaizhi. *Dangdai zhongguo jundui de junshi gongzuo* [Contemporary Chinese Army's military work], vol. 2, Beijing: Zhongguo shehui kexue chubanshe, 1989.

Han Jingchun. "Tabian qingshan ren weilao – Ji yuan guojia minzhengbu fubuzhang Zhuo Xiong" [Crossing the blue hills adds nothing to one's years – A story about former Vice Minister of the Civil Affairs Zhuo Xiong], *Laoyou* [Old friends], no. 3, 2005, pp. 4–6.

Hao Zaijin. *Zhongguo mimi zhan – Zhonggong qingbao he baowei gongzuo jishi* [China's secret war – A true account of China's intelligence and security work], Hong Kong: Liwen chubanshe, 2006.

Harding, Harry. "The Chinese State in Crisis, 1966–9," in Roderick MacFarquhar, ed., *The Politics of China*, 2nd ed., New York: Cambridge University Press, 1997, pp. 148–247.

He Libo. "Xia Xi yu Xiang-e-xi suqu 'sufan'" [Xia Xi and the "suppression against counterrevolutionaries" in Hunan-Western Hubei Soviet base areas], *Wenshi jinghua*, no. 2 (2006), pp. 22–9.

He Ting (ed.). *Pan Yan jiangjun jinian wenji* [Collected works in commemorating General Pan Yan], Beijing: Haichao chubanshe, 2000.

He Tingyi. *Wo shouxi de lingxiu he jiangshuai* [The leaders and army generals with whom I am familiar], Beijing: Changzheng chubanshe, 1999.

Heinzig, Dieter. *The Soviet Union and Communist China, 1945–1950: The Arduous Road to the Alliance*, Armonk, NY: M. E. Sharpe, 2004.

Hu Lianhe, Hu Angang, and Wang Lei. "Yingxiang shehui wending de shehui maodun bianhua taishi de shizheng fenxi" [Empirical analysis of change and trend of social contradictions that affect social stability], in *Shehui kexue zhanxian* [Frontline of social science], 4 (2006), pp. 175–85.

Hu Wei. "Siren yiqu fengfan changcun – Shenqie huainian Shi Yizhi tongzhi" [His legacy lives on though he is gone – Deeply yearning for comrade Shi Yizhi], in Chen Feng, ed., *Xue yu huo de lilian – Shi Yizhi jinian wenji* [Tempered by blood and fire – Collected works commemorating Shi Yizhi], Beijing: Zhongguo wenhua yishu chubanshe, 2005.

Huang Huoqing. *Yige pingfan gongchan dangyuan de jingli* [The experience of an ordinary Communist Party member], Beijing: Renmin chubanshe, 2000.

Huang, Jing. *Factionalism in Chinese Communist Politics*, New York: Cambridge University Press, 2000.

Huang Kecheng. *Huang Kecheng zishu* [The autobiographical notes of Huang Kecheng], Beijing: Renmin chubanshe, 1994.

Huang Yao and Zhang Mingzhe. *Luo Ruiqing zhuan* [A biography of Luo Ruiqing], Beijing: Dangdai zhongguo chubanshe, 1996.

Huang Yifan. "Dongluan zhichu – Liu Zhijian zai 'wenge' chuqi de jingli he zaoyu" [Beginning of turbulence – Experience and lot of Liu Zhijian in the early of the "Cultural Revolution"], in Li Yong and Wen Lequn, eds., *'Wenhua da geming' fengyun renwu fangtan lu* [Collected interviews of the people of the moment in the "Cultural Revolution"], Beijing: Zhongyang minzhu xueyuan chubanshe, 1993, pp. 1–39.

Huang Zheng. *Wang Guangmei fangtan lu* [Interview with Wang Guangmei], Beijing: Zhongyang wenxian chubanshe, 2006.

Hubei sheng di fang zhi bian zuan weiyuanhui (ed.). *Hubeisheng zhi: Junshi* [Annals of Hubei Province: Military]. Wuhan: Hubei renmin chubanshe, 1996.

Jackson, Robert. *International Trotskyism, 1929–1985: A Documented Analysis of the Movement*, Durham, NC: Duke University Press, 1991.

Jackson, Robert, and Carl G. Rosberg. *Personal Rule in Black Africa: Prince, Autocrat, Prophet, Tyrant*, Berkeley: University of California Press, 1982.

Jan, George P. "The Military and Democracy in China," in Stuart S. Nagel, ed., *Handbook of Global Political Policy*, New York: CRC Press, 2000, pp. 211–30.

Ji Min. "Zhou Enlai chuli Taiwan wenti de zuihou zhutuo" [The last advice of Zhou Enlai for dealing with Taiwan issues], *Zongheng*, no. 1, 2002, pp. 9–12.

Jiang Feng et al. *Yang Yong jiangjun zhuan* [A biography of General Yang Yong], Beijing: Jiefangjun chubanshe, 1991.

Jin Chongji and Chen Qun. *Chen Yun zhuan* [A biography of Chen Yun], 2 vols. Beijing: Zhangyang wenxian chubanshe, 2005.

Joffe, Ellis. "The Chinese Army in Domestic Politics: Factors and Phases," in Li Nan, ed., *Chinese Civil-Military Relations: The Transformation of the People's Liberation Army*, New York: Routledge, 2006, pp. 8–24.

——. *Party and Army: Professionalism and Political Control in the Chinese Officer Corps, 1949–1964*, Cambridge, MA: Harvard University Press, 1971.

Jue Shi. "Zhou Enlai yu kangzhan chuqi de changjiang ju" [Zhou Enlai and the Yangtze Bureau in the early period of the Sino-Japanese War], *Zhonggong dangshi yanjiu* [Research of CCP history], no. 2, 1988, pp. 10–18.

Junshi kexueyuan junshi lishi yanjiusuo [Research Institute of Military History of the PLA Military Academy], *Zhonghua renmin gongheguo junshi shiyao* [Outline of PRC military history], Beijing: Junshi kexueyuan chubanshe, 2005.

Junshi kexueyuan junshi tushuguan [Military library of the CCP Military Academy]. *Zhongguo renmin jiefangjun zuzhi yange he geji lingdao chengyuan minglu* [The PLA organizational evolution and the list of leadership members at different levels], Beijing: Junshi kexue chubanshe, 1990.

Kang Sheng. "Chanchu rikou zhentan minzu gongdi de Trotskyist feitu" [Sweep away the Trotskyist bandits – the Japanese agents and the national public enemies], in *Jiefang* (Liberation), no. 29 (January 28, 1938) and no. 30 (February 8, 1938).

Kang Shijian. *Zhongguo renmin jiefangjun dangwei zhi* [The party committee system in the PLA], Beijing: Guofang daxue chubanshe, 1995.

Kenez, Peter. *A History of the Soviet Union from the Beginning to the End*, New York: Cambridge University Press, 1999.

Lam, Willy. "China Flaunts Growing Naval Capabilities," in *China Brief*, vol. 9, no. 1, January 12, 2009.

Lau, Siu-kai. "Pragmatic Calculations of National Interest: China's Hong Kong Policy, 1949–1997," in Suisheng Zhao, ed., *Chinese Foreign Policy: Pragmatism and Strategic Behavior*, Armonk, NY: M. E. Sharpe, 2004, pp. 91–106.

Lau, W. K. Raymond. "Sociopolitical Control in Urban China: Changes and Crisis," *British Journal of Sociology*, 52, no. 4 (December 2001), pp. 605–20.

Lee, Ching Kwan. "Pathways of Labor Activism," in Elizabeth J. Perry and Mark Selden, eds., *Chinese Society: Change, Conflict and Resistance*, 3rd ed., New York: Routledge, 2010, pp. 57–79.

Lee, Hong Yung. *From Revolutionary Cadres to Party Technocrats in Socialist China*, Berkeley and Los Angeles: University of California Press, 1991.

Leng Meng. *Baizhan jiangxing: zai Liu Bocheng, Deng Xiaoping, Xu Xiangqian huixia* [Star among the generals with hundred battles: Under the leadership of Liu

Bocheng, Deng Xiaoping, and Xu Xiangqian], Beijing: Jiefangjun wenyi chubanshe, 1997.

Lewis, John Wilson, and Litai Xue. *Imagined Enemies: China Prepares for Uncertain War*, Stanford, CA: Stanford University Press, 2006.

Li, Cheng. "The New Military Elite: Generational Profile and Contradictory Trends," in M. Finkelstein and Kristen Gunness, eds., *Civil-Military Relations in Today's China: Swimming in a New Sea*, Armonk, NY: M. E. Sharpe, 2007, pp. 48–73.

Li, Cheng, and Lynn White. "The Sixteenth Central Committee of the Chinese Communist Party: *Hu Gets What?*" in *Asian Survey*, 43, no. 4 (July–August 2003), pp. 553–97.

Li Desheng. *Li Desheng huiyilu* [Memoirs of Li Desheng], Beijing: Jiefangjun chubanshe, 1999.

Li Dingyuan. "Kaiguo shangjiang renmin gongchen" [The colonel general who is one of China's founding fathers], in *Chaohu chenkan* [Chaohu morning journal], 3 parts, September 7, 2009 (part 1), September 14, 2009 (part 2), September 21, 2009 (part 3).

Li Haiwen and Wang Yanling. *Shiji duihua – Yi xinzhongguo fazhi dianjiren Peng Zhen* [Centurial dialogue – Reminiscing the founder of the PRC law and legal systems Peng Zhen], Beijing: Qunzhong chubanshe, 2002.

Li Jiaji and Yang Qingwang. *Lingxiu shengbian shisan nian – Mao Zedong weishi Li Jiaji fangtan lu* [Thirteen years at the site of the leader – Interview with Mao Zedong's guard Li Jiaji], vol. 1, Beijing: Zhongyang wenxian chubanshe, 2007.

Li Jianjun and Ji Hongjian. "Shenmi de '8341'" [Mysterious "8341"], in *Junshi lishi* [Military History], no. 3 (2004), pp. 53–4.

Li Jianming. "Lun dang lingdao xiaode sifa duli" [On legal independence under the leadership of the Party], in *Zhengzhi yu falu* [Political science and law], no. 2 (2003), pp. 33–41.

Li Jing. *Rujiang Xiao Hua* [Scholarly General Xiao Hua], Beijing: Jiefangjun wenyi chubanshe, 1998.

Li Jinming. "He Long fennu zhizhi jizhong 'sutuo'" [He Long indignantly stopped the I campaign "suppressing Trotskysts" in the central Hebei], in *Laonian shibao* [Senior times], April 11, 2008.

Li Junting and Yang Jinhe. *Zhongguo wuzhuang liliang tonglan, 1949–1989* [Overall elucidation of China's armed forces, 1949–1989], Beijing: Renmin chubanshe, 1992.

Li Laizhu. *Zhu: Wode rensheng lu* [Refining: The road of my life], Beijing: Zhongyang wenxian chubanshe, 2002.

Li Ming. "Shuli zhengfa wei" [Sorting out the CCP Political and Legal Commission], *Zhongguo xinwen zhoukan* [Chinese news weekly], no. 20, 2010, p. 13.

Li Rui. *Lushan huiyi shilu* [True record of the Lushan plenum], Zhengzhou: Henan renmin chubanshe, 1995.

Li Wei. "The Security Service for Chinese Central Leaders," in *The China Quarterly*, no. 143 (September 1995), pp. 814–27.

Li Weihan. *Huiyi yu yanjiu* (Recollection and Research), vol. 1, Beijing: Zhonggong dangshi ziliao chubanshe, 1986.

Li Wenqing. *Jinkan Xu Shiyou,1967–1985* [A close observation on Xu Shiyou, 1967–1985], Beijing: Jiefangjun wenyi chubanshe, 2002.

Li Xuefeng. "Wo suo zhidao de 'wenge' fadong neiqing" [The inside story that I know about how the "Cultural Revolution" was launched], in Zhang Hua and Su Caiqing, eds., *Huishou "wenge"* [Recollection of the "Cultural Revolution"], vol. 2, Beijing: Zhonggong dangshi chubanshe, 2000, pp. 603–16.

Li Yanke, Li Jianjun, and Ji Hongjian. "Jinlu xiongfeng – Jiefangjun mou jingweishi de fazhan yange ji zhandou licheng" [Awe-inspiring crack force: The revolution and combat course of a guard division of the PLA]. *Junshi lishi* [Military history], no. 1, 2006, pp. 60–3.

Li Yimeng. *Li Yimeng huiyilu* [Memoirs of Li Yimeng], Beijing: Remin chubanshe, 2001.

Li Yimin. *Li Yimin huiyilu* [Memoirs of Li Yimin], Changsha: Hunan renmin chubanshe, 1986.

Li Yu. "Fendou de zongzhi – xin zhongguo jianyu de wushi si nian" [Pursued objective – Fifty-four years in new China's prisons], in *Fazhi ribao* [Legal system daily], December, 28, 2003.

Li Zhimin. *Li Zhimin huiyilu* [Memoirs of Li Zhimin], Beijing: Jiefangjun chubanshe, 1993.

Li Zhisui. *Mao Zedong siren yisheng huiyilu* [Memoirs of Mao Zedong's private doctor], Taipei: Shibao wenhua chuban qiye gufen youxian gongsi, 1994.

Liang Bing. *He Zhengwen jiangjun* [General He Zhengwen], Beijing: Zuojia chubanshe, 2004.

Liang Qi. "Dangqian chaban shehei 'baohu san' zhiwu fanzui anjian de nandian ji duice" [Difficulties and strategies for current initiatives in investigating job-related crimes that involve the "protecting umbrella" for underground societies], *Renmin jiancha* [People's procuratorate], no. 7, 2003, pp. 34–7.

Liao Hansheng. *Liao Hansheng huiyilu* [Memoirs of Liao Hansheng], Beijing: Jiefangjun chubanshe, 2003.

Lieberthal, Kenneth. "The Great Leap Forward and the Split in the Yan'an Leadership," in Roderick MacFarquhar, ed., *The Politics of China: The Eras of Mao and Deng*, New York: Cambridge University Press, 1997, pp. 87–147.

Liebman, Benjamin L. "China's Courts: Restricted Reform," in Donald C. Clarke, ed., *China's Legal System: New Developments, New Challenges*, New York: Cambridge University Press, 2008.

Lin Jiajie. "Wenge zhong de Beijing weishuqu silingyuan Wu Zhong" [Commander Wu Zhong of Beijing Garrison Command in the Cultural Revolution], *Sichuan dangshi* [Party history of Sichuan], no. 4, 1994, pp. 19–22.

Ling Yun. "Kang Sheng weihe zhizao 'mousha Su Mei an'" [Why did Kang Sheng create the case of "Murdering Su Mei"], in Sun Mingshan, ed., *Lishi shunjian* [An instant in history], pp. 90–105.

"Lishi de shenpan" bianjizu. *Lishi de shenpan, xuji* [Historical Trial, sequel], Beijing: Qunzhong chubanshe, 1986.

Liu Guangren, Zhao Yimin, and Yu Xingqiang. *Feng Jiping zhuan: Jingdu gong'an juzhang* [A biography of Feng Jiping: Director of bureau of public security in the capital], Beijing: Qunzhong chubanshe, 1997.

Liu Han and Huang Yao. *Luo Ruiqing zhuan* [A biography of Luo Ruiqing], Beijing: Dangdai zhongguo chubanshe, 1995.

Liu Huaqing. *Liu Huaqing huiyilu* [Memoirs of Liu Huaqing], Beijing: Jiefangjun chubanshe, 2004.

Liu Xiaonong. "Er-yu-wan suqu – Baiqueyuan sufan" [The Hubei-Henan-Anhui base area – Suppression of counterrevolutionaries in Baiqueyuan], *Wenshi jinghua*, no. 1, 2006, pp. 19–28.

Liu Xingyi. *Yang Qiqing zhuan* [A biography of Yang Qiqing], Beijing: Qunzhong chubanshe, 2006.

Liu Ying. *Liu Ying zishu* [The autobiographical notes of Liu Ying], Beijing: Renmin chubanshe, 2005.

Liu Yong. "Zhongguo qingbao shi shang de 'wuchong jiandie'" [The "pentahedral agent" in Chinese intelligence history], *Lianzheng liaowang* [Honesty outlook], no. 2, 2005, pp. 52–3.

Liu Yuan and He Jiadong. "'Siqing' yituan" [Doubt about the "Four Clean-up" campaign], in Wang Guangmei and Liu Yuan, ed., *Nisuo bu zhidao de Liu Shaoqi* [Liu Shaoqi whom you don't know], pp. 88–124.

Liu Zhe. "Li Zongren huiguo de lingyi lishi jianzheng ren" [Another historical witness for Li Zongren's return to China], *Wenshi chunqiu*, no. 4, 2001, pp. 58–60.

Liu Zhende. "Jiyao mishu de huiyi" [Recollections of a confidential secretary], in Huang Zheng, ed., *Liu Shaoqi de zuihou suiyue* [The last years of Liu Shaoqi], Beijing: Zhongyang wenxian chubanshe, 2006, pp. 61–125.

Lo, Carlos Wing-hung. *China's Legal Awakening: Legal Theory and Criminal Justice in Deng's Era*, Hong Kong: Hong Kong University Press, 1995.

Lu Xueyi, (ed.). *Beijing shehui jianshe liushi nian* [Sixty years of Beijing social construction], Beijing: Kexue chubanshe, 2008.

Lu Zhengcao. *Lu Zhengcao huiyilu* [Memoirs of Lu Zhengcao], Beijing: Jiefangjun chubanshe, 2007.

Lujun di sanshiba jun [The Thirty-Eighth Army Corps of the PLA], *Lujun di sanshiba jun junshi* [The military history of the Thirty-Eighth Army Corps], Beijing: Jiefangjun wenyi chubanshe, 1993.

[Luo] Diandian. *Hongse jiachu dang'an* [Archives of red families], Haikou: Nanfang chuban gongsi, 1999.

——. *Feifan de niandai* [Those extraordinary years], Shanghai: Jiefangjun chubanshe, 1987.

Luo Gan. "Zhengfa jiguan zai goujian hexie shehui zhong danfu zhongda lishi shiming de zhengzhi zeren" [Political and law organizations undertake political responsibilities of historical importance in constructing a harmonious society]. *Qiushi* [Truth seeking] (March 2007), pp. 3–10.

Ma Licheng. "Liu Suola songwo 'Liu Zhidan'" [Liu Suola sent me the book of "Liu Zhidan"], *Zhongwai wenzhai* [China and foreign digest], no. 15, 2010, pp. 38–9.

Ma Shexiang. "Mao Zedong zai Shaoshan 'Dishui dong'" [Mao Zedong at the "Dishui Hole" of Shaozhan], *Hubei wenshi* [Hubei literature and history], 4 (2000), pp. 1–14.

MacFarquhar, Roderick, John Fairbank, and Denis Twitchett. *The Cambridge History of China: The People's Republic, Part 2: Revolutions within the Chinese Revolution, 1966–1982*, New York: Cambridge University Press, 1991.

——. *The Origins of the Cultural Revolution: The Coming of the Cataclysm 1961–1966*. New York: Columbia University Press, 1999.

Mao Taiquan et al. *Guofang buzhang chenfu ji* [The ups and downs of a defense minister], Beijing: Jiefangjun wenyi chubanshe, 1997.

Mao Zedong. *Mao Zedong wenji* [Collected works of Mao Zedong], Beijing: Renmin chubanshe, vol. 2, 1993, vol. 7, 1999.

————. *Jianguo yilai Mao Zedong wengao* [Mao Zedong's manuscripts since the founding of the state], 13 vols., Internal Publication, Beijing: Zhongyang wenxian chubanshe, 1987–98.

————. "Zong qianwei dabian de yi fengxin (12/20/1930)" [A letter General Front Committee replies for the charges, December 20, 1930), in Zhongguo renmin jiefangjun zhengzhi xueyuan, ed., *Zhonggong dangshi jiaoxue cankao ziliao* [Reference materials of the CCP party history education], 14, pp. 634–7.

Meisner, Maurice. *Mao's China and After: A History of the People's Republic*, 3rd ed., New York: Free Press, 1999.

Miller, L. Alice. "Institutionalization and the Changing Dynamics of Chinese Leadership Politics," in Cheng Li, ed., *China's Changing Political Landscape: Prospects for Democracy*, Washington, DC: Brookings Institution Press, 2008, pp. 61–79.

Ming Jin and Shi Hui. "Dongluan zhongde 'mohe' – 'Wenhua dageming' zhongde Chen Xianrui jiangjun" ["Grinding" in turmoil – General Chen Xianrui in the "Cultural Revolution"], *Dangshi tiandi* [Field of party history], no. 6, 1995, pp. 10–14.

Moise, Edwin. *Tonkin Gulf and the Escalation of the Vietnam War*, Chapel Hill: University of North Carolina Press, 2004.

Möller, Kay. "Diplomatic Relations and Mutual Strategic Perceptions: China and the European Union," in Richard L. Edmonds, ed., *China and Europe since 1978: A European Perspective*, New York: Cambridge University Press, 2002, pp. 10–32.

Mu Fengyun. "Wode wenge shengya" [My life in the Cultural Revolution], in Sun Mingshan, ed., *Lishi shunjian* [an instant in history], vol. 2, Beijing: Qunzhong chubanshe, pp. 541–63.

————. "Zoujin yinbi zhanxian" [Getting close to the underground front], in Zhu Chunlin, ed., *Lishi shunjian* [An instant in history], Beijing: Qunzhong chubanshe, 1999, pp. 387–97.

Mu Xin. *Chen Geng tongzhi zai Shanghai: Zai zhongyang teke de douzheng jingli* [Comrade Chen Geng in Shanghai: Battle experience in the central committee's Special Services Division], Beijing: Wenshi ziliao chubanshe, 1980.

Mulvenon, James C. "Chinese C4I Modernization: An Experiment in Open-Source Analysis," in James C. Mulvenon and Andrew N. D. Yang, eds., *A Poverty of Riches: New Challenges and Opportunities in PLA Reresearch*, Santa Monica, CA: RAND, 2003, pp. 193–208.

Nathan, Andrew J. *China's Transition*, New York: Columbia University Press, 1997.

National Geographic Society. *National Geographic Atlas of China*, Washington, D.C.: National Geographic, 2007.

Nie Junhua. "Xin zhongguo chengli chuqi zhengwu yuan de sheli yu chexiao" [Establishment and abolishment of the Government Administrative Council in the early PRC], *Dangshi bolan*, no. 6, 2009, pp. 7–10.

Nie Rongzhen. *Nie Rongzhen huiyilu* [Memoirs of Nie Rongzhen], 3 vols., Beijing: Jiefangjun chubanshe, 1984.

Ouyang Qing. *Baizhan jiangxing Xie Zhenhua* [Star of generals who experienced hundred battles – Xie Zhenhua]. Beijing: Jiefangjun wenyi chubanshe, 2001.

Ouyang Yi. *Ouyang Yi huiyilu* [Memiors of Ouyang Yi], Beijing: Zhonggong dangshi chubanshe, 2005.

Pei, Minxin. *China's Trapped Transition: The Limits of Developmental Autocracy*, Cambridge, MA: Harvard University, 2006.

Peng Dehuai. *Peng Dehuai zishu* [The autobiographical notes of Peng Dehuai], Beijing: Renmin chubanshe, 1981.

Peng Xianzhi and Jin Chongji. *Mao Zedong zhuan (1949–1976)* [A biography of Mao Zedong], vol. 2, Beijing: Zhongyang wenxian chubanshe, 2003.

Perry, Elizabeth J., and Merle Goldman. *Grassroots Political Reform in Contemporary China*, Cambridge, MA: Harvard University Press, 2007.

Pollack, Jonathan D. "Short-Range Ballistic Missile Capabilities," in Steve Yui-Sang Tsang, ed., *If China Attacks Taiwan: Military Strategy, Politics and Economics*, New York: Routledge, 2006, pp. 47–59.

Priestland, David. *The Red Flag: A History of Communism*, New York: Grove Press, 2009.

Qi Li. *Mao Zedong wannian shenghuo jishi* [Record of events of Mao Zedong's later life], Beijing: Zhongyang wenxian chubanshe, 2004.

Qi Li ed. *Shaan-Gan-Ning bianqu shilu* [True accounts from the Shaanxi-Gansu-Ningxia Border region], Yan'an: Jiefang she, 1939.

Qian Jiang. "Jianguo chuqi de jiefangjun zongcan moubu" [The PLA General Staff Department in the early PRC]," *Dangshi bolan*, no. 7, 2003, pp. 17–21.

Qiao Jinwang. "Lao Qiao a, wenhua da geming ba wo lei kua le" [Old Qiao ah, the Cultural Revolution has tired me out], in Cheng Hua, ed., *Zhou Enlai he tade mishumen* [Zhou Enlai and his secretaries], Beijing: Zhongguo guangbo dianshi chubanshe, 1992, p. 428–54.

Qin Fuquan. "Bo Gu yu Pan Hannian guanxi de beihou" [Behind the relationship of Bo Gu and Pan Hannian], *Yanhuang chunqiu*, no. 10, 2006, pp. 20–6.

Qu Aiguo. *Baizhan jiangxing – Wu Zhong* [Star of generals who experienced hundred battles – Wu Zhong], Beijing: Jiefangjun wenyi chubanshe, 2000.

Quan Yanchi. *Lingxiu lei* [Tears of leaders], Hohehaote: Neimenggu renmin chubanshe, 2004.

———. *He Long yu Lin Biao zhimi* [Mystery of He Long and Lin Biao], Huhehot: Neimenggu renmin chubanshe, 1997.

———. *Longkun – He Long yu Xue Ming* [The stranded dragon – He Long and Xue Ming]. Guangzhou: Guangdong luyou chubanshe, 1997.

———. *Weixing: Yang Chengwu zai yijiu liuqi* [Tour in disguise: Yang Chengwu in 1967], Guangzhou: Guangdong luyou chubanshe, 1997.

———. *Zouxia shentan de Mao Zedong* [Mao Zedong stepping down from holy altar], Huhehot: Neimenggu renmin chubanshe, 2004.

———. *Zouxia shentan de Zhou Enlai* [Zhou Enlai stepping down from holy altar], Beijing: Guangming ribao chubanshe, 2004.

Radzinsky, Edvard. *Stalin: The First In-Depth Biography Based on Explosive New Documents from Russia's Secret Archives*, trans. H. T. Willetts, New York: Anchor Books, 1996.

Richelson, T. Jeffrey. *A Century of Spies*, New York: Oxford University Press, 1997.

———. *Foreign Intelligence Organizations*, Cambridge, MA: Ballinger Publishing, 1988.

Saich, Tony. "Development and Choice," in Edward Friedman and Bruce Gilley, eds., *Asia's Giants: Comparing China and India*, New York: Palgrave Macmillan, 2008, pp. 227–41.

San Mu. "Zuo Quan de liesi yu zixu wuyou de 'tuopai' xianyi" [Zuo Quan's heroic death and unwarranted suspect as a member of "Trotskystic faction"], *Wenshi jinghua*, no. 2, 2003, pp. 24–9.

Schram, Stuart R., and Nancy Jane Hodes. *Mao's Road to Power: Revolutionary Writings 1912–1949*, Armonk, NY: M. E. Sharpe, 1995.

Scobell, Andrew. *China's Use of Military Force: Beyond the Great Wall and the Long March*, New York: Cambridge University Press, 2003.

Seymour, James D., and Richard Anderson. *New Ghosts, Old Ghosts: Prisons and Labor Reform Camps in China*, Armonk, NY: M. E. Sharpe, 1998.

Shambaugh, David. "The Soldier and the State in China: The Political Work System in the People's Liberation Army," *CQ*, 127 (September 1991), pp. 527–68.

_____. *Modernizing China's Military: Progress, Problems, and Prospects*, Berkeley: University of California Press, 2002.

Sheng Renxue. *Zhang Guotao wenti yanjiu ziliao* [Research materials of Zhang Guotao case], Chengdu: Sichuan renmin chubanshe, 1982.

Sheng Xue. *"Yuanhua an" heimu* [Unveiling the "Yuan Hua case"], Hong Kong: Mirror Books, 2001.

Shi Dongbing. *Zuichu de kangzheng – Peng Zhen zai "wenhua da geming" qianxi* [The last resistance – Peng Zhen in the eve of the Cultural Revolution], Beijing: Zhonggong zhongyang dangxiao chubanshe, 1993.

Shi Zhe. *Mao Zedong de fanyi: Shi Zhe yanzhong de gaoceng renwu* [Interpreter of Mao Zedong: The high-level figures in the eyes of Shi Zhe], Beijing: Renmin chubanshe, 2005.

_____. *Zai lishi juren shengbian: Shi Zhe huiyilu* [At the side of a historical colossus: Memoirs of Shi Zhe]. Beijing: Zhongyang wenxian chubanshe, 1991.

Shirk, Susan L. *The Political Logic of Economic Reform in China*, Berkeley: University of California Press, 1993.

Shu Ping and Xiao Mingxing. "Luo Ruiqing dajiang yu zhongguo renmin gong'an budui de zujian" [Senior General Luo Ruiqing and the establishment of the Chinese People's Public Security Forces], *Wenshi chunqiu*, no. 7, 2005, pp. 4–7.

Shu Yun. *Dajiang Luo Ruiqing* [Senior General Luo Ruiqing], Beijing: Jiefangjun chubanshe, 1998.

_____. "Huimou 1971: Zaitan 'wuqiyi gongcheng' zhimi" [Recall 1971: Reevaluate the myth of "Project 571"], *Shidai wenxue* [Times literature], no. 4 (2004), pp. 4–40.

_____. *Lin Biao shijian wanzheng diaocha* [The complete investigation on Lin Biao's incident], vol. 1, New York: Mirror Books, 2006.

_____. "Mao Zedong de da jingweiyuan Luo Ruiqing" [Mao Zedong's chief guard Luo Ruiqing], in *Hainei yu haiwai* [At home and overseas], no. 9 (1997), pp. 5–13.

_____. "Xin zhongguo diyiren gong'an buzhang Luo Ruiqing" [First public security minister Luo Ruiqing], *Dangshi bolan*, no. 4 (2004), pp. 17–20.

_____. "Zhongjiang Zheng Weishan pingfan de qianqian houhou" [Before and after Lieutenant General Zheng Weishan's rehabilitation], *Dangshi Bolan*, no. 1 (2002), pp. 17–21.

Sima Lu. *Zhonggong lish de jianzheng: Sima Lu huiyilu* [Witness of the CCP history: Memoirs of Sima Lu], Hong Kong: Mingjing chubanshe, 2004.

Snow, Edgar. *The Long Revolution*, London: Hutchinson, 1973.

Song Wen. *Yige zhongguo jiandie de huiyi* [Recollections of a Chinese spy], Hong Kong: Mirror Books, 2010.

Song Yongyi (ed.). *Zhongguo wenhua dageming wenku* [Chinese Cultural Revolution library], Hong Kong: Center for China's Research and Service of Hong Kong Chinese University, 2002.

Su, Chi. *Taiwan's Relations with Mainland China: A Tail Wagging Two Dogs*, New York: Routledge, 2009.

Su Weimin, "Yang Shangkun tan zai zhongyang bangongting ershi nian" (Yang Shangkun talked about his twenty years in the Central General Office), in *Bainian chao* (Hundred year tide), no. 7 (2008), pp. 17–23.

Sukma, Rizal. *Indonesia and China: The Politics of a Troubled Relationship*, London: Routledge, 1999.

Sun, Y. Ivan, and Wu Yuning. "The Role of the People's Armed Police in Chinese Policing," *Asian Journal of Criminology*, 4, no. 2, (2009), pp. 108–28.

Sun Yi. *Sun Yi jiangjun zishu* [General Sun Yi's personal account], Shenyang: Liaoning renmin chubanshe, 2001.

Sun Yuting. "'Daoqie zhongyang dang'an guan hexin jimi' an zhenxiang" ["Truth of the case of 'stealing the top secrets from the Central Archive'"], in Sun Mingshan, ed., *Lishi shunjian* [An instant in history], vol. 2, Beijing: Qunzhong chubanshe, 2001, pp. 187–98.

Swaine, Michael D. "Chinese Decision-Making Regarding Taiwan, 1979-2000," in David M. Lampton, ed., *The Making of Chinese Foreign and Security Policy in the Era of Reform, 1978–2000*, Stanford, CA: Stanford University Press, 2001, pp. 289–336.

———. "Civil-Military Relations and Domestic Power and Policies," Paper Presented at the Conference on "Chinese Leadership, Politics, and Policy," November 2, 2005.

———. *The Military and Political Succession in China: Leadership, Institutions, Beliefs*, Santa Monica, CA: RAND, 1995.

———. *The Role of the Chinese Military in National Security Policymaking*, rev. ed., Santa Monica, CA: RAND, 1998.

Tan Qilong. *Tan Qilong huiyilu* [Memoirs of Tan Qilong], Beijing: Zhonggong dangshi chubanshe, 2003.

Tanner, Scot Murray. "How China Manages Internal Security Challenges and Its Impact on PLA Missions," in Roy Kamphausen, David Lai, and Andrew Scobell, eds., *Beyond the Strait: PLA Missions Other Than Taiwan*, Carlisle, PA: Strategic Studies Institute of the U.S. Army War College, 2009, pp. 39–98.

———. "The Institutional Lessons of Disaster: Reorganizing the People's Armed Police after Tiananmen," in James C. Mulvenon and Andrew N. D. Yang, eds., *The People's Liberation Army as Organization*, Santa Monica: RAND, 2002, pp. 587–635.

Tanner, Scot Murray, and Eric Green. "Principals and Secret Agents: Central versus Local Control over Policing and Obstacles to 'Rule of Law' in China," in Donald C. Clarke, ed., *China's Legal System: New Developments, New Challenges*, New York: Cambridge University Press, 2008, pp. 90–120.

Tao Dazhao. *Jiang zhi meng: cong tiedao youjidui zou chulai de Zheng Ti jiangjun* [Dream from a general: General Zheng Ti who came from the Railway Guerrilla Force], Beijing: Jiefangjun chubanshe, 2005.

Tao Siju. *Xinzhongguo diyiren gong'an buzhang: Luo Ruiqing* [First PRC public security minister: Luo Ruiqing], Beijing: Qunzhong chubanshe, 1997.

————. *Gong'an baowei gongzuo de zhuoyue lingdaoren Xu Zirong zhuan* [A biography of Xu Zirong – The outstanding leader of guard and public security], Beijing: Qunzhong chubanshe, 1997.

Tao Zhuwen. "Lishi xuanwo zhong de Chen Xianrui" [Chen Xianrui in the eddy of history]. *Dangshi bolan*, no. 8 (2001), pp. 14–26.

————. "Wen Yucheng chenfu lu" [Rise and fall of Wen Yucheng], *Dangshi tiandi* [Field of party history], no. 10 (2000), pp. 14–18.

Teiwes, Frederick C. *Politics and Purges in China: Rectification and the Decline of Party Norms, 1950–1965*, 2nd ed. Armonk, NY: M. E. Sharpe, 1993.

————. "Politics at the 'Core': The Political Circumstances of Mao Zedong, Deng Xiaoping and Jiang Zemin." *China Information*, 15, no. 1 (2001), pp. 1–66.

————. *Politics at Mao's Court: Gao Gang and Party Factionalism in the Early 1950s*, Armonk, NY: M. E. Sharpe, 1990.

Teiwes, Frederick C., and Warren Sun, *The Formation of the Maoist Leadership: From the Return of Wang Ming to the Seventh Party Congress*, London: Contemporary China Institute School of Orient, 1994.

————. *The Tragedy of Lin Biao*, Honolulu: University of Hawaii Press, 1996.

Tian Bingxin, "Zhou Yushu: Zaozao baoxiao dasheng ti" [Zhou Yushu: Announce the dawn daily and crow loudly], in *Hainan jinji bao* [Hainan economic daily], December 12, 2005.

Tian Min and Xu Jianchuan (ed.). *Gonghui da cidian* [The big dictionary of labor union], Beijing: Jingji guanli chubanshe, 1989.

Titov, A. "Kangri zhanzheng chuqi zhonggong lingdao neibu liangtiao luxian de douzheng, 1937-1939" [Two line struggle within the CCP leadership in the early period of the anti-Japanese war], in *Gongchan guoji yu zhongguo geming – sulian xuezhe lunwen xuanyi* [Comintern and Chinese Revolution – Selected and translated work of the Soviet scholars], trans. Xu Zhengming and Xu Junji, Chengdu: Sichuan renmin chubanshe, 1987, pp. 356–7.

Tong Xiaopeng. *Fengyu sishi nian* [Forty years of wind and rain], 2 vols., Beijing: Zhongyang wenxian chubanshe, 1997.

————. *Shaoxiao lijia laoda hui – Tong Xiaopeng huiyilu* [I left home young and return old – Memoirs of Tong Xiaopeng], Fuzhou: Fujian renmin chubanshe, 2000.

Tourison, Sedgwick. *Secret Army, Secret War: Washington's Tragic Spy Operation in North Vietnam*, Annapolis, MD: Naval Institute Press, 1995.

Tu Qiao. *Yuan Geng zhuan: Gaige xianchang, 1978–1984* [A biography of Yuan Geng: Scene of reform, 1978–1984], Beijing: Zuojia chubanshe, 2008.

Van de Ven, Hans J. "Introduction," in Tony Saich and Hans J. Van de Ven, eds., *New Perspectives on the Chinese Communist Revolution*, Armonk, NY: M. E. Sharpe, 1995, pp. xiii–xxii.

————. "New States of War: Communist and Nationalist Warfare, and State Building, 1928–1934," in Hans J. Van de Ven, ed., *Warfare in Chinese History*, Leiden, The Netherlands: Brill Academic Publisher, 2000, pp. 321–96.

————. *War and Nationalism in China, 1925–1945*, New York: RoutledgeCurzon, 2003.

Wakeman, Frederic, Jr. "Models of Historical Change: The Chinese State and Society, 1839–1989," in Kenneth Lieberthal ed., *Perspectives on Modern China: Four Anniversaries*, Armonk, NY: M. E. Sharpe, 1991, pp. 68–102.

————. *Policing Shanghai, 1927–1937*, Berkeley: University of California Press, 1995.
————. *Spymaster: Dai Li and the Chinese Secret Service*, Berkeley and Los Angeles: University of California Press, 2003.
Wang Binbin. "Jiaru Gu Shunzhang meiyou beibu" [If Gu Shunzhang had not been captured], *Tongzhou gongjin* [In the same boat], no. 4 (2008), pp. 41–4.
Wang Dongxing. *Wang Dongxing huiyi: Mao Zedong yu Lin Biao fangeming jituan de douzheng* [The recollections of Wang Dongxing: The struggle between Mao Zedong and Lin Biao's counterrevolutionary clique], Beijing: Dangdai zhongguo chubanshe, 1997.
Wang Fan et al. *Zhiqing zheshuo* [Said by insiders], vol. 1, Beijing: Zhongguo qingnian chubanshe, 2000.
Wang Fan and Dong Ping. *Hongqiang tonghua: wojia zhuzai zhongnanhai* [Fairy tales within the red wall: My family lived in the Zhongnanhai], Beijing: Zuojia zhubanshe, 2003.
————. *Hongqiang yisheng: Wo qingli de Zhongnanhai wangshi* [Doctors behind the red wall: Past events that I have personally experienced in Zhongnanhai], Beijing: Zuojia chubanshe, 2006.
Wang Fang. *Wang Fang huiyilu* [Memoirs of Wang Fang], Beijing: Zhejiang renmin chubanshe, 2005.
Wang Fuyi. *Xiang Ying zhuan* [A biography of Xiang Ying], Beijing: Zhonggong dangshi chubanshe, 1995.
Wang Hao. *Yige laobing xinzhong de Chen Yi yuanshuai* [Marshal Chen Yi in the heart of old soldiers], Shanghai: Shanghai wenyi chubanshe, 1996.
Wang Jianying. *Zhonggong zhongyang jiguan lishi yanbian kaoshi* [Textual research of historical evolution of CCP central organizations], Beijing: Zhonggong dangshi chubanshe, 2005.
————. *Zhongguo gongchandang zuzhishi ziliao huibian: Lingdao jigou yange he chengyuan minglu* [A collection of reference materials about the CCP organization history: The evolution of the leadership structure and the list of its members], Beijing: Zhonggong zhongyang dangxiao chubanshe, 1995.
Wang Jun. "Kang Sheng zai zhongyang shehui bu" [Kang Sheng in the Social Affairs Department], *Bai nian chao*, no. 5 (2003), pp. 21–9.
Wang Ming. "Rikou qinlue de xinjieduan yu zhongguo renmin douzheng de xinshiqi" [The new stage of the Japanese invasion and the new era of Chinese people's struggle], in *Jiefang* [Liberation], no. 26, December 4, 1937.
"Wang Ming jufa 'lun chijiu zhan' qianhou" [Before and after Wang Ming refused to publish "The Sustained and Protracted Warfare"], in *Laonian shenghuo bao* (Senior lives), July 2, 2010.
Wang Nianyi. *1949–1989 nian de zhongguo: Da dongluan de niandai* [China 1949–1989: The years of great turmoil], Henan: Henan renmin chubanshe, 1990.
————. "'Wenge' mantan [Informal discussion of the "Cultural Revolution"], *Ershiyi shiji* [Twenty-first century], 97 (October 2006), pp. 36–54.
Wang Shaoguang. "China's Expenditure for the People's Armed Police and Militia," in Nan Li, ed., *Chinese Civil-Military Relations: The Transformation of the People's Liberation Army*, London: Routledge, 2006, pp. 151–60.
Wang Shoudao. *Wang Shoudao huiyilu* [Memoirs of Wang Shoudao], Beijing: Jiefangjun chubanshe, 1988.

Wang Yong. "Minxi genju di 'shehui minzhu dang' yuan'an" [The false case "Social Democratic Party" in the western Fujian base areas], *Yanhuang chunqiu*, no. 2 (2004), pp. 27–31.

Wang Zhongfang. *Lian yu* [Purgatory], Beijing: Qunzhong chubanshe, 2004.

Weatherley, Robert. *Politics in China since 1949: Legitimizing Authoritarian Rule*, New York: Routledge, 2006.

Wei Xiaolan. "'Woxin tian zong hui liang' – Kang Sheng mishu tan 'Sa Tao shijian'" ["I believe daylight will come" – Kang Sheng's secretary discusses the "Sa Tao Incident"], *Bainian chao* [Hundred-year tide], 9 (2007), pp. 52–6.

Wen Guang. "Pan Hannian yuan'an de qianqian houhou" [Before and after the unjust case of Pan Hannian], in Zhonggong shanghai shiwei dangshi yanjiushi, ed., *Pan Hannian zai Shanghai* [Pan Hannian in Shanghai], Shanghai: Shanghai renmin chubanshe, 1996, pp. 413–34.

Wen Hong. "Guanyu Futian shibian ji Jiangxi suqu sufan wenti" [Concerning the Futian Incident and the issue of suppressing counterrevolutionaries in Jiangxi Soviet base areas], in *Jiangxi wenshi ziliao xuanji* [Selected materials of Jiangxi literature and history], vol. 2, 1982.

Wen Yu. *Zhongguo zuohuo* [China's left disaster], Beijing: Chaohua chubanshe, 1993, *Wenhui bao* [Wenhui daily], December 6, 2006.

White, Gordon. *Riding the Tiger: The Politics of Economic Reform in Post-Mao China*, Stanford, CA: Stanford University Press, 1993.

White, Lynn T. *Local Causes of China's Intellectual, Legal, and Governmental Reform*, Armonk, NY: M. E. Sharpe, 1999.

Williams, Philip F., and Yenne Wu. *The Great Wall of Confinement: The Chinese Prison Camp through Contemporary Fiction and Reportage*, Berkeley: University of California Press, 2004.

Womack, Brantly. *The Foundations of Mao Zedong's Political Thought, 1917–1935*, Honolulu: University Press of Hawaii, 1982.

Wu De. "Lushan huiyi he Lin Biao shijian" [Lushan plenum and Lin Biao affairs], in Zhang Hua and Su Caiqing, eds., *Huishou "wenge"* [Look back the "Cultural Revolution"], Beijing: Zhonggong dangshi chubanshe, 2000, pp. 1019–45.

Wu Faxian. *Suiyue jiannan – Wu Faxian huiyilu* [Difficult years – The memoirs of Wu Faxian], vol. 2, Hong Kong: Beixing chubanshe, 2006.

Wu Jicheng and Wang Fan. *Hongse jingwei: zhongyang jingweiju yuan fujuzhang Wu Jicheng huiyilu* [Red Guards: Memoirs of former deputy director of the Central Guard Bureau Wu Jicheng], Beijing: Dangdai zhongguo chubanshe, 2003.

Wu Jixue. *Hongqiang huiyi* [Memory within red wall], vol. 1, Beijing: Zhonggong dangshi chubanshe, 2004.

Wu Lie. *Zhengrong suiyue* [The eventful times], Beijing: Zhongyang wenxian chubanshe, 1999.

Wu, Tien-wei. "The Chinese Communist Movement," in James Chieh Hsiung and Steven I. Levine, eds., *China's Bitter Victory: The War with Japan, 1937–1945*, Armonk, NY: M. E. Sharpe, 1997.

"Wu Zhong zhuihuailu" bianxiezu zhu (ed.). *Wu Zhong zhuihuailu* [Memoirs that bring Wu Zhong to mind], Shaoguan: Guangdong renmin chubanshe, 1993.

Wuhan shi difangzhi bianzuan weiyuanhui [Compiling Commission of Wuhan Local Annals]. *Wuhan shizhi: Junshi zhi* [Annals of Wuhan: Military annals], Wuhan: Wuhan University Press, 1989.

Xiao Ke. "Hong er, liu juntuan huishi qianhou – Xiangei Ren Bishi, He Long, he Guan Xiangyiny tongzhi" [Before and after the joint force of the Second Army Group and Sixth Army Group – Dedicated to comrades Ren Bishi, He Long, and Guan Xiangying], *Jindai shi yanjiu* [Research of contemporary Chinese history], no. 1 (1980), pp. 1–38.

_____. "Zhongyang suqu chuqi de sufan yundong" [Suppressing campaign in early period of the central Soviet base areas], in *Dangshi yanjiu ziliao* [Research materials of party history], no. 5 (1982).

Xiao Nong. "Yijiu wuwu nian Rao Shushi de wenti weihe shengji e'hua?" [Why did the 1955 Rao Shushi case escalate and deteriorate?], *Dangshi wenyuan* [Literary circles of CCP history], no. 11 (2005), pp. 35–8.

Xin Junsheng. "Wogei Xu Zirong dang mishu" [I was Xu Zirong's secretary], in Sun Mingshan, ed., *Lishi shunjian* [An instant in history], vol. 3, Beijing: Qunzhong chubanshe, 2004, pp. 361–410.

Xinghuo liaoyuan bianjibu. *Zhongguo renmin jiefangjun jiangshuai minglu* [Name list of the PLA generals and marshals], vol. 2, Beijing: Jiefangjun chubanshe, 1991.

Xiong Lei. "1976 nian, Hua Guofeng he Ye Jianying zenyang lianshou de" [1976, how did Hua Guofeng and Ye Jianying become allies?], *Yanhuang chunqiu*, 10 (2008), pp. 1–8.

Xiong Xianghui. *Wode qingbao yu waijiao shengya* [My intelligence and diplomatic careers], Beijing: Zhonggong dangshi chubanshe, 2006.

Xu Enzeng. "Wohe gongchandang zhandou de huiyi" [Recollections of my battle against communists], in Xu Enzeng et al., eds., *Xishuo zhongtong juntong* [Detailed discussions on the Central Investigation Department and the Military Statistics Bureau], Taipei: Zhuanji wenxue chubanshe, 1992, pp. 117–275.

Xu Guangshou. "Chen Duxiu 'hanjian' shijian shimo" [Beginning and end of Chen Duxiu "traitor" case], *Dangshi zonglan* [Over the party history], no. 2 (2007), pp. 41–6.

Xu Jiatun. *Xu Jiatun xianggang huiyilu* [Xu Jiatun's Hong Kong memoirs], vol. 1, Hong Kong: Xianggang lianhe bao youxian gongsi, 1993.

Xu Linxiang and Zhu Yu. *Chuanqi jiangjun Li Kenong* [Legendary General Li Kenong], Hefei: Anhui renmin chubanshe, 1999.

Xu Ping. "Zhonggong bada yilai de lijie zhongyang zhengzhiju changwei" [Members of the Politburo Standing Committee since the Eighth Party Congress], *Dangshi bolan*, no. 7 (2003), pp. 22–5.

Xu Xiangqian. *Lishi de huigu* [Historical recollection], vol. 1, Beijing: Jiefangjun chubanshe, 1984.

Xue Qingchao. "Angshou yu gaofeng yu digu zhijian – Li Desheng danren zhonggong zhongyang fuzhuxi qianhou" [Strut between peak and valley – Before and after Li Desheng became a vice chairman of the CCP Central Committee], *Lingdao kexue*, no. 11 (2002), pp. 30–3, no. 15 (2002), pp. 32–5.

Yan Mingfu. "Wokan Kang Sheng" [My view of Kang Sheng], *Lingdao wencui* [Literature collection of leadership], no. 8 (2005), pp. 139–44.

Yan Youmin. *Gong'an zhanxian wushi nian* [Fifty years on the public security front], Beijing: Qunzhong chubanshe, 2005.

Yang Chengwu. *Yang Chengwu jiangjun zishu* [The autobiographical notes of General Yang Chengwu]. Shenyang: Liaoning renmin chubanshe, 1997.

Yang Jing. *Wangshi* [The past], Beijing: Jiefangjun chubanshe, 1985.

Yang Jingming. "Wo he Zhao Guowei" [Zhao Guowei and I], in Sun Mingshan, ed., *Lishi shunjian* [An instant in history], vol. 3, Beijing: Qunzhong chubanshe, 2004, pp. 570–614.

Yang Kuisong. "Reconsidering the Campaign to Suppress Counterrevolutionaries," *CQ*, 193 (March 2008), pp. 102–21.

Yang Shangkun. "Guanyu 'ershiba ge ban buer shiweike' wenti" [Concerning the issue of "28 and a half Bolsheviks"], *Bainian chao* [Hundred-year tide], no. 8 (2001), pp. 10–22.

———. *Yang Shangkun huiyilu* [Memoirs of Yang Shangkun], Beijing: Zhongyang wenxian chubanshe, 2001.

———. *Yang Shangkun riji* [Yang Shangkun's diaries], 2 vols., Beijing: Zhongyang wenxian chubanshe, 2001.

———. *Zhuiyi lingxiu zhanyou tongzhi* [Recollecting leaders, comrades-in-arms, and comrades], Beijing: Zhongyang wenxian chubanshe, 2001.

Yang Shuanwen. "Wujing budui 'zhifa quan' chutan" [A preliminary exploration on the "law enforcement power" of the armed police], *Wujing gongcheng xueyuan xuebao* [Journal of Engineering College of Armed Police Force], 20, no. 1 (2004), pp. 39–40.

Yang Yize. "Shilun wujing budui de tedian" [A discussion of the characteristics of the armed police force], *Wujing xueyuan xuebao* [Academic Journal of the Chinese People's Armed Police College], no. 1 (1997), pp. 55–8.

Yang Yuying. "Wohe Zhou Xing," in Sun Mingshan, ed., *Lishi shunjian* [An instant in history], vol. 2, Beijing: Qunzhong chubanshe, 2001, pp. 477–520.

Yang Zhaolin. *Baizhan jiangxing – Su Zhenhua* [Star of generals who experienced hundred battles – Su Zhenhua], Beijing: Jiefangjun wenyi chubanshe, 2000.

Yao Jinguo. "Futian shibian shi ruhe dingxing wei fangeming shijian de" [How was Futian Incident determined a counterrevolutionary event?], *Bai nian chao*, no. 3 (2008), pp. 58–60.

Yao Jinguo and Su Hang. *Zhang Guotao zhuan* [A biography of Zhang Guotao], Xi'an: Shaanxi renmin chubanshe, 2007.

Yao Yizhe and Chen Yuhong. *Li Kenong chuanqi* [Legendary General Li Kenong], Beijing: Xinhua chubanshe, 1999.

Ye Yonglie. *Chen Boda zhuan* [A biography of Chen Boda], vol. 2, Beijing: Renmin ribao chubanshe, 1999.

Ye Zilong. *Ye Zilong huiyilu* [Memoirs of Ye Zilong], Beijing: Zhongyang wenxian chubanshe, 2000.

You, Ji. *The Armed Forces of China*, New York: I. B. Tauris & Co. Ltd., 1999.

———. "Sorting Out the Myths about Political Commissars," in Nan Li, ed., *Chinese Civil-Military Relations: The Transformation of the People's Liberation Army*, New York: Routledge, 2006, pp. 89–116.

Yu Boliu. "Mao Zedong yu donggu geming genju di de bujie zhiyuan" [Mao Zedong had an indissoluble bond with the Donggu revolutionary base areas], *Dangshi wenyuan* [Literature circle of party history], no. 3 (2008), pp. 4–15.

Yu Jianrong. "Dangqian woguo quntixing shijian de zhuyao leixing jiqi jiben tezheng" [Major types and basic features of current mass incidents in China], in *Zhongguo zhengfa daxie xuebao* (Journal of China University of Political Science and Law), 6 (2009), pp. 114–20.

Yu Ruxin. "1969: duisu zhanbei zhongde junwei banshizu, Lin Biao yu Mao Zedong" [1969: The CMC Administrative Group, Lin Biao, and Mao Zedong during the war preparation against the Soviet Union], in Ding Kaiwen, ed., *Bainian Lin Biao* [The centennial of Lin Biao], Hong Kong: Mirror Books, 2007, pp. 312–48.

Yu Sang. "Zhao Cangbi tongzhi zhuanlue" [A brief biography of Zhao Cangbi], in Yu Sang (ed.), *Zhao Cangbi zhuanlue ji jinian wenji* [A brief biography of Zhao Cangbi and collected works commemorating Zhao Cangbi], Beijing: Qunzhong chubanshe, 2004, pp. 3–114.

Yuan Renyuan. *Zhengtu jishi* [Actual record of my life journey], Changsha: Hunan renmin chubanshe, 1985.

Zeng Chenggui. "Lun 1927 nian zhonggong zhongyang jiancha weiyuanhui de chuangli" [On the creation of the CCP Supervision Commission in 1927], *Xuexi yu shijian* [Studies and practices], no. 12 (2008), pp. 5–9.

Zhang Bingwu. "Liu Shaoqi zai 'wenhua dageming' zhong de yixie qingkuang" [Some information about Liu Shaoqi during the "Cultural Revolution"], in Zhongyang wenxian yanjiushi dier bianyanbu, ed., *Huashuo Liu Shaoqi – Zhiqingzhe fangtan lu* [Talking about Liu Shaoqi – Interview with insiders], Beijing: Zhongyang wenxian chubanshe, 2000, pp. 387–91.

Zhang Guotao. *Wode huiyi* [My reminiscence], 3 vols., Hong Kong: Mingbao yukan chubanshe, 1973.

Zhang Jiakang. "Wang Ming yu zhongyang fenting kangli de shi ge yue" [Ten months in which Wang Ming stood up to the center as an equal], *Dangshi zongheng* [Over the party history], no. 9 (2007), pp. 19–22.

Zhang Ning. *Ziji xie ziji* [One writes oneself], Beijing: Zuojia chubanshe, 1998.

Zhang Qihou. "Zhonggong jianzheng wushi nian gong'an bu fazhan yange" [Development and evolution of Ministry of Public Security in the CCP fifty years of nation building], in Zhongguo dalu wenti yanjiu suo, ed., *Zhonggong jianzheng wushi nian* [CCP fifty years of nation building], Taipei: Zhengzhong shuju gufen youxian gongsi, 2001, pp. 247–88.

Zhang Shude. "Mao Zedong wei 175 jiangjun pingfan de qianqian houhou" [Before and after Mao Zedong rehabilitated 175 generals], *Dangshi bolan*, no. 3 (2001), pp. 11–17.

Zhang Xingxing. "Zhongguo jundui da caijun yu xin shiqi jingji jianshe" [Great disarmament of China's army and economic development in the new era], *Dangdai zhongguo shi yanjiu* [Research of contemporary Chinese history], 13, no. 1 (January 2006), pp. 21–8.

Zhang Yaoci. *Zhang Yaoci huiyi Mao Zedong* [Zhang Yaoci recalls Mao Zedong], Beijing: Zhonggong zhongyang dangxiao chubanshe, 1996.

Zhang Yunsheng. *Maojiawan jishi: Lin Biao mishu huiyilu* [The true account of Maojiawan: Memoirs of Lin Biao's secretary], Beijing: Chunqiu chubanshe, 1988.

Zhang Zhen. *Zhang Zhen huiyilu* [Memoirs of Zhang Zhen], vol. 1, Beijing: Jiefangjun chubanshe, 2003.

Zhang Zhenglong. *Zhanjiang* [Combat general], Beijing: Jiefangjun chubanshe, 2000.

Zhang Zishen. *Zhanjiang yu tongshuai – Yang Chengwu zai Mao Zedong huixia de sishiba nian* [Combat general and commander – Yang Chengwu's forty-eight years under Mao Zedong's leadership], Shenyang: Liaoning renmin chubanshe, 2000.

Zhao Hua, "Zuohao budui bu jingshang wenti qingli jiancha gongzuo de jidian renshi" [Some understandings about handling well with the the liquidation and examination for putting an end to the army's non-commercial activities], in *Wujing houqing* [Logistics of the People's Armed Police], no. 3 (2002), p. 62.

Zhao Ming. "Cong lishi de shenchu zoulai: mantan zhuanxing shiqi de dangdai zhongguo zhengzhi yu sifa gaige" [Coming from history: On relationship of China's judicial system reform and political system reform]," in *Zhengfa luncong* [Politics and law forum], no. 3 (2008), pp. 3–14.

Zhao, Quansheng, and Guoli Liu. "China Rising: Theoretical Understanding and Global Response," in Quansheng Zhao and Guoli Liu, eds., *Managing the China Challenge: Global Perspectives*, New York: Routledge, 2009, pp. 3–22.

Zhao Ziyang. *Gaige licheng* [Journey in the course of reform], Hong Kong: New Century Media and Consulting Co. Ltd., 2009.

Zheng Chaolin. *Zheng Chaolin huiyilu – 1919–1931* [Memoirs of Zheng Chaolin, 1919–1931], Beijing: Dongfang chubanshe, 1996.

Zhonggong shanghai shiwei dangshi yanjiushi (ed.). *Pan Hannian zai Shanghai* [Pan Hannian in Shanghai], Shanghai: Shanghai renmin chubanshe, 1996.

Zhonggong yanjiu zazhishe [Journal Press of Researching CCP] (ed.). *Zhonggong wenhua dageming zhongyao wenjian huibian* [Compilation of the CCP central documents issued in the Cultural Revolution], Taipei: Shanghai yinshuachang, 1973.

Zhonggong zhongyang dangshi yanjiushi diyi yanjiubu [First Research Unit of the CCP Central Party History Research Office] (ed.). *Liangong (bu), gongchan guoji yu zhongguo suwei'ai yundong* [The Soviet Communist Party [Bolshevik], Comintern and Chinese Soviet movement], 14 vols., Beijing: Zhongyang wenxian chubanshe, 2002.

Zhonggong zhongyang jilu jiancha weiyuanhui bangongting [General Office of the Central Discipline Inspection Commission]. *Zhongguo gongchandang dangfeng lianzheng jianshe wenxian xuanbian* [Selected documents on the CCP's work style and clean government], vol. 4, Beijing: Zhongguo fangzheng chubanshe, 2001.

Zhonggong zhongyang wenxian yanjiushi [CCP Central Document Research Office], *Deng Xiaoping nianpu, 1975–1979* [Chronicle of Deng Xiaoping, 1975–1979], 2 vols., Beijing: Zhongyang wenxian chubanshe, 2004.

_____. *Mao Zedong nianpu (1893–1949)* [Chronicle of Mao Zedong, 1893–1949], Beijing: Zhongyang wenxian chubanshe, 1993.

_____. *Ren Bishi zhuan* [A biography of Ren Bishi], rev. ed., Beijing: Zhongyang wenxian chubanshe, 2004.

_____. *Zhou Enlai nianpu – 1898–1949* [Chronicle of Zhou Enlai, 1898–1949], Beijing: Zhongyang wenxian chubanshe, 1990.

_____. *Zhou Enlai nianpu – 1949–1976* [Chronicle of Zhou Enlai, 1949–1976], 3 vols., Beijing: Zhongyang wenxian chubanshe, 1997.

Zhonggong zhongyang zuzhi bu [CCP Organization Department] et al. (eds.). *Zhongguo gongchandang zuzhi shi ziliao* [Materials of the CCP organizational history], 9 vols. and 4 ancillary vols., Beijing: Zhonggong dangshi chubanshe, 2000.

Zhongguo renmin gong'an shigao bianxie shaozu [Writing group of draft of Chinese people's public security history]. *Zhongguo renmin gong'an shigao* [Draft of Chinese people's public security history], Beijing: Jingguan jiaoyue chubanshe, 1997.

Zhongguo renmin jiefangjun zhengzhi xueyuan [The PLA Political Institute] (ed.). *Zhonggong dangshi jiaoxue cankao ziliao* [Reference materials of the CCP history education], vol. 14, Beijing: Zhongguo renmin jiefangjun zhengzhi xueyuan, 1985.

"Zhongguo renmin jingcha jianshi" bianxiezu. Zhongguo renmin jingcha jianshi [A brief history of Chinese policing], Beijing: Jingguan jiaoyue chubanshe, 1989.

Zhongyang dang'an guan [Central Archive] (ed.). *Zhonggong zhongyang wenjian xuanji* [A selection of the CCP Central Committee documents], 18 vols., Beijing: Zhonggong zhongyang dangxiao chubanshe, 1991.

Zhongyang dang'an guan and Jiangxi sheng dang'an guan (eds.). *Jiangxi geming lishi wenjian huiji*, 1930, 2 [Complilation of Jiangxi revolutionary historical documents issued in 1930, part 2], internal publication, Beijing: Zhongyang dang'an guan, 1988.

Zhongyang tongzhan bu [Central Department of United Front], *Zhonggong zhongyang kangri minzhu tongyi zhanxian wenjian huibian* [Compiled Documents of CCP Central Anti-Japanese National United Front], vol. 2, Beijing: Dang'an chubanshe, 1985.

Zhou Chunlin. *Zhou Chunlin huiyilu* [Memoirs of Zhou Chunlin], Beijing: Zhonggong dangshi chubanshe, 2005.

Zhou Degao. *Wo yu zhonggong he jiangong* [My career with the CCP and Khmer Rouge and Red], written by Zhu Xueyuan, Hong Kong: Tianyuan shuwu, 2007.

Zhu Fang. "Political Work in the Military from the Viewpoint of the Beijing Garrison Command," in Carol Lee Hamrin and Suisheng Zhao, eds., *Decision-Making in Deng's China: Perspectives from Insiders*, Armonk, NY: M. E. Sharpe, 1995, pp. 118–132.

Zhu Yuanshi et al. *Wu De koushu: Shinian fengyu wangshi – Wozai Beijing gongzuo de yixie jingli* [Wu De's dictating: Past events with ten-year hardship – Some experiences when I worked in Beijing], Beijing: Dangdai zhongguo chubanshe, 2004.

Index

CPSIA information can be obtained at www.ICGtesting.com
Printed in the USA
BVOW04s0619120215

387360BV00049B/964/P